D1096366

MUNICIPAL BONDS
Planning, Sale, and Administration

Lennox L. Moak

Municipal Finance Officers Association

To Bonnie Helen
to whom the debt is increased
with no hope of amortization

FOREWORD

Lennox L. Moak has authored numerous publications for the Municipal Finance Officers Association (MFOA) on subjects as diverse as taxation, budgeting and the general practice of local government finance. It is safe to say, however, that his heart and overwhelming interest lie in the field of governmental debt administration. MFOA is pleased to publish Moak's most recent work on this subject.

I have had the pleasure of knowing and working with the author for more than 10 years. We are continually indebted to Len's ability to share his knowledge through keen ability to organize detailed and complex information through his writing.

Moak was for almost 30 years a lecturer in public finance at the Wharton School of Finance, University of Pennsylvania. Moak has served as president of the Philadelphia Bureau of Municipal Research and director of the Eastern Division of the Pennsylvania Economy League. He was the first director of finance in the City of Philadelphia, 1952–54, and for more than a decade before that, he was executive director of the Bureau of Governmental Research of New Orleans. Moak returned to the City of Philadelphia in 1972–77 as the director of finance. During this period, Moak was elected to the MFOA Executive Board and served as association president in 1976–77.

In the 12 years I have served the association, no one has inspired me more than Len Moak. In his preface Moak expresses appreciation for my patience with this publication's development. In most instances, my patience is best explained by my concern that someday state and local government finance officers may not have the advantage of Moak's experience and expertise in governmental finance. I deeply respect his knowledge and appreciate his many contributions to MFOA.

As in all other books authored by Moak, the opinions expressed in the text and responsibility for factual accuracy rest entirely with him. Although MFOA has sponsored this publication, the recommendations herein have not been officially adopted by the association.

We are indebted to Moak for another contribution to his favorite area of governmental finance—governmental debt administration.

Donald W. Beatty
Executive Director
Municipal Finance Officers Association

PREFACE

By any measure 1938 was a watershed year for me:

I enticed the lady of my dreams into what has proved to be a tremendously rewarding marriage for me—but, I am sure, a frequently trying one for her.

I departed my first professional love of public school teaching to try my hand at the study and practice of public administration and public finance.

I moved from Texas to New Orleans and became associated with those seeking to rescue state and local government from some of the more oppressive forces of political dictatorship and imaginative theory.

In the examination of a financial statement of the Orleans Levee Board, I learned that somehow $496,000 had been paid for services in connection with the refunding of about $5 million in bonds.

And I quickly became fully acquainted with Albert M. Hillhouse's volume, *Municipal Bonds: A Century of Experience,* and the companion work by him and Carl H. Chatters, *Administration of Local Government Debt.*

Within two years we had five prominent New Orleans citizens in the federal penitentiary, half the $496,000 back in the Levee Board's treasury, and I had learned a great deal not only about bonds but about Louisiana public affairs and politics—some of the scars of which I still carry both visibly and invisibly to this day.

Until that time I had barely known the meaning of the word "bond." However, a lifelong interest in mathematics came immediately into play when the U.S. Special Prosecutor launched into his approach to *present value of future money.* Somewhat dimly at first, but with greater clarity as time progressed, I comprehended the views he was expressing. The more I comprehended, the more I expressed doubts concerning the ease with which present value might be explained to the jury. His response was to the effect that jurors did not necessarily need to understand. They only had to come to the realization that the concept was of importance and had validity. Moreover, that the existence of the Series E Savings Bond would be quite sufficient to carry the day. Whereupon he proceeded to try the case with great flourishes—sometimes expressed correctly in mathematical terms and sometimes not. In like manner did the battery of defense counsel, witnesses and occasionally the judge himself, expound at length. But O. John Rogge, the Special Prosecutor, knew his trade; he won his case including all appeals—all the way to the U.S. Supreme Court.

My conclusion was that a subject about which so little was known but which could produce such significant results was indeed worthy of occasional attention from an erstwhile student of public finance and mathematics. Now several file drawers overflow with calculations on the subject [some useful, most useless]. I have learned that in the affairs of men the translation between (a) money-in-hand and (b) money promised to be paid at a future date or dates is one of the most complex of all financial subjects. Although eventually reduced to deceptively simple arithmetical expressions, the realities are usually composites of a host of interacting factors.

From the standpoint of the debtor, the object is to secure the greatest amount of money in hand for the payment or sum of payments agreed to be made at a future date or dates. From the standpoint of the investor, the opposite is true: to secure the greatest amount of payments in the future in return for the use of the money and its eventual repayment, taking into consideration the risk involved.

State and local governments in the United States range widely in their ability and sophistication as both borrowers and as investors. They do not pay salaries nor provide other emoluments of office which begin to approach those of large financial organizations or officers of more general corporations with significantly lesser responsibilities.

Financial officers of many state and local governments have sought to bolster their limited in-house staff capabilities through increased reliance upon contractual relationships with "financial consultants." Following the problems arising in New York in 1975 this field has mushroomed as the growing list of those in the field indicates. Some of the firms have genuine competence and are doing a genuinely excellent job for their clients. On the other hand, even casual examination of the results of sales data shows clearly that in numerous cases large avoidable losses are being incurred by issuers despite their use of financial consultants. There is no easy answer to this problem in the short run. Eventually competitive forces will doubtless drive many of the incompetent firms out of business. In any case, no financial advisor who does not reasonably comprehend a wide variety of the considerations of present value of future money as this relates to the design of municipal bond issues should be long considered or tolerated.

In this connection, the new-found interest in the zero coupon type of bond may well prove to be a major market development. If so, we will require the development of substantial knowledge, literature, and in-service training for all concerned lest we unwittingly make major expensive errors during the early years of its use.

Would that space considerations should have permitted broader treatment of many topics than has been feasible and that mental agility had permitted presentations with greater clarity at many points. As noted below, I am indebted to many for their contributions but the errors of omission, commission, and emphasis are the responsibility of the author.

IN APPRECIATION

Only as one brings to a conclusion a volume of this character does he reflect upon the host of persons to whom he has turned for assistance in so many ways. Let it be remembered that except for their help either the work would not have been completed or would have been less well done.

In Development and Criticism of Plan of Organization of Materials: Harlan E. Boyles, Treasurer, State of North Carolina; Jefferson M. Moak, Secretary, Philadelphia Historical Commission; John E. Petersen, Director, MFOA's Governmental Finance Research Center, Washington, D.C.; John M. Urie, Director of Finance, Kansas City, Missouri.

In Review and Criticism of the Manuscript (wholly or selected parts): E. George Cross III, Special Assistant to the Secretary of the Treasury; William J. McCarthy, Vice President, Fitch Investors Service, Inc.; Lynn M. Moak, Director of Research, Office of Lieutenant Governor of Texas; Val C. Mogensen, Executive Assistant Director of Finance, City of Philadelphia; and Allan S. Olsen, Special Officer, Department of Community Affairs, State of New Jersey.

For Technical Assistance on Numerous Points: G. Edward DeSeve, Director of Finance, City of Philadelphia; Samuel Katz and Martin Dorph, Public Financial Management, Inc.; Stanley Pardo and Gregory Hickock, Blyth Eastman Paine Webber, Inc.; Joseph B. Sturges, Esq., Saul, Ewing, Remick & Saul; and Wade S. Smith, Moody's Investors Service, Inc.

For Provision of Materials and Assistance in Securing Access to Them: Freda Stern Ackerman, Moody's Investors Service, Inc.; Ellen Brennan, Pennsylvania Economy League;

Hyman C. Grossman, Standard & Poor's Corporation; Jean Rousseau, Merrill Lynch Pierce Fenner & Smith Inc.; and John J. Winders, *The Bond Buyer.*

To three other groups genuine appreciation is also extended.

For Financial Assistance: The work was made possible through the combined generosity of F. Eugene Dixon, Jr. and the MFOA Publications Fund. Although the latter may hope to recoup its investment from sales, the contribution of the former is another of the hundreds of instances of Mr. Dixon's use of his resources in support of projects in the public interest.

In the Preparation of the Manuscript: Throughout its preparation I have had the benefit of the unexcelled secretarial services of Lois Hammer who has not only produced excellent copy but more importantly has identified numerous points of inconsistencies and error that required further attention. Also, as the book moved toward its final phases, I was once again able to depend on Kathryn K. Gordon as editor and critic. Rebecca Russum and her staff in the editorial office in Chicago have done yeoman work in seeing the manuscript through the printer.

And Donald Beatty: We part almost where we came in. In 1970 the precursor volume, *Administration of Local Government Debt,* was just being published as Don joined MFOA as its Executive Director. I looked forward to working with him as an MFOA author, little expecting that I would shortly be back as a working finance officer, would join his board and have an opportunity to work with him as an officer of MFOA. It has been a most rewarding experience. For a variety of reasons I have failed to meet the original deadlines on this volume and Don has been unfailingly understanding. Now that he is to pursue his professional work elsewhere, *bon voyage*—with great appreciation!

Lennox L. Moak
Philadelphia, Pennsylvania
April 21, 1982

TABLE
OF CONTENTS

TABLES

Appendix Tables

Exhibits

Chapter 1
THE DEBT AND SECURITIES
OF STATE AND
LOCAL GOVERNMENTS

Perhaps the best overview of the amount of state and local government debt outstanding is contained in the series of publications generally known as the *Flow of Funds* statements[1] issued by the Board of Governors of the Federal Reserve System. Under the board's classification, the outstanding debt as of December 31, 1980, may be summarized as follows:

	(Amount in billions)	Percent of Total
Total	$361.5	100.0
Liability	337.8	88.5
Obligations in market	312.5	86.4
Long-term	296.7	82.1
Short-term	15.8	4.4
U.S. Government	7.6	2.1
Trade debt	17.8	4.9
Non-liability debt (pollution control)	23.6	6.5
Exhibit: Total Securities		
[$361.5 − ($17.8 + $7.6)]	336.1	93.0

The foregoing constitutes the best available statement of the aggregate amounts of credit market and trade debt in the names of state and local governments. Yet, it does not differentiate various types of *on behalf of* debt issued in the names of these governments but in no sense an actual liability chargeable against their regular revenues—whether general, utility, or those of social insurance systems. No comprehensive data provide a basis for segregation of the genuine liability debt of these governments from the other elements of debt issued largely for housing, health facilities, nonprofit institutions of higher learning, and several forms of economic development.

Finally, this statement includes those elements of public housing and urban renewal debt marketed by state and local governments which in all other respects are general or special obligations of the United States Government.

Against the outstanding debt reported above, state and local governments held large sums as direct offsets. Most of these were in debt service funds, sinking funds, and in trusteed accounts related to advance refunding of bonds. At the close of the fiscal years ending in the 1979–1980 period, the Bureau of the Census reported $59.5 billion held as offsets to debt. [These amounts did not include cash held in operating funds which may

---

[1] The Board of Governors of the Federal Reserve System publishes the *Flow of Funds* statements on a quarterly basis, with this data being in highly preliminary form. It provides an annual update early each year and a further annual update in midyear, usually in August. See bibliography for a listing of the reports in this series. See Chapter 16 for discussion of possible omissions of large amounts of tax-exempt debt issued for small industrial developments, especially for claims of the Congressional Budget Office as to the amounts of such debt.

have constituted offsets to debt, especially to short-term debt. Nor did they include $33.2 billion held by bond funds of state and local governments.][2]

Therefore, if it had been feasible to measure the net liability debt of state and local governments at the end of 1980, after taking into account offsets and *on behalf of* debt, the amount was probably about $250 billion. However, from a marketing point of view, the entire $362 billion, except for the $25.4 billion in trade debt and debt to the United States Government, was in the hands of investors or of the state and local governments themselves.

In addition, the *Flow of Funds* statements do not take into account large amounts of other types of obligations of state and local governments, especially the following:

1. Current compensation accrued but not yet payable
2. Unfunded pension and other deferred compensation, e.g., various types of accumulated compensable leave of employees
3. Obligations to other state and local governments
4. Tax-exempt mortgage loans of industrial development agencies of state and local governments where debt is not represented by bonds

With respect to warrants payable and amounts due under judgments and other claims there are no data available on a national basis concerning these elements of indebtedness by state and local governments.

The focus of this volume is on the type of debt included in the $312.5 billion of obligation debt that took the form of credit market instruments at the end of 1980 as reported in the *Flow of Funds* statements—specifically on the liability aspect of that debt. Much of the data makes no differentiation between the *on behalf of* debt and the liability debt of these governments.

This chapter provides selected information about: (1) the trends in outstanding debt; (2) the distribution of debt among different types of governments; (3) gross and net debt; (4) the purposes of the debt; (5) the security pledged; (6) relationship of debt service to available revenues; and (7) the amounts of debt being issued.

GROWTH IN AMOUNTS OF DEBT OUTSTANDING

In 1902 the amount of outstanding debt of state and local governments as determined by the Bureau of the Census[3] stood at $2.1 billion, or about $27 per capita. By 1927 it

---

[2] Of interest in this regard are not only the $59.5 billion in debt offset funds and the $33.2 billion in bond [proceeds] funds but also the additional $109.4 billion of cash and securities being held in various funds not related to the insurance systems of these governments. It is apparent that substantial amounts were on hand to help retire short-term debt incurred for working capital purposes as well as surplus funds which are pledged under general obligation or limited obligation bonds but which are retained in operating funds. (See U.S. Bureau of the Census, *Governmental Finances in 1979–80*, p. 54.)

Also of interest in this regard are the securities held by state bond banks and other agencies issuing their own securities in lieu of those acquired from local governments. It appears that the $6.4 billion of state and local securities being held by these governments at the end of their 1979–1980 fiscal years does not include these securities.

[3] The Bureau of the Census publications on governmental finance are listed in the bibliography. It is important to note the basis upon which data are reported for state and local governments:

For state governments, data are for the fiscal year ending in the year carried in the title to the annual publication, e.g., *State Government Finances in 1978* carries data for 46 states with a June 30 fiscal year; for Alabama and Michigan, September 30; for New York, March 31; and for Texas, August 31. For local governments the data is for the fiscal year ending at June 30, 1978, or at any time during the preceding twelve months. This means that for local governments with a fiscal year ending at December 31, 1977, the data would be reported in the 1977–78 series; for school districts that end their fiscal year at August 31, 1977, their data would also be included in the 1977–78 data; for other governmental units, the same rule would apply. Therefore, year-end data or operational data for the fiscal year contained in the reports of the

had jumped to $14.9 billion—$125 per capita. During the Great Depression, capital spending—except for that financed by the federal government—largely dried up. With the onset of World War II, and especially after the entrance of the United States into that war in late 1941, there was a dearth of manpower and materials available for any type of public improvements except those of an emergency character closely related to the war effort.[4]

At the end of World War II, the nation was confronted with the results of a 15-year drought of capital spending, a significant growth in the population, and major relocations from rural to urban centers. Moreover, the pent-up demand for housing, the changing character of transportation, and the shift of manufacturing from multistory to single-story structures with ample open space all combined to produce a huge demand for additional public and private facilities. In response to that demand, accentuated by inflation, the debt of state and local governments increased rapidly during the period 1946–1960.

Data on the trends in outstanding debt are derived primarily from surveys of the Governments Division of the Bureau of the Census published in a number of annual volumes and from the more comprehensive *Census of Governments* published at five-year intervals.[5] The *Flow of Funds* statements rely heavily on updated estimates based upon Bureau of the Census data and on data furnished by the Public Securities Association and *The Bond Buyer*. The two statements are essentially interlocking. The debt of state and local governments in the *Flow of Funds* statements is prepared on a year-end basis and updates (with revisions) the amounts developed by the Bureau of the Census. Occasionally, there are differences which require explanation or admission of discrepancy.[6]

Trends in Total Debt

The *Flow of Funds* data, summarized in Table 1, provide the most comprehensive available picture of outstanding debt of state and local governments. The aggregate amount outstanding increased from $16.1 billion in 1946 to $361.5 billion in 1980. For the 1946–1980 period the compound average annual rate of increase was 9.6 percent. This growth rate corresponded closely to that for the 1946–1970 period (9.9 percent) and for the 1970–1980 period (8.8 percent). When the pollution control debt is deducted, the annual rate of increase for 1970–1980 period drops to 8.1 percent.

Trade debt increased more rapidly during the 1970s than did total credit market instruments—10.8 percent per annum vs. 8.8 percent. This was due to the fact that price increases were quickly reflected in trade debt but slowly affect long-term debt as old debt is retired and superseded by new debt. In like manner, the trend for short-term debt reflects

---

Bureau of the Census do not constitute information for a discrete period. Some of the other financial series of the Bureau of the Census are for discrete periods or dates, as is its employment series.

This fiscal year approach of the Bureau of the Census has made it difficult to establish direct comparisons between such data and data presented in the *Flow of Funds* statements, that compiled by the Public Securities Association, and other reports by the Board of Governors of the Federal Reserve System, the Comptroller of the Currency, and the Federal Deposit Insurance Corporation—all of which tend to report on a calendar year basis.

[4] The 1970 edition of the author's predecessor volume, *Administration of Local Government Debt,* included information commencing at much earlier dates. Those data are of potential interest only to historians and are therefore not included here.

[5] Of some interest here are the holdings of short-maturity debt of state and local governments by commercial banks. For example, as of December 31, 1977, the insured commercial banks held obligations of state and local governments in the amount of $16.8 billion for securities maturing in less than one year. This compared to $18.4 billion one year earlier. See Board of Governors of the Federal Reserve System, Federal Deposit Insurance Corporation, and Office of the Comptroller of the Currency, *Assets and Liabilities: Commercial and Mutual Savings Banks, December 31, 1977. 1977 Report of Income,* p. 14.

[6] A recent entry into the field is the Municipal Securities Rulemaking Board which gathers a limited amount of information in connection with its assessment of fees against underwriters. It has not published any statistics based upon the data received.

Table 1

Debt and Securities of State and Local Governments as of December 31
Selected Years, 1946–1980
Flow of Funds Basis

(amounts in billions of dollars)

Year	Total (2) + (9)	Liabilities of State and Local Governments							Liabilities of Nonfinancial Corporations[1]	Exhibit:	
		Total	Trade Debt	Credit Market Instruments						Total Credit Market Debt (4) + (9)	Total Securities (6) + (9)
				Total	U.S. Govt. Loans	Obligations of State & Local Govts.					
						Total	Long-term	Short-term			
	(1)	(2)	(3)	(4)	(5)	(6)	(7)	(8)	(9)	(10)	(11)
1980	361.5	337.9	17.8	320.1	7.6	312.5	296.7	15.8	23.6	343.7	336.1
1978	308.6	291.0	14.6	276.4	6.5	269.9	257.7	12.2	17.6	294.0	397.6
1976	259.7	250.5	12.1	238.2	7.8	230.3	215.9	14.5	9.2	247.4	239.5
1974	223.5	219.4	10.3	209.2	5.6	203.6	184.8	18.8	4.1	213.3	207.7
1972	189.6	189.0	7.6	181.4	5.5	175.9	160.1	15.8	.6	182.0	176.5
1970	155.6	155.6	6.4	149.2	4.8	144.4	131.1	13.3	—	149.2	144.4
1960	74.5	74.5	2.5	72.0	1.2	70.8	67.3	3.5	—	72.0	70.8
1950	26.2	26.2	1.3	24.9	.6	24.4	23.1	1.3	—	24.9	24.4
1946	16.1	16.1	.8	15.4	.5	14.9	14.6	.3	—	15.4	14.9
Annual Compound Percentage Increase											
1946–1980	9.6	9.4	9.6	9.3	8.3	9.4	9.3	12.4	na	11.1	9.6
1946–1970	9.9	9.9	9.1	9.9	9.9	9.9	9.6	17.1	na	9.9	9.9
1970–1980	8.8	8.1	10.8	7.9	4.7	8.0	8.5	1.7	na	8.7	8.8

Sources: Board of Governors of the Federal Reserve System, *Flow of Funds Accounts, 1946–1975: Annual Total Flows and Year-End Assets and Liabilities* (December 1976), pp. 107–109; *Flow of Funds Accounts, 1968–78: Assets and Liabilities Outstanding* (September 1981), pp. 11, 15.

[1] The amounts reported in this column relate solely to pollution control debt guaranteed by private corporations; they do not include tax-exempt debt issued for other *on behalf of* guarantors, e.g., industrial development debt, and facilities for nongovernmental profit and nonprofit corporations in such fields as hospitals, health facilities, and higher education.

the current price structure. Short-term debt increased very rapidly until the mid-1970s when it reached a peak of about $19 billion, followed by dramatic decreases. However, by 1980 bond market disruptions produced a return to wider use of BANS.

Constant Dollar Trends. When the data are converted to constant dollars, the decrease is all the more dramatic. To illustrate, the *Flow of Funds* data have been adjusted on the basis of the consumer price index with the results presented in Table 2. On a per capita constant dollar basis, the amount of outstanding security debt in 1980 was somewhat below the level which prevailed during the 1972–1980 period. These data are easily subject to misinterpretation. They help to provide a measure of the economic load being carried; however, by deflating debt incurred at earlier dates one tends to obscure the fact that, if such earlier debt were continued in the table at the values when issued, there would be increases—perhaps even more dramatic than those shown in current dollars in Table 2.

As has been noted, the *Flow of Funds* data are developed largely as updates to information secured by the Bureau of the Census in its various surveys of the finances of state and local governments. It is appropriate, therefore, to present the data concerning the growth in outstanding debt as reported by the Bureau of the Census. From Table 3 it is seen that the rates of growth are slightly lower than those reported by the *Flow of Funds* statements, due in part to the timelag. However, this information shows that there has been a similar pattern of growth to that previously outlined.

Table 2

State and Local Government Securities Outstanding as of December 31
Selected Years, 1946–1980
Current and Constant Dollars
Flow of Funds Basis

Year	Total Securities Outstanding (billions)		Civilian Population	Per Capita Security Debt	
	Current Dollars	Constant Dollars[1] 1967 = 100		Current Dollars	Constant Dollars[1] 1967 = 100
	(1)	(2)	(3)	(4)	(5)
1980	336.1	136.1	225.6	1,490	603
1978	287.5	147.2	216.6	1,327	688
1976	239.5	140.5	213.0	1,124	660
1974	207.7	140.8	209.7	990	672
1972	176.5	140.8	206.5	855	682
1970	144.4	124.2	201.7	716	616
1960	70.8	79.8	178.1	398	448
1950	24.4	33.8	150.8	162	224
1946	14.9	25.5	138.3	108	184
Annual Compound Percentage Increase					
1946–1980	9.6	5.1	1.4	8.0	3.6
1946–1970	9.6	6.8	1.6	8.2	5.2
1970–1980	8.8	1.0	1.1	7.6	(.2)

[1] The consumer price index is used as deflator.

Sources: U.S. Bureau of the Census, *Historical Statistics of the United States from Colonial Times until 1970*, pp. 8, 210; *Statistical Abstract of the United States, 1979*, pp. 6, 483; *Current Population Reports* Series p. 25, No. 903 (September, 1981); *Supra.* Table 1.

Table 3

Gross Outstanding Debt of State
and Local Governments
Selected Years, 1946–1980
Bureau of the Census Basis

Year	Amounts (amounts in billions of dollars)			Percentage Distribution	
	Total	State	Local	State	Local
	(1)	(2)	(3)	(4)	(5)
1980	336	122	214	36	64
1978	280	103	177	37	63
1976	241	85	156	35	65
1974	207	72	134	35	65
1972	175	54	121	31	69
1970	144	42	102	29	71
1960	70	19	51	27	73
1950	24	5	19	22	78
1946	16	2	14	14	86

Annual Compound Percentage Increase

1946–1980	9.4	12.9	8.4
1946–1970	9.6	13.5	8.6
1970–1980	8.9	11.3	7.7

Sources: U.S. Bureau of the Census, *Historical Statistics of the United States, Colonial Times to 1970*, pp. 1127, 1130, 1132; *Governmental Finances in 1969–70*, pp. 19, 28; *in 1971–72*, p. 19; *in 1973–74*, p. 28; *in 1975–76*, p. 27; *in 1977–78*, p. 55; *in 1979–80*, p. 55.

NB: For fiscal year basis used by the Bureau of the Census see Appendix F.

State and Local Shares of the Debt

From Table 3 it is noted that there has been a dramatic shift in the respective shares of the state and local governments in the amounts of their total debt outstanding in the years since 1946. Thus, at that time, the state governments accounted for only 14 percent of the total; whereas, in 1980 this had risen to 36 percent. In terms of rates of growth, in each period examined it is noted that the state governments' outstanding debt rose more rapidly than that of the local governments, e.g., 11.3 percent vs. 7.7 percent in the 1970–1980 period.

Of course, a small portion of the growth of state government debt has been in the form of governmental lessee debt issued for local governments and another smaller portion has been due to state issuance of bond-bank types of debt for the benefit of local governments. Yet, it appears that the basic patterns of growth at the state level, even after correction for these factors, show a major rate of increase that exceeds the rate that would apply for local governments on a corrected basis.

Gross and Net Debt

The *Flow of Funds* statements of outstanding debt are concerned only with gross debt, largely because the Board of Governors of the Federal Reserve System focuses upon

Table 4

Outstanding Debt and Debt Offsets of State and Local Governments
Selected Years, 1946–1980
Bureau of the Census Basis

(amounts in billions of dollars)

Year	Total	Long-term Debt				Short-term Debt	
		Total	Debt Offsets	Net Long-term		Amount	As a Percent of Total
				Amount	As a Percent of Total		
	(1)	(2)	(3)	(4)	(5)	(6)	(7)
1980	335.6	322.5	59.5	263.0	82	13.1	3.9
1978	280.4	269.0	43.8	225.2	84	11.4	4.1
1976	240.1	221.3	26.0	195.3	88	18.8	7.8
1974	209.6	190.0	16.0	174.0	92	16.7	7.8
1972	174.5	158.8	11.4	147.4	93	15.7	9.0
1970	143.6	131.4	9.5	121.9	93	12.2	8.5
1960	70.0	66.8	5.2	61.6	92	3.2	4.6
1950	24.1	23.5	na	na	na	.9	.4
1946	15.9	15.7	na	na	na	.2	.1
Annual Compound Percentage Increase							
1946–1980	9.3	9.3	na	na	—	13.1	—
1946–1970	9.6	9.3	na	na	—	18.7	—
1970–1980	8.9	9.4	20.1	8.0	—	0.7	—

Sources: U.S. Bureau of the Census, *Historical Statistics of State and Local Government Finances, 1902–1953,* p. 21; *Government Finances in 1969–70,* pp. 28, 29; *in 1971–72,* pp. 28–29; *in 1973–74,* pp. 28–29; *in 1975–76,* pp. 18, 27; *in 1977–78,* p. 53; *in 1979–80,* pp. 54, 55.
NB: For fiscal year basis used by the Bureau of the Census see Appendix F.

economic and monetary factors. On the other hand, the Bureau of the Census seeks to present information useful in relating outstanding debt to other factors, e.g., revenues and expenditures of the governments. Accordingly, in Table 4, data are presented on both gross and net long-term debt outstanding. In 1960, the first year for which full data are reported, moneys held by state and local governments as offsets to long-term debt amounted to about 8 percent of such debt; by 1980, the offsets were estimated at 18 percent. [These offsets to outstanding debt consist of a combination of debt service funds and various other set-asides.] The increase in these offset funds reduced the annual compound rate of increase in long-term debt during the 1970–1980 period from 9.4 percent to 8.0 percent. However, one of the most important factors in this reduction was the tremendous increase in advance refunding of debt—especially of nonguaranteed debt—and its associated debt reserve funds.

Purposes of Outstanding Long-term Debt

The most recent data available as to the purposes of outstanding long-term debt are from the *1977 Census of Governments;* these are summarized in Table 5. Education accounted for 23.2 percent; utilities, 16.3 percent; and housing and urban renewal, 6.7 percent. Unfortunately, more than a third of the debt is reported in the "Other and unallocable" category.

Table 5

Outstanding Long-term Debt of State and Local Governments, By Purpose 1977

(amounts in billions of dollars)

	Amounts			Percentages of Total		
	Total	State	Local	Total	State	Local
	(1)	(2)	(3)	(4)	(5)	(6)
Total	246.8	87.2	159.6	100.0	100.0	100.0
Education	57.3	19.3	38.0	23.2	22.2	23.8
Highways	19.3	16.7	2.7	7.8	19.1	1.7
Housing & urban renewal	16.5	6.9	9.6	6.7	7.9	6.0
Sewage	7.9	1.7	6.1	3.2	2.0	3.9
Hospitals	6.0	3.3	2.7	2.4	3.7	1.7
Airports	3.4	.3	3.1	1.4	.0	1.9
Parks & recreation	3.2	1.4	1.8	1.3	1.6	1.1
Water transportation & terminals	2.3	.6	1.7	.9	.6	1.1
Utilities	40.2	3.3	36.8	16.3	3.8	23.1
Electric power	18.0	3.2	14.8	7.3	3.7	9.3
Water supply	16.9	.1	16.8	6.8	.2	10.5
Transit	5.0	—	5.0	2.0	—	3.1
Gas	.3	—	.3	.1	—	.2
Other & unallocable	90.8	33.7	57.1	36.8	38.7	35.8

Source: U.S. Bureau of the Census, *1977 Census of Government,* Vol. 4, No. 5, p. 35.
NB: For fiscal year basis used by the Bureau of the Census see Appendix F.

This robs the remainder of the data of a part of its validity inasmuch as a full distribution would likely affect the reported categories. Moreover such important segments as housing and redevelopment are not separately identified.

For state governments, the largest identifiable functions for outstanding debt are education and highways; at the local level of government, it is education and utilities.

Short-term Debt

Trends in the amounts of short-term debt outstanding of state and local governments are shown in Table 6—at December 31 in the *Flow of Funds* statement and at the fiscal year-end by the Bureau of the Census. The *Flow of Funds* shows that the amounts outstanding increased from $2.4 billion in 1957 to a peak of $18.9 billion in 1975—a 12.1 percent compound annual growth; in Bureau of the Census data, the increase was from $2.2 billion to $19.8 billion—13.0 percent.

With the crisis in New York City in 1975, there was a strong shift in the policies of the State of New York and its local governments away from short-term debt, bringing a decrease from $9.0 billion in 1975 to $2.8 billion in 1980. The ratios of short-term debt to total debt in New York decreased from more than 20 percent in the mid-1970s to less than 5 percent in 1980.

For the other states, their local governments, and the District of Columbia, the level has rarely reached as much as 5 percent of total debt outstanding and in 1980 stood at 4.3 percent. Those governments also decreased their reliance upon short-term debt from $10.8 billion in 1975 to $8.0 billion in 1978 but increased to $10.3 billion in 1980.

In constant dollars, using the consumer price index as a deflator, the peak in outstanding short-term debt was in the $12/$13 billion range in the mid-1970s. By 1980 this had decreased to less than half that level.

Table 6

Outstanding Short-term Debt of State and Local Governments as of Year End Selected Years, 1957–1980

(amounts in billions of dollars)

Year	Current Dollars				Constant Dollars[1]	
	Flow of Funds	Bureau of the Census			Flow of Funds	Bureau of the Census
		Total	New York[2]	All Other		
	(1)	(2)	(3)	(4)	(5)	(6)
1980	15.8	13.1	2.8	10.3	6.4	5.3
1978	12.2	11.4	3.4	8.0	6.3	5.8
1976	14.5	18.8	8.3	10.5	8.5	11.0
1975	18.9	19.8	9.0	10.8	11.7	12.3
1974	18.8	16.7	7.6	9.1	12.7	11.3
1972	15.8	16.1	7.5	8.6	12.6	12.8
1967	8.0	7.0	2.2	4.8	8.0	7.0
1962	3.7	3.7	.9	2.8	4.1	4.1
1957	2.4	2.2	.6	1.6	2.8	2.6
Annual Compound Percentage Increase						
1957–1980	8.5	8.1	6.9	8.4	6.6	3.5
1957–1975	12.1	13.0	16.2	11.2	8.3	9.0
1975–1980	(3.6)	(8.6)	(26.3)	(1.0)	(12.8)	(18.3)

[1] The consumer price index is used as the deflator, 1967 = 100.

[2] State and local governments in the State of New York.

Sources: Board of Governors of the Federal Reserve System, *Flow of Funds Accounts 1946–1975: Annual Total Flows and Year-End Assets and Liabilities* (December 1976), pp. 107–109; *Flow of Funds Accounts 1968–1978: Assets and Liabilities Outstanding* (September 1981), p. 45; p. 13; U.S. Bureau of the Census, *Governmental Finances in 1972–73*, p. 19; *in 1973–74*, pp. 42–43; *in 1974–75*, pp. 57–58; *in 1975–76*, pp. 58–59; *in 1977–78*, pp. 53, 58; *in 1979–1980*, pp. 53, 58; *1977 Census of Governments*, V. 6, No. 4, pp. 72, 105.

NB: For fiscal year basis used by the Bureau of the Census see Appendix F.

Security Pledged

Periodically, the Bureau of the Census presents estimates of the amounts of outstanding state and local government debt classified on the basis of security pledged for the debt, i.e., on the basis of either full faith and credit or nonguaranteed debt. Data for 1957 and 1980 are summarized by level of government and by type of local government in Table 7. At the state government level, there has been only a modest change in the percentage of full-faith-and-credit debt outstanding—down from 48.1 percent in 1957 to 41.2 percent in 1980. On the other hand, at the local level there has been a dramatic decrease in the percentage of full-faith-and-credit debt, from 70.0 percent to 49.6 percent.

Expressed in other terms, the rate of growth of full-faith-and-credit debt at the local level during the 23 years was at an average of 6.0 percent compounded. This compares to a growth in nonguaranteed debt at the rate of 10.1 percent during the same period. Within the local government category, it is noted that the greatest amount of nonguaranteed debt is now in special districts; however in terms of the rate of growth the counties have now outstripped both municipalities and special districts. These changes occured at a time when state debt was growing more rapidly than local debt.

Table 7

Outstanding Long-term Debt of State and Local Governments by Security Pledged and Level of Government 1957 and 1980 Bureau of the Census Basis

(amounts in billions of dollars)

	State Govern- ments	Local Governments Total	Munici- palities	Special Dis- tricts	School Dis- tricts	Counties	Townships
	(1)	(2)	(3)	(4)	(5)	(6)	(7)
Total							
Amounts: 1980	119.8	202.6	82.3	55.9	29.0	31.5	3.9
1957	13.5	37.3	18.2	6.0	8.9	3.4	.9
Annual Compound Percentage Increase	10.0	7.6	6.8	10.2	5.3	10.9	6.6
Full-Faith-and-Credit							
Amounts: 1980	49.4	100.4	39.6	10.4	29.0	18.0	3.5
1957	6.5	26.1	12.3	1.2	8.9	2.9	.8
Annual Compound Percentage Increase	9.2	6.0	5.2	9.8	5.4	8.3	6.6
Nonguaranteed							
Amounts: 1980	70.5	102.2	42.8	45.5	—	13.5	.4
1957	7.0	11.2	5.8	4.8	—	.5	.1
Annual Compound Percentage Increase	10.6	10.1	9.1	10.3	—	15.4	6.2
Full-Faith-and-Credit as Percentage of Total							
1980	41.2	49.6	48.1	18.6	100.0	57.1	89.7
1957	48.1	70.0	67.9	20.0	100.0	85.3	87.5

Sources: Bureau of the Census, *Census of Governments, 1957,* Vol. 3, No. 5, p. 24; *Governmental Finances in 1979–80,* pp. 53, 64.
NB: For fiscal year basis used by the Bureau of the Census see Appendix F.

Distribution of Debt Among Local Governments

From Table 7, the differential rates of growth of total debt among the different types of local governments during the 23-year period can also be observed. Thus, it is noted that the rates of growth for special districts and counties have been significantly greater than for the other categories. Surprisingly, the school districts grew at the lowest rate; however, their rate of increase in debt is due to more intensive use of governmental lessee debt in a number of states.

DEBT SERVICE COSTS AND REVENUES FROM OWN SOURCES

Table 8 presents information for selected years on revenues from own sources and presumptive debt service costs. The Bureau of the Census reports interest as an item of expense and the amounts of long-term securities retired by state and local governments.

Table 8

Revenues from Own Sources and Estimated Debt Service Payments
State and Local Governments
Selected Years, 1960–1980
Bureau of the Census Basis

(amounts in billions of dollars)

Year	Interest on Debt	Long-term Debt Retired	Total Debt Service (1) + (2)	Total Revenues from Own Sources[1]	Debt Service as a Percent of Revenues from Own Sources[1] (3) ÷ (4)
	(1)	(2)	(3)	(4)	(5)
1980	17.6	17.4	35.0	321.7	10.9
1978	14.0	16.7	30.7	263.6	11.6
1976	11.7	11.3	23.0	213.2	10.8
1974	8.8	10.0	18.8	175.2	10.7
1972	6.9	8.2	15.1	142.9	10.6
1970	5.1	7.0	12.1	115.5	10.5
1965	3.0	5.0	8.0	76.7	10.4
1960	2.0	3.5	5.5	53.3	10.3
Annual Compound Percentage Increase					
1960–1980	11.5	8.3	9.7	8.4	
1960–1970	9.8	7.2	8.2	8.0	
1970–1980	13.2	9.5	11.2	10.8	

[1] This statement of revenues from own sources excludes revenues of liquor stores and trust funds.
Sources: U.S. Bureau of the Census, *Historical Statistics of the United States, Colonial Times to 1970*, p. 1125; *Statistical Abstract of the United States, 1948*, pp. 378, 380, 390; *1962*, p. 419; *1966*, pp. 422–423; *Governmental Finances in 1972–73*, pp. 18–19; *in 1977–78*, p. 16; *in 1979–80*, p. 16.
NB: For fiscal year basis used by the Bureau of the Census see Appendix F.

These cannot be fully reconciled with the amounts of debt outstanding when adjusted from one year to the next by adding new debt issued and subtracting the debt retired; however, for the purpose of establishing general relationships, the data is the best available.

During the years 1970–1980, the compound average annual rate of increase in revenues of state and local governments from their own sources amounted to 10.8 percent. During this same period, the estimated debt service rose at a rate of 11.2 percent. As a result, debt service as a percent of revenues from own sources increased from 10.5 percent in 1970 to 10.9 percent in 1980.

These relationships are distorted by the significant increase in *on behalf of* debt. The moneys received as revenues in relation to such debt are almost precisely equal to the debt service. As this element of debt service has increased in proportion to the total, the relationships between revenues from own sources and debt service requirements have been distorted.

DEBT ISSUED

This portion of the chapter is devoted to the presentation of information concerning the long-term debt issued in selected recent years for which information is available. The principal topics explored are (1) the numbers, sizes, and aggregate amounts of debt issued;

(2) the purposes of such debt; (3) the type of governmental issuer; (4) method of sale, i.e., competitive vs. negotiated; and (5) security pledged for new long-term debt.

On a national basis, annual statistics concerning the amounts of debt issued by state and local governments from 1960 through 1980 are derived from three basic sources: *The Bond Buyer;* the Bureau of the Census; and the Public Securities Association (formed from the Investment Bankers Association of America) which gathered data concerning municipal bonds prior to the separation of the public securities group from the general investment group.

Unfortunately, the different sources gather data for different fiscal periods and through different information channels. This process produces results which are sometimes easily reconciled as to the probable reasons for the differences. In other years, the differences are so great as to leave open to question just which source or trend line offers the best view of the manner in which gross sales are changing.

Long-term Debt

Table 9 shows the amounts of long-term debt issued for selected years, 1960–1980, as reported by the Bureau of the Census, *The Bond Buyer,* and the Public Securities Association. In the earlier years there was considerable difference between the three sources; for

Table 9

Long-term Debt Issued by State and Local Governments
Selected Years, 1960–1980

(amounts in billions of dollars)

Year	Total Debt Issued			Refunding Debt		New Issue Debt	
	Bureau of the Census	*The Bond Buyer*	Public Securities Association	*The Bond Buyer*	Public Securities Association	*The Bond Buyer*	Public Securities Association
	(1)	(2)	(3)	(4)	(5)	(6)	(7)
1980	42.3	47.1	47.8	1.6	1.8	45.5	46.0
1978	40.0	46.2	48.4	9.3	11.9	36.6	36.6
1976	31.7	33.8	35.3	3.5	3.2	30.3	32.1
1974	23.2	22.8	24.3	.6	.8	22.2	23.5
1972	21.9	22.9	23.6	1.6	1.6	21.3	22.0
1970	12.8	17.8	18.1	.1	.2	17.7	18.0
1965	11.2	11.1	11.1	na	na	na	na
1960	8.0	7.2	7.1	.1	.1	7.1	7.0
Annual Compound Percentage Increase							
1960–1980	8.7	9.8	10.0	na	na	9.7	9.9
1960–1970	4.8	9.5	9.8	na	na	9.6	9.9
1970–1980	12.7	10.2	10.2	na	na	9.9	9.8

Sources: U.S. Bureau of the Census, *Governmental Finances in 1972–73,* p. 19; in *1976–77,* p. 14; *in 1977–78,* p. 16; *in 1979–80,* p. 16; Lennox L. Moak, *Administration of Local Government Debt,* p. 95; The Bond Buyer, *Statistics on State and Local Government Finances,* Vol. 10, p. 5; Vol. 17, p. 5; *The Weekly Bond Buyer* Vol. 227, No. 4630 (January 11, 1982), p. 19; Public Securities Association, *Municipal Market Developments,* February 28, 1975, Table 1; April 21, 1977, Table 1; March 28, 1978, Table 1; February 11, 1981, Table 1; Investment Bankers Association, *Municipal Bulletin,* No. 60, February, 1973, Table 1.

NB. *The Bond Buyer* and Public Securities Association data are on a calendar year basis; the Bureau of the Census data are on the basis of the fiscal years of governments involved as set forth in Appendix F to this volume.

1976 there is substantial agreement; however, for 1980 there is a broad difference between the Bureau of the Census and the other two—doubtless due largely to the differences in reporting dates.

Only for recent years does the Bureau of the Census segregate refunding bonds from the total bonds issued. Refunding issues were of relatively minor importance until the heyday of advance refunding in the mid- to late-1970s, when they exploded from 3 percent of total long-term debt issued in 1974 to about 20 percent in 1977 and 1978. In 1980 advance refundings were again low due both to the new arbitrage rules and to the generally higher levels of interest costs.

The percentage rates of growth of debt issued during the 1970–1980 period were recorded at 12.7 by the Bureau of the Census, 10.2 by *The Bond Buyer,* and 10.2 by the Public Securities Association. On a net basis, after excluding refunding debt, the percentage rates were 9.9 and 9.8, respectively, for *The Bond Buyer* and the Public Securities Association.

In constant dollar terms there was a decrease in the amount of new issue debt when the *Engineering News Record* Construction Price Index is used as a deflator.[7] On this basis, the $46 billion of new issue debt issued in 1980 would purchase only about $17 billion of construction in place compared to the $18 billion for 1970. If one takes into account that in 1980 the *on behalf of* debt accounted for a much greater proportion of total new issue debt than in 1970, it is found that the constant dollar new issue debt proceeds available for conventional public investments by state and local governments decreased substantially. [The use of the *Engineering News Record* Building Cost Index would produce a somewhat higher constant dollar amount for 1980 than 1970 in terms of new issue debt; however, it is believed that the greatest percentage of new issue debt proceeds of local governments for their own facilities goes to items classified as *construction* rather than *buildings* by the *Engineering News Record.*]

The Purposes of Debt Issued. A study of Table 10 leads to some very significant conclusions concerning the trends in the purposes for which debt is issued. The data from the Public Securities Association [and its predecessor agencies] is particularly revealing as to changes between 1970 and 1980:

	1970	1980	(billions of dollars) Increase (Decrease)	
			Amount	Annual Compound Percentage Increase
Education	5.0	4.5	(.5)	(1.0)
Transportation	3.2	2.6	(.6)	(2.1)
Utilities and conservation excluding electric & gas	3.5	5.6	2.1	4.8
Recreation and general public services	.4	1.4	1.4	13.3
Other and unclassified	5.3	7.1	1.8	3.0
Subtotal general purpose	17.4	21.2	4.8	2.0
Primarily *on behalf of* debt				
Housing	.5	15.1	14.6	40.6
Hospitals & health	na	3.5	3.5	na
Industrial aid	.1	5.0	4.9	49.3
Electric & gas	na	3.4	3.4	na
Subtotal	.6	27.0	26.4	49.0
Total	18.0	46.0	28.0	9.8

[7] See various issues of *Engineering News Record* for source data.

Table 10

The Purposes of Long-term Debt Issued by State and Local Governments
Selected Years, 1970–1980

(amounts in billions of dollars)

	1980	1978	1976	1974	1972	1970
As Reported by The Bond Buyer						
Total	47.1	46.2	33.8	22.8	22.9	17.7
Schools	4.8	6.2	5.2	4.9	5.3	5.0
Water and sewer	3.5	4.5	3.3	2.1	2.8	2.3
Highway, bridge & tunnel	1.1	1.9	1.6	1.0	2.1	1.5
Gas & electric	4.8	6.0	4.5	1.5	nr	nr
Hospitals	3.6	3.1	2.7	1.3	nr	nr
Industrial	1.5	.6	.4	.3	.5	.1
Pollution control	1.4	3.5	2.7	2.2	nr	nr
Housing	14.3	—	—	.5	1.0	.1
Veteran's aid	—	1.2	.6	.7	.3	.2
Other	10.9	19.3	13.0	8.4	11.0	8.6
As Reported by The Public Securities Association:[1] *New capital only*						
Total	46.0	37.6	32.1	23.5	22.1	18.0
Education	4.5	5.0	4.9	4.7	5.0	5.0
Transportation	2.6	3.6	2.6	1.7	3.0	3.2
Roads & bridges	1.1	1.3	1.6	.8	1.7	1.5
Ports & airports	.9	1.4	.7	.3	.5	.7
Other	.7	.6	.3	.7	.8	.9
Utilities & conservation	8.0	9.0	9.4	5.6	4.7	3.5
Pollution control	.6	.5	2.3	1.7	.6	na
Water & sewer	2.9	3.3	2.9	2.0	2.4	2.2
Electric & gas	3.4	4.5	na	na	na	na
Other	1.1	.9	4.3	1.9	1.6	1.2
Public housing	15.1	5.7	2.7	1.7	1.9	.5
Hospitals	3.5	2.3	2.3	.8	.5	na
Industrial aid—general	1.5	.8	.5	.5	.3	.1
Industrial aid—pollution control	2.2	2.7	—[2]	—[2]	—[2]	na
Public services	.8	.5	.4	.2	.5	.4
Recreation	.6	.7	na	na	na	na
Other classified & unclassified	7.1	7.3	9.3	8.3	6.2	5.3

[1] Data prior to 1975 are from predecessor organization, the Investment Bankers Association.
[2] Under utilities & conservation.
Sources: The Bond Buyer, *Statistics on State and Local Government Finance,* Vol. 16 (April 1976), p. 8; vol. 18 (June 1980), p. 8. Public Securities Association, *Municipal Market Developments,* Table 4 of issues dated February 28, 1975, April 21, 1977, March 29, 1978, February 11, 1981. Investment Bankers Association, *Municipal Bulletin,* Table 2 of Nos. 56 and 60.

These data clearly show that in the conventional functional areas the increase in borrowing has been at a very slow compound growth rate of 2.0 percent per annum as contrasted with a 49.0 percent rate of increase for the *on behalf of* financing, with the electric and gas utilities included in this group. The 1981 data of *The Bond Buyer* indicates that these trends have continued; the amounts of housing debt decreased sharply but this was largely offset by increases in electric utility financing.

Debt Issues: Number and Size. The numbers of issues of long-term debt for selected years in the 1970–1980 period as reported by *The Bond Buyer* and the Public Securities Association are shown in Table 11. Although the two sources differ, there was a decrease in the number of issues sold between 1960 and 1970. However, the numbers for recent years are considerably above those of the mid-1970s, especially in the data of the Public Securities Association—up from 4,814 in 1974 to 5,389 in 1980.

Table 11

Number and Size of Long-term Debt Sales
Selected Years 1960–1980

Year	The Bond Buyer	Public Securities Association				
		Total	Size of Issues (in millions of dollars)			
			Over 100	25–99	1–24	Under 1
	(1)	(2)	(3)	(4)	(5)	(6)
1980	5,550	5,389	94	257	2,968	1,964
1978	5,061	5,695	70	338	3,058	2,267
1976	4,768	4,920	44	256	2,794	1,826
1974	4,287	4,814	27	165	2,171	2,451
1972	5,103	4,740	na	na	na	na
1970	4,701	4,336	na	na	na	na
1960	6,529	6,414	na	na	na	na

Sources: *The Weekly Bond Buyer,* January 15, 1979, p. 36; *The Daily Bond Buyer,* January 9, 1980, p. 14. The Bond Buyer, *Statistics on State and Local Government Finance,* Vol. 16 (June 1978), p. 7; Vol. 5 (April 1957), p. 5. Public Securities Association, *Statistical Yearbook: Municipal Securities Data Base: The New Issue Market in 1978,* Table H-3; *Municipal Market Developments,* February 11, 1981, Table 6B. Investment Bankers Association of America, *Statistical Bulletin,* No. 6, p. 4; No. 18, p. 4; No. 30, p. 2; No. 60 (February 1973), p. 1.

The only data concerning size of issues is that of the Public Securities Association. As might be expected, in part due to inflation, the number of issues of over $100 million has increased dramatically during the 1974–1980 period—up from 27 to 94. Large increases were also noted in the $25–$99 million group, up from 165 to 257; and the number of issues in the $1.0–$24.9 million range increased about 37 percent. Only those issues of less than $1 million decreased.

Type of Sale. Commencing in 1973 *The Bond Buyer* has tabulated the amounts of long-term loans issued by competitive vs. negotiated sales. In dollar value the record may be summarized as follows:[8]

Year	Amounts (billions)			Percentage of Total	
	Total	Competitive	Negotiated	Competitive	Negotiated
1980	$47.1	$19.5	$30.8	41.4	58.6
1978	46.2	21.5	24.7	46.5	53.5
1976	33.8	19.5	14.3	57.6	42.4
1974	22.8	16.6	6.3	72.5	27.5

The increase in the percentage of volume at negotiated sale from 27.5 in 1974 to 58.6 in 1980 represents a substantial shift from competitive to negotiated sales.

[8] The Bond Buyer, *Statistics on State and Local Government Finance,* Vol. 19, p. 5.

In terms of the dollar amounts of long-term bonds issued, the relative importance of the state governments has grown rapidly during the 1970s. In 1970 the Bureau of the Census reported that state governments accounted for less than one third—only $3.9 billion of the $12.9 billion sold. By 1978 this had risen to 42.5 percent although by 1980 the percentage dropped to 38.8. Within the local government group, municipalities accounted for just under half of the amounts issued with the remainder being distributed among other units of local government, predominantly the special districts and authorities.[9]

Table 12

Security Pledged for Debt Issued by State and Local Governments
Selected Years, 1970–1980

| (amounts in billions of dollars) | | | | |
	1980	1978	1976	1970	Annual Compound Percentage Increase 1970–80
Amounts					
Public Securities Association					
Total	47.8	48.4	35.1	18.0	10.3
General Obligation	12.9	17.8	18.0	11.9	.8
Revenue	33.9	30.6	17.1	6.1	18.7
The Bond Buyer					
Total	47.3	46.2	33.8	17.8	10.3
General Obligation	12.3	17.9	16.9	11.8	.4
Revenue	30.8	28.3	16.9	6.0	17.8
Bureau of the Census					
State Governments only	16.4	17.0	13.9	3.9	15.4
Full-Faith-and-Credit	4.5	5.8	6.4	2.5	6.1
Nonguaranteed	12.0	11.2	7.5	1.4	24.0
Percentage Distribution					
Public Securities Association					
General Obligation	29.1	36.7	51.3	66.1	
Revenue	70.9	63.3	48.7	33.9	
The Bond Buyer					
General Obligation	34.7	38.7	50.0	66.3	
Revenue	65.3	61.3	50.0	33.7	
Bureau of The Census					
State Governments only					
Full-Faith-and-Credit	29.1	34.1	46.0	64.1	
Nonguaranteed	72.9	65.9	54.0	35.9	

Sources: U.S. Bureau of the Census, *State Government Finances; in 1976*, p. 7; *in 1978*, p. 9; *in 1980*, p. 9. *Statistical Abstract of the United States, 1978*, p. 301. *The Weekly Bond Buyer*, Vol. 227, No. 4630 (January 11, 1982), p. 19; Public Securities Association, *Municipal Market Developments*, 1979, and Moak, February 11, 1981, Tables 2A and 2B.

NB: Data of the Public Securities Association and *The Bond Buyer* are on a calendar year basis; Bureau of the Census data are on a fiscal year basis for individual governments (see Appendix F).

---

[9] U.S. Bureau of the Census, *Governmental Finances in 1972–73*, p. 19; *in 1979–80*, p. 53; *County Government Finances in 1972–73*, p. 8; *City Government Finances in 1962–73*, p. 8; *Finances of Public School Systems in 1977–78*, p. 12; *1977 Census of Governments*, Vol. 3, No. 3, p. 9.

For 1978 the Public Securities Association reported that of new capital debt issued the state governments accounted for $5.4 billion (excluding statutory authorities)—14.4 percent of the total. Issues by other units of government were as follows: Counties, $3.0 billion (8.0 percent); municipalities, $7.9 billion (21.1 percent); school districts, $2.6 billion (7.0 percent); special districts, $1.7 billion (4.5 percent); and statutory authorities, both state and local, $16.7 billion (44.7 percent).[10]

Security Pledged. Table 12 presents data on the security pledged in respect to the debt issued by state and local governments for selected years, 1970–1980. Data from both the Public Securities Association and *The Bond Buyer* show that although there was an increase in general obligation debt issued between 1970 and 1980, the sharp decrease in 1980 brought the totals back close to the amounts issued in 1970. Substantially the full increase of 1980 over 1970 was in the revenue bond field—an annual rate of increase in the 17–18 percent range. The result was that, whereas general obligation debt accounted for about two-thirds of the money value of new issues in 1970, it had decreased to less than one-third by 1980. Bureau of the Census data tended to confirm these reported trends.

Short-term Debt

The trends in the amounts of short-term debt outstanding were discussed earlier in this chapter. Table 13 presents data concerning the amounts of short-term debt issued in

Table 13

Short-term Debt Issued by State and Local Governments
1970–1980

(amounts in billions of dollars)

Year	*The Bond Buyer* Data					Public Securities Association Data
	Total	Public Housing Authorities	Renewal Project Notes	All Other Amount	All Other Percent	
	(1)	(2)	(3)	(4)	(5)	(6)
1980	26.5	15.6	.4	10.5	40	27.7
1979	20.6	9.7	.6	10.0	48	21.7
1978	21.6	9.1	1.1	11.5	53	21.4
1977	21.3	9.2	1.6	10.5	49	24.8
1976	21.9	8.1	2.8	11.0	50	21.9
1975	29.0	7.3	4.1	17.6	61	29.0
1974	29.0	6.8	4.6	17.6	61	29.5
1973	24.7	6.6	4.4	13.6	55	24.7
1972	25.2	6.5	4.2	14.1	56	25.3
1971	26.3	6.0	4.0	16.3	62	26.3
1970	17.9	4.6	3.8	5.5	31	17.8
Annual Compound Percentage Increase 1970–1980	4.0	13.0	(25.2)	6.7	na	4.5

Sources: *The Bond Buyer, Statistics of State and Local Government Finance,* Vol. 17 (June 1979), p. 5. *The Weekly Bond Buyer,* Vol. 22, No. 4630 (January 11, 1980) p. 19. Public Securities Association, *Statistical Yearbook: Municipal Securities Data Base: The New Issue Market in 1978,* Tables V-1, *Municipal Market Developments,* February 28, 1975, Table 1; March 19, 1978, Table 1; February 11, 1981, Table 1.

[10] Public Securities Association. *Statistical Yearbook: Municipal Securities Data Base: The New Issue Market in 1978,* Tables V-1. V-4, V-5.

recent years reported by *The Bond Buyer* and the Public Securities Association. That table shows a moderate increase for the period as a whole, rising from $17.9 billion in 1970 to $26.5 billion in 1980. Then in 1981 *The Bond Buyer* reported a further increase to $34.3 billion, thereby exceeding the levels in the mid 1970s when the State of New York and the City of New York were such heavy borrowers in the short-term market.

During the 1970–1980 period there was a decrease in the short-term borrowing for urban renewal purposes as the community development grant program superseded the previous loan and the grant program of the federal government for urban renewal purposes. On the other hand, the amounts of short-term loans for public housing continued to increase—to $15.6 billion in 1980 and to $20.1 billion in 1981.

The "all other" category comprehends all the RANS, TANS, and BANS as well as the other borrowings by state and local governments that came to the attention of *The Bond Buyer* and the Public Securities Association; however, it probably includes few of the short-term loans negotiated by state and local governments with commercial banks or other private placements. For 1980 *The Bond Buyer* reported $10.5 billion and for 1981 $14 billion in the "all other" category of short-term loans known to it.

CONCLUSIONS

From the materials presented, it is apparent that the outstanding state and local government debt in current dollars continued to increase at a substantial rate during the 1970s. Yet considerable care must be exercised in evaluating the raw data presented due to the factors that tend to distort the meaning of the information:

1. Population has continued to increase at a moderate rate; shifts in population between rural and urban areas have been rather limited but population density within urban areas has continued to become less, and this spreading has produced requirements for additional facilities. Regional shifts impose substantial added requirements in the areas to which population is rapidly shifting.

2. Inflation tends to cause most of the raw data to produce distortions that cannot easily be corrected except through application of appropriate deflators to produce something approaching the constant dollar concept.

3. Large amounts of the additional debt issued in the mid- and late-1970s was for advance refunding of previously issued debt. The patterns of defeasing preexisting bond issues differed, with some requiring less than the par amount of the debt being refunded and other patterns interjecting refunding debt equal to twice the debt it replaced—so that for a period of time there were three outstanding dollars of debt for the one original dollar.

4. In several important fields public policy resulted in the extension of tax-free debt benefits to a number of activities which were not under the management and control of the state and local governments involved. Generally, this type of debt is known as *on behalf of* debt. There are some data concerning the amounts issued but almost no data as to the amounts of such debt that are outstanding in recent years.

5. Information sources upon which the research must depend in relation to state and local government debt generally flows from the Bureau of the Census, from trade associations, or from *The Bond Buyer*. Considerable discrepancy exists in the sources upon which these rely and, in the case of the Bureau of the Census, the reporting dates do not bring information onto a comparable, at-date basis. These differences lead to some lack of clarity as to the actual picture. The agency that is in the best position to require the submission of information on a comprehensive, accurate, and timely basis is the Municipal Securities Rulemaking Board, and it still has under consideration the matter of the extent to which it should supplement or supplant some of the existing data sources.

6. The very high interest rates commencing in 1980 and extending generally to the completion of this book early in 1982 have resulted in some lessening of the average life of many bond issues. Also, a noticeable shift to short-term debt by use of BANS, RANS, and TANS, as well as the introduction of commercial paper for issues of municipal debt, have become new characteristics of the market.

Chapter 2
STATE AND LOCAL GOVERNMENT DEBT AND THE ECONOMY

State and local government finance has a significant, albeit limited, role in the national economy. It follows that the debt element of such finance also has a significant, but limited, role in that economy. Both are recognized as elements worthy of consideration by the principal federal agencies concerned with different aspects of national development: The Board of Governors of the Federal Reserve System, the Treasury Department, the Department of Commerce, and the Congress. The debt of state and local governments also has significance to economic activity levels, although the identification and quantification of such impacts are difficult. If the Reagan Administration's "new federalism" program is substantially adopted the role of the state and local governments will be markedly increased in importance.

RELATIONSHIP TO OTHER ECONOMIC INDICATORS

During the period 1960–80 the gross national product increased at a compound annual rate of 8.6 percent compared to a 7.8 percent compound annual rate for the financial liabilities of the general funds of state and local governments as reflected in Table 14. A comparison between the rates of change for the federal government and the state and local governments for the 1960s shows a federal increase of 2.7 percent versus 7.6 percent; however, in the 1970s, the federal government led state and local governments—9.4 versus 8.0 percent.

Expressed in other terms, in 1960 and again in 1970, the financial liabilities of the general funds of state and local governments amounted to almost five percent of the aggregate financial liabilities outstanding in the national economy. By 1980 this percentage had decreased to 3.8.

These indicators confirm other data that state and local governments have not been expanding their debt at a rate of growth comparable to the expansion of the general economy expressed in current dollars. If the *on behalf of* debt could be identified and netted out from the total state and local government debt, it would be found that the genuine liabilities of these governments have increased at a significantly slower rate than the remainder of the economy. If all data could be adjusted to a constant dollar basis, the liability debt of state and local governments in their general funds (*Flow of Funds* concept), probably showed a net decrease during the 1970s.

A comparison between the growth rates of state and local government liabilities and those of the United States Government in the period 1960–1970 shows a much higher rate of growth for state and local governments (7.6 percent per year) than for the U.S. Government (2.7 percent per year). On the other hand, from 1970 to 1980 the federal government's debt increased 9.4 percent compared to 8.0 percent for state and local governments.

A comparison of the financial liabilities of state and local government with the gross national product (GNP) in selected years shows the following:

Table 14

Financial Liabilities of Major Economic Sectors as of December 31, Selected Years, 1960–1980

(amounts in billions of dollars)

	1980	1978	1976	1974	1972	1970	1960	Annual Compound Percentage Increase 1970–1980	Annual Compound Percentage Increase 1960–1970
Total	8,934	7,187	5,663	4,643	3,964	3,209	1,529	10.8	7.7
State and Local Government General Funds	338	291	250	220	189	156	75	8.0	7.6
Percent of total	*3.8*	*4.1*	*4.4*	*4.7*	*4.8*	*4.9*	*4.9*		
Other Sectors	8,576	6,896	5,413	4,423	3,775	3,053	1,454	10.9	7.7
Financial	3,919	3,128	2,481	2,027	1,757	1,376	608	11.0	8.5
Nonfinancial	3,349	2,686	2,064	1,768	1,464	1,192	519	10.9	8.7
U.S. Government	848	719	591	421	393	345	264	9.4	2.7
Foreign	470	363	278	208	162	138	64	13.0	8.0

Sources: Board of Governors of the Federal Reserve System, *Flow of Funds Accounts, 1946–1975, Annual Flows & Year-End Liabilities*, pp. 98–121; *Flow of Funds Accounts: Assets and Liabilities Outstanding, 1957–1981* (September 1981), pp. 4–25.

(amounts in billions of dollars)			
	Gross National Product	Liabilities of State and Local Governments	
		Amount	As a Percent of GNP
1980	2,626	338	12.9
1978	2,108	296	14.0
1970	982	156	15.9
1960	506	75	14.8
1950	286	26	9.1

The relatively low ratio of state and local government liabilities to the GNP in 1950 was a reflection of the very low level of debt outstanding for these governments at the end of World War II. By 1960, however, this liability debt had reached 14.8 percent of GNP and by 1970 rose to 15.9 percent. By 1980, it decreased to 12.9 percent of GNP. To some extent this decrease is illusion: The GNP is expressed in current dollars and fully reflects inflation, while state and local debt outstanding represents an accumulation from two or three decades. On the other hand, the demand on the economy to support the debt has been marginally reduced.

IMPORTANCE OF STATE AND LOCAL GOVERNMENT DEBT IN THE NATIONAL ECONOMY[1]

Aside from meeting their current cash requirements, the cumulative effect of state and local government debt on the national economy is substantial: First, when issued, the debt can either support the current fiscal policy objectives of the federal government or act partially to thwart them; secondly, state and local securities constitute significant financial assets in portfolios of private institutions and individuals.

When state and local governments borrow and spend for their own account, they have an effect on the level of economic activity. The economic impact of spending financed from borrowing depends on which type of investor buys the bonds. If nonbank investors acquire municipal debt, the total supply of money in the economy remains unchanged. Ownership of the money simply shifts from the lenders to the borrower governments. Although the net economic impact on the national economy may be limited when nonbank lenders are involved, it is essential to recognize the effect of the debt on the economy of the state or the locality. In many situations, the debt instrument is a device by which capital is attracted to states and communities with acute needs for new capital infusion. The effects of this new capital will produce both short-term and long-term economic consequences quite different from borrowing of a similar amount of money by a government situated in a region with surplus capital available. And, if state and local government debt is purchased by commercial banks, the money supply is expanded immediately by the amount of the purchase and the ultimate economic impact of such actions on a cumulative basis can be substantial.

Nonbank Investors

Nonbank investors give up money in exchange for financial assets when they purchase municipal bonds. Although they may later reconvert these bonds to money in the secondary

---

[1] This portion of Chapter 2 is an update and revision of materials originally prepared in 1970 by William F. Statts, formerly Secretary, Federal Reserve Bank of Philadelphia, and appearing in Lennox L. Moak, *Administration of Local Government Debt*, pp. 28–36. The author takes full responsibility for the restatement of the material.

market, they forego spending or alternative investment opportunities for the period the money is invested in municipal bonds. Hence, the money that nonbank investors channel into municipal securities represents savings or the conversion from other assets.

On the other side of the transaction, governmental borrowers give pledges against the future in the form of promises to pay from future income. When proceeds of bond sales are spent on currently produced goods and services, the gross national product is increased. Of course, the same effect on the GNP would be obtained if other spenders borrowed such funds from nonbank investors.

The loans to state and local governments by nonbank investors are generally not inflationary because they produce no increase in the nation's money supply. Ownership of money is simply transferred from private to governmental entities. When proceeds are spent, the money is shifted back to the private sector. Thus, the total of the private holdings of money (except for interim interest) is the same after the borrowing and spending as it was before these transactions occurred. The persons holding the money after the transactions differ from those holding it before because those who buy the bonds are not generally the same as those from whom goods and services are purchased by use of bond proceeds. But, from the standpoint of aggregate national effect, the important consideration is that the total money supply held outside the banking system remains unchanged—even though nonbank investors emerge from the transaction owning additional financial assets in the form of municipal bonds. The process is likely to have resulted in substantial transfers from one locality to another; however, the net national economic effect is generally negligible.[2]

Commercial Bank Investors

If commercial banks, instead of nonbank investors, purchase state and local government debt, the economic impact may be significantly different because money supply *may* be increased. If the banks have excess reserves—that is, if their cash and deposits in Federal Reserve Banks exceed the required percentage of deposits—they may purchase municipal bonds simply by creating deposit money. For the banking system as a whole, the balance sheet effect of a purchase of $1 million of municipal bonds is as follows:

Assets	Liabilities
+ $1 million municipal bonds	+ $1 million deposits

Although this transaction results in increased deposits and, therefore, an increased money supply, similar results would occur if banks bought other types of securities or made loans directly to the public; however, many banks may be more willing to buy municipal bonds than other types of securities. Therefore, expansion in the money supply may depend, to a limited extent, on the availability of state and local bond issues and the terms of such availability. Banks may also purchase municipal bonds from nonbank investors in the secondary market. The effect of such transactions on money supply would be the same as purchasing securities directly from the borrowing government.

If banks have no excess reserves, they can buy additional municipal debt by selling an equivalent amount of other securities to the nonbank sectors of the economy or by reducing loans by the same amount. Selling securities and reducing loans causes the public's deposits (and the money supply) to decline. However, when banks purchase state and local securities, deposits and money supply are again increased to prior levels. Hence, in the absence of excess reserves, the net effect of bank purchases of municipal debt is no different from purchases by the nonbank sector.

---

[2] These are more or less immediate effects. However, inasmuch as the money is now in different private hands and may be spent for purposes quite different from those for which the investors might have used the funds, they are likely to be collateral side effects. The multiplier effect may operate differently than it would have without the exchange, thereby producing different economic consequences.

The Federal Reserve System can (and may) supply reserves to the banking system in order that banks can purchase municipals without drawing down excess reserves or liquidating loans or other investments. If new reserves are used to acquire municipal debt, deposits are increased initially by the amount of the purchase of state and local obligations. But, because banks would need to hold reserves equal to only a fraction of these new deposits, the total money supply can be expanded by an amount that is considerably larger than the initial purchase of municipal debt.

The same effect occurs if banks buy other securities or make loans based on their new reserves. As shown in Table 15, in the period from 1965 to 1971, commercial banks increased their holdings of municipal securities from 11 percent to 15 percent of their deposits; however, the ratio declined thereafter. By 1976, the ratio dropped to 12 percent and remained at that level through 1980. This contraction of bank emphasis on holdings of state and local government securities after 1971 has been a significant factor in marketing the new securities of these governments. The rate at which commercial banks have increased their holdings of the securities of state and local governments has been irregular during the 1970s, characterized by significant net acquisitions in the years 1970–1974 and 1976–1980 but very low net acquisitions during the 1974–1976 period. These changes were due in part to Federal Reserve actions directed toward controlling the money supply.

An Overview

Most of the economic impact of deficit financing of state and local governments tends to be procyclical—that is, borrowing and spending tend to increase as general economic conditions improve and to decrease as total economic activity slows. Such behavior by state and local governments reinforces both the direction and the pace of changes in the level of the nation's economic activity. It tends to accentuate cyclical swings rather than dampen them. It does not serve the objectives of fiscal policy directed toward stabilization of economic growth patterns.

State and local governments usually borrow more during periods of rapid economic growth when interest rates are relatively high and less when economic activity is expanding at a slower pace and interest rates are lower. Two factors help to account for this: (1) Public officials believe it easier to obtain voter authorizations during boom periods when the public mood is exuberant (provided inflation is not rampant) and (2) increased construction of residential and commercial buildings and rising costs associated with more prosperous periods cause greater demand for public facilities such as streets, sewer lines, and fire equipment.[3]

However, when interest rates become very high, borrowing by state and local governments drops sharply. Thus, in 1969, when interest rates increased to quite high levels, sales of municipal bonds declined. This occurred again in 1979, 1980, and 1981. The extent to which this decline was due to high interest rates is not known; however, it is known that a considerable portion of the decline was attributable to displacements, i.e., the inability of some state and local governments to borrow within interest rate limitations imposed by law. A similar effect has been noted in other periods of high interest rates; however, added sales from concurrent expansion of the market into new areas tend to obscure those trends. Again, in the early part of 1980, record-high interest rates caused many governments to reduce their demands for long-term capital financing and use short-term financing pending a stabilization of the market.[4]

---

[3] Frank E. Morris, "Impact of Monetary Policy on State and Local Governments: An Empirical Study," *The Journal of Finance,* Vol. 15 (May 1960), p. 233.

[4] The full degree of decline was obscured by several areas of marked expansion in the municipal market. Principal among these were the emergence of financing for single-family housing through issuance of state and local government bonds; a broadening of the use of these bonds for industrial development; for hospital financing; for pollution control; and especially for financing nuclear power developments.

Table 15

Financial Assets and Security Investments of Commercial Banks as of December 31, 1965–1980[1]

| | | (amounts in billions of dollars) | | |
| Year | Financial Assets | Investments | | Other Financial Assets |
		Total	State and Local Government Obligations Only	
	(1)	(2)	(3)	(4)
1980	1,245	322	147	922
1979	1,161	284	134	878
1978	1,056	268	125	788
1977	936	257	114	679
1976	845	250	105	595
1975	786	228	102	558
1974	757	199	100	563
1973	696	188	95	508
1972	616	183	90	423
1971	545	169	82	376
1970	489	148	70	341
1969	453	126	59	325
1968	439	136	59	303
1967	395	124	50	271
1966	335	104	41	231
1965	336	103	37	233
Investments as a Percentage of Financial Assets				
1980		26	12	74
1979		24	12	75
1978		25	12	75
1977		27	12	73
1976		30	12	70
1975		29	13	71
1974		26	13	74
1973		27	14	73
1972		30	15	70
1971		31	15	69
1970		30	14	70
1969		28	13	72
1968		31	13	69
1967		31	13	69
1966		31	12	69
1965		31	11	69

[1] Consists of only U.S. chartered commercial banks. It excludes their domestic affiliates, Edge Acts corporations, agencies and branches of foreign banks and banks in U.S. possessions.

Source: Board of Governors of the Federal Reserve System, *Flow of Funds Accounts, 1946–1975* (December 1976), pp. 117–118; *Flow of Funds Accounts, Assets and Liabilities Outstanding, 1957–1980* (September, 1981), pp. 20–21.

The importance of state and local government debt in the United States economy stems not only from the process of debt issue and related spending but also from the role of such debt as part of the nation's stock of financial assets, i.e., marketable securities. In order for the economy to function efficiently, there must be an adequate supply of sound marketable securities which can act as a store of wealth (for the holder) and, through the banking system, as a support for large portions of the nation's money supply.[5]

As a part of their savings program, individuals and institutions generally hold some of their assets in forms which can be quickly converted to cash as needed. One form in which wealth can be held is cash. But cash is a nonearning asset; so, most investors attempt to hold relatively small amounts of cash. Another form is real property; but at times it cannot be converted quickly to cash on advantageous terms. Consequently, individuals and institutions look to marketable securities as a suitable form in which to hold savings. Many investors have found state and local government debt to have qualities which enable it to satisfy certain of their needs. For example, tax-exempt bonds provide an attractive income (particularly for investors in the higher income tax brackets). Such bonds generally carry little risk other than that associated with market changes in interest levels and they usually can be liquidated readily through a rather well-developed secondary market.

When banks make loans or invest in securities, they create demand deposits that currently make up a very large portion of the nation's money supply. For example, when a bank buys a municipal bond, it usually pays for the security by crediting the seller's demand deposit account for the amount of purchase, thereby increasing the money supply. The security then becomes part of the bank's assets and helps to back up the value of the deposits. Much of the money expansion carried out by banks involves loans to individuals and businesses. Although these loans provide good earnings for banks, they are not always fully liquid or of high quality. Consequently, in order to provide some protection for deposits, banks are required to channel some of their funds into marketable securities such as federal debt and into state and local government debt—as happened in the period prior to 1971. Periods of very high interest rates (usually periods of more constricted money supply) ordinarily result in liquidation of some of these securities producing decreases in the percentages of assets invested in municipal bonds.

BORROWING AND THE STATE AND LOCAL ECONOMY

Measuring the impact of individual state and local government debt on the economy of the areas they serve is difficult. An immediately favorable impact is derived from the expenditure of bond proceeds. But, as current revenues are used to amortize the debt, a negative impact on the economy is produced.

The uses to which the moneys are put determine the long-term effects on the operations of the government and its requirements for operating revenue. For example, the replacement of an obsolete motor vehicle service shop operating inefficiently should pay dividends by reducing the cost of motor vehicle maintenance and improving the efficiency of functions depending on such equipment, e.g., police patrol. A well-designed office building or hospital can contribute to improved efficiency or better patient care. Modernization of elevators or reduction in energy requirements can produce dividends. On the other hand, increases

---

[5] As of December 31, 1980, the *Flow of Funds* estimate of credit market debt outstanding was $4,651 billion, of which $313 billion (7.37 percent) was state and local government securities. The importance of these securities is doubtless significantly greater than the indicated percentage in terms of providing liquidity to the market. Thus, the total of all negotiable securities was $1,685 billion, with state and local government securities accounting for 18.6 percent. Moreover, given the attractiveness of tax-exempt securities to certain portions of the market that are particularly active, their importance is further enhanced. For data cited, see Board of Governors of the Federal Reserve System, *Flow of Funds Accounts: Assets and Liabilities, 1969–1979* (February, 1980), p. 511.

in the inventory of facilities for recreation, libraries, and health as well as hospitals and nursing homes, can be counted upon to produce demands for larger—not smaller—operating budgets.

Throughout the history of the states and their local governments, there are illustrations of the use of public funds—both current revenue and borrowed money—to facilitate economic development within the community. Although the examples are myriad, several aspects of governmental borrowing being utilized to effect a change in the state and local economy are noteworthy; viz., borrowing for transportation facilities, industrial aid, housing, and urban renewal financing.

In the early history of the nation there was some use of public moneys for development of street and road systems and for the facilities required for water-borne commerce. With the coming of the canals, the use of public credit in one form or another was expanded— through direct expenditures, tax adjustments, or subsidies of other types. Development of the railroads brought keen competition, especially among the cities, for inclusion in the plans of as many railroad builders as feasible. This brought numerous variations in the use of public powers, property, and money. In some instances, large subscriptions to the stock of railroads was made from current or borrowed funds, e.g., the City of Cincinnati's interest in a railroad now leased to the Southern Railway. The period from the close of the Civil War until the Great Depression of the 1930s was characterized by rapid expansion of public investments in railroads and water-borne commerce facilities. Following World War II, as air transport became a predominant mode of long-distance, intercity travel, local governments developed air terminal facilities—usually with the initial investment depending on general obligation bonds, although a few cities began full revenue bond financing in the 1950s. Only in the 1960s and 1970s did airport owners begin to require the patrons and air carriers to pay the full cost of airports and air terminals including debt service. Even so, under governmental ownership almost all airport facilities are fully tax-exempt—in contrast to most privately owned railroad terminal properties. These investments have generally proved sound providing direct access to the mainstream of national and international travel. Even so, only a few communities have been able to recapture the full original investment of their tax funds directly from airport operations.

In the instance of industrial aid, Mississippi in the early 1930s instituted a program under which various types of industrial facilities could be financed from debt of the state and local governments with the facilities leased to industrial firms that agreed to bring jobs to the communities involved. The program initially moved slowly outside the boundaries of Mississippi; however, in the 1950s and 1960s it expanded at such a rate that Congress in 1969 imposed significant restrictions. More recently, there has been a moderate expansion in tax-exempt financing of large segments of industrial physical development. This use of state and local government debt (usually fully self-supporting) has provided a means of retaining industrial activity that might have moved elsewhere and, occasionally, of attracting industry from other places. However, as the process has become more nearly universal, the differential advantages originally enjoyed in some states now tend to be nullified as most states offer similar programs.

The use of tax-exempt debt to finance housing has been an evolving process commencing with the Housing Act of 1937. Initially restricted to low-rent public housing projects, it has from time to time been expanded. For a brief period in the late 1970s it encompassed the entire housing market. Although policies are still in process of evolution, it appears that the financing of housing through use of tax-exempt debt will be somewhat broadened but is likely to be associated with housing for lower and lower-middle income groups.

Debt financing of urban renewal has taken several forms, including the loans made by renewal agencies under federal guarantees until that program was replaced in the mid-1970s. Tax-increment financing is one type of loan used for this purpose. Other kinds of loans made by development agencies have also been used in the urban renewal process, including many of the more recent loans for rehabilitation of facilities in central cities. A significant portion of state and local government debt is accounted for by the extension of tax-exempt financing to nonprofit hospitals, private institutions of higher learning, pollution control, and other kinds of programs operated outside government. It does not appear that the initial approval of these uses of tax-exempt financing has taken fully into account the impact of this additional debt on the municipal bond market's interest levels, nor have local issuers fully understood the specific impact of these types of financing on interest costs for other tax-free debt in the same community.

The introduction in October 1981 of the "All-Savers Certificates," primarily to benefit the thrift institutions, offers a major additional supply of tax-exempt securities in the marketplace. Although the major source of initial investments in these certificates was primarily through shifts of funds from taxable investments [in the thrift institutions and otherwise], it appears inevitable that should the practice be continued beyond the initially authorized period of 15 months and if the term of such certificates is extended to genuinely long-term periods, this new credit market instrument will have a significant adverse impact upon the interest payable by state and local governments upon moneys borrowed for conventional public purposes.

As will be pointed out in Chapter 7, for any given level and pattern of local, state, and federal taxation, there is an upper limit at which state and local government debt can be marketed on the basis of safety of investment.

Chapter 3
CLASSIFICATION OF DEBT

Among the more widely used systems of classification of state and local government debt are the following:

Form of the debt, i.e., the classification by the type of instrument evidencing debt

Functions for which the debt is created, e.g., to acquire capital facilities or to meet current expense

Purposes for which the proceeds are used, e.g., provision of facilities required for health programs, fire protection programs, transportation

Issuer, e.g., states, municipalities, school districts, counties, or public authorities

Term during which the debt is to be outstanding, i.e., short-term or long-term

Security pledged for payment of the debt and interest thereon.

The Forms of Tax-exempt Debt

The debt of state and local governments appears in a number of forms. Although this volume is limited largely to debt represented by notes and bonds, it is appropriate to identify and briefly comment upon each of the forms in order that the full picture may be in focus.

1. Trade debt
2. Warrants
3. Notes
4. Bonds
5. Unfunded deferred compensation
6. Obligations to other governments
7. Tort claims, judgments, and other claims

Trade Debt

Trade debt consists principally of accounts payable, i.e., amounts due for goods and services for which payment has not been made. Ordinarily, trade debt is very short-term; however, in periods of financial stress, elements of trade debt can remain outstanding for months or even for years, as some did during the Great Depression. It includes vouchers payable and also, on a conceptual basis, includes obligations for goods and services rendered by persons other than employees, whether or not invoiced. Important though trade debt is to the operations of state and local governments, its administration is not generally deemed to be within the purview of debt administration, partially because trade debt is so short-term and is ordinarily not interest bearing.

Warrants

In 1980 the Municipal Finance Officers Association, relying heavily upon the prior work of the National Committee on Government Accounting (NCGA)[1], defined a warrant in these terms:

> An order drawn by the legislative body or an officer of a governmental unit upon its treasurer directing the latter to pay a specified amount to the person named or to the bearer. It may be payable upon demand, in which case it usually circulates the same as a bank check; or it may be payable only out of certain revenues when and if received, in which case it does not circulate as freely.[2]

Beyond the simple warrant payable, one finds two other forms of the warrant:

Registered Warrant. This is a warrant which, due to a present lack of funds, is registered by the paying officer for future payment and which is to be paid in the order of its registration. In some cases, such warrants are registered when issued; in others, when first presented to the paying officer by the holders.[3]

Time Warrant. A time warrant is a negotiable obligation of a governmental unit having a term shorter than bonds and frequently tendered to individuals and firms in exchange for contractual services, capital acquisitions, or equipment purchases.[4] In the case of a simple warrant that is paid promptly upon presentation, the form is essentially that of a check and is processed through the banking system in much the same manner; warrants are considered as short-term debt.

Notes

A note is essentially a written acknowledgment of a debt due. It may constitute an unconditional promise to pay, or it may be a conditional promise to pay in support of which only specified resources of the issuer are available for the purpose. The note is usually a simple form of debt acknowledgment; it is usually a negotiable credit market instrument inasmuch as it is payable either to the bearer or to the order of the initial holder. Notes are customarily interest bearing. Of the several forms of notes used as evidence of debt by state and local governments, the two most common are:

Tax Anticipation Notes (TANS). These are notes (sometimes called warrants) which are issued in anticipation of the collection of taxes, usually retirable only from tax collections, and frequently only from the proceeds of the tax levy whose collection they anticipate.[5]

Bond Anticipation Notes (BANS). These are short-term interest-bearing notes issued by a governmental unit in anticipation of bonds to be issued at a later date. The notes are retired from the proceeds of the bond issue to which they are related.[6]

---

[1] The National Council on Governmental Accounting is the successor to the National Committee on Government Accounting, which, in turn, developed from the Municipal Finance Officers Association's (MFOA) Committee on Municipal Accounting, established in 1933. The NCGA is independent of the MFOA in terms of selection of its membership and conduct of its program of developing generally accepted accounting principles for state and local governments. It is related to the MFOA in the sense that most of its budget has heretofore either been financed by MFOA or under grants secured by MFOA. The future role of NCGA is not altogether clear at the time of publication of this volume inasmuch as there is the impending creation of the new Governmental Accounting Standards Board (GASB) under the arrangements announced early in 1982 by the Financial Accounting Standards Board. Presumably NCGA will be continued indefinitely but its role will have to be modified and redefined.

[2] The 1968 edition of *Governmental Accounting, Auditing, and Financial Reporting* was authored by the National Committee on Governmental Accounting and published by MFOA. The 1980 edition is both authored and published by MFOA. The text of the statement bears one series of page numbers and the appendices bear a separate series, cited here as, e.g., Appendix B, p. 77.

[3] Ibid., p. 71.

[4] Ibid., p. 76.

[5] Ibid., p. 75.

[6] Ibid., p. 56.

In addition to these two forms, revenue anticipation notes (RANS) are encountered with increasing frequency. They are ordinarily issued in anticipation of nontax revenues. One of the principal contemporary uses is to obtain cash to pay obligations for the provision of services under arrangements with another government. However, other forms of delayed payment, e.g., in the operation of governmental enterprises, account for the increasing use of RANS.

Commercial Paper

Commercial paper has long been used by private corporations as a means of meeting short-term requirements for cash. Commercial paper is issued to the general credit markets being based upon letters of credit obtained by the issuer from a recognized commercial bank. The term of the paper is not more than 270 days and thereby avoids the necessity in private cases for the development of disclosure statements required by the Securities and Exchange Commission. It is being adapted to use by state and local governments; commencing in 1977 and expanding considerably in 1981 [albeit still with less than 20 issuers at December 10, 1981].

The commitment by the commercial bank(s) is essential to viability of this type of credit instrument. The volume outstanding in early December, 1981, amounted to $1.25 billion.

Bonds

The largest amount of state and local government debt (with the possible exception of unfunded deferred compensation obligations) takes the form of *bonds*. The MFOA has defined a bond in these terms:

> A written promise to pay a specified sum of money, called the face value or principal amount, at a specified date or dates in the future, called the maturity date(s), together with periodic interest at a specified rate.[7]

Bonds themselves can, in turn, be classified as temporary bonds or permanent bonds. They can also be classified as bearer bonds or registered bonds.

Temporary or Permanent. Prior to the development of the present systems for expeditious preparation of the definitive bonds, delays in engraving sometimes required the printing of temporary bonds, which were exchanged for permanent bonds as soon as these were available. This practice is now virtually extinct. Today almost all bonds are issued in permanent form, i.e., in the form which they will maintain until matured or until an exchange is made from coupon to registered bonds, or vice versa.

Bearer Bonds or Registered Bonds. The large majority of state and local government bonds are issued as *bearer bonds*. These bearer bonds and their attached coupons are negotiable instruments and may be transferred without notice to the issuer. The *registered bond* is one in which the ownership is entered on the books of the issuer or its paying agent. If the bond is registrable as to both principal and interest, interest is paid automatically to the owner of record on each interest payment date, much as are the dividends on stock and interest on corporate bonds. In some cases the bond may be registrable as to principal only, as a protection against theft or other loss.

A *certificate of indebtedness* is similar to a bond. The precise differences are defined under the laws of the state in which issued. Another form is the *equipment trust certificate* (of indebtedness) which is issued frequently in the acquisition of mobile equipment. These certificates are, in commercial practice, issued by the trustee and not the eventual obligor. This form has not been broadly used in state and local governments; however, various

---

[7] Ibid.

types of lease/rental/purchase arrangements tend to provide substitutes—usually avoiding the formal classification of debt.

Unfunded Deferred Liabilities

Contemporary deferred benefits cover a wide range, e.g., (1) pensions; (2) accrued annual leave and compensable portions of unused sick leave; (3) provisions for injury benefits, including workmen's compensation; (4) life insurance contracts; (5) health and welfare benefits payable after termination of employment; and (6) unemployment compensation after separation.[8] Until the present century, almost no provision was made for funding of any of these liabilities. Gradually, during the period following World War I, it became customary in many governments to fund pension liabilities for teachers and some other groups of employees, although other governments continued to pay these from current income or current employee contributions. Even though the pension reserves of state and local governments exceeded $183 billion in 1980,[9] few of these governments have established sufficient reserves to fund fully the accrued liabilities relating to active and retired employees. Ordinarily, their balance sheets have not reflected unfunded liabilities either for pensions or for other deferred compensation and benefits. Many do not maintain their records in a form permitting easy valuation of the deferred benefits. And even fewer governmental units maintain formal reserves for such debt other than pensions.

Almost any liberalization of pension benefit plans both increases the rates of normal cost and greatly increases the amounts of unfunded liability. The aggregate value of these unfunded liabilities is huge. It may significantly exceed the aggregate amounts of outstanding bonded debt of these governments. The unfunded pension liabilities arise from a failure to maintain reserves with a present value (PV-1)[10] equal to the present value of benefits payable at future dates associated with the past service of active or retired employees. Many governments have attempted to avoid unfunded accrued liabilities by the payment of "normal costs," i.e., costs accruing for current service, as such costs arise. They also have programs for liquidation of unfunded accrued liabilities over a period of years. During periods of relative economic stability, such systems have generally served well. However, during periods of rapid inflation, the assumptions on which previous funding was carried out frequently prove too low, especially in terms of the rates used in projecting increases in employee compensation as well as costs arising from indexing pension costs. As a result, systems well on their way toward controlling unfunded liabilities frequently encountered new unpaid liabilities.

Intergovernmental Obligations

For 1979–80 the Bureau of the Census reported aggregate revenues of state and local governments from their own sources at $299 billion. Simultaneously, their intergovernmental receipts amounted to $166 billion [including some duplication of moneys from federal to state governments that were subsequently transferred to local governments]. The ratio of intergovernmental revenues [including some for utility and insurance trust purposes] to general revenue from their own sources amounted to more than one dollar in each three received.[11] Large portions of these intergovernmental payments are made substantially

---

[8] These liabilities are, in a sense, more important than those represented by bonded debt. Their unfunded amounts represent negative patrimony bequeathed by each generation to the next. In the case of bonded debt, there is ordinarily a positive patrimony accumulation in the form of physical facilities—inasmuch as their depreciated value usually exceeds related unamortized debt. But, in the case of the unfunded liabilities for pensions and other debt discussed here, the amounts involved constitute net negative patrimony.

[9] U.S. Bureau of the Census, *Governmental Finances in 1979–80*, p. 18.

[10] For a discussion of present value systems see Appendix B.

[11] U.S. Bureau of the Census, *Governmental Finances in 1979–80*, p. 17.

at the time the recipient governments are obliged to make payments for the services being financed from intergovernmental revenue. But there are numerous instances in which these payments do not correspond to the timing of payments by recipient governments for services being financed. In such instances of mismatch in the times of receipt and disbursement, there are likely to be significant debtor/creditor transactions. In the case of local governments (the principal recipients of aggregate transfers), there is frequently both inconvenience and considerable cost in furnishing cash to meet current outgo in advance of receiving associated revenues.

The concern here is the effect of these payments on the debt transactions of recipient governments. A senior government failing to make timely payment has an outstanding debt. The junior government has an accounts receivable asset; however, it also has a working capital problem that frequently can be managed only through an increase in the amount of its outstanding short-term debt.

Torts, Judgments, and Other Claims

The final category of debt recognized here is that representing torts, judgments, or miscellaneous claims arising from the operations of the government. Ordinarily, these are not recognized in the balance sheet as debt until the settlement amount has been determined by agreement or by judgment entered against the government. Historically, the doctrine of sovereign immunity protected state and local governments against most claims in relation to damages sustained as a result of governmental operations. However, during the past two decades, through a combination of legislative and judicial action, the protections formerly afforded by sovereign immunity have been virtually eliminated. As a result, the debt of state and local governments arising from claims has risen rapidly.

Classification by Function

Debt may be classified as to the ends for which it is incurred, e.g., (1) provision of working capital, (2) temporarily financing current or accumulated operating deficits, (3) acquisition of equipment, (4) acquisition of land and other fixed assets, or (5) payment of deferred compensation and other liabilities.

Providing Working Capital

All enterprises require working capital.[12] Unincorporated businesses and professional service groups combine equity capital and borrowed funds; profit-oriented corporations use equity capital (proceeds from the sale of stock and accumulations of undistributed profits) and loans secured by their assets; nonprofit corporations utilize contributed equity capital and loans; state and local governments have no equity capital except accumulations of surplus or prepayment of revenues. The remainder of working capital must come from taxes, revenue anticipation notes, or either intra- or inter-governmental loans. Most of the short-term loans to state and local governments are to provide working capital, pending the realization of taxes or other revenues for the fiscal year; some are bond anticipation loans.

Some state and local governments are able to maintain sufficient surplus funds to meet their cash requirements pending receipt of the current year's revenues; others are not. The calendar for realizing revenue in relation to that for making disbursements within the fiscal year is critical. Realization of the local property tax is frequently delayed until

---

[12] Working capital consists of cash and other assets which are immediately convertible to cash and are available to meet day-to-day cash flow requirements in operating funds.

late in the fiscal year. In 1979–80 property taxes accounted for about half of the general revenue of local governments from their own sources—$65.6 billion of a total of $130.0 billion, or about 50.5 percent.[13] For many the percentage was much higher.

At the state government level, many elements of revenue are not realized until relatively late in the fiscal year, e.g., final payments of personal income taxes. For either a state or local government that accrues revenues not yet realized, smaller cash balances in relation to the amount of surplus are inevitable. Delays in timely receipt of payments from other governments imposes added requirements for working capital.

Resort to TANS or RANS becomes a necessity for many local and state governments.

Funding Operating Deficits

State and local governments are generally required to adopt balanced budgets; however, when plans fail, deficits are likely to result. These can become so large that it is not feasible to liquidate the full amount in the following year's budget. In such cases floating debt develops, frequently requiring liquidation over a period of years through the use of funding loans.

Equipment Acquisition

In private, profit-oriented enterprises equipment acquisition is considered a capital outlay to be depreciated over its useful life. However, in governmental operations (other than governmental enterprises) depreciation accounting is not used.[14]

Most governments appear to finance equipment purchases directly from their operating funds or through internal "equipment rental funds." But some have turned in increasing degree to financing portions of their equipment requirements through commercial rentals, lease-purchase agreements, or equipment loans. Where the loans are direct, the expense is recorded as debt service; where loans are funded through special authorities or outside of the using entity, the cost will appear as equipment rental.[15]

Physical Facilities Acquisition

The bulk of the long-term debt of state and local governments is incurred to finance the acquisition of land, structures, fixed equipment in buildings, and the inventory of movable equipment incident to initial occupancy of new structures.

Deferred Compensation Obligations

A major part of the debt which state and local governments have incurred relates to deferred compensation arrangements described earlier in this chapter.[16]

---

[13] U.S. Bureau of the Census, *Governmental Finances in 1979–80*, p. 17.

[14] MFOA, *Governmental Accounting, Auditing, and Financial Reporting* (1980) Appendix B, pp. 57, 62. Capital outlays are defined as "expenditures which result in the acquisition of or addition to fixed assets," with fixed assets being "assets of a long-term character which are intended to continue to be held or used, such as land, buildings, machinery, furniture, and other equipment." This note is appended: "The term does not indicate the immobility of an asset, which is the distinctive character of a 'fixture.'"

[15] State and local governments frequently use installment purchases or lease-purchase agreements to acquire some types of equipment, e.g., parking meters and computers. For a general discussion of different aspects of the use of lease financing for tax-exempt governments, see F. Glenn Nichols, "Debt Limitations and the Bona Fide Long-Term Lease with an Option to Purchase: Another Look at Lord Coke," *Urban Lawyer, The National Journal of Urban Law,* Vol. 9, No. 2 (Spring, 1977), pp. 11–28; Harold E. Rogers, Jr., "Municipal Debt Restrictions and Lease-Purchase Financing," *American Bar Association Journal,* Vol. 49 (Jan., 1963), pp. 31–37; Jon Magnusson, "Lease-Financing by Municipal Corporations as a Way Around Debt Limitations," *George Washington Law Review,* Vol. 25, No. 3 (March, 1957), pp. 41–60.

[16] There are no generally accepted actuarial standards under which pension and other liabilities are evaluated. As a result, the statements showing unfunded deferred compensation plans produce data that

Classifications by Purpose to Which the Proceeds are Applied

The following purpose classifications are provided by the Bureau of the Census, *The Bond Buyer,* and the Public Securities Association.

The Bureau of the Census in the *1977 Census of Governments*[17] presented information as to long-term outstanding debt at the end of the fiscal year 1976–77 as follows:

Education
   State institutions of
     higher learning
   Local schools
   Other
Highways
   State toll facilities
   Other
Housing and urban renewal
Sewerage
Hospitals

Airports
Parks and recreation
Water transport
   and terminals
Utilities
   Electric power
   Water supply
   Transit system
   Gas supply
   Other and
     unallocable

For 1978 *The Bond Buyer*[18] used the following classifications:

School
Water and sewer
Highway, bridge & tunnel
Gas and electric
Hospital

Industrial
Pollution control
Veterans' aid
Other
Public housing authority (used only on
   an historical base for issues sold prior
   to 1975)

For 1979 the Public Securities Association[19] used the following classifications:

Education
   Elementary and secondary
   Colleges and universities
   Other
Transportation
   Roads and bridges
   Ports and airports
   Other
Utilities and conservation
   Pollution control
   Water and sewer
   Electric and gas
   Other

Social welfare
   Public housing
   Hospitals
   Other
Industrial aid
   Pollution control
   Industrial
   Other
Public services
   Recreation
   Other

---

are rarely comparable from one jurisdiction to another. Moreover, as the assumptions change from time to time the evaluations of the gross liabilities of the same government may be significantly restated. During periods of rapid inflation, assumptions concerning the average rates of future compensation payable are likely to be grossly understated. For a comprehensive discussion of the problems of valuation, see Howard E. Winklevoss and Dan M. McGill, *Public Pension Plans,* pp. 183–316.

[17] U.S. Bureau of the Census, *1977 Census of Governments,* Vol. 4, No. 5, p. 35.

[18] *The Bond Buyer, Statistics on State and Local Government Finance, 1978,* p. 8.

[19] Public Securities Association, *Municipal Market Developments,* February, 1980, Table 4 and paper dated July 7, 1977, by Public Securities Association and the Municipal Finance Study Group, School of Business, State University of New York at Albany, entitled, "Data Descriptions for the Long Term Municipal Bond File."

The effect of these multiple classification categories is to provide a quite substantial body of data to the student of municipal bonds. On the other hand, in the absence of a suitable degree of standardization, it is not feasible to identify important characteristics of the debt, e.g., the amounts of *on behalf of* or governmental lessee debt being sold. The computer data file maintained by the Public Securities Association in cooperation with the Municipal Finance Study Group, School of Business, State University of New York at Albany, has a much more extensive set of classification codes relating to the use of proceeds. For example, in the file, the education group is divided into eight categories, as is social welfare but, for reporting purposes, a lesser number of categories is used.

Classification by Issuer

The Bureau of the Census classifies certain of its debt data on the basis of issuer, using the following classifications:

> State (includes the state, state agencies, authorities, etc.)
> Local
>> Municipalities
>> Townships
>> Counties
>> School districts
>> Special districts (including local authorities, commissions,
>> governmental non-profit corporations)

The Bureau of the Census data includes as state debt the bonds issued by state authorities for use by local governments, e.g., state public school building authorities and state bond banks. Thus, in 1979–80, total debt outstanding for local school *purposes* was about $32 billion, but about one-ninth of this was classified as state debt because it was issued by a state agency or authority.[20]

The Public Securities Association's computer data file uses the following classifications; however, there are variations from time to time as to which are used in reporting:

State	Statutory authorities
County	State housing finance agency
Municipality, city, borough	Local housing and urban renewal authority
Town, township, village	thority
School district	State health, hospital or educational facilities authority
Special district	facilities authority
State municipal bond bank	Local health, hospital or educational facilities authority
	State electric or utility authority
	Local electric or utility authority
	Local authority, other
	State authority, other
	Local industrial development agency

The Bond Buyer does not have an independent classification for this purpose. It uses the data of the Bureau of the Census.

Maturity Date of Debt

The Municipal Finance Officers Association defines debt in two categories insofar as the term of the debt is concerned:

---

[20] Among the states relying heavily on such state agency financing of local school building costs are California, Delaware, Georgia, Maryland, Pennsylvania, and Virginia. See U.S. Bureau of the Census, *Governmental Finances in 1979–80*, p. 53.

Short-term Debt. Debt with a maturity of one year or less after the date of issuance. Short-term debt usually includes floating debt, bond anticiption notes, tax anticipation notes, and interim warrants.

Long-term Debt. Debt with a maturity of more than one year after the date of issuance.[21]

The Bureau of the Census defines these terms in the following manner:

Short-term Debt comprises interest-bearing debt payable within one year from date of issue, such as bond anticipation notes; bank loans; and tax anticipation notes and warrants; this category also includes similar obligations having no fixed maturity date, even where outstanding over one year, if payable from a tax levied for collection in the year of their issuance. Excluded are non-interest-bearing warrants, accounts payable, and other non-interest-bearing short-term obligations.

Long-term Debt consists of all debt payable more than one year after date of issue, including bonds, judgments, mortgages, and the like. Tax-anticipation warrants or notes outstanding more than one year are considered short-term if they are payable from a specific tax levied for collection within the year.[22]

A review of these two sets of definitions indicates that they are substantially the same in concept; however, the Bureau of the Census omits certain non-interest-bearing obligations from its definitions of short-term debt that are apparently included in the MFOA definition.

A review of statistics relating to short-term debt insofar as it relates to bond anticipation notes raises a question concerning the character of debt represented by debt that is issued in the form of short-term debt but which is rolled over year after year to the point that the actual maturity falls several years after the initial issuance. This has occurred in some jurisdictions in various states, e.g., New Jersey[23] and Ohio. Effectively such debt becomes long-term although it continues to be short-term in classification.

Term Bond Issues and Serial Bond Issues

In one sense almost all state and local government debt is term debt, i.e., it has a fixed maturity date. More frequently, bond issues consist of serial maturities. In any event, each debt instrument ordinarily has a fixed date at which the issuer agrees to monetize the principal due. The issuer may have reserved the right to redeem (mature) the entire principal at an earlier date than that on which it is obliged to do so. Moreover, the issuer may reserve the right to retire portions of the debt in advance of its normal maturity date. A debt contract may carry provisions under which the maturity date for all of the outstanding principal and unpaid interest is accelerated to the present date in case of default in making any payment due.

Some debt instruments, e.g., a note secured by a mortgage, may require interim payments—usually applied first to accrued interest and then to principal. In case of defaults in governmental enterprise bonds, it is customary to apply available net income first to accrued interest. Payments of principal are made only when accrued interest has been fully paid.

Before proceeding with the discussion of term bond issues vs. serial bond issues, it is appropriate to consider MFOA definitions of selected terms.[24]

---

[21] MFOA, *Governmental Accounting, Auditing, and Financial Reporting* (1980) Appendix B, pp. 67, 73.
[22] U.S. Bureau of the Census, *Classification Manual, Governmental Finances,* dated March 1976, pp. 70–71, which was issued in conjunction with the *1977 Census of Governments.*
[23] New Jersey Tax Policy Committee, *The Use and Costs of Public Credit,* pp. 28–32.
[24] MFOA, *Governmental Accounting, Auditing, and Financial Reporting* (1980) Appendix B, pp. 73, 76.

Term Bonds. Bonds the entire principal of which matures on one date. Also called sinking fund bonds.

It follows that a term bond issue is an issue of debt in respect to which each of the *term bonds* composing the *term bond issue* have the same maturity date.

Serial Bonds. Bonds the principal of which is repaid in periodic installments over the life of the issue.

Serial Annuity Bonds. Serial bonds in which the annual installments of bond principal are so arranged that the combined payments for principal and interest are approximately the same each year. (The author does not use this term. In lieu thereof, the term "equal annual debt service bonds" is used.)

Deferred Serial Bonds. Serial bonds in which the first installment does not fall due for two or more years from the date of issue.

Debt Service Fund. A fund established to finance and account for payment of interest and principal on all general obligation debt, serial and term, other than that payable exclusively from special assessments and revenue debt issued for and serviced by a governmental enterprise. Formerly called a SINKING FUND.

Beyond the foregoing definitions it is appropriate here to provide working definitions for some other terms:

Term Bond Issue with Sinking Fund. A bond issue in respect to which the issuer regularly sets aside moneys in a sinking fund which, together with the compound earnings thereon, are expected to be sufficient to "sink" the principal at maturity.[25]

Block Term Bonds. A block of bonds within a combined serial/term bond issue having the same nominal maturity date but under agreement that substantial portions of the "block-term" maturity will be redeemed prior to the stated maturity.

The phrase *block term maturity* is not currently in use but it is needed to describe the phenomenon frequently occurring in relation to bond issues originally planned as serial bonds issues but whose pattern is altered in the course of the sale, especially during negotiated sales. It arises from the fact that frequently the syndicate receives few orders for certain maturities, e.g., the 16th–19th maturities, while there is a good demand for others, e.g., the 20th maturity. Thereupon the unpopular maturities are consolidated with those normally occurring in the 20th year. All the bonds will bear the coupon rate that would have been applicable to the bonds maturing in the 20th year; however, the contract typically provides that the maturities will, in fact, continue substantially as originally planned. That is, a portion of the bonds in the block-term maturity will be called on the 16th anniversary, additional ones on the 17th anniversary, etc. There seems to be limited rationality to the use of the block-term bond beyond: (1) providing a break in the yield curve, and (2) affording purchase of a larger total block of bonds. The phrase *block-term bonds* seems to be useful in the identification of this phenomenon.

In the 19th and early 20th centuries, most public and private debt in the United States was issued as term debt. Periodic payments of interest were made but no payments to reduce the principal. Federal and corporate bonds are still issued largely as term debt, generally without a requirement for accumulation of a sinking fund during the life of the

---

[25] The terms, "float a bond issue" and "sink the debt" are gradually falling into disuse; however, until World War II the process of issuance of bonds was generally referred to as "floating the debt" or "floating a bond issue." As the debt was retired, or as provision was made for its retirement by accumulation of assets to "sinking" the debt, the fund in which these assets were accumulated was known as the "sinking fund." In many communities special boards or commissions were created to manage such funds, sometimes called "commissioners of the sinking fund."

debt to mature the debt upon its due date. Typically, the debt is rolled over at maturity by issuance of substitute long-term debt.

During the early part of this century, there was a marked change in practice in respect to both private debt and the debt of state and local governments. Initially, this took the form in state and local governments of requirements for the development of sinking funds from which the debt could be retired at maturity. Gradually, this gave way to the issuance of serial bonds for these governments and to requirements for periodic payments in respect to mortgages, installment credit, and personal loans. Alternatively, term bonds were frequently issued for such projects as toll roads but with requirements for redemption of portions of the debt from the earnings of the enterprise.

Security Classifications

Two systems of classification are in use in relation to long-term debt of state and local governments: Those of the Bureau of the Census and the Public Securities Association in concert with the Municipal Finance Study Group of the School of Business of the State University of New York at Albany.

The Bureau of the Census describes its concepts in the following terms:

Full Faith and Credit Debt. All long-term obligations for which the credit of the government, implying the power of taxation, is unconditionally pledged. This category is further subclassified under two headings, as follows:

(a) **General Obligations.** Full faith and credit debt other than that payable initially from nontax revenue (but including debt payable in first instance from particular earmarked taxes).

(b) **Debt Payable Initially from Specified Nontax Revenue.** Long-term debt amounts payable in the first instance from some specific source of nontax revenue (such as pledged toll highway revenues, recoupment of loans made in credit operations, or particular intergovernmental revenue sources) but payable from taxes or other available resources if pledged sources are insufficient.

Nonguaranteed Debt. Long-term obligations payable *solely* from pledged specific sources, such as earnings of plants or activities, or special assessments, and which do not constitute obligations against any other resources of the government if the pledged sources are insufficient. Includes "revenue bonds" payable *solely* from earnings of toll highway facilities, college dormitories, utilities, sewage disposal plants, and the like.[26]

The Public Securities Association classification guide calls for the following categories in its computer file, not all of which are used in its annual statistical reports:

A. General obligation
  1. Unlimited tax
    a. Without qualification
    b. Secured by general revenues
    c. Secured by special assessments
  2. Limited tax
    a. Without further qualification
    b. Secured by general revenue source
    c. Secured by special assessments
  3. Other

---

[26] U.S. Bureau of the Census, *Classification Manual, Governmental Finances* (March 1976), pp. 71–72.

B. Revenue bonds
1. Utility revenues
2. Quasi-utility revenues, e.g., parking, bridges and colleges
3. Special tax revenue, e.g., a dedicated tax backing up a revenue pledge
4. Lessee revenue, e.g., rentals, schools, and mortgages
5. Utility revenue, further secured by special tax revenues
6. Miscellaneous, e.g., secured by severance tax revenues
C. Other, e.g., PHA federally guaranteed issues sold after January 1, 1963[27]

In addition to the foregoing classifications for long-term debt, the Public Securities Association provides these classifications for short-term debt:

A. Urban renewal
B. Local housing agencies
C. Anticipation notes
1. Tax anticipation notes (TANS) and revenue anticipation notes (RANS)
2. Bond anticipation notes (BANS)
3. Other

Moody's Investors Service does not directly define general obligation bonds but states that ". . . 'general obligations' (which) are defined as validly issued and legally binding evidence of indebtedness secured by the full faith, credit and taxing power of the issuer."[28] For revenue bonds Moody's provides this definition:

The term **revenue bonds** is used loosely to identify bonds of a political subdivision or governmental agency which are payable solely from some specified source other than the general taxing power of the issuer, and to distinguish such bonds from general obligations (indebtedness secured by the full faith, credit and taxing power). The term customarily is not associated with certain other types of non-general obligations, viz: 1-Special assessment bonds or certificates (payable solely from assessed benefits) although the term has so been applied on a few occasions . . . ; 2-warrants, certificates, or other evidences of indebtedness issued in anticipation of collection of imposts of the general property tax (although long-term anticipatory borrowing associated with other types of taxes, notably the gasoline tax, frequently is classified as revenue debt).[29]

Moody's provides the following classification of revenue bonds based upon source of payment:

A. Utility
1. Bridge, tunnel or toll highway
2. Electric light and power
3. Gas
4. Public transportation
5. Off-street parking facilities
6. Water
7. Multiple purpose, the more common combinations being electric and water, water and sewer
B. Quasi-utility
1. Airport
2. Dock and terminal

---

[27] Public Securities Association and the Municipal Finance Study Group, School of Business Administration, State University of New York at Albany, paper entitled, "Data Descriptions for the Long Term Municipal Bond File," (July 7, 1977), p. 6.
[28] Moody's Investors Service, Inc. *Municipal & Government Manual, 1977,* p. vi.
[29] Ibid., p. 214. [The 1980 edition of the manual no longer carries any definition of revenue bonds.]

     3. Hospital
     4. Public market
     5. Public garage
  C. Non-utility
     1. Gasoline tax, cigarette tax, beer tax, utility excise tax, etc.
     2. Rental of public buildings
        a. To another governmental agency
        b. To the public generally
           (1) Educational facilities
           (2) Recreational facilities
        c. To private persons or corporations[30]

This classification is not used in the collection or reporting of statistics.

CONCLUSIONS

The classification systems described in this chapter have evolved over a period of years based on the needs of different groups served.

As it stands today, the result is confusion—confusion among specialists in public finance, economists, public officials, investors, dealers, and others working in the field.

A part of the confusion is inevitable. Given the huge array of issuers and the breadth of their authority to develop debt instruments to meet their respective needs or preferences, many of the elements of classification cannot be perfect. In other words, as long as one is dealing with custom-made bond issues there is no set of standard classifications that will neatly comprehend all bond issues.

On the other hand, various shifts in the market make the historic classification systems especially vulnerable. This vulnerability extends to almost every aspect of classification— whether the term of the debt, purposes to which the proceeds are allocated, the security pledged, or the issuers.

If, indeed, it is worth the efforts that annually go into the collection, compilation, and publication of statistics, it seems that it would be worth a major effort to develop a set of fairly detailed classifications reflecting the realities of the present-day municipal bond market. As it stands, the economist can no longer make a great deal of sense out of the data as a measure of the debt in relation to revenues and resources of state and local governments, especially in view of the amounts of *on behalf of* financing. The political scientist trying to comprehend the significance of different governmental debt patterns, based upon levels of government, necessarily becomes confused. The investor can no longer depend upon such short-hand phrases as "general obligation" or "revenue bonds" to describe the security that may be involved. The issuers frequently may be confronted with reduced market attractiveness of their offerings because of a lack of comprehension of just what the security is.

All are much too busy to take the time to attempt to make *de novo* analyses.

Commencing in 1976 the Municipal Securities Rulemaking Board has, from time to time, considered the possibility of mounting a research program that would utilize some of the data it is gathering (or is in a position to gather) on an official basis. The MSRB is best situated to take the leadership in the development of a new classification system. Such a system could provide for fairly narrow classifications; computer print-outs could then be organized to report under different patterns of groupings to meet specialized needs.

---

[30] Ibid.

Chapter 4
DEALERS AND INVESTMENT BANKERS

In order for the issuers of municipal securities to receive cash for their bonds and notes, the seller and the investor must be brought together. The process by which this occurs is the subject of this chapter. As in other financial markets, sales may be directly to the investor; however, most initial sales are conducted through markets operated by dealers in municipal securities. Beyond the primary market, i.e., initial sale to the investor, a secondary market operates in which outstanding securities are traded. In the typical municipal bond sale and in many short-term notes sales, the entire issue is sold to dealers who reoffer the securities through their networks to investors. In some sales, the issuer sells directly to the investor.

Sales directly to investors may occur in several ways: (1) By issuance of notes or bonds to commercial banks; (2) by private placement with investors, either directly or through dealers; (3) by sale to investors at competitive sales; or (4) by over-the-counter sales. Discussion of the sales of bonds by the issuer is reserved for Chapter 17; the concern here is principally with the role of dealers in municipal securities, whether acting in an underwriting capacity as investment bankers, dealing in the secondary market, or acting as an agent in the acquisition or disposition of municipal securities.

DEALERS

The primary function of the dealer in municipal securities is to buy and sell. In other words, the dealer "takes a position" in the securities, i.e., he has either a "long" position in that he owns securities being held for sale (maintenance of an inventory of securities), or he has a "short" position in which he has agreed to sell and deliver securities not yet owned by him. The dealer's planned profit in such cases is the spread between the price paid by him and the sales price. Dealers also accept orders from investors for the sale or purchase of securities with compensation on a commission basis. Some dealers undertake to "make a market" in selected securities, i.e., they quote bid and asked prices.

Municipal bond dealers who deal only in municipal securities are known as "sole municipal dealers." There are relatively few such dealers. A second category of dealer is the dealer department of commercial banks; the third is the firm that deals in a wide range of corporate, municipal, and government securities.

The services of municipal dealers are indispensable to the issuers of tax-exempt securities. Although substantial amounts of securities, especially short-term securities, are initially placed as loans from the commercial banks and by direct sales to other investors, the bulk of both the short-term and almost all of the long-term securities is sold through dealers. Virtually the entire secondary market, so essential as a support for the primary market, is carried on through the dealer network.

Dealer Firms

Historically, investment banking firms were unincorporated. A few were individual proprietorships; most were partnerships. Until 1953 the rules of the New York Stock Exchange required that dealer firms be unincorporated. However, in that year the rule was changed and the shift from partnerships to corporate forms of organization commenced. Since 1953 many firms have changed to the corporate form of organization.

Investment Banking Partnerships

The investment banking firm organized on a partnership basis consists solely of natural persons. Each member of the partnership has a defined interest. Each regular partner participates in the profits and losses of the firm according to his partnership interest. He is bound by the articles of the partnership agreement—thereby being responsible not only for his actions but also for those of his partners. Ordinarily, the full estates of all partners are at risk in fulfillment of the obligations undertaken in the partnership.

The partnership interests in some firms include not only the traditional *active* partners but also a class known as *limited* partners. The active partners establish policy, carry on the business, and participate in profits and losses. By contrast, the interest of limited partners is solely financial. They invest money in the firm and their investment returns as well as their liabilities are defined by the terms of the limited partnership agreement. This class of partnership has two purposes: (1) To facilitate continued participation in the firm by former active partners and (2) to attract new capital.

Corporate Investment Banking Firms

As the magnitude and scope of the operations of investment banking firms have expanded and the consolidation of firms through mergers has accelerated during the past decade, the operations have generally become much more complex. The principal reason for incorporation include: (1) Requirements for huge additional amounts of capital;[1] (2) improved methods of operation for firms of increased size and diversity; (3) facilitating the sale of the firm; (4) disassociation of ownership from management; (5) limitation of personal liability associated with partnership. In recent years a number of the investment banking firms have been acquired by other corporations, e.g., Shearson by American Express Company due in part to the need of the firms for capital.

Commercial Banks

Prior to the adoption of the National Banking Act of 1933, commercial banks were permitted wide latitude in dealing in municipal securities. Under that legislation they were prohibited from dealing in securities which did not bear the full faith and credit of the issuer, implying access of the issuer to taxing power (including property taxation). Although the restrictions have been relaxed to some degree, commercial banks are still foreclosed from underwriting or dealing in large portions of the municipal bond market.

After several decades of vigorous and successful opposition to the commercial banks, the nonbank underwriters [acting through the Public Securities Association] withdrew their opposition in November 1981, portending early revenue bond underwriting by banks.

ROLE OF THE INVESTMENT BANKER IN COMPETITIVE SALES

Although the major portion of municipal securities has been sold at negotiated sale in recent years, the competitive market is still a very significant portion of the full market.[2]

---

[1] From 1953 until 1970, the total assets of security dealers rose from $4.6 billion to $16.2 billion and by 1980 amounted to $33.5 billion according to the Board of Governors of the Federal Reserve System, *Flow of Funds Accounts, 1946–1975*, pp. 128–130; *Flow of Funds Accounts: Assets and Liabilities Outstanding: 1957–1980* (September, 1981), p. 29.

[2] See Chapter 1.

This section of this chapter is concerned with the role of the investment banker in competitive sales.

Formation of the Syndicate

When an investment banking firm learns that a government may be planning to sell a bond issue at public sale, it is likely to set in motion an effort to participate significantly in the sale, especially if this issuer has not previously sold bonds of this type. If suited by size and specialization, the firm may take the lead in the formation of a syndicate. If unsuited, it may approach another firm to undertake the lead in formation of a syndicate in which the first firm will participate. If these alternatives are foreclosed, membership in some other syndicate may be sought.

On some occasions, syndicates are formed months or years in advance of the time the bonds are offered for sale. Thus, when there is serious discussion of the creation of a new public entity likely to issue bonds at public sale, or when an existing entity is known to be considering a new type of security, e.g., revenue bonds for enterprises formerly financed only from general obligation bonds, a syndicate may be formed promptly.

In most bond sales, however, the new issue will be by a government that has previously sold bonds. A firm may have participated in a previous submission of bids on the same type of bonds of the issuing jurisdiction. If so, it is likely to participate in the historic account. However, each sale of debt produces a new syndication. Even for issuers frequently in the market, a new sale results in a re-formation of the syndicate for the most recent issue. The membership of the successive syndicates may be remarkably similar in composition; it is likely to show change from the preceding one. This is especially true of the participations of the different members of the syndicate, i.e., their relative standings within the group. These re-formed syndicates are sometimes referred to as "traditional accounts" or "historical accounts" and may continue for decades. However, when the size of the bond issues being offered changes markedly or when there is a major shift in the relative strength of the member firms, traditional syndicates may cease to function. New firms may seek to be included in one of the historic syndicates, may form a new syndicate, or become a member of a new syndicate being formed under the leadership of another firm.

At the time of the organization of the syndicate, a formal agreement is entered into by representatives of member firms. The content of syndicate agreements has been more or less standardized into a few basic patterns which set forth the terms of the agreement, including the amount of participation which each firm has undertaken in the syndicate and the duration for which the account is being organized.[3]

The number of firms taken into a syndicate for a competitive sale is determined by the size of the issue, the conditions of the market, the size of the participation each member is willing to accept, and relationships among the investment banking group. Usually, the membership is limited to the number required comfortably to underwrite the bonds; however, strong firms can sometimes gain admission even when unneeded. The assumption is that, if the syndicate can develop strength sufficient to underwrite, it will also have the capacity to distribute the bonds if the syndicate is awarded the issue.

The syndicate consists of a manager (or management group) and a number of members who participate in the pricing, risk bearing, and distribution of the bonds.[4] If there is only one manager, he determines who will be invited into the syndicate; if there are several comanagers, the group makes the determination.

If there is a group of comanagers, one is designated as the lead manager. He keeps

---

[3] Perhaps the best summary available of the different types of accounts is contained in Public Securities Association, *Fundamentals of Municipal Bonds* (1981), pp. 69–70.

[4] The procedures described in this section generally apply when the account is large, e.g., 15 or more members. When the number is smaller, less formal procedures are frequently used.

Exhibit A

Reoffering Yield Advertisement

In the opinion of Bond Counsel, under existing statutes and court decisions, interest on the 1980 Series A Bonds is exempt from Federal income taxes. Furthermore, in the opinion of Bond Counsel, under existing statutes the 1980 Series A Bonds and the interest payable thereon are exempt from taxation directly imposed thereon by the State of Utah.

NEW ISSUE   February 13, 1980

$100,000,000

UTAH HOUSING FINANCE AGENCY

SINGLE FAMILY MORTGAGE PURCHASE BONDS, 1980 SERIES A
(FEDERALLY INSURED OR GUARANTEED OR PRIVATELY INSURED MORTGAGE LOANS)

Dated: February 1, 1980   Due: July 1, as shown below

The Bonds are redeemable prior to maturity as set forth in the Official Statement.

Interest is payable semiannually on January 1 and July 1 in each year, commencing July 1, 1980. The 1980 Series A Bonds will be issued as coupon bonds in the denomination of $5,000 each, registrable as to principal only, or as fully registered bonds in denominations of $5,000 or any authorized multiple thereof. Coupon 1980 Series A Bonds, unless registered as to principal, and interest thereon are payable, at the option of the holder, at the corporate trust office of First Security Bank of Utah, N.A., Salt Lake City, Utah, the Trustee, or at the principal office of Chemical Bank, New York, New York, the Paying Agent. Coupon 1980 Series A Bonds, registered as to principal, and registered 1980 Series A Bonds are payable at the corporate trust office of First Security Bank of Utah, N.A., Salt Lake City, Utah, the Trustee.

MATURITY SCHEDULE

$72,890,000 SERIAL BONDS

Amount	Maturity	Interest Rate	Amount	Maturity	Interest Rate	Amount	Maturity	Interest Rate
$1,000,000	1981	6.30%	$3,990,000	1988	6.85%	$3,685,000	1995	7.60%
1,255,000	1982	6.40	3,990,000	1989	6.90	3,595,000	1996	7.70
3,455,000	1983	6.45	3,930,000	1990	7	3,585,000	1997	7.80
3,590,000	1984	6½	3,920,000	1991	7.10	3,500,000	1998	7.90
3,840,000	1985	6.60	3,895,000	1992	7¼	3,460,000	1999	7.95
4,075,000	1986	6.70	3,860,000	1993	7.40	3,440,000	2000	8
3,995,000	1987	6.80	3,730,000	1994	7½	3,100,000	2001	8

$27,110,000 8¼% TERM BONDS DUE JULY 1, 2011

PRICE OF ALL BONDS 100%
(Accrued interest to be added)

The Bonds are offered only by means of the Official Statement, copies of which may be obtained from such of the undersigned as may legally offer these Bonds in this State. Bonds of particular maturities may or may not be available from the undersigned or others at the above prices on and after the date of this announcement.

Blyth Eastman Paine Webber
Incorporated

Burrows, Smith and Company

Bache Halsey Stuart Shields   BancNorthwest   Bank of America NT & SA   The Bank of California, N.A.
Incorporated

Bankers Trust Company   Bear, Stearns & Co.   A. G. Becker   Alex. Brown & Sons   The Chase Manhattan Bank, N.A.
Warburg Paribas Becker

Chemical Bank   Citibank, N.A.   Continental Bank   Crocker National Bank   Dillon, Read & Co. Inc.
Continental Illinois National Bank
and Trust Company of Chicago

Donaldson, Lufkin & Jenrette   Drexel Burnham Lambert   Ehrlich-Bober & Co., Inc.   The First Boston Corporation
Securities Corporation   Incorporated

The First National Bank of Boston   First Chicago   First Pennco Securities, Inc.   Goldman, Sachs & Co.
The First National Bank of Chicago

Harris Trust and Savings Bank   E. F. Hutton & Company Inc.   Kidder, Peabody & Co.   Lazard Frères & Co.
Incorporated

Lehman Brothers Kuhn Loeb   Matthews & Wright, Inc.   Merrill Lynch White Weld Capital Markets Group
Incorporated   Merrill Lynch, Pierce, Fenner & Smith Incorporated

Morgan Guaranty Trust Company of New York   W. H. Morton & Co.   The Northern Trust Company
(Div. of American Express Co.)

John Nuveen & Co.   Oppenheimer & Co., Inc.   L. F. Rothschild, Unterberg, Towbin   Salomon Brothers
Incorporated

Shearson Loeb Rhoades Inc.   Smith Barney, Harris Upham & Co.   United California Bank
Incorporated

Weeden & Co.   Wertheim & Co., Inc.   Dean Witter Reynolds Inc.
Div. of Moseley, Hallgarten, Estabrook & Weeden Inc.

Commercial Security Bank   The Continental Bank and Trust Company   Tracy Collins Bank and Trust Company
of Salt Lake City

Valley Bank & Trust Company   Walker Bank & Trust Company   Zions First National Bank

the appropriate records and maintains contact with all of the members of the syndicate prior to submission of a bid. If the syndicate is successful, this lead manager will also handle the necessary job of "running the book," i.e., the records of sales and apportionment of the bonds among the various members of the syndicate, as will be discussed later in this chapter.

The participation in the account of each member is determined primarily by the manager or comanagers. This is usually done through a bracket system, with the assignments to brackets being dependent in large measure upon the size, standing, and historical sales performance of the firms. From Exhibit A, it is noted that the management group consists of the first two firms listed. The next group consists of 42 firms and the final group of 6 firms.

Generally, the members in a given bracket have equal shares of interest and liabilities, known as "participations." A member can ask for a larger participation or accept a smaller one; this decision is usually that of the syndicate manager. If the manager succeeds in obtaining assent of each expected member as to the proposed participations, the total of the issue is covered. If the manager is not successful, one of the following occurs:

1. The syndicate members are prevailed upon to accept larger participations than initially planned
2. Members are added
3. The syndicate merges with another syndicate in order that their underwriting capabilities are adequate to cover the issue
4. The account is disbanded without submitting a bid
5. Members may bid without being fully syndicated and then adjust participations if they are successful in buying the issue

Many firms have strong views concerning their position and participation in the account as these help to determine the relative standings of firms in the investment banking field. Thus, a dealer accustomed to acceptance as a "major" participant may refuse to accept a minor level of participation as this would be interpreted by others as an indication of weakness.[5]

Agreeing upon the Price to be Bid

In all sales of bonds, a price must be established at which the buyer is willing to purchase and the issuer is willing to sell. In competitive sales of bonds, members of the syndicate must reach internal agreement as to coupon rates (i.e., the interest applicable to each maturity) and the price to be bid for the bonds. Once all bids have been reviewed, the issuer ascertains the best bid and decides whether to accept it.

An actual meeting of either the full membership (or of a representative portion) of the syndicate must take place, with some members exercising proxies for those not in attendance. With the progress in electronic communication, the meetings now frequently take place through conference telephone, telex, and other wire arrangement. Only in highly complex offerings are meetings required of the full membership. On some occasions, the terms of bidding are determined in a single pricing session; on other occasions, additional sessions or telephone conferences are required. When the market is highly volatile, changes may be made within the final minutes before closing time for submission of bids.

The bid for a bond issue is a specific total dollar price at a specific coupon rate (or rates for serial bonds). In agreeing upon the terms of a bid, the syndicate first determines the yields at which the bonds may be offered to investors; this is followed by agreement

---

[5] Although there is no fixed "pecking order" among dealers, each dealer is likely to be keenly aware of his position among his competitors. There is a continuous striving for position but this appears to be done within a fairly well understood, unwritten code among dealers. Within each level of participation in a syndicate, firms are listed in alphabetical order.

upon the proposed spread between the bid price and the reoffering yield price for the bonds, i.e., the planned gross profit. When the syndicate members have agreed upon these two matters, the manager recommends the coupon rate structure to be used and the premium (or discount, where allowed) to be bid. In the case of serial bonds, the syndicate agrees upon the reoffering yield rate for each maturity. If any member wishes to have coupons of one or more maturities at or near the end of the schedule set at rates significantly below the par reoffering yield rates for the maturities involved, he must make this known at the syndicate meeting, as a special reoffering yield is required for the discount bonds. When agreement is reached on the foregoing points, the dollar price to be bid is determined in light of the approved coupon schedule.

In some states, e.g., New Jersey and Ohio, bidders in many sales are limited to a single coupon rate for the entire serial bond issue. In such cases, the establishment of the single coupon rate to be bid may become more difficult because of the impact upon penalty yields.[6] Inasmuch as term bonds bear only a single coupon rate, they are simpler to price.

Syndicate Pricing for Bid Purposes

Table 16 illustrates how interest coupon rates are converted into prices and yields for purposes of reoffering and allowance of profit.

To understand the pricing of a municipal bond issue, it is necessary to interpose a brief statement concerning the manner in which the price is determined. The price is a function of three variables: (1) The coupon rate; (2) the term of the bond; and (3) the yield rate. Once the planned reoffering yield rate for a maturity has been determined, the present value (PV-1) of the principal and the present value of the interest (PV-1) are computed using the yield rate as a basis of discount. All calculations are made on the basis of semiannual periods with the result that a bond maturing in five years with a coupon rate of 5.50 percent and a yield rate of 4.35 percent will be on the basis of 10 periods, a 2.275 coupon rate and 2.175 yield rate. The calculations are made under the following (PV-1) formulae:

$$\text{Present value of principal} = \frac{1}{(1+i)^n} \times \$1{,}000 = \frac{1}{(1.02175)^{10}} \times \$1{,}000 = \$\ 806.41$$

$$\text{Present value of interest} = \frac{1 - \dfrac{1}{(1+i)^n}}{i} \times (c) \times (p)$$

$$= \frac{1 - \dfrac{1}{(1.02175)^{10}}}{.02175} \times .0275 \times \$1{,}000 \qquad = \underline{\ 244.77}$$

Price $\qquad\qquad\qquad\qquad\qquad\qquad\qquad\qquad\qquad = \$1051.18*$

When: i = semiannual yield rate $\qquad$ p = principal
$\qquad$ c = semiannual coupon rate $\qquad$ n = number of semiannual periods

* In most trades for medium and small lots the price would be rounded to "105.10" producing a price quoted as $1051.00.

Therefore, assuming that the bond was purchased at par, the gross profit per $1,000 for this maturity becomes $51.18 per $1,000 par value. When the reoffering yield rate exceeds the coupon rate, as in the 17th and 19th maturities in Table 16, the reoffering

---

[6] A penalty yield rate is a yield above that which would normally apply to a given maturity should all bonds be reoffered at par. The general concept of penalty rates is included in Chapter 12.

Table 16

Gross Profit Schedule for a $20,000,000 Bond Issue[1]

Years to Maturity	Maturities (000)	Coupon Rate (Percent)	Reoffering Yield Rate (Percent)	Reoffering Price Per $1,000 Par Value	Gross Profit or (Loss)	
					Per $1,000 Par Value	Total for Maturity
	(1)	(2)	(3)	(4)	(5)	(6)
1	$ 1,000	5.50	3.20	$1,022.45	$22.45	$ 22,450
2	1,000	5.50	3.50	1,038.31	38.31	38,309
3	1,000	5.50	3.80	1,047.77	47.77	47,773
4	1,000	5.50	4.10	1,051.17	51.17	51,168
5	1,000	5.50	4.35	1,051.18	51.18	51,180
6	1,000	5.50	4.60	1,046.70	46.72	46,722
7	1,000	5.50	4.80	1,041.20	41.20	41,203
8	1,000	5.50	5.00	1,032.64	32.64	32,637
9	1,000	5.50	5.20	1,021.34	21.34	21,345
10	1,000	5.40	5.25	1,011.55	11.55	11,556
11	1,000	5.50	5.50	1,000.00	—	—
12	1,000	5.60	5.60	1,000.00	—	—
13	1,000	5.70	5.70	1,000.00	—	—
14	1,000	5.80	5.80	1,000.00	—	—
15	1,000	5.90	5.90	1,000.00	—	—
16	1,000	6.00	6.00	1,000.00	—	—
17	1,000	6.00	6.10	989.51	(10.49)	(10,490)
18	1,000	6.25	6.20	1,005.38	5.38	5,377
19	1,000	6.25	6.30	994.51	(5.49)	(5,494)
20	1,000	6.35	6.35	1,000.00	—	—
Subtotal	$20,000					$353,747
Premium						1,028
Total	$20,000					$352,719

Average interest costs (percent): NIC   5.85357
TIC   5.81686

[1] Assumptions (1) Reoffering yield rates from Pattern B, Appendix Table A.
    (2) Bids required to be not less than par.
    (3) Bonds are callable @ par 10 years from date of issue.
NB. In all debt service tables where price computations are shown, values have been computed on formula basis, without rounding as is frequently done in municipal bond trading.

price is below par, i.e., at a discount. Therefore, the syndicate would sustain a loss of $10.49 per $1,000 par value on the 17th maturity and $5.49 per bond[7] on the 19th maturity. When the yield rate and the coupon rate are identical, the bond is sold at par. Assuming the syndicate paid par for the bond issue, there is no gross profit on such a bond, e.g., the 11th through the 16th and the 20th maturities in Table 16.

If the entire $20 million in Table 16 were purchased at par, the gross profit would become $353,747, or approximately $17.69 per $1,000 of principal involved. The marketing cost thereby becomes 1.769 percent of the par value involved.[8]

---

[7] For many years most bonds were sold in denominations of $1,000. Although denominations are now at the $5,000 or higher level, it is still customary to use the term "bond" to denote $1,000 of par value.

[8] The term "issuance cost" comprehends the full cost to the issuer for the sale, except for the value of time and overhead costs of officials and employees. It ordinarily includes: (1) The "spread" (also called "production" or "gross profit") between the price paid for the bonds and the price expected to be realized

In almost all issues requiring a par bid, a lump-sum premium is offered by the bidder. This is usually a small amount and constitutes a fine adjustment in the effective interest costs.[9] If the bond issue is purchased at a discount, no premium is involved as all adjustments are made in the amount of the discount bid. In Table 16 it has been assumed that a premium of $.028 has been offered. This adjusts the gross profit (spread) downward from $17.69 to $17.64 per bond.

Purchase of the Bonds

The syndicate bid must be in full conformity to bid requirements. Assuming that the bidding specifications call for a security deposit (usually in the one to two percent range), the manager makes arrangements for posting the deposit—either through requiring a deposit from each member or by securing a loan in the name of the syndicate.

The bid form itself constitutes an offer; its acceptance establishes a contract of sale[10] for the bonds at the price and under the conditions specified. Immediately upon award of the bonds to the successful bidder, the syndicate sets its sales machinery in motion. At the time bids are opened, *Munifacts*[11] furnishes to its subscribers the results of bidding and the yield rates at which the bonds will be reoffered. Normally, the investment bankers in Wall Street already know who bought the issue and are busily reoffering the bonds simultaneously with the opening of the bids. Such reoffering is informal and subject to acceptance of the bid.

Reoffering of the Bonds for Sale to Investors

At the moment the successful syndicate knows that it has bought the bonds, the race is on among members of the syndicate for sale to their customers.[12] Many investors, especially institutional investors, make purchases regularly from more than one dealer. Therefore, if two or more of the members in the syndicate have the same investor as a regular customer, the sale may go to the one who first approaches the investor—assuming that they have equal standing with the investor; or, it may become a group sale, as explained below.

Dealers are understandably secretive concerning their customer relations. Ordinarily, no reports are made to the managers of the syndicate concerning the names of investors

---

by the syndicate if all bonds are sold at the planned yield rate; (2) legal and financial fees; (3) the cost of the feasibility report, if any; (4) printing and advertising; and (5) out-of-pocket expenses incident to holding sales meetings with dealers and underwriters. The costs of elections and other expenses associated with authorization of the bonds are not ordinarily included in the term "issuance costs."

[9] At earlier times, e.g., in the 1920s, the issuer often predetermined the coupon rate at which the bonds were offered at competitive bidding. These were usually set at a rate somewhat above the projected bid rate in order to provide some flexibility for the bidder obliged to bid par for the bonds. In some cases, they were set deliberately high with a view to producing a larger premium at the bidding. Different jurisdictions followed different practices in application of the premiums, generally choosing from one of the three basic alternatives: (1) Augmenting the money available for capital outlays; (2) application in full against the debt service first payable on the bond issue; or (3) deposit in the sinking fund with its use acting to decrease projected annual debt service costs over the life of the issue.

[10] The "sale" at this point is actually a conditional sale on a "when, as, and if issued" basis and subject to receipt of a satisfactory legal opinion.

[11] *Munifacts* is a wire service offered by *The Bond Buyer*. All large and many smaller dealers subscribe to this very useful service. By this process, the industry gains information on a national basis in a timely manner. Orders for new issues or repricing of older outstanding bonds can follow immediately.

[12] Frequently, bidders supply the details of their bids to *Munifacts* in advance of the opening of the bids. On occasion, this has resulted in circulation of the bids in the trade before they are opened—a practice which has resulted in confusion among some issuers.

to whom sales are made or the amounts sold to them. This is an expected characteristic of a business that is so highly competitive. The competition among members of the syndicate for sales of an issue is all the keener because the price for the initial sale of a specific issue of bonds is fixed. All dealers must sell bonds of a given maturity at identical prices—except to the extent that the syndicate affords special consideration to some large institutional buyers which maintain dealer departments.

In the formation of the syndicate and preparation of the bid, agreement will have been reached concerning the price or yield upon which each maturity will be sold, the amount of "concession" that will be permitted, and the "order period"[13]—the time during which members of the syndicate are permitted to place their orders for specific bonds with the manager who is maintaining the book for the sale. The order period begins at the moment the syndicate knows it will purchase the bonds. It may run for as little as an hour or for much longer periods.

During the order period, each member plans its order for bonds with the manager, but no allotments of bonds are confirmed until after the close of the period. The purpose of the order period is to prevent a few members, and particularly the manager, from selling all or a large part of the issue, or selling out the most popular maturities before the other members have an opportunity to order bonds. It also is supposed to afford some opportunity to investors, regardless of size, to purchase bonds in which they may be interested.

If the issue proves very attractive, the amount of the subscriptions will exceed the amount of the bonds available. Thereupon, the manager has a delicate problem in appropriately allotting the bonds among the members. Sometimes rules are established at the price meeting to provide a guide to the manager on the allotment; but, usually it is left to his discretion. In allotting bonds where there is a conflict among orders, i.e., orders for more than the number of bonds available for a given maturity, the manager is expected to work for the benefit of the whole account—rather than the benefit of any individual member. Thus, he may give preference to a large order over a small one, or to the order which he believes will "put the bonds away," i.e., place them with an investor who is likely to hold them for a considerable period of time, rather than with a dealer outside the account who is buying them for speculative or trading purposes (for "mark-up"). This system of reoffering will frequently appear on the financial pages in substantially the form shown in Exhibit A.

A problem is sometimes posed as to which syndicate member will be allowed the commission on the purchase of a large block of bonds by an investor. Such a large buyer, who would otherwise be approached by numerous dealers, customarily will speak directly to the manager and request that his purchase be entered as a "group sale." He thus avoids numerous calls and the need for making an unwelcome choice among a number of dealers with whom he frequently does business. If this request is approved, no take-down profit[14] goes to any member of the syndicate. Rather, the profit goes to the account and is shared by all members in proportion to their participations. Often such sales are agreed to at the final price meeting. Another practice is for large investors to designate the distribution of the sales among dealers designated by the investor.

---

[13] An order period is the time within which each member of the syndicate signifies the number of bonds of each maturity each wishes to acquire from the account. This will be a combination of the bonds each member has sold and those which he believes he can sell or wishes to hold in inventory. Bonds are added to inventory based on a judgment that the bonds will shortly advance in price, thereby enabling the dealer to realize an additional profit. Generally, during the period of syndication, each dealer is obliged to sell only at the price designated by the syndicate.

[14] "Take-down" is, in fact, a commission paid by the syndicate to a member for selling bonds. It varies according to the amount of profit in the deal and averages about one-third of gross profit. Take-down for the more easily sold maturities (usually the shorter maturities) will be less than take-down for the harder to sell maturities (usually the longer ones).

Other Considerations

In addition to the sales made by the members of the syndicate, a considerable portion of the total sales may be produced by dealers who are not members. This is accomplished by authorizing a specified "concession" to nonmember dealers to encourage them to assist in the distribution of the bonds. The profit margin established by the syndicate in such circumstances is binding upon all members of the syndicate in their dealings with nonmember dealers. Concessions are frequently stated in terms of a fraction of a percent of the price of a bond, e.g., a $1,000 bond that may be priced for resale to the investor at $1,052.50 might be offered to a nonmember dealer at a concession of $\frac{1}{2}$ or $\frac{3}{4}$, enabling him to purchase it for $1,047.50 or $1,045.00.[15]

Each new sale of municipals takes place within the context of unsold portions of other new-issue bonds and of the amount of bonds available in the secondary market. The opinion of the syndicate is a professional judgment of the market for the new issue at the time of sale. It takes into account the full range of general market factors as well as specific factors seen by the syndicate in marketing the issue under immediate consideration. Finally, it reflects to some degree the amounts of unsold securities, if any, owned by the major members of the syndicate.

It is the view of the investment bankers that, once having purchased the securities, delay enhances the risk of loss. Therefore, the syndicate is anxious to sell the bonds it has purchased as promptly as possible—preferably on the day of purchase. Even a small adverse change in the market can greatly reduce, or wipe out, the anticipated gross profit on the sale. Conversely, the syndicate is obliged to sell the bonds at the advertised yield. Hence, it cannot reprice the bonds to take into account a favorable market change following purchase of the securities. Indicative of the magnitude of the impact of relatively small changes, if the bonds in Table 16 were reoffered at 10 basis points higher yield on each maturity, i.e., 3.30 percent on the first and 3.60 on the second, etc., the spread would be reduced to $208,515. After sales commissions and costs are paid, the members of the syndicate may realize little, if any, net profit from their work in distributing the $20 million in bonds.

The syndicate may have properly judged the general market on the day of sale but may have misjudged the attitude of investors toward the particular securities. Or, there may have been a last minute adverse development of some type that depreciated the value of the securities just purchased. Under these circumstances, the syndicate must either reprice the securities in order to sell them or dissolve the syndicate. Should the syndicate be dissolved, each member must take its pro rata share of the unsold bonds, as determined under the syndicate agreement. Thereafter, each member of the dissolved syndicate establishes the prices at which it can sell its share of bonds.

The volume of new offerings in the investment market varies widely from day to day, from week to week, and from month to month. Thus, in 1980, new long-term loans reported by *The Bond Buyer* ranged from a low of $2.4 billion in March to a high of $6.0 billion in June. But in other years, e.g., 1975, the range is much narrower—$2.0 to $3.4 billion. In these circumstances, the investment bankers must maintain organizations for sales and incur other elements of expense sufficient to cope with very large volumes while having much lower workloads during the slack months. Secondary market transactions also reflect wide monthly and seasonal variations.

Participation in the Preparation of a Disclosure Statement

Issuers are generally required by the underwriters to prepare a disclosure statement as a prerequisite to the purchase of bonds. It has become customary for the representatives

---

[15] Concessions are made by the syndicate for nonmember firms to encourage distribution through such nonmember firms.

of the syndicates in the larger issues to become involved in the preparation of such statements by accepting an *underwriters' counsel* agreeable to them. It is advisable that the issuer seek to secure agreement in advance among the known potential bidders upon the underwriters' counsel in order that the preparation of the disclosure statement can proceed in an orderly manner.[16]

ROLE OF THE INVESTMENT BANKER IN NEGOTIATED SALES

With the dramatic shift from competitive to negotiated sales, many finance officers are confronting new and added responsibilities. Negotiation offers both interesting potentials and major challenges to the issuer and its representatives. The general problems are discussed in Chapter 17; the focus here is upon some of the differences in the role played by the investment banker in negotiated and competitive sales.

Formation and Function of the Syndicate

Whereas in a competitive sale the role of the issuer is passive insofar as syndicate formation and performance are concerned, the reverse is true in negotiated sales where the role of the issuer is critical. The choice of negotiation has been the issuer's choice. Having made this choice, the responsibility for protecting the public interest passes fully to the issuer. No longer can refuge be taken in the protections afforded by competitive bidding. If the negotiation fails or if the public interest is not adequately protected, it is the issuer's fault unless circumstances make it impossible to negotiate a successful sale. Under these circumstances, the choice of the leadership of the investment banking syndicate, the choice of the remainder of the syndicate, the gross compensation, and the pattern of distribution of that compensation are matters of concern of both the issuer and the members of the syndicate. And, of course, the interest costs to be paid are of paramount importance. The discussion of these matters is reserved for Chapter 19 which deals with the conduct of the sale from the standpoint of the issuer.

The function of the syndicate in the negotiated sale is basically that of working cooperatively with the issuer and with investors to bring about a sale under reasonable terms.

The investment banking syndicate in a negotiated sale has a responsibility to bring to the attention of the issuer every aspect of the design of the issue which the syndicate believes will facilitate the sale of the issue on terms that are advantageous to the issuer—consistent, of course, with the profit objective of the members of the syndicate. In developing the program for sale of the bonds, the issuer has a right to expect the management of the syndicate to have intimate knowledge of the market and investor preferences.

Among the results that the issuer should seek in a negotiated sale is a commitment that every effort will be made by members of the syndicate to place the bonds with investors likely to "put them away." That is, to place the bonds in such a manner that they will be held for at least a reasonable time by the investors—not merely be placed on a speculative basis to reappear at an early date.

No enforceable contract can be made to the effect that the members of the syndicate, especially members of the management of the syndicate, will maintain an interest in the securities and help to facilitate secondary market[17] exchange of the securities. On the other hand, in cases in which the issuer is contemplating future financings that may be of interest to the members of the syndicate, it is appropriate to make it clear that an

---

[16] See Chapter 18 for a general discussion of disclosure.

[17] The secondary market is properly defined as the market in which bonds are traded after confirmation of the initial sale to the purchaser (usually an investor) by a member of the underwriting syndicate, or by the manager of the syndicate to a dealer that has purchased the bonds, even though not a member of the syndicate.

evaluation of their performance will extend to secondary market operations in respect to outstanding securities that have been sold through these firms.

Beyond the foregoing, the functions of the syndicate in a negotiated sale are similar to those in a competitive sale.

THE SECONDARY MARKET

The attention of finance officers is likely to be focused on the primary market. It is there that they see their bonds purchased by syndicates. To a degree to which they are not ordinarily aware, the prices they receive for their bonds when issued are greatly influenced by the prices being accorded to their outstanding bonds and to similar bonds outstanding. Although many investors in municipal bonds purchase them with the intent of holding them to maturity, a larger percentage of the purchasers do not. Moreover, even for those having such intent, circumstances change and the original decision to hold onto the bonds is altered. Due to these factors, the investor takes into consideration the liquidity of the bonds as a part of his investment decision. He has a rightful concern about his ability to sell the bonds promptly at a reasonable price should he find it appropriate to sell. The market through which such sales occur is referred to as the *secondary market*.

Nature of the Market

The secondary market for most municipal bonds is a vastly different market from that for either equity or debt corporate securities. It also differs materially from the market for bonds of the U.S. Government and its agencies. Insofar as a basic market is concerned, only in the case of the relatively small number of bond issues known as "dollar bonds" and for other issues for which dealers from time to time seek to "make a market" is there anything resembling the market for private securities or that for government bonds.

Several reasons help account for the absence of an organized market comparable to that for other securities, among which the principal are: (1) The wide diversity in security actually pledged for different municipal securities, (2) the prevailing use of serial bonds and (3) the diversity of coupon rates. These latter two factors result in a relatively few bonds of the same coupon rate maturing at the same time. Thus, even in a large municipal bond issue, the maximum amount of bonds likely to be maturing in a single year, except for term bonds or block-term bonds, is a few million dollars. For most bond issues the current volume of trading in respect to a given maturity is too small to warrant an attempt to maintain a market so finely tuned to reflect an acknowledged price level for given maturities of each issue. Moreover, minor differences in security pledged by the same issuer may be sufficient either to confuse the secondary market or to warrant differential yield rates for different issues.

Another factor is the tendency to trade municipal bonds on a yield basis, rather than on a price basis. The use of the yield basis permits an easier comparison between different bonds than does a price basis. Even so, the effects of capital gains taxes rob even the yield basis of some of its meaning for tax-exempt bonds.

Structure of the Market

The secondary municipal market is not an organized market in the same sense as the stock market. The operations in this market have only recently begun to come under substantial regulation through the operation of the Municipal Securities Rulemaking Board (MSRB). The rules of the MSRB are enforced by the National Association of Securities Dealers (a trade association operating under the oversight of the Securities and Exchange Commission) for its members, by the Securities and Exchange Commission itself for sole municipal dealers, and by the Comptroller of the Currency for the Federal Reserve System or the Federal Deposit Insurance Corporation for bank dealers.

The major center for trading in municipals is New York; although, with the increase in population and wealth, other regions are developing significant regional strength which enables them to handle issues of considerable size. This is especially true of the larger banks headquartered outside New York. In any event, nationwide trading does not flow through New York to the extent that trading in stocks still so flows. One reason for this lies in the fact that the vast majority of bonds in the market are bearer bonds, i.e., they are negotiable instruments which pass directly from seller to buyer or from dealer to dealer without going through a transfer agent for each trade as does each trade in stock and corporate bonds.

Dealers in the Secondary Market

Many of the larger investment firms and banks that underwrite municipals maintain municipal trading departments. In fact, under the rules of the MSRB they are virtually obliged to do so. Within the overall market, some security dealers and numerous commercial banks rarely or never participate in an underwriting. Also, there are municipal bond brokers who do no underwriting but who are active in the secondary market.

In addition to the investment banker dealers, the commercial banks comprise an active portion of the secondary market as investors. As of December 31, 1980, the commercial banks held $149 billion of state and municipal securities—about 44 percent of the aggregate amount outstanding. Only a very small portion of these holdings could be classified as inventory for trading purposes. On the other hand, the banks do trade widely in these securities in the sense that they are more or less constantly buying or selling for their investment account as well as for their trading accounts. Under 1975 legislation and the MSRB rules, the banks are now obliged to differentiate between their two kinds of holdings and their dealer activities must be conducted by a separately identifiable department.

Some dealers and dealer banks undertake to "make a market" for a given number of securities. By this is meant that the dealer assumes a position in a given security, i.e., the dealer acquires an inventory of a considerable number of bonds of the same or related issues. Thus, the dealer firm or dealer department may "make a market" for one or more issues of a single issuer or a number of issuers. Generally, those wishing to sell bonds will find a ready buyer from those who "make market" in that security. Conversely, those interested in purchasing such bonds go to the dealer as a specialist in the issue concerned.

Municipal Bond Brokers

As there are no security exchanges dealing in municipals, the dealers throughout the country conduct most of their business by wire (occasionally by correspondence). In this process of nationwide trading, municipal bond brokers play an important role. Largely concentrated in New York City, they trade only with dealers and not with investors. They act solely as brokers. They do not take a position, i.e., buy or sell for their own account. They bring dealers together, adding better information for liquidity in an otherwise cumbersome market. Accordingly, the broker never loses money on a position if the market moves but only foregoes profits lost because of missed trades. He only loses money on "fails," i.e., transactions not completed. The active municipal bond broker has a relatively small staff of traders who are in constant wire communication with dealers throughout the country. Brokers endeavor to know what bonds the dealers have to offer and what they seek to purchase.

In a way, municipal bond brokers serve the function of an exchange. A dealer who has an order to buy (or sell) a quantity of a particular bond calls a broker who knows which dealers are likely to have an interest in buying or selling such a bond. When the broker finds an interested dealer and a satisfactory price can be agreed upon, the broker will either buy for the account of the purchaser or sell for the account of the seller, without revealing the identity of either. For this service, the broker obtains a very small commission; however, his volume is ordinarily large. Frequently, he will find many bids or offerings from which to select the best for the inquiring dealer, and he may trade an entire list of bonds for a dealer. An active broker can save time and money for dealers and considerably broaden their market.

Methods of Trading

The investor buying or selling municipal bonds usually does so through a commercial bank or a securities dealer. There are instances where one individual or institution buys from another but such instances are few. One of the limiting factors on direct sales between investors is the absence of a quoted market. Inasmuch as the municipal market is essentially a professional market, buyers and sellers generally need professional guidance on market value of bonds traded, with consequent protection afforded thereby.

For the investor having access to a qualified dealer, the purchase of municipal bonds usually presents no problems other than those of selection and price. For the seller, the alternatives may include:

1. Sale to a dealer, acting as a principal, at an agreed price
2. Placing an order with a dealer who, under a commission arrangement, is to seek the best price
3. Establishing a price on a consignment to a dealer with a commission arrangement
4. Advertising for bids either directly or through a dealer

Choice of the method to be used depends largely upon the size of the transaction and the judgment of the dealer. Most orders are handled by either of the first two methods. An active dealer maintaining an inventory of municipals will offer to buy bonds from the holder at a price the dealer believes will afford a reasonable profit upon resale. If the number of bonds is too great for the dealer to buy for his own account, he may arrange joint secondary accounts with other dealers to handle the trade. If the dealer does not want to take the bonds into the firm's trading position, the best bid available from other dealers may be sought and a trade made on a commission basis.

In either case, it may be assumed that the investor has confidence in the judgment and integrity of the dealer. If not, or if the investor has his own ideas of the market value, he may set a price and give the dealer a commission for finding a buyer and handling the transaction. The hazard here is that the investor's idea may be wide of the market; accordingly, he may have a long wait before he sells his bonds or may not be able to sell them at all at his indicated price level, whereas sales by either of the first two methods are usually executed promptly. Alternatively, he may offer them too cheaply.

The fourth method—advertising for bids—is used infrequently. It is not a feasible alternative for the average investor due to its cost, the delay involved, and potential adverse impact on the market if a large amount is involved.

Some bond issues, usually larger issues of general market bonds, are traded on the basis of specific dollar price, rather than on the basis of yield. All are term bond issues. Any bond may be so traded; however, the group regularly traded in this manner is usually limited to bonds of about 30 issuers, embracing a total of 50 or 60 separate issues. The bid and asked prices are quoted daily in *The Bond Buyer*. In addition, a number of other issues and issuers are similarly handled through *The Blue List* offerings but only on the offered side.

Once a yield basis for a trade has been agreed upon (except for the dollar bonds), the dollar price (PV-1) is determined by computers using the formula set forth earlier in this chapter. The price is computed as of the day of intended settlement and accrued interest to that date is added. Of course, the bond may be offered on a price basis, in which case the only remaining factor is determination of accrued interest. If the buyer wishes to convert the price to a yield basis, this is also done by computer. Settlement and delivery are normally scheduled for the fifth business day following the date of the trade. Unless otherwise stated, it is understood that the bonds are in coupon form and are accompanied by or bear an acceptable legal opinion (now frequently printed on the bonds). Anything less than $25,000 is considered an odd lot and usually will not bring as good a price as a regular lot. Registered bonds are less marketable than bearer bonds, and generally sell at lower prices—due to the nuisance, time, and expense in securing a prompt change in registration or of exchanging registered bonds for bearer bonds. Accordingly, an owner of registered bonds usually arranges the conversion to coupon bonds in advance of the offer to sell.

Financing the Market

In the secondary market, most municipal bonds are sold to dealers acting as principals. When they remain in the dealer's hands overnight or longer (for days or weeks), temporary financing is required. The $1.1 billion inventory of municipal bonds held by the dealers at the close of 1980 helps to indicate the size of the holdings—some of which were, of course, bonds unsold from purchases in the primary market; however, inasmuch as they do not enter inventory until settlement date, only a relatively small amount of such bonds is likely to appear in inventory.

Any dealer active in municipals ordinarily carries an inventory of bonds for sale. This inventory he finances in part from the firm's capital, but the business would rarely be profitable if the firm were obliged to rely solely upon its own capital. An active dealer will often carry an inventory of a value many times that of the firm's capital. If the dealer is an investment firm, this inventory is usually carried by bank loans or customer credit balances. Thus, at the end of 1980, the *Flow of Funds* statement estimated that security brokers and dealers had security credit from banks of $17.2 billion against net equity of about $2.4 billion at a time when their financial assets exceeded financial liabilities by $3.3 billion.[18] Sale and repurchase agreements have also been used by some firms to finance their inventories. If the dealer is a bank, its inventory is financed in the same manner as the bank's investments and loans. Availability of bank credit is essential to a satisfactory functioning of the municipal market.

The dealer firms have increasingly become incorporated and some of them have become held largely by other corporations that can provide greater capital.

Judging the Market

The Blue List. An essential tool of the present-day municipal market is *The Blue List of Current Municipal Offerings,* commonly referred to simply as *The Blue List.* This is a publication issued after the close of each day's business which contains a list of offerings by dealers in state and local government tax-exempt bonds.[19] It now also contains as additional features:

Housing authority bonds	New issue delivery dates
Industrial development bonds	Federally sponsored bonds
Pollution control bonds	Prerefunded bonds
Notes [short-term]	Corporate bonds
Tax-exempt investment trusts	Preferred stocks

---

[18] Board of Governors of the Federal Reserve System, *Flow of Funds Accounts: Assets and Liabilities Outstanding, 1957–1980* (February, 1981), p. 29.

[19] *The Blue List* maintains a wire service that shows, on a continuous basis throughout the day, changes in offerings as they are entered into the computer in New York.

The list is distributed primarily to dealers on a subscription basis. A single issue may carry more than 15,000 listings, ranging in amount from a few thousand dollars to more than $10 million on a single line. In most municipal departments of banks and in most active dealers' offices, the careful examination of *The Blue List* is a required daily routine.

The monthly range of municipal offerings in *The Blue List* is very wide, due in part to listings being included for unsold balances of certain difficult-to-sell new-issue securities.

Considering the great diversity of municipal bonds and of municipal bond investors and the wide geographical range of both the primary and secondary markets, it is perhaps surprising that the market does such an efficient job in bringing the buyers and sellers together in the secondary market and the issuers and investors together in the primary market. If the secondary market be judged by the spread between bid and asking prices, it probably functions best in blocks of $100,000 or more of bonds of well-known and well-respected names, when those bonds are selling near par. It is not so efficient for bonds of low credit rating and of little-known names. It is often unsatisfactory for odd lots and for bonds selling at substantial discounts from par. The costs of a trade may be at less than $2.50 per $1,000 par value under the most favorable conditions or as much as $40 or $50 when the bond is difficult to move. Although bids for bonds which are not in demand may often seem low to the bondholder, this does not necessarily mean that they are unreasonable bids in light of market conditions. When there have been no recent sales and when the issuer is not well known, the dealer may be obliged to hold the bond for a long time and eventually sell it cheaply. Moreover, small lot sales frequently involve as much time and processing cost as large lots; hence, the cost for the small lot is likely to be a greater percentage of the par value involved.

For the typical public finance officer, the most readily available means of maintaining knowledge of the market is through local banks and other dealers, the columns of *The Bond Buyer,* and *The Blue List.* If the issuer has a financial advisor, he can ordinarily provide independent advice concerning the current market value of securities of the issuer. In the examination of prices and yields, one must be cognizant of the impact of the federal and state capital gains tax and of the state capital gains and income taxes upon the prices of bonds. When bonds are selling below par, capital gains taxes are important; otherwise, one may be misled as to the after-tax yield involved. Generally, the lower the coupon rate in relation to the yield rate, the more important capital gains taxes become.

Market Regulation

Until 1975 there was relatively little regulation of the municipal market on a national basis. States varied in the degree to which they sought to supervise operations. Following the problems in New York in February 1975, Congress amended its security laws to establish the Municipal Securities Rulemaking Board. Its rules now cover many of the practices of municipal bond dealers but it has no power over issuers.[20]

---

[20] See Commerce Clearing House, Inc., *Municipal Securities Rulemaking Board Manual* and the annual reports of the Municipal Securities Rulemaking Board.

Chapter 5
THE INVESTORS

In the decade of the 1970s more then $300 billion in long-term, tax-exempt bonds were issued. When the huge amounts of short-term financing are added, the total amount of financing for the decade rose to the magnitude of $500 billion.[1] Most issuers pay relatively little attention to the investors who purchase and hold their bonds. They are much more aware of the investment bankers through whom the bonds are distributed in the market. Many do not realize that, without the market for their securities provided by the present group of holders, it would be necessary to find alternative investors and also greatly to modify their capital programs and financing operations. Finding these other investors is difficult. The prices at which they could be induced to purchase and hold municipal securities vary with their tax status, investment objectives, and available alternatives for investment.

Although the typical issuer of municipal bonds cannot be expected to maintain a current grasp of significant developments in the market, such issuers cannot afford to be totally ignorant of a factor so important in planning their capital programs and debt issuance activities. The function of this chapter is to provide an elementary introduction to the subject, i.e., the shifting patterns of ownership of municipal securities. The chapter commences with an identification of the principal sectors and the volume of financial assets of each. It comments briefly upon the relationship between the tax status of municipal securities and the attraction of these securities to different economic sectors. It concludes with comparing the changing patterns in the ownership of municipals to the financial assets of these sectors.

THE FINANCIAL SECTORS OF THE ECONOMY AND THEIR FINANCIAL ASSETS

Until the mid-1960s, there were no composite accounts reflecting the financial assets and liabilities of different sectors of the economy. Much progress has since been made in economic reporting with numerous governmental and nongovernmental organizations, economists, and others participating in the development of data systems. One of the results is a series of publications that appear under the general title of *Flow of Funds,* officially described thusly:

> The flow of funds system of national accounts is designed to bring the many financial activities of the U.S. economy into explicit statistical relationship with one another and into direct relation to data on the nonfinancial activities that generate income and production.[2]

The presentation is viewed essentially as an econometric model, reflecting development on an historical basis. It is not offered as a precise statement of accounts. As a consequence,

---

[1] *The Bond Buyer,* January 9, 1980, p. 14, shows a total of $308 billion long-term debt and $236 billion of short-term issues.

[2] Board of Governors of the Federal Reserve System, *Introduction to Flow of Funds* (Washington, D.C., 1975), p. 2.

it evolves and is refined over time as more elements of actual data supplant estimates required to produce model outputs on a current basis. As the data for a given year matures, adjustments in the previous statement for the same year are required. Generally, these follow-up changes are of limited relative significance although they are sometimes substantial in absolute terms for some accounts. The system of reporting affords a useful basis for a general appreciation of levels of financial assets of sectors of the economy, quarterly changes in levels, and the manner in which each sector and subsector invests its financial assets— including investments in the securities of state and local governments.

Before discussing the financial assets of economic sectors, it is appropriate to differentiate between financial and nonfinancial assets. Financial assets consist of intangible personal property, including: Money; life insurance reserves of households; bank deposits, both demand and time (savings); various types of equity and debt credit market instruments, i.e., shares in corporations, bonds, and notes. Nonfinancial assets consist of such items as land, improvements to the land, structures, and tangible personal property—household goods, inventories, motor vehicles, farm machinery, and other tangible personal property. [See Exhibit B for definitions of the economic sectors used by the Federal Reserve System.]

Absorption of the debt issued by state and local governments occurs from the investment of financial assets by different sectors of the economy. It is therefore appropriate to view the total financial assets in our national economy. To do this, data from the *Flow of Funds* statement are summarized in Table 17. [In a sense, the $10,747 billion of financial assets shown in Table 17 is misleading because there are significant duplications between sectors. For example, a commercial bank will show state and local government obligations as a part of its assets but the value of the stock of the banks and deposits therein will appear in the asset statements of other sectors that own such stock or deposits. Hence, the importance in Table 17 is not so much the distribution of financial assets among the sectors but rather the extent to which each sector is an owner of the obligations or other debt of state and local governments. Yet, the aggregate amount of financial assets of the individual sectors, together with their investment policies, help to determine the amounts of state and local government obligations which can be absorbed by the respective sectors and by the economy as a whole.]

The sector holdings of state and local government debt and the relationships of such holdings to the financial assets of the sector are shown in Table 17. From that table it may be seen that the combined nonfinancial sectors at the end of 1980 had invested only 1.8 percent of their financial assets in such debt as compared to 5.9 percent for the domestic financial sectors.

In the individual sectors, it is found that the nonlife (casualty) insurance companies found state and local government debt most attractive—having invested 45 percent of total financial assets in these securities. Next came the commercial banks with 12 percent and open-end investment trusts with 10 percent. Beyond these sectors, it is found that others had invested less than 1/30th of their financial assets in state and local governments and that many had no such holdings in their asset portfolios.

The sectors of the economy holding measurable amounts of state and local government securities are identified in Table 17 in column 2. In some of these sectors, almost all entities within the sector hold at least some municipal securities, e.g., the commercial banks; in others, e.g., households, only selected portions of the sector have an interest in this type of investment. Interest is stimulated by after-tax return in relation to risk and other opportunities for investment return. This emphasizes the tax status of municipals for some sectors. In others, e.g., personal finance companies and real estate investment trusts, the only interest likely to be shown is transitory and limited to occasional purchases of short-term securities.

In all instances, however, the availability of financial assets defines the limits within which interest can be expressed through purchase. Thus, the rapid growth in recent years of the assets of casualty insurance companies has helped to make available a huge amount

Table 17

Financial Assets of Economic Sectors and their Holdings of State and Local Government Obligations as of December 31, 1980

(amounts in billions of dollars)

	Financial Assets	Holdings of State and Local Government Obligations	
		Amount	As a Percent of Financial Assets
	(1)	(2)	(3)
Total	10,747	361.5	3.4
Domestic: Nonfinancial	6,057	109.4	1.8
Households, personal trusts & nonprofit corps.	4,494	74.2	1.7
Business	1,040	21.3	2.0
Corporate	958	21.3*	2.2
Other	82	—	—
Farm	25	—	—
State and local government general funds	216	6.5	3.0
U.S. Government	307	7.6	2.5
Domestic: Financial	4,251	252.2	5.9
Commercial banking	1,387	149.2	10.8
Commercial banks	1,245	149.2	12.0
Domestic affiliates of commercial banks	30	—	—
Edge Act corporations and agencies of foreign banks	101	—	—
Banks in U.S. possessions	11	—	—
Private nonbank financial agencies	2,383	103.0	4.2
Saving and loan associations	630	1.2	.1
Mutual savings banks	172	2.4	1.4
Credit unions	69	—	—
Life insurance companies	470	6.7	1.4
Other insurance companies (casualty)	180	81.1	45.1
Private pension funds	287	—	—
State and local govt. pension funds	198	4.1	2.1
Finance companies	199	—	—
Real estate investment trusts	6	—	—
Open-end investment trusts	64	6.4	10.0
Money market funds	74	—	—
Security brokers and dealers	34	1.1	3.3
Monetary authority	174	—	—
Agencies and mortgage pools sponsored by U.S. Government	307	—	—
Foreign Sector	439	—	—

* Comprised of $3.5 billion of securities and $17.8 billion of trade debt.
Source: Board of Governors of the Federal Reserve System, *Flow of Funds Accounts: Assets and Liabilities 1957–1980* (September 1981), pp. 9–29.

Exhibit B

Defined Economic Sectors Used by Board of Governors of the Federal Reserve System

Households include—in addition to persons as members of households—personal trusts and nonprofit organizations serving individuals, such as foundations, private schools and hospitals, labor unions, churches, and charitable organizations. . .

Farm business covers all farming activities in the United States including corporate farms.

Nonfarm noncorporate business consists of partnerships and proprietorships in nonfinancial enterprises, including individuals' rental activities and the professions.

Corporate nonfinancial business comprises all private corporations not specifically covered in financial sectors. It includes holding companies and closed-end investment companies on a consolidated basis, and it includes real estate firms.

State and local government—General funds comprise all political subdivisions of the United States, and all corporations, enterprises, debt-issuing authorities, and trust funds operated by these subdivisions, other than employee retirement funds; these last are shown separately as a financial sector.

Commercial banks cover all banks in the 50 States, as defined by the coverage of all-bank statistics in annual reports of the Comptroller of the Currency. The sector excludes banks in U.S. territories and possessions, which are a separate sector.

Domestic affiliates of commercial banks are mainly holding-company parents of banks and nonbank subsidiaries of bank holding companies.

Foreign banking agencies are a combination of Edge Act corporations and agencies of foreign banks. Edge Act corporations are subsidiaries of U.S. banks engaged in international banking under Section 25 of the Federal Reserve Act.

Banks in U.S. territories and possessions . . . consist of those currently published by the FDIC. It includes branches of U.S. and foreign banks in these areas.

Savings and loan associations are mutual and stock institutions chartered by States and the Federal Government to accept share capital inflows and to lend primarily in mortgages. The group consists of associations covered in Federal Home Loan Bank Board statistics, including noninsured associations.

Mutual savings banks are institutions operated under savings bank charters in 19 States with deposit insurance from FDIC.

Credit unions are employee organizations related to individual firms or agencies that are organized under State or Federal charter to accept share funds from members and to lend consumer credit to members. The group consists of all State and Federal credit unions in statistics published by the Bureau of Federal Credit Unions in the Department of Health, Education and Welfare.

Life insurance companies are those covered in the Life Insurance Institute's *Fact Book* but excludes fraternal orders. Government life insurance programs are also excluded; they are in the U.S. Government sector account.

Other insurance companies are the fire, casualty, and other companies covered in *Best's Aggregates and Averages*.

Private pension funds are defined in the annual statistics on self-administered pension funds published by the Securities and Exchange Commission. They include retirement funds of nonprofit organizations and multiemployer plans shown in those data.

State and local government employee retirement funds are the group of such funds reported in the *Census of Governments*.

Finance companies comprise sales finance, consumer loan, and commercial finance companies covered in the Federal Reserve's 5-year Censuses of Finance Companies. This group also includes mortgage companies.

Real estate investment trusts (REIT's) are a relatively new form of intermediary that, through 1960 legislation, are exempt from Federal corporate income tax provided they distribute most of their ordinary income to shareholders and provided most of their investments and gross income

---

Exhibit B *(continued)*

are from real estate or mortgages. They can be either open end or closed-end, but in practice all trusts created so far have been closed-end companies.

Open-end investment companies (mutual funds) are the group reported by the Investment Company Institute. Closed-end companies are consolidated with the nonfinancial corporate business sector.

Security brokers and dealers are based on aggregates for such firms registered with the Securities and Exchange Commission.

Monetary authorities consist of the Federal Reserve System and certain monetary accounts of the Treasury: the gold account, the silver account, and an account constructed to record other currency liabilities of the Government and the assets behind those liabilities.

Federally sponsored credit agencies are a financial sector consisting of five types of specialized lending institutions that had originally been created by the Government and owned by the Government to varying extents. Government equity has been fully retired, and they are now excluded from the Governmental budget accounts as private institutions. . . . The agencies are:

> Federal home loan banks
> Federal National Mortgage Association
> Federal land banks
> Federal intermediate credit banks
> Bank for cooperatives

U.S. Government covers, for all years, the agencies and funds that are in the Government's unified budget as of 1969, except the District of Columbia. Included are the Exchange Stabilization Fund, employee retirement funds, life insurance funds, and all corporations that are wholly or partly owned by the Government . . . The sector does not include the Federal Reserve System and certain treasury monetary accounts that constitute the monetary authority sector, and it does not include a set of sponsored credit agencies. [See above.]

Rest of the world* is as defined in the balance of payments statement for the United States, and the data in this sector account are from that statement, with financial transactions classified into flow of funds categories and nonfinancial transactions as published in the income and product accounts.

Source: Board of Governors of the Federal Reserve System. *Introduction to Flow of Funds* (February 1975). pp. 34–38.

*Subsequent to 1975 a new category—money market funds—was added and the *Rest of the world* category was redefined as the *Foreign sector.*

---

of additional money for investment. And, it happens that the combination of tax and other factors has resulted in the investment of very large portions of these increased financial assets in municipal bonds. Thus, in the period 1969–1975, investments in municipal securities by this group accounted for 68 percent of their growth in financial assets, and in the period 1974–1979, more than half their increase in financial assets was used to increase their holdings of municipals.

This type of relationship between financial assets and investment practices of different segments of the economy are of major importance to the issuers of municipal securities.

TAX STATUS OF MUNICIPAL SECURITIES

Although there are various tax shelters under federal, state, and local laws, and although some sectors of the economy are exempt from taxation in respect of all or portions of their property and/or income, it is the tax-exempt feature of state and local government securities that makes them attractive to taxable economic sectors at the relatively low yield rates at which they sell.[3] The degree of their interest is much influenced by the

---

[3] The United States Internal Revenue Code of 1954 in Section 103 defines the basic exemption of interest on state and local government obligations as a part of gross income for purposes of determining liability under corporate and individual income tax provisions of the code.

characteristics and objectives of their business operations, their profitability, and the opportunity costs involved in the selection of financial investments. For those who are taxed, it becomes a question as to the relationship of the after-tax yield of the taxable investments vis-à-vis the yield of tax-exempt investments.

Even within those sectors holding tax-exempt securities, portions of the sector invest very little in these securities. Thus, nonprofit corporations and individuals of low and moderate taxable income (both important parts of the household sector) have minimal holdings while others in the sector are substantial investors. On the other hand, while the U.S. Government gains no advantage from the tax status of municipal bonds, from time to time it has substantial holdings for other policy reasons. There is no effective central reporting of the holdings of certain federal agencies of credit market instruments or of the amounts of outstanding loans to state and local governments. The *Flow of Funds* statements do contain information concerning U.S. Government loans to state and local governments, e.g., $6.6 billion reported as of the close of 1977. However, this amount is distorted by the substantial amounts advanced to the state employment security operations that were in deficit positions in their unemployment compensation operations.

Federal Tax Exemptions

Since the enactment of the United States income tax in 1913, the interest paid on obligations issued by state and local governments has generally been deemed to be free from federal income taxation. When fully operative, the exemption has the effect of greatly increasing the after-tax income for numerous investors. The effects vary, depending upon how the provisions of federal tax law apply to different investment sectors and on profitability of the investor at the time. Thus, in the case of individuals, at the same time the law provides tax exemption for interest on municipal bonds, it gives tax preferences or exemptions to other elements of income (e.g., long-term capital gains, accelerated depreciation, and depletion allowances and the All Savers Certificates) as well as encouraging some types of investments through tax credits.

The subject of federal tax exemption is much too complex to treat even superficially here; however, summary comments on a few aspects of federal tax policy as they relate to the treatment of income from state and local government debt may help to explain some of the trends reported in this chapter.

Bonds Sold at Discount on Initial Sale. When bonds are originally sold by the issuer at a discount and subsequently reoffered by the syndicate to the investor at a discount no greater than the average discount at which purchased, such discount is amortized over the life of the bonds and is treated as the equivalent of nontaxable interest income. If the original holder disposes of the bonds prior to their maturity, the original discount must be apportioned in relation to the share of the life of the bonds during which they are held by each owner. [See Chapter 17 for further discussion of original issue discount.]

For example, assume that a 30-year $1,000 bond is issued at a 5 percent discount (i.e., at $950 per $1,000 par value), and sold at that discount to the investor. If the investor should dispose of the bond on the 10th anniversary, at a price of $966.67 or more, he will be permitted one-third of the $50 discount ($16.67) as tax-free income. If he sells the bond at par, the $16.67 may be treated as tax-free income while the remaining $33.33 is treated as a long-term capital gain. If he retains the bond until maturity, he may deduct the entire $50.00 as appreciation in value and as tax-free income. Should he sell the bond at $966.67, and the secondary purchaser then holds the bond to maturity, he can claim the $33.33 (or any amount up to $33.33 if purchased at another discount level) as tax-free income. Should the original holder sell the bond at less than $966.67, the differential between that amount and the sale can be claimed as a long-term loss.

Bond Issues Purchased at Par or Above. If an investor purchases a bond at a discount which is a part of an issue purchased at par or above by the syndicate, the investor may not treat the increase in value as tax-free income. Rather, the investor is obliged to report the difference between the purchase price and the redemption price (or sales price if sold prior to redemption) as a capital gain to be taxed as other capital gains.

If he purchases a 20-year bond bearing 2 percent coupon rate to provide a pretax yield of 6.00 percent, the price will be $306.56 for the principal plus $231.15 for the interest, or $537.70. If he is in the 46 percent capital gains tax bracket, the eventual capital gains tax will be $65.19 [($1,000 − $537.70 × .46 × .30656)]. Therefore, in present value terms (PV-1), the purchaser is in fact paying the $537.70 + $65.19 = $602.89. Inasmuch as a 2.00 percent bond priced to yield only 5.25 percent would be priced at $600.53, the effective after-tax yield is only about 5.225 percent, rather than 6.00 percent.

Alternatively, if the purchaser insisted upon an after-tax yield of at least 6.00 percent, the bond would have to be priced to yield about 7.10 percent. The price drops to $461.81— a loss to the seller of $75.89.

In like manner, if a 7.00 percent bond due in 7 years sold in a market in which a par yield of 11.00 percent would be appropriate without tax considerations, a corporate taxpayer in the 46 percent capital gains tax bracket would be obliged to require a yield of 12.35 percent on the bond in order to obtain an after-tax yield of 11.00 percent. This would mean that a bond priced at $808.21 at an 11.00 percent yield would have to drop in price to about $755.60 to cover the present value of the anticipated capital gains tax.

These examples show that the federal taxes on capital gains are of major importance to those trading in municipal bonds priced below par when such pricing is not a part of a *whole issue* discount at the time of original sale by the issuer.

Bonds Originally Purchased at Par. When a bond is purchased at par but is subsequently traded at a yield rate in excess of the coupon rate, the seller is entitled to treat the loss as a capital loss for income tax purposes. If, for example, the investor purchases a 4.00 percent, 30-year bond at par and five years later sells it to yield 5.00 percent, he will sustain a long-term loss of $141.80. He may count this loss as a long-term capital loss to be offset against long-term capital gains or to be offset against current regular income to the extent permitted by current law.

Bonds Sold at a Premium at Original Sale. In the case of tax-exempt bonds initially sold to the investor at a premium, the investor must amortize the premium against the interest from the tax-exempt security. He may not amortize it against other income and claim the full coupon interest as tax-exempt income. Nor can it be treated as a capital loss. This rule also applies with respect to premiums paid by any successive owner of the security.

The effect of this is that, in the case of a bond with a 6.00 percent coupon due in 7 years purchased to yield 4.40 percent, the purchaser would be obliged to pay a premium of $95.50 on a $1,000 bond. Should he hold the bond until maturity, he would have received an effective tax-free yield of 4.40 percent. He would, in fact, have received $420 in interest over the period for which he held the bond, from which he would be obliged to absorb the premium of $95.50. In order to amortize the premium of $95.50 the investor must set aside $8.00 per semiannual period from a gross income of $30.00. Thereby, he derives only $22.00 per period on the $1,000 net investment ($1,095.50 − $95.50). Hence, over the life of the bonds he obtains a tax-free income of $308.00 (14 × $22). The issuer will have paid $420 in interest but only $308 will have been tax-free income to the investor.

Substantially the same rule applies to interim purchasers in that they must amortize the premium against the tax-exempt interest. The purchaser is not permitted to treat the premium as a capital loss to offset capital gains or as a deduction from taxable income.

Taxation at the State and Local Levels

In the early years of state income taxation, the rates were relatively low—even on the upper levels of income; however, these rates have increased appreciably. Now the top bracket is well above 10 percent in about one-sixth of the states. In addition to income taxes, in some states ad valorem taxes on intangible personal property are imposed.

All state and local governments exempt from taxation the municipal bonds issued in the state of residence of the taxpayer. However, personal income taxes usually apply to income derived from bonds of other states and their local governments. Some local governments impose local income taxes on the same basis.

The effect of state (or state and local) income taxes upon investment decisions is significant. For example, make these assumptions:

1. That three states (Connecticut, New York, and Texas) are each offering $100 million in local government bonds of identical quality and market acceptability.

2. That the demand for the Texas and New York bonds within their own states is sufficient to absorb more than three-fourths of the bonds issued by their own local government but that the Connecticut market can absorb only half of the bonds being issued by its local government, with the result that it must depend upon the New York residents in order to make the sale a success.

3. That the effective rate of taxation in New York upon out-of-state municipal bonds is 15 percent.

Under these circumstances, the 6.00 percent bonds offered by the Texas and New York local governments could be absorbed at that rate. However, the rate on the Connecticut local government's bonds would have to be increased to 7.02 percent in order that the New York investor receive an equivalent after-tax return available from the bonds being issued by the local government of New York.

As a practical matter, the effect upon the coupon rate would be much less, since customers would be obtained elsewhere in the national market to take up some of the bonds not absorbed in Connecticut and to take them up at a lower yield rate. Thereby, the Connecticut issuer would not be obliged to pay the full penalty yield, and the New York investor would have to absorb part of the tax.

The market cannot price the bonds of every issuer to suit the internal market of that particular state. Rather, it is obliged to do its pricing against general market conditions. Bonds thereby become relatively more or less attractive, depending upon the relationship between the tax structures of the state of issue and the state of residence of the investor.

PATTERNS OF OWNERSHIP OF STATE AND LOCAL GOVERNMENT SECURITIES

The attractiveness of municipal bonds to investors vis-à-vis alternative investments is dependent upon the tax status of the investor. For those elements of the economy such as nonprofit corporations (including foundations), tax-exempt pension funds, and the state and local governments themselves, the effective yield to be derived from taxable securities is usually much too high for them to purchase tax-exempt securities.

Table 18 shows the distribution of ownership of state and local government obligations at five-year intervals, commencing in 1965. From that table it is apparent that the major holdings of these obligations have been concentrated in three sectors: Commercial banks, households, and nonlife insurance companies. In the aggregate these three sectors accounted for 86 percent of the obligations outstanding in 1965 but this increased to more than 90 percent throughout the 1970s and for the end-of-the-year data for 1980.

Conversely, investor interest in other sectors has generally lagged. Only investments by the state and local governments themselves [largely in New York after 1975] have helped to sustain even the minor role of these sectors. As has been shown in Table 17, many of the economic sectors with large financial assets have not been attracted to the ownership of state and local government obligations inasmuch as they have found more attractive avenues for the investment of their funds.

Individual Sector Trends

Data in Tables 18 and 19 enable one to trace the trends in individual economic sectors during the past 15 years. These are commented upon briefly below.

Commercial Banks. The domestic commercial banks have found state and local government obligations attractive investments during all periods since World War II and have consistently constituted the largest single sector holder of these obligations. As the amount of the obligations in the market has increased, the commercial banks generally increased their holdings; however, their holdings as a percentage of the total peaked in the 1972 and 1973 period at slightly above half all such outstanding obligations.

Commercial banks are usually obliged to limit their acquisitions of state and local government obligations during periods of economic stress or during periods when the Federal Reserve System is placing pressure upon the banks to hold down the money supply. In such periods some commercial banks find it necessary to sell off portions of their municipal security portfolios—or at least to allow them to mature without making correspondingly large reinvestments of moneys obtained through such liquidation.

This process, together with changes in profitability in the banks and availability of other tax-preference or tax-exempt items, helps to explain the fact that these banks at the end of 1980 accounted for 44 percent of outstanding municipal obligations as contrasted

Table 18

Holdings of State and Local Government Obligations as of December 31, By Major Economic Sectors
Selected Years, 1965–1980

(amounts in billions of dollars)					Increase During Period		
	1965	1970	1975	1980	1965–1970	1970–1975	1975–1980
Total	100.3	144.4	223.8	336.6	43.8	79.4	112.3
Major holders	86.5	133.5	204.3	310.4	47.0	70.8	106.1
Commercial banking	38.8	70.2	102.9	149.2	31.4	32.7	46.3
Households	36.4	46.0	68.1	80.6	9.6	22.1	12.5
Direct holdings	36.4	46.0	68.1	74.2	9.6	22.2	6.1
Through mutual funds	—	—	—	6.4	—	—	6.4
Casualty and other nonlife insurance companies	11.3	17.0	33.3	81.1	5.7	16.3	47.8
Other holders	13.7	11.1	19.5	25.5	(2.2)	8.4	6.0
State and local governments	4.8	4.4	6.9	10.6	(.4)	2.5	3.7
General funds	2.2	2.4	5.0	6.5	.2	2.6	1.5
Retirement funds	2.6	2.0	1.9	4.1	(.6)	(.1)	2.2
Life insurance companies	3.5	3.3	4.5	6.7	(.2)	1.2	2.2
Nonfinancial corporations	4.6	2.2	4.5	3.5	(2.4)	2.3	(1.0)
Mutual savings banks	.3	.2	1.5	2.4	(.1)	1.4	.9
Savings and loan associations	—	.1	1.5	1.2	.1	1.4	(.3)
Security dealers	.5	.9	.6	1.1	.4	(.3)	.5

Source: Board of Governors of the Federal Reserve System, *Flow of Funds Accounts, Assets and Liabilities Outstanding, 1957–80* (September 1981), pp. 38–39.

Table 19

Percentage Distribution of Holdings of State and Local Government Obligations as of December 31, by Major Economic Sectors Selected Years, 1965–1980

	1965	1970	1972	1974	1976	1978	1980
Total	100.0	100.0	100.0	100.0	100.0	100.0	100.0
Major holders	86.2	92.5	92.5	93.3	89.9	90.7	92.4
Commercial banking	38.7	48.6	51.0	48.7	44.3	42.9	43.8
Household	36.3	31.9	27.4	29.8	29.5	24.9	24.0
Direct holdings	36.3	32.9	27.4	29.8	29.3	24.0	22.1
Through mutual funds	—	—	—	—	.2	.9	1.9
Casualty and other nonlife insurance companies	11.3	11.8	14.1	14.8	16.2	21.9	24.1
Other sectors	13.7	7.7	7.3	6.7	10.1	9.4	7.6
State and local governments	4.8	3.0	2.1	1.7	4.5	3.9	3.2
General funds	2.2	1.7	1.0	1.3	3.0	2.5	1.9
Retirement funds	2.6	1.4	1.1	.2	1.4	1.4	1.2
Life insurance companies	3.5	2.3	1.9	1.6	2.3	2.2	2.0
Nonfinancial corporations	4.6	1.5	2.4	2.3	1.4	1.3	1.0
Mutual savings banks	.3	.1	.2	.4	1.0	1.1	.7
Savings and loan associations	—	.1	.1	.2	.5	.5	.4
Security dealers	.5	.6	.5	.3	.4	.3	.3

Source: Board of Governors of the Federal Reserve System, *Flow of Funds Accounts, Assets and Liabilities Outstanding, 1957–80* (September, 1981), pp. 38–39.

with the high in the 51/52 percent range in 1972 and 1973. Another factor in this process has been the shift in issuance of bonds from the general obligation type to bonds falling within the broad revenue classification. Inasmuch as the banks are precluded from underwriting or trading in most of the revenue bond classifications, the supply of bonds open to them has not increased commensurately with the general amount of municipal debt outstanding.

The decline of the intensity of commercial bank participation in the municipal bond field has produced significant marketing problems for municipal bonds and has helped to create the distorted [and sometimes inverse] yield curves that predominated the market in late 1980 and almost all of 1981. Finally, commercial banks had apparently gradually extended the average life of the municipal securities that they held. When the pressures developed on restriction of the money supply during the 1980–1981 period (and to some extent earlier), a number of larger banks sustained very large losses in the disposition of their low-coupon bonds during periods of high interest rates and more or less forced liquidations.

Households. The household sector holdings have continued to increase in dollar amount—from $36 billion in 1965 to $81 billion in 1980; however, in terms of a segment of the market, holdings have generally declined from more than 36 percent in 1965 to only 24 percent in 1980—including amounts held through mutual funds as well as direct holdings.

With the changes in individual income tax rates early in 1981—especially with the reduction of the aggregate rates for very high income taxpayers—the attractiveness of municipal bonds will decrease vis-à-vis taxable securities. Moreover, the 1981 legislation created a number of other attractive alternatives for tax-exempt and tax-sheltered income. These factors will doubtless encourage still further inroads upon interest by the household sector in the purchase and holding of municipal bonds.

Casualty Insurance Companies. Throughout the period under consideration the nonlife insurance companies have very significantly increased their holdings of state and local government obligations—up from $11 billion in 1965 to more than $81 billion in 1980. As a percentage of the total of such obligations outstanding, their holdings have more than doubled, up from 11 percent in 1965 to 24 percent at the end of 1980.

State and Local Governments. Although state and local governments have increased their holdings of municipal securities from $4.8 billion in 1965 to $10.6 billion in 1980, this increase has not kept pace with overall growth in these securities. As a matter of fact, percentage holdings decreased from 4.8 in 1965 to 1.7 in 1974. Although an increase in amounts and a temporary increase in percentages occurred in 1976, this was due wholly to the fact that with the New York crisis pension and other funds were induced to purchase large amounts of these securities in order to help avoid default by New York City and difficulties for New York State government. Without the public pension fund purchases in New York as well as the investment of some other state and local government funds there in these securities, this sector would doubtless continue to show insignificant holdings.[4]

The holdings of municipal securities by the general funds of state and local governments derive largely from the state bond banks and state purchases of locally issued securities, e.g., the Texas water resource agencies. In each of these cases, the senior agencies purchase the securities of the junior governments and then issue their own securities to the market. In effect, this constitutes a duplication of the dollar amounts of outstanding securities. In some instances, state or local governments have other occasions to purchase municipal securities.

Other Sectors. The holdings of the remainder of the sectors are important in the absolute and provide a welcome strengthening of the total market. On the other hand, they accounted for less than 5 percent of the total absorption of outstanding securities in 1980. Of this group, the life insurance companies have shown considerable return to the market during recent years, increasing absolute holdings from $3.3 billion in 1970 to $6.7 billion in 1980. In the same period, mutual savings banks have gone from less than $0.2 billion to $2.4 billion. Also, the savings and loan associations have shown considerable interest, especially since 1974.

Conversely, the nonfinancial business corporations appear to have been in and out of the market over the years. By 1965 they held $4.6 billion, or about 4.6 percent, of the aggregate outstanding. But this decreased sharply to $2.2 billion in 1970. It rallied to $4.5 billion by 1975 but has dropped in percentage terms since then. Broker and dealer holdings are largely dictated by positions taken in "making a market" for the bonds and by the amounts of unsold securities held by them at any given time, due to general market conditions.

Holdings by Economic Sectors Vis-à-Vis Financial Assets of Each Sector

The final measure of interest in the securities of state and local governments by the several economic sectors in relation to their financial assets is presented in Table 20.

---

[4] The *Flow of Funds* estimate for total holdings was $4.1 billion at December 31, 1980. The Bureau of the Census showed $4.0 million at the end of the fiscal year in the 1979–80 period, with New York City accounting for $3,457 million and the State of New York for an additional $438 million—leaving less than $126 million being held by pension funds in other states. Bureau of the Census, *Finances of Employee-Retirement Systems of State and Local Governments in 1979–80,* pp. 5–7, 23.

Table 20

Holdings of State and Local Government Obligations as a Percent of Financial Assets by Economic Sectors as of December 31, 1970, 1975, and 1980

	Financial Assets (amounts in billions of dollars)			Holdings of State & Local Govt. Obligations			Holdings as a Percent of Financial Assets		
	1970	1975	1980	1970	1975	1980	1970	1975	1980
	(1)	(2)	(3)	(4)	(5)	(6)	(7)	(8)	(9)
Total	*	*	*	144.4	233.8	336.6	na	na	na
Major holders									
Commercial banking	505	834	1,386	70.2	102.9	149.2	12.9	12.3	10.8
Households**	1,936	2,563	4,494	46.0	68.1	80.6	2.4	2.7	1.8
Casualty & other non-life ins.	50	77	180	17.0	33.3	81.1	34.0	43.2	45.1
Other holders									
State and local govts.	132	228	415	4.4	6.9	10.6	3.3	3.0	2.6
General funds	72	123	217	2.4	5.0	6.5	3.3	4.1	3.0
Retirement funds	60	105	198	2.0	1.9	4.1	3.3	1.8	2.1
Life insurance cos.	201	280	470	3.3	4.5	6.7	1.6	1.6	1.4
Nonfinancial corps.	370	558	958	2.2	4.5	3.5	.6	.8	.5
Mutual savings banks	79	121	172	.2	1.5	2.4	.3	1.2	1.4
Savings & loan assns.	176	338	629	.1	1.5	1.2	.1	.4	.1
Security dealers	16	19	34	.9	.6	1.1	5.6	3.2	3.3

* Aggregating financial assets of all sectors for purposes of this table would lead to inappropriate interpretation of relationships. For example, much of the ownership of the other sectors is by the household sector and would, therefore, represent duplications in aggregate financial assets through multiple counting of such assets.
** Household sector data for 1975 and 1980 includes mutual fund assets and holdings of state and local government obligations.
Source: Board of Governors of the Federal Reserve System, *Flow of Funds Accounts: Assets and Liabilities 1957–80* (September, 1981), pp. 8–29.

Commercial Banks. In 1970 the commercial banks invested 13 percent of their financial assets in state and local government securities. This decreased to 12.3 percent in 1975 and to 10.8 percent in 1980. Changes in investment patterns of commercial banks are a reflection of many factors, including the fact that loan losses associated with unsuccessful ventures have affected the after-tax income of banks and, consequently, their appetite for tax-exempt municipal securities. Also important is the fact that from time to time banks are obliged to liquidate substantial portions of their holdings in order to realize cash.

Of course, the holdings of banks as a group fail to reflect the large differences among different banks and among groups of banks of different sizes. Thus, at the end of 1977, it was found that the highest investment ratios of commercial banks in municipal securities were in those with assets in the $25–$999 million bracket. For the smaller and for the larger banks (again as groups), the investment ratio in municipal securities was significantly below the middle group.[5]

[5] Board of Governors of the Federal Reserve System, Federal Deposit Insurance Corporation, and Office of the Comptroller of the Currency, *Assets and Liabilities: Report of Income for Commercial and Mutual Savings Banks, December 31, 1977,* pp. 118–119. At December 31, 1977, 16 percent of commercial bank

To some extent, the holdings of commercial banks may have been influenced by the reduction of the short-term debt outlined in Chapter 1. Moreover, as newly marketed debt has shifted more to nonguaranteed debt, banks have been largely excluded as the average life of the issues has increased materially. Finally, the commerical banks are holders of a substantial portion of the smaller tax-exempt industrial development mortgage debt not generally reflected in these data.

Households. The holdings of state and local government securities by households are very important to the municipal market; however, they represented only 1.8 percent of the sector's financial assets at the end of 1980—down from 2.7 percent five years earlier.

A considerable portion of municipal bonds reported in the household sector are accounted for by the trust departments of commercial banks. Thus, at December 31, 1978, they were reported to have held $28.8 billion of municipal securities, primarily for the account of personal trusts. These holdings amounted to about one-eighth of the total assets of such trusts and to more than one-third of municipals held by the household sector. Thus, the commercial banks are important customers of municipal issuers not only when investing for their own account but also when acting as trustees. The municipal bond funds have become important intermediaries in holding municipal bonds, with participation in such funds largely accounted for by the household sector.[6]

Casualty Insurance Companies. In terms of the percentage of financial assets invested in municipal securities, none of the sectors exceeds the casualty insurance companies. This group has increased its holdings at a rapid annual rate and has also increased the percentage of its assets invested in municipals. Even in years such as 1974 when the financial assets of this sector actually declined, the holdings of municipal securities continued to increase.

Life Insurance Companies. The life insurance companies' commitment to tax-free bonds has never been great in relation to their financial assets. Even so, following the changes in federal tax law affecting them in 1959, their interest declined even further and has apparently not been rekindled by the higher yields available in recent markets. Although they occasionally buy these securities, their investments in recent years have consistently stood well below two percent of financial assets.

Mutual Savings Banks. The mutual savings banks had a pattern of disinvestment in these tax-exempt securities in the 1957–1967 decade, followed by a mild return in recent years.

Other Sectors. The trends in the other sectors are not particularly important. They appear to come in and go out with various pressures and markets. The presence of the savings and loan associations in this field in recent years is still minimal; however, their rather substantial pool of assets makes them an inviting possibility for the future.

MUNICIPAL BOND FUNDS

Municipal bond funds date from 1961, when the firm of Ira Haupt & Co. organized the first such fund. From that modest beginning the total has increased very significantly as have the type and function of the municipal bond funds. Today there are several distinct categories of municipal bond funds, including:

1. *The Unit Trust Fund.* In the unit trust fund, a decision is made in advance concerning the size of the portfolio to be acquired and certificates of beneficial interest are sold, normally in units of $1,000. The explicit unit investment fund collects interest and distributes this from time to time to the holders of the beneficial interest certificates. More recently, some of these funds provide for monthly payment of interest and others provide for reinvestment of interest in additional unit trust funds organized by the owners.

---

holdings of municipal securities were scheduled to mature within one year; an additional 28 percent before the end of the fifth year; and three-fourths of all municipal securities held scheduled to mature in less than ten years.

[6] David Tyson, *The Daily Bond Buyer,* November 20, 1979, p. 16.

As the bonds held by the unit trust fund mature, principal is redistributed to the owners unless they have entered into agreements to have such reinvested by the managers in new unit trust funds.

Owners of unit investment beneficial interest certificates who wish to dispose of these during the life of the fund may sell them through the manager of the fund if that manager maintains a secondary market in the securities. If the manager does not maintain such secondary market, the owner may surrender the certificates to the fund and be paid the principal of his investment depending upon the market value of the securities in the fund that must be liquidated in order to meet the requirements for surrendered certificates. Should the number of surrendered certificates become substantial in relation to the full size of the fund, the management has the right—under specified conditions—to liquidate the fund and distribute the assets among the remaining certificate holders.

Many of these funds are in existence today. About a dozen of the larger investment banking firms regularly operate such funds which are organized from time to time as demand requires.

In addition to the general unit trust funds operating at a national level, a number of regional firms now maintain [either independently or in association with national investment banking firms] specialized funds that invest only in securities arising within a given state. The advantage here is that the investor is able to enjoy exemption not only from federal income taxes on the income but also from state taxes on such income where the state laws permit.

2. *Managed Mutual Funds.* Until 1976 Congress did not allow the pass-through of tax-exempt interest in managed municipal bond funds, i.e., open-ended municipal mutual funds. In that year the law was amended and since then the managed municipal bond fund has operated in much the same manner as the managed municipal stock funds in which such significant amount of the investments in stocks are made.

The funds operate on a strictly open-ended basis and prices are determined by the market value of the securities held.

Again, about a dozen of the larger operators of mutual funds now offer participation by investors in the managed mutual municipal bond funds. Units of participation are usually about $1,000 at the outset; however, inasmuch as the value of the units varies from time to time depending upon market conditions, one is obliged to buy or sell at prices dictated by the market. These funds have different features, including provisions for reinvestment of interest as earned or for periodic distribution of earnings as the investor elects.

These funds operate on a no-load basis with the managers receiving a management fee determined by the contract involved in the organization and operation of the fund.

The managed mutual municipal bond funds differ in specialization. Some appeal to those concerned with high current tax-exempt yield; accordingly they purchase only high-yield securities. Others emphasize the safety of securities by purchasing only very high quality bonds. The maximum security is afforded by those funds which purchase only bonds which are accepted as insurable quality by AMBAC [American Municipal Bond Assurance Corporation]. Under these insured funds, the holders of beneficial interest certificates hold the equivalent of triple-A securities, with only a minimal risk of loss inasmuch as huge insurance reserves stand behind the insured funds.

The managed funds also specialize in different maturities. Some are concerned primarily with long-term bonds. Some are specializing in intermediate term securities, with an average life of eight or nine years. A few are in short-term securities with an average remaining life of only about one year while still others are in the "money market" range of about 90 days maximum.

From the standpoint of investors these municipal bond funds offer several advantages:

1. They permit investments at unit levels approximating $1,000, rather than the traditional $5,000 amounts of individual bonds or the $25,000 trading unit.

2. Higher degrees of specialization in investment are possible, depending upon the investment objectives of the investor.
3. The investor is able to hedge his risk to a greater extent by virtue of the substantial number of different issuers' bonds that are included in the typical portfolio.
4. Liquidity is frequently greater than for some kinds of municipal bonds, especially those of smaller or not so well known issuers in whose bonds no one maintains an active secondary market.

Among the disadvantages is the fact that investment decisions are largely delegated to the managers of the funds and, in the case of the open-ended mutual municipal bond funds, the investor is obliged to live with the decisions of the managers or to liquidate.

The municipal bond funds have become a huge factor in the marketing of new municipal bonds. The underwriters must be cognizant of the attractiveness of securities that they purchase to these funds and in some instances are obliged, especially in negotiated sales, to tailor some features of their bids to the known wishes of the municipal bond funds.

Where municipal bond funds are managed by the same underwriters that are purchasing the bonds of the issuer, special care is required to avoid any conflict of interest between the functions of the underwriters in the underwriting capacity vis-à-vis their responsibilities as fund managers.

The only comprehensive official national data concerning the holdings of state and local government obligations by money market funds is the information provided by the *Flow of Funds* statements, which first identified these funds as a separate reporting entity in 1974 and provided the first data on their tax-exempt holdings in 1976 as $0.5 billion. This has increased very rapidly so that by 1978 the total was $2.7 billion and at the end of 1980 $6.4 billion. The preliminary data for 1981 shows a substantial addition which is likely to provide a total in excess of $10 billion sometime in 1982.

Indicative of the growth in the importance of such funds was the report of increase in their holdings of short-term debt of state and local governments by the bond funds during 1981—up from $2.5 billion to $5.9 billion.[7]

---

[7] *The Weekly Bond Buyer,* Vol. 117, No 4633. (February 1, 1982), p. 58.

Chapter 6
FACTORS AFFECTING INTEREST RATES PAYABLE: GENERAL CONSIDERATIONS

Factors affecting interest rates payable by governmental borrowers are discussed in this and succeeding chapters. Here, the focus is on general considerations including bond ratings; the succeeding chapter focuses on more definitive factors. The principal factors are identified and a brief commentary is provided concerning their impact on the market for tax-exempt securities. These factors are not of equal importance in credit analysis—whether applied to a number of issuers concurrently or to the same issuer over longer periods of time. Some have a continuous, significant impact on the market; others have irregular consequences—ranging from almost nil to dominance, depending upon the contemporary circumstances.

Money is generally timid; old money is more timid; and old money being invested by fiduciaries is excessively timid. Accordingly, psychology is a major factor in the securities market. Although leaders are prepared to create initiatives and to accept the associated risk and the reward, the timid prefer the safe harbor. They prefer the comfort of the company of the crowd—the reassurance that they are not standing alone on strange ground and that they will not be held accountable for being other than the prudent man. Governmental debt managers must be mindful of these psychological factors if they are to operate successfully in the broad securities market from which they are to derive the funds required for the operations of their governments.

POLITICAL AND ECONOMIC CONDITIONS

Political and economic conditions and prospects influence the world money markets. These conditions range from abject depression (early 1930s) to unbridled optimism (late 1960s) to befuddlement (1980–1981). The conditions and the moods they generate are the major determinants of the market. Within the basic general conditions, patterns of economic constraints are designed by those who seek to control the course of events. National economic policies ordinarily seek to shape the outlook and thereby to create both perceptions and realities; they seek to channel affairs in a manner that harmonizes with the current national objectives.

Since World War II, the actions of the United States have been of major significance in world political and economic circles—albeit at somewhat more reduced levels of influence today than in the 1945–1963 years. The abrupt actions of the Organization of Petroleum Exporting Countries (OPEC) in 1974 produced worldwide shock waves that continue as major determinants. OPEC made it clear that certain highly important initiatives were no longer the exclusive prerogative of the West. No longer could the United States, the NATO group, or these in combination with Japan, make the same kinds of binding economic determinations to which they had been so long accustomed. OPEC sharply modified conventional wisdom. It continues as a significant factor in both the domestic and international policies of the free world.

One writes with discernibly less confidence concerning many aspects of economics than he did a decade ago. The capacity of the Federal Reserve System to manage the rates of inflation and the levels of economic activity continues to be significant but more drastic actions are required today than a decade ago to achieve similar results. Indeed, many challenge the extent to which U.S. federal policies can produce the political, economic, and social objectives upon which the nation so confidently embarked before 1970. A new spirit of humbleness seems to be the order of the day.

The next several pages present the conventional views concerning the role and methods of the Federal Reserve System as it is presumed to interact on the marketplace in influencing the interest market for debt securities. Even so, the jury is still out. Its verdict may be that these statements are more nearly those of an economic historian than those of the successful prognosticator of the way the system will operate in the next decade.

Transitory Developments. The marketplace acts both rationally and irrationally. It is greatly affected by the timidity of money, or at least the timidity of many investors—especially at the point of purchase. Issuers are obliged to take into account the effects of transitory developments on the prevailing atmosphere in the marketplace. There may be a mid-East war; a Cuban confrontation; an insurrection in an African nation; a Soviet adventure into the affairs of another country; or a major political upset at home. Each such event has considerable impact on the current attitude of investors; but, viewed from historical perspective, only a few are likely to have major long-term policy effects. Yet, for the issuer and the investor selling or purchasing bonds during such periods of upheaval, the effects on the value of securities being sold or acquired are long-term.

The able public finance officer knows that during such troubled periods numerous investors withdraw to the safe harbor of highest quality, short-term commitments; hoard gold, silver, or diamonds; and maintain substantial amounts of idle cash or foreign bank accounts. Analysts frequently seem obliged to take precautionary measures during periods of stress by downgrading doubtful credits, including some that are basically sound but temporarily in disfavor due to transitory developments.

Litigation. Our society has become very litiguous; each day seems to produce new ventures by old and new groups seeking to secure some advantage through litigation. When litigation is directed to the issuer—even when not directly associated with matters of debt—it may have adverse effects on interest levels for the government selling securities.

Federal Monetary Policy

Within the framework of national and world economic conditions, a principal determinant of the availability and cost of credit in the United States is national monetary policy. The Congress has vested in the Federal Reserve System the responsibility for maintaining monetary and credit conditions deemed to help promote a sustainable rate of economic growth, full employment, a stable price structure, and an international balance-of-payments equilibrium. In determining monetary policy, the Federal Reserve examines not only domestic economic factors but also foreign economic conditions. In a world of instantaneous communication and extensive world trade, national economies are remarkably interactive as has been repeatedly demonstrated by OPEC. The position of the dollar vis-à-vis other currencies is high priority radio and television news today; whereas, at earlier periods, this would have warranted no mention. Monetary developments in foreign countries have an impact on domestic financial conditions, and vice versa. Thus, in the absence of artificial barriers to the flow of capital, high interest rates abroad may draw funds from the United States until domestic interest rates must respond in search of an equilibrium; or, the converse may happen, thereby producing a downward pressure on domestic rates. Even so, availability and cost of credit within the United States are greatly influenced by domestic factors, e.g., consumer demands, the labor movement, and tax policies. Three general tools of monetary policy are used by the Federal Reserve System: (1) open market operations, (2) discount policy, and (3) reserve requirements.

Open market operations involve the purchase and sale of U.S. government securities in the market. When the Board of Governors of the Federal Reserve System believes that economic activity is not expanding rapidly enough, the Federal Reserve buys securities, thereby increasing the money supply and commercial bank reserves and exerting downward pressure on interest rates. Conversely, if economic activity is increasing at a rate the Board believes will accentuate inflation, it sells federal government securities. This produces some reduction in money supply and bank reserves, which tends to push interest rates up.

Economists have generally accepted this as classical theory; however, the past decade has shown that there are significant limitations on the extent to which the Federal Reserve can maintain planned interest rate levels solely through open market operations in the face of the combined weight of other components in the national and international marketplace. New tools for control of consumer credit are being relied upon to a greater degree.

Discount policy refers to the availability and cost of borrowing by commercial banks from Federal Reserve Banks. Willingness of the Federal Reserve to lend and the interest rate (discount rate) charged have some effect upon the nation's monetary environment. When Federal Reserve authorities find that the pace of economic activity is accelerating beyond a prudent and sustainable rate, they are likely to raise the discount rate. Following an announcement of an increase in this rate, market participants usually push up other interest rates, including those on municipal bonds and other tax-exempt debt—especially on the shorter maturities.

On the other hand, when economic activity needs to be stimulated, monetary authorities may lower the discount rate. This usually causes some decrease in the rates on other money and capital market debt. Even so, economists differ on the degree to which the changes in interest rates genuinely affect economic activity and also the period for which higher rates must be maintained in order to achieve the objectives sought.

Reserve requirements for commercial banks that are members of the Federal Reserve System constitute the third general instrument of monetary policy available to the Federal Reserve officials. Reserve requirements (expressed as a percent of deposits) determine the maximum expansion of deposits which the banking system can effect on a given base of reserves. If economic conditions result in a determination by the Federal Reserve that a restrictive monetary policy should be in force, it may raise reserve requirements within limits prescribed by the Congress. Such increases may cause the banking system to reduce deposits by curtailing lending and investing activities that, in turn, reduce the money supply. Because the supply of lendable funds is reduced, interest rates tend to be pushed up when reserve requirements are raised. Conversely, reduction in required reserves enables the banking system to create more money and credit and this tends to cause lower general interest rate levels in all financial markets.

Restrictive monetary policy is likely to be applied during periods of booming economic activity when normal demands for credit are great or in periods of high inflation. Therefore, interest rates may be already rising and credit availability becoming tighter when the Federal Reserve moves to a more restrictive policy. Consequently, the total impact on credit cost and availability is not that of monetary policy alone but also that of demand and supply forces in the general market.

Two other observations are in order at this point. First, the impact of Federal Reserve decisions upon the tax-exempt interest rates is likely to be greater if the commerical banks in general have a significant role in the municipal bond market than when they have a reduced participation. For example, during the 1973–1977 period, widespread commercial bank losses from foreign exchange and real estate financing activities diminished their need for tax-exempt income and decreased the availability of funds for this type of investment. Secondly, the effects of Federal Reserve policies appear to have somewhat greater immediate impact upon shorter-term vs. longer-term investment policies of those who purchase tax-exempt securities—partially due to the relatively high concentration of commercial banks on the shorter-term securities of state and local governments. However, protracted pressure inevitably causes the effects to be greatest in the availability of long-term investors. Given the huge purchasing power of the banks, both for investment on their own account and in performance of their fiduciary responsibilities, one cannot be oblivious to both their independent views and the extent to which those views may be influenced by Federal Reserve actions.

Federal Fiscal Policy

Monetary policy usually is not expected to carry the burden of economic stabilization alone. Fiscal policy has a potent role. Fiscal policy involves elements that constitute the financing of the federal budget. Thus, fiscal policy is concerned with both the purposes and levels of spending; the sources used to finance the budget; the extent to which surpluses are developed or deficits encountered; and, in the case of deficits, the manner in which such deficits are monetized. Ideally, fiscal and monetary policy have the same objectives. Yet, with monetary policy somewhat insulated from day-to-day political policy, it is not surprising that the two frequently do not appear to be on the same wave-length, especially when the more political elements of the governmental process are pursuing objectives discernibly different from those of the monetary authority.

The principal tools of fiscal policy in the United States are the federal government's taxation and spending operations. When the federal government engages in deficit financing, i.e., it pays out more than it takes in within a given period of time (regardless of the purposes of such expenditures), these deficits must be monetized immediately. This process ordinarily acts to stimulate increases in personal and business income; produces increased demand for goods and services; and may result in an increase in the money supply. Usually, the process also tends to produce some restatement of the price structure, including the rates paid as compensation to workers. In other words, it facilitates inflation. Pursuit of such a policy is sometimes deliberate with a view to the stimulation of the economy; sometimes it is a reflection of weak political leadership that is unwilling to confront the forces of inflation; sometimes it becomes a way of life in which debtors see it as the only way in which to liquidate heavy debts short of default.

Deficits or surpluses can be attained through modification of the tax structure, changes in spending levels, or by a combination of tax and spending adjustments. Selection of the means used depends upon the socio/political value judgments of executive and legislative leadership, conditioned by grass-roots views. For example, prior to 1930 the general view in the United States was that the role of government in the search for answers to major public problems should be minimal. Except for national defense, public education, transportation, public safety and a few other areas, governmental involvement tended to be minimal.

During the succeeding half century, there has been a continual expansion of the role of government at all levels in the United States—largely on the assumption that the combination of the groups pressing for added spending and increased regulation represented the aggregate public will. Suddenly, the California "Proposition 13" referendum on the property tax in 1978 demonstrated sharply that political leadership had misinterpreted the "consent of the governed." The shock waves are still being emitted at this writing, and it is much too early to assign meaningful interpretations to the potential long-term effects that may be involved in the taxpayer revolt.

The Increased Importance of State and Local Government Finance

Until recent years there has been a tendency to ignore or to downplay the role of state and local government finance in discussions of national fiscal policy. In some respects, this doubtless has been due to the relatively small role occupied in earlier years and also the fact that these governments long operated with substantial independence both of the federal government and of each other. Despite the aggregate size of their operations when viewed compositely, they have frequently been ignored in economic discussions. This view is not warranted today. Information contained in Tables 21 and 22 shows that in 1980 the general revenues of these governments accounted for:

About four-tenths of all taxes and general revenues of all governments in the United States

About one-half total governmental revenues of the nation

Somewhat less than half of all governmental expenditures and more than half of the general expenditures of all governments

More than one-fourth of the outstanding governmental debt

In terms of average annual compound growth rates over the 30-year period, 1950–1980, the rate of increase for state and local governments outstripped the developments at the federal level in each of these categories. For example, tax revenues increased 9.2 percent vs. 8.0 percent for the federal government; general expenditures, 9.7 vs. 7.8 percent; and debt at more than double the rate of that of the federal government—9.2 vs. 4.3 percent. During the 1970–1980 period, the rates of growth for total expenditures were at the same level; however, for general expenditures the state and local governments exceeded the federal rate—10.9 vs. 9.5. In revenues state and local rates exceeded those of the federal government in total, tax, and general revenues. Only in the category of growth of debt did the federal rate exceed that of the state and local governments.

Thus, even if the federal fiscal policy is controlled, the increasingly important fiscal aspects of state and local governmental finance still must be confronted. This is especially true in relation to debt policies. A balanced federal budget is understood to be one in which total cash receipts and total cash outgo are equal, thereby stabilizing the level of federal government debt outstanding. If the same policy were applied to state and local governments, this would mean that new debt issued during the year would have to be offset by debt retirements (or, in an economic sense, by a combination of debt retirement and accumulation of liquid assets) sufficient to forestall an increase in net liabilities.

The Reagan Administration has espoused a policy of reduced federal expenditures, largely in the areas of federal financing of state and local government expenditures. There has already been sufficient execution of this policy to suggest that state and local governments will confront further responsibilities for financing their own operations in the future.

Those concerned with the nuances and realities of public fiscal policy can no longer safely restrict their concern to the federal level. The importance of state and local governments in these respects is now too great to be ignored.

In a genuine federal system there is an immediate contradiction when national fiscal policy is extended to control the fiscal policies of the states and their local governments. Such control could lead to the abolition of what remains of our federal system of checks and balances.[1] The Bureau of the Census national data on governmental surpluses, especially on state government surpluses, is confusing because the Bureau of the Census aggregates are essentially cash receipts and disbursements rather than surplus or deficit as used in an accounting and budgetary sense by state and local governments. Thus, a surplus defined as an excess of cash receipts from current sources over cash disbursements fails to take into account and to give appropriate weight to the differences attained in different types of funds, e.g., general funds, special funds, and insurance trust funds. A "surplus" in an insurance trust fund may, in fact, be a deficit under reasonable pension fund accounting

---

[1] One finds some basis for speculating whether the thrust of the U.S. Department of the Treasury in seeking controls over state and local government debt policies under the guise of controlling arbitrage or of controlling public purpose in certain *on behalf of* debt is interested in the amounts of revenue allegedly lost on tax-exempt bonds or whether the real thrust is to secure control of the fiscal policies of these governments.

Table 21

Governmental Revenues in the United States
Selected Years, 1950–1980

(amounts in billions of dollars)

	Total[1]	Federal	State and Local	
			Amount	Percent of Total
	(1)	(2)	(3)	(4)
TOTAL REVENUES				
1980	932.2	565.5	451.5	48.4
1978	731.7	431.3	371.6	50.8
1976	571.2	324.8	303.3	53.1
1970	333.8	205.6	150.1	45.0
1960	153.1	99.8	60.3	39.4
1950	66.7	43.5	25.6	38.4
Annual Compound Percentage				
Increase: 1950–1980	9.2	8.9	10.0	
1970–1980	10.8	10.6	11.6	
GENERAL REVENUES FROM OWN SOURCES				
1980	716.6	417.3	299.3	41.8
1978	565.6	319.2	246.4	43.6
1976	438.3	237.7	200.6	45.8
1970	272.5	163.6	108.9	40.0
1960	130.6	87.1	43.5	33.3
1950	58.5	40.1	18.4	31.4
Annual Compound Percentage				
Increase: 1950–1980	8.7	8.1	9.7	
1970–1980	10.2	9.8	10.6	
TAX REVENUES				
1980	574.2	350.8	223.5	38.9
1978	468.2	274.5	193.6	41.3
1976	361.2	201.4	156.8	43.4
1970	232.9	146.1	86.8	37.3
1960	113.1	77.0	36.1	31.9
1950	51.1	35.2	15.9	31.1
Annual Compound Percentage				
Increase: 1950–1980	8.4	8.0	9.2	
1970–1980	9.4	9.2	9.9	

[1] Data in this column excludes intergovernmental transfers.

Sources: U.S. Bureau of the Census, *Historical Statistics of the United States: Colonial Times to 1979,* pp. 1121–1126; *Governmental Finances in 1976–77,* pp. 14–17; *in 1977–78,* pp. 13–16; *in 1979–80,* pp. 13–17.

NB: For fiscal year basis used by the Bureau of the Census, see Appendix F.

Table 22

Governmental Expenditures and Indebtedness in the United States
Selected Years, 1950–1980

(amounts in billions of dollars)

	Total	Federal	State and Local	
			Amount	Percent of Total
	(1)	(2)	(3)	(4)
TOTAL EXPENDITURES				
1980	958.6	617.2	434.1	45.3
1978	745.4	479.3	346.8	51.0
1976	625.1	391.1	304.2	48.7
1970	333.0	208.2	148.1	44.5
1960	151.3	97.3	61.0	40.3
1950	70.3	44.8	27.9	39.7
Annual Compound Percentage				
Increase: 1950–1980	9.1	9.1	9.6	
1970–1980	11.2	11.5	11.4	
GENERAL EXPENDITURES				
1980	723.1	355.8[1]	369.1	51.0
1978	564.3	268.8[1]	297.0	52.6
1976	477.3	220.6[1]	256.7	53.8
1970	275.0	143.7[1]	131.3	47.7
1960	128.6	76.7[1]	51.9	40.4
1950	60.7	37.9[1]	22.8	37.6
Annual Compound Percentage				
Increase: 1950–1980	8.6	7.8	9.7	
1970–1980	10.2	9.5	10.9	
GROSS DEBT (FISCAL YEAR-END)				
1980	1,249.9	914.3	335.6	26.9
1978	1,060.9	780.4	280.4	26.4
1976	871.8	631.3	240.5	27.5
1970	514.5	370.9	143.6	27.9
1960	356.3	286.3	70.0	19.6
1950	281.5	257.4	24.1	8.6
Annual Compound Percentage				
Increase: 1950–1980	5.1	4.3	9.2	
1970–1980	9.3	9.4	8.9	

[1] Federal general expenditures determined by elimination of insurance trust payments from total of direct expenditures. Intergovernmental expenditures are thereby eliminated.

Sources: U.S. Bureau of the Census, *Historical Statistics of the United States: Colonial Times to 1979,* pp. 1121–1126; *Governmental Finances in 1976–77,* pp. 14–17; *in 1977–78,* pp. 13–15, 32, 34, 53; *in 1979–80,* pp. 13–17.

NB: For fiscal year basis used by the Bureau of the Census, see Appendix F.

because liabilities are accruing at a greater rate than assets. Nevertheless, it may be reported as a surplus in cash flow consolidated data.

Taxation in Management of the Economy

Most economists seem to conclude that taxation can have a major impact upon the levels at which the economy functions.[2] Others have limited confidence in the extent to which the economy can be managed through taxation—not so much because of the absence of cause/effect relationships as the difficulties of obtaining prompt, appropriate, and sustained action.

Conventional wisdom suggests that, when governments wish to stimulate the economy, they can do so by promptly adjusting the levels of personal taxation downward—thereby increasing net expendable income. Conversely, when they wish to slow down the economy, they may be able to increase the levels of personal taxation and thereby decrease the money available for expenditure. In like manner, business enterprise can be stimulated and directed through changes in tax treatment. On a theoretical level there is considerable force to these arguments. Generally, those who wish to manage the economy through this avenue tend to select the federal personal income tax as the tax that can be most readily adjusted and likely to have the greatest significant early impact.

A decrease in personal taxation has the effect of increasing expendable income. A very large percentage of tax cuts find its way almost immediately into the spending patterns—especially for middle and lower income families. The economy is stimulated. Conversely, tax increases (especially withholding or sales tax increases) discourage expenditures and therefore slow down the economy.

The rates of expansion or contraction of the economy derived from these changes in taxation vary greatly in different sectors of the economy. Thus, in the short run, the increase in demand for consumer goods is likely to be quickly stimulated. Changes in residential construction starts and major business investments may come more slowly.

Decreases in income tax levels for middle- and upper-income groups tend to increase the amounts of money available for investment. On the other hand, such decreases reduce the advantages provided by the tax-exempt feature of municipal bonds. Increases in income tax levels produce converse results. In both cases, it is difficult to determine the net effect.

The Supply of Tax-preference Investments. Within any given level of total demands for credit vis-à-vis monetary supply and within any given level of taxation, the differentials between the levels at which taxable and tax-exempt securities may be sold is determined [on a grade for grade basis] largely by the extent of the tax-preference investments available.

Thus, if almost all securities should become tax-exempt, the demand for them would be relatively low in relation to the taxable yields of comparable quality. The spread between taxable and nontaxable interest levels would become less and less because there would be insufficient numbers of taxable investors available to whom the tax-exemption had a major value. Conversely, if the supply of tax-exempt bonds and tax-preference investments were greatly decreased, the competition between investors would become much keener and the price of the tax-exempt bonds would decrease as the yields rose.

Although there can be no precise measurement of the impact of the addition or subtraction of large amounts of tax-exempt or tax-preference securities, it is clear that the introduction of the All Savers tax-exempt certificates late in 1981 had a significant effect in helping to close the gap between taxable and nontaxable securities of comparable value. As is explained elsewhere in this volume, the huge amounts of *on behalf of* tax-exempt obligations have acted markedly to increase the volume of new money tax-exempt securities being

---

[2] Concern here is with the relationship of taxation to the economy. Later, attention will be directed to the effects of specific kinds of taxes upon investor interest in municipal bonds.

offered, with consequent adverse effects upon the interest rates which state and local governments would alternatively enjoy for their investments in conventional public facilities.

SOME GENERAL FACTORS AFFECTING INVESTOR CHOICES

Within the framework of prevailing general market conditions, large numbers of investment decisions are made each business day. The factors dictating these decisions are influenced by logic, astrology, prejudice, ignorance, hunches, information, and misinformation.

The objectives of investors change from time to time with their positions in life, age, rates of inflation, and a host of other factors. Investment advisors will testify to moodiness that seems frequently to be the most important factor in decision making—perhaps more important than the entire gamut of more rational decision-making factors.

Individual investments are frequently made on the basis of impulse buying, i.e., purchases are made on the spur of the moment triggered by chance gossip, a telephone call, or a bit of advertising or mail approach appealing at the time rather than as a result of a deliberative process. On the other hand, well-operated institutional investment programs are usually the result of substantial research, discussion, group decision making, and other processes designed to establish investment objectives and programs for their achievement.

Quality of Investment

It is axiomatic that the investor wishes to protect the principal invested. This can be done by placing currency in a safety deposit box; however, as in the parable, no income is earned. Moreover, in an inflationary economy, the value melts away. The investor is also concerned about the level of income generated during the period of the investment. Knowing that return varies inversely with the risk taken, the investor must balance risk against indicated return.

A comparison of the return on an investment of $1,000 at par in Aaa, A, and Baa grade 25-year bonds during 1978 (low yield) and October 1981 (high yield), with reinvestment of income at the same effective internal rate of return as the coupon rate, produces the following values at maturity (VAM):

	Aaa	A	Baa
Low Yield Bonds			
Coupon/reinvestment rates	5.70	6.10	6.70
VAM	4,076	4,492	5,194
Excess VAM over Aaa bonds	—	416	1,118
Percentage excess	—	10.20	27.44
High Yield Bonds			
Coupon/reinvestment rates	12.00	12.80	13.35
VAM	18,420	22,237	25,301
Excess VAM over Aaa bonds	—	3,817	6,881
Percentage excess	—	20.72	37.36

From the foregoing it is apparent that the conservative investor is obliged to pay a considerable premium for the safety of his investment. Thus, in the low yield illustration, if the A-Grade investor should lose no more than one-tenth of his investments, he would presumably be about equal at the maturity to the gains achieved by the Aaa-Grade investor. As to the Baa-Grade investor, he could lose a full one-fourth of his aggregate investments and still be equal at maturity to the Aaa-Grade investor. At the high yield rates, the A grade investor would gain one-fifth and the Baa investor more than one-third.

Current Income

Many investors are more concerned about current income from investments than they are about yield to maturity. Accordingly, they are usually less interested in securities sold at high premiums or sizeable discounts. If interested, they require additional (penalty) yields as a consideration for accepting them. Thus, a security that is selling at a substantial discount may have a good yield to maturity but an inadequate rate of current income to meet the requirements of the investor. This comparison helps to illustrate the point of the returns on a $100,000 investment scheduled to mature in 20 years:

Investor	Annual Coupon Rate	Price Per Bond	Par Value of Security Pur- chased	Current Annual Return	Yield to Maturity	
					Gross	Net for 46% Capital Gains Taxpayer
A	7.00	$1,000.00	$100,000	$7,000	7.00	7.00
B	3.00	511.45	195,523	5,866	7.90	7.05

From the foregoing it can be seen that, although the after-tax yield to maturity for the two investors is approximately the same, the current income of "B" is significantly less than for "A"—about one-sixth less. Therefore, if the investor requires current optimum income, the security offered at a discount will be less attractive.

In most recent years, the yield rates for longer-term bonds significantly exceeded those for the shorter-term bonds. Depending upon the current configurations of the yield curve and the degree of inflation that is bearing upon the market, the yield of 25-year securities in current dollars is sometimes twice that on securities due a year from date. In other markets, it has been as little as 10 or 11 percent.[3] These differentials help to determine the rates in the primary municipal bond market, as set forth more fully in a subsequent chapter.

Opportunity for Appreciation in Value

Except for municipal bonds purchased at a discount, the opportunities for appreciation in value over the purchase price depend upon a decrease in the yield-to-maturity rate vis-à-vis that at which the security was purchased. Among the circumstances in which a capital gain can be realized are:

1. A General Decline in Market Interest Rates. Thus a bond due in 20 years bearing a 6.60 percent coupon rate which was purchased at par will increase in value if the general interest levels decline. Therefore, if the bond can be sold on its first anniversary date at a 5.00 percent yield to maturity, it will have increased in price to $1,164, providing the investor a 16.4 percent pretax profit. If the owner is subject to capital gains taxation, that profit will be at the long-term federal rate—still leaving a considerable net return in addition to the current income or, if the coupon rate were 12.5 percent and within a year the yield rate dropped to 9.00 percent, the market value of the bond would increase by 27 percent to $1,271.

2. Yield Curve Appreciation. Reference has been made earlier to the importance of the yield curve in municipal bond investments. If one assumes a continuation of the same "normal" yield curve pattern and level throughout the life of a bond the value tends to increase to a high point followed by gradual return to par at the maturity date.

---

[3] During late 1979 and early 1980 it was found that the yield on three-year securities not only exceeded those maturing at earlier dates but also some of those maturing at later dates.

To illustrate, assume that a $1,000 bond is purchased at par in a period when the par yield rate was 6.60 percent and that during the life of the bond yield rates at specimen dates were as shown below for that bond. In such case, on the bond's 5th anniversary date, the price would have reached $1,028 under a 6.35 yield and on the 15th anniversary, $1,104. Thereafter the price would decline and eventually reach par just prior to maturity. Sale at these premium prices would produce substantial capital gains to the original investor. A similar pattern is evident in a much higher interest rate level that is also illustrated below. In the latter case, the price never rises so high as in the lower rate bond; however, it is sustained at somewhat higher levels in its final years prior to maturity.

Years to Maturity	Low Interest Rate Market		High Interest Rate Market	
	Yield	Price	Yield	Price
25	6.60	$1,000.00	12.15	$1,000.00
20	6.35	1,028.09	12.00	1,011.28
15	5.90	1,069.05	11.70	1,031.47
10	5.25	1,103.99	10.70	1,087.77
5	4.35	1,100.14	9.90	1,087.08
3	3.80	1,078.69	8.75	1,088.04
1	3.20	1,020.31	8.00	1,039.14
0	—	1,000.00	—	1,000.00

3. Improvement in the Quality of the Security Held. Communities and states are continuously changing. Many of these changes act to offset each other; however, the cumulative effects over a period of years are likely to be either discernibly positive or clearly negative. The population shifts during the 1970s to the sun belt areas correlated with an improved credit position for many jurisdictions there and a generally decreased viability of the economy in regions from which population shifted. The improved credit of an issuer is usually recognized in the marketplace, resulting in a lower yield curve vis-à-vis general market levels.

Even when the general credit of the issuer remains unchanged there can be improvement in the basic security lying behind a given credit market instrument. A record of improved budgetary and general financial management can help improve the credit of a general purpose government. A governmental enterprise may generate much higher net income than was projected at the time of the sale of its bonds. With this increased revenue the enterprise can (1) create new facilities that will generate additional net income; (2) accelerate retirement of outstanding debt; or (3) create additional reserve funds—all of which will be viewed favorably by investors. Governmental lessee debt can be strengthened by changes in the law governing the flow of funds from the state or local governments on a more favorable basis.

4. Advance Refunding. In advance refunding operations, outstanding bonds being defeased are frequently placed in triple-A credit status by investment of refunding bond proceeds in either U.S. Government securities or certificates of deposit. The new rating accorded the bonds can cause the price of the bonds to increase materially.

5. Impending Call. For bonds subject to call, the price can rise in anticipation of the early redemption of the bonds—especially for low coupon bonds selling at discounts.

6. Increase in Income Tax Rates. An increase in income tax rates by the federal government is likely to increase the value of outstanding tax-exempt bonds because of their increased pretax equivalent in taxable bonds. State income tax increases can have similar effects although these are somewhat diluted because many of the bonds are owned by nonresidents.

The Potential for Losses

Offsetting the opportunities for gain by investment in municipal securities are the potentials for loss. In many periods of financial pressure the price of outstanding securities has decreased but at no time in recent history has the market dropped so rapidly and for such a continuous period as from mid-1980 until the fall of 1981—with only brief respites along the way.

As the interest rates generally reached unprecedented levels the prices of low coupon securities dropped precipitously. Thus, a 6 percent coupon bond due in 20 years that had been selling near par might quickly experience substantial decreases in value. When the market went to a 12 percent yield for a 20-year bond, the price dropped to $549 on a $1,000 par value bond. Holders who for any reason were obliged to (or elected to) sell had to absorb colossal losses. And, this occurred not only with individuals but also with many commercial banks, institutional investors and investment bankers.

Moreover, as the yield curve went flat and then inverted for some parts of the maturity schedule, holders of relatively short-term maturities, who conventionally are protected by the low yield rates in that time bracket, also lost huge amounts.

Finally, as the Reagan Administration has reduced the higher income tax levels from 70 percent to 50 percent and made other reductions along the line together with broadening numerous advantages for investment in other areas, the pressures for higher interest returns on tax-exempt municipal securities have increased substantially. The result has been a market judgment that it will be a long time before there is a return to the yield rate levels illustrated in Patterns A and B, Appendix Table A.

Moreover, the sustained shifts in the economy and the relocation of many elements of economic productivity away from their traditional centers—especially in the Northeast quadrant—portend long-term readjustments in those areas, including losses for investors who acquired their securities at a time when their economic outlook was much brighter.

The effects of these recent experiences will doubtless be somewhat muted when a stable market recurs; however, they will probably linger long in the memory of those who incurred great losses in recent years.

Inflation

Consideration of the effects of inflation is significantly different for two groups of investors: (1) Financial institutions and others concerned solely with the accounting concept of monetary transactions signifying ownership and (2) investors planning to use the income or principal for purchase of goods and services.

The first group is little affected by changes in the purchasing power of the currency. They have assets and liabilities represented in accounting entries known as dollars. They have incurred liabilities payable in dollars. They fulfill their liabilities by payment in currency, without reference to its purchasing power. For this group there is only limited interest in the value of the currency; there is little direct risk arising from decreased purchasing power of the currency, although there may be significant risks arising from general economic disruption associated with long-term high rates of either inflation or deflation.

The second group consists of natural persons, institutions obliged to operate from accumulated endowment and other reserve funds, and others who may be in a trustee capacity with interest in the welfare of those for whom they act. They see the value of their accumulated reserves, pensions, and other fixed-dollar income diminish.[4] This inevita-

---

[4] Consider, for example, the school teacher who in 1934 decided to put aside 6 percent of his annual pay for a period of 20 years in order to assure a retirement income equal to 23 percent of his 1934 income. The policy recently matured. The author receives his $15 per month and each month reflects upon alternatives foregone by that decision.

bly produces a reluctance to accept fixed-dollar securities at the same rates of return that would be acceptable during periods of price stability. As a result, the interest demanded on new issues of municipal bonds increases.

Availability of a Secondary Market

The general need for an effective secondary market has been discussed in Chapter 4. It is necessary here only to emphasize the extent to which the availability of such a market influences investment decisions. If investors can anticipate prompt and equitable disposition of their securities in a viable secondary market, no penalty yields will be assessed on this score. Conversely, if the issue is little known or if it is difficult to secure an equitable appraisal, the investor may impose stiff penalty yields as a protection against the difficulties that may be encountered at a future date, i.e., for risk undertaken. The issuer has relatively little influence over the availability of a secondary market for its securities; however, this can be taken into consideration in planning the bond issue. The design of the bond issue in a manner that some bonds are being called and redeemed through the use of sinking funds helps to create a secondary potential for the lesser-known issues. Selection of underwriters with a view to their continuing interest in the securities also helps in a modest way to facilitate secondary market arrangements. The use of term bonds may provide a better-known security.

Term of the Loan

The term of the loan has a significant impact upon the interest costs to be paid under most market conditions. When the yield curve is flat, the cost at the time of issue is affected only by the amortization period chosen. More important is the market characterized by a high incidence yield curve coupled with an equal annual debt service arrangement. The capitalization (PV-2) of an equal annual debt service payment under Pattern B of Appendix Table A for a 30-year serial loan produces an effective, average interest rate much higher than capitalization for a 20-year loan. Thus, as shown in Appendix Table C, the NIC for a 20-year loan is 5.8145 percent and for a 30-year loan is 6.4106 percent. Under these market conditions, the issuer will wish to determine the probable effective average interest rate for different terms of the contemplated bond issue in making a decision as to the financing plan to be used.[5]

EVALUATION OF SECURITY RISK: RATINGS

The amount of *interest* payable on a new issue of bonds is influenced by several independent factors, including:

1. The issuance costs
2. The cost of the use of money, exclusive of risk
3. Compensation for risk of:
   a. Taxes payable
   b. Inflation
   c. Default

Most of these matters (as applied to the primary market) have been discussed elsewhere in this volume; concern here is related primarily with the risk of default.

---

[5] If the bond issue is a term issue, the same factors are present but in the form of the rate at which the sinking fund proceeds can be invested. For a further discussion of the impact of the yield curve upon costs, see Appendix E.

The evaluation of risk associated with the security pledged is the function of the investor and the credit analysts[6] upon whom the investor depends.

Default as applied to municipal bonds is a difficult term to define inasmuch as it is used in a number of different senses. In all cases, default includes failure to pay upon presentation at maturity either interest or principal on debt. In some cases, the term is used to encompass failures of debtors to make timely payments to trustees of amounts due under the terms of indentures for revenue bonds or failure to make timely deposits with the agencies administering sinking funds for general obligation bonds. Moreover, the term is sometimes applied to a failure to make timely increases in rates for use of facilities in governmental enterprises, to follow recommendations of consulting engineers, or to transfer funds from one account to another.[7] From the standpoint of the investor, these and other failures to meet the terms of contract influence the attractiveness of a security.

Defaults which are technical or cured within a very short period of time are likely to involve inconvenience and perhaps potential loss to the bondholder; they may besmirch the previously impeccable reputation of the issuer. Technical defaults sometimes occur without being recorded as defaults. Thus, an issuer may be tardy in making a deposit with the trustee or the sinking fund commission without any impact, or even without the knowledge of the bondholder. Failures to act within prescribed time limits to cure coverage requirements or to abide by other terms of the contract that do not affect the timely receipt by the bondholder of interest or principal may also not be recorded as defaults. However, any failure by the issuer or by the issuer's paying agent or trustee to make payment on demand of a coupon or bond that is due is a default that is noted and one which can have long-term adverse effects on the credit of the issuer, or, if the fault lies with the paying agent or trustee, on the reputation of both the issuer and the agent or trustee. A default cured within a short period of time may have only limited adverse effects; a default that is protracted or one that results in full loss by the bondholder of the principal and interest payable commencing with the date of default constitutes a severe blow to the issuer—one that may have continuing adverse effects for decades. Thus, a default by the State of Louisiana in the 1870s was still being well remembered by some credit analysts more than a half-century later.

The Function of the Credit Analyst

The function of the credit analyst is principally that of estimating the degree of risk the investor is assuming in relation to potential default by the issuer, especially failure to meet scheduled payments of interest and principal. The analyst seeks to determine the relative potential for default. If formal credit ratings are assigned, they constitute expressions of the analyst's view of this relative risk.

The analyst works in the field of the prospective. Although he may have the advantage of historical performance, the investor's interest is in relation to the future; interest in past performance is limited to the extent to which that historical performance may provide a guide to the future.

Credit Ratings

Two national organizations regularly issue ratings on a wide range of municipal bond issues: Moody's Investors Service and Standard & Poor's. Fitch's Investors Service provides analyses and ratings for selected municipal securities; it is especially active in the health facility field and in certain municipal notes. The two principal agencies offer these rating grades for bonds:

---

[6] Credit analysts may be employees of the investor; credit rating agencies; analysts associated with underwriters; independent analysts selling their services on a consulting basis; authors of newsletters; or columnists in financial or other journals.

[7] See general discussion in Wade S. Smith, *The Appraisal of Municipal Credit Risk*, pp. 243–245.

	Moody's	Standard & Poor's
Best quality	Aaa	AAA
Excellent	Aa	AA
Upper medium	A and A 1	A and A—
Lower medium	Baa and Baa 1	BBB
Marginally speculative	Ba	BB
Very speculative	B, Caa	B
Default	Ca, C	D

These rating agencies now issue ratings only on bonds in respect to which the issuer pays a fee at the time of issuance of the bonds. In addition to the rating system for bonds, Moody's maintains a rating service for short-term debt, with ratings of M-1, M-2, M-3, and M-4 denoting various levels of quality of these instruments.[8]

Beyond the letter ratings, each of the agencies issues reports on bonds rated at the time of their issue. From time to time, the agencies make a comprehensive review of the credit of major issuers and, occasionally, of selected smaller issuers. These reviews may result in reconfirming ratings previously established; they may increase the rating; or they may decrease the rating. Such reviews result in reports on the factors that have been considered and set forth the reasons for the actions being taken.

Moody's issues an annual two-volume report entitled *Municipal & Government Manual* providing substantial amounts of information concerning the financial affairs of the governments issuing bonds rated by it. It also issues a weekly review of the municipal market. Standard & Poor's *Creditweek,* a commentary upon the credit market conditions, provides general information regarding credit analysis data on major municipal and corporate bond issues arriving on the market.

The factors taken into account by the rating agency analysts encompass virtually the full gamut of the operations of the issuer; the economy upon which the issuer relies for support of the debt being considered; and pertinent social and management factors. High in the list of factors being considered are trends in population, employment, wealth, and income; the organization and management of the government; the history (especially the recent history) of the financial affairs of the government; the performance of governmental enterprises in relation to projections previously made. And, any other matters likely to influence the ability of the issuer to continue to meet the financial obligations undertaken in respect to the debt being rated are taken into account to the extent feasible.[9]

The two principal rating agencies are commercial enterprises. They provide an evaluation of the credit risk for the benefit of the investor. They also serve the issuer in the sense of providing an independent assessment of the credit-worthiness of the bonds being rated. The rating service is financed from a combination of the sale of services to investors and fees charged the issuer for the review and rating of the new bond issue. Without credit ratings, both the primary and secondary market would function less efficiently and probably at considerable additional costs.

From time to time, the ratings have been the subject of protracted, and sometimes bitter, dispute between issuers and the rating agencies. Congressional committees have reviewed the subject on several occasions and the rating services have been the subject of a report by The Twentieth Century Fund.[10] There have been recurring proposals for the establishment of an official federal agency that would rate bonds; however, no such proposal has ever advanced significantly on the Congressional calendar.

Impact of Ratings on Interest Rates

The effect of ratings upon interest rates is pronounced. At the same time, one finds a considerable amount of spread in the reoffering yields for any given maturity date among

---

[8] For a description of the rating classes used by Moody's and Standard & Poor's, see Appendix D.

[9] For a review of the factors taken into account, see Wade S. Smith, *The Appraisal of Municipal Credit Risk.*

[10] The Twentieth Century Fund, *The Rating Game: Report of the Twentieth Century Fund Task Force on Municipal Bond Credit Ratings.*

bonds accorded identical ratings. This spread is sometimes pronounced, with bonds in the next lower rating in one category attaining a better market position than bonds carrying higher ratings. Moreover, the two organizations frequently differ in ratings of a given credit.

Even with these differences, a government whose bonds are reduced in rating will almost inevitably be obliged to pay a higher interest rate on subsequent sales vis-à-vis the previous levels of costs for parity bonds. Conversely, when ratings are increased, the prices of the bonds outstanding are likely to increase as a result of higher ratings. Therefore, from the point of view of the issuer, the attainment and maintenance of a good or excellent rating is highly desirable.

Prior to the initiation of the fee system for rating, the rating agencies would not provide ratings for some issues, frequently due to the absence of sufficient reliable information being supplied to the rating agency or to the agency's lack of confidence in data being furnished. With the use of fees for rating, this becomes a purchased service and the incidence of refusal by the agencies to rate bonds has become much less, partially because those willing to pay the fee will provide required information.

Of course, no issuer is obliged to secure a rating. The bonds may be issued on an unrated basis. A variety of reasons account for the unrated bonds; however, the principal reason tends to be a belief by the issuer that the bonds can be more favorably marketed without a rating than with the rating likely to be assigned.

Presentations to Rating Agencies

Given the significant importance of ratings, it is surprising that many issuers devote so little time to preparation of presentations made to the credit analysts. Prior to the issuance of the MFOA disclosure guidelines,[11] the data presented was usually limited to that called for in schedules supplied by the agencies. Frequently, these were not prepared in full or with sufficient attention to detail and accuracy. Since the issuance of the guidelines, the amount of information furnished and the quality of the information appear to have improved materially; however, persons engaged in rating agency work suggest that the millenium has not been reached.

Other Informational Sources

Beyond the ratings provided by the two principal national firms, information is provided in some states by various types of organizations (generally known as municipal bond councils) largely sponsored by dealers. Some of these organizations seek to provide ratings for new issues arising in their areas; others provide various types of useful information to dealer members without formal rating. Organizations exist in a number of states, with those serving Texas, North Carolina, South Carolina, Tennessee, and Michigan, being among the more active.

---

[11] See discussion in Chapter 18.

Chapter 7
FINANCING CAPITAL COSTS: SOME BASIC CONSIDERATIONS

This chapter examines the general aspects of policy development in financing capital improvements. The four cornerstones of debt policy are discussed briefly and a number of other factors are examined.

THE CORNERSTONES OF DEBT POLICY

Sound debt policy rests upon these four cornerstones:

1. A proper determination of capital facility needs[1]
2. The ability and willingness to pay for the facilities and for the programs to which they relate
3. An understanding of the economic rental for each facility
4. The rate of accumulation of community patrimony

There is extensive literature about the need for capital facilities and the ability to pay for them; however, there is a dearth of information on the economic rental of public facilities, and almost no literature on patrimony accumulation.

The Need for Capital Facilities

Capital facilities exist to facilitate the conduct of *operating programs*. Except as monuments and contributions to art, there is no other legitimate justification for their acquisition and maintenance. State and local governments exist to provide services which vary widely in their need for capital facilities. Thus, public water supply systems are capital intensive; they require reservoirs, aqueducts, filtration plants, distribution networks, shops, meters, and both mobile and stationary equipment. By contrast, social services, e.g., a marriage counselling service, ordinarily have very low capital facility components—an office, furniture, and perhaps access to a park bench on a mild day suffice.

Public administration has overcompartmentalized the capital program process as if it were severable from the operating program—frequently, as if they were unrelated. The capital program process is an integral part of the comprehensive operating process. One can find a body of literature on long-term capital programs but there is a dearth of attention to the more important subject of comprehensive, long-term operating programs.

Long-term capital programs can be wisely and efficiently developed and executed only as incident to comprehensive long-term operating programs. Unfortunately, the process is frequently reversed through development of capital facilities with little appreciation of the operating requirements to be served. Officials and employees responsible for the operations are thereby confronted with the Procrustean bed syndrome—being obliged to fit

---

[1] The term *capital facility* is used in this chapter to comprehend the aggregate of land, structures, and equipment being used at a given location, assuming that it has a useful life of more than one year. It embraces both stationary and movable equipment.

the program into the facility, rather than having the facility designed to serve operating requirements.[2]

A point to be considered in relation to capital programs is ownership vs. availability of the capital facilities. From the standpoint of the operating official, the need is for *availability* as required, whether the user be a surgeon, a librarian, or a social worker, the availability of the facility for use as needed should be sufficient; ownership should be relatively inconsequential to them.[3] On the other hand, ownership may be a major factor in determination of public policies affecting the rate at which the rental on such facilities is paid. A complete separation of the concepts of *use* and *ownership* is essential to a full understanding of the economic rental and patrimony accumulation as they relate to provision of capital facilities.

Returning to the capital program, the identification of needed facilities should be developed from the comprehensive, long-term operating program. Therefore, the first cornerstone is a proper determination of need, integrated with plans for both operation and the physical development of the community. This relationship to community development is especially pertinent to primary local governments.

Ability and Willingness to Pay

The second major cornerstone of debt policy is the *ability* of the community to pay for the community service—that is, for both its operating and capital components. Inasmuch as economic capacity is not uniformly distributed, communities vary widely in their ability to pay for services and their associated capital programs. Moreover, ability to pay can change dramatically within relatively short periods of time. Consequently, the view of ability to pay as it relates to long-term financing of capital programs must take into account the possibilities of adverse economic developments. For example, the migrational patterns of the 1970s have left many older cities with decreased population, employment, and economic activity. Some facilities constructed in earlier decades are no longer required. Yet, most communities have amortized only a part of these facilities. Debt service payments and some other costs continue. The ability to pay is a factor of major importance in the design of a public debt program. It is of major concern to any lender and to credit analysts. Ability to pay is determined by the wealth of the community and its level of economic activity in relation to the demands on such resources. The ability to pay is also influenced by the organizational patterns of local government within a state. Some states have wisely restricted the number and types of local governmental units and have sought to bring about reasonable relationships between the geographical area served by political subdivisions and the social and economic community being served. Others have allowed unfettered balkanization. This has fragmented economic capacity to the point that ability to support debt has been unnecessarily jeopardized.

Beyond the ability to pay, *willingness* to pay is an important ingredient—a subject

---

[2] Given the compartmentalization required in large-scale enterprise, the prerogative and responsibility for general policy development and coordination rests with the apex of the administrative pyramid. Inasmuch as governmental programs are designed to serve broad areas of community life, there is a need for intimate coordination between the physical, economic, and social development of the community and the rendition of its services. Accordingly, most primary local governments have authority to use the police power related to land use in the development and enforcement of comprehensive physical community development plans. Those governments which have opted to exercise controls over physical development of a community can improve the efficiency of this operation through the integration of the capital programming and community development planning processes.

[3] Experience has shown that ownership is one of the most dependable means of assuring that facilities are available for use as needed. As a consequence, ownership is frequently sought as the means to assure the availability of facilities as needed. Consequently, there is a resistance to ownership and control of such facilities outside the unit requiring their use—whether such ownership and control be by another department, another unit of government, or by private owners. Ownership frequently lessens the number of negotiations required for immediate availability, thereby reducing administrative friction. However, ownership on a departmental basis can lead to inefficient use of community assets because of the tendency toward hoarding.

to which too little attention has been directed. Prior to 1970 there was a relatively high rate of increase in per capita GNP (on a constant dollar basis). A considerable portion of this could be pre-empted as taxes and other charges by governments, still leaving the worker with a sense of upward mobility beyond governmental services. However, during the 1970s the per capita GNP (after inflation and after taxation) grew at a slower rate. Not only the ability but also the willingness of citizens to support expanded governmental programs and facilities diminished markedly. The experience with the taxpayers' rebellion in California and elsewhere is a definite indication of the public mood. Accordingly, it is necessary to take into account both *ability* and *willingness* to pay.

Economic Rental

The concept of *economic rental* as used in this volume comprehends the full *accruing* cost of ownership and occupancy or use during the accounting period. It is independent of cash flows. Thus, some portions of economic rental may be fully prepaid, e.g., the cost of the acquisition of a building; some may be amortized over the useful life of the facility; and payment for some may be deferred long beyond the time during which the economic rental accrued. Timing of payment in relation to timing of accrual of economic rental affects public patrimony accumulation.

A sound debt policy requires a comprehensive appreciation of economic rental of the facilities being acquired. Some aspects of economic rental are applicable solely to the structure itself, whether in use or merely in existence. Other aspects of economic rental are more immediately related to the fact that the facility is in use.

The portion of economic rental accruing without reference to use of the facility includes depreciation, interest on undepreciated investment, ground rent, portions of insurance, payments in lieu of tax payments, maintenance, operating costs, and provision for demolition. The portion of economic rental related to use involves most operating costs of the facility itself, internal maintenance, rehabilitation, and tenant alterations.

1. *Depreciation.* A schedule of depreciation covering the full life of the facility is required. This schedule should be fully realistic in relation to the rate appropriate for each period of the life of the facility. The schedule should not be warped by the arbitrary acceleration of depreciation which occurs in private enterprise accounting related to maximizing profits, cash flows, and tax preferences. Nor should it be related to the practice of accelerating genuine depreciation in the manner frequently found in public enterprise accounting deemed necessary to provide cash flow to redeem outstanding bonds at a more rapid rate than the bona fide rate of depreciation.

2. *Interest.* The interest on the unamortized investment in structures is an element of economic rental. This interest can be precisely the same as the interest payable on outstanding debt only if the retirement of debt is precisely equal to the depreciation component of economic rental accruing. Ordinarily, debt is retired before the useful life of the facility is terminated. For the purpose of determining interest as a component in economic rental, interest runs on all unamortized investment, i.e., on the gross less depreciation. [The interest on unamortized rehabilitation and tenant alterations is more appropriately related to an interest component incident to use as distinguished from original development costs.]

3. *Insurance.* Insurance on the structure relates to all hazards not directly related to occupancy. The insurance may be provided by a commercial carrier or it may be on the basis of self-insurance.

4. *Exterior Maintenance.* Maintenance is included in the costs relating to the structure without reference to use, i.e., primarily exterior maintenance. This is necessary because much of the interrelationship is between the level of external maintenance and the depreciation rate for the structure. Internal maintenance is largely a function of use.

5. *Operating Costs.* Only small portions of operating costs, e.g., external security ar-

rangements or maintenance of grounds and roadways, pertain to the structure itself. The remainder is related to the use of the facility.

6. *Payments in lieu of Taxes.* A number of services are provided to property by local governments without reference to use of the property. Thus, police and fire protection are elements of the cost of owning a structure. In the same manner, the demand charges for certain utilities as well as access charges for use of the streets may be appropriately assessed as costs of ownership of the facility. These charges related to ownership should be included in base economic rental.

7. *Provision for Demolition.* If the structure is one that is likely to be demolished at the end of its useful life, the cost of demolition should be included in basic economic rental and apportioned over the life of the structure.

8. *Ground Rent.* Economic rental encompasses the interest payable on the cost of the site. It also includes amortization of the cost of site development, e.g., demolition of pre-existing structures as well as earth movement required for development of the new structures. Ground rent, therefore, consists of interest on the original investment and amortization of those elements of investment in the site that will not enhance its value if and when demolition of the structure is required.

The foregoing constitute the principal elements of economic rental related to ownership of ground and structures. In addition, there are those elements (mentioned earlier) that become elements of the economic rental related to occupancy. In single occupancy facilities these are all apportioned to a single activity, e.g., a public library or playground. In multiple occupancy they are apportioned among the users.

The pertinency of economic rental in the development of a capital program is the creation of data necessary to determine the full cost of programs. Without such information the process of planning operating programs cannot go forward with the same confidence; because, lacking such information, it is not feasible to make fully responsible judgments as to whether the program(s) giving rise to the need for the facility can be afforded.

Having determined the costs of economic rental for each year of the expected life of a facility, the owner must address the question of how these costs will be paid. The rate of payment impinges upon the final cornerstone discussed here: Patrimony accumulation.

In the course of determining the rate at which economic rental is to be incurred, the owner must also give attention to the periods of probable nonuse of the facility and the apportionment of the cost of economic rental accruing during such periods to those periods of actual use. If the owner has a number of facilities that are more or less interchangeable, e.g., a number of public school buildings, the apportionment of vacancy charges may best be handled on a group basis rather than on an individual facility basis, inasmuch as a direct charge to the facility chosen for temporary deactivation may be very high and could apply to an alternate structure had it been chosen for vacancy instead of continued occupancy. Thus, economic rentals relating to the vacancy of several buildings in a school system may be more appropriately apportioned among the whole group of such buildings rather than to the individual vacated structures.

Patrimony Accumulation

Each generation[4] inherits a patrimony from the preceding generation consisting of various assets and liabilities. A major portion of this patrimony is the physical plant and land associated with it. The value of this portion of the patrimony consists of the net difference between the present bona fide value of the assets and the outstanding debt pertaining to such physical assets.

---

[4] For purposes of this discussion, a generation is considered as one group that is successor to another. It may be the group of people living here today vis-à-vis those living here yesterday. It may be those living here this year vis-à-vis those residing here last year. Or, it can relate to any other period of time. It is not limited to the conventional concept of the span of time from the birth of the father until the birth of the son.

In the aggregate, public patrimony consists of a combination of the net worth of tangible and intangible assets. Most of the tangible assets and many of the intangible assets can be valued in terms of currency; some cannot, e.g., museum treasures such as the original copy of the Declaration of Independence. The "going business" attributes of social and political organization are not subject to evaluation in monetary terms.

The concern with public patrimony in this discussion is limited to public lands and public facilities and their associated liabilities. If the outstanding debt is precisely equal to the depreciated value of capital facilities, the value of patrimony associated with these elements is zero. If, during a given period of time (herein called "generation"), the liabilities are reduced in a greater amount than the assets are amortized under the kind of depreciation discussed above, there is a *positive* accumulation of patrimony. Conversely, if the liabilities are reduced at a slower rate than the depreciation rate, there is a *negative* accumulation of patrimony during such period. Hence a building with a 50-year life that is paid for in 25 years is almost assuredly producing a positive patrimony accumulation during most of the first 25 years of its life and a negative patrimony accumulation during each of the final 25 years of its life.

The foregoing discussion of patrimony is fully applicable only in periods of stable value of the currency. This, of course, is not realistic inasmuch as the value of currency is always fluctuating. Generally, over longer periods of time, there is a deflation in the value of currency (price inflation). It is therefore appropriate to restate costs and outstanding debt in terms of the current purchasing power of dollars for similar types of capital expenditure. Only in this manner can comparisons with contemporary costs be accomplished. However, it should be understood that the restatement does not provide an actual growth in patrimony in constant dollar terms.

Historical Precedent. The long-term trend of patrimony accumulation in the United States has been positive, even after adjustment for price changes. Most, if not all, decades have seen a net increase in the patrimony passed on at the end of the decade compared to that at the beginning of the decade. This has not been true in every community. Ghost towns offer testimony to negative patrimony accumulation during a part of their history; shifts in population on a more general scale, e.g., away from Oklahoma during the 1930s and contemporary losses in many older urban areas, help produce negative patrimony.

The concern here is twofold: (1) Measuring the amount and direction of patrimony accumulation and (2) exploring its relationship to the debt policies of state and local governments. The first topic is the relationship between economic rental and the amortization of debt. Thus, if at the end of 30 years the depreciated value is 60 percent of original cost and all debt has been liquidated along with current provision for other costs, the full 60 percent represents net accumulated patrimony.

The use of patrimony accumulation as a concept in the development and execution of debt policy is of significance here. The basic policy questions relating to patrimony accumulation appear to be these:

1. During which periods should the policy be one of positive accumulation and during which periods is negative accumulation appropriate?
2. During periods of either positive or negative accumulation, what rates should apply? Should they be constant or variable? Under what criteria?
3. Should overall policies of accumulation take into account the method of financing? Especially financing from grants-in-aid?
4. What kinds of price deflators should be used in order to bring about substantial equity between investments made during different patterns of price change?

Positive Accumulations of Patrimony. A positive accumulation of patrimony occurs only when there is a *prepayment* of economic rental. This can arise in the year in which a grant is received and used for acquisition of a public facility. But, for the future years, the depreciation of the facility produces negative accumulation. The principal policy question at that point is whether to accept the negative accumulation or to seek to overcome it by positive accumulation in respect to other structures.

The positive accumulation of patrimony is most frequently achieved through a deliberate retirement of debt at a more rapid rate than the bona fide depreciation rate. [Retirement of debt in this sense comprehends not only actual retirement but also the accumulation of reserves allocated to eventual retirement of the debt.] Typically, these debt retirement schedules have been determined in a highly unsophisticated manner. The retirement schedules for most debt are on a basis of either equal annual principal retirement or equal annual debt service. In both cases, the final maturity is likely to be arbitrarily selected and significantly in advance of the date at which the life of the facility has been exhausted. If there is a relationship to economic rental, it is more likely to be accidental than carefully planned.

Eventually—when the full life of the facility has expired and demolition has occurred—a point of zero accumulation is reached, assuming that all liabilities have been discharged before demolition. Positive or negative accumulation, therefore, occurs only during the life of the facility. It occurs in respect to the rate of amortization of liabilities during the life of the facility as compared to the rate of amortization of the value of the facility.[5]

Negative Patrimony Accumulation. Inevitably, there are periods of negative patrimony accumulation; for example:

1. *Amortization of Grant-in-Aid Financing.* Facilities of a government that are provided in part or in whole by grants-in-aid from other governments should be entered into the patrimony balance sheet. At the time of acquisition of these facilities there will have been a significant unearned increase in the community patrimony. As the facility is used, the patrimony is decreased unless reserves are established for eventual renewal or alternative facilities are being financed on a basis of payments for use substantially above the economic rental level appropriate for such facilities. The larger the amount of grants used for capital outlays during one period, the greater the likelihood of negative patrimony in the periods immediately following.

2. *Conversion from "Pay-as-You-Acquire" to "Pay-as-You-Use."* When a community converts from "pay-as-you-acquire" (either partially or wholly) to "pay-as-you-use," there will usually be a sustained period of negative patrimony accumulation, even if a policy of modest positive accumulation is pursued in respect of new acquisitions. The community is "expending" portions of the equity developed by previous generations of users. Even though the current users are making full payment of economic rental (and even partial prepayment) for the new facilities being developed, the amortization of the pre-existing acquisitions constitutes a charge in the patrimony balance sheet. The same effects occur to a lesser degree as the term for amortizing debt is extended beyond the life of the facility.

3. *Failure to Provide Reserves.* Negative patrimony accumulation also occurs when there is a failure to provide for accumulation of proper levels of reserves required under economic rental concepts.

4. *Technological Obsolescence.* Unforseen developments can render facilities obsolete in a much shorter time than anticipated. Portions of the obligations remain outstanding, but the facility may have ceased to have any utility or may have significantly reduced utility.

---

[5] This author hastens to admit that during his periods of service as a public finance officer and as advisor to various governments he did not pursue the course advocated here. This failure was a failure in perception because, until the leisure available for the preparation of this volume came along, he had not taken the time to think through the theoretical base suggested here. This leaves open the question as to how far he might have been able to proceed along the recommended lines should he have had the perception and the methods worked out in time for use in one or more of those tours of duty.

5. *Catastrophe.* Although a suitable insurance charge has been suggested, if insurance is carried as self-insurance, an untimely disaster can produce a heavy and unexpected charge upon the patrimony account.

If there has been an orderly accumulation of patrimony, the account will doubtless have sufficient reserves to absorb the shock effects of the foregoing types of negative patrimony developments and still leave a net positive balance. On the other hand, if the positive balance is low or nonexistent, difficulties may shortly be encountered.

Policy for Accumulation of Patrimony. Reference has already been made to the policy to be followed in the accumulation of a positive patrimony. Generally, investors are favorably impressed with large accumulations of net equity, are discouraged by small accumulations, and are generally quite negative about negative accumulations.

Patrimony can be accumulated only through acceleration of payment of portions of economic rental to a point in advance of the time when earned. Given this circumstance, the question recurs as to the pattern of accumulation being sought by the community, both as to the amounts and the rates of accumulation involved. Policymakers must understand any accumulation by a "generation" means that the current "generation" of users is being obliged to prepay a portion of the economic rental for a future generation. Moreover, given the likelihood of long-term inflation, the prepayments are required to be made in currency of greater purchasing power (and, therefore, of greater value to most taxpayers) than the replacement dollars at a later date.

Against this is the fact that the accumulation of reserves against unforeseen demands on current income is always a prudent approach to take during periods of reasonable economic activity. Once again, this calls for formulation of a policy that is well understood by those responsible for debt management.

It is not the function of this author to suggest the patterns appropriate at given times for specific communities. On the other hand, it is strongly urged that pre-existing policies of decision making on highly arbitrary basis of a specific term of years coupled with either equal annual principal retirement or equal annual debt service be supplanted by a much more sophisticated view of this matter including studies of PV-2 capitalization.

The foregoing discussion outlines the four cornerstones on which effective debt policy can be developed. The articulation of a sound debt policy requires not only definition but also effective follow-through. Good debt policies can be developed without the formalities set forth above as to the cornerstones; however, there is likely to be more confidence if both a theoretical and practical base have been developed.

Capital Facilities' Cost and Inventory Records. With these matters in mind, the examination of some of the more concrete aspects of debt policy are in order. Moreover, the maintenance of the records of economic rental, patrimony accounts, and occupancy costs for structures are critical management tools. Before proceeding it is appropriate to emphasize the need for comprehensive inventories of capital facilities. Such inventories should be current in all respects, fully computerized under classification systems that permit instant retrieval, and also current as to the use of each facility. The investment in movable equipment of all types (especially mobile equipment) should be known at all times. Replacement cycles should reflect optimun life cycles for each type of equipment. The optimum life cycle needs to be determined in light of the total impact of continuing the ownership and operation of present equipment as contrasted to the probable alternative costs involved in replacement of the equipment. This, in turn, consists of (1) the more or less direct cost of ownership of the equipment and (2) the indirect impact of the equipment on efficiency of overall operations.

Insofar as the equipment itself is concerned, one must address the amortization of the original investment and the cost of keeping the equipment in a reasonable status of operation vis-à-vis its functions. Insofar as the impact upon operations is concerned, one is obliged to take into account the costs of loss of use of manpower, e.g., the refuse truck crew when the truck breaks down, and all of the associated costs that arise from the inefficient performance of the equipment. Unfortunately, most of the equipment accounts reflect only a part of the more or less direct costs and fail to reflect any portion of the indirect costs—even though these indirect costs may be vastly greater than the direct costs.

Not only is it necessary to know when individual items of equipment—lemons or damaged items—should be withdrawn from inventory but also the effects of mixtures of makes and models vs. full replacement of identified segments of the fleet, e.g., refuse compactors, will permit lower training, parts inventory, and maintenance costs.

RECENT TRENDS IN CAPITAL OUTLAYS OF STATE AND LOCAL GOVERNMENTS

The Bureau of the Census prepares annual estimates of the capital outlays of state and local governments. Table 23 shows that in current dollars capital outlays increased from $30 billion in 1970 to a plateau of about $45 billion in 1975–1978, followed by a sharp increase to $63 billion in 1980. However, in constant dollars, there was a net decrease in outlays during the 1970s.[6]

Table 23

Capital Outlays of State and Local Governments
1970–1980

Year	Total	Construction	Equipment	Land and Existing Structures
	(amounts in billions of dollars)			
	(1)	(2)	(3)	(4)
1980	62.9	51.5	--------11.4--------------	
1979	53.2	43.3	---------9.9--------------	
1978	44.8	36.2	---------8.6--------------	
1977	44.9	36.1	5.6	3.2
1976	46.5	38.3	5.4	3.2
1975	44.8	36.4	5.1	3.4
1974	38.1	30.5	4.2	3.4
1973	35.3	28.2	3.7	3.3
1972	34.2	28.1	3.1	3.0
1971	33.1	27.0	3.0	3.2
1970	29.7	24.3	2.8	2.6
Annual Compound Percentage Increase				
1970–1980	7.8	7.8	-------7.8---------------	

Sources: U.S. Bureau of the Census, *Governmental Finances in 1972–73*, p. 18; *in 1976–77*, p. 16; *in 1979–80*, p. 52; *in 1979–80*, p. 51; *Historical Statistics of the United States: Colonial Times to 1970*, p. 1127.
NB: For fiscal year basis used by the Bureau of the Census, see Appendix F.

---

[6] The building cost index of the *Engineering News Record* (ENR) increased from 866 to 2017 between 1970 and 1980 (8.82 percent annual compound rate) and the construction costs index from 1445 to 3376 (8.86 percent). Therefore, the average annual compound rate of increase was about 9 percent. If this rate is used as a deflator, the $51.5 billion of construction (building and construction as used by ENR), the value in 1970 dollars drops to $21.8 billion, or a decrease in constant dollars of 10 percent below the 1971 rate of $24.2 billion.

During the 10-year period about four-fifths of the total capital outlays went for construction, with the remainder going for equipment and acquisition of land and existing structures. It is noted that the compound annual rate of increase for the 1970–1980 period for construction was only 7.8 percent. Given the high rates of inflation (especially in building and construction) during this period, it is apparent that the expenditures for construction increased at a much lesser rate than necessary to maintain the level in constant dollars. In 1970 capital outlays of $30 billion accounted for about 20 percent of total state and local government expenditures. By 1980 outlays of $63 billion amounted to only about 17 percent of total expenditures, representing a slower rate of growth for capital costs.

The purposes for which capital outlays are made are summarized in Table 24. In 1980 transportation functions absorbed more than one-third of the $63 billion. Utilities were next with $14 billion and education third with $11 billion. The remainder was widely distributed among other functions. In terms of rates of growth during the decade, utilities led the list with an average annual compound growth rate of 15 percent, followed by

Table 24

Expenditures of State and Local Governments for Capital Outlays by Function
Selected Years, 1970–1980

	1980	1978	1976	1970	Annual Compound Percentage Increase 1970–1980
	(amounts in billions of dollars)				
Total	62.9	44.8	46.5	29.7	7.8
Education	10.7	8.7	10.1	7.6	3.5
Local schools	7.4	5.7	6.5	4.7	4.2
Institutions of higher learning	3.0	2.6	3.0	2.7	1.1
Other	.4	.4	.6	.3	2.9
Transportation	23.0	15.4	16.7	12.2	6.5
Highways	19.1	12.9	14.2	10.8	5.9
Air transportation	1.4	.8	.8	.7	7.2
Water transportation	.6	.3	.4	.3	7.2
Transit	1.9	1.4	1.3	.4	16.9
Utilities	14.3	8.6	8.1	3.5	15.1
Water	3.3	2.1	2.2	1.2	10.6
Sewage	6.3	4.4	4.0	1.4	16.2
Electricity	4.6	3.0	1.8	.8	19.1
Gas	.1	.1	.1	.1	—
Health & hospitals	2.4	1.9	1.8	.8	11.6
Parks & recreation	2.0	1.6	1.3	.7	11.1
Natural resources	1.1	.6	1.1	.8	2.2
Housing & urban renewal	2.2	1.4	1.4	1.3	5.4
All other	7.0	6.6	6.1	2.9	9.3

Sources: U.S. Bureau of the Census, *Governmental Finances in 1969–70*, p. 25; *in 1975–76*, p. 24; *in 1977–78*, p. 51; *in 1979–80*, p. 51.
NB: For fiscal year basis used by the Bureau of the Census, see Appendix F.

health and hospitals and then by parks and recreations [both in the 11 to 12 percent range]. Growth in transportation was at the 6.5 percent level and education at only 3.5 percent. Given the increase in building and construction costs averaging over 9 percent per annum, any rate of increase below that level constituted an actual decline in constant dollar capital outlays.[7]

FINANCING OF CAPITAL OUTLAYS: CURRENT REVENUES VS. CAPITALIZATION OF REVENUES

Governmental capital outlays are financed in part from current revenues, i.e., "pay-as-you-acquire," and partly through the capitalization of future income, i.e., "pay-as-you-use." Perhaps the greatest single decision confronted in the development and execution of public debt policy is the choice of the mix of current revenue and debt that is to be used. During the past several decades there have been wide fluctuations in the mix.

The views held concerning public finance during the 1800s were influenced to a large degree by the tremendous growth and expansion of the nation. Moreover, during that period, the mechanisms of debt and financing were still in their infancy as applied to state and local governments. Even so, during the period immediately following the Civil War, state and local government debt was being used not only to finance the capital facilities of those governments but also to provide developmental assistance to transportation, especially to the railroads. As the municipal bond market began to come of age in the period following World War I, a full-scale debate arose as to the extent to which loans or current revenues should be used. Milwaukee and some other local governments opted for heavy reliance upon current revenues; others depended largely on the proceeds of long-term loans—many of them for 50-year terms. The Great Depression of the 1930s caused a reevaluation of the trends, and it became an article of faith with many persons concerned with improved local government to insist upon either full "pay-as-you-acquire" or at least to provide for very sizeable "down payments" in capital outlay financing. This reflected the difficulties encountered in meeting heavy fixed debt service charges during that period of significantly reduced revenue for many of these governments. Moreover, the average effective life of bond issues was significantly reduced. The reduction in reliance on long-term debt was abetted by the huge loans and grants under various federal government programs, especially the Public Works Administration and the work-relief program under the Civil Works Administration and the Works Progress Administration. Capital outlay programs were severely curtailed. During World War II, however, some governments developed "Post War Reserve Funds" to help finance capital outlays that had been foregone during 15 years of war and depression.

Even so, numerous factors combined after World War II to reestablish reliance on "pay-as-you-use" as the dominant pattern of capital financing. Chief among these were:

1. The backlog of needs arising from low levels of capital facility outlays between 1930 and 1946
2. A rapidly expanding population commencing in the early 1940s
3. Shifts in population from rural to urban, among regions, and from central cities to suburbia with consequent demands for a full range of facilities
4. Reduction in overcrowded housing as a result of the spreading out into single-family occupancy by family groups who had long lived crowded together in single households
5. The expansion of the economy
6. Increased public demand for higher levels of public service and facilities, e.g., pollution abatement, health and hospital facilities, trafficways, public transportation

---

[7] Ibid.

One by one, most of those cities which, during the 1930s, had moved toward "pay-as-you-acquire" reversed their policies. They had no practical alternative, particularly the rapidly growing communities. Although the pressure of large capital spending was a factor in these decisions, many persons were convinced that an equitable sharing in the cost of providing public facilities required a heavy reliance upon "pay-as-you-use" approaches. The view was accepted that each generation should be expected to pay its own economic rental by spreading most of the costs over longer, rather than shorter, periods.

The following arguments deserve consideration in the decision-making process relating to the choice of methods of financing capital outlays.

Arguments for "Pay-as-You-Acquire"

These are the principal arguments for a "pay-as-you-acquire" policy:

1. *Fiscal Responsibility.* The community and its leaders must confront the fiscal realities immediately by providing amounts ranging from a "down payment" to a full financing from current revenues. This kind of action discouraged irresponsible spending—both as to the number and types of projects as well as scope, design, and costs of such projects. In other words, they should maximize patrimony accumulation.

2. *Flexibility.* The community will have reserved unto itself a much greater flexibility in periods of economic adversity in that it has fewer fixed costs. It may reduce capital outlays with an immediate reduction in tax rates and service charges without adversely affecting current operations. Even if current operations must be curtailed, the shock will be much less.

3. *Reduced Interest.* A substantial saving in interest payable on outstanding debt is effected. Over a period of years, this saving can be used to finance additional facilities, to reduce tax rates and service charges, or expand operations.

4. *Improved Borrowing Terms.* Such funds as must be borrowed can be borrowed under more favorable terms, i.e., lower interest costs.

5. *Patrimony.* A greater patrimony is accumulated in the form of paid-up equity in public facilities.

6. *Borrowing Capacity.* The capacity to borrow—within both legal and economic limits—is husbanded against periods of greater need.

Arguments in Favor of "Pay-as-You-Use"

Advocates of "pay-as-you-use" offer these arguments:

1. *Reduced Current Payments.* In an expanding economy (excluding the effects of inflation), per capita income increases. Therefore, payment of a reasonable annual charge for the "rental" of a facility can be made less burdensome over a period of years than through full payment at the time of acquisition.

2. *Acquisition as Needed.* The capacity of the community, especially a new community or a declining one, to provide funds from current revenue for immediate construction is severely limited. Accordingly, it is desirable to proceed with the acquisition of facilities as needed. This can be done only through a "pay-as-you-use" policy.

3. *Intergenerational Equity.* Each generation of users of a facility should be obliged to pay a fair economic rent for use of the facilities it enjoys. The certainty of these payments constitutes a deterrent to over-building because the community knows the annual debt service must be paid, whereas a generation not accustomed to such payments may find it easy to incur too much debt. The man who has had experience with the problems of servicing and repayment of a large personal loan is more knowledgeable as to the requirements debt imposes than is one who has always been debt-free. Distribution of costs among generations of highly migratory users can be best accomplished through a policy of "pay-as-you-use."

4. *Repayment in Cheaper Dollars.* The use of "pay-as-you-use" permits payment of portions of the debt service in cheaper dollars.

Overhanging all discussions of this subject are two other considerations of which little cognizance is taken:

1. *Opportunity Costs.* Money taken from taxpayers as accelerated economic rental either (a) reduces the alternative opportunities for expenditure or investment of those funds by the taxpayers in other directions, or (b) imposes upon them the carrying of larger debts in their private affairs and at higher interest rates than would be necessary should they be able to retain larger amounts of current income for personal use. Moreover, the public expenditures can be funded under lower tax free interest rates.

2. *Deflation of Currency.* It is an historical fact that all nations sooner or later debase their currency. The American economy has been characterized by long-term price inflation, i.e., deflation of the value of the currency. The dollars in which the funds are repaid will, on the average, be of a lesser value than those which are borrowed in the first place. When the rate of inflation approaches the rate of interest for tax-free securities, the effective interest charge is significantly reduced. During periods when the inflation rate exceeds the interest rate, the debt service may, in constant dollars, drop to the point that interest becomes negative. That is, no effective interest is being charged in the sense that the dollars used to pay interest and to repay principal are so reduced in value that combined payments of interest and principal to the investor have less purchasing power than that of the dollars invested. However, in considering matters of inflation and deflation, it is necessary to examine the reliability of the indices used to measure these trends. Unfortunately, the consumer price index is an inaccurate index of change in real costs. It shows only price changes; it does not take into account costs arising from changes in the quality, quantity, or character of goods and services being purchased.

Thus, the transportation component of the consumer price index will reflect changes in the quality of private automobiles and of other elements of transportation, as well as the prices of providing items or services at original levels. As automobiles have become air conditioned, provided with improved safety and other features, all of this has been charged to the consumer price index whereas large portions of the change are appropriately chargeable to changes in the *standard* of living rather than the *cost* of living. The same is true in respect of food, household appliances, energy consumption, and many other aspects of the consumer price index. The tremendously increased health services are all charged up to cost of living—none allocated to standard of living.

In the case of many facilities acquired in the 1960s, payment of principal and interest charges in the 1970s and 1980s is resulting in total debt service being less than acquisition costs in constant dollars of the year of acquisition.

The community and its public officers will necessarily ponder these considerations from time to time. They are matters upon which there are no permanent answers—only decisions to guide actions of the present and near future. Yet, the decisions concerning what is to be financed from current revenue and what is to be financed from the capitalization of future revenue continue to be among the most important underlying decisions of any government at any time. To the extent that the decision is to finance through capitalization of future revenues, decisions are then required as to the patterns in which the debt is to be issued, secured, and serviced. Before moving to those more definitive aspects of the administration of state and local government debt, it is appropriate to take a further look at the basic subject of capital outlays, their relationships to governmental operations, and the use of capital programming.

CAPITAL OUTLAYS AND THE REVENUE STRUCTURE

Capital outlays are financed from revenues—either immediately or over a period of time. Therefore, it is appropriate briefly to review the sources of revenue on which state and local government operations rely for financing their liability debt. Revenues of these governments are derived from four basic sources: taxation, service charges, miscellaneous revenues, and intergovernmental revenues. To varying degrees all four of these sources can be used in the financing of capital outlays. Some intergovernmental revenues are available for financing capital outlays; others are not. For example, categorical grants for highway purposes by the federal government to the state governments are very largely designed for capital facility outlay as are federal grants to local governments for airport development and for water pollution abatement. Laws authorizing or levying taxes frequently designate the functions for which they may be used. There is rarely any legal restriction upon the extent of use of *current* revenue for capital outlays; however, there are numerous restrictions concerning the extent to which future taxes may be capitalized.

Governmental enterprise operations are likely to be capital intensive with most of the revenue from service charges. Miscellaneous revenues are rarely the identified source of capital outlay financing on either a current or capitalized basis. Yet, they may contribute significantly to the general support of the capital outlay elements of the ongoing programs of the government.

Taxation

There are only three basic sources of taxation: Wealth, income, and business transactions. A careful examination of any tax is likely to indicate that it is closely related to one of these concepts.

Taxation of Wealth. The taxation of property, i.e., title to items with a market value, comes in many forms. The form best known to local government is the "property tax" on real property and, in some states, selected categories of personal property. This tax has been the mainstay of local government for centuries, due in large part to the clearly apparent presence and general availability of measures of value, especially for real property. Other forms of taxation of wealth include such taxes as inheritance, gift, and estate taxes— none of which is widely used at the local level of government.

The advantages and disadvantages of reliance upon the property tax are so well known to finance officers that it is unnecessary to dwell upon them here. However, it is appropriate to note that both taxpayers and local governments have become increasingly dissatisfied by the historically high degree of reliance on property taxes. This discontent developed because of both practical and theoretical reasons:

1. Many categories of real property or its owners have been exempt from taxation.
2. Assessment practices are subject to criticism on both theory and practice. Acceptable bases for valuation are difficult to attain, especially during periods when increases in market value significantly exceed increases in family income.
3. Rates of taxation in many communities constitute a very high percentage tax when related to cash or imputed income from property. Thus, property may yield annual rentals of 9 to 12 percent of value; but, the real estate tax may be equal to 2 or 3 percent of market value, thereby becoming the equivalent of 17 to 33 percent of gross receipts.
4. For low income persons and other persons on fixed income, the property tax constitutes a high percentage of income, especially in an inflationary economy.
5. There is mounting organized resistance to increases in property taxes.

It is not surprising, therefore, that local officials in many states have sought vigorously to substitute other forms of taxation and income for the local property tax. The Proposition 13 and other taxpayer revolt attitudes during the late 1970s gave convincing proof of the desire of citizens to move away from property taxation—or perhaps to limit all taxation.

At the state level, the general ad valorem property tax has almost disappeared; however, other forms of taxation on wealth still abound—e.g., capital stock taxes, severance taxes, estate and gift taxes.

Income Taxation. The income tax at the state and local levels of government has spread rapidly since World War II, when fewer than half the state governments had income taxes and only Philadelphia had a local income tax. By 1980, 44 state governments were levying individual income taxes and 46 levied corporate income taxes; local income taxes were in effect to some degree in the District of Columbia and 10 states.[8]

At the state level, the taxes vary in both scope and rate structure characteristics. At the local level, they have been generally restricted to earned income; however, in a few cases, the tax has been extended to elements of unearned income.

Taxation of Transactions. The general and selected sales taxes, gross receipts taxes, license taxes, utility taxes, and occupancy taxes are generally held to fall within this category. These kinds of taxes are widely used at the state level, with some of them also constituting important sources of revenue for the local governments in those states that allow substantial flexibility to their local governments.

Service Charges

The second major element of income for state and local governments derived from their own sources are service charges, the best known being for water, electric, gas, and transit services. These are usually set aside in separate categories because the services tend to be monopolistic whether performed under private or governmental ownership. A great many governments impose charges for such services as school lunches, parking, museums, and the collection and disposal of refuse and waste water. As the services of state and local governments have expanded and as the pressures for moneys to finance these functions have grown, increasing amounts and percentages of state and local governmental revenues from their own sources are secured from service charges or from a combination of service charges and other miscellaneous revenue.

Miscellaneous Revenues

Under the Bureau of the Census revenue classification system, the following items are included in the miscellaneous category of *general* revenue:

Special assessments
Sale of property
Interest earned
Fines and forfeits
Rents and Royalties
Donations from private sources
Net lottery revenue
Miscellaneous general revenues not otherwise classified, e.g., insurance adjustments from prior year, escheats, profits from sales of securities, and unclaimed moneys.

The Bureau of the Census places revenues from the operation of liquor stores and insurance trust operations in separate categories outside the general revenue classification.

Intergovernmental Revenues

The Bureau of the Census has defined intergovernmental revenues in these terms:

Intergovernmental revenue includes grants, shared taxes, and contingent loans and advances for support of particular functions or for general financial support, any significant and identifiable amounts received from other governments as reimburse-

---

[8] U.S. Bureau of the Census, *Governmental Finances in 1979–80*, pp. 18–26; *City Government Finances in 1979–80*, pp. 12–67; and *State Government Finances in 1980*, pp. 23–33.

ment for performance of governmental functions, and any other form of revenue representing the sharing by other governments in the financing of activities administered by the receiving government. Intergovernmental revenue excludes amounts received from the sale of property, commodities, and utility services to other governments. All intergovernmental revenue is classified as general revenue.[9]

The amount of intergovernmental revenue available for and used for capital outlays is not ascertainable.

Trends in Revenue

From Table 25 it is noted that the rate of increase in intergovernmental revenue from the federal government to state and local governments was greater than for most of the other revenue categories. This was in part triggered by the initiation of general revenue sharing in 1972–73; however, other factors were also involved, including the change from categorical loan and grant programs to block grant programs for community development in 1975. This produced an acceleration of federal payments as the older system was phased out. Of course under the initial proposed "new federalism" of the Reagan Administration, those sources would be markedly reduced. Taxes for state and local governments had a compound rate of increase of 9.9 percent per annum in the 1970–1980 period. Within the tax group, the greatest percentage increases were for individual and corporate income taxes—14.6 and 13.6 respectively. The rate of increase of 7.2 percent for property taxes was the lowest. The greatest increase was for current charges and miscellaneous revenues— at the astounding rate of 27.7 percent per annum.

Revenues Not Available for Debt Service. Generally, grants from the federal government are not available to support debt service, although certain payments for housing and, at an earlier time, for urban renewal were fundable. In like manner, the revenues from liquor store operations and from insurance trust proceeds of state and local governments are not generally subject to anticipation in the form of debt. The degree of availability of the remainder of the revenue stream in support of debt varies widely among state and local governments.

How Much Debt in Relation to Revenue?

Policymakers are confronted with not only the four cornerstones of debt policy but also with the question of how much of future revenue should be anticipated as debt service charges. This question cannot be answered on a basis of any neat formula, such as a percentage relationship to the value of taxable real property or to governmental income.

To borrow so little that public facilities are not provided as needed produces adverse effects. In some cases, e.g., the timely development of aviation facilities, this can result in a by-passing of the community by industry or other elements of economic development. Conversely, an overload of debt can produce burdensome local taxes and charges that result in economic dislocation and decay.

Upon the degree of correctness or degree of error reflected in the decision will depend much of the future welfare of the community. This is a heavy responsibility in which the chief finance officer should take the lead. He should provide the facts and his conclusions for the benefit of other key officials.[10]

---

[9] U.S. Bureau of the Census, *Classification Manual, Governmental Finances,* p. 20. On the basis of the definition, it appears that intergovernmental revenue is all treated as general revenue, including that made available for financing capital outlays for utilities. Thus, the general revenue classification includes elements of income that are otherwise reported in the expenditure categories as public utility expenditure.

[10] See D. J. Date, *Municipal Debt Carrying Capacity Study.* This report provides broad statistical measures of various factors of importance in the development of debt policy for Canadian cities, with special emphasis upon New London, Ontario.

Table 25

Revenues of State and Local Governments
1970–1980

(amounts in billions of dollars)				
	1980	1978	1976	1970	Annual Compound Percentage Increase 1970–1980

	1980	1978	1976	1970	Annual Compound Percentage Increase 1970–1980
Amounts					
Total revenue	451.5	371.6	304.7	150.1	11.6
Total general revenue	382.3	316.0	256.2	130.8	11.3
Intergovernmental revenue (Federal only)	83.0	69.6	55.6	21.9	14.3
General revenue from own sources	299.3	246.4	200.6	108.9	10.6
Taxes	223.5	193.6	156.8	86.8	9.9
Property	68.5	66.4	57.0	34.1	7.2
Individual income	42.1	33.2	24.6	10.8	14.6
Corporate income	13.3	10.7	7.3	3.7	13.6
Sales & Gross Receipts	79.9	67.6	54.5	30.3	10.2
Other	19.7	15.7	13.3	7.9	9.6
Current charges	44.4	34.7	29.3	{ 6.6	{ 27.7
Miscellaneous	31.5	18.0	14.5		
Utility revenue	22.4	17.3	12.6	6.6	13.0
Liquor store revenue	3.2	2.8	2.6	2.0	4.8
Trust fund revenue	43.7	35.6	33.4	10.7	4.1
Exhibit: Intergovernmental Revenues of States to Local Governments	81.3	69.6	56.2	na	na
Percentage Distribution					
Total revenue	100.0	100.0	100.0	100.0	
Total general revenue	84.7	85.0	84.1	87.1	
Intergovernmental revenue (Federal only)	18.4	18.7	18.2	14.6	
General revenue from own sources	66.3	66.3	65.8	72.6	
Taxes	49.5	52.0	51.5	57.8	
Property	15.2	17.9	18.7	22.7	
Individual income	9.3	8.9	8.1	7.2	
Corporate income	2.9	2.9	2.4	2.5	
Sales & Gross Receipts	17.7	18.2	17.9	20.2	
Other	4.4	4.2	4.5	5.3	
Current charges	9.8	9.4	9.6	{ 4.4	
Miscellaneous	7.0	4.8	4.8		
Utility revenue	5.0	4.7	4.1	4.4	
Liquor store revenue	.7	.8	.9	1.3	
Trust fund revenue	9.7	9.6	11.0	7.1	

Sources: U.S. Bureau of the Census, *Governmental Finances in 1972–73*, p. 18; *in 1975–76*, pp. 17, 19; *in 1977–78*, p. 18; *in 1979–80*, p. 17.

NB: For fiscal year basis used by the Bureau of the Census, see Appendix F.

FRAMEWORK FOR DECISION

A strong central finance officer helps produce the most satisfactory level of performance. At the same time it is recognized that the finance functions are typically distributed among many offices and departments, rather than being under a cohesive pattern of direction. Regardless of the pattern of organization, policy in respect to debt does exist and it is modified from time to time. The question is whether it is developed in the most effective manner or is merely the product of random, uncoordinated actions. Somewhere in almost every government, there is an officer concerned about basic financial policies. He may be an assistant to the mayor, a director of administration for a governor, a deputy superintendent of schools, or the comptroller in a public enterprise operation. To a considerable extent, debt policy must be formulated and espoused by the chief executive and leaders in the legislative body.

One of the difficulties in the development of financial policies is the tendency, especially in the field of debt, to rely upon various crutches provided by law and precedent. Frequently, a public official is willing to use the existence of a legal limitation as a reason or excuse for not developing an effective debt policy statement. There is a willingness to accept the law as refuge without adequate analysis of the advantages and disadvantages of alternative courses of action. Until and unless one is willing to forego these crutches he is never obliged to develop his own concepts of what constitutes the best policy for the community being served. Although fanciful, it is recommended that those concerned with development of debt policy occasionally put aside all thoughts of existing legal and historical constraints and evolve their own model as to how they would state debt policy if there were no legal constraints.

In order to comprehend the extremely wide range of considerations involved in the formulation of a comprehensive debt policy, it is helpful for a moment to assume that the task is to develop each point on a *de novo* basis. Perhaps this can best be done under these assumptions:

1. There are no legal limits, inhibitions, or injunctives concerning the amount of debt, its term, purpose, interest rates to be paid, form of debt, or any other feature
2. There are no executive or administrative regulations or directives
3. Outstanding debt may be called or advance refunded at will
4. There are no legal limits upon the kinds of taxes, service charges, or their rates
5. There are no limits or mandates in relation to the kinds of services, facilities, and programs or levels at which the government may choose to deliver them

Given this flexibility, how would one proceed to develop a comprehensive, long-term debt policy for the government? Among the avenues to be explored would be these:

1. What are the present and reasonably foreseeable unmet service requirements? In what system of priorities will these requirements be satisfied? What will be the requirements for physical facilities, both to expand the total inventory and to provide for replacement or renewal of existing facilities as they wear out or become obsolete?

2. What are the present and prospective economic resources?

3. What is the present revenue structure and what is its impact upon the present and potential economic development? What is the potential for adjustment in the revenue structure in light of the economy and of public attitudes?

4. In providing for financing of needed capital facilities, to what degree should reliance be placed upon a "pay-as-you-acquire" vs. a "pay-as-you-use" approach to financing?

5. Under what patterns of patrimony accumulation is the system to function?

6. What kinds of debt shall be used to meet each of the requirements?

Only when those responsible for debt policy have confronted such problems and sought solutions without the crutches of artificial constraints are they obliged to cope with the realities implicit in the development of a responsible financial policy, including such decisions as: (1) Levels of taxation and expenditure; (2) the optimum mix of current and capital expense; (3) the extent to which concepts of economic rental and patrimony accumulation should govern public investment and debt amortization policies; and (4) the benefits secured and the liabilities incurred by use of *on behalf of* debt.

Only when these and other pertinent questions are answered in the *abstract* is it feasible to develop policy objectives best for the community—policies to which leadership is willing to commit itself. To accept as a "given" all those laws, regulations and precedents—good, bad, and indifferent—that others have collectively imposed is to consign one's self to a restricted and frequently a passive role. Genuinely effective public officials are willing to confront the tough policy problems and search for meaningful answers. This is one of the challenges that attracts able people to the job in the first place.

If they are willing to develop a set of policy factors on a *de novo* basis, they can create policy objectives toward which to aim.

To attempt to develop a desirable policy within the preexisting limitations and restraints is too inhibiting. It invites the waste of valuable time and energy in devising ways by which to overcome the accepted barriers. It leaves little time in which to develop constructive initiatives in debt policy; it is likely to produce a warped set of policy elements.

After the theoretical debt policy outline has been evolved, the objectives can be adjusted to the realities of the immediate situation. Realistic evaluations of the potentials for overcoming unproductive constraints can be made. Action programs to overcome these undesirable constraints can be planned and execution sought. The next bond issue must be planned within the existing law and basic framework of historical precedents and currently outstanding debt and debt service requirements; but, this can be done within a framework of how it will contribute to the revised policy objectives.

THE GOVERNMENTAL ENTITY FOR FINANCING

Prior to 1945, only a limited number of routes were open to state and local governments insofar as the entity to be used in the issuance of debt. With the exception of a few authorities, the states, municipalities, townships, school districts, and counties were obliged to issue their own debt. The intervening years have been characterized by two major developments for funding of capital outlays:

1. There has been expanded reliance upon special districts, authorities, corporations, or other agencies to perform governmental functions previously assigned directly to the basic governmental units. Many of the newer units have relied heavily upon governmental enterprise debt.
2. In a number of the states, the basic units of government now use governmental lessee debt for important parts of the funding operations.

These developments lead to questions as to why authorities and special debt issuance agencies have grown in such profusion and what are the advantages of their use vis-à-vis the more forthright general obligation of governmental enterprise debt.

Typically, special agency debt has been used to escape constitutional or statutory constraints; take advantage of debt laws providing greater flexibility than those relating to general obligation bonds; accommodate to the blandishments of the sales efforts of investment bankers seeking negotiated sales; and take advantage of some state or federal support available for special purpose debt that is not easily handled within the conventional pattern of funding.

In some states, the laws, at different times, have provided for lessee debt that is better secured than the general obligation bonds of the same government. As the casualty insurance companies became a more significant factor in the market, their interest in lessee bonds expanded because of higher yields, greater use of term bonds with larger blocs available, and because they were not in competition with the commercial banks for this group of securities. Many of them believed that they could interpret the financial statements of both governmental enterprise and governmental lessee debt with greater ease than they could the general financial statements of the state and local governments. Accordingly, they were less dependent on the rating agencies. Also, the fees associated with governmental lessee debt appear to be somewhat higher than those for more conventional issues. In some states bond banks, or their equivalent structures, offered new avenues for sale of debt. In any event, today in many states both the state and the local levels of government have more than one avenue available in the issuance of their debt. Most of them still have the option of general obligation bonds; many can utilize either enterprise or lessee debt; some can use bond banks.

Also, authorities and other special agencies in many cases become the only viable agencies for moving across state lines or even across the boundary lines of local governments in metropolitan areas. Although most students of public administration have long advocated that governments in metropolitan areas be reconstituted to coincide more closely with the social and economic conurbations, during the period since World War II, only a few cities took any basic steps in this direction. The principal ones were Miami/Dade County; Nashville/Davidson County; Indianapolis/Marion County; Baton Rouge/East Baton Rouge Parish; and Jacksonville/Duval County. The resurgency of county governments in some states has helped, e.g., New Castle County (Del.) and Suffolk County (N.Y.). Elsewhere, it has been largely through special agencies that some functions have been metropolitanized.

It has also been found that, in some circumstances, larger amounts of total debt can be marketed by use of a number of agencies acting in specialized directions than can be issued through a single government or type of instrument. This has proved especially true in some of the larger metropolitan areas and in a few of the state governments.

The Issuer's Responsibility. When these alternatives are available [or when they may be enacted into law with relative ease] it becomes the responsibility of the debtor government to explore with the utmost care the different patterns of debt issuance available and to select those that will not only meet immediate requirements but will also best serve the community in the long run. This kind of decision requires the evaluation of numerous specialized factors. Some types of evaluation require a high degree of specialization in municipal bond finance.

SELECTING THE SECURITY TO BE PLEDGED

Among the critical decisions in planning the financing of capital outlays through debt is selection of the security to be pledged. This decision is closely associated with that of the selection of the governmental unit to act as issuer. Frequently, the beneficiary government is limited to acting as issuer; sometimes the beneficiary government has a fairly wide choice. If the choice is a potential within the state but currently not available to the beneficiary government, strong leadership from that government may be sufficient to secure authority to broaden the flexibility available.

The conventional categories for broad classification of the debt of state and local governments on the basis of security pledged are:

1. General obligation bonds, or full-faith-and-credit bonds
2. Revenue bonds, or nonguaranteed debt

These have been discussed, along with more comprehensive definitions, in Chapter 3. Within the broad classifications of general obligation and revenue debt it is appropriate to take into consideration some of the advantages and disadvantages of each.

Full-Faith-and-Credit Pledge

Among the advantages of the full-faith-and-credit security pledge are:

1. It is frequently the strongest pledge available to the issuer and will usually produce the lowest effective interest cost.

2. There is a minimum of money held in debt service reserves and special reserves associated with most other debt.

3. Most full-faith-and-credit debt requires electoral approval, imposing a restraint on the exercise of discretion by public officers.

4. The exclusive reliance on this pledge enables the government to maintain a simple debt structure which, in turn, facilitates understanding as to the character and amount of the debt payable from taxes and other general revenues of the government.

5. The administrative aspects of planning and execution of the borrowing are simplified and frequently less costly than in most other forms of debt.

6. The exclusion of self-supporting general obligation debt from gross debt in determining debt chargeable against general obligation debt limits offers substantial flexibility in debt management.

The disadvantages of the full-faith-and-credit pledge include:

1. Exclusive reliance upon full-faith-and-credit debt can result in an unwise overburdening of the pledge. Thus, when large investments in governmental enterprises are required, the aggregate debt can dilute the full-faith-and-credit pledge to the point that the credit position of the community is endangered. If all self-supporting debt is placed outside the full-faith-and-credit orbit, that pledge can be much more meaningful.

2. Total reliance on full-faith-and-credit debt can result in a failure to maintain sharp lines of demarcation between self-supporting debt and a combination of self-supporting and tax-supported debt for certain types of governmental enterprises. Thus, the community that supports both water supply and waste water disposal from service charges must maintain this as a public policy. But, if these are only partially supported from service charges, there may be a tendency to play a bit of politics. When the enterprise is separately funded and this is fully demonstrated by the accounting system, the governing body may find it more appropriate to maintain charges at an appropriate level—even in the face of opposition—because it is necessary to meet contractual obligations relating to the enterprise debt. Moreover, if the enterprise fails to produce sufficient revenues, the general taxpayers are likely to be protected against being obliged to make up the deficit—unless a general public policy is adopted under which self-support is abandoned.

3. The requirement for referendum frequently associated with full-faith-and-credit debt can result in delay or long-term deferment of capital financing necessary to carry into effect elements of the capital program essential to community well-being.

4. Exclusive use of the full-faith-and-credit pledge denies access by the issuer to that portion of the bond market willing to assume somewhat greater risks for potentially greater gains offered in other forms of financing.

5. As generally construed, the full-faith-and-credit pledge implies the use of unlimited ad valorem taxing power at the local level of government and broad taxing powers at the state level, although this is not always true. This pledge, when applied to all debt of a government, can impose a severe tax burden upon the owners of taxable property. A few state governments, e.g., Louisiana and Pennsylvania, after long use of special tax and lessee financing, have reverted largely to general obligation financing for their principal debt issues.

Revenue Bonds

The current broad classification of so-called revenue bonds includes at least these distinct categories:

1. *Governmental Enterprise Financing.* Bonds for capital facilities of public utilities and a wide variety of other kinds of enterprises including parking, sports facilities, convention facilities, waste water treatment, office buildings, and many others.

2. *Special Tax and Limited Tax Bonds.* Numerous kinds of special tax or limited tax bonds are not general obligation bonds. Hence, under a system in which revenue bonds include everything other than general obligation bonds, they must be included here.

3. *Government Lessee Bonds.* Although these bonds are revenue in form, they are actually tax-supported debt created as lessee debt, frequently to avoid or overcome problems incident to debt limits or to voter actions upon proposed debt; or, they have been created to facilitate the strengthening of the credit of certain issuers.

4. *Federally Supported State and Local Government Debt.* Various kinds of federally supported housing debt take the form of revenue debt but they are essentially a substitute for federal debt. The Congress agrees to support certain tax-exempt debt for programs of concern to it, rather than increasing the federal debt and making direct grants for the capital purposes involved.

5. *Special Assessment Debt.* Special assessment debt is used to help finance various kinds of local improvements where the costs are assessed against the benefited property.

6. *On Behalf of Debt.* Initiated as a means of providing tax-exempt financing for industrial development, *on behalf of* debt has been extended to certain aspects of airport and water-borne commerce facilities; pollution control financing; financing of facilities for private, nonprofit institutions of higher learning; hospital and some other health facility financing; and, most recently, financing of the single family housing market in some states.

It is appropriate to review the advantages and disadvantages relating to a number of these categories. This section also provides an opportunity to add some explanatory comments concerning some of the above categories.

Governmental Enterprise Debt

Among the advantages of governmental enterprise debt are:

1. *Conservation of General Obligation Borrowing Power.* The substitution of revenue bonds for general obligation debt in financing of governmental enterprises acts to preserve the unused general obligation borrowing power for use in tax-supported projects or in those other revenue-producing projects that fail to produce sufficient revenues to warrant revenue bond financing.

2. *Improved Credit Position.* The use of revenue bonds for enterprise financing produces an improved credit position in some circumstances for both revenue and guaranteed debt. In other words, if the credit position of the general obligation financing has been overloaded, the revenue bond offers an opportunity for relieving the pressure upon that credit. Simultaneously, a well-designed revenue bond can enjoy a better market position than the general obligation bond of the same issuer. Over time, the issuer may find that both the revenue bonds and general obligation bonds improve their positions in the marketplace and with the rating services.

3. *More Equitable Cost Distribution.* The use of revenue bonds for governmental enterprise financing tends to require that the costs of the enterprise be borne exclusively from revenues generated by the enterprise. Thereby, the costs are assessed among users of the enterprise—generally in proportion to their use of the service—instead of being the responsibility of taxpayers.

4. *Discipline in Spending.* Inasmuch as governmental enterprises are obliged to meet public demands for service at reasonable costs, there is a discipline associated with this type of financing that is not present in general obligation financing. In general obligation financing it is frequently difficult to associate the cost of the service with the source of financing.

5. *Expansion of the Market.* Inasmuch as many investors (especially casualty insurance companies) prefer revenue bonds over general obligation bonds, the use of revenue bonds for governmental enterprise financing tends to open up to the issuer portions of the market that are not readily available when all financing is restricted to general obligation bonds.

6. *Expanded Flexibility and Responsibility.* The use of revenue bonds increases the degree of flexibility enjoyed by public officials in the conduct of public business. It can also act to increase a sense of responsibility for their actions, rather than passing some of it off to the electorate through referenda.

7. *Better Accounting and Reporting.* Many of the investors in revenue bonds make their own analyses of the credit behind their investments; some demand better accounting and reporting of financial operations on a current basis.

8. *Improved Operation and Maintenance.* Frequently, the governmental enterprise bond indenture carries with it requirements for elements of supervision of budget, maintenance, and other phases of management not present in general obligation financing.

9. *Assured Amortization Schedules.* The revenue bond must be amortized during the useful life of the facility inasmuch as this is the only source of funds for such amortization. As a result, the pressures are greater for amortization well in advance of the termination of such life, thereby increasing the level of patrimony accumulation.

Among the disadvantages to be considered are:

1. *Potentially Higher Interest Costs.* Generally, revenue bonds tend to carry higher interest costs than general obligation bonds of the same issuer.[11]

2. *Excessively Rapid Amortization.* Many revenue bond indentures require that all of the net revenues be applied to a reduction in the debt, or to the creation of reserve funds therefor. The effect is to produce heavy prepayments of economic rental by the earlier generations of users.

3. *Avoidance of Electoral Action.* The history of public debt in the United States at all levels tends to show that the electorate is fiscally more conservative than are its representatives in government. The avoidance of electoral action removes this discipline.

4. *Imbalance in the Capital Program.* Availability of revenue bond financing is frequently seized upon by administrators of those programs as a reason why their capital program should be more generously financed and more or less automatically approved inasmuch as no taxes are involved. This can lead to extravagance and also can produce an imbalance in the physical development program in which the revenue bond-financed programs are given unwarranted priority.

5. *Potential Defaults.* Although the community is not obliged to make payments for defaults in enterprise revenue bonds, actual or potential default can have carry-over adverse effects in the credit markets on the issuer's general obligation debt.

6. *Higher Issuance Costs.* Governmental enterprise revenue bonds are usually accompanied by higher issuance costs than the counterpart general obligation financing. Legal fees, financial fees, consulting engineers, and feasibility reports produce additional costs.

7. *Restricted Market.* The historic restriction against revenue bond underwriting by commercial banks [now likely to be repealed] may have curtailed the revenue bond market.

8. *Expanded Use of Negotiated Sale.* Governmental enterprise revenue bonds are sold more frequently through negotiation than counterpart general obligation debt. Many issuers are not adequately staffed to engage in effective negotiation with the professionals of the investment banking community. The result may be somewhat higher interest costs.

---

[11] The search is for the lowest interest costs, especially in respect of those bonds where the debt service is payable largely by citizens of the community and where the charges are broadly distributed within the community. In some cases, analysis will show that the aggregate costs are less under universal use of the general obligation pledge; in other cases, it may be determined that the lowest interest costs can be secured only through a combination of general obligation and revenue financing. Only intensive inquiry will reveal the *current* answer. With changing conditions, the equation also changes and requires reapplication to the new circumstances.

Limited Tax and Special Tax Bonds

Considerable amounts of debt are secured by a limited ad valorem tax or by some other tax, e.g., an excise tax on tobacco, alcoholic beverages, motor fuels, or an income tax. The use of the limited tax bond frequently occurs because of the difficulty of overcoming constraints on general obligation debt—either because of constrictive debt limits or because of requirements for electoral approval. Occasionally, it is used because it commands a better credit market acceptance than general obligation bonds, e.g., the debt issued by the Board of Administration in Florida for certain school district purposes.

The advantages of limited tax and special tax bonds that do not carry a general obligation security pledge include:

1. *Raising Money Through Funding Without Resort to the Pledge of Full-Faith-and-Credit.* In periods of economic adversity, the general revenues of the government remain available for support of the ongoing services of the government.

2. *Avoidance of Debt Limits.* Ordinarily, the limits as to the amounts of such debt to be incurred are determined by the marketplace in light of the coverage provided for debt service on proposed bonds, rather than by some arbitrary formula.

3. *Taxation of Nonresidents.* In the case of taxes that fall upon both residents and nonresidents, the special tax bond may provide a means of requiring nonresidents to participate more equitably in the development of facilities that are to be used by both residents and nonresidents.

The disadvantages of limited tax and special tax bonds include:

1. *Potentially Higher Interest Costs.* The interest cost on limited tax or special tax debt is likely to be higher than that required under a pledge of full-faith-and-credit.

2. *Necessity of Reserves.* Frequently, reserve funds will be required as part of limited tax financing, thereby either (a) withholding or deferring delivery to the public of the immediate benefits that could be financed from funds allocated to reserves, or (b) increasing the tax rate to a higher level than would otherwise be required.

3. *Limitation of Investors.* The limited tax bond may unnecessarily restrict the number of investors to whom the bonds can be sold.

4. *Lack of Flexibility.* The limited tax or special tax must ordinarily be continued at the pledged rate for the life of the bonds, thereby denying flexibility in the revenue structure.

Governmental Lessee Financing

Many state and local governments now engage in lessee financing to meet a part of their need for capital funds. This type of financing has been available in some states for almost a half century; however, in most states utilizing governmental lessee debt, the practice commenced after World War II.

The essence of the arrangement is for an authority or governmentally related corporation to be created with the function of constructing public facilities to be leased to other governments. The agency providing the facilities issues bonds secured by the lease-rentals from the taxing authority needing facilities. In most cases, the law directs the special public agency to deed the facility to the related taxing entity when the debt is retired. The legal theory developed in Pennsylvania (and gradually adopted by the courts in some other states) was that the debt of the issuer was not debt of the lessee government. The lease accepted by the taxing authority as lessee was construed not to be debt. It was construed to be off-balance sheet financing. As such, the debt incurred by the issuer was not subject to any of the constraints imposed upon the lessee government. The effect of this process in most states using it has been effectively to evade constitutional debt limits for the purposes for which the legislature permits governmental lessee debt.

The advantages and disadvantages are similar to those outlined above for governmental enterprise debt. Beyond these, on the positive side, there is the consideration of being able to move expeditiously. For some local governments, the use of governmental lessee debt has provided access to the market on more favorable terms than would have been available under local debt issuance—especially in economically distressed school districts.

On the disadvantage side, in addition to those cited for governmental enterprise debt, it is found that the appointed members of the authorities or building corporations may seek to usurp some of the powers normally assigned to elected governmental officers. Increased complexity of governmental structure, relationships, and administrative expense almost inevitably result.

Federally Supported Debt

Commencing with the 1937 Federal Housing Act and under a number of other acts, the federal government pursued a policy of encouraging the use of federally guaranteed, tax-exempt, long-term and short-term debt to finance selected capital facilities. The federal government could have issued its own bonds and made payments for these projects as grants in the years when the money was expended; however, it preferred to keep this debt out of the debt structure of the U.S. Government. Moreover, inasmuch as the debt was sold at very low interest rates, this acted to reduce requirements for current appropriations. Eventually, the federal government lost more than it saved through the use of this type of arrangement because it meant that more tax-free debt was outstanding.

One of the advantages of this type of debt was that it constituted a "risk-free" tax-exempt bond (in terms of the possibility of eventual nonpayment). Comparisons between such debt and that issued as taxable debt for the same term of years by the United States helped to provide an accurate gauge of the value of tax exemption for AAA debt.

Special Assessment Debt

The use of special assessment debt to finance improvements wholly or partially assessable against benefited property is an ancient, well-known form of local government debt. Special assessments have been used to finance a wide range of improvements including streets, public utilities, sanitary and storm sewers, sidewalks, street lights, and other special improvements. Conventional special assessment debt is supported solely by the pledge of the special assessments being funded; however, in some states, special assessment debt enjoys varying degrees of support from tax or general revenue funds. The advantages of special assessment debt include:

1. *Amortization Period.* Special assessment debt permits property owners to amortize assessments against their property over a period of years. Without this arrangement, many public improvements would have to be foregone inasmuch as the property holders would find it difficult to meet the full assessments in lump-sum amounts.

2. *Protection of General Borrowing Capacity.* Even if special assessments must be augmented by general revenues in order to finance the projects, the use of special assessment debt enables the issuer to expand the public improvement program while preserving equivalent general borrowing capacity.

3. *Protection of Taxing Power.* Availability of special assessment debt encourages the use of benefit charges as a means of financing. This, in turn, encourages payment for beneficial improvements by the persons benefited, rather than relying on general taxpayers to finance these improvements.

Among the disadvantages of special assessment debt are:

1. *Taxability.* Property owners are not entitled to a deduction from income of amounts payable as special assessments in determining federal income tax liability. However, if the improvements were financed from local taxes, deduction is permitted in determining taxable income. Although this is not a direct fiscal concern of the issuer, it is a concern to a government seeking to protect the interests of its citizens.

2. *High Risk.* The history of defaults in special assessment debt tends to make this a relatively high risk with higher interest costs. Property owners using special assessment bonds as a means of funding their assessments are frequently charged incremental interest to help cover defaults by other property owners.

3. *Defaults.* Many local governments have found it necessary to come to the aid of special assessment debt to avoid or cure defaults.

4. *Restricted Market.* The market for the debt is restricted—partly because there is ordinarily no organized secondary market for special assessment debt.

5. *Administrative Costs.* The cost of administration of the special assessment payments is relatively high.

6. *Premature Subdivision.* Use of special assessment debt can facilitate premature subdivision of land.

On Behalf of Debt

The foregoing categories of tax-free debt generally involve the performance of functions carried out largely by government. There remains the increasing body of tax-exempt debt where the states and local governments are acting only as agents for the de facto debtors— or rather the guarantors of debt issued by the public agency involved.

During recent years *on behalf of* debt has been a major source of new, tax-exempt debt issues.[12] Indeed, along with the advance refunding debt, it accentuated the bloated markets of 1975–1981. State and local governments authorizing arrangements for *on behalf of* debt frequently fail to comprehend the full economic significance of such debt. Especially, they have frequently failed to analyze the impact of such debt upon the debt issued by state and local governments for more conventional purposes.

At any given market level of interest rates there is presumably a given amount of money available for investment in tax-free bonds. If the volume of debt being offered rises, more investors must be brought into the market in order to be able to absorb the increased offerings. This is usually accomplished by increasing the yields in order to improve the relative attractiveness of tax-free bonds. Conversely, if the supply of tax-free debt is below the money available for investment at those rates, competition among investors tends to drive the interest rates down.

Moral Obligation Bonds

A number of states have issued bonds that are known as "moral obligation bonds." These bonds have typically been issued by agencies of the state under legislation that implies that the state will come to the aid of such debt if default is threatened. A favorite pattern has been to require that a debt service reserve fund be created from the proceeds of the bonds sold. If the income of the agency from its normal sources is insufficient to meet debt service costs as they become due, money is temporarily advanced from the debt service reserve fund to make payments due. The legislation under which the debt is issued would, in these circumstances, state or imply that the succeeding legislative sessions would make appropriations sufficient to restore the debt service reserve fund to its original level. These pledges are not enforceable against the legislature, and any session of the legislature that elects to forego such payments has the legal right to do so. On the other hand, it is assumed that, inasmuch as the state legislature has authorized such debt under

---

[12] The Public Securities Association reported that in 1980 lessee revenue bonds (governmental lessee and *on behalf of* lessee) amounted to $23.7 billion of the total $33.9 billion of revenue bonds issued in that year. This may also be compared to total revenue and general obligation issues of $47.8 billion for the year. The extent to which the lessee debt was for governmental lessee purposes is not known; however, the sharp increase from $6.8 billion in 1976 to $15.1 billion in 1977, to $15.2 billion in 1978, and to $23.7 billion in 1980, strongly suggests that most of the increase was *on behalf of* financing.

these terms, it has incurred a "moral obligation" under which the state should make appropriations, as needed, to meet the shortfalls in revenue needed for debt service.[13]

Concluding Comments on the Choice of Security Pledged

The choice of the type of security (or combination of types) to be pledged is one of the most important decisions in the entire process of the planning and sale of debt. Public officials are under a strong obligation to design their debt in a manner that is most beneficial to the community. Ordinarily, this means securing the lowest net interest cost on the debt to be issued; however, in some circumstances, this can be achieved by accepting a higher interest cost upon some types of debt in order to protect the rate that will apply to other debt.

In the design of the debt structure, it is essential that one view it as a *system*. Unfortunately, many state and local governments have permitted the development and use of different patterns of issuance without integration of the parts into a rational system. Rather, the results have come from numerous uncoordinated actions—each perhaps fulfilling an immediate objective (sometimes quite narrow) but without understanding the impact of these actions upon the overall pattern of debt for the government. Such uncoordinated debt management leads to unnecessary expense.

Unwise constitutional limitations relating to general obligation debt have frequently forced these governments to resort to alternative forms of debt—especially lessee debt. On some occasions, the alternatives have been more expensive than would be a rational use of general obligation financing. The continued patterns of use of the indirect type of debt are frequently testimony to the indifference and ignorance of executives and legislators. The experience in Louisiana in the development, over a period of four decades, of a highly irrational system of debt security arrangements eventually led that state to a wholesale revision of its security arrangements during the 1968–1974 period.

One of the problems in comprehensive revisions lies in the fact that underwriters, bond counsel, financial advisors, and others frequently develop relationships that are comfortable and profitable. They resist changes that would disturb these relationships.

No single pattern can be prescribed that will be best in all situations. The effective finance officer has an obligation to know the workable alternatives for each type of situation (or to have such knowledge immediately available through qualified consultants). Armed with such knowledge, leadership can be assumed in working out policies that are best for the government.

---

[13] See Wade S. Smith, *The Appraisal of Municipal Credit Risk*, pp. 92, 386.

Chapter 8
POLICIES RELATING TO
SHORT-TERM DEBT

Although policies relating to long-term debt are in some respects applicable to short-term debt, the two fields are significantly different. Until a few years ago discussions of debt policies were usually limited to long-term debt.

This lack of interest in short-term debt arose largely from the fact that the public sale of short-term notes was restricted to a few large jurisdictions and the federally guaranteed notes of public housing and renewal agencies. Other short-term debt was primarily in the form of loans made by commercial banks directly to state and local governments.

Developments during the 1970s markedly modified almost all concepts and conditions concerning short-term debt. The change was largely associated with the difficulties that arose from the very heavy reliance upon short-term debt by the City of New York and to a lesser degree by the State of New York. The city's problems reached the crisis stage when in February 1975 it was no longer able to market its short-term debt. Underwriters, investors, and credit analysts became acutely aware of the critical character of accessibility to short-term credit markets. Public finance officers found that their presumed easy access to that market no longer existed and in some cases disappeared altogether.

They confronted illiquidity!

Attention was no longer focused on the ability of an issuer to balance the budget but on his capacity to meet his obligations on a timely basis during the next few months. Monthly cash flow statements became a requirement in many bond disclosure statements; the focus was upon the creditability of the official statements concerning generation of cash as needed by the government. A number of developments helped to produce pressure upon the short-term cash position of governments as these came to the forefront of official and investor attention.

The years 1980 and 1981 brought a different kind of crisis. It arose from the general short supply of money triggered by Federal Reserve policies. Short-term rates increased very rapidly and inverted yield curves were not uncommon.

Tables 6 and 9 (Chapter 1) summarize data of the Bureau of the Census on the outstanding short-term debt of state and local governments at the close of their respective fiscal years. When the short-term debt data of these governments is related to the total revenues from their own sources, it is found that in 1960 the $3 billion in outstanding short-term debt was equal to 5.9 percent of revenues from their own sources. By 1970 this stood at 9.5 percent of revenues from their own sources. Although the total outstanding short-term debt continued to rise during the first half of the 1970s, it gradually decreased as a percentage of revenues. Thus, by 1976 it stood at 7.5 percent. It then decreased to 3.6 percent by 1980 but increased in 1981.[1] These data include debt for not only short-term working capital but also amounts needed under bond anticipation notes. There are no data that separate the operating from the capital short-term debt. Therefore, one cannot be sure just what the gross relationships portray.

---

[1] U.S. Bureau of the Census, *Statistical Abstract of the United States, 1978,* p. 296, *Governmental Finances in 1979–80,* pp. 16, 53.

Table 13 (Chapter 1) shows that the issuance of short-term debt as reported in *The Bond Buyer* series has declined from the peak of $29 billion in 1974 to a level of about $21/22 billion in the 1976–1979 period and then increased to $26 billion in 1980 and $34 billion in 1981. Given the large proportions of short-term debt (especially that placed directly with commercial banks) which does not find its way into *The Bond Buyer* data, it must be presumed that the annual volumes of short-term debt issued are substantially above the levels indicated by that source.

Generally, state and local governments increase their net short-term debt during the April 1–September 30 period and decrease it during the October 1–March 31 period. Doubtless, this is partially reflective of property tax payment schedules.[2]

LIQUIDITY

Liquidity is that status in which a government has sufficient cash available to meet cash demands as they arise. Illiquidity occurs when the government is not able to meet cash demands on a current basis.[3] The four principal determinants of liquidity are:

1. The pattern for realization of revenues
2. The pattern for disbursements
3. Cumulative cash balances carried forward from prior periods
4. Availability of temporary loans in anticipation of the realization of revenues

It is noted that each of these four concepts relates to cash. They are not concerned with fund condition, the amounts of unappropriated surplus, or the amount of surplus or equity in enterprise or enterprise-type operations.

The Pattern for Realization of Revenues

Revenues generated from a government's own sources consist of taxes and nontax sources. The remainder of revenue is largely in the form of intergovernmental payments. The calendar upon which these are due and upon which actually received are key elements of the maintenance of liquidity. In the case of tax revenues, the most important for local governments has been the general property tax. Historically, the real property tax was collected in the fall of the year in order that the payment dates would correspond to periods of favorable cash flow for taxpayers—a holdover from an agricultural economy. Other types of taxes for local and state governments were also paid on an annual basis. These have included business license taxes and income taxes, especially prior to the inauguration of withholding tax practices commencing in 1939 in Philadelphia (and extended by the federal government and some state governments in the early 1940s). Sales taxes and other excises have generally been remitted immediately following the month in which taxable sales are made.

With the extended reliance of state and local governments upon intergovernmental revenue, practices have varied from prepayment of some grants, to payments more or less as earned, and on to payments significantly after the time of state and local disbursements that are intended to be financed, in part, from payments from senior governments.

Analyses of revenue and expenditure flows show for which portions of the year the government has not received a pro rata share of its budgeted income—either in relation to the time that has elapsed or in relation to the disbursements required, or both.

---

[2] See quarterly statements of *Flow of Funds* statements, e.g., Board of Governors of the Federal Reserve System, *Flow of Funds Accounts, 1st Quarter, 1980, Seasonally Adjusted and Unadjusted*, p. 34.

[3] For purposes of this discussion, liquidity or illiquidity do not embrace the concepts of delay in paying warrants. This matter is discussed in Chapter 19.

The Pattern for Disbursements

Patterns of disbursements for recurring expenditures for goods and services are likely to be spread rather evenly throughout the year. Payments for debt service, remission of taxes collected by other governments, and payments for employee benefits may be made in one lump sum for the entire year or in irregular patterns. These latter types of disbursements are likely to produce uneven patterns of cash requirements in the operating budgets.

Cash Balances from Prior Periods

The working capital of various funds in governmental operations that is carried forward from one fiscal period to the next is a significant factor in determining liquidity. If the government is in a position to carry forward large cash balances that will cover excesses of cash requirements, the problems of liquidity may be minimal or nonexistent. Conversely, if the government is not in a position to carry forward significant cash balances as operating capital, it becomes necessary to look elsewhere in order to avoid default in meeting obligations as they fall due.

Availability of Temporary Loans

The final major determinant of liquidity is the availability of temporary loans in anticipation of nontax revenues (RANS). These may be internal loans from other funds within the government or they may be external loans. However, they are frequently the only source from which the government is able to realize needed cash.

Accounting Procedures

Aside from these fundamental factors in liquidity and illiquidity, one is obliged to take into account the impact of the accounting system upon liquidity. In order to do this, it is perhaps easiest to review the options available. Both revenues and expenditures can be treated on a cash basis, on a full accrual basis, or by some combination of, or adjustment to, the cash and accrual systems.

The federal government operates on a cash basis, i.e., it takes revenues into account when received and expenditures into account when disbursements are made. State and local governmental enterprise operations are usually on full accrual accounting, i.e., revenues are recorded as earned and expenditures are recorded as goods and services are delivered. Under such a system, all revenues are recorded as "earned" after reservations for amounts considered noncollectable; expenditures relate to the time goods and services are received, rather than when paid.

For the operating funds of state and local governments, other than enterprise operations, it became customary during the 1930s to adopt a so-called "modified accrual system" under which revenues were recorded as received and expenditures recorded on a full accrual basis. Moreover, in many cases, the budgetary accounting systems provided for a "reserve for encumbrances" as one of the items of liability in arriving at fund condition, i.e., statement of surplus available for appropriation. The effect of this system was to improve the working capital position even though substantial amounts of taxes and other revenues were not received in the year in which they were due. It is theoretically possible to operate on the basis of accrual of revenues and treat expenditures only on a cash basis; however, no governments are known to be operating under that system at the present time.

Although the "modified accrual" system does not guarantee sufficient cash from which to meet requirements, from the point of view of cash management, it is a conservative system. A number of accounting firms and some others in the field of state and local government finance have recently emphasized full accrual systems as *the* appropriate system for governmental accounting. Frequently, they have done this without a realization of the impact such actions would have on the cash flow operations of these governments or the difficulties imposed in the political and public relations arena of justifying the revenue increases necessary to provide working capital when the balance sheet showed substantial amounts of unappropriated surplus available.

OVERCOMING ILLIQUIDITY

In order to overcome the basic problems of illiquidity, some combination of these steps is indicated.

1. Acceleration within the fiscal year of realization of locally administered taxes and other revenues
2. Prompt settlement of intergovernmental receivables
3. Adjustment of the bases of accounting
4. Development of a working capital reserve fund

The steps are simple of enumeration but frequently difficult of attainment. They are likely to involve problems of acceptance by both the local political leadership and the general public. Although the soundness of financial condition is much improved by good working capital reserves and likely to improve the position of the government in the credit markets, the temptation to a future group of office holders to have a "cheap drunk" by dissipation of the working capital account is an ever-present threat. As such, it becomes a discouragement to those who might otherwise work to achieve a sounder working capital position.

Calendars for Locally Administered Revenues

Strong executive leadership supported by good legislative leadership can modify the local tax calendar to overcome some of the principal elements of lag. Due dates for payment of property and other taxes can be accelerated in order to provide for an earlier realization within the fiscal year. However, if this process is not to set the stage for another round of adjustment of the fiscal year in an effort to gain one-time budgetary advantages, the adoption of a quarterly or monthly payment system is appropriate to avoid enticements for those seeking another one-shot advantage.

For property taxes, the law can require periodic payments—either as payments of ascertained taxes due or as prepayment on an estimated basis with the final amount determined when the assessments and tax rates have been established. Savings and loan associations, banking institutions, and others can be required to make periodic remissions of tax deposits made under mortgage arrangements. For income taxes, sales taxes, and some other taxes, provision can be made for accelerated payments or deposits by employers or vendors of such taxes substantially as collected.

Settlement of Intergovernmental Accounts

There is need for a comprehensive national policy in respect to timely settlement of intergovernmental accounts. The national policy should include requirements that senior governments make interim payments corresponding closely to outgo by the recipient governments in any program where the senior government has a financial interest or responsibility. Such a system of current payment based upon cash flow requirements can overcome much of the difficulty. Adjustments required (in the light of completed final accounting verification and audit) can be made retrospectively.

Representatives of the senior government should be prohibited from withholding timely payment of funds for services that are jointly financed. If penalties are to be assessed for noncompliance with operating requirements, this process should be independent of the routine payment cycle. In many circumstances, quasi-judicial administrative processes should apply. Administrative appeal or arbitration panels should hear complaints and be empowered to assess reasonable penalties in explicit amounts for noncompliance; however, the tremendous power now exercised by nameless senior government employees should cease.

A senior government failing to make timely settlement of accounts should pay interest on the funds temporarily withheld. Conversely, when a recipient government draws funds in advance of the date earned, it should be responsible for payment of interest on such funds. Interest rates should reflect the cost (or value) of money in the marketplace. Such policies would not apply to minor amounts. They would take into account requirements for working capital balances. Such policies would have the effect of reducing the working capital problem of recipient governments arising from the joint or full financing of programs by the senior government and would provide equity between governments. The objective is to produce a cash flow among governments closely corresponding to the outgo in related accounts.

Pending the adoption of comprehensive measures, governments relying to a significant degree on transfers of funds from senior governments should designate an officer explicitly responsible for development and maintenance of constructive relationships with these senior governments. A cooperative approach to a more equitable system of timely payment should markedly improve federal-state-local relations.

Accounting Procedures

As a long-term advocate of responsible home rule, this author is always reticent to recommend procedures that become straight-jackets for state and local governments. Senior governments do not have a monopoly on wisdom—even though their agents frequently seek to exercise monopolies in the prescription of rules. Yet, the pressures from some accountants and from some other sources may make it wise for state governments to establish the major principles governing the manner in which receipts of the state and its local governments shall be recorded as revenues. Generally, it appears that the modified accrual systems widely used during the past four decades have served state and local governments well in their general funds.

The requirements in enterprise operations are different. Full accruals may be appropriate for such revenues; however, some general rules concerning the cash budget may be in order to forestall strains upon working capital funds. In general, the thrust should be toward maintenance of reasonable working capital funds and discouragement of budgetary gimmicks that threaten this objective. There should be effective prohibitions against gimmick changes that produce temporary advantages to a current group of office-holders while simultaneously creating continuing problems for the government in the future, e.g., a change in the fiscal year in order to take advantage of a one-time book surplus.

A modified accrual accounting system for the general operations of the government (but not for governmental enterprise operations) appears to be the wisest course available. With locally generated revenues treated on a cash receipts basis, intergovernmental payments and expenditures on an accrual basis, and with reserves for encumbrances recorded as accrued liabilities, the objective of maintenance of desirable working capital cash is best served. This approach does not satisfy the advocates of full accrual accounting. They seem to prefer full accrual of revenues receivable, after allowances for noncollection, and to want to reduce the use of reserves for encumbrances where goods and services have not been delivered at the close of the accounting period. Yet, the full accrual system requires the maintenance of large amounts of unappropriated surplus if suitable working capital cash is to be available.

Most laws and public policy in most jurisdictions require that unappropriated surplus be taken into account as a resource in the preparation of the budget for the succeeding year and that taxes be levied in amounts only sufficient to balance the budget. If this rule is followed, there is an inevitable cash shortage at many points during the year and usually at year-end. These shortages must be covered by internal or external loans and eventually they are likely to adversely affect the position of the government in the credit markets.

Conversely, if the government attempts to maintain an unappropriated surplus sufficient to meet working capital requirements, political leaders are obliged to shoulder the burden of voting additional taxes in the face of the availability of large amounts of unappropriated surplus. In most communities, the pressures will eventually be sufficient to render such a course politically unacceptable. At that point, the government is back to the position of being dependent upon short-term loans to carry on its operations and to avoid default on its long-term loans. The temptations are almost too great during periods of stress and the one-time advantages are but harbingers of a worse tomorrow.

SOURCES OF FUNDS FOR TEMPORARY LIQUIDITY

Pending achievement of long-term favorable cash flow solutions, it is necessary to develop cash by obtaining loans from either internal or external sources.

The Use of Internal Funds

The aggregate amounts of cash and securities held by state and local governments at the close of their 1979–1980 fiscal years is reported by the Bureau of the Census to have been $408 billion. Of this, $206 billion was in insurance trust funds; $92 billion in bond funds or debt offset funds; and $109 billion in other funds—primarily operating funds.[4] Of course, these funds were distributed in widely varying patterns among the state and local governments. Some had large amounts of working capital; some had little or none. Some had substantial moneys in bond funds and little in operating funds. Some had large amounts in enterprise and other special funds but were without net available cash in other operating funds.

A review of all the funds subject to the control of a government is likely to reveal considerable cash balances (excluding proceeds of temporary loans) from time to time in selected accounts while at the same time shortages may exist in others. This suggests the need for consolidated cash accounts. The sources of internal loans to cash-short accounts are most likely to be other operating funds; however, in some governments, use by consolidated cash accounts of temporary loans from bond funds to operating funds may be appropriate. The policies controlling the use of internal loans are frequently established by state law and the provisions of bond contracts. A factor involved in illiquidity in some operating funds has been the tendency of state legislatures and local governing bodies to adopt requirements or to enter into contracts with provisions necessitating excessive segregation of moneys into separate funds and separate bank accounts. The purposes of these actions vary. In some cases, the benefits derived from such segregation are reasonably commensurate with the disadvantages imposed on cash management. In others, the benefits may be minimal—accruing largely to commercial banks.

---

[4] U.S. Bureau of the Census, *Governmental Finances in 1979–80,* p. 54. Of interest in this respect is that the reported balances at the end of the 1976–77 fiscal years amounted to $271 billion. As of December 31 of 1977, insured commercial banks held deposits of state and local governments in the amount of $68.1 billion, or almost one-fourth of the total cash and security assets of these governments. See U.S. Bureau of the Census, *1977 Census of Governments,* v. 5, no. 5, "Compendium of Governmental Finances," pp. 74–75; Board of Governors of the Federal Reserve System, Federal Deposit Insurance Corporation, and Office of the Comptroller of the Currency, *Assets and Liabilities: Report of Income for Commercial and Mutual Savings Banks* (December 31, 1977), p. 16.

The public policy issues should be fully identified and comprehensively evaluated. Policies can then be developed, taking into account the requirements of good cash management as well as the benefits of special protection to portions of the moneys of the government. The costs and the benefits can be compared and a policy adopted in the light of such an evaluation.

External Short-term Loans

TANS and RANS have been the most common types of loans used to produce operating capital for state and local governments. Many of these loans are placed directly with the banks; others are sold through the general credit markets.[5]

The Board of Governors of the Federal Reserve System reports the investments of a substantial group of large commercial banks that make weekly reports to federal banking officials. Among the investment categories used for reporting is one for the obligations of states and political subdivisions, which is subdivided into two categories: (1) "Tax warrants, short-term notes, and bills" and (2) "other." The first category is concerned with short-term and the second with the long-term obligations of these governments. As of December 31, 1977, this group of large commercial banks held $51.9 billion of state and local government obligations of which $8.7 billion (16.8 percent) were short-term. If that ratio were typical of overall commercial bank practices, the total short-term obligations held by all commercial banks would have been about $19.1 billion. On the other hand, if holdings of short-term debt are viewed as a percentage of total loans and investments, the indicated total holdings of all commercial banks would have been $17.6 billion. These amounts may be compared with the $11.6 billion estimate contained in the February 1980 *Flow of Funds* statement for December 31, 1977.[6] Therefore, it appears that the larger banks may have been used to a somewhat greater degree than the smaller banks as a source for these short-term loans.

The extent of holdings of short-term obligations of state and local governments by investors other than commercial banks is not known; however, there is some evidence of considerable holdings by the nonfinancial corporations and other economic sectors.

Direct Bank Loans. The use of the direct bank loan is frequently the simplest and easiest course, especially for local governments. Ordinarily, the negotiations are between public officials and bank officials, with no need for the development of a formal disclosure statement or advertisement—and may be without public announcement.

Bank loans offer flexibility in terms of the time (or times) at which money is to be taken down and repaid as well as adjustment in amounts. Commitments can be secured to advance moneys on a schedule deemed appropriate beforehand, and, if circumstances change in the course of the year, the terms can ordinarily be renegotiated within reasonable limits. The direct bank loans do not involve a separately identified element of cost for sale of the notes, as is the case with notes offered in the general market. On the adverse side, there is likely to be a commitment fee.

---

[5] This discussion of short-term debt has deliberately omitted the field of municipal commercial paper. This method of borrowing may become a wave of the future; however, the experience to date is too limited to warrant evaluation here. According to the September 17, 1980, issue of Standard & Poor's news letter, *Perspective,* municipal commercial paper was first introduced in 1974 when a Virginia agency sold $20 million in connection with a pollution control project. The problems of New York City in early 1975, involving in large degree a reexamination of huge use of short-term credit, acted to abort the use of municipal commercial paper. However, by mid-1980, several issues of substantial size had been marketed, including the Government Development Bank for Puerto Rico, the Illinois Education Facilities Authority ($60 million), the Salt River Project Agricultural Improvement and Power District in Arizona ($200 million), and the South Dakota Housing Development Authority ($15 million). Other large issues were in prospect.

[6] See Board of Governors of the Federal Reserve System, *Annual Statistical Digest, 1973–1977,* pp. 70, 77. See also Board of Governors of the Federal Reserve System, *Flow of Funds Accounts, 1957–1980: Assets and Liabilities Outstanding* (September 1981), p. 39. In August 1978, the *Flow of Funds* set this amount at $18.5 billion but subsequently adjusted it downward to $11.6 billion.

Despite the cordiality of relations between the banks and the public officials of the community, the banks are in business for profit. Accordingly, while they may consider a loan to the state or local government a form of civic obligation, they are obliged to charge interest rates that produce a profit. Therefore, negotiations should be arms-length transactions in order to assure that reasonable rates are obtained. The government has an obligation to consider the terms offered by the banks; it also has an obligation to get the best rate attainable.

Sale of Notes. For state and local governments that have never issued short-term debt to the securities markets, there may be no reasonable yardstick concerning the market position to be accorded to their short-term loans. The yield rates on outstanding or new-issue bonds maturing within a year or two may afford some guideline as to their relative credit position; however, this is not a fully satisfactory gauge because the amount of such bonds in the market at any given time is small when related to the amounts invested in short-term loans for working capital purposes. Due in part to the large volume, the yield rates upon short-term loans are likely to be higher.[7]

Even for governments which can easily obtain their full requirements for cash from the commercial banks, it is occasionally desirable for most short-term borrowers to offer notes to the general securities market. Such sales offer several potential benefits:

1. They demonstrate that the government has access to credit markets other than the commercial banks with which it normally does business. Although the commercial banks will ordinarily be in a position to supply the short-term capital during periods of scarce funds, they sometimes find this difficult. Accordingly, the prudent issuer will wish to maintain a demonstrated access to the general capital market. Publicly issued notes are rated by Moody's if the issuer so requests. The demonstrated record of performance, created at times when other alternatives are available, may prove useful during periods of tight money or unforeseen emergencies.

2. The capital market sometimes offers rates lower than those offered by the local banks. The degree of participation of a given bank (or group of banks) in the short-term securities of the instant government varies with the bank's own cash position as of the time the loan is negotiated. Other banks and other investors have different cash positions and objectives. As a result, even though there may be considerable issuance costs for notes offered to the general market, that market may be able to offer the needed funds at a significantly lesser cost than the rate obtainable from a single bank or a consortium of local banks. In other circumstances, the converse may be true.

3. Sales to the general market provide benchmarks for comparison of rates between the securities of this government and that being paid by other governments. Such information will be useful to the issuer in planning future sales of RANS, TANS, and BANS.

As will be discussed in a subsequent chapter, sales to the market of notes can be conducted on either a negotiated or competitive basis. If done on a competitive basis, the sale can be on an "all or none" basis or on a so-called "Dutch auction" basis. Under the former, all notes are awarded to a single bidder; under the latter, minimum amounts from each bidder are established and the notes are then awarded among the bidders to those offering the lowest rates until the full amount of notes being offered is placed.

Commercial Paper and Demand Notes. Two recent developments in the short-term loan market for state and local government securities relate to the use of commercial paper and demand notes. In the case of commercial paper, the pattern is one which follows the general pattern long accepted in respect to private corporations that borrow upon their general credit. The demand is generally assumed to mature within the short-term range, i.e., one year; however, it can be matured by the owner in shorter periods at his

---

[7] To some extent, the attractiveness of short-term bonds arises from the pattern of semiannual interest income as contrasted with income payable only at maturity in the case of most notes. Thus, a 5.00 percent rate for a note for one year with interest payable at maturity becomes 5.0625 percent for a one-year bond $(1.025)^2$.

option. A method of inducing the investor to forego demand for settlement has been the introduction of the variable rate concept insofar as the interest payable. The effect is to help the investor to maintain earnings commensurate with the changes in the yardstick rates used for purposes of escalation or deescalation of the rates of return on these demand notes.

Both the commercial paper and demand markets for state and local governments are such recent developments that as of the closing date for this book, it was not feasible to offer any evaluation of the experience or even to secure comprehensive data concerning the extent of use geographically, by types of governments, or amounts involved, although some of the larger municipal bond funds were being reported as investing as much as 10 percent of their assets in demand tax-exempt variable rate notes.

When and How Much to Borrow

The government obliged to depend on external short-term loans is confronted with two decisions: When to borrow and how much to borrow. These decisions rest on a combination of current circumstances, projected needs, and the opportunity for gain from arbitrage. However, before considering potential arbitrage, a determination should be made as to the cash needs during the upcoming fiscal year. This is done in light of a detailed cash flow statement showing all anticipated cash income and cash outgo. Each major and moderate-sized revenue source is carefully examined for yield during each month. For critical months, analyses may be on a weekly or even, occasionally, on a daily basis. Similar projections are made for each major element of cash requirement, with special attention to debt service requirements.

The working draft cash flow statement should reflect the cumulative experience gained in estimating income by source over a period of years and likewise from experience with patterns of cash requirements. The working paper statement should be as realistic as possible. There is no room for a fudge factor at this stage. It should take into account previous working paper projections and the basis for each element of the projection as well as carefully documented actual experience. Over time, a substantial body of knowledge will be accumulated which can produce highly accurate projections for typical years.

The working paper projection will not ordinarily become the official projection. Like averages of rainfall or temperature, there is rarely a wholly typical year. Variations in economic conditions and emergencies can produce significant variations from the experience norm. Accordingly, it is necessary to introduce flexibility into the process by providing for conservative estimates of the rate of realization of income and liberal estimates as to the rates of disbursement, i.e., some acceleration beyond cumulative actual experience. Moreover, a further reserve element is desirable in order to avoid the likelihood of being obliged to return to the market during the year for a greater amount of temporary financing than originally anticipated. Such a safety margin may not produce a net added cost because of the opportunity to invest temporary balances at rates that are generally higher than those being paid for tax-exempt, short-term loans. A return to the market for greater amounts than set forth in the original public plan is likely to produce adverse effects in terms of credibility in capital markets.

In making projections of disbursements, attention is required to large payments that can distort cash flows *within* the month, or even within weekly periods. Typically, debt service payments are due on the first day of the month and they may be huge in some months. Biweekly pay periods can produce large demands that cannot be reasonably deferred beyond due date. Pension payments made early in the month that happens to have major income later in the month can also produce crises. Cash disbursement projections must take into account past patterns of each category of expense. The government will receive little criticism from its lenders if the rate of disbursements on a cumulative basis is less at checkpoints than projected; however, if disbursements are significantly greater than shown in the projections, confidence may be shaken. Lack of confidence can produce or accentuate crises.

Beyond the more or less mandatory patterns of disbursements, the government can develop some flexibility in the rate of disbursements. The crudest form of flexibility is a simple delay in payment of vendors. However, if this becomes a pattern, it will also become one of the most expensive possible ways in which to "borrow" money. It results in a decrease in the number of firms willing to do business as suppliers. This decreased competition, coupled with the practice of increasing bid prices to compensate for slow payment, imposes additional costs. Some other types of payments, especially payments of social security and pension costs to other governments, may offer limited degrees of flexibility—without incurring late penalties. The competent money manager will take these fully into account.

Where pension funds are self-administered and the system includes employee deductions, there is a potential for two kinds of flexibility: (1) The time at which the employee contributions are remitted and (2) the time at which the government makes its contributions to the pension funds. Delay of such payments as long as feasible can enhance the short-term earnings; however, early payment to the pension fund permits immediate investments at long-term taxable rates. Inasmuch as these rates are usually higher than the cost of money to the government, the interest earnable upon these early payments during the current year represents a gain that is recapturable—either immediately or over a period of years in terms of the amount of net pension contributions required. In other words, if the government can borrow money temporarily at 8 percent for the year and pay $50 million to the pension fund at the beginning of the year where such funds can earn 10 to 11 percent during the current year, there may have been a gain of $2.0 to $2.5 million for the year.[8] In like manner, prepayment of certain debt service costs to sinking funds may provide potential gains. These kinds of earnings are not considered arbitrage under current regulations.

Potential for Arbitrage

In weighing the alternatives to be pursued, especially the alternatives of maximizing the use of internal funds vs. the use of borrowed funds, the potentials for arbitrage under alternative loan programs should be carefully weighed. Pursuit of the arbitrage pattern requires careful advanced planning. It has risks; it also has handsome potential rewards. The opportunity for arbitrage through short-term working capital loans is illustrated in Table 26. From this table, it is apparent that during eight of the twelve months there is projected a negative balance in the operating fund, ranging from $1.2 million to $27.2 million.

Under Plan A approach, the bank advances loans as required and is repaid as promptly as cash flow permits. Operating under this plan, the government will realize an estimated $371,000 in interest earnings and will pay an estimated $544,000 in interest charges for a net interest cost of $173,000.

Under alternative Plan B, the government borrows $30 million at the outset of the year for the entire year at an 8.5 percent interest rate, producing a gross interest charge of $3.0 million for the year. It is able to invest portions of the money for longer periods and therefore is able to earn a 10.0 percent average rate as compared to earnings averaging 9.5 percent under Plan A. The aggregate earnings of interest for the year on these balances amount to $3,000,000, thereby producing a net interest income under Plan B of $696,000. When this is compared with the net cost of $173,000 under Plan A, it is obvious that the government is able to achieve a net advantage of $869,000 by use of Plan B rather than Plan A.

---

[8] Local pension fund accounting practices will determine when the gain is taken into account insofar as budgetary impact is concerned.

Table 26

Potential Arbitrage from Operating Capital Loans

(amounts in thousands of dollars)

						Months							Totals for Year
	1	2	3	4	5	6	7	8	9	10	11	12	
Operations Excluding Loans													
Opening balance	10,500	(1,200)	(3,200)	800	(1,200)	(3,200)	(19,200)	(27,200)	(24,200)	(2,200)	17,800	17,800	10,500
Receipts	3,300	6,000	14,000	10,000	7,000	4,000	5,000	12,000	30,000	40,000	12,000	6,000	149,300
Total available	13,800	8,000	10,800	10,800	5,800	800	(14,200)	(15,200)	5,800	37,800	29,200	23,800	159,800
Disbursements	15,000	8,000	10,000	12,000	9,000	20,000	13,000	9,000	8,000	20,000	12,000	13,300	149,300
Closing balance	(1,200)	(3,200)	800	(1,200)	(3,200)	(19,200)	(27,200)	(24,200)	(2,200)	17,800	17,800	10,500	10,500
Operations: Plan A													Average
Minimum Loan													
Loan balances	1,200	3,200				19,200	27,200	24,200					6,800
Invested balances			800	1,200	3,200				2,200	17,800	17,800	10,500	3,908
Interest earned[1]													391
Interest paid[2]													544
Net interest													173
Operations: Plan B													Average
Maximum Loan													
Loan balances	30,000	30,000	30,000	30,000	30,000	30,000	30,000	30,000	30,000	30,000	30,000	30,000	30,000
Invested cash	28,800	26,800	30,800	28,800	26,800	10,800	2,800	5,800	27,800	47,800	47,800	40,500	27,108
Interest earned[3]													3,000
Interest paid[4]													2,304
Net interest costs													(696)
Gain, B over A													869

[1] @ 9.50 percent
[2] @ 8.00 percent
[3] @ 10.00 percent
[4] @ 8.50 percent

In any given fiscal year, there is a possibility that reinvestment rates for the borrower government during the final months of the year may be less than those being paid for the loans, thereby producing a loss in that year. On the other hand, over a period of years, the average will almost inevitably produce an arbitrage profit under pursuit of Plan B type of operations. As a matter of fact, the spread between the rates being paid by the tax-exempt borrower and that receivable from taxable securities may be appreciably higher than the amounts used in the illustration, however, this must be examined closely in each case.

The foregoing does not constitute a recommendation that a government deliberately arrange its affairs in order to use short-term loans to meet working capital requirements. There are incontrovertible advantages to a cash flow that make such loans unnecessary; however, if they are necessary, a decision is required as to when and how much to borrow and when to repay.

The Warrant System

A considerable number of state and local governments continue to operate under the warrant system. Under this arrangement, the appropriate officer(s) issues warrants upon the treasurer for payment for goods and services. When the treasury is liquid, the warrants pass through the banking system in the same manner as checks and are honored on presentation by the commercial banks to the treasurer. If the treasury is unable to make payment on a current basis, the banks may hold the warrants pending the ability of the treasurer to honor them.

When the banks expect delays in payment, they ordinarily discount the warrants upon acceptance. In such circumstances, the original holder has the option of retaining the warrant until the treasurer is prepared to pay or of discounting the warrant. Alternatively, the government's treasurer may maintain compensating balances in other accounts with the commercial banks as offsets to the warrants being held by them, thereby avoiding discount of the warrants.[9]

Except in the payment of interest and principal requirements of bonded debt, the warrant system provides a ready means by which loans can be forced from those who render service or sell goods to these governments. Vendors or employees must take into account potential losses from temporary delays in payment (or discounting required for current payment) in establishing the rates to be charged or paid. Of course, vendors are likely to adjust prices to compensate for the use of money and to do so at taxable interest rates. Employees may demand added compensation to offset the losses. Should this happen, a double cost is incurred from elevated pension and other costs dependent on wage and salary levels.

The system avoids direct negotiation of loans from the banks or security markets. Disadvantages lie in the rates of interest likely to be charged; general concern over the liquidity position of the government when warrants are not honored on a current basis; and the inability of the government to take advantage of its tax-free interest rights in financing the temporary forced loans.

Long-term Working Capital Loans

One method of providing a solid working capital fund is to issue long-term bonds for this purpose and to amortize such debt as an operating cost over a period of years. The plan is a simple one in which long-term bonds are sold and the proceeds placed in a working capital fund—either as an independent fund or as a member of the consolidated

---

[9] This is an unnecessarily expensive method. The government could invest its available balances, borrow at lesser rates, and develop the equivalent of significant arbitrage advantages.

cash account. Thereinafter, the operating account borrows these amounts on terms at least equal to the costs of carrying the long-term debt. The rate for the long-term debt is likely to be greater than the rates at which short-term loans could have been obtained; however, during the periods of the year in which the operating fund has either a cash surplus or low demand on the consolidated cash account for loans, the excess can be invested at taxable short-term rates.

One of the advantages of the plan is that, over a period of years, the operating budget actually provides the cash with which fully to fund the working capital reserve and does so at relatively small incremental costs for any one year. This approach appears to have a great deal of merit and warrants fuller exploration than has been given to it by most governments confronted with recurring working capital problems. It is, however, highly desirable that any such working capital accounts be surrounded with appropriate restrictions to avoid misuse of the funds.

Temporary Use of the Proceeds of Bonds or BANS

Those governments using consolidated cash accounts that comingle bond proceeds and operating funds can use bond proceeds or bond anticipation notes to help provide temporary funds for working capital requirements. However, this form of consolidated cash management is available in only a minority of governments. The more frequent pattern is one in which proceeds of bonds and BANS must be segregated not only on a fund basis but also on a bank account basis. Such segregation has advantages in the sense that the integrity of the accounting procedures is enhanced and the risks of unavailability of moneys for the explicit purposes for which the bonds were issued are minimized. On the other hand, such segregation produces high degrees of inflexibility in money management and invites the potentiality of added costs that may not be warranted in relation to the *actual,* rather than the *presumed,* risks that arise from a more flexible policy.

Inasmuch as the subject of mingling of the proceeds of one bond issue with those of another or with operating funds impinges upon the whole subject of cash flow, the governmental unit must also make policy decisions upon that point. Frequently, the procedure is mandated either by law or by bond contract. However, effective public officials do not allow themselves to become permanent prisoners of inadequate law. They abide by the law until changed; in the meantime, they work assiduously for needed change. In any event, the first major policy question in dealing with cash flows incident to the use of the proceeds of bonds and BANS rests upon the patterns under which moneys will be managed. If the consolidated cash account has the right to advance moneys to member capital funds on a short-term basis, the need for bond anticipation notes is likely to be reduced. Conversely, provision of working capital through a consolidated cash account in which bond proceeds are deposited may require the issuance of bond anticipation notes taking into consideration the working capital requirements of funds. Frequently, BANS can be issued at lower costs than TANS or RANS. In such circumstances, the matter of flexibility in the *temporary* application of the proceeds of bond anticipation notes becomes germane.

BOND ANTICIPATION NOTES

BANS are usually sold under these circumstances:

1. The amount of the long-term debt needed has not been precisely determined; BANS are issued temporarily to finance the project pending determination of the precise amounts of permanent financing required. In some respects, this form of financing is similar to that used in many private capital projects. Arrangements are made at the outset for long-term financing but the final amount of such financing may be contingent upon the actual

cost of the facilities being developed. Construction loans are negotiated to provide temporary financing pending the completion of the project and the consummation of the long-term financing.

2. The amount of long-term bonds to be issued is known; however, the issuer believes that financing on a temporary basis is better because of unsettled market conditions in respect of long-term debt.

3. The amount of long-term financing is known; however, the development of the disclosure statement and perhaps some elements of final ministerial actions by the legislative body make it desirable to secure prompt temporary financing, with permanent financing to follow.

4. The law may permit the funding of interest during construction if the debt is first issued as bond anticipation debt but may foreclose such funding if the debt is initially issued as long-term debt.

5. Officials may seek to take advantage of provisions of the law that permit deferring the issuance of permanent financing for one or more years after the facility is partially or wholly in use. Through the use of bond anticipation notes, they are able to defer initial principal payments.[10]

6. The rate of issuance of other long-term debt may be so great for a period of time that it is not feasible to raise all of the money needed for capital purposes through the sale of long-term bonds. The market may be supersaturated for this issuer. The only recourse is through the issuance of BANS in the hope that a circumstance will soon occur that will permit the issuer to catch up on long-term funding requirements.[11]

7. The law may require that the debt, at least in temporary form, shall be issued before contracts are let.

In addition to the foregoing capital-related uses of funds, there may also be a basis for issuance to provide working capital for operating funds, as noted above.

To Use or Not to Use BANS

BANS were widely used in some states in the 1960s and even more widely used during the first half of the 1970s.[12] With the problems in New York and the threat of problems elsewhere in the wake of the New York crisis, the use of BANS has been markedly constricted. Many governments have reduced or eliminated their use. Yet, BANS offer a sound system for achieving many legitimate objectives in capital fund management. However, when a practice is associated in the minds of investors and citizens with acts they believe to be fiscally irresponsible, a holiday from their use is indicated.

The investor in BANS knows that the timely repayment of the obligation he holds is dependent upon the capacity of the issuer either (1) to sell long-term securities related to the BANS or (2) to issue substitute BANS at the maturity date of the ones outstanding. In either situation, where the access of the debtor government to the long-term market is even marginally uncertain, investors are likely to charge premium rates for BANS in relation to TANS, RANS, or long-term debt securities. In only a few instances do BANS carry an obligation of the holder to accept long-term bonds in exchange for the BANS.

---

[10] The contrast between a government that commences repayment of principal on bonds issued at the outset of construction and a government able to defer issuance of bonds until well after the completion date of the project can be a significant item. Moreover, the BANS can usually be issued at short-term rates and, in a stable market, this reduces the current budgetary requirements, assuming that funding of interest during construction is not being permitted.

[11] The use of BANS in these circumstances can involve large risks, as proved to be the case in the City of New York. The future may not provide a better opportunity than afforded by the current market. The eventual conversion of BANS to bonds may involve significantly higher costs. In extreme circumstances, there may be major difficulty in marketing the bonds at any rate of interest.

[12] New Jersey. *Report of New Jersey Tax Policy Committee, Part IV*, "The Use and Costs of Public Credit." pp. 28–32.

It is not customary for state and local governments to negotiate long-term financing agreements (commitments) to become effective at the completion date of the facility, as is the practice for the major portions of private construction. As a result, the holder of BANS is in a more exposed position than is the bank or lender furnishing short-term moneys in financing private construction. Perhaps practice will eventually evolve to the point that it is feasible to arrange long-term financing for public structures in advance of the time of need therefor in much the same manner as long-term mortgage commitments are now available in private finance. If this occurs, a more extensive use of BANS is likely to prove beneficial and market acceptance much improved.

Chapter 9
SECURING SPECIALIZED SERVICES

The development and execution of a successful debt policy requires a high level of competence in a variety of specializations. Although different in general obligation and revenue bond financing, there is considerable overlap between the two areas. Among the specialties required are: (1) Knowledge of the law; (2) information about the financial markets, especially the bond market; (3) an opinion on the feasibility of governmental enterprise operations; (4) familiarity with the character of the bonds or notes offered and the most advantageous general structure for the bond or note issue; (5) knowledge of the best ways in which to package the detailed features of the bond issue; (6) acquaintance with the appropriate trustee and fiscal agency arrangements; and (7) know-how in bond printing. Beyond the development of the foregoing, further skills are required at the time of sale and in the administration of outstanding debt.

Large issuers of tax-exempt debt are likely to develop many specialized services on an in-house basis; medium and smaller sized issuers depend upon consultants for most of these specialized services. Moreover, marketing considerations frequently dictate that in-house competence be supplemented by use of well-recognized independent consultants.

FINANCIAL ADVISORY SERVICES

The planning and sale of a bond or note issue may appear to be a simple undertaking. In the not-too-distant past this was true for the typical general obligation bond. However, appearances are deceiving. Today, the planning and sale of all debt of state and local governments involves complexities which tend to increase with the passing of time.

There is a danger that the issuer will view the issuance of debt as merely a series of routinized steps that can be easily mastered through limited experience. Few assumptions are likely to be more erroneous. Successful planning and execution of a single bond issue almost always require the services of experienced, competent personnel. The more frequent and the more complex the fundings, the greater the need for competent staff and usually for consulting assistance. To proceed without the benefit of competent financial services is to invite development of an unwise plan that will prove faulty in execution. Such errors result in unnecessarily high interest and other costs to the community.

The Need

The need for competent financial services is clear. If these are not available on an in-house basis, they should be provided through a combination of staff and consultants. The need for competent financial services in relation to the issuance and administration of debt has become more acute with various market developments, including: Widespread use of advance refunding; expanded frequency and scope of federal treasury regulation; the growth in governmental lessee and *on behalf of* debt; high interest levels and frequent tight money markets; and general instability in the market of the type that prevailed in

135

1975 due to problems in New York and, commencing in 1980, with efforts to control inflation. Each of these has posed new problems for public officials concerned with debt policies and the issuance of debt. Some of the problems were turned into opportunities by governments well-situated to take advantage of the situations as they arose.

In much of this volume, attention is focused on policy problems requiring resolution. Both decision and execution can be on the basis of informed judgment or can be made on the basis of pseudo knowledge or blind acceptance of precedent. It is difficult to find financial advisors with the breadth of personal competence and experience needed for effective advice on such a wide range of subjects. The genuinely able ones are few in number. Their services are expensive. Unfortunately, some who offer to serve have quite limited capacity. The need for services falls into two broad categories:

1. The general policy issues concerned with levels of debt appropriate for the community and the types of debt to be used
2. The cost of financing, i.e., interest, issuance costs, and related costs

The competent financial advisor should be able to provide to the issuer a comprehensive statement of the choices available on each aspect of policy requiring resolution. For each alternative presented, pros and cons together with a recommendation and the reasons therefor are requisites of good service. Beyond the policy issues, the advisor should assist the issuer in these areas:

1. Presentation to the rating agencies
2. Timing of the sale
3. The probable range of interest costs for different alternative potential means of financing
4. Reasonableness of fees for other specialized services
5. Suitability of fees for the underwriters
6. The call provisions appropriate for the bond issue
7. Structure of the bond issue
8. Bidding requirements and other terms of public sale
9. Conduct of negotiated sales
10. Evaluation of bids
11. Evaluation of the performance of members of the syndicate in negotiated financing

Beyond these matters, there is another group of decisions likely to influence the cost to the issuer. Although these are treated in greater depth elsewhere in this volume, it is appropriate to recall them here:

a. The credit market position to be accorded the debt
b. Choice of security to be pledged
c. Use of competitive vs. negotiated sale
d. Patterns of coupons permitted and par vs. discount bids
e. Evaluation of bond counsel services
f. Evaluation of services of trustees and paying agents
g. Fund structure required and its contribution to cash management
h. Bidding requirements
i. Preparation of disclosure document
j. Selection of feasibility analysts
k. Evaluation of efforts to expand and sustain primary and secondary markets
l. Settlement
m. Postsettlement analyses for use in subsequent sales

The enumeration reminds one of the breadth of knowledge and experience required for mature advice if the issuer is to be properly served.

Role of Issuer's Staff

Only in large jurisdictions can adequate in-house staff be developed and maintained. Unless the jurisdiction comes to market four or more times a year, such an undertaking is probably not cost efficient. A more effective pattern is to assign responsibility for general oversight of debt administration to one of the principal members of the finance staff. His services can be supplemented by a combination of in-house and consulting services.

The staff of the issuer is usually oriented to the internal government tasks incident to obtaining necessary legislative and administrative approvals, coordinating timetables for the sale with the capital spending requirements, and gathering materials for the official statement. In contrast, the majority of the work of the financial advisor relates to external relationships and factors. That is, he relates the needs of the issuer to capital markets in order that the lowest costs of financing can be obtained. The work program of the consultant, prepared at the outset of each planned financing by the joint action of the debt manager and the advisor, will serve these purposes:

1. Establishment of a basis for scheduling all activities of planning the issue as well as setting forth the framework for assignment of responsibilities to the advisor and to the staff of the issuer
2. Outlining the scope of services to be provided by the advisor which can become the basis for the contract and for compensation of the advisor and for evaluating performance by him
3. Clarifying for the staff the tasks required of it and establishing the timing of such performance

Free Services

The acronym TINSTAFL ("There is No Such Thing as a Free Lunch") applies in financial advisory services. With the exception of crisis situations and a few extraordinarily public spirited individuals or organizations, there is little likelihood of securing good quality free services. Advisory committees can provide generalized policy assistance. Local banks and representatives of investment banking firms may provide limited free consultation; however, this cannot be depended on as an alternative to effective in-house or contractual consultative services.

Frequently, an investment banker will incur considerable costs either on a promotional or contingent basis. A significant amount of service may be provided as an investment in good will looking toward the likelihood of a contract as managing underwriter in a negotiated sale. If not named as a managing underwriter, services provided will be free to the issuer; however, at the critical points in the negotiation the issuer will find that there is no advisor on its side of the table. Moreover, the underwriter cannot be reasonably expected to subsidize the issuer by continued or repetitive free services.

Limited free assistance can be obtained from university personnel and from nonprofit organizations if they have personnel with expertise in various aspects of debt financing; however, in the long run, the issuer will find that there is no substitute for either a full in-house capability or a combination of staff and professional advisors.

Sources for Professional Assistance

Essentially, there are three sources for professional assistance as financial advisors: State agencies, underwriters of municipal securities, and independent advisory firms not engaged in underwriting municipal securities. Each of these sources has its strengths; each has its weaknesses. The issuer is obliged to make a choice based upon evaluation of the particular services required and the capability of the persons available through contract.

Despite the significance of local government debt, few of the states provide technical services to those governments in debt administration. Their emphasis has been upon the more negative and controlled functions; almost none upon the positive, creative and rewarding aspects of debt management. Among the states acting positively have been Florida, Louisiana, Michigan, New Mexico, North Carolina, Oregon, Tennessee, Virginia, West Virginia, and Washington.[1] The state services range from comment as requested to actual issuance of local government securities by an agency of the state. Each of these services constitutes a distinct alternative for use by the local governments of the respective states.

The North Carolina Local Government Commission. Although a number of states require approval of a state government agency as a prerequisite to issuance of bonds by local governments, only in the State of North Carolina is the sale of local government bonds conducted by a state agency. The Local Government Commission, created by statute in 1931, conducts the sale of all bonds of municipal and county governments and all local special districts.[2]

The sales for the year ending June 30, 1979, were:

(dollar amounts in millions)					
	Schools	Utilities	Other	Total	Number of Sales
General Obligation Bonds of Local Governments					
Counties	$25.5	$10.2	$13.4	$ 49.2	15
Cities and towns		28.0	7.1	35.3	35
Special districts		0.1		0.1	1
Subtotal	$25.5	$38.4	$20.6	$ 84.6	51
Revenue Bonds Sold by Negotiation for:					
Medical Care Commission				$ 60.5	5
Power agencies				550.0	2
Industrial and pollution control authorities				91.4	37
Subtotal				$701.9	44
Total bonds sold				$786.5	95
Notes For Local Governments					
Bond anticipation notes				$ 45.8	71
Grant anticipation notes				0.8	1
Subtotal				$ 46.6	72
Total				$833.1	166

---

[1] See Municipal Finance Officers Association of United States and Canada, *Watching and Counting: A Survey of State Assistance to and Supervision of Local Debt and Financial Administration* (1977).

[2] The Commission consists of nine members, of whom four (State Treasurer, State Auditor, Secretary of State, and Secretary of Revenue) are ex-officio. Three members are appointed by the Governor and serve at his pleasure. One of the three appointed members must have had experience as a chief executive officer or member of the governing body of a city or town, and one must have had experience as a member of the governing body of a county. One member is appointed by the Lt. Governor and one member is appointed by the Speaker of House. The State Auditor, State Treasurer, Secretary of Revenue, and Secretary of State constitute the executive committee of the Commission with power to act when the Commission is not in session. A deputy to the State Treasurer acts as Secretary to the Commission.

The statute provides that, before any bonds or notes can be issued by a county or municipality, an application must be filed with the Commission for its approval.[3] If approved by the Commission, the proposed bonds or notes may then be submitted to the voters. Once the bonds have been approved by the Commission and by the voters, the governing authority of the issuer requests the Commission to sell the bonds or notes. The Commission holds public sales of bonds on each Tuesday (holidays excepted) when there are bonds to be sold or warrants to be offered. The sale on any given Tuesday may consist solely of the bonds of a single municipality or county if the issue is of substantial size. On the other hand, the Commission frequently conducts sales of several smaller issues on the same day. Each issue is separately offered and bid. Separate awards are made for each issue sold.

Among the advantages of the North Carolina system are:

1. Close supervision of local funding plans which adds to the attractiveness of the securities offered
2. Provision of adequate statistical information to prospective bidders concerning the finances of each government
3. Technical assistance in the planning of the bond issues, especially for the smaller local governments
4. Regularity of issues emanating from the Commission, thereby encouraging interest by investment bankers
5. Convenience of bidding at a single accessible city (Raleigh)
6. Groupings of issues to provide a package of offerings that is usually sufficient to attract the attention of syndicates that would otherwise forego an interest in bidding

Patterns of Assistance in Other States. In addition to the sales by the State of North Carolina, three other types of state marketing of local government debt are now practiced:

1. The use of governmental lessee bonds—primarily for local school building financing, e.g., Pennsylvania and Virginia
2. The use of state bond banks—e.g., Maine, New Hampshire, Vermont and Alaska
3. State purchase of local government or special agency debt—e.g., Texas

These categories are discussed elsewhere in this volume.

Hawaii issues state general obligation bonds from which the state makes sums available to the counties for capital improvements. The state thereupon withholds from the real property tax (administered by the state government) amounts necessary to pay the debt service on the sums that have been advanced to the local governments.

In two circumstances, the State of Florida sells and services bonds issued on behalf of local governments: (1) Local (county) school districts may authorize the State Board of Education to sell bonds secured by the county's portion of state motor vehicle license funds; (2) county governments may authorize the Florida Development Commission to issue bonds for improvements within the county, to be paid from the county's portion of a special two-cent statewide motor fuels tax. In the case of highway revenue bonds, each county's bonds are rated separately according to the degree of coverage and other factors provided by the county's portion of the motor fuels taxes. These elements of debt are serviced by the State Board of Administration.

Underwriting Firms. The underwriting firms must have fully current information concerning the market. They are in the market each day risking their capital; they must know the current market or they will soon be bankrupt. They are intimately engaged in

---

[3] For legal provisions relating to the Local Government Commission and its responsibilities in respect to the sale of bonds of local governments, see Chapter 159 of the General Statutes of North Carolina.

all aspects of underwriting. They know the investors first-hand and are obliged to carry on continuing relationships with the rating agencies in respect to various bonds in which they are interested.

On the other hand, unless they have an organized municipal bond advisory service, the personnel available to perform the advisory functions will be used in other phases of their operations, including business development. The profit to be derived from a man-day used in development of a new negotiated sale is likely to be much greater than the profit to be derived from the sale of the services of such personnel as advisors. Therefore, in the application of its resources, the underwriter is cognizant of the relative profit to be developed from advisory operations vis-à-vis other operations in the municipal finance field, especially in underwriting. This is not to suggest that the advisory staff of underwriters is incompetent; however, it is to state that the issuer should be cognizant of the realities confronted by the underwriting firm. Thus, the issuer must be in a position to demand a suitable level of service including, where appropriate, interaction and accessibility to the underwriting personnel of the organization.

The issuer must weigh how firm the advisor will be in presenting a strong position for the issuer in dealing with other underwriters. Any underwriting firm that acts as an advisor is involved in simultaneous relationships with many other dealers in syndicates of which they are both members. Hence, insistence upon independent advice is essential.

Only dealers are likely to have the depth of knowledge of market conditions to serve that aspect of the financial advisory role; however, they simultaneously have other relationships that are also important to them. Strong underwriters can perform both roles.

The Independent Financial Advisory Firm. The independent financial advisory firm can bring a fully independent view in working with the problems of the issuer. Such firms do not deal, underwrite, or act as brokers. They may have broad experience in the field of public administration and public financing management that can rarely be obtained from the underwriter acting as advisor. The conditioning developed as a result of effective public service with other governments may prove invaluable to the issuer. Moreover, the independent advisor has an opportunity to specialize in being an advisor, i.e., developing this as his specialized professional competence whereas others combine this and other work. Because of its extensive involvement, there is usually greater opportunity for keeping abreast of developments in the broader field of public finance. The fully independent firm can be independent in all respects from other interests in the municipal bond market. As such, the independent firm can serve without being obliged to take into account the impact of its stance on other relationships in the field.

The small independent firm cannot have at its command the full range of information and services available to the larger investment banking firms in maintaining current knowledge about the market. Sheer differences in size permit specialization and pooling of information in the larger firms in addition to the larger firm's broader first-hand knowledge.

The Use of Commercial Banks as Professional Advisors. A number of commercial banks, particularly in New England, provide financial advisory services under the heading of "fiscal agency arrangements." Often, these arrangements combine the roles of trustee, paying agent, depositary bank, and financial advisor.

If the staff available within the bank is capable of providing high quality financial advisory services, this relationship can be effective. In some cases, the provision of trustee services or paying agent services is the primary focus of these arrangements. Other commercial banks have developed departments or subsidiary corporations of one-bank holding companies that serve as financial advisors. In such situations, the comments made earlier concerning dealer investment banking firms may or may not be relevant, depending upon the bank's role in the market.

Care is required in making an objective evaluation of the services to be provided. An after-the-fact review of the value of the services is essential, especially where the relationship is one of long standing and more or less automatically renewed.

Steps in Making a Choice

The first step in acquiring the services of a financial advisor is to review the potential sources of such service. This can commence with a review of experience of nearby jurisdictions and inquiries of professional organizations. Examination of some of the more recent official statements of other jurisdictions provides a good source. The *Directory of Municipal Bond Dealers of the United States*[4] provides a comprehensive listing of financial advisors.

From these sources a preliminary list of potentials may be developed and a request for proposals issued to the selected firms. The requests for proposals should elicit information on the following points:

1. *Experience.* A description of recent experience with financings, with emphasis on those similar to that contemplated by the issuer

2. *Personnel and Assignments.* Information concerning the personnel to be available and particularly of the project manager to be assigned

3. *Services.* A description of the services intended to be performed with the benefits to be derived by the issuer from each service offered

4. *Financial Statement.* The financial statement of the advisor for the two preceding years

5. *References.* The names of individuals associated with issuers who have been served by the advisor in the past two years and who may be familiar with the work of the advisor

6. *Copies of Official Statements.* Specimen copies of several official statements of different jurisdictions where the firm has acted as financial advisor; examination of these will provide useful information in the process of evaluation

These requests for proposals should be accompanied by a statement from the issuer describing the financing contemplated, recent (three years') experience of the issuer in selling bonds of this general type, problems heretofore encountered or difficulties foreseen in the current proposed offering, and any other items that will enable the advisor to comprehend the problems confronted by the issuer. Interested firms should be invited to comment briefly upon how their experience relates to the problems identified.

From the proposals received, the issuer should prepare a short list of the more promising potentials. Interviews should be arranged in which the issuer elicits greater information about the ability of the firm to function effectively in the financing contemplated. Of particular interest will be methods of operation, work to be performed, and the terms of contract as to compensation and participation or nonparticipation in underwriting of the bonds. The period for which the contract is to run is important. It should be sufficiently long to encompass the full financing program being contemplated, yet with the right of termination at the option of either party under specified conditions.

The issuer must decide which type of advisory service can provide it with the best results. Within the framework of that decision, a selection of the advisor is made. In the process of deciding, the issuer will want to know precisely which personnel of the advisory firm will work on his account. A list of qualified senior personnel does not assure that these persons will be available for servicing this account. The issuer should press the advisor to name the individual who would be the principal for this account and to provide names and work assignments of other personnel to be used. Interviews with key prospective personnel may be appropriate. With this knowledge, greater confidence can be reposed as to the manner in which the assignment will be handled.

A Caution. There are investment banking firms that provide advisory services on a basis which enables them at the last moment to withdraw as advisor and become an active principal in the syndicate seeking to purchase the bonds. The Municipal Securities Rulemaking Board has discussed this subject in relation to its Regulation G-23 stating:

---

[4] Published semiannually by the *The Bond Buyer.* It lists all dealers, including dealer departments of commercial banks, by states and cities within states. It also carries a separate section listing bond counsel.

> . . . The Board continues to believe that there is a *prima facie* conflict of interest when a municipal securities professional acts as both financial advisor to the issuer and purchaser of the issuer's securities in a negotiated sale . . .[5]

In no case should an issuer enter into an arrangement with a financial advisor knowing that the firm intends to switch sides of the table and become an underwriter. In a competitive sale, this can give the underwriter an unwarranted advantage over other underwriters. Although a temporary advantage may be gained by the issuer in a single sale, lessened competition in the future is likely to be very costly. One or more of these circumstances may occur:

1. Compensation already received for financial advisory services may enable the firm to bid an amount lower than other bidders
2. Insider knowledge of the issuer's affairs allows the underwriter to explain special situations or security features to potential customers in a competitive sale situation
3. Inasmuch as the advisor has assisted in the preparation of the time table for the issue, such an advisor who becomes a bidder can begin presale efforts even before the public advertisement is placed to the disadvantage of competitive syndicates
4. At the time of the sale, the issuer has no advisor on his side of the table upon whom to rely

The potential conflict is even greater in a negotiated sale. Here, an advisor brings a transaction to a certain point as an agent of the issuer (for which he may or may not be paid a fee). Thereupon, the advisor may seek to change sides of the table by attempting to become the principal underwriter. The willingness of an underwriter to engage in such tactics places the issuer at a tremendous disadvantage and raises questions concerning the ethical character of the whole so-called advisory relationship. To eliminate the potential for this situation, a financial advisor should be precluded by the terms of the agreement from participating as underwriter or in any manner other than that of advisor until a stipulated period following the sale of the bonds, e.g., 30 days. The issuer may subsequently decide (in certain highly unusual situations) to concur in a modification in such terms; however, this should occur only in unforeseen emergency situations where the use of the advisor as an underwriter becomes the only practical way in which to sell the bonds in a timely manner.

Compensation

The general bases of compensating financial advisors are two: (1) An agreed hourly rate for different levels of personnel, plus out-of-pocket expenses, with an upset total amount payable under the contract; or (2) a fee based on the number of bonds in the sale. The issuer will wish to become informed concerning the current levels of compensation by inquiry of other issuers and also by requirement for disclosure of the fees being charged by this advisor in other contemporary business of a more or less comparable character.

BOND COUNSEL

Purchasers of bonds require conformity to all pertinent legal requirements including (1) a legally constituted issuer; (2) valid authorization of the bond issue; (3) adherence by the issuer to prescribed precedures; (4) disclosure of litigation, if any, that might affect the validity of the bonds; (5) correctness of the signatures on the bond; and (6) other procedural matters. Beyond these is the need for certification that the interest is tax-exempt

---

[5] Municipal Securities Rulemaking Board, Rule G-23.

under the federal internal revenue code and regulations of the U.S. Treasury Department as well as under the laws of the state in which issued.[6] It is customary to require an unqualified approving opinion of bond counsel on these matters as a prerequisite to the delivery of the bonds.

The practice of using bond counsel developed out of the widespread irregularities in municipal bonds during the latter part of the 19th century. Investors found that some of the instruments they had purchased in good faith were fraudulent. In other cases, the bonds were declared invalid because of the issuer's failure to comply with the procedures specified in the law governing the sale of municipal bonds. Owners found themselves essentially without recourse except against the persons from whom they had purchased the securities. The situation produced an atmosphere of suspicion and undermined confidence in municipal bonds. In order to assure themselves of the validity of bonds in which they were interested, some investors employed counsel to research pertinent points and to give opinions concerning their validity. Gradually investment bankers, and later the issuers, employed attorneys with outstanding reputations for ability and integrity in the municipal bond field to provide opinions as to the validity of the bonds at the time of sale. The practice is now almost universal.

The acceptability of opinions of counsel by investment banking syndicates and investors is wholly a matter of trust in the capability and integrity of the individuals and firms involved. There is no separate licensing of bond attorneys. It was not until 1978 that the first national association of counsel involved in offering opinions in this field was organized.

In the early part of this century only a few attorneys specialized in this field. As the market for municipal bonds expanded, the number of attorneys who offer opinions with respect to the legality of bond issues has also increased. Thus, the Bond Buyer's *Directory of Municipal Bond Dealers of the United States* for 1955 listed only 115 law firms as bond counsel; in 1968, 124 firms; in 1979, more than 300 firms. This growth has occurred despite the fact that the number of bond issues has remained remarkably stable in recent years. Among the factors accounting for the increase have been the larger size of the issues and the greater complexities of many of them. Moreover, the introduction in 1975 of the disclosure statements as a more or less required procedure increased the demand. Finally, a considerable number of the firms act as bond counsel for the issuers and, on other occasions, as underwriter's counsel or as advisors directly to commercial banks or other investors.

At one time the firms were largely concentrated in Philadelphia, New York, and Chicago. Today, they are much more widely situated. The firms range in size from single attorneys specializing in municipal bonds to firms with as many as 30 partners listing municipal bonds as a specialty.

Bond counsel ordinarily maintain checklists of items requiring attention in the course of their work on a bond issue. Many of these relate to the procedural aspects of authorization, security, and sale of the bonds. Always there is the matter of tax exemption. This has become increasingly important in the light of the complex U.S. Treasury Department regulations concerning arbitrage. Some indication of the scope of the matters involved may be gleaned from examination of Exhibit C, a partial checklist of documents involved in the closing of a bond sale. In some types of revenue bonds, the contracts run to hundreds of pages—all of which must be fully understood, checked, and approved by bond counsel insofar as they relate to the security and tax-exempt status of the bonds.

For Whom Does Bond Counsel Work?

In the early history of bond counsel opinions, the counsel was responsible solely to the investor. With the development of the municipal bond market, bond counsel became

---

[6] These are marketing requirements. The bond counsel will participate in the development of the disclosure statement but issues no opinion concerning its completeness nor correctness.

an appointee of the issuer and was usually paid by the issuer. During the period following World War II, bond counsel frequently sought to assume a position of neutrality between the investor and the issuer in order to stress the independence of their opinions, even though appointment and payment continued to be by the issuer.[7]

During the period between 1950 and 1975, it appeared that the bond counsel were on the way to becoming substantially independent of all parties—the issuer, the underwriter, and the investor. But, with the New York crisis in 1975, this changed abruptly. Underwriters quickly sent their counsel (recruited largely from a combination of experienced bond counsel and lawyers who had practiced before the Securities and Exchange Commission) to the sessions where the disclosure statements were being prepared. The bond counsel was obliged to become closely identified with the interests of the issuer in order that the disclosure statements could be worked out satisfactorily. These sessions frequently became adversary proceedings with the issuer and his bond counsel on the one side and the underwriters and their counsel on the other. Although it was the disclosure statement of the issuer (similar to the SEC "due diligence" requirement in corporate sales), its content and tone were frequently dictated by the counsel for the underwriters—all in the interest of protecting the underwriters from unwarranted attacks in court. The role of the bond counsel once again became clearly identified with the issuer and remains so today.

Method of Selection

From the standpoint of the issuer, the objective is to secure the opinion of a bond counsel who commands wide respect among investment bankers and investors but who is willing to promote the interest of the issuer within appropriate limits. The choice of a firm that may have an excellent reputation and capacity in many other fields of law but which does not have an established reputation in the municipal bond field can lessen the interest of investment bankers and investors who do not feel comfortable with opinions of the counsel selected.

Service as bond counsel is lucrative. From time to time, local public officials or others politically active undertake to require the appointment of bond counsel largely on the basis of political considerations. The typical pattern is to provide for joint counsel, one of which is an established bond counsel. If an experienced counsel is still in the picture, investors and underwriters are likely to continue their interest; however, on occasion, the appointments become so blatant that either underwriters or investors withdraw their interest in the sale. This process acts, in the long run, to expand the field of bond counsel and has brought along some very competent attorneys into the municipal bond arena. On the other hand, it has also been the source of unnecessary costs and embarrassment on occasion.

Compensation of Bond Counsel

The fee to be paid to bond counsel is usually a matter for negotiation between the counsel and the issuer. The amount of the fee should be conditioned upon the amount and complexity of the work required; however, it is more frequently a function of the size of the bond issue. Issuers should keep informed concerning the going rates being paid to bond counsel by other governments issuing similar kinds of bonds and involving similar amounts of work. If there is a financial advisor in the picture, he can be used to secure the information. Care is required to avoid the doubling of fees where co-counsel are involved.

---

[7] Ordinarily, the bond counsel is paid directly by the issuer; however, in a few jurisdictions, it is still customary for the issuer to designate the counsel but to require the underwriters to make the payment as a part of their expense in underwriting the issue. Also, the practice still exists under which the bidder names and pays the bond counsel, e.g., some local governments in Oklahoma.

Participation by Regular Counsel

The question often arises as to whether the regular legal counsel of the issuer should receive extraordinary compensation for services in relation to the issuance of bonds. No universal rule can be stated. If the transactions involved in the issuance are more or less routine, no special compensation should be payable—even though these may involve work by the regular counsel. Normally, the regular fee for representing the issuer should embrace this work as well as other types of legal work. On the other hand, where the issuance of debt involves the expenditure of a substantial amount of time by the regular counsel, either additional fees or the engagement of additional personnel appears warranted. The ground rules should be established at the time the regular counsel is employed.

Underwriter's Counsel

The matter of counsel for the underwriter is not a responsibility of the issuer. Yet, in competitive bond sales, the issuer is confronted with the necessity of proceeding with the preparation of the preliminary official statement, including the disclosure materials. To do so without the involvement of counsel for the potential underwriters is to invite the possibility of difficult problems of development of a disclosure statement between the sale and settlement dates. Moreover, it is to the advantage of the issuer and underwriter to have a comprehensive preliminary statement available during the sales period. Accordingly, it is frequently advisable for the issuer to take the initiative with the known syndicates likely to submit bids with the objective of naming an underwriter's counsel to participate in the preparation of the disclosure statement. This may result in attendance of several different counsel, one for each potential bidder, or, of a single counsel acceptable to all of the potential bidding syndicates—a procedure that simplifies preparation of the disclosure statement.

OTHER SPECIALIZED SERVICES

Beyond the financial advisor and bond counsel, the issuer will require additional specialized services—with the amounts and types depending upon the circumstances. Thus, in the case of governmental enterprise debt, a consultant is needed to prepare the feasibility report. In all cases, there is a need for a bond printer and a paying agent (except where the issuer is paying agent). In some circumstances, the issuer may expand the responsibilities of the commercial bank to the point that it becomes the fiscal agent of the issuer. In many revenue bonds, especially those issued under indenture, there is need for a trustee to perform certain responsibilities directed largely to the benefit of the investor—even though the trustee is named by the issuer at the outset.

The Fiscal Agent and Paying Agent

The paying agent acts in the limited capacity indicated by the title; the fiscal agent performs a larger role, including some, or all, of the following functions:

1. Representing the issuer at delivery of the bonds
2. Making timely payment of interest and principal from funds provided by the issuer
3. Providing replacement bonds for those lost or destroyed
4. Registering bonds and making exchange for bearer bonds as required
5. Maintaining basic records concerning coupons and bonds that have been paid
6. Cancelling paid bonds and coupons
7. Safekeeping duplicate or blank bonds

      8. Supervising the cremation of cancelled bonds and coupons

      9. Processing routine correspondence and inquiries concerning outstanding bonds

   10. Performing other responsibilities required to enable the issuer to avoid direct handling of many of the routine transactions

In the New England states, the fiscal agent also authenticates the bonds by certifying that the signatures are valid, thereby providing a guarantee against forgery and counterfeiting. Also, as noted earlier, New England banks sometimes provide some, or all, of the fiscal advisory functions to the issuer. Relatively few governments have assigned the full range of these responsibilities to the fiscal agent, except where the fiscal agent is also the trustee.

Historically, in many governments, the treasurer has been the paying agent. Today, one finds fewer governments which vest these responsibilities in officers of the government; the trend has been toward performance of many of these functions by a designated corporate fiscal agent. Still more recently, some issuers allow the successful bidder to designate either the paying agent or copaying agent. There has also been a tendency to provide for at least the copaying agent in one of the major financial centers to facilitate the timely processing of payments.

Agreement with Fiscal Agent. When a fiscal agent or paying agent is designated, the designation should be by written contract defining the functions and relationships. Of major importance are: Time for remission of funds to the agent; arrangements for investment of temporary balances for the account of the issuer; fees payable; accounting to be provided; and any other aspects of the undertaking.

Preparation of the Bonds

The issuer is expected to supply bonds and notes in a form providing a high degree of protection against counterfeiting or alteration. Inasmuch as bonds and notes are bearer instruments, they are fully negotiable. Ordinarily, the bonds are printed from engraved plates containing designs that are difficult to duplicate, and with special papers and ink for added protection. Modern methods of photographic reproduction make it increasingly difficult to protect fully against counterfeiting. However, the issuer should select a firm noted for its reliability in bond printing to afford maximum protection. Modern signature machines have robbed the process of the manual signature of much of the protection it previously afforded.

Chapter 10
AUTHORIZATIONS AND LIMITATIONS

An indispensable prerequisite to successful marketing of debt is an authorization conforming in all respects to the provisions of law. Without certification of such compliance by bond counsel, investors will not accept delivery of the bonds. Although the law differs from state to state, each bond issue must have a specific authorization, usually by the governing body of the issuer. It may also require electoral approval, and, in the case of local governments in some states, it may require approval of a state officer, board, or commission. The instrument authorizing the bonds is variously designated as a law, ordinance, resolution, or local law; however, within municipal bond circles, such an instrument is referred to simply as the *bond resolution*.

General obligation bond resolutions are frequently required to be submitted to the electorate for approval. Until recently, at least one state required that such approval be limited to property taxpayers and that the majority was not only the number of taxpayers but also a majority of the assessed value voted by such property taxpayers. In some jurisdictions, revenue bonds are required to be approved by the voters; however, the general pattern is to permit the governing authority to authorize revenue bonds without reference to a voter referendum, except where such local ordinances are subject to referendum in response to popular petition.

The first substantial hurdle in adopting the bond resolution is the legal limit upon the amount of debt that may exist at any given time.[1]

Bond resolutions constitute the basic authority to borrow. They specify the purposes for which the moneys are to be used either in general or specific terms. The bond resolution can constitute the appropriation for the purposes and/or projects in the amounts specified, or it may leave the appropriation to a subsequent action. Bond resolutions sometimes require that proceeds of each bond issue be kept segregated in separate bank accounts. Some fail to authorize investment of balances temporarily held, thereby permitting free use by depositary banks. Few provide the degree of flexibility in money management essential for best results, e.g., the use of consolidated bond funds or consolidated cash accounts. These and numerous other aspects of debt administration are controlled in varying degree by the bond resolution; however, some debt administrators do not comprehend the extent to which a bond resolution can control their future actions. A more or less automatic reenactment of policies established at some previous time under quite different conditions provides an inadequate basis for current actions.

Timing of Bond Authorizations

The timing of authorizations for general obligation bonds is influenced by such factors as the term of the administration in office; the availability of borrowing margin within

---

[1] A frequent pattern is to include as "existing debt" all outstanding debt plus authorized but unissued debt, reduced by the amount of recognized debt offsets—usually consisting of some combination of sinking funds, debt service reserve funds, self-sustaining debt, and debt to be retired from appropriations already made for the current fiscal year.

debt limits; the regular election calendar; the status of plans for construction; and the urgency of the need for authorizations against which the commitments required to complete a project can be made.

The time left to the administration in office has a major impact on bond authorizations. For officials who have just taken office there is usually a need to deliver on political commitments made in the course of their election campaigns. The officials are anxious to get on with the execution of these programs. As a result, the largest bond authorizations are likely to be sought during the first year of the term of the newly elected officials. Occasionally, large authorizations are also sought near the end of the term in the hope of awarding contracts for projects which will then have to be built—even if during the succeeding term of elected officers.

In those cases in which bond authorizations must be approved by the electorate, attention to the calendar of regularly scheduled elections during the term of the administration is necessary. Although the administration may have the authority to call special elections, the cost of conducting such elections is significant and most administrations will wish to avoid the special election process. In like manner, officials may prefer to offer bond proposals in elections in which the bond proposals are not likely to become issues insofar as candidates are concerned.

The availability of borrowing margin for debt controlled by debt limits is critical. Frequently, the slow rate of increase in assessments has resulted in marked strain on debt limits—to the point that the issuer is obliged to plan the timing of authorizations carefully to assure that they will fall within the debt limits prescribed.

The status of plans in relation to bond authorization is critical. If the bond resolution is offered before completion of the plans, it can become the financial envelope into which the project design must fit. If the envelope is too small, the project may be contorted. Conversely, if one awaits the completion of the plans before securing authorization, significant delay may occur in commencement of the undertaking.

CONTENT OF THE BOND RESOLUTION

The primary function of the bond resolution is to authorize the creation of debt. However, within the limits permitted by state constitutions and laws, the content of the bond resolution is left largely to the governing body of the issuer. Once the bond resolution is adopted in final form, it becomes the embodiment of the policy decisions for the bonds to be issued. Among the matters that can be covered in the bond resolution are:

1. The scope of expenditures to be paid from the bond proceeds
2. The amount of the authorization
3. The breadth of the authorization
4. The basis for appropriation of bond proceeds
5. Features of the bonds to be issued
6. Conditions under which the bond sale is to be conducted
7. Management of the bond proceeds
8. Adjustments in allocation of proceeds and "sunset" provisions

In other words, the bond resolution provides a basic framework within which bonds are to be issued and proceeds applied—subject only to superior constitutional, statutory, or charter provisions.

Scope of the Bond Resolution

In planning the bond resolution, the first determination is that of the scope of the resolution in terms of the purposes to be comprehended. The scope of the bond resolution (or resolutions) will be affected by whether the resolution is subject to referendum or adopted solely upon the responsibility of the governing body. If the latter choice prevails, bond resolutions can be adopted over a period of time, with each covering those matters appropriate for action at the time. If the bond resolution requires voter approval, the planners are obliged to determine (1) the number of bond resolutions to be submitted at a given time and (2) the scope of each of the resolutions. Scope is related to the number of purposes and the grouping of purposes in each resolution. It is not concerned with the amount of the bonds to be authorized.

A critical aspect of decision making regarding the scope of a bond resolution or a family group of related resolution referenda is public and political attitudes toward the capital program and selected projects or functions to be financed under the resolution or family of resolutions. Thus, approvals for playgrounds, libraries, and recreation centers may be easy to secure; programs for stadia, housing of minorities, or opera houses may be controversial. Inasmuch as a number of different functional expenditures can be grouped within a single resolution, the debt planners must take into account the problems in securing voter approval.

The Amount of Authorization

A second major element in planning the bond resolution is the aggregate amount of bonds for which authorization is sought under the current resolution. If more than one resolution is to be presented either to the governing body or to the voters, a corollary consideration is the number of resolutions and the distribution of authorizations among the resolutions and referenda. One approach is to provide for the full group of authorizations in the same resolution; however, inasmuch as some of the purposes may be quite popular while others are controversial, it may be appropriate to arrange the loans in several different proposals. Morover, provisions of law or other considerations may make it desirable to split the authorizations into several packages. Among the factors involved are:

1. *Borrowing Margin.* Bond resolutions being planned for approval at a given election must take into account the availability of unused borrowing margin comprehended by the debt limit. If there is little available borrowing margin, only partial financing of some projects can be provided at present—with the remainder to be provided at subsequent times. The examination of the available borrowing margin should extend not only to the immediate situation but also should involve projections for the next several years in relation to probable needs.

Although it may be desirable to provide full financing for major projects before these are commenced, this may not be feasible due to borrowing capacity limitations. Current authorizations may have to be restricted to the amounts necessary to provide financing for the current period, with supplemental authorizations to come at later times. The current resolutions will have to provide ongoing financing to bring to successful conclusion projects already under construction.

2. *The Aggregate Size.* Voters are sometimes overwhelmed by very large authorizations at a single election. A careful examination of probable editorial and political support and opposition needs to be made before a decision is made to ask for record- or near record-sized authorization packages.

3. *Stockpiling Authorizations.* The stockpiling of authorizations is frequently sought by administrations in order that they can have great flexibility as to which projects will be advanced at a given time. Although such large unused authorizations may provide comfort to the administration, they may constitute a source of major concern to credit analysts and investors. Generally, it is not advisable to ask for authorizations several years in advance of the time at which they will be required. Moreover, unused authorizations preempt elements of borrowing capacity that may be needed for other projects. It becomes awkward to be unable to proceed with authorized projects and, at the same time, be

unable to secure authorization for new high priority projects because of the stockpiled authorizations.

Breadth of Authorizations

The breadth of bond authorizations is a major determinant of the extent to which the bond authorization may be viewed as a source of financing for a comprehensive capital programming and capital budgeting process vis-à-vis a situation in which the act of authorization becomes tantamount to the capital budgeting process. The question is whether the bond authorization process will minutely determine the use of the proceeds or will leave this to a more comprehensive capital programming and capital budgeting process.

Generally, political leadership is reluctant to submit to the electorate debt proposals that do not contain basic allocations of the proposed bond proceeds. In some cases, detailed and ironclad determinations have been considered necessary to obtain approval at the polls. One of the difficulties in making explicit determinations derives from the fact that plans have not developed to finality prior to electoral action. Therefore, the definitive amounts either force the project to be finally planned and executed within an arbitrary authorization envelope or force the officials to return for subsequent supplemental authorizations to complete the undertaking. The narrow authorization either leaves various portions of the original authorizations unused or offers a challenge to administrators to find ways to exhaust the funds in order that they not be "lost."

A number of communities have substituted fairly broad purpose designations by categories, e.g., health, recreation, libraries, or streets, and have coupled these with tandem bond authorizations for the same general categories. Thereupon, a given project may be financed in part from the 198x authorization and the remainder from portions of the 198y and 198z authorizations. A variation is to provide general categories of expense but provide unused amounts that may be distributed by the governing authority among the other categories contained in the same authorization.

The analogy between the bond authorization and the revenue ordinance is again appropriate. The revenue ordinance makes available a given number of dollars in support of the operating budget—regardless of the purposes to which these dollars are apportioned. Broad scale bond resolutions come closer to this approach by providing a given number of dollars in support of the capital budget process, leaving determination as to detailed purpose and project to the capital budget processes.

Appropriation of Bond Proceeds

Generally, the bond resolution constitutes a legal authorization for executive officials to incur debt within the limits prescribed in the resolution. The authorization may constitute an appropriation[2] or it may (as in the case of the congressional authorization process) stop short of that step. The difference is subtle but important to both the governing body and the administration. The critical issue is whether the bond resolution constitutes:

1. Solely an authorization to borrow for the purposes indicated, or
2. An authorization to borrow plus an appropriation for the projects involved

If the former, a subsequent appropriation is required before obligations can be incurred or expenditures made. The decision between the alternative methods constitutes an important determinant insofar as the character of the capital program and capital budget procedures are concerned.

---

[2] The MFOA in *Governmental Accounting, Auditing, and Financial Reporting* (1980), Appendix B, p. 55, defines appropriation as "An authorization granted by a legislative body to make expenditures and to incur obligations for specific purposes."

The Capital Budget Approach. For jurisdictions wishing to make the formal capital programming and capital budgeting processes effective, the capital budget should become the sole means of capital appropriations. The bond authorization is thereby viewed as analogous to revenue in the operating budget. It constitutes a source of funding that is not tied to explicit appropriations. For those governments pursuing this pattern, the separation of the sources of funding from the projects being funded is reminiscent of the development in operating budgeting in which the large number of dedicated funds and narrow tax levies of a half-century ago gave way to more flexible and effective contemporary practices. These governments have developed this process to the point that the authorization of a bond issue is construed as an important general step in the funding for a capital budget.

As governments increase in size and complexity, it becomes increasingly difficult to specify in detail each of the myriad projects which together make up the community's capital program. Thus, whereas a small unit of government may find it appropriate to identify the reconstruction of a four-block section of a sewer as a capital project, in larger jurisdictions the capital program and capital budget would become unmanageable in size and complexity should such a level of detail be included. Moreover, in periods of marked increase of capital funds from senior governments and the high rates of inflation, it became more difficult accurately to estimate the costs of many projects as well as the shares of financing likely to be available from the different funding sources.

It is the view of this author that, for governments with reasonably good capital programming and capital budgeting processes, the various bond authorizations should be viewed as elements of financing for the capital budget—in much the same manner as the sales tax, the parking lot tax, the parking meter charges, fines and fees, and earnings on cash balances in operating funds are considered as parts of the general revenue package needed to balance a general expenditures program.

Features of the Bond Issue

Within the limit of the powers of the governing authority, the features of the bonds to be sold are largely predetermined by the terms of the resolution. The bond resolution becomes the vehicle by which the issuer expresses debt policies. Having made such a determination in the bond resolution, the governing authority is impotent to adjust the features specified in the resolution, especially in those cases in which the authorization process includes action by the electorate. Under these circumstances, the debt manager and all others concerned with debt administration will wish to review carefully each aspect of the bond resolution prior to final action by the governing body to assure that the features prescribed are in harmony with agreed policy.

Regulating the Bond Sale

The bond resolution can control various aspects of the bond sale, e.g., maximum and minimum coupon rates, maximum effective interest rates, basis of determining the best bid, time of the sale, type of sale to be conducted, and the date of the bonds. Once again, the debt manager and others concerned should review each aspect of the bond resolution governing elements of the bond sale that are within the discretion of the governing authority.

Management of Bond Proceeds

In many jurisdictions, the bonds must be sold before contracts can be executed for the work to be financed from bond proceeds. In such cases, long periods of time are likely to elapse between the time the money is borrowed and disbursed. Subject to statutory

requirements, the bond resolution can contain provisions regulating elements of the management of bond proceeds pending disbursement. Most of these problems are discussed in
Chapter 8 as a part of the policies relating to short-term debt. The extent to which the
fund managers can effectively manage the proceeds of the bond issue is largely contingent
upon the provisions of law and the bond resolution governing deposit, investment, interfund
loans, consolidated bond funds, and consolidated cash accounts.

Adjustment in Allocations and "Sunset" Provisions

It is rarely possible to execute plans for financing capital programs and capital budgets
precisely as contemplated in the authorization. If the resolution permits reasonable latitude
in adjusting allocations, the governing authority can administer the bond authorizations
within the substantive intent of the bond resolution and, at the same time, avoid problems
arising from rigid resolution provisions.

Under the broader type of authorization, the debt manager has the authority to allocate
the proceeds of various bond issues to provide financing for appropriations comprehended
by the purpose clauses of the resolution. Alternatively, the bond resolution should permit
the governing body to adjust allocations in a manner consistent with the purposes comprehended by the resolution. This can be accomplished by inclusion of a provision under
which the governing body can reallocate proceeds found unnecessary for any of the enumer-
ated purposes to one or more other purposes comprehended by the resolution.

There is a final point: The "sunset" provisions. Frequently, times change sufficiently
that the original intent cannot be carried out. The bond resolution should authorize the
governing body to cancel unneeded portions of authorizations and to dispose of unneeded
cash balances from bond sales.

DEBT LIMITATIONS

The pattern of limitations of the amounts of debt of the state governments themselves
and of their local governments varies from state to state and among different kinds of
local governments in most states.

Limitations on the States

The most recent comprehensive data concerning such limitations is that prepared by
ACIR (Advisory Commission on Intergovernmental Relations) as of 1976.[3] It was found
that 11 states[4] imposed no limits upon the legislatures as to the amount of debt to be
authorized; however, in most of these, extraordinary majorities in each house of the legislature were required to authorize debt. Of the states that imposed limitations, eleven required
a referendum to create any debt beyond nominal amounts[5] and fifteen required referenda
when debt authorizations exceeded amounts stipulated in the constitutions of the individual
states.[6] Seventeen of the states imposing limitations in some manner permitted the issuance
of refunding bonds without further voter action.

These limitations were directed to "debt of the state." In many states, various kinds

---

[3] Advisory Commission on Intergovernmental Relations, *Significant Features of Fiscal Federalism: 1976–
77 Edition, Volume II—Revenues and Debt,* pp. 82–96.

[4] Connecticut, Delaware, Illinois, Louisiana, Maryland, Massachusetts, Minnesota, Montana, New Hampshire, Tennessee, and Vermont.

[5] Alabama, Alaska, Florida, Illinois (alternate to three-fourths majority), Michigan, New York, Oklahoma,
Pennsylvania, South Carolina, Virginia, and Washington.

[6] California, Colorado, Idaho, Iowa, Kansas, Kentucky, Louisiana, Maine, Missouri, New Jersey, New
Mexico, North Carolina, Rhode Island, Washington, and Wyoming.

of agency and authority debt have been construed not to be "debt of the state" and, in that sense, not subject to the constitutional limitations.

Limitations on Local Governments

The 1976 ACIR study showed a widely different pattern of constitutional limitations on the general obligation debt of local governments. There was variation both from state to state and among different types of jurisdictions within many of the states. Four states (Alaska, Florida, Nebraska, and Tennessee) imposed no limitations as to the amount of such debt, although referenda were required in three of them.

In most of the states, constitutional limits were expressed in terms of percentages of assessed value of taxable real property. The assessment base used was the local assessed value in some cases, state-equalized value or market value in others. Three states (Connecticut, Hawaii, and Indiana) had no constitutional requirements for referenda; five (Massachusetts, New Jersey, New York, Tennessee, and Washington) required referenda only under designated circumstances. For those requiring referenda, a simple majority was required in 32 states, with the others imposing extraordinary majorities.

It is emphasized that these are *constitutional* limitations only. Many states imposed additional limitations by *statute*. Moreover, these limitations relate only to general obligation debt of the local governments. A study of the constitutional provisions relating to nonguaranteed debt would doubtless reveal a much different pattern.

A different pattern of statutory limitations is revealed in a study of *The Weekly Bond Buyer*.[7] As of the close of 1981 it found that no rate limitations were imposed upon either state or local governments in 16 states:

Arizona	Massachusetts	Pennsylvania
Connecticut	Montana	Rhode Island
Indiana	New Jersey	Utah
Kentucky	New York	Vermont
Louisiana	North Dakota	Virginia
		Wisconsin

At the same time it found limitations for only a few elements of debt in five states:

Colorado	local agency debt
Georgia	local agency and local revenue debt
Nebraska	urban renewal notes
New Hampshire	urban renewal and housing notes
North Carolina	local obligation debt

In other states that imposed limitations the practices varied widely. In some cases limitations were imposed on an overall basis, e.g., Tennessee at 18 percent.

---

[7] John McCorry, "25 States Change Caps on Debt Interest in '81," *The Weekly Bond Buyer,* Vol. 227, No. 4631 (January 18, 1982), p. 8.

Chapter 11
SCHEDULING DEBT ISSUANCE AND REPAYMENT

Capital programs must be developed within the constraints of debt policy. The policy may be a well-defined one that is set forth in law and statements adopted by the issuer. Or, it may be little more than reacting to the pressures of the moment. If the policy is not defined, the capital program and the capital budget[1] become the vehicles for control of important elements of debt policy.

DEFINING CAPITAL COSTS

From an accounting point of view, capital costs are usually defined in very broad terms, e.g., the MFOA definition:

Expenditures which result in the acquisition or addition to fixed assets.[2]

Unfortunately, many who deal with capital costs fail to apply the definition as intended. As a result many of the costs are either omitted or understated in the capital accounts. As applied to the acquisition of a facility, e.g., a highway bridge, they include all outlays relating to preliminary planning, engineering, site acquisition, construction, insurance, use of equipment, temporary use of property to facilitate construction (even though not permanently a part of the site), protective services specially required on site (including inspection), preparation for opening, and general administrative expenses. In the latter category are many of the central services of the governmental entity that are frequently paid from the operating budget without reference to the source of the funds for financing them.

One of the principal elements of capital outlays frequently overlooked in the statement of the cost consists of financing prior to opening date. Private enterprise takes care to capitalize these financing costs and usually to capitalize much of the other expense that may be paid from the operating budget in the case of governments. Capital programs and capital budgets are consequently frequently understated.

A further effect, especially for those costs payable from general obligation bonds associated with nonenterprise projects, is markedly to understate the degree of "pay-as-you-acquire" in the course of financing the project. This is emphasized by the considerations brought out in Table 27 which compares the outlays under two alternatives:

I. A financing of a highway bridge where the entire costs are paid from the proceeds of bonds, with funds during construction being provided by the sale of BANS

II. A financing under a combination of general obligation bonds issued at the beginning of the construction period, contributions in various forms from the current revenues of the issuer, and expenses borne through the use of property for the benefit of the project

---

[1] There are always capital programs and capital budgets. They may be produced through a highly formalized process or they may be developed through a series of informal, uncoordinated actions. Compositely they constitute the capital program and capital budget of the governmental unit until a change is made.

[2] MFOA, *Governmental Accounting, Auditing, and Financial Reporting* (1980), Appendix B, p. 57.

The best comparison between the two approaches is to determine the difference in the aggregate outstanding debt plus contributions to opening date taken from data in Table 27:

		(in thousands of dollars)		
		I	II	(I) − (II)
A.	Outstanding debt	16,645	12,375	4,270
B.	Use of property	—	450	(450)
C.	Use of revenues			
	1. For direct expenses	—	1,175	(1,175)
	2. For payment of interest [$4,853,000 paid less $3,248,000 earned]	—	1,605	(1,605)
	3. Principal paid	—	630	(630)
D.	Imputed interest [$96,000 + $1,013,000 + $588,000]	—	1,697	(1,697)
	Total	16,645*	17,932	(1,287)

* Inasmuch as there was no imputed interest or actual interest paid from revenues prior to opening date transactions in Col. 1, lines 12–21 of Table 27 are recorded in net total.

From the foregoing it is apparent that under the postulated circumstances the use of the full financing approach produces an advantage of almost $1.3 million. This, however, is not the principal purpose of this illustration. Rather, the purposes are:

1. To demonstrate the degree of "pay-as-you-acquire" which is likely to be present under a combined financing alternative
2. To demonstrate that analyses of this type are important in order to comprehend the values which may be involved in the choice between alternative methods of financing.

As to the latter, it is unfortunately true that many officials and citizens who are interested in methods of financing fail to understand the full ramifications of the alternatives under consideration. There is a great likelihood of oversimplification of the combined financing method and to assume that the amount of outstanding debt as of opening date constitutes the *de facto* difference in results obtained—usually with little recognition of the costs which have been incurred in order to attain the differentials in outstanding debt.

Patrimony Considerations. All of this would constitute a contribution to the community patrimony as of opening date—before the community had any use of the facility for which the payments were being made. Therefore, the residents (or former residents) would have made an advance contribution to the project of about one-third of the costs required to bring the bridge to completion and to place it in operation. This constitutes a major form of "pay-as-you-acquire," although it is rarely recognized as such in general obligation financing.

This is further reflected in the fact that under Alternative I, the outstanding debt at opening of $16,645,000 means that the full costs are yet to be amortized—as compared to outstanding debt of $12,375,000 in general obligation bonds to be amortized.

From an economic accounting point of view, projects have both costs and benefits beyond the effects during the construction period. Although these will not be recorded in the patrimony accounts of the issuer—except to the degree that the issuer is obliged to compensate for damages—they should be taken into account in the development of the capital program. Both the benefits likely to be gained on a long-term basis and costs repre-

---

[3] The differences between the aggregate costs of $16,645,000 for I and the $17,932,000 for II derive largely from higher earnings on temporary balances under I; however, the result is also influenced by the fact that under II some of the heavy bond interest pertaining to the middle and later maturities is reflected during this period for that alternative.

Table 27

Comparative Statement of Costs for Highway Bridge Under
Alternative I: Full Debt Financing
Alternative II: Combined Debt, Current Revenue, and In-kind Financing

(amounts in thousands of dollars)

		Alternative I: Full Debt Financing	Alternative II:			
			Total	General Obligation Bonds	Current Revenues	Use of Property
		(1)	(2)	(3)	(4)	(5)
Direct Capital Acquisition Costs						
1	Preliminary planning	100	100	—	100	—
2	Site acquisition	1,150	1,150	1,000	—	150
3	Engineering	975	975	900	75	—
4	Rental of real property	150	150	—	—	150
5	Construction	10,030	10,030	10,030	—	—
6	Insurance	300	300	200	100	—
7	Equipment rental	700	700	550	—	150
8	Protective services	200	200	—	200	—
9	Preparation for opening	100	100	—	100	—
10	General administrative costs	600	600	—	600	—
11	Subtotal	14,305	14,305	12,680	1,175	450
Financing Costs						
12	BANS: Amount issued	23,000	—	—	—	—
13	Proceeds used for interest	8,280	—	—	—	—
14	Proceeds used for direct capital acquisition	14,305	—	—	—	—
15	Proceeds used for discount	345	—	—	—	—
16	Subtotal	22,930	—	—	—	—
17	Excess BANS proceeds	70	—	—	—	—
18	Interest earned on temporary investments	6,707	—	—	—	—
19	Net bond proceeds required	16,225		12,680	—	—
20	Bond discount	417	325	325		
21	Amount of bonds to be issued	16,645		13,005	—	—
Other Costs and Credits						
22	Interest paid on bonds to opening date	—	4,853	—	4,853	—
	Interest earnings foregone due to					
23	Advances to pay principal	—	96	—	96	—
24	Advances to pay interest	—	1,013	—	1,013	—
25	Advances to pay expenses	—	588	—	400	188
26	Subtotal (22) – (25)	—	6,550	—	6,362	188
27	Less interest earned on temporary investments	—	3,248	—	3,248	—
28	Net interest to opening date	—	3,302	—	3,114	188
29	Debt principal retirement to opening	—	—	(630)	630	—
30	Net to opening date	16,645	17,932	12,375	4,919	638

sented by economic disruption, e.g., taking of land or buildings belonging to employers in the community, are now understood to have potentially major, long-term economic consequences that require careful evaluation in reaching site decisions.

PLANNING CASH FLOWS FOR CAPITAL OPERATIONS

In Chapter 8 attention was focused on cash flow requirements with particular attention to operating funds; the focus here is upon cash flows in connection with the execution of capital budgets. In order to assure availability of cash in a timely manner, detailed cash flow estimates are required.

The cash requirements schedule can be on a project-by-project basis; or (in the case of larger governments operating under flexible cash management programs) it can be on a composite basis showing the aggregate disbursements for all of the projects during the period covered.

Whether prepared on a project or a composite basis, the schedule of probable cash outlays should be on a monthly basis. In certain critical periods, weekly or daily projections are appropriate. These can be developed from the architectural or engineering projections of the rates of expenditure for individual projects or from composite experience in financing entire capital programs. In the latter case, attention must be given to the impact of very large projects with expenditure rates different from the general mix of projects. Thus, if a major airport expansion or transit line extension is proceeding, it is necessary to make separate projections. Subsequently, these can be consolidated with the results from other projects to produce a useful composite.

In preparation of estimates of cash receipts, money should be identified as to both source and timing, for example:

1. Financing from operating funds
2. Temporary advances to capital funds from operating or other funds
3. Proceeds of bond issues previously sold
4. Cash contributions from other governments, either as general subventions for the project or in the form of contractual participation. (The schedule of expenditures should identify those elements of the project being carried out on a joint basis with other governments when the moneys are payable directly to contractors by others. Such participation needs to be noted against the possibility of delays or default by others that may impose risks upon this government in maintaining the viability of the project.)
5. Cash payments receivable from private persons in support of the project as contributions or assessments (The schedule of expenditures should take these into account as elements of cash flow.)
6. Proceeds from the sale or value arising from reassignment of any property to be released as a result of this project
7. Interest earned on temporary balances

Schedules of projected cash requirements should be reviewed monthly and revised at least quarterly. If the plan calls for operating with small cash balances, more frequent review and revision are in order.

Once the schedule reflecting these anticipated cash receipts is related to the projected cash requirements, the amounts and timing of any cash delinquencies will become apparent. At this juncture, a decision may be required in the case of project-by-project financing as to when the bonds required for this undertaking shall be issued. Project-by-project funding is frequently arranged under a schedule providing for simultaneous execution of the major contracts and the sale of the bonds. Under such schedules, it is usually necessary to provide for temporary financing for those expenses that have been incurred prior to the sale of the bonds. In some such ventures, the architects, engineers, and other consultants may have financed their own costs pending the sale of the bonds;[4] in others, the government may have to obtain temporary advances from other funds, negotiate temporary loans from commercial banks, or issue bond anticipation notes.

In any event, the money managers must decide when bond proceeds are expected and how temporary financing is to be arranged. The decision as to the date for sale of the bonds is one of when they will be sold in relation to requirements for cash. The government has three potential courses: (1) Full long-term financing in advance of making major expenditure commitments; (2) sequential sales timed to produce cash as the project proceeds; or (3) temporary loans in anticipation of the sale of the long-term securities. It is appropriate to consider these courses of action:

Early Permanent Funding

The major advantage of early permanent funding is that both the issuer and the contractors know that the moneys are in hand with which to meet obligations as they fall due; the issuer also knows the pattern of interest costs for the project are fixed. Moreover, there is no question of access at future dates when the financial markets may be disturbed and access difficult.

The early permanent funding requires sound management of cash balances arising from the sale of bonds. Depending on market conditions, the interest earned on the balances may be greater or less than the interest being paid on the long-term debt. Ordinarily, it is not difficult to make a small profit because of the spread between tax-free interest rates and the opportunities for short-term investment at taxable rates. However, it can become a problem when the yield curve has a high incidence or when general interest rate levels decline sharply after sale of the bonds.

Early issuance of general obligation bonds causes the time clock to begin to run in relation to time for interest and bond retirement payments. This results in accelerated payments from the operating budget but has the advantage of increasing available borrowing margin.

Sequential Sales

For some projects, e.g., a large power plant, it may not be appropriate to issue the full amount of bonds needed for the project as a single bond issue. To attempt to do so may overload the market, resulting in significantly higher interest costs over the life of the bonds. In such large projects, the issuer may prefer to schedule sales on a sequential basis in the hopes that the market will be able to absorb the debt being issued at more favorable rates. The use of sequential sales requires frequent reexamination in light of the progress of the project, the market conditions, and other demands for capital by the issuer. Such sales can be coupled with interim short-term financing or they can be planned in a manner that helps to avoid the use of interim financing.

Temporary Funding

Chapter 8 has discussed various aspects of short-term financing. The principal advantage lies in the ability of the issuer to accumulate costs, including interest during construction, before being obliged to fix the amount of the long-term bond issue. A second advantage, in many circumstances, is the deferment of any payments of principal and interest until

---

[4] Generally, such practice should be avoided as the carrying costs and risk costs are likely to be much higher than when payment is made currently.

the project has been completed and is in operation. This is of especial importance to revenue bond projects and is sometimes indispensable.

In the matter of deferment, some governments have used BANS in order to delay debt service on permanent financing as an operating budget cost—in some cases until several years after the completion of the project in order to secure the political advantages of use of the facility without being obliged to make current payments of debt service from operating funds.[5]

A further advantage of temporary financing is afforded by the fact that the interest rates on short-term loans are usually significantly below those payable on long-term financing. Hence, use of temporary financing may act to hold down the total cost of the undertaking. Moreover, it may afford a greater opportunity for arbitrage profits.

The principal disadvantage of heavy reliance on temporary financing lies in the uncertainty of the market in which long-term financing must be eventually arranged. Under normal access conditions, the issuer should be able to sell long-term bonds with relative ease or be able to roll-over short-term BANS as needed. However, in unfavorable markets this may become either difficult or virtually impossible. Moreover, the conversion of short-term debt to long-term debt may occur at times when long-term interest rates are much higher than at the outset of the project.

Multiple Project Financing

In a sense, the remarks above relate to the financing of independent projects; however, the same general considerations occur in multiple project financing. Assume that the government is carrying on a more or less level capital expenditure program at about $75 million per year and that, at any given time, the amount of unliquidated contracts is about $115 million. If the government pursues a policy of early funding involving three $25 million bond sales, such early sales could result in maintenance of balances in the range of $100–$125 million.

Alternatively, if the three $25 million sales were conducted only shortly in advance of the need for cash, the range of cash balances would probably be at the $10/40 million level. The net gain or loss between the two courses of action would be measured by the opportunity for arbitrage and the success with which it was pursued.

The principal advantages of maintenance of low balances are: (1) Existence of lower amounts of outstanding debt, (2) deferring the time at which principal repayment commences, and (3) avoidance of potential losses on short-term investments. The disadvantages are: (1) A dependency upon immediate access to the market, especially in periods of unsettled times or difficulty with this issue and (2) reduced possibility for arbitrage.

SIZE AND FREQUENCY OF BOND SALES

Although both size and frequency of bond sales influence the rates at which bonds may be marketed, little of a definitive nature is known as to the effect of either upon such rates. Expert opinion varies widely. The two concepts are usually interactive but they may operate independently.

The Size of Issues

Smaller and medium sized issues seem to sell more easily and at perhaps lower interest costs than larger issues. At the other extreme, dealers know that, in some situations, they

---

[5] This practice was widely followed by local governments in New Jersey in the 1960s. See *Report of the New Jersey Tax Policy Committee,* Part IV, "The Use and Costs of Public Credit," pp. 28–32.

cannot market the bonds because the issue proposed is too large for absorption and therefore beyond amounts underwriters are willing to accept as inventory. As a general rule, once the size of the issue has become sufficiently large to permit the development of an appropriate marketing effort, each significant increment of size is likely to increase the basic level of the yield curve if a sufficient number of investors are to be attracted. A factor frequently overlooked by issuers in this regard is the impact of state and local tax laws upon the marketability of the bonds of the state and its local governments. This is especially true if the size makes it necessary to sell large amounts outside the state of issue.

Sufficiency of Size. One of the factors in determining the attractiveness of size rests upon the need for large investors to have access to large blocks of bonds. The conventional serial bond issue of smaller size is not likely to provide a sufficient number of bonds in a given maturity range to be attractive to the very large investors. As a consequence, these investors may easily ignore the bonds of the issuer solely because they have become accustomed to purchases in blocks of a size beyond those available in most serial bond issues. Therefore, it behooves the issuer to make careful evaluation of the size of the bond issues being offered. There is no single size continually appropriate, even for a single issuer. The appropriateness of size is a professional judgment and should be related both to the issuer's needs and to market conditions.

Frequency of Sales

Many believe that the market functions best for the issuer when sales are at intervals of not less than six months. Annual sales of bonds with identical security are preferable unless the size of the issue becomes so great that market absorption becomes a problem. Municipal bonds are marketed, in part, on the basis of the psychological factor of scarcity. Many salesmen emphasize the need to purchase now inasmuch as there will be no opportunity in the near future for purchase of these bonds. When the next bond sale is only a short time away, this factor is removed, or reduced, as a marketing consideration. Continual availability of bonds in the primary market may also adversely affect the price for bonds in both the primary and the secondary markets.

In planning bond sale programs, it is desirable to develop tentative sale schedules for two or three years in advance in order to provide a framework for other decisions. Where comprehensive capital programming is being done, tentative bond sale schedules should take into account the amounts reflected in the capital program. A compromise between the ideal size of issues and the frequency of issues is required to secure the best market reception of such issues. In periods of tight money supply, variations on the theme will be necessary. When each sale of a series is announced, it is advisable to state the period, e.g., 90 days or 180 days, that is expected to intervene before the next sale.

AVAILABLE DEBT RETIREMENT PATTERNS

The patterns for retirement of debt may, for purposes of this discussion, be grouped under the following general headings:

1. Serial bonds
    a. Fixed retirement schedules
        (1) Equal annual maturity
        (2) Equal annual debt service
        (3) Irregular maturity patterns
    b. Contingent mandatory accelerated maturity of portions of bonds
    c. Optional accelerated maturity of all or portions of the debt

2. Serial bonds coupled with *block-term* bonds
   a. Mandatory accelerated retirement of portions of *block-term* bonds
   b. Payment of *block-term* bonds at their stated maturity date
3. Term bonds
   a. Retirement at maturity date
      (1) From sinking funds accumulated on a mandatory basis
      (2) From general assets or proceeds of roll-over bonds
   b. Mandatory accelerated retirement
   c. Optional accelerated retirement

The choice of the pattern or combination of patterns to be used in the administration of the debt of any issuer involves a major professional and technical marketing judgment on behalf of the issuer. This in turn should be based upon a comprehensive understanding of the impact of the decision on the cost of the money being borrowed. No issuer should be obliged uniformly to conform to a single pattern for retirement of bonds. Such rigid requirements are, however, frequently written into state laws or into outstanding bond contracts. They should be eliminated.

On the other hand, issuers who enjoy a wide range of discretion in planning of their debt must be fully advised concerning the cost implications of the various alternatives. Otherwise, very expensive decisions may be made on the basis of ignorance and blind following of preexisting patterns.

First, by way of definition of the alternatives:

The Equal Annual Maturity Serial Bond. The equal annual maturity bond is one under which the issuer is obliged to retire an equal, or approximately equal, amount of principal during each year of the life of the bonds, usually commencing with a date approximately one year from date of issue but sometimes with deferment of the initial maturity for two or more years from date of issue.

The Equal Annual Debt Service Serial Bond. The serial bond under which maturities are scheduled in a manner that the sum of the principal and interest requirements during each year of the life of the bond issue are approximately the same is known as an equal annual debt service bond.

The Irregular Maturity Serial Bond Issue. Occasionally, serial bond issues are sold under which there is an irregular maturity pattern. This may be to rearrange the aggregate debt service schedule for the issuer or it may be geared to anticipated patterns of projected net revenues which are to be available for payment of interest upon, and eventual maturity of, the debt.

Contingent Mandatory Acceleration of Serial Bonds. Many bond issues, especially governmental lessee bonds and *on behalf of* bonds carry with them provision for excess coverage and a requirement that under specified circumstances all or portions of such excess be used to accelerate the maturity of portions of the serial debt. The content of this provision is of major importance to the issuer and may be of major importance to individual investors. Thus, from the standpoint of the issuer it is desirable to maintain substantial flexibility in the manner in which the bonds to be retired are acquired. If the issuer is limited to calling the bonds and to calling them in inverse order, such issuer is deprived of the opportunities which may exist in purchase of bonds in the open market or through tenders at prices more favorable than those afforded by mandatory call. Generally it is advisable to retain all three options—as well as that of continuing to accumulate moneys in the reserve funds where this is profitable.

Optional Acceleration of Maturity of Serial Bonds. Under some bond contracts the issuer retains the right to use portions of the excess revenues and/or reserve funds in which to acquire portions of the bonds on an optional basis for the purpose of cancelling them. From the standpoint of the issuer such flexibility is desirable; however, from the standpoint of the investor whose bonds are not acquired such flexibility may act against him in due course. Thus, if in the 10th to 12th year the issuer uses portions of reserve funds to acquire bonds it is true that the debt is reduced; however, should the issuer encounter difficulties in meeting ordinary debt service requirements in year 15–17, the fact that some bonds have already been retired in advance of maturity may constitute little comfort to the holders of the bonds still outstanding.

Serial/Block-Term Bonds. A serial bond issue in which portions of what would constitute the normal serial pattern of maturities are grouped into a single maturity is designated by this author as serial bonds with *block-term* features. Thus, the bonds normally maturing during the 16th through the 20th years may be grouped into a single "term" maturity in the 20th year. Usually, this is accompanied by a provision under which the issuer is obliged to call a portion of the bonds in advance of their scheduled maturity date. Thus, during each of the years 16–19, acceleration of payment of portions of the 20-year *block-term* bonds thereby leaves for redemption on the 20th anniversary only the amount of bonds that would have been scheduled for retirement at that time under the normal serial schedule. Accelerated payment of *block-term* bonds may be by lot, open market purchase, or tender. [Alternatively, a few bond contracts give the issuer the option of calling the bonds in advance of such *block-term* maturity date or of accumulation of a sinking fund for their payment on their scheduled formal maturity date.] This type of bond is usually issued when there is a significant incidence to the yield curve and use of the yield/coupon rate for the 20th maturity increases the cost to the issuer and attractiveness to the investor.

Mandatory Sinking Fund Term Bonds. All bonds in a term bond issue carry the same maturity date. Traditionally, municipal term bond contracts provide for mandatory accumulation of a sinking fund through periodic contributions. The amounts of these periodic contributions were established and, from time to time, modified under sinking fund accumulation tables designed to produce at maturity date deposits and accumulated earnings equal to that required to "sink" the debt.

Non-Mandatory Sinking Fund Bonds. In private corporate practice it is not customary for the issuer to accumulate a sinking fund for retirement of term-bonded debt. Rather, the expectation is that the debt will either be rolled over through the issuance of a new bond issue or retired from treasury cash if financial conditions are appropriate.

Mandatory Accelerated Retirement Term Bonds. Certain types of enterprise debt (especially the toll road bonds) are associated with projects having variable annual income from use of the facility. The bonds are likely to be issued in the form of term bonds but with a requirement that all or designated portions of the net revenues (after provision for payment of interest on the debt) be used to accelerate retirement of portions of the debt. Ordinarily, the issuer has the option of purchase of the debt in the general market, acquisition from tenders made by bondholders, or (failing acquisition of sufficient bonds from these sources) call by lot from among the outstanding bonds.

Optional Accelerated Retirement. Any of the foregoing patterns can be coupled with various optional call rights of the issuer under which portions or all of the debt may be retired in advance of the scheduled maturity date. Such options must be included in the bond contract at the time the debt is issued.

SELECTING THE DEBT RETIREMENT PATTERN

Within the limits imposed by law, the choice of a pattern for retirement of the debt will depend largely upon combinations of these factors:

1. The life of the facility
2. Concepts of economic rental and patrimony accumulation

3. Net revenues available to secure revenue bonds
4. Economic development prospects
5. Prevailing reoffering yield curve and level to be applied to this bond issue
6. Desired pattern of regeneration of borrowing capacity
7. Operating and maintenance costs and the costs of programs to be conducted in conjunction with the facility
8. The potentiality for arbitrage

The Life of the Facility

A critical determinant of the maximum period for amortization of debt relating to a facility is the time at which its useful life is expected to be exhausted. The law frequently imposes upon some official the responsibility for certifying that the financing period for the facility is within the expected life of the facility. These certifications are usually made with only limited attention to the economic realities involved. Thus, the life of several new buildings may be set at 50 years with only the most superficial attention to differential characteristics that help to determine the period of probable usefulness of each. Even with the most careful assessment of factors, determination of the probable life is fraught with many potential pitfalls when one considers these matters:

1. *Structural Characteristics.* Absent fire, wind, water, earthquake, and electrolytic action or intentional damage to a property in war or civil conflict, some reasonably maintained structures are likely to have a structural life of several hundreds of years. A lack of care in operation and maintenance, especially that required to prevent the adverse effects of moisture and frost, can greatly reduce the potential life.

2. *Obsolescence.* The design of a facility has a significant impact upon its useful life. Thus, the Brooklyn Bridge has sufficient width that as the width of vehicles using the bridge has changed, the utility of the bridge has continued at a high level. In contrast, the highway portion of the Huey P. Long Bridge above New Orleans constructed in the 1930s is now hazardous because of the narrow traffic lanes. Likewise, buildings for educational and other purposes can be designed in such a manner that their utility is largely depleted decades before structural requirements indicate abandonment. The question is one of functional obsolescence.

3. *Need.* Among the more difficult elements to assess are the wide swings in need for particular structures. Thus, as birth rates increase or decrease, one finds a shortage or surplus of classrooms. As population shifts or changes its composition, facilities that are still structurally sound and functionally acceptable are retired from use because of lack of demand.

4. *Operation.* Physical facilities respond to the intensity of use and the quality of operation just as do motor vehicles. A careful and sensitive operator of a motor vehicle gets thousands of added hours of satisfactory operation beyond those available to the abusive operator. Likewise, a fixed asset facility responds to care or abuse.

5. *Maintenance.* Without a comprehensive and effective maintenance program, most facilities deteriorate at a rapid rate, especially if roof, walls, and windows are not kept in order. Full maintenance keeps the facility in a condition that will not materially reduce its utility on this account.

6. *Rehabilitation.* Given the changes in technology as well as the inability of routine maintenance to cover all facets of a structure, the time comes in which basic rehabilitation and modernization are required if the structure is not to be either effectively written off or dropped to a much lower class of operation. Changes in lighting, heating, air conditioning, vertical passenger movement and other factors are involved. Many office buildings constructed in the 1920s that have been well-maintained and, from time to time, appropriately rehabilitated are still very useful structures. Others built at later dates are downgraded or ready for demolition.

Economic Rental

The general concepts of economic rental have been discussed in Chapter 7. No fully sound policy for amortization of the debt created in the acquisition of a facility can be developed without taking into consideration other aspects of economic rental incident to the occupancy or use of a facility. The principal components of economic rental for facilities owned by governments are:

1. Depreciation and obsolescence
2. Interest
3. Operating and insurance costs
4. Maintenance (including development of reserves for, or amortization of, deferred maintenance and rehabilitation)

Concepts of economic rental should be carefully differentiated from concepts of acquisition or liquidation of patrimony—a subject discussed later in this chapter. Although there are almost endless complications in the development of sound estimates of the economic rental to be applied to each individual year, a reasonably accurate set of estimates can be prepared to fit a given set of circumstances. Generally, such estimates initially assume a zero inflation rate; these can subsequently be adjusted to current purchasing power of the dollar.

To illustrate costs involved and selected potential patterns of debt liquidation, Tables 28 and 29 have been developed, using interest rates reflected in Pattern C of Appendix Table A. These tables show financing for an office building constructed by an authority that leases the building at rates sufficient to provide for operation, maintenance (including rehabilitation, as required), and amortization of the debt. Several patterns are used in the illustrations. These are based on yield/coupon rates shown in Appendix Table A and may be summarized as follows:

Pattern C: Liquidation of debt over a period of 100 years from net rentals
Pattern C-1:   Liquidation of debt over a period of 50 years from net rentals which have been increased modestly to permit accelerated amortization
Pattern C-2:   Liquidation of debt over a 50-year period in equal annual principal installments
Pattern C-3:   Liquidation of debt over a 50-year period with equal annual debt service

Table 28 is the basic table. It shows the gross rental, amounts provided for (1) operation, (2) maintenance, and (3) debt service. The assumptions involved in the development of Table 28 may be summarized as follows:

1. A gross rental of $1,000,000 per year plus a small net auxiliary income ($551 per year) during the first 10 years in the 100-year amortization. Thereafter, the rental decreases on a gradual basis to about $900,000 in the 20th year, $656,000 in the 50th year, $590,000 in the 75th year, and $533,000 in the final (100th) year.
2. Costs of operation commence at $125,000 per year and increase at an annual compound rate until reaching the level of $250,000 in the 50th year, which level is maintained during the second 50 years.
3. Maintenance and rehabilitation expenses are paid from a reserve into which $25,000 is placed in the first year and which is increased gradually to $225,000 in the 40th year. Thereafter, the charge remains at $225,000 until the 100th year.
4. The inflation rate is zero.
5. The cost of the building is $10,000,000, including insurance costs for the debt.

6. The coupon rates are the yield rates assumed in Pattern C, Appendix Table A.
7. Depreciation is computed on the basis of the sum of the digits.

On the basis of these assumptions, it may be seen from Table 28 that under Alternative C some 21.4 percent of the debt is retired during the first decade, 22.4 percent during the second decade and gradually decreasing amounts until near the end of the schedule when $1,435,000 is retired during the final 25 years of life.

This type debt retirement schedule is dictated by the amount of available net revenue. As shown below, this results in some peculiar patterns of patrimony accumulation. [It is noted that the full available revenue is capitalized in Table 28. Of course, in an enterprise revenue bond issue it would be necessary to provide some excess coverage; however, in this illustration it is assumed that the governmental lessee arrangement would permit marketing with only a 100 cover.]

One of the astounding findings reflected in Table 28 is that if the debt had been issued under Pattern C-1 on a basis of a 50-year amortization schedule, the actual rental required to liquidate the debt during the first 50 years would have been moderately less

Table 28

Cash Flows in Operation, Maintenance, and Servicing of Debt
$10,000,000 Office Building

Years	Gross Revenue	Operating Costs	Maintenance Costs	Available for Debt Service	Principal	Interest	Debt Outstanding End of Period
	(1)	(2)	(3)	(4)	(5)	(6)	(7)
Pattern C:							
100-Year Amortization							
0	—	—	—	—	—	—	10,000
1–10	10,555	1,332	629	8,594	2,135	6,459	7,865
11–20	9,805	1,530	1,024	7,250	2,239	5,011	5,626
21–30	9,305	1,758	1,669	5,878	1,816	4,062	3,809
31–40	7,805	2,021	2,241	3,543	1,035	2,508	2,774
41–50	7,055	2,322	2,250	2,483	557	1,926	2,217
Subtotal 1–50	44,525	8,963	7,813	27,748	7,783	19,966	2,217
51–75	16,388	6,250	5,625	4,513	782	3,731	1,435
76–100	15,138	6,254	5,625	3,263	1,435	1,828	—
Subtotal 51–100	31,525	12,500	11,250	7,776	2,217	5,559	—
Total 1–100	76,051	21,463	19,063	35,525	10,000	25,525	—
Pattern C-1:							
50-Year Amortization							
0	—	—	—	—	—	—	10,000
1–10	10,547	1,332	629	8,586	2,210	6,376	7,790
11–20	9,797	1,530	1,024	7,242	2,382	4,861	5,408
21–30	8,797	1,758	1,669	5,366	2,095	3,274	3,313
31–40	7,797	2,021	2,241	3,535	1,600	1,935	1,713
41–50	7,047	2,322	2,250	2,475	1,713	762	—
Total 1–50	43,985	8,963	7,813	27,209	10,000	17,208	—

(amounts in thousands of dollars)

than that required during the same years under the 100-year amortization plan. This derives from the fact that when capitalizing flows of money for long periods of time with even moderate incidence in the yield curve, gradually so much of the cash flow to accommodate the longer-term debt is preempted that it squeezes to near the zero point the amount available for servicing debt that may, under other schedules, be maturing in the earlier years and at lower coupon rates. Thus, under Pattern C-1, the total debt service for the first 50 years is $27,209,000 as compared to $27,748,000 under Pattern C. Therefore, adherence to the shorter schedule is actually beneficial to the issuer. (See effects demonstrated in Appendix Table D.)

Alternative 50-Year Amortization Patterns

Tables 28 and 29 provide information concerning 50-year amortization patterns as a substitute for the 100-year amortization plan initially presented. From Pattern C-1 presented in Table 28, it is interesting to note that the 50-year amortization of the debt can be achieved at a cost slightly less than the cost of a 100-year amortization. This arises from the fact that the action of the yield curve is to increase moderately the average interest

Table 29

Debt Service for $10,000,000 Bond Issue under Alternative Patterns of 50-Year Amortization

(amounts in thousands of dollars)

Years		Debt Service Requirement			Debt Outstanding End of Period		
		Pattern C-1	Pattern C-2	Pattern C-3	Pattern C-1	Pattern C-2	Pattern C-3
		(1)	(2)	(3)	(4)	(5)	(6)
0		—	—	—	10,000	10,000	10,000
1–10:	Total	8,586	8,441	7,586	7,790	8,000	9,657
	Range	880/835	899/788	759			
	Average	859	844	759			
11–20:	Total	7,242	7,152	7,586	5,401	6,000	9,015
	Range	780/665	744/654	759			
	Average	724	715	759			
21–30:	Total	5,369	5,763	7,586	3,313	4,000	7,756
	Range	607/462	640/611	759			
	Average	537	576	759			
31–40:	Total	3,535	4,307	7,586	1,713	2,000	5,200
	Range	399/315	497/364	759			
	Average	354	431	759			
41–50:	Total	2,475	2,824	7,586	—	—	—
	Range	262/230	250/215	759			
	Average	248	282	759			
Total:	Total	27,287	28,487	37,929			
	Range	880/230	899/215	759			
	Average	544	670	759			

NB: Yield/coupon rates are from Pattern C in Appendix Table A.

costs in the 100-year plan over the 50-year plan and that, in the process of capitalization, this has the effect of reducing the aggregate debt service cost during the first 50 years from $27,748,000 under the 100-year plan to $27,209,000 under the 50-year plan. And, of course, the full $35,525 in debt service during the second 50 years of the life of the building is eliminated.

Under the equal annual debt principal payment plan shown in Pattern C-2, debt service payments during the first 10 years would be slightly less than under C-1 as they would also be in the second decade; however, during the remaining three decades, the debt service costs [and net available revenues for debt service] would increase moderately above those in C-1—thereby necessitating the lessee government to increase its rentals moderately.

When an equal annual debt service pattern for 50 years is examined, it is found that, during the first decade, there would be a significant decrease in rental payments required; however, in each of the succeeding decades the aggregate rentals would have to increase sharply. Again, inasmuch as this is a governmental lessee arrangement, the decision would become one of when the lessee government wished to make its higher rental payments and the pattern of patrimony accumulation it wished to follow.

Patrimony Accumulation

From Table 30 the impact of the different patterns of amortization of debt in relation to the depreciated value of the building is illustrated. From this table it is seen that, under Pattern C, the accumulation of patrimony at any given time in the life of the building is relatively low, reaching its peak (insofar as end of decades are concerned) when the building is about 30 years of age. At that point accumulated patrimony is $1.1 million. Under Pattern C-1, accumulation is more rapid and reaches its peak at the end of 50 years with the debt paid off and a residual value of $2.5 million shown. This same accumulation at the end of 50 years is, of course, also applicable to C-2 and C-3, inasmuch as their debt is also liquidated by the end of 50 years.

However, it is significant that under Pattern C-3 (the equal annual debt service alternative) there is a negative accumulation of patrimony to a point well beyond the 40th year. In other words, in order to hold down debt service payments, debt is being reduced at a significantly slower rate than the rate at which depreciation is running on the property. Such a pattern is of genuine concern to those who are interested in patrimony accumulation—especially important to investors who must look to accumulated patrimony as at least a part of their security in governmental enterprise operations.[6]

Availability and Capitalization of Revenues

Most debt is secured by capitalization of expected future revenues.

Unfortunately, those whose experience is largely limited to tax-supported debt frequently overlook this fact. Or, perhaps they are focusing upon the fact that taxes have to be levied to support a given amount of debt, rather than viewing the debt in the proper

---

[6] The foregoing discussion of patrimony has been based upon conventional concepts of treating interest as expense in the year in which it accrues. A case can be made for the view that the interest and principal portions of amortization should not be separately treated—at least in discussions of patrimony and perhaps also in some other respects. Unless the earlier "generation" acquires the facility and pays the interest on the money required, there would be no facility inherited by the current generation. Therefore, should the current generation demand the use of the facility, it would be obliged to make the very heavy interest payments arising in the early years of the life of the facility it creates. Accordingly, it seems that the conventional concepts of both interest and accumulation (or liquidation) of patrimony require further examination in order to achieve intergenerational equity. It is to be remembered that much of the present value (PV-1) of an outstanding bond is likely to arise from the interest component yet to be paid.

Table 30

Depreciation, Outstanding Debt, and Patrimony Accumulation under Alternative Financing Plans

(amounts in thousands of dollars)

	Years						
	1–10	11–20	21–30	31–40	41–50	51–75	76–100
Depreciation							
Percent of investment	18.9	16.9	15.0	13.0	11.0	18.8	6.4
Amount during period	1,811	1,633	1,495	1,297	1,099	1,881	644
Depreciated value at end of period	8,109	6,416	4,921	3,624	2,525	644	—
Outstanding Debt *End of Period* Pattern							
C	7,865	5,626	3,805	2,774	2,217	1,435	—
C–1	7,790	5,401	3,313	1,713	—	—	—
C–2	8,000	6,000	4,000	2,000	—	—	—
C–3	9,657	9,015	7,756	5,200	—	—	—
Patrimony *Accumulated During Period**							
C	214	579	323	(266)	(542)	(1,881)	781
C–1	319	700	589	303	614	(1,881)	(644)
C–2	109	310	611	703	901	(1,881)	(644)
C–3	(1,548)	(1,048)	(240)	1,259	4,100	(1,881)	(644)
Cumulative Patrimony *at Close of Period**							
C	214	793	1,116	850	308	781	—
C–1	319	1,019	1,608	1,911	2,525	644	—
C–2	109	419	921	1,624	2,525	644	—
C–3	(1,548)	(2,595)	(2,835)	(1,575)	2,525	644	—

* Differentials in gross rentals between plans are ignored. Should these be taken into consideration, values would be substantially modified for C–1, C–2, and C–3. It is also appropriate to call attention to the vastly different effects of high interest rates upon PV-2 capitalization which result in 50-year and even some 25-year (or still less) periods of capitalization being unwise, as is discussed on pp. 166–168.

NB: For discussion of alternative patterns, see text associated with Tables 28 and 29.

perspective of its being a capitalization of anticipated future revenues—whether earned revenue from governmental enterprises, taxes and other revenues already in place, or the anticipation of the levy and collection of future taxes.

The special considerations involved in the planning of governmental enterprise debt are discussed in Chapter 14; however, it is appropriate to point out here that availability of revenue, especially net revenue after provision for operation and maintenance, becomes a principal controlling factor in the rate at which debt retirement may be scheduled. If the rates are established on the basis of economic rental, they may closely parallel the results outlined above in Table 28. Ordinarily, however, rates of liquidation are established on a basis that will provide for acceleration of amortization as hedges against (1) periods in which there may be a short-fall of revenue and (2) errors in assumptions as to depreciation, operating and maintenance costs, and accelerated obsolescence.

In any event, it is the availability of revenues that establishes the upper limit at which the debt may be amortized. The actual schedule of mandatory amortization will usually be over considerably longer periods than full capitalization of revenues for defined periods in order to provide a margin of safety.

The Technique of Capitalization (PV-2). For ease of calculation, the typical quick method is to assume a single coupon rate applicable to the entire number of years and to carry out the capitalization under this formula:

$$\text{Principal} = \frac{1 - \dfrac{1}{(1+i)^n}}{i} \times A$$

When: i = interest rate per period (as decimal fraction)
n = number of periods
A = amount per period being capitalized

Thus, if the interest rate is 6.00 percent and the number of periods is 20 and the amount per period is $1,000,000, the principal becomes $11,469,921.22. But, if the interest rate is 5.00 percent, the amount of principal becomes $12,462,210.34.

This is a rather crude method of calculation. A much superior method is to use the yield curve and calculate values for each of the years under a formula that takes into account individual projected coupon rates, e.g., those presented in Appendix Table A. The formula to be applied in determining the amount of principal where coupon rates vary from year to year is:

$$\text{Principal for Year} = \frac{x - y}{(1 + i)}$$

When x = amount of revenue available for debt service for current year
y = amount of interest payable in succeeding year
i = coupon rate for this year

When this formula is applied to the 20th year the result is:

$$\text{Principal for Year} = \frac{\$1,000,000.00 - 0}{(1 + .0605)} = \$942,951.43$$

For the 19th year:

$$\text{Principal for Year} = \frac{\$1,000,000.00 - \$57,048.57}{(1 + .06)} = \$889,576.82$$

As this process is repeated for years 18, 17, etc., it is found that the sum of the amounts of principal supportable, i.e., present value (PV-2) becomes $11,690,860.73.

When the issuer has computer services available, a simple computer program may be developed. Thereafter, the debt planner may test different patterns of reoffering yield rates, terms of years, and amounts available for debt service until a pattern fitting the current needs is determined.

When a level debt service is the objective for the new bond issue, once a determination is made as to the amount of debt that can be supported by a debt service of $1,000,000 per year, one can then determine the debt service required to produce net proceeds of a desired amount after allowance for the cost of issuance. Thus, if the cost of issuance is assumed to be 2.00 percent of the aggregate principal developed over a 20-year capitalization under Pattern "A," the amount of debt service required to support a capital project need of $17,500,000 would become:

$$\text{Annual debt service} = \frac{(\$17,500,000) \div (1 - .02)}{\$11,690,861} \times \$1,000,000 = \$1,527,445$$

Integration with Existing Debt Service Requirements

In most cases, the debt service on newly created debt will be merged almost immediately upon the issuance of the new debt into the aggregates of debt service on previously outstanding debt. Recognition of this continuum requires that the debt service pattern for each new increment of debt be designed with a full understanding of the impact it will have upon the new aggregates—both immediately and in the light of future funding requirements. Insofar as the relationship to existing debt service is concerned, there is need for a full review of that pattern. If there are irregularities, perhaps the pattern for the new debt can be modified partially or fully to overcome these irrationalities. The pattern of the maturities and debt service can be determined, taking into account patrimony objectives. If the past policy has been one of materially increasing patrimony from year to year, within some periods of the life of the community, review may produce changes in policy, with consequent impact upon debt service arrangements.

Economic Development of the Community

The rate of development of the economy of a community varies significantly from periods of rapid expansion, to stability, and to contraction. These are frequently interspersed. In estimating future revenues of state and local governments, the amounts (in constant dollars) will have a significant relationship to levels of local and national economic activity. However, the relationship is not one in which revenues correlate precisely with economic change.

Those responsible for planning a bond issue should take into account projections of the economy of the community for the life of the planned bond issue. Thus, if the issuer is in an area which is growing and has good economic prospects, a longer-term bond issue is likely to be much more easily supportable than one for a community with a declining economy. In the latter, it may be better to plan amortization during a much shorter period of time in order to hold interest costs to reasonable levels.

Impact of the Reoffering Yield Curve

The present value of the revenue flow is markedly influenced by:

a. The general level of the yield curve, and
b. The incidence of the yield rate curve

From Table 31 it is noted that in the case of bond issues maturing over a 10-year period Pattern B produces the highest capitalized value—due to the relatively low interest rate level, coupled with a high incidence to the yield curve, thereby providing money during the early years at relatively low costs. On the other hand, for the longer-term bond issues (30 or more years) the capitalized value of $1,000,000 per year under Pattern A produces higher present values than does capitalization under B. In like manner, as the interest rate levels increase in Patterns C, D, and E, the capitalized values decrease.

A very high level of interest and incidence produces a pattern of total capitalized values at much less than those which may have existed under a Pattern A market only a few months or years previously.[7]

Although the issuer is unable to control either the basic level of interest rates or the yield curve [except to the extent that improvement in credit position may improve rating

---

[7] Such a pattern of capitalization can result in a minor error in statement of present value (PV-2) because there are differentials in the semiannual payments of interest and these have a minor effect upon a true statement of present value (PV-2); however, for the purposes at hand, these differences are ignored. (See also Appendix Table D.)

and market acceptance], the issuer does have a responsibility to review most carefully the impact of the prevailing yield rate incidence and interest level in determining the *term* of the bonds to be sold. A study of lines 10, 15 and 20 will show that after the 20th year under Pattern E, the amount of net additional proceeds to be derived from capitalization of revenue for additional years is so low that issuers should strenuously seek to avoid such long-term capitalization. Thus, for a capitalization of 30 years vs. 20 years, the additional $10,000,000 capitalized revenue produces only $279,000 in additional present value—an increase of only 3.9 percent. No knowledgeable and wise issuer will make such an extension in such a market unless absolutely obliged to do so. Yet, many— through ignorance—did sell into such a long-term market.

Although there are no fixed guidelines for determining the point at which it is unwise to extend the term of a bond issue—or, rather to limit it—a good rule of thumb may be:

Table 31

Principal Generated by Capitalization of $1 Million Annually under Alternative Reoffering Yield Patterns and Number of Years of Capitalization under PV-2

(amounts in thousands of dollars)

Line	Item	Number of Years Capitalized				
		10	20	30	40	50
	Aggregate capitalized value					
1	Yield pattern A	7,571	11,690	13,770	14,676	15,115
2	Yield pattern B	7,813	11,708	13,292	13,910	14,115
3	Yield pattern C	7,255	10,867	12,381	12,985	13,182
4	Yield pattern D	7,453	10,827	11,951	12,238	12,272
5	Yield pattern E	5,766	7,120	7,399	7,448	7,426
	Incremental gain in capitalized value over previous period					
6	Yield pattern A	7,571	3,589	2,080	916	419
7	Yield pattern B	7,813	3,895	1,589	615	205
8	Yield pattern C	7,255	3,612	1,514	604	197
9	Yield pattern D	7,453	3,374	1,124	287	34
10	Yield pattern E	5,766	1,354	279	49	(22)
	Incremental amount of principal generated as a percentage of revenue capitalized for period					
11	Yield pattern A	75.7	35.9	20.8	9.1	4.4
12	Yield pattern B	78.1	39.0	15.9	6.2	2.1
13	Yield pattern C	72.6	36.1	15.1	6.0	2.0
14	Yield pattern D	74.5	33.7	11.2	2.9	.3
15	Yield pattern E	57.7	13.5	2.8	.5	(.2)
	Principal generated as a percentage of aggregate revenue capitalized					
16	Yield pattern A	75.7	59.5	45.9	36.7	30.2
17	Yield pattern B	78.1	58.5	44.3	34.8	28.2
18	Yield pattern C	72.6	54.3	41.3	32.5	26.4
19	Yield pattern D	74.5	54.1	39.8	30.6	24.5
20	Yield pattern E	57.7	35.6	24.7	18.6	14.8

For yield patterns see Appendix Table A and for details see Appendix Table D.

If the capitalization of an additional year's revenue does not produce a net increase in present value for the bond issue of at least 10 percent of the incremental revenue, it appears to be wise to limit the issue to the number of years already capitalized.

There will be circumstances which mitigate use of this rule; however, policy-makers should have such rules clearly in mind and should have available appropriate computer programs which will enable them quickly to comprehend the effects of different interest rate markets upon decisions relating to the term of bond issues.

A further view of the impact of interest rate levels and the pattern of yield curve incidence is afforded by the cost of debt service under the A/E alternatives as applied to amortization periods of 10, 20, and 30 years—all as reflected in Table 32. From that table it is seen that, whereas the low levels of interest and incidence produce interest equal to only 23 percent of total debt service in the 10-year maturity group, this rises to 26 percent in the moderate range for Pattern C and to 39 percent in the high interest rate level. In the 30-year group, interest for Pattern A amounts to 93 percent of principal,

Table 32

Debt Service Requirements for a $10,000,000 Equal Annual Maturity Bond Issue under Alternative Yield Patterns and Periods of Amortization under PV-2

(amounts in thousands of dollars)

Amortization Period in Years	Yield/Coupon Patterns				
	Low Interest Rates		Intermediate Interest Rates		High Interest Rates
	Low Yield Curve Incidence A*	High Yield Curve Incidence B*	Low Yield Curve Incidence C*	High Yield Curve Incidence D*	Moderate Yield Curve Incidence E*
	(1)	(2)	(3)	(4)	(5)
Debt Service					
10	12,976	12,603	13,462	13,138	16,295
20	16,020	15,949	16,964	16,955	23,185
30	19,260	19,602	20,755	21,174	30,099
*Net Interest Cost Rates***					
10	5.64	4.96	6.52	5.93	11.67
20	5.88	5.81	6.78	6.77	12.70
30	6.09	6.31	7.05	7.32	13.08
Aggregate Coupon Interest Payable					
10	2,976	2,603	3,462	3,138	6,295
20	6,020	5,949	6,964	6,955	13,185
30	9,260	9,602	10,755	11,174	20,099
Coupon Interest Payable As Percent of Debt Service					
10	22.9	20.7	25.7	23.9	38.6
20	37.6	37.4	41.0	41.0	56.9
30	48.1	49.0	51.8	52.8	66.8

* For yield/coupon rates see Appendix Table A.
** Computed on assumption that 10-year bond issues are sold at discount of 1.2 percent, 20-year bond issues sold at discount of 1.50 percent, and 30-year bond issues sold at a discount of 1.75 percent—all to cover issuance costs.

whereas in the 30-year group, interest for Pattern E amounts to 201 percent of principal. Annual debt service for Patterns A and B ranges downward from just under $1,300,000 for a 10-year amortization to about $650,000 for a 30-year payout. Patterns C and D decrease from $1,300,000 in 10 years to $700,000 for 30 years. Pattern E, with its higher rates, requires $1.6 million for 10-year amortization and about $1.0 million for a 30-year payout.

Regeneration of Borrowing Capacity

Within any given debt limit, the regeneration of borrowing power is a function of the rate at which outstanding debt is being liquidated. The more rapid the rate of retirement, the more rapid the regeneration of borrowing authority. This factor is not of great significance to those governments operating under very liberal debt limits. The importance of regeneration of borrowing capacity during the 1970s with rapid inflation has been principally related to whether the assessed values have kept pace with the change in market values of property. Where debt limits have risen in relation to these changes in market value, the probability is that the community has encountered no difficulty with its legal borrowing capacity. In those circumstances, the legal borrowing capacity has probably risen more rapidly than the need for capital funds. On the other hand, where the legal borrowing limit has not risen rapidly, due to slow adjustments in assessed values to correspond to inflation, difficulties have doubtless been encountered. In any event, debt managers will wish to take into account the immediate and long-term impact of their debt repayment schedules upon the rate of regeneration of unused borrowing capacity. In doing so, the choice among plans will need to be carefully reviewed and evaluated to assure that borrowing capacity required at future dates will be available in reasonable amounts.

Operating and Maintenance Costs

In the discussion of Table 28, attention was focused upon the desirability of taking operating and maintenance costs of each new facility into account as decisions are being made in respect of the capital program and the debt service schedule. One can develop a debt service pattern without reference to the operation and maintenance costs; however, to do so ignores important elements of facility costs. A careful analysis may lead to lease, rather than acquisition—especially when the continual need for the facility over its full physical life may be uncertain.

With the revenue/expenditure squeeze becoming progressively tighter, greater attention is needed to the implications of operating and maintenance costs of facilities, both in terms of the impact they have upon the operating budget and of the effects those impending costs may have upon the rate at which the issuer wishes to plan the retirement of debt. (A related subject is the cost of the programs to be conducted in the facilities. Some are not affected; a few are decreased; but many, e.g., recreation and cultural programs, are likely to require significant increases in program funding.)

Opportunity for Arbitrage

A final consideration in development of the schedule for retirement of the debt is the potential for arbitrage between the rates at which the government may borrow money and the returns receivable through investment. Prior to 1969 little attention was given to opportunities for arbitrage. As state and local governments have exploited arbitrage income fully, the resistance of the U.S. Treasury has increased. Current arbitrage regulations have severely circumscribed the potential. Yet, there are many who believe that as these regulations are litigated there will be changes that will again afford to the issuers a much broader degree of flexibility.

TERM BONDS OR SERIAL BONDS

An earlier chapter has provided general definitions of term bonds and serial bonds. The past half-century has seen a major shift from the use of term bonds to serial bonds. Some of the factors responsible for change were valid; some were not. It is appropriate to examine some of these briefly because the same arguments are likely to occur in any decision to return to the use of term bonds with sinking fund accumulation in the debt management program.

The Decline in the Use of Term Bonds

During the 1930s, several factors combined to produce a massive shift of new debt issues from term bond issues to serial bond issues. Among the more important of these factors were:

1. *Misunderstanding as to Interest Actually Paid.* Rather surprisingly, one of the fallacies that arose was the amount of interest actually paid. Some persons asserted that, under a term bond, substantially more interest was being paid than was the case. The misunderstanding is illustrated by the following example involving a loan of $1,000,000 at 6.00 percent to be amortized in six equal semiannual installments with sinking fund balances also earning 6.00 percent.

Period	Semiannual Payment	Term Bond Account			Serial Bond Account	
		Interest	Sinking Fund Deposit	Sinking Fund Accumulation	Interest	Principal
1	184,597.50	30,000	154,597.50	154,597.50	30,000.00	154,697.50
2	184,597.50	30,000	154,597.50	313,832.93	25,362.07	159,532.42
3	184,597.50	30,000	154,597.50	477,845.41	20,585.01	164,012.48
4	184,597.50	30,000	154.597.50	646,778.28	15,664.63	168,932.86
5	184,597.50	30,000	154,597.50	820,779.12	10,596.66	174,000.84
6	184,597.50	30,000	154,597.50	1,000,000.00	5,376.62	179,220.88
Total	1,107,585.00	180,000	927,585.00	1,000,000.00	107,585.00	1,000,000.00

Several things are clear from the tabulation:

a. In both cases the principal was repaid
b. The nominal amount of the interest in the case of the term bond appears to be significantly greater than that under the serial bond
c. The actual amount of interest is the same—$107,585.00. In the case of the serial bond it is obvious. In the case of the term bond, the sinking fund deposits of $927,585.00 become $1,000,000.00 through total earnings of $72,415 over the life of the bonds. When this is subtracted from the nominal interest of $180,000, the net interest becomes $107,585.00

2. *Sinking Fund Mismanagement.* Various instances of mismanagement of sinking funds were disclosed during the 1930s. Some of these were caused by persons who unloaded securities of low market value upon sinking funds at prices much above market prices. Some mismanagement arose from good faith purchases at market value which subsequently turned sour. Moreover, in many cases the hard-pressed state and local governments did not have the money to make timely payments to the sinking funds, nor could they raise it. Managers of the funds were frequently obliged to use moneys that had been set aside

for eventual payment of principal in order to make current interest payments. Bank failures accentuated the losses of sinking funds.

3. *Declining Interest Rates.* Interest rates declined dramatically—especially in the years following 1932. Opportunities for investment by sinking fund managers at rates originally postulated dried up. Managers were obliged to call upon state and local treasuries for larger periodic deposits to the sinking funds to offset losses in projected earnings. This came at a time when those treasuries were already in great difficulty.

4. *The Yield Curve.* The yield curve applied to municipal bonds showed an increased incidence, i.e., spread between the early years and the later years. This meant that, where term bond issues were being sold, the interest rate for the long-term bonds was at the highest point on the curve. Moreover, the yield was lowest during the periods of greatest sinking fund investments. Resort to the serial bond issue enabled the issuer to take advantage of the lower rates in the earlier years of the span of years being covered and to avoid the vicissitudes of future market uncertainties.

5. *Average Life of Bonds.* The average nominal life of the bond issue was greatly reduced in the case of the serial bond issue. In stating the amounts of outstanding debt, this proved attractive to many investment analysts. (Of course, the net debt outstanding— gross less sinking fund assets—was not materially affected.)

6. *Investor Preference.* The serial bond issues became more attractive in many invest- ment market situations because of the opportunity to appeal to different segments of the market—short-, medium-, and long-term.

7. *Discipline for Issuers.* Many investors and financial analysts take a dim view of the wide latitudes provided to public officials in debt management. The discipline demanded in a fixed debt service schedule for serial bonds was attractive to them. From their point of view, it eliminated the problems of sinking fund administration and imposed upon issuers a clearly defined obligation to meet interest and principal payments on the basis of an easily defined standard. Failures by issuers became immediately apparent as defaults. The penalties implicit in defaults caused issuers to make extra efforts to meet both interest and principal payments from revenues as they fell due. Moreover, many issuers found the new fixed debt service comforting. It eliminated fluctuations incident to sinking fund administration.

Various combinations of these factors produced a major shift to the use of serial bond issues. By 1940 term bonds had virtually disappeared from the general obligation list of new securities. Although still used in revenue financing, there was an increasing tendency toward use of mandatory retirement schedules in relation to term bond issues, which in effect made them *block-term* serial bonds without sinking funds.

Advantages and Disadvantages

The advantages and disadvantages of using different patterns of term and serial bond issues can be stated in terms of their contributions to the following objectives:

1. Maximizing the principal to be derived from payment of a given level of debt service
2. Providing flexibility in administration of outstanding debt
3. Broadening of market appeal
4. Minimizing the amount of bonds outstanding
5. Improving the secondary market

An examination of the contribution of each alternative is reviewed in relation to these objectives.

Objective No. 1: High Principal Production. The term bond issue with a full operation of the sinking fund frequently offers the best relationship between debt service paid and principal generated. However, this depends upon the rates at which sinking fund assets may be invested.[8] In turn, the reoffering yield curve operative at the time such investments are made and the ability of the issuer to invest in longer-term securities that can be sold to other sinking funds as different term issues mature, will help to determine whether this is a best alternative. Moreover, the advantages will depend, in part, upon the interest levels applicable to the debt of the issuer. Where the issuer's credit position is relatively low, the potential for arbitrage between use of funds for direct retirement of debt vis-à-vis investment and accumulation in a sinking fund will be less than for issuers enjoying a relatively high credit position. When serial bonds are used, there are the usual advantages previously ascribed to them either as base-rate serials, as serial/block-term bonds, or as serials with adjusted reoffering yield rates.

Objective No. 2: Flexibility in Debt Service Management. Public officials frequently seek ways in which to defer until *mañana* fiscal responsibilities belonging to the present. When the management of the invested sinking fund is lodged with the public officials (rather than with fiscal agents) they sometimes short-change debt service appropriations for term bonds with the knowledge that formal default will not necessarily occur. They may expect sinking fund commissioners to meet interest payments from accumulated sinking fund reserves, if necessary to avoid default. Or, perhaps the underappropriation extends only to failure to make appropriation for the proper sinking fund deposit. Current interest is appropriated but accrued deficits are developing in the sinking fund. The serial bond issue avoids this situation. The officials are required to make appropriations or face the penalties arising from default.

In periods of great emergency, e.g., the early 1930s, the fact that much of the debt was term debt helped to avoid a large number of defaults that would have occurred had the debt of all state and local governments been of the straight serial bond issue type with its lock-step demands for payment. This leaves it a judgment call.

Objective No. 3: Broad Market Appeal. In order to market bonds being offered, the issuer should maintain the flexibility needed to tailor the issue to the current demands of the market (to the extent feasible). Thus, during some periods, commercial banks may be significantly increasing their holdings of municipals but largely within the maturities during the first 10 years. Simultaneously, the casualty insurance companies may be strong net purchasers of the longer-term securities—especially of term bonds or block-term bonds so frequently associated with revenue bond issues.

Such conditions invite the use of serial bonds for the first 10 maturities and a term bond with sinking fund (without mandatory acceleration of the retirement of bonds) for the remainder of the issue. However, there may be sufficient strength in the remainder of the market to permit advantageous scheduling of a portion of the bonds on a serial basis between the 10th and 20th year with strong interest in term bonds at the 25th or 30th year.

The combination of the treasury rulings on arbitrage and the provisions of law relating to serial bonds have acted to deny many issuers the kinds of flexibility needed to enable issuers to function with full efficiency. Moreover, relatively few finance officers and/or their financial advisors are easily at home with the financial calculations—frequently being dependent upon computer programs developed for other purposes. Issuers generally have a paucity of knowledge concerning the actual demands in the market for bonds of different maturities. Even the most able and determined negotiator for the issuer has difficulty in securing adequate information as to the possible market for bonds of maturities that will have to be sold largely to the household sector purchasers. The results of the preliminary offerings are skewed by the interest shown by large buyers because the smaller buyers

---

[8] Currently, the U.S. Treasury seeks to inhibit the use of invested sinking funds by asserting that earnings by these funds constitute "use of bond proceeds" and, therefore, that earnings in excess of the rates payable on the bonds constitute arbitrage.

may not be canvassed. The result may be added interest costs imposed by the *block-term* bond approach described in a later chapter.

Opinion differs concerning the impact of the use of the term bond upon the yield rate at which the bond can be sold. Some authorities believe that a large amount of bonds with a long maturity is likely to result in a higher coupon rate because of the difficulty of securing ample supply of customers at a given point in time. Others hold that, except for exceedingly large issues, this is no problem. Indeed, they believe that, on some occasions, the term bond can be sold at lower yield rates than can the final maturities in a group of serial bonds with somewhat similar maturities.

These factors change from time to time. Accordingly, issuers are best served when they develop current opinion on these matters for their jurisdictions at the time of each sale. In some instances, the only way to determine the relative impact is to offer the bonds under alternative plans; however, this can become awkward and may discourage bidding.

Objective No. 4: Minimizing Outstanding Debt. In serial bond issues, portions of the debt are being retired each year. This acts to reduce the amount of bonds in the hands of investors. Under economic supply and demand theory this smaller amount of outstanding bonds should result in a greater demand (and hence lower yield rate) for new bonds being sold. Doubtless this is true for issuers with very large amounts of debt outstanding vis-à-vis the depth of the market in their bonds.

Objective No. 5: Improvement of the Secondary Market. Inasmuch as the price one pays in the primary market is largely influenced by the view taken of the securities of the same issuer in the secondary market, it is advisable to seek to improve the market position of the issuer in the secondary market. For the larger issuers, this can, in part, derive from the encouragement of an active market in its securities. The market can respond marginally better to term bonds than to serial bonds because of the greater number and frequency of sales of identical bonds—thereby measuring a wider variety of opinion concerning the appropriate yield rate for the security. Thus, the so-called "dollar bonds" have some secondary market advantages not enjoyed by most other municipal securities. This factor indicates a need for more term bonds in order that the market will have a better opportunity to operate with respect to securities of a given issuer. No comprehensive data on this point are available.

FINANCING COST OF ISSUANCE

The elements of the cost of issuance of a bond issue consist of the following: (1) administrative costs; (2) advertising and printing, (3) legal fees, (4) financial advisory fees, (5) feasibility study costs, and (6) services of the investment banking syndicate in distribution of the bonds. Assertions are made, from time to time, that certain elements of costs are absorbed by the syndicate, rather than by the issuer. There should be no mistake: The issuer pays for the full range of costs incident to issuance of debt unless the syndicate misjudges the market and is obliged to absorb costs that it planned to recover.

On the other hand, there are important questions as to *how* the costs are to be paid. The basic sources of funds for payment of issuance costs are:

1. The operating budget
2. The present value (PV-1) of the excess of coupon interest over the reoffering yield rate
3. Sale of the bonds at discount

Use of the Operating Budget

To the extent that the issuer finances all, or portions, of the issuance costs from the operating budget, it is presumed that these are being paid from current revenues. This constitutes a part of the "pay-as-you-acquire" type of financing to which reference has been made at the beginning of this chapter in conjunction with the discussion of Table 27. Therefore, to the extent that the issuer elects to pay portions of the issuance costs from the operating budget (current revenues), a down-payment is being made in that amount.

Present Value of Excess Interest Payments

A second method of payment is to provide for payment of excess interest in respect to some, or all, of the maturities, the excess being the payment of coupon rates in excess of the yield rates at which the bonds are reoffered. The amounts of these excesses are converted to present value (PV-1) pricing of bonds by the syndicate as they are reoffered. Except when the practice results in penalty yield rates, this is an acceptable manner in which to make the payments. It has the effect of holding down the statement of the par value of the aggregate amount of bonds being offered vis-à-vis the sale of bonds at discount for the purpose of paying large parts of the issuance costs.

Payment of Issuance Costs Through Sale of Bonds at Discount

The final way in which to pay the issuance costs not borne from the current operating budget is to sell the bonds to the syndicate at a discount, e.g., 1.50 or 2.00 percent below the par value. This enables the issuer to reoffer all of the bonds at par to the investors—a practice that is preferred by almost all investors. The actual payment of the issuance costs is thereby spread over the life of the bonds through amortization of the discount and through payment of interest on the par value, rather than on the sale-to-syndicate value.

Various aspects of the differential advantages and effects of the latter two methods are discussed in Chapter 12.

ZERO COUPON DEBT

Before leaving the subject of scheduling debt issuance and repayment it is essential to provide a brief overview of the matter of zero coupon debt.

In most financial transactions, interest payable for the use of money is expected to be paid on a current basis although many deviations from this basic pattern may be observed by those who study the capital markets. In the case of conventional term bonds issued by private corporations, payment of interest is a current charge even though there is rarely any sinking fund developed for the payment of principal at maturity. Rather, such profit-oriented corporations are likely to depend upon rolling the debt over at maturity through the issuance of alternative bonds where proceeds are used in part to retire bonds as they become due and in part for other corporate purposes.

For state and local governments the term bond issued in the early and mid-19th century tended to be issued in similar manner, without provision for accumulation of a fund from which to sink the debt at its maturity; however, problems encountered from time to time by such jurisdictions brought a shift after the Civil War to one under which the issuer was expected to make payment into a sinking fund which, together with earnings thereon, would be sufficient to pay the debt at maturity. Payment of interest was deemed to be a current charge and was ordinarily paid currently from the general revenues of the issuer although during periods of depression some jurisdictions met interest charges at least partially from accumulated sinking funds.

With the progressive reliance upon serial bonds commencing in the early 20th century and accelerating as a result of problems encountered in sinking fund administration during the Great Depression of the 1930s, there was a broad shift to payment of not only interest but also portions of the principal of debt on an annual basis. Interest paid was in more or less direct relationship to the outstanding debt and was paid as earned except in those occasional instances in which the coupon rate schedule was severely skewed in relation to the time at which interest was earned.

A significant exception to payment of interest as earned by governments occurred in the case of certain U.S. Government securities, especially the Series E Saving Bonds which were introduced during the 1930s. In that case the investor purchased the bond at its fully discounted amount and the payment of all interest was deferred until the maturity of the bond—or at the time it was surrendered under the terms of the bond contract. This was a zero coupon bond. Thus the $25 savings bond issued at that time was generally sold for $18.75 and was due 10 years from date of issue. The $6.25 in interest payable at maturity produced an interest rate return of 1.4488053 per semiannual period, or about 2.90 percent per annum as such rates are generally expressed in the trade.

The advantage to the zero coupon bond from the standpoint of the issuer was that the cost of administration was decreased because of the absence of need for current administration of the program, except for redemption of bonds in advance of maturity. Interest was recorded when paid in the accounts of the U.S. Government inasmuch as its budgeting and accounting were both on a cash receipts and disbursement basis. From the point of view of the investor there was no need for handling relatively small amounts of periodic interest receipts and the costs in time and delays in reinvestment of such funds.

The only near approach to the zero coupon bond for state and local governments was in the form of TANS, RANS, and BANS upon which the interest was frequently payable at maturity and was incorporated into the face amount of the notes with adjustments made by way of discount at the time of sale.

As will be demonstrated in Table 41 (in Chapter 13) there is a significant financial advantage to the issuer in True Interest Costs rates under the zero coupon pattern of capitalization of a given flow of money vs. the capitalization through the conventional pattern involved under PV-2 capitalization of the same stream of money for the same period of time. The degree of advantage is largely influenced by the slope (incidence) of the reoffering yield curve applicable to conventional serial coupon bonds.

At least during the past several decades there were no issues of long-term zero coupon bonds sold by state and local governments in the United States. In a considerable number and percentage of the bond issues offered at competitive sale, there was a skewing of the coupon rates in a manner that frequently resulted in near zero rates on the final maturity or maturities, the 1/20th of 1 percent coupon being a favorite.

During early 1982 there was an initial marketing of a bond issue by the Massachusetts Transportation Authority consisting of conventional coupon bonds and of some zero coupon bonds, with the latter designed in a manner that they fell under the U.S. Treasury ruling of entitlement to the "original issue discount" treatment of the discount (except for that used to cover issuance costs) being allowed as tax-exempt interest.[9] There are a number of advantages to the tax-exempt issuer as well as to the corporate issuer of zero coupon bonds and in the years immediately ahead this type of bond is doubtless due for much more careful examination and use by tax-exempt issuers. Numerous problems also must be resolved incident to its use. The development has come too late for the author to undertake a comprehensive analysis for this book, which was too far advanced at the time of the Massachusetts sale.

---

[9] See William J. Ryan. "High Municipal Bond Interest Rates Fuel Rebirth of Zero Coupon Issues." *The Weekly Bond Buyer,* Vol. 227, No. 4641 (March 29, 1982), pp. 1, 54. Also see discussion of zero coupon bonds in Appendix B.

Chapter 12
DETERMINING LOWEST EFFECTIVE NET INTEREST COSTS

There are few subjects in the technical aspects of debt policy in respect to which a greater number of errors are made than those concerned with determination of the effective interest costs. Despite the availability of ample information on the subject, a majority of debt managers still seem not to understand the issues. As a result, they continue to pursue policies that are unnecessarily costly to their governments.

In a negotiated bond sale, the determination of the average interest cost is for two purposes: (1) Ascertaining that the rate is within any limits set by law and (2) providing management and the public with information concerning the cost of moneys that are being borrowed. In competitive sale, the determination of an average interest rate has an additional purpose: (3) Determining the *best* bidder, i.e., the bidder offering the lowest effective interest costs. For reasons set forth in this chapter, this is of critical importance to the issuer.

Best Bid Determination Imperative in Competitive Sales

The primary purpose of the competitive sale is to enable the issuer to select the *best* bid. The best bid under conventional bidding procedures is determined on the basis of the lowest effective simple interest cost.

The problem is to assure a valid system for determining the effective interest costs represented by each bid. When the bidder is permitted to designate the coupon rate for each maturity, it is essential that the effective interest costs be determined through the use of *compound,* rather than *simple,* interest. Simple interest techniques almost always result in a distortion of the actual rates. They act to encourage the bidder to take advantage of the issuer's naiveté, thereby causing unnecessary expense.

With the bids in hand, the issuer makes a determination of the average interest rate payable under each bid in accordance with the rules established in the formal offering of the bonds for sale. Under prevailing law and custom in the United States, it is determined under one of two patterns:

1. The aggregate interest, adjusted for premiums offered or discounts sought, payable over the life of the bonds is divided by the aggregate amount of the bonds sold times the average life of the issue. The result is known as *net interest cost* (NIC)—sometimes referred to as *average net interest cost* (ANIC).

2. Determination of a rate at which each payment of debt service can be discounted to present value (PV-1) with a resultant total equal to the money received by the issuer in exchange for the bonds. The method in the literature of statistics is referred to as the *internal rate of return* (IRR). It is more commonly referred to as the *true interest cost* (TIC) method and sometimes also referred to in the United States as the *Canadian Method.*

The Christopher Columbus Investments

In a previous chapter, it has been suggested that, on some occasions, a flight of fancy helps to free the mind from its imprisoning stereotypes; that it helps to facilitate understanding of underlying basic considerations. The reader again is invited to indulge in such an exercise through review of the following apocryphal story:

> Christopher Columbus returned from his first trip to America on March 15, 1493. (That much is true.)
>
> He made two $1.00 investments at 8.00 percent, each maturing on March 15, 1993— one at simple interest and one compounded semiannually.
>
> At maturity the value of these two investments will be:
>
> a. At simple interest . . . . $ 41.00
> b. At compound interest $106,839,836,600,741,746.12

By way of comparison, $106.8 quadrillion is equal to about 115,000 times the U.S. Government public debt as of September 30, 1980.

Within the past decade, many issuers have sustained avoidable losses by the sale of their bonds under *simple,* rather than *compound,* interest procedures in the evaluation of the *best bid.*

This practice continues, perhaps in somewhat lesser degree, to be followed by numerous issuers who otherwise regularly exhibit sophisticated knowledge in money management. No responsible finance officer would execute either a purchase or a sale of securities for the pension or other funds on the basis of simple interest. Yet, for incomprehensible reasons, many follow the outmoded methods that are detrimental to their communities by conducting competitive sales on the basis of NIC (simple interest) calculations. In this era when someone is willing to litigate almost everything, it is surprising that public interest law groups have not litigated the matter—holding officials personally responsible for avoidable losses.

UNDERSTANDING NIC AND TIC[1]

It is necessary that every public debt officer comprehend the arithmetic principles and the procedures in the determination of NIC and TIC. The method of computations for conventional NIC are simple; the principle underlying TIC is simple but somewhat complex in execution.

NIC

Measurement of net interest cost was originally applied to term bond issues, each of which carried a single coupon rate and single maturity date. The formula is simple:

$$NIC = \frac{\text{Aggregate Interest Payable} \begin{array}{l} + \text{Discount} \\ - \text{Premium} \end{array}}{\text{Par Value of Issue} \times \text{Average Life}}$$

Thus, in the case of a $5,000,000 five-year term bond issue sold at par, with a 6.00 percent coupon:

---

[1] This chapter has deliberately used reoffering yield patterns which are characteristic of periods in the market characterized by:

    a. A relatively low level of interest rates
    b. A relatively high incidence to the yield curve
    c. A marked stability in the market which enables the competitive elements of the market to become more finely tuned and to operate more successfully than during periods of great instability such as those existing in the latter parts of 1980 and 1981.

The use of the lower interest rate levels does not in any manner affect the importance of the points discussed or of the adverse effects upon the issuer that continues to incur the unnecessary penalty yields.

$$\text{NIC} = \frac{\$1,500,000}{(\$5,000,000 \times 5)} = .060000 \text{ or } 6.00 \text{ percent}$$

If the same bond issue were sold at a discount of $10,000:

$$\text{NIC} = \frac{\$1,500,000 + \$10,000}{(\$5,000,000 \times 5)} = .060400 \text{ or } 6.04 \text{ percent}$$

If the bond issue were sold at a premium of $5,000:

$$\text{NIC} = \frac{\$1,500,000 - \$5,000}{(\$5,000,000 \times 5)} = .059800 \text{ or } 5.98 \text{ percent}$$

This system was carried over into the determination of NIC for serial bonds as they were introduced. The aggregate interest payable was calculated, the average life of the par value of bonds issued determined, and the formula applied.

When the formula was applied to term bonds, the amount of the distortion in the true interest cost rate was relatively small because interest was being paid at the same rate throughout the life of the bonds. The only distortion arose when discounts or premiums were involved. These affected the actual money available and, therefore, affected the average life of the money available for *use* as contrasted to the par value of the bond issue. Thus, if a premium were bid, the issuer had the advantage of additional money to *use;* conversely, if a discount were bid, the issuer had a lesser amount of money available for *use.*

TIC Interest

The function of TIC is to ascertain a rate of discount which, when applied to *each* dollar payment of debt service, will produce an aggregate amount that will precisely equal the money delivered to the issuer at settlement. The formula for discount of each amount is the basic present value (PV-1) formula:

$$\text{pv} = \frac{1}{(1 + i)^n} \times A$$

when: i = semiannual interest rate used for discounting
n = number of semiannual periods from issue date to the payment date for the amount
A = amount of debt service payable at the *end* of n semiannual periods.

In order to illustrate the points that have been made in respect of NIC and TIC, assume that a serial bond issue is sold, maturing in five annual installments with the coupon rates indicated below:

Year	Bonds Outstanding Prior to Retirement	Maturities	Coupon Rate	Total Interest
1	$ 5,000,000	$1,000,000	5.00	$265,500
2	4,000,000	1,000,000	5.20	215,500
3	3,000,000	1,000,000	5.35	163,500
4	2,000,000	1,000,000	5.45	110,000
5	1,000,000	1,000,000	5.55	55,500
Totals	$15,000,000	$5,000,000		$810,000

Again, assume that one bid provides for purchase at par, one at a discount of $10,000, and one at a premium of $5,000. The results from application of NIC are:

	Average Net Interest Costs: Conventional NIC Percentage
For the par bid	5.40000
For the premium bid	5.36667
For the discount bid	5.43333

Before computer technology was generally available, the calculation of TIC was a very complex and time-consuming operation. Computers bring the calculation of TIC into easy availability at almost any sale conducted at almost any hour or place.

The computation of TIC is made through iteration. Using the NIC value as a starting point, a rate above the NIC rate and a rate below the NIC rate are selected. Each is tested to determine whether the results they produce bracket the target amount, i.e., the amount to be delivered at settlement for the bonds. Assume that the rates selected for testing are 5.40 percent and 5.39 percent. The tentative present value (PV-1) results using one-half the annual rates would be:

For 5.40 percent, the discounted value	$4,999,319
For 5.39 percent, the discounted value	5,000,665

An intermediate rate is then tested to produce a value nearer to the $5,000,000 target. Through iteration it is found that the rate of 5.39494 percent produces the target amount. Applying this procedure to a sale of the $5,000,000 with the same coupon rates but with a premium of $5,000 and a discount of $10,000, the following semiannual values are determined at the indicated rates.

Semiannual Period	Debt Service	Present Value (PV-1) at Indicated Rates		
		Par Sale	Premium of $5,000	Discount of $10,000
TIC rate		5.39494	5.35785	5.46930
1	132,750	129,263	129,287	129,216
2	1,132,750	1,074,025	1,074,413	1,072,248
3	107,750	99,481	99,634	99,373
4	1,107,780	995,870	996,590	994,429
5	81,750	71,563	71,628	71,434
6	1,081,750	922,080	923,079	920,079
7	55,000	45,650	45,708	45,534
8	1,055,000	852,657	853,890	850,191
9	27,750	21,839	21,874	21,767
10	1,027,750	787,572	789,003	784,726
Total	5,810,000	5,000,000	5,005,000	4,990,000

Under the foregoing approaches, the values under conventional NIC and TIC may be summarized as follows:

	NIC	TIC
Par	5.40000	5.39494
Premium of $5,000	5.36667	5.35785
Discount of $10,000	5.43333	5.46930

It is noted that in the foregoing example, the TIC is less than NIC in a par sale. When the sale is at a premium, TIC is lower than NIC; under the discount bid, TIC is greater than NIC.

In almost all circumstances TIC will be different from NIC; however, as will be illustrated later in this chapter, it is sometimes greater and sometimes less—depending upon a combination of the amounts paid and the times of such payments. The discussion which follows will illustrate how coupon arrangements can be manipulated to produce results that are disadvantageous to the issuer.

THE PRICING OF A MUNICIPAL BOND

The price of a noncallable municipal bond consists of the present value (PV-1) of the principal plus the present value (PV-1) of the interest. The price represents the sum of the two values, separately determined. The same semiannual yield rate is applied in determining the value of the principal and of the semiannual interest payments. The formulae for determining the values for a noncallable bond being reoffered at par rate are:

$$\text{Principal: } pv = \frac{1}{(1-i)^n} \times \$1,000$$

$$\text{Interest: } pv = \frac{1 - \dfrac{1}{(1+i)^n}}{i} \times (c) \times \$1,000$$

When: $i = \frac{1}{2}$ yield rate
$c = \frac{1}{2}$ coupon rate
$n =$ number of semiannual periods from date to maturity

Thus, in the case of a bond due 10 years from date, with a 5.25 percent coupon rate and a 5.25 percent yield rate, the present values are:

$$\text{Principal} = \frac{1}{(1.02625)^{20}} \times \$1,000 \qquad\qquad = \$\ \ 595.58$$

$$\text{Interest} = \frac{1 - \dfrac{1}{(1.02625)^{20}}}{.02625} \times .02625 \times \$1,000 \qquad = \$\ \ 404.42$$

Price $= \$1,000.00$

If, however, the 7th maturity bears a coupon rate of 6.60 percent and the reoffering yield rate is 4.80 percent, the result becomes:

$$\text{Principal} = \frac{1}{(1.024)^{14}} \times \$1,000 \qquad\qquad = \$\ \ 717.46$$

$$\text{Interest} = \frac{1 - \dfrac{1}{(1.024)^{14}}}{.024} \times .033 \times \$1,000 = \qquad 388.49$$

Total Value $= \$1,105.95$

For a bond acquired at par from the issuer, this represents a profit of $105.95 on the $1,000 for the syndicate.

On the other hand, if an 18-year bond has a coupon rate of 4.50 percent and a yield rate of 6.20 percent, the present value (PV-1) amounts become:

$$
\begin{aligned}
\text{Principal} &= \$333.18 \\
\text{Interest} &= \underline{483.98} \\
\text{Total value} &= \$817.16
\end{aligned}
$$

In this latter circumstance, if the syndicate purchases the bond at par and sells at $817.16, it will have sustained a loss of $182.84. This will have to be made up from profits developed from other maturities as is illustrated in Table 33 (Column 6). Moreover, unless the sale is to an investor exempt from capital gains taxation or to an investor prepared to balance this capital loss with taxable gains from other transactions, a penalty yield will be assessed in the manner explained below.

The Operation of the Penalty Yield Rates in Respect to Premium Prices

When bonds are priced significantly above par, investors frequently demand a premium yield (price) adjustment. Thus, in the example of the year-7 bond priced at $1,105.95 for a $1,000 bond with a 6.60 percent coupon and a 4.80 percent yield, the syndicate may find it necessary to reoffer the bond at a higher yield, e.g., 4.90 percent, in order to attract buyers. When the bond is repriced on a 4.90 yield basis, it is found that the price decreases to $1,099.72—a loss of $6.23 to the seller. Thus, the 0.10 percent added to the 4.80 par yield rate becomes a *penalty yield increment.*

If the syndicate is to maintain its gross profit objective, the $6.23 must be passed back to the issuer in the form of an increase in coupon rates somewhere in the schedule if the issue is sold at par, or through an addition to the discount if the bond issue is sold at a discount. Although the adjustment is not made with a minute preciseness, the approximate amount is taken into account.

The Operation of Penalty Yield Rates for Discount Bonds

Reference has been made to the fact that bonds reoffered at discount prices ordinarily involve payment of federal capital gains taxes (and in some cases, state capital gains taxes). These are payable by the investor at the time of maturity (or earlier, if sold at a profit).

It has been shown above that a $1,000 bond due in 18 years with a coupon rate of 4.50 percent and a par yield rate of 6.20 percent would be priced at $817.16—producing a capital gain at maturity of $182.84 before taking into account the capital gains tax payable. For the corporate taxpayer, long-term capital gains are included as a part of ordinary taxable income and are currently taxed at a rate of 46 percent. [An alternative method is available but not considered here.] The tax would be $84.11 on the $184.84 gain. The present value (PV-1) of this tax at the par yield rate of 6.20 percent is $28.02. This is the equivalent of the new investor giving up 4.05 percent of the amount he is investing. Naturally, the investor will not make such a sacrifice as long as other investment opportunities are available without such loss. He will require an adjustment in the yield sufficient to provide the after-tax yield of 6.20 percent available from competitively priced bonds.

In order to compensate the investor for the burden of the capital gains tax, the yield is adjusted (and, in the process, consideration is given to the capital gains tax on the adjustment). Eventually, it is determined that a yield of 6.56 percent, rather than the original 6.20 percent will be required. The bond is now repriced at $784.05. This will involve a discount of $215.94 or $33.10 more than the discount would have been had the bond been priced without the capital gains tax factor.

In these circumstances, the issuer is required to make further adjustments in the coupon rates (or amount of the discount) sufficient to sustain the profit objective of the syndicate. (See Appendix E for method of calculation.)

Impact of State and Local Taxes

Ordinarily, no state or local income taxes are payable by a resident on the interest on tax-exempt bonds issued by his state government or by its local governments. However, this exemption frequently does not extend to income from bonds issued in other states nor to personal property taxes on such bonds. Capital gains on tax-exempt bonds are usually taxable by state and local governments without reference to the state in which issued.

Pricing to Call Date

When bonds are callable prior to maturity and the coupon rate is greater than the yield rate, the bonds are usually priced to call date rather than to maturity date. Thus a noncallable bond maturing in 12 years is priced on the basis of 24 semiannual periods; if the bond is callable after 10 years, the pricing would be on the basis of only 20 semiannual periods. If a call premium is payable, the present value (PV-1) of the call premium will be added to the price if the bond is selling at or below par.

All of the foregoing factors are to be kept in focus in the examination of the six illustrative alternatives (V-1 to V-6) shown in Tables 33–38. The factors have varying degrees of impact on the effective interest rate.

Zero Coupon Debt

In zero coupon bonds, no interest is paid on a given bond between the date of its issue and the date of its maturity.[2] For zero coupon bonds arranged to provide an equal annual debt service, the face value of the bond is established in a manner that the sum of all bonds maturing on a given date is approximately equal to the number maturing on each other date. A discount rate is applied to each maturity from the reoffering scale that is to be used in the sale of the bonds (presumably with the bonds being sold to investment bankers at discounts which will enable them to reoffer the bonds at prices that provide for the appropriate yield).

Each bond is price under PV-1, i.e.

$$\text{Price} = \frac{1}{(1+i)^n} \times \$1,000$$

The sum of the prices times the value of the debt service scheduled for each maturity constitutes the money in hand delivered to the issuer, after adjustment for the cost of issuance.

As is illustrated in Table 41 in Chapter 13, the net interest costs expressed in TIC terms is substantially below the TIC for conventional serial bonds.[3] As explained in the preceding chapter, zero coupon bonds for municipalities are only beginning to make their appearance in the market and much learning is required concerning this new instrument.

---

[2] The maturity of the bond is accelerated through call by the issuer, or it may be paid prior to maturity if the owner has and exercises a right of earlier surrender. In the latter case, the owner is usually required to pay a penalty for redemption prior to maturity.

[3] An interesting variation on the theme was provided by the "premium bonds" sold by the City of New Orleans in the 1870s. These bonds were of $20.00 denomination, with an interest rate of 4.00 percent, with interest payable as simple interest at maturity, with 1 percent of the bonds maturing each six months for 50 years. The result was that only one percent of the holders realized a full 4.00 percent rate—those whose bonds were drawn and paid at the first maturity. The effective rate steadily decreased thereafter to 3.39 for those paid at the 10th anniversary, to 2.79 percent on the 25th anniversary, and 2.21 percent on the 50th anniversary. Attractive premiums were paid semiannually based on drawings by lot among the holders.

Effect of the Yield Curve

In the determination of interest costs, the yield curve is critical. A yield curve is developed by plotting the yield values for a series of years on a graph and connecting the points. The yield curve may have a high or low incidence. Thus, Pattern A in Appendix Table A illustrates a low rate of incidence during the first 20 years while Pattern B offers a much higher rate of incidence. Occasionally, during very tight short-term money markets, the curve may be inverted for the short maturities. Also, at times it is almost flat because of the lack of differential between short-term and long-term rates. The par (basic) yield curve is the set of values which apply to a sale in which the bonds are all reoffered at or near par. The yield curve applied to a given bond issue is frequently warped through the application of penalty yield points due to either prices above 105 percent of par or to discount prices to compensate for capital gains taxation.

As applied to a specific bond issue, the yield curve represents the yield to maturity rates at which a bidder proposes to reoffer a given issue of bonds if each were reoffered at par. Other bidders preparing par yield curves for the same bonds at the same time are influenced by the same basic market conditions and will, therefore, follow the same configuration; however, the second bidder's yield curve may reflect a belief that the particular bonds command a more favorable or a less favorable position in the market than the other yield curves prepared simultaneously for the same bond issue.

In order to illustrate the dollar effect of two separately prepared yield curves of two bidders for the same bond issue, assume $10,000,000 in bonds are being offered to mature at the rate of $1,000,000 per year. Bidders X and Y submit offers shown below with coupon rates equal to yield rates. For the early years, Y assumes that the combination of general market conditions and the market position of this bond issue requires 10 basis points higher yield for the first six years and 15 basis points higher yield for the remaining four years than X does. In order to understand the dollar significance of the higher Y bid, it is necessary to price the bonds at the yield rates offered by X. When this is done, the results are as follows:

Year	Maturity	Yield Rates Used in Development of Bids Offered		Additional Interest Payable under Y	Value of Bonds Carrying Coupon Rates under Y when Priced at Yields under X
		X	Y		
1	1,000,000	4.50	4.60	12,000	1,000,967
2	1,000,000	4.75	4.85	11,000	1,001,887
3	1,000,000	5.00	5.10	10,000	1,002,754
4	1,000,000	5.20	5.30	9,000	1,003,570
5	1,000,000	5.40	5.50	8,000	1,004,331
6	1,000,000	5.60	5.70	7,000	1,005,037
7	1,000,000	5.70	5.85	6,000	1,008,559
8	1,000,000	5.80	5.95	4,500	1,009,493
9	1,000,000	5.90	6.05	3,000	1,010,359
10	1,000,000	5.95	6.10	1,500	1,011,184
Total	10,000,000			72,000	10,058,141

In other words, Y is asking that the issuer pay an additional $72,000 which has a present value (PV-1) of $58,141 or $5.81 per bond, when valued under X yield rates.

Different bidders may have moderately different views concerning the incline in the curve appropriate to the current circumstances. Two bidders might agree on a yield rate of 5.25 percent for year-4 but differ for year-20, with one ending his yield curve at 6.10 and the other at 6.20.

The basic configurations of a par yield curve at a given time on a given day for high-grade bonds, are likely to be very similar because they tend to represent market conditions. On the other hand, differences do exist due largely to judgments as to the direction in which the basic trend for the remainder of the day and the near future will move. The patterns of yield curves set forth in Appendix Table A would occur at substantially different times. The change from the one pattern to a markedly different pattern occurs over a period of time, usually with relatively minor adjustments from one day to the next. However, occasionally, there is a sharp change in the market with a very noticeable shift within hours.

Fitting the Basic Yield Curve to a Given Bond Issue. The manager of each syndicate in a competitive sale of municipal bonds develops a proposed yield curve for that bond issue. When completed and accepted by the syndicate members, it is the lowest yield basis at which the syndicate can agree and represents their collective judgment of the yields at which the bonds can be successfully marketed. Having developed the yield curve it proposes to use in marketing the bonds (if it becomes the successful bidder), the next job is to reach agreement within the syndicate as to the amount of gross profit to be sought, i.e., the spread between the amount to be paid for the bond issue and the aggregate amount expected to be received from the sale of the bonds by the syndicate. If the bidding specifications permit a discount bid, the syndicate will offer to purchase the bonds at a price sufficiently below par to enable it to reoffer all of the bonds at par on the yield curve and achieve its spread from the discount. If, for example, the syndicate concludes that on a $20,000,000 issue it expects to make a gross profit of 2.00 percent, it will offer to purchase the bonds at a discount of 2 percent, i.e., it will agree to pay $19,600,000 for the bonds. In that case, coupon rates bid will usually be identical with the yield curve rates of the bidder.

On the other hand, if the bidding specifications require a *par bid,* i.e., a bid which offers settlement in an amount at least to the par value of the bonds, the bidder will develop a schedule of coupon rates that are higher than the yield rates for selected maturities. The bonds with the higher coupon rates will be sold at profits sufficient to aggregate the projected $400,000 in spread.

Although the yield curve of the successful bidder is made public through reoffering of the bonds, the reoffering scales of the other bidders are not usually made public. Even so, sophisticated investors will usually know whether the other bids were substantially in line with the successful bidder or whether there were significant differences. If the differences have been minor, the effect of the other bids will have been supportive of the judgment of the successful bidder, thereby aiding the syndicate in the sale of the bonds at the planned yield rates. On the other hand, if there is a considerable difference between the successful bid and the next higher bid, the sophisticated investor will likely conclude that the yield rates offered are too low. If all the bonds cannot be sold at the established reoffering yield rates, the syndicate will be dissolved. Thereupon, members are obliged to take their agreed shares of the unsold bonds and to sell them subsequently at such prices as they find feasible.

Effects of Premiums and Discounts at Reoffering

The foregoing discussion has been concerned with bonds sold to investors at par, or marginally above or below par. What happens when the bonds are sold at prices significantly above or significantly below par? Two different patterns emerge.

The Bonds Reoffered at a Significant Premium. When bonds are sold at prices above par, there is generally little investor resistance as long as the premium is relatively small, e.g., less than 5 percent ($1,050 per $1,000 par value). As prices rise above 105 percent of par, many investors complain and some refuse to buy without further inducement in the form of additional yield, i.e. the *penalty increment*. As the prices rise higher, penalty yields increase in an irregular pattern, depending largely on the portion of the market to which the securities are being sold. For example, banks generally do not resist premiums to the same extent as do individual investors. Hence, it is not unusual to find that, for bonds reoffered at prices above par, most of the spread is generated from the first 10 maturities—the area in which the banks are most interested.

Individual Maturities Reoffered at Discount. Bonds of selected maturities at discounts will eventually require taxable investors to pay federal capital gains taxes and may also involve state capital gains taxes, whether issued within or outside the state of residence of the owner. As indicated earlier, the investor usually refuses to purchase municipal bonds involving potential gains taxation unless the price is adjusted downward to assure an after-tax yield approximating the tax-free par yield rate for the same bond. In this manner, the seller absorbs the present value (PV-1) of the capital gains tax. If the seller is the issuer, the issuer is obliged to absorb the present value (PV-1) arising from the penalty yield. Usually, pricing takes into account federal capital gains taxes but, where state income or capital gains taxes are high, these may also be factored into the price. Within the context of these restraints, it is appropriate to examine each of six alternatives.

Conventional Par Bid

Alternative V-1 (Table 33) represents a conventional par bid requiring all bonds to be purchased as a part of the serial bond issue. V-1 develops the gross profit on the first 10 maturities, in a manner that holds penalty yields to a minimum.[4] Under V-1, bonds maturing after call date are all reoffered at par. As a result, the reoffering and par yield rates shown in Column 4 of Table 33 are identical in all but four years.

This bid results in an indicated spread between purchase price and reoffering price of $405,891 (Column 6), with a premium of $5,891 offered. This brings the net amount realized to $20,005,891. The gross coupon interest payable is $12,370,000 which produces a spread of $400,000 after allowance for the premium. Total debt service under this alternative becomes $32,370,000. V-1 results in conventional NIC of 5.8877 percent and a TIC rate of 5.8543 percent.

Reoffering Selected Maturities at Discount

Alternative V-2, illustrated in Table 34, assumes the same bidding specifications as Alternative V-1. However, under Alternative V-2, the bidder seeks an NIC advantage over V-1 by decreasing the coupon rate for the final three maturities to 4.50 percent and increasing the coupon rates on the first ten maturities. The result is a skewing of the *time* at which interest is paid by the issuer, thereby readjusting the present value (PV-1) of both the principal and interest. Thus, the interest payable in the first year increases from $1,154,000 to $1,262,000.

---

[4] There is no absolute rule concerning the point at which penalty rates will be applied in the pricing of bonds above par. Different dealers and investors have widely varying ideas of what is appropriate. For purposes of Tables 33–38 it has been assumed that, if the price is less than 105 percent of par value, no penalty rate will be assessed. Beyond 105 percent, it is assumed that a penalty of 5 basis points (.005 percentage points) is added to the reoffering yield for each increase of 5 percent (or fraction thereof) in the price. Thus, a bond priced at $1,075 would carry a 5 basis point penalty; a bond priced at $1,137 would carry a 10 basis point penalty, etc.

Table 33

Debt Service on Equal Annual Maturity 20-Year Conventional Serial Bond Issue Sold under a Par Bid Requirement—Conventional Bid
Alternative V-1

(amounts in thousands of dollars)

Year	Maturi-ties	Par Yield Rate[1]	Penalty Yield	Reof-fering Yield Rate[2]	Coupon Rate	Profit (Loss)	Interest
	(1)	(2)	(3)	(4)	(5)	(6)	(7)
1	1,000	3.20		3.20	5.60	23	1,154
2	1,000	3.50		3.50	5.60	40	1,098
3	1,000	3.80	+ .05 =	3.85	5.60	49	1,042
4	1,000	4.10	+ .05 =	4.15	5.60	53	986
5	1,000	4.35	+ .05 =	4.40	5.60	53	930
6	1,000	4.60	+ .05 =	4.65	5.60	49	874
7	1,000	4.80		4.80	5.60	47	818
8	1,000	5.00		5.00	5.60	39	762
9	1,000	5.20		5.20	5.60	28	706
10	1,000	5.25		5.25	5.55	23	650
11	1,000	5.50		5.50	5.50	—	595
12	1,000	5.60		5.60	5.60	—	539
13	1,000	5.70		5.70	5.70	—	484
14	1,000	5.80		5.80	5.80	—	426
15	1,000	5.90		5.90	5.90	—	368
16	1,000	6.00		6.00	6.00	—	310
17	1,000	6.10		6.10	6.10	—	250
18	1,000	6.20		6.20	6.20	—	188
19	1,000	6.30		6.30	6.30	—	127
20	1,000	6.35		6.35	6.35	—	64
Total	20,000					406[3]	12,370

[1] The par yield rates are identical to those reflected in Pattern B of Appendix Table A.

[2] The reoffering yield rates shown in italics in Column 4 are penalty yield rates reflecting the penalty yield rates shown as additions between the par yield rates in Column 2 and the reoffering yield rates.

[3] A premium of $5,891 is offered to bring the average gross profit per bond to 2 percent of par value.
Average interest rates: NIC 5.8877
TIC 5.8543

As the syndicate retails the bonds, it is obliged to take an aggregate loss of $703,000 on the final three maturities (Column 6 for years 18, 19, and 20). In order to compensate for this loss, the coupon rate for each of the first nine maturities is raised from the 5.60 percent shown under V-1 to 7.25 percent and a somewhat similar adjustment is made in the 10th maturity (Column 5). In the process, additional losses are sustained by the issuer because the syndicate is obliged to provide for two sets of *penalty yields*, i.e., the difference between the values shown in Columns 2 and 4 of Table 34. These penalty yields occur in respect to maturities in each of the years 2-10 and 18-20.

Despite the loss being sustained by the issuer, the aggregate interest payable under V-2 is $145,000 less than under V-1 before adjusting for the difference in premium offered on the two issues—$12,225,000 vs. $12,370,000. Therefore, under the NIC basis the bonds would be awarded to V-2 with an NIC of 5.8208 percent vs. 5.8877 percent for V-1.

Table 34

Debt Service on Equal Annual Maturity 20-Year Serial Bond Issue
Sold under Par Bid—Skewed Coupon Bid
Alternative V-2

(amounts in thousands of dollars)

Year	Maturi- ties	Par Yield Rate[1]	Penalty Yield	Reof- fering Yield Rate[2]	Coupon Rate	Profit (Loss)	Interest
	(1)	(2)	(3)	(4)	(5)	(6)	(7)
1	1,000	3.20		3.20	7.25	39	1,262
2	1,000	3.50	+ .05 =	3.55	7.25	71	1,189
3	1,000	3.80	+ .05 =	3.85	7.25	95	1,117
4	1,000	4.10	+ .10 =	4.20	7.25	111	1,045
5	1,000	4.35	+ .10 =	4.45	7.25	124	972
6	1,000	4.60	+ .10 =	4.70	7.25	132	899
7	1,000	4.80	+ .10 =	4.90	7.25	138	827
8	1,000	5.00	+ .10 =	5.10	7.25	140	755
9	1,000	5.20	+ .10 =	5.30	7.25	138	682
10	1,000	5.25	+ .10 =	5.35	6.85	115	609
11	1,000	5.50		5.50	5.50	—	541
12	1,000	5.60		5.60	5.60	—	486
13	1,000	5.70		5.70	5.70	—	430
14	1,000	5.80		5.80	5.80	—	373
15	1,000	5.90		5.90	5.90	—	315
16	1,000	6.00		6.00	6.00	—	256
17	1,000	6.10		6.10	6.10	—	196
18	1,000	6.20	+ .35 =	6.55	4.50	(215)	135
19	1,000	6.30	+ .40 =	6.70	4.50	(234)	90
20	1,000	6.35	+ .50 =	6.85	4.50	(254)	45
Total	20,000					401[3]	12,225

[1] The par yield rates are identical to those reflected in Pattern B of Appendix Table A.

[2] The reoffering yield rates shown in italics in Column 4 are penalty yield rates reflecting the penalty yield rates shown as additions between the par yield rates in Column 2 and the reoffering yield rates.

[3] A premium of $836 is offered to bring the average gross profit per bond to 2 percent of par value.
Average interest rates: NIC 5.8208
  TIC 5.93028

The Single Coupon Rate Alternative

Alternative V-3 (Table 35) illustrates the results of a bid under specifications requiring a single coupon rate applicable to all maturities.[5] A bid of 5.875 percent enables the bidder to pay $20,006,552 at settlement and develop a profit at 2.00 percent per bond. The gross spread of $406,552 is adjusted to $400,000 by a premium of $6,552. The single coupon rate requirement adds three separate cost elements to the issuer:

1. Penalty yield for maturities in year-3 through year-8 to pricing:
   5 basis points with aggregate value of $14,768

---

[5] Among the states in which a single coupon rate is widely used by local governments are Indiana, Ohio, Massachusetts, New Jersey, and New York.

Table 35

Debt Service on Equal Annual Maturity 20-Year Serial Bond Issue Sold under Requirements for Par Bid and Single Coupon Rate Alternative V-3

			(amounts in thousands of dollars)				
Year	Maturi-ties	Par Yield Rate[1]	Penalty Yield	Reof-fering Yield Rate[2]	Coupon Rate	Profit (Loss)	Interest
	(1)	(2)	(3)	(4)	(5)	(6)	(7)
1	1,000	3.20		3.20	5.875	26	1,175
2	1,000	3.50		3.50	5.875	45	1,116
3	1,000	3.80	+ .05 =	3.85	5.875	57	1,057
4	1,000	4.10	+ .05 =	4.15	5.875	63	999
5	1,000	4.35	+ .05 =	4.40	5.875	· 66	940
6	1,000	4.60	+ .05 =	4.65	5.875	63	881
7	1,000	4.80	+ .05 =	4.85	5.875	60	822
8	1,000	5.00	+ .05 =	5.05	5.875	54	764
9	1,000	5.20		5.20	5.875	47	705
10	1,000	5.25		5.25	5.875	48	646
11	1,000	5.50		5.50	5.875	29[3]	587
12	1,000	5.60		5.60	5.875	21[3]	529
13	1,000	5.70		5.70	5.875	13[3]	470
14	1,000	5.80		5.80	5.875	6[3]	411
15	1,000	5.90		5.90	5.875	(2)	352
16	1,000	6.00		6.00	5.875	(13)	294
17	1,000	6.10	+ .025 =	6.125	5.875	(26)	235
18	1,000	6.20	+ .05 =	6.25	5.875	(40)	176
19	1,000	6.30	+ .05 =	6.35	5.875	(52)	117
20	1,000	6.35	+ .05 =	6.40	5.875	(59)	59
Total	20,000					407[4]	12,338

[1] The par yield rates are identical to those reflected in Pattern B of Appendix Table A.
[2] The reoffering yield rates shown in italics in Column 4 are penalty yield rates reflecting the penalty yield rates shown as additions between the par yield rates in Column 2 and the reoffering yield rates.
[3] Priced to first call date.
[4] A premium of $6,552 is offered to bring the average gross profit per bond to 2 percent of par value.
Average interest rates: NIC 5.8719
TIC 5.8705

2. Penalty yield to accommodate capital gains taxes for maturities in year-17 through year-20 with an aggregate value of 18,483
3. Penalty for maturities in year-11 through year-14 arising from price to call date for bonds having coupon rate in excess of yield rate, with an aggregate value of 9,257
Total penalty $42,508

The NIC rate is 5.8719 percent and the TIC rate, 5.8705 percent.

Coupon Rate Limitations

Many issuers believe they can foreclose the tendency of bidders to indulge in discount reoffering of the type shown under Alternative V-2 by introducing a prohibition against

Table 36

Debt Service on Equal Annual Maturity 20-Year Serial Bond Issue Sold under Requirement for Par Bid and No Decrease in Coupon Rate after 11th Maturity
Alternative V-4

(amounts in thousands of dollars)

Year	Maturities	Par Yield Rate[1]	Penalty Yield	Reoffering Yield Rate[2]	Coupon Rate	Profit (Loss)	Interest
	(1)	(2)	(3)	(4)	(5)	(6)	(7)
1	1,000	3.20		3.20	6.90	36	1,240
2	1,000	3.50	+ .05 =	3.55	6.90	64	1,171
3	1,000	3.80	+ .05 =	3.85	6.90	86	1,102
4	1,000	4.10	+ .05 =	4.15	6.90	100	1,033
5	1,000	4.35	+ .10 =	4.45	6.90	109	964
6	1,000	4.60	+ .10 =	4.70	6.90	114	895
7	1,000	4.80	+ .10 =	4.90	6.90	117	826
8	1,000	5.00	+ .10 =	5.10	6.90	117	757
9	1,000	5.20	+ .10 =	5.30	6.90	113	688
10	1,000	5.25	+ .10 =	5.35	6.90	119	619
11	1,000	5.50		5.50	5.50	—	550
12	1,000	5.60	+ .05 =	5.65	5.50	(13)	495
13	1,000	5.70	+ .05 =	5.75	5.50	(23)	440
14	1,000	5.80	+ .05 =	5.85	5.50	(33)	385
15	1,000	5.90	+ .10 =	6.00	5.50	(49)	330
16	1,000	6.00	+ .15 =	6.15	5.50	(66)	275
17	1,000	6.10	+ .15 =	6.25	5.50	(78)	220
18	1,000	6.20	+ .15 =	6.35	5.50	(90)	165
19	1,000	6.30	+ .15 =	6.45	5.50	(103)	110
20	1,000	6.35	+ .15 =	6.50	5.50	(111)	55
Total	20,000					410[3]	12,320

[1] The par yield rates are identical to those reflected in Pattern B of Appendix Table A.

[2] The reoffering yield rates shown in italics in Column 4 are penalty yield rates reflecting the penalty yield rates shown as additions between the par yield rates in Column 2 and the reoffering yield rates.

[3] A premium of $9,622 is offered to bring the average gross profit per bond to 2 percent of par value. Average interest rates: NIC 5.8621
TIC 5.9267

any decrease in coupon rates after a given point—either throughout the issue or after a given point in time, e.g., the midpoint. The limitation is usually successful; however, a determined bidder can submit a V-4 type bid, while conforming to most bid specifications. It has been shown under V-2 that, with a spread of 2.75 percent between the highest and lowest coupon rate, substantial losses can be produced. In Alternative V-3, it is shown that the single coupon bid requirement also produces losses. V-4 (Table 36) tests the premise based on a prohibition against an increase in coupon rates after midpoint in the series. The coupon rate for V-4 is set at 6.90 percent during the first 10 years and 5.50 percent during the second 10 years. This produces an NIC of 5.8621 percent and a TIC of 5.9267 percent.

It also produces penalty yield rates for 18 of the 20 maturities; only year-1 and year-11 are exempt. The penalty yields in several of the years is as much as 15 basis points.

Sales of Bonds by the Issuer at Discount

When an entire bond issue is sold at a sufficient discount, the profit for the underwriter can be derived from either (1) the discount alone with all bonds reoffered at par, or (2) a combination of discount and profit differentials between the coupon and reoffering yield rates. An examination of reported results of negotiated bond sales shows that in discount sales it is customary to reoffer all of the bonds at or near par. This reflects the decided preference of most investors for acquisition at par and removes any need for adjustments in par yield, thereby also avoiding all penalty yields.

Alternative V-5 (Table 37) illustrates the sale of a bond issue at a 2.00 percent discount with par reoffering. The aggregate amount of the bonds sold has been increased from the $20,000,000 in the preceding tables to $20,408,160 in order that, after a discount of approximately 2.00 percent ($408,160), a settlement of $20,000,000 will be produced—the same

Table 37

**Debt Service on Equal Annual Maturity 20-Year Serial Bond Issue
Sold at 2.00 Percent Discount—Conventional
Alternative V-5**

Year	Maturi- ties[1]	Par Yield Rate[2]	Reof- fering Yield Rate[2]	Coupon Rate	Profit (Loss)	Interest
	(1)	(2)	(3)	(4)	(5)	(6)
1	1,020	3.20	3.20	3.20	—	1,054
2	1,020	3.50	3.50	3.50	—	1,021
3	1,020	3.80	3.80	3.80	—	985
4	1,020	4.10	4.10	4.10	—	946
5	1,020	4.35	4.35	4.35	—	905
6	1,020	4.60	4.60	4.60	—	860
7	1,020	4.80	4.80	4.80	—	813
8	1,020	5.00	5.00	5.00	—	764
9	1,020	5.20	5.20	5.20	—	713
10	1,020	5.25	5.25	5.25	—	660
11	1,020	5.50	5.50	5.50	—	607
12	1,020	5.60	5.60	5.60	—	551
13	1,020	5.70	5.70	5.70	—	493
14	1,020	5.80	5.80	5.80	—	435
15	1,020	5.90	5.90	5.90	—	376
16	1,020	6.00	6.00	6.00	—	316
17	1,020	6.10	6.10	6.10	—	255
18	1,020	6.20	6.20	6.20	—	192
19	1,020	6.30	6.30	6.30	—	129
20	1,020	6.35	6.35	6.35	—	65
Total	20,408				408[3]	12,140

(amounts in thousands of dollars)

[1] The actual amount of maturities is $1,020,408 for each year and the interest and debt service amounts reflect that amount of principal.

[2] The par yield rates are identical to those reflected in Pattern B of Appendix Table A.

[3] Inasmuch as all bonds are sold at a 2.00 percent discount, the profit is derived from the discount.

Average interest rates: NIC 5.8557
TIC 5.8578

Table 38

Debt Service on Equal Annual Maturity 20-Year Serial Bond Issue
Sold at 2.00 Percent Discount—Skewed Coupon Bid
Alternative V-6

(amounts in thousands of dollars)

Year	Maturities[1]	Par Yield Rate[2]	Penalty Yield	Reoffering Yield Rate[3]	Coupon Rate	Profit (Loss)[4]	Interest
	(1)	(2)	(3)	(4)	(5)	(6)	(7)
1	1,020	3.20		3.20	5.55	23	1,186
2	1,020	3.50	+.05 =	*3.55*	6.30	54	1,130
3	1,020	3.80	+.05 =	*3.85*	6.30	70	1,065
4	1,020	4.10	+.05 =	*4.15*	6.30	80	1,001
5	1,020	4.35	+.05 =	*4.40*	6.30	86	937
6	1,020	4.60	+.05 =	*4.65*	6.30	87	872
7	1,020	4.80	+.05 =	*4.85*	6.30	87	808
8	1,020	5.00	+.05 =	*5.05*	6.30	83	744
9	1,020	5.20	+.05 =	*5.25*	6.30	76	680
10	1,020	5.25	+.05 =	*5.30*	6.20	71	615
11	1,020	5.50		5.50	5.50	—	552
12	1,020	5.60		5.60	5.60	—	496
13	1,020	5.70		5.70	5.70	—	439
14	1,020	5.80		5.80	5.80	—	381
15	1,020	5.90		5.90	5.90	—	321
16	1,020	6.00		6.00	6.00	—	261
17	1,020	6.10		6.10	6.10	—	200
18	1,020	6.20	+.35 =	*6.55*	4.50	(219)	138
19	1,020	6.30	+.40 =	*6.70*	4.50	(239)	92
20	1,020	6.35	+.50 =	*6.85*	4.50	(259)	46
Total	20,408					408	11,963

[1] The actual amount of maturities is $1,020,408 for each year and the interest and debt service amounts reflect that amount of principal.

[2] The par yield rates are identical to those reflected in Pattern B of Appendix Table A.

[3] The reoffering yield rates shown in italics in Column 4 are penalty yield rates reflecting the penalty yield rates shown as additions between the par yield rates in Column 2 and the reoffering yield rates.

[4] The profit under this bid consists of a discount of 2.00 percent of the par value of the bonds plus adjustments reflected in Column 5 for individual maturities.

Average interest rates: NIC 5.7731
TIC 5.9254

as the earlier issues in this series (except for premium adjustments). Because the size of the issue is increased moderately, the gross profit objective rises from $400,000 to $408,160—still at the level of $20 per $1,000 par value. The result is an NIC of 5.8557 percent and a TIC of 5.8578 percent.

Alternative V-6 (Table 38) combines the sale at discount with a bid in which the bidder seeks the same type of advantage shown in V-2, by use of 4.50 percent coupon rates for year-18 through year-20 maturities. In order to do this, the bidder is obliged to set the coupon rates at 5.55 percent for the first year; 6.30 for years 2–9; and 6.20 for the 10th maturity. Penalty yields of .05 percent are required in year-2 through year-10

Table 39

Summary of Results Obtained in Six Alternatives Illustrated in Tables 33–38

(amounts in thousands of dollars)

Line	Item		The Par Bids			The Discount Bids	
		V-1 Table 33	V-2 Table 34	V-3 Table 35	V-4 Table 36	V-5 Table 37	V-6 Table 38
		(1)	(2)	(3)	(4)	(5)	(6)
	I. Results Under Bidding Processes Outlined						
	A. Principal						
1	1. Par Value	20,000	20,000	20,000	20,000	20,408	20,408
2	2. Premium (discount)	6	1	7	5	(408)	(408)
3	3. Net Proceeds	20,006	20,001	20,007	20,005	20,000	20,000
4	B. Interest	12,370	12,225	12,338	12,320	12,140	11,963
5	C. Debt Service (1) + (4)	32,370	32,225	32,338	32,320	32,548	32,372
6	Bond years	210,000	210,000	210,000	210,000	214,286	214,286
	Average Interest Costs						
7	NIC	5.8877	5.8208	5.8719	5.8621	5.8557	5.7731
8	TIC	5.8543	5.9303	5.8705	5.9267	5.8578	5.9254
	II. Interest Costs Payable Before and After Call Date						
9	To call date	9,020	9,353	9,106	9,295	8,722	9,038
10	After call date	3,350	2,867	3,231	3,025	3,418	2,925
11	Total	12,370	12,225	12,338	12,320	12,140	11,963

and penalty yields of 35, 40, and 50 basis points, respectively, for year-18, year-19, and year-20 to compensate for the capital gains taxes payable.

SUMMARY OF THE RESULTS OF THE BIDDING PROCESS

Under par bid specifications, V-2 would be the winner under NIC processes inasmuch as it has a decided advantage over the others—5.8208 percent compared to 5.8621, 5.8719, and 5.8877 for V-4, V-3, and V-1, respectively. However, quite different results are obtained under TIC calculations. The order is substantially modified, with V-1 in a commanding lead position with 5.8543 percent and V-2 in fourth place with 5.9303 percent. Inasmuch as TIC is a much better gauge of the relative advantages of different bids, the issuer would find it appropriate to adopt TIC under these circumstances. These results are reflected in Table 39.

If the bidding permitted discount bids, V-6 would have the major advantage under NIC over V-5—5.7731 percent vs. 5.8557 percent. But, it would be at a major disadvantage under TIC calculations, 5.9254 vs. 5.8578 percent.

Effect on Potential Savings in Refunding

Assuming that the bond issues are to be callable on the 10th anniversary, the potential saving from refunding is directly related to the amount of interest payable after that date and the times at which it is payable. The greater the amount of interest to be paid per callable bond outstanding, the greater the potential for saving through refunding after call date is likely to be. From Table 39 it is seen that the aggregate amounts of interest payable after call date vary substantially, depending upon the alternative used. The amounts become:

Alternative	Interest Payable after Call Date	Principal Outstanding	Interest Payable after Call Date per $1,000,000 Outstanding
V-1	3,350,000	10,000,000	335,000
V-2	2,867,000	10,000,000	286,700
V-3	3,231,250	10,000,000	323,125
V-4	3,025,000	10,000,000	302,500
V-5	3,418,340	10,204,080	334,997
V-6	2,925,487	10,204,080	286,698

By this measure, V-1 and V-5 offer the most favorable alternatives, followed closely by V-3. The least favorable are V-2 and V-6, with V-4 falling in the middle range of potential for savings in refundings. Although one does not design bond issues solely for the purpose of future refunding, good design requires that the potentials for savings under refunding be taken into consideration. If, for example, a 10 percent net reduction in future interest costs were obtainable, the potential savings under V-2 and V-6 would be distinctly less than those obtainable under the other alternatives.

THE CAPITALIZATION TEST

Although the foregoing advantages under TIC are impressive, they are not easy to interpret as to dollar impact. The best test is afforded through capitalization of the debt service under the various plans to determine which produces the greatest amount of cash in hand (PV-2) at settlement date for the issuer in return for the debt service the issuer would pay under the bid. Table 40: Part A illustrates both the technique and results of such capitalization as applied to V-2. From Column 1 of Table 40: Part A, it can be seen that the amount of principal to be received is $20,000,000 and in Column 3, the debt service is $32,225,000—both as shown in Table 34.

The next step is to ascertain the amount of principal supportable by the pattern of debt service if the amounts were capitalized into a municipal bond issue. The results on an annual basis are shown in Column 4 using coupon rates for V-2A equal to the par yield rates shown in Tables 33–38. The aggregate amount of principal supportable on this basis is $20,543,330. The debt service for each year for V-2 is equal to that for V-2A; however, there is an aggregate increase of principal in the amount of $543,330 and a corresponding decrease in the amount of interest payable under V-2A. But, inasmuch as the issuer has made provision for an average profit of $20 per bond for V-2, it is necessary to provide an identical profit under V-2A. This is done by discounting the principal of $20,543,330 by the amount of $410,867. Therefore, the issuer would receive $20,132,463 at settlement, which can be compared to the $20,000,836 received under V-2. Thus, the realizable value of the debt service payable under V-2 is $131,627 more than the issuer would receive should that bid have been accepted.

Similar calculations have been made for each of the other alternatives and the results can be summarized as follows:

	(amounts in thousands of dollars)				
Alternative	Capitalized Value	Less: Discount	Value at Settlement	Amount Realizable under Tables 33–38	Gain under PV-2 (4) − (5)
(1)	(2)	(3)	(4)	(5)	(6)
Par Bids					
V-1	20,415	408	20,007	20,006	(1)
V-2	20,543	411	20,132	20,001	131
V-3	20,446	409	20,037	20,007	30
V-4	20,540	411	20,129	20,010	119
Discount Bids					
V-5	20,408	408	20,000	20,000	—
V-6	20,528	411	20,118	20,000	118

The significance of this tabulation is that, for the par bids, the value under capitalization for V-1 is substantially identical with the values under the amounts shown in the tables.

Under this analysis approach, it is revealed that V-2 has a present value (PV-2) of $131,000 greater than the amount being delivered to the issuer should V-2 be accepted (as would be required under NIC). Failure to obtain this additional amount at settlement constitutes a loss to the issuer. The tabulation also shows that V-3 (the single rate bid) involves a loss of about $30,000. The effort to discourage discount through bid limitations or declines in coupon rates after call date in V-4 provides $119,000 fewer dollars in hand than the PV-2 approach. For the original discount bids, the manipulation of coupons under V-6 produces a loss of $118,000.

Reduced Debt Service. One final calculation in this series is presented in Table 40: Part B. The amounts shown in Columns 4 and 6 of Table 40: Part A are reduced sufficiently to produce $20,000,000 at settlement to the issuer by use of the discount bid for the full issue and through use of par yield reoffering of all bonds. A review of Table 40: Part B

Table 40: Part A

Capitalization of Debt Service In Table 34—Alternative V-2
Based on Coupon Rates Equivalent to Par Yield Rates

(amounts in dollars)

Year	Values of V-2 (From Table 34)			Values of V-2A			Increase in Amounts of V-2A over V-2	
	Maturities	Coupon Rate	Debt Service	Maturities	Coupon Rate	Debt Service	Maturities (4)–(1)	Interest
	(1)	(2)	(3)	(4)	(5)	(6)	(7)	(8)
1	1,000,000	7.25	2,260,000	1,216,351	3.20	2,260,000	216,351	(216,351)
2	1,000,000	7.25	2,189,500	1,182,774	3.50	2,189,499	182,774	(182,774)
3	1,000,000	7.25	2,117,000	1,151,671	3,80	2,117,000	151,671	(151,671)
4	1,000,000	7.25	2,044,500	1,122,935	4.10	4,044,500	122,935	(122,935)
5	1,000,000	7.25	1,972,500	1,096,475	4.35	1,972,000	96,475	(96,475)
6	1,000,000	7.25	1,899,500	1,091,672	4.60	1,899,500	71,672	(71,672)
7	1,000,000	7.25	1,827,000	1,048,469	4.80	1,827,000	48,469	(48,469)
8	1,000,000	7.25	1,754,500	1,026,295	5.00	1,754,500	26,295	(26,295)
9	1,000,000	7.25	1,682,000	1,005,110	5.20	1,682,000	5,110	(5,110)
10	1,000,000	6.85	1,609,500	984,876	5.25	1,609,500	(15,163)	15,163
11	1,000,000	5.50	1,541,000	968,082	5.50	1,541,000	(31,917)	31,917
12	1,000,000	5.60	1,486,000	966,327	5.60	1,486,000	(33,672)	33,672
13	1,000,000	5.70	1,430,000	964,441	5.70	1,430,000	(35,558)	35,558
14	1,000,000	5.80	1,373,000	962,414	5.80	1,373,000	(37,585)	37,585
15	1,000,000	5.90	1,315,000	960,234	5.90	1,315,000	(39,765)	39,765
16	1,000,000	6.00	1,256,000	957,888	6.00	1,256,000	(42,111)	42,111
17	1,000,000	6.10	1,196,000	955,361	6.10	1,196,000	(44,638)	44,638
18	1,000,000	4.50	1,135,000	952,638	6.20	1,135,000	(47,361)	47,361
19	1,000,000	4.50	1,090,000	966,702	6.30	1,090,000	(33,297)	33,297
20	1,000,000	4.50	1,045,000	982,605	6.35	1,045,000	(17,395)	17,395
Total	20,000,000		32,225,000	20,543,330		32,225,000	543,330	(543,330)
Discount	—			(410,867)			(410,867)	
Net	20,000,000			20,132,463			132,463	(543,330)

shows that the aggregate principal produced (Column 4) is $20,408,000. After a discount of 2 percent, or $408,000, this results in delivery to the issuer of $20,000,000 at settlement. The debt service for such a sale is shown in Column 6; the effect on overall debt service is reflected in Column 9. Under this alternative plan, the issuer pays an aggregate of $212,000 less debt service than under Plan V-2, while receiving almost identical amounts at settlement.

The foregoing offers a condensed statement of the problems involved in determining the best bid. It also offers a basis for redesign of procedures and specifications by those issuers that continue to hold to the NIC basis for award of competitive bids. In these illustrations, the issuer could make savings in the range of 6/10ths of 1 percent of the par value of the issue in present value terms in V-2, V-4, and V-6.[6]

---

[6] For other views concerning this entire subject, see Center for Capital Market Research, University of Oregon, in cooperation with Municipal Finance Officers Association of the United States and Canada, *Improving Bidding Rules to Reduce Interest Costs in the Competitive Sale of Municipal Bonds* (1977).

Table 40: Part B

Comparison of Debt Service on $20,000,000 in Bonds With Debt Service Shown in Table 34 and with Net Proceeds of $20,408,000 Bond Issue Sold at 2.00 Percent Discount Issued Under Pattern V-2A Shown in Table 40: Part A

(amounts in thousands of dollars)

Year	Values of V-2 (From Table 34)			Values for Alternative V-2B			Increase (Decrease) in Amounts of V-2B over V-2		
	Maturities	Coupon Rate	Debt Service	Maturities	Coupon Rate	Debt Service	Maturities	Interest	Debt Service
	(1)	(2)	(3)	(4)	(5)	(6)	(7)	(8)	(9)
1	1,000	7.25	2,260	1,208	3.20	2,247	208	(221)	(13)
2	1,000	7.25	2,190	1,174	3.50	2,175	174	(189)	(14)
3	1,000	7.25	2,117	1,145	3.80	2,103	145	(159)	(14)
4	1,000	7.25	2,044	1,115	4.10	2,031	116	(129)	(13)
5	1,000	7.25	1,972	1,089	4.35	1,959	89	(102)	(13)
6	1,000	7.25	1,900	1,065	4.60	1,887	65	(77)	(12)
7	1,000	7.25	1,827	1,042	4.80	1,815	42	(54)	(12)
8	1,000	7.25	1,754	1,020	5.00	1,743	20	(31)	(12)
9	1,000	7.25	1,682	998	5.20	1,671	(2)	(10)	(11)
10	1,000	6.85	1,610	978	5.25	1,599	(22)	11	(11)
11	1,000	5.50	1,541	962	5.50	1,531	(38)	28	(11)
12	1,000	5.60	1,486	960	5.60	1,476	(40)	30	(10)
13	1,000	5.70	1,430	958	5.70	1,421	(42)	33	(9)
14	1,000	5.80	1,373	956	5.80	1,364	(44)	35	(9)
15	1,000	5.90	1,315	954	5.90	1,306	(46)	37	(9)
16	1,000	6.00	1,656	953	6.00	1,248	(48)	40	(8)
17	1,000	6.10	1,196	949	6.10	1,188	(51)	43	(8)
18	1,000	4.50	1,135	946	6.20	1,128	(54)	46	(7)
19	1,000	4.50	1,090	960	6.30	1,082	(40)	32	(7)
Total	20,000		32,225	20,408		32,012	408	(196)	(212)
Discount	—		—	(408)		—	(408)		
Net	20,000		32,225	20,000		32,012	0		

Single Coupon Rate Requirement

For two reasons the single coupon rate requirement in effect in several states is inadvisable: (1) In all circumstances it requires that almost all of the bonds be offered at either a premium or a discount; and (2) in many market situations, this results in either penalty yields or in adjustment of yields to pay the present value (PV-1) of the capital gains tax. In the case of callable bonds, the single bid rate is likely to increase the inefficiency as shown under V-3. In the first case, it is basically a nuisance but doubtless adds to the cost of distribution in ways that cannot easily be quantified; in the second case, it is a demonstrable waste arising from penalty yields. Except in the case of almost flat yield curves, single rate coupons should be avoided. Moreover, a careful review of potential impact in the case of callable bonds is needed.

Responsibility of Financial Advisors and Bond Counsel

With their increased use, it becomes imperative that the financial advisors be held accountable for the introduction of methods that provide the best protection to the issuer.

This includes ability on the part of the financial advisor to cope with the problem of the best method of determining effective interest costs. Frequently, the law requires only that the issuer make the award to the bidder offering the lowest *effective* interest costs. The bond counsel issues opinions to the effect that the issuer has complied with the law. When the law does not require the use of NIC, the bond counsel is probably making an incorrect certification.

RECOMMENDED SPECIFICATIONS FOR AVERAGE INTEREST COST DETERMINATIONS

The basic objective is to secure the best available par yield curve and to couple this with avoidance of penalty yields—whether due to the high pricing at reoffering for the early maturities or to providing for payment of capital gains taxes on final or near final maturities. The achievement of a good par yield position depends upon the many considerations discussed elsewhere. The avoidance of penalty yields is largely a technical problem to which the solution is primarily in the use of TIC. Issuers confronted with NIC constraints should move promptly to have these eliminated. Frequently, the bond counsel will find that it is feasible to substitute TIC in situations heretofore believed to require NIC.

Par + NIC

If the issuer is constrained by law to use both the par settlement and NIC, there is relatively little that can be done until the constraint is removed. Efforts to restrict discount bids on the final maturities are only partially effective as they can be largely thwarted by the determined bidder. Even so, it is worth the try because it will doubtless discourage many skewed bids—especially for discount bonds for only a few maturities.

Equal Annual Debt Service + NIC

If the issuer is offering bonds on the basis of substantially equal annual debt service with the bidder fixing the schedule of maturities, NIC can ordinarily be safely used. In the process of providing substantially equal annual debt service, the bidder seeks to avoid penalty bids. Within the framework of the par bid yield rates and the gross profit objective, the bidder will be attempting to secure the same objective as the issuer—the highest present value (PV-2) for a given level of debt service. The bidder seeks to drive down the average debt service, and thereby the interest charge, in order to win the bid.

TIC Bids

The preferable basis for determining the lowest average net interest cost is TIC. It virtually forces the bidder to eliminate penalty bids if this is possible within the other constraints set by the issuer. It functions with impartiality between bonds bid at par, at a premium, or at a full-issue discount.

Full-Issue Discounts

In most circumstances, the full-issue discount sale is preferable to the par bid inasmuch as it facilitates reoffering of all bonds at or near par. Thereby, all penalty yield increments can be avoided.

DETERMINING THE BEST BID THROUGH CAPITALIZATION

The objective of this chapter has been to point out the importance of selecting a system for evaluating bids that will enable the issuer to obtain and accept the best bid. The differentials in interest costs outlined in the illustrations may appear as statistical abstractions to most readers. However, additional dollars in hand (PV-2) at settlement are not abstractions. They are the name of the game.

Under conventional patterns of bond sales, the roles of the issuer and the bidder may be stated thusly:

Issuer: Determines amount of principal sought and prescribes detailed rules of bidding.

Bidder: Determines debt service schedule by ascertaining the coupon rates to be affixed to each maturity, the amount of premium (or discount) to be bid, and thereby the pattern of debt service to be payable. In equal annual debt service offerings, the bidder may also determine the maturity schedule.

The issuer may influence the manner in which the bidder performs by the rules established. Bidders determine the appropriate par yield curves, the amount of gross profit, and the coupon rates to be applied—and, in some cases, the maturity schedules. The issuer tabulates the bids and makes an award on the basis of the lowest average net interest cost, under either NIC or TIC.

The Reverse Approach

Consider the possibility of reversing a part of the roles of the issuer and the bidder:

Issuer: Determines the amount of money to be available in each year as debt service and the maturity dates.

Bidder: Determines the amount of money in hand to be delivered to the issuer at settlement.

As to specifications, the issuer has to name only the amount of debt service payable each year and the date(s) on which maturities will fall.

The objective of the issuer is to obtain the maximum amount of principal at settlement that the best bidder can deliver through capitalization of the specified amounts of debt service. Thereupon, the bidder is free to use serial bonds, block-term bonds, zero coupon, or term bonds.[7] The bidder can plan to reoffer bonds above or below par, fix coupon rates in any pattern deemed advantageous, and otherwise tailor the offering to meet the twin objectives of satisfying investors and producing maximum amounts of principal for the issuer. The bidder can take advantage of the "original issue discount" doctrine if specifications permit or the issuer can offer specifications under which the bidder could in effect be purchasing two or more bond issues.

In some respects this type of bidding is approached in those bond issues selling under equal annual debt service constraints; however, in that case, the amounts of principal are predetermined by the issuer. Under this proposal, the issuer would place no formal limit on the amount of principal. If the highest amount offered under the best bid was deemed too low, all bids would be rejected in the same manner as is now done if the lowest interest cost is deemed to be too high. Alternatively, the issuer could establish a minimum

---

[7] The yield curve tends to obviate the use of full-term bonds unless the issuer has specified an investment rate for the sinking fund which acts in favor of that alternative and takes this into consideration in determining the effective interest cost. (Insofar as this author knows, this has never been done.)

amount of cash in hand that was acceptable. The issuer would, of course, continue to prescribe other features, e.g., call options.

This alternative approach would have the advantage of maximum simplicity for the issuer in determining the best bid. It would obviate all the arguments about NIC or TIC. It would obviate many of the factors discussed in the succeeding chapter about coupons. On the other hand, the issuer would have to be reasonably attuned to the probable par yield curve to be applied to its bonds and to the probable amount of gross profit to be sought in order to construct the debt service schedule against which bidding is to occur, especially if minimum acceptance bids were specified.

Chapter 13
COUPONS, CALL OPTIONS, DENOMINATION, AND REGISTRABILITY

Four of the major features of bond issues to be determined in advance of advertisement of a conventional competitive sale are:

1. The permitted pattern of coupons
2. The option for redemption of all, or portions, of bonds prior to their stated maturity date
3. The denominations in which the bonds are to be issued
4. The extent to which the bonds may be registered and, if registered, the circumstances under which they may be reconverted to coupon bonds

Similar determinations must be made in the course of negotiated sales.

THE COUPON

The great majority of municipal bonds are bearer bonds with coupons attached. As such, the issuer rarely knows who owns outstanding bonds. Payment of interest is made through surrender of detached coupons. Each coupon is in specific dollar amounts due at a stated date—almost always at semiannual intervals. When the bond is sold to the investor at par, the coupon and yield rates are identical. When tax-exempt bonds are sold to the investor at a premium, the premium must be amortized only against the tax-exempt coupon income. If the investor buys the bonds at a discount, a part of the yield is obtained from the coupon and a part from the increase in value at maturity.

Functions of Coupons

The use of coupons facilitates attainment of two objectives:

1. *Current Payment of Interest.* The coupon provides a method of payment of all, or part, of the interest to the bondholder on a current basis.

2. *Privacy for Investors.* The coupon facilitates maintenance of the *privacy* desired by many investors. In the view of some, maintenance of privacy is antithetical to the concept of full disclosure of everything to everybody. On the other hand, the founding fathers saw fit to provide against unwarranted searches and seizures. The use of the bearer bond with coupons enables the investor to enhance the likelihood of privacy. In the minds of numerous investors in municipal bonds, this is a value worth preserving in a society that progressively invades privacy of the individual.

The bearer bond does not require disclosure to the tax-enforcement bureaucracy—except for state taxes or capital gains taxes. There is still a great host of Americans who take the view that their personal affairs are *personal;* and that their affairs should not be open to the scrutiny of bank clerks or governmental or private bureaucrats—subject to gossip and unauthorized leaks to the press. They know that many legally mandated confidential relationships do not remain confidential. They find great consolation in the fact that the tax-exempt coupon permits a degree of privacy not available in most other types of investments. To this end, they are prepared to accept the annoyance incident to processing coupons.

Inefficiency of Coupons

The use of coupon bonds is a manifestly inefficient way in which to handle the payment of interest. The corporate practice of mailing checks at appropriate intervals to the owners of record is more efficient—especially in a computer age. Much of the processing of coupons is still handled manually through the banking system and paying agents as items for collection.

The inefficiency extends both to the out-of-pocket administrative costs for the issuer and the cost to the investor from delays in the settlement of accounts on interest due.[1] When one considers that many millions of coupons must be processed every six months, there is little wonder that numerous efforts have been made to encourage more widespread use of registered bonds or to make payments that can be processed mechanically through the banking system. Despite the inefficiency of the coupon bond, it continues to be the most popular means of settlement of interest. The matter of the *form* of the coupon is discussed later in this chapter.

Determining Coupon Rates

Except in those states in which the entire bond issue must be sold at a single interest rate, substantial flexibility is afforded to the bidders in competitive sales in establishing the coupon rates for each maturity. The degree of flexibility is subject to requirements of law and is regulated by the issuer in bidding specifications. In negotiated sales, the pattern of coupon rates suggested by the syndicate can be accepted, or a different pattern can be developed through negotiation.

As set forth in Chapter 12, each bidder may offer a different pattern of coupons. In par bid sales, coupon rates must exceed the reoffering yield rates for some maturities in order to develop the required gross profit. In establishing the specifications for bidding, the issuer normally has flexibility in determining these aspects of coupon rate patterns: (1) The maximum rate, (2) the minimum rate, (3) spread between the minimum and maximum rates, (4) the total number of rates, (5) the number of rates applicable to a single maturity, (6) the fractional interest rates, and (7) limitations on decreases in coupon rates.

Maximum Coupon Rate. The fixing of a maximum coupon rate is primarily to help control the pattern of debt service. Bonds can, of course, be sold at competitive sale without any maximum coupon rate limit. Occasionally, the absence of this limit has resulted in absurdly high coupon rates on the early maturities—the highest being the 50 percent rate established on certain bonds of the State of Minnesota in the early 1970s.

Unnecessarily high coupon rates at the front end of the maturity schedule produce three adverse effects:

1. The issuer is obliged to prepay large portions of the interest in relation to the time earned
2. High penalty reoffering yield rates almost always result because of the high prices on such maturities; high penalty yield rates also appear in some of the later maturities due to the capital gains tax considerations
3. It reduces or eliminates the capacity of the issuer to attain implicit potential savings in case a portion of the issue is refunded

---

[1] In efficient governmental cash management systems, these delays can be turned to the advantage of the issuer through short-term investment of cash balances in bond and coupon redemption accounts.

The pattern of restrictions on maximum coupon rates should be at a level that enables bidders to develop the necessary spread between the purchase and sale price of the bond issue with a minimum use of penalty yields. If the bonds are callable, the ceiling should be sufficiently high to permit generation of all of the spread on the noncallable portion of the issue.

The establishment of maximum coupon rates carries with it hazards that are sometimes not foreseen. Thus, if maximum rates are set too low, a no-bid situation becomes inevitable. If the bonds are callable, it can produce a sacrifice of values for the bonds with coupon rates higher than yield rates for bonds maturing after the first call date.

Minimum Coupon Rates and Coupon Spread Limitations. Specifications for bond issues rarely include an explicit minimum coupon rate. However, many issuers specify a limit on the spread between the highest and the lowest coupon rates to discourage absurdly deep discounts at reoffering. Limits on coupon rate spread frequently discourage discount reofferings of some maturities. When used, the coupon spread limitations are expressed in terms of a range of interest rates, e.g., a spread of not more than two percentage points between the highest and lowest coupon fixed by the bidder. At best, the coupon spread limitation is a palliative—not a cure. The use of TIC forces the bidders to eliminate rates that produce unnecessary penalty yields.

Number of Coupon Rates. There is no economic justification for limiting the number of coupon rates to be used in respect to a bond issue. No positive result is obtained; negative results frequently occur from penalty yields required in the pricing of a considerable portion of the bond issue. This observation extends to laws that impose single coupon limitations. Although the practice of limiting the number of coupon rates was once fairly widespread, it is being phased out.[2]

Split Rate Prohibition. Ordinarily, bidding specifications prohibit the use of more than one coupon rate for a single maturity. Although no historical documentation has been found on the point, it appears to arise from marketing considerations. From the standpoint of the issuer, the printing job is simplified by the use of only a single rate per maturity as are certain calculations in respect of debt service for the issue.

Fractional Interest Rate Intervals. In earlier periods, it was customary to limit the number of fractional rates that could be used—usually to multiples of $\frac{1}{4}$ of 1 percent. It was thought that this provided a sufficient flexibility for marketing purposes. As late as a decade ago, a considerable number of issuers still invoked the $\frac{1}{4}$ of 1 percent rule. At the other extremity, some bidders at that time were permitting bids on the basis of $\frac{1}{100}$ of 1 percent for coupon purposes.

When bonds are traded on a yield basis, it is almost always in multiples of $\frac{1}{20}$ or $\frac{1}{8}$ of 1 percent. When traded on a price basis, trading is usually in terms of multiples of $\frac{1}{8}$, e.g., $97\frac{7}{8}$ or $99\frac{3}{4}$, which usually produces fractional yields. It is desirable to facilitate the reoffering of all (or the largest portion feasible) of the bond issue at par. In order to do this, bidders should have the full flexibility afforded by the use of $\frac{1}{20}$ or $\frac{1}{8}$ of 1 percent. There are no demonstrable general market advantages to narrower or broader limits; however, in some private placement situations, a different rule may be warranted.

Prohibiting Decreased Coupon Rates. For those persisting in the use of NIC for award of bonds sold at competitive sale, the 1970s brought a growing limitation in coupon rates in an attempt to discourage payments in lieu of the capital gains tax and the penalty reoffering yield rates implicit in reoffering some maturities at a discount. The device used is a prohibition against setting the coupon rates for certain maturities below the rates established for the immediately preceding maturity.

Some issuers extend the prohibition to all maturities (usually producing a single coupon

---

[2] A study by the author of all advertised sales during the period January 16–March 15, 1968, showed that, of the 330 sales, about 10 percent imposed a single coupon rate. An additional 25 percent established limits as to the number of coupons, ranging from two to seven different rates. See Moak, *Administration of Local Government Debt,* p. 265.

bid rate); in other cases, the prohibition extends only to the final half or third of the maturity periods.[3] It is likely that this process has discouraged such discount bidding, although no comprehensive study has been made of the results achieved. On the other hand, a bid which uses a single interest rate for the final portion of maturities (as illustrated in Table 36) can still result in stiff penalty yields while conforming to the restriction.

When this type of restriction is applied only to the final one-third of the maturity periods, there is limited adverse effect and a greater likelihood of discouraging the discount bids. On the other hand, when the restriction is applied to the entire issue of bonds, it is likely to require offering some bonds at penalty yield rates that could have been advantageously reoffered at par yield rates (see Table 35). This is especially true in the case of callable bonds if coupon rates exceed yield rates after the first call date, thereby forcing the pricing of the bonds to such call date.[4]

The use of TIC in determining the best bid, with the range of coupons left to the bidder's discretion, is doubtless the best approach when award is made on the basis of average interest rates.

Legislatively Mandated Coupon Rate Ceilings

Legislatively mandated ceilings on interest rates usually take the form of either a maximum coupon rate or a maximum average interest rate for the bond issue. One (or both) of these purposes is sought:

1. A limit on the interest rates which lenders will charge
2. A public policy ceiling on rates at which debt can be incurred

As to the first, market interest rates are not significantly affected by maximum interest rate limitations on bonds offered for sale. Legislative limitations may be partially effective in regulated debt financing, e.g., mortgage and personal loans; but, they have little influence on rates competitively set. Investors tend to ignore the bonds that do not offer yields commensurate with the prevailing market. Although there may be minimal influence on interest rates, the usual effect is not to lower costs but to produce a no-bid market response.

On the other hand, limitations on interest rates designed to foreclose borrowing when the interest rate levels rise above the prescribed limit constitute an enforceable public policy. The objective is to prohibit the issuance of debt at interest levels judged by the lawmakers to be too high. The history of such policy efforts shows that, if rates continue at high levels for a period of time, the legislative bodies are likely to yield in the face of pressure for access to the market by the issuers.

As to the techniques to be used, maximum coupon rates constitute a rather crude tool. It is likely that they will result in a combination of penalty yield rates for many maturities in order to attempt to comply with the mandate. This is especially true when the yield curve is sharply inclined. It can produce the kinds of adverse results illustrated under the single coupon bond issues in the preceding chapter (Table 35). Legislatures would be more effective in pursuit of this objective should they consistently state the limit in TIC terms—perhaps at levels related to the average life of the bond issue. Recent experience shows that legislative bodies were frequently obliged to retreat from previous efforts to control overall interest payable by local governments. Many of them have abandoned all limits.[5]

---

[3] See Center for Capital Market Research, University of Oregon, and the Municipal Finance Officers Association, *Improving Bidding Rules to Reduce Interest Costs in the Competitive Sale of Municipal Bonds* (1977: University of Oregon, Eugene, Oregon), pp. 43 ff.

[4] Thus, in Table 35, it is noted that the 11th through the 14th maturities are priced to call date with consequent adverse effect on the aggregate profit for these maturities.

[5] For a tabulation of contemporary interest rate ceilings, see annual editions of The Bond Buyer's *Statistics on State and Local Government Finance*.

The Zero Coupon Loan

The zero coupon type of loan has been discussed briefly in Chapter 12. It is characterized by payment of interest at maturity in the form of appreciation in value of the money advanced by the lender. The issuance of noninterest-bearing warrants by state and local governments constitutes a type of zero coupon loan—even though the warrant may shift formal responsibility to the payee for payment of interest by forcing either a discounting of the warrant or an extension of nominally interest-free loans. Banks have frequently used a long-term version of the discounted loan in connection with certain types of transactions, e.g., in advance refunding of municipal bonds, they have sold their certificates of deposit on a discounted basis in order to assure that funds will be available to meet interest and maturity requirements on prerefunded bonds.

Despite certain theoretical and actual beneficial results from the use of zero coupon loans by state and local governments, they do not generally use them. There are also certain theoretical and actual disadvantages to such a system. Table 41 illustrates the present value (PV-2) to be derived from the capitalization of $1,000,000 per semiannual period over 20 years through the implicit method used in determining the amount of bonds supportable by a given stream of money in development of a municipal bond issue. It also illustrates the present value of the same debt service obtained by discounting each $1,000,000 installment of debt service at the semiannual coupon (yield) rate applicable to the period. Part A of Table 41 is developed in relation to the values shown in Pattern B of Appendix Table A. Part B contains a summary comparison of the results that would be obtainable under each of the A/E patterns under Appendix Table A.

From Table 41: Part A it may be observed that under the conventional method of capitalization a value of $23,627,000 is developed.[6] This may be computed to $24,197,000 under the zero coupon method of capitalization used under PV-3. It is apparent that an advantage of $570,000 is obtained under the zero coupon method—representing a gain in principal of 2.41 percent for the identical semiannual debt service of $1,000,000. From Part B it is also observed that a similar gain is derived under Alternative Pattern D and even greater gain from Pattern E—the very high coupon/yield pattern. Conversely, when the yield curve is relatively flat—as in Patterns A and C—the differential in the two systems of capitalization becomes relatively modest. Of course, if the yield curve were absolutely flat, the values would be identical.

The advantages to investors of the zero coupon type of investment include:

1. An automatic reinvestment of earned interest precisely upon the dates when compounding occurs. Thereby the investor is not confronted with the losses which frequently occur in the conventional processing of coupons and reinvestment operations.
2. The zero coupon approach assures the investor a guaranteed rate of return on his investment over its entire life as contrasted to his being obliged to accept the market risk involved in the reinvestment process each six months. [Of course, conventional YTM calculations assume a continuation of the reinvestment rate throughout the life of the security and immediate reinvestment even though this is never likely to occur.]
3. For investors who do not have a need for current income, the zero coupon bond offers a convenient manner in which to accumulate capital toward defined objectives, e.g., retirement income or payment of a deferred liability such as college tuition. Through purchase of bonds of given maturity dates matching the investor's objectives, this becomes the equivalent to the purchase of long-term certificates of deposit under which interest is all payable at maturity.

---

[6] See discussion in Chapter 12, especially in connection with Table 40: Part A, concerning the methodology of such capitalization.

Table 41: Part A

Comparative Present Value of $1,000,000 Per Semiannual Period for 20 Years under Capitalization as Conventional Serial Bonds and Capitalization under Zero Coupon

Semiannual Period	Semiannual Yield Rate	Amounts of Principal under	
		Conventional Serial Bond Capitalization (PV-2)	Discount at Yield Rate (Zero Coupon) (PV-3)
	(1)	(2)	(3)
1	1.525	$ 364,018	$ 984,979
2	1.60	369,569	968,751
3	1.675	375,482	951,387
4	1.75	381,772	932,958
5	1.825	388,453	913,540
6	1.90	395,542	893,212
7	1.975	403,057	872,055
8	2.05	411,017	850,150
9	2.1125	419,443	828,494
10	2.175	428,304	806,405
11	2.2375	437,620	783,948
12	2.30	447,411	761,188
13	2.35	457,702	739,363
14	2.40	468,458	717,464
15	2.45	479,701	695,537
16	2.50	491,454	673,624
17	2.55	503,740	651,768
18	2.60	516,585	630,010
19	2.6125	530,017	612,625
20	2.625	543,863	595,575
21	2.6875	558,140	572,968
22	2.75	573,140	550,553
23	2.775	588,901	532,828
24	2.80	605,243	515,424
25	2.825	622,190	498,347
26	2.85	639,767	481,602
27	2.875	658,000	465,193
28	2.90	676,918	449,127
29	2.925	696,548	433,405
30	2.95	716,922	418,031
31	2.975	738,072	403,008
32	3.00	760,029	388,337
33	3.025	782,830	374,018
34	3.05	806,511	360,054
35	3.075	831,109	346,443
36	3.10	856,667	333,187
37	3.125	883,223	320,282
38	3.15	910,823	307,729
39	3.1625	939,514	296,925
40	3.175	969,227	286,431
Total		$23,627,001	$24,196,947
Total Interest Cost		16,372,999	15,803,053
Total Debt Service		$40,000,000	$40,000,000
Average interest rates (percent): NIC		5.7967	7.9677
TIC		5.7303	5.4404

N.B. Semiannual rates developed from Pattern B, Appendix Table A.

Table 41: Part B

Conventional Coupon Capitalization and Zero Coupon Capitalization of $1,000,000 Per Semiannual Period under Alternatives A/E

(amounts in thousands of dollars)

	Alternatives from Appendix Table A				
	A	B	C	D	E
Amount capitalized	40,000	40,000	40,000	40,000	40,000
Principal realized by capitalization					
Under conventional coupon pattern	23,573	23,627	21,924	21,855	14,350
Under zero coupon pattern	23,775	24,197	22,139	22,441	15,028
Advantage gained by capitalization through zero coupon over conventional coupon					
Amount	203	570	214	585	678
Percent	.86	2.41	.98	2.68	4.72
Internal Rate of Return (TIC)					
Under conventional coupons	5.76848	5.73032	6.66311	6.70297	12.76388
Under zero coupons	5.65385	5.44040	6.59834	6.36860	12.01947
Difference	.10463	.28992	.06476	.33437	.74441

On the other hand, an investor who acquires a zero coupon bond is confronted with certain actual and potential disadvantages, including:

1. The rate of return is fixed and if the interest rates move to higher levels the investor is confronted with the likelihood of significant decreases in market prices for the bonds held.
2. There is no current income. Only through sale of the security can any cash be derived prior to maturity unless the issuer can be induced to make provision for some earlier redemption.

From the standpoint of the issuer, new accounting procedures are necessary in order to reflect interest costs as they accrue. Moreover, adjustments may also be necessary in order to reflect the net amount of principal represented by these outstanding bonds—with the amount being adjusted on each reporting date to reflect changes in value. Depending upon the character of the debt service plan developed in conjunction with zero coupon bonds, the issuer may be obliged to establish and administer a rather complex system of sinking fund or other debt service reserves to assure that sufficient funds will be on hand at the time of the maturity of the instruments. Such sinking funds may become a necessity in order to help assure the investor that he will not be wholly dependent upon the current year's appropriation corresponding to the year of maturity of his bonds.

Supplemental Coupons

From time to time, issuers sell bonds on the basis of dual or two-part coupons for early maturities, a practice that is also referred to as providing supplemental (or *B*) coupons. Supplemental coupons are usually detached by the syndicate at the time of sale of the bonds and promptly discounted as *taxable* instruments and at *taxable* interest rates.

If the *A* coupon is set at the par yield rate, the practice has the advantage of permitting a reoffering of the bonds at par—thereby avoiding penalty yield rates arising from marketing at prices significantly above par. On the other hand, when the supplemental coupon is discounted at taxable interest rates, the present value (PV-1) is much less than when discounted at significantly lower tax-free rates. Thus, assuming that a 7.00 percent coupon would be attached to a bond due in five years with the par reoffering yield rate being 5.00 percent, the initial pricing would be considered as $1,087.52. If this pricing resulted in a change in the reoffering yield rate to 5.05 percent, the bond would be priced at $1,085.22. The syndicate would have $85.22 in hand as spread.

However, if the coupon rate were split into a 5.00 percent coupon and a 2.00 percent coupon, the syndicate may be obliged to discount the supplemental coupon at a rate of 8.00 percent. Thereupon, the value of the 2.00 percent coupon would be only $81.11. A loss of $4.11 per bond would be involved—to be allocated to the issuer if the gross profit of the syndicate is to be maintained.

Indexed Interest Rates

During the rapid escalation of interest and inflation rates in the mid-1970s, there was discussion of indexed interest rates. Again, in 1980 and 1981, record interest rates revived such discussions for tax-free debt. Although there has been some use of indexed rates for private debt, they have only recently appeared in a few municipal bond issues.

Micro-encoded Substitutes for Coupons

For several years East Brunswick, New Jersey, has offered an alternative to conventional coupons as a means of payment of interest on tax-exempt bonds. It has recognized that the conventional system imposes an expense on both the banking system and the issuers of tax-exempt bonds. It also constitutes a nuisance for the investor. Further, it is more difficult and expensive to maintain a proper reconciliation of the accounts relating to coupons and to cancelled bonds. A considerable number of outstanding bonds are lost or misplaced each year. Substitute securities are issued. Unless there is a means of identification both of the coupons paid and of the bonds themselves at maturity, the issuer may make some duplicate payments. Moreover, the quality of commercial reproduction equipment has improved to the point that the likelihood of fraud arising from bogus bonds and coupons is increased.

One of the problems encountered has been that the coupons do not represent money under the Uniform Commercial Code and Federal Reserve Regulation J—both of which treat coupons as noncash items. East Brunswick has overcome these problems by issuing both bonds and coupons on check-sized, micro-encoded paper. The interest payment is in the form of a series of postdated checks that can be processed by the banking system as cash transactions. Therefore, they are subject to full computer processing both in the banking system and in the maintenance of records relating to the bond issue.

This system has been in operation in East Brunswick for several years and is reported to be in use by a number of other jurisdictions—including Spotswold, Piscataway, the Princeton Board of Education, and Trenton in New Jersey, as well as Aurora, Colorado. Although the experience has not been evaluated by any broadly representative group, it offers a promising potential that warrants the most careful review by each issuer pending such general evaluation.[7]

Conclusions as to Coupon Rates

In the light of the foregoing discussion and that in Chapter 12, these conclusions are offered concerning coupon rate practices:

1. *To Compensate Investment Bankers.* Par bid requirements force the issuer into a position of accepting coupon rates on certain maturities in excess of the reoffering rates to provide the spread necessary to generate the gross compensation to the syndicate. This practice is likely to result in penalty yield rates unless the issuer works out a pattern designed to avoid high premiums in the pricing of the bonds. Generally, bonds sold at a discount enable reoffering at par, thereby avoiding penalty yields.

2. *Maximum Coupon Rates.* If NIC bid procedures are used, the establishment of a well-planned, maximum coupon rate discourages manipulation of the bidding through the use of discount reoffering rates for the final maturity, or group of maturities. The maximum coupon rate limitations may aid in enforcement of policies relating to maximum interest rate policies. The rates must be designed in a manner that does not foreclose generation of sufficient spread for the underwriters, especially in high interest rate periods for equal annual debt service issues.[8] Moreover, such rates should seek to avoid penalty yields.

3. *Coupon Spread Limitations.* Limits on the spread between the highest and lowest coupon rates help to control the amount of discount at which selected maturities may be reoffered. However, if poorly planned, they can result in penalty yields for some maturities.

4. *Maximum Effective Interest Costs.* If state legislatures wish to establish maximum effective interest costs, these maximums should be established on the basis of average effective TIC interest rates and not by limiting maximum coupon rates.

5. *Number of Coupon Rates.* There appears to be no valid reason for limiting the number of coupon rates. Single coupon requirements should be eliminated.

---

[7] For a general discussion of micro-encoding, see L. Mason Neely, "Can the Municipal Bond Market be Broadened to Reach the Average Citizen?" *Municipal Management: A Journal,* 1978–1979, pp. 143–150. Neely took the initiative in development of these procedures as they relate to East Brunswick, shortly after becoming Director of Finance there in 1974.

[8] In high interest rate markets, equal annual debt service requirements act to produce low amounts of maturities in the early years. Maximum interest rates, if poorly designed, can result in no-bid situations because of the inability of the syndicate to develop a bid under which sufficient gross profit can be obtained.

6. *Coupon Rate Intervals.* In order to provide maximum flexibility in establishing coupon rates and to encourage reoffering of the maximum number of bonds at par, it is desirable to allow wide flexibility in establishing rates by use of multiples of $\frac{1}{20}$ and $\frac{1}{8}$ of one percent.

7. *Supplemental Coupons.* Supplemental coupons should be avoided because of the inefficiency arising from discount of these at the higher taxable coupon rates whereas discount at the lower tax-free rates can usually be arranged in the absence of the supplemental coupon. Occasionally, the split coupon is useful, especially when the option is excessively high penalty yields. This should be monitored by expert financial advisors.

8. *Micro-encoded Payments.* The initial experience and the logic of the use of micro-encoded, check-type bonds and coupons offer advantages warranting careful examination and potential use by issuers.

THE USE OF THE CALL OPTION

Each bond of a state or local government has a specified maturity date, i.e., a date at which the issuer is obliged to redeem the bonds. However, bond contracts frequently permit the redemption of all, or portions, of the outstanding bonds at dates in advance of the specified maturity date. Some bond contracts require the issuer to retire portions of the bond issue in advance of the stated maturity date.

The *optional* prepayment of principal (in advance of the specified maturity date) is a *right.* If reserved, this must be done at the time the bond contract is being consummated.[9] Unless such right is reserved in the bond contract, the issuer can accelerate the maturity only with the consent of the bond holder, or by readjustment in default or debt reorganization proceedings. Bonds redeemable prior to maturity are referred to as *callable, optional,* or *redeemable*—usually on an interchangeable basis.

Purposes of the Call Feature

The call option is ordinarily inserted to enable the issuer to achieve one or more of the following objectives:

1. Voluntary reduction of outstanding debt
2. Accommodation of mandatory debt reduction features of indenture
3. Achievement of a reduction in interest costs through refunding
4. Defeasing existing contractual obligations in relation to outstanding debt
5. Voluntary reorganization of the debt

Voluntary Reduction of Outstanding Debt. The call option affords an opportunity for the use of excess revenues in the acceleration of the maturity of the debt on a voluntary basis. There is limited use of the call option for this purpose, inasmuch as the issuer can ordinarily secure a higher rate of return on moneys invested in taxable securities than can be saved through acceleration of retirement of outstanding debt. Moreover, even though the reduction of outstanding debt does not show a net interest advantage, sometimes reduction of outstanding debt strengthens the market for new debt being issued.

---

[9] There is, however, one case involving the issuance of $8,500,000 in highway bonds by Maricopa County, Arizona, in 1919 and 1921. Apparently, the County believed that, despite the fact that the bonds appeared to mature serially through 1951, under legislation effective at the time of the issue of the bonds, the County had an automatic right to refund outstanding bonds at such time as it should elect. Such an election was made by the County in 1941, and after four years of litigation in the state courts of Arizona and in the United States Court for the District of Arizona and the U.S. Circuit Court of Appeals, Ninth District, the right of the County to issue the refunding bonds was eventually sustained. See *Washington v. Maricopa County et al.* Mem. 327 US 799; 66 S.Ct. 900, 90:1024. Also 90 Law Ed., No. 878; 143 F. 2d 871; 152 F. 2d 556; 327.

Mandatory Debt Reduction. Many revenue bond indentures require mandatory reduction of debt through the use of designated excess revenues. Absent a call option for this purpose, the issuer would be obliged to accomplish such reductions through market purchases regardless of price.

Refunding to Achieve Interest Savings. The opportunities for refunding at an interest saving arise from three circumstances:

1. A general decrease in interest rates
2. The operation of the yield curve in markets usually prevailing under which longer-term debt can be advantageously refunded even though the basic interest market is very similar to that in which the bonds were initially sold
3. Improvement in the credit position of the issuer, arising either from basic improvement in economic conditions or from a record of successful operation of a governmental enterprise

These matters are discussed in Chapter 21.

Defeasing Existing Bond Contracts. In commencing a governmental enterprise, it is frequently necessary to include in the original indenture various kinds of restrictive provisions in order to be able to float the initial bond issue. As the enterprise matures and proves its earning capacity, it may prove inconvenient for the issuer to continue to operate under the existing indenture. However, until the existing restrictions can be defeased, the issuer is obliged to conform to each of the conditions imposed, e.g., retrospective or prospective earnings tests in the issuance of additional parity bonds, or requirements that disproportionate shares of current revenues be applied exclusively to liquidation of outstanding debt. At the time of initial financing, the issuer may have had little discretion as to the terms under which loans were being obtained; however, as the enterprise proves successful, the issuer may seek to defease the outstanding debt in order to eliminate the restrictive covenants.

Voluntary Reorganization of the Debt. Under some circumstances it is desirable to be able to reorganize outstanding debt to achieve these current objectives:

1. Defeasing the current indenture
2. Consolidation of debt
3. Transfer of debt obligations as functions are shifted from one government to another
4. Integration of debt service on new debt with that on outstanding debt

In each of these and other circumstances, the availability of a call provision can facilitate the operation and, in some cases, may reduce the costs involved.

Beyond these, there are occasions for reorganization such as those confronted by many older school districts today. They have high debt service costs in the 1980s and much lower costs in the 1990s. A new pattern of debt service costs may be appropriate. Call provisions can facilitate such reorganization.

Reservation of the Option to Call

The reservation of the call option was widespread in bonds issued prior to World War II;[10] however, with the drastically lower interest rates during the 1940s and 1950s,

---

[10] A perusal of the literature shows that the number of surveys of the inclusion of call features in bond contracts is limited. For many years *The Bond Buyer* published an analysis of *Municipal Bond Sales*. A review of these annual editions of 1920–1936 inclusive was reported by the Committee on Municipal Debt Administration in 1938. It showed that 5.21 percent of both number of issues and amount of bonds sold in the period contained a call feature. At least some of the 5,158 callable issues examined were sold by governments in 46 of the 48 states. The most frequent use of the call feature was, in terms of the number of issues, in Colorado (418), Kansas (502), Nebraska (946), and Pennsylvania (616). The largest volume was in Pennsylvania, with $317.8 million of a total of $862.4 million of total callable issues. See Committee on Municipal Debt Administration, Municipal Finance Officers Association, *The Call Feature in Municipal Bonds* (1938), pp. 14–15, 113–114.

the practice fell largely into disuse. At the same time, term bonds were supplanted by serial bonds and the average life of all debt was drastically reduced, thereby reducing the portions of bond issues available for refunding. With the return of higher interest rates in the mid-1960s and the accentuation of these rates after 1974, the popularity of the call feature has returned.

Cost of the Call Option

There is no organized body of knowledge or professional opinion concerning the effect of a call option on the reoffering yield curve. Samplings of the opinions of underwriters and other professionals active in the municipal bond market reveal divergent views. Under these circumstances, it is not feasible to discuss the cost of the call option in definitive terms. Yet, a review of some points helps to clarify some aspects of the importance of the call option to both the issuer and the investor.

The issuer and the investor have diametrically opposite interests in this area. Except for advantages the investor may gain through advance refunding,[11] any potential advantage gained by the issuer represents a corresponding disadvantage by the investor. Thus, the issuer can give significant call protection to the investor either in the form of deferring the call date or offering substantial premiums payable for exercise of the call option; however, the greater the protection afforded, the less the advantage to the issuer if the call option is exercised. The call option can affect the pricing of the callable bonds either by a general adjustment in the reoffering yield curve or through specific adjustments in prices for those maturities that are priced to call date.

If one assumes, for purposes of illustration, that an investor has the option of purchasing at date of issue a 20-year bond bearing a 6.35 percent coupon rate under terms that are (a) noncallable, (b) callable on or after 10th anniversary date at par, or (c) callable on or after 10th anniversary date @ $102\frac{1}{2}$, he is obliged to ponder the relative value of the three bonds should he decide to sell at some future date. For purposes of illustration the investor would rationally make a number of assumptions as to what might happen. One set of assumptions he might explore is disposition in markets represented in the tabular material immediately below (in which the yield to maturity rates are based upon data from Appendix Table A).

Years to maturity	18	14	10	6	3
Years to next call date	8	4	$\frac{1}{2}$	$\frac{1}{2}$	$\frac{1}{2}$
Coupon rate	6.35	6.35	6.35	6.35	6.35
Yield to maturity rate	6.20	5.80	5.35	4.60	3.50
Price for a bond that is:					
Noncallable	1,016.13	1,052.24	1,076.67	1,090.85	1,080.50
Callable at par	1,009.35	1,019.39	1,004.87	1,008.55	1,014.10
Callable @ $102\frac{1}{2}$	1,024.69	1,039.28	1,029.27	1,032.99	1,038.57
Advantage (disadvantage) of noncallable bond over:					
Bond callable @ par	6.75	32.85	71.80	82.30	66.40
Bond callable @ $102\frac{1}{2}$	(8.56)	12.96	47.45	57.86	52.28

Under the circumstances postulated, the investor would know that should he sell the bonds two years hence, the noncallable bond would be priced at $1,016.13; the bond

---

[11] Lower- and medium-quality bonds that are refunded on an advance refunding basis usually experience a significant increase in quality and price.

callable at par, at \$1,009.35, and that callable with a premium of $2\frac{1}{2}$ percent would bring \$1,024.69. The differences obtainable are relatively minor and would not materially influence his judgment.

On the other hand in examining the situation at the mid-point of the life of the bonds, it would be found that the noncallable bond would have a *then* price advantage of \$71.80 over the bond callable at par and a \$47.45 advantage over that callable @ $102\frac{1}{2}$. Similar differentials are present at other times.

It is, however, emphasized that these differentials are being computed at a *future* date in respect to the date of issue of the bonds. Accordingly, should they be reduced to present value at the time of sale, the amounts would all be much less than that provided in the illustrative materials—with the actual amount depending upon the discount rate used. Thus if a 6.20 percent discount rate were used against the \$66.40 to be derived on a sale in the last column, the present value of the \$66.40 would be only \$23.52; however this might be of sufficient importance to cause the investor to avoid the bond callable at par in this illustration.

Decision to Reserve Call Option

The decision to reserve or not to reserve the call option is one to be made at the time the bond sale is planned. Current opinion should be sought as to the probable costs of the feature (as penalty yields). Analysis should be made of the potential costs vs. contingent benefits at a future date. On balance, it appears a call option should be included in almost all circumstances for bonds maturing more than 10 years from date of issue. In periods of low interest rates, the cost is doubtless nil because of the low probability of exercise of the option; in periods of high interest costs, the cost of the option is not known although it is probably well below the potential benefits to be gained. In any event, the analyses should include a present value (PV-1) statement of all of the costs and potential benefits. Otherwise, erroneous conclusions are likely because of a failure to bring data into a common frame of reference.[12]

Kinds of Call Features

The use of a call feature requires determination of the following:

1. The portion of the bond issue which will be made callable
2. The premium or pattern of premiums, if any, to be paid for the privilege of call
3. The notice required for exercise of the call

Portion of the Issue to be Made Callable. Prior to World War II, when 30-, 40-, and 50-year term bonds were common, the period between issue date and call date was found to be 12.5 years for bonds sold in 1931—the highest year for which data have been compiled. For 1925, the average term to call date was 7.00 years and in 1936, it was 5.3 years. When serial bonds were viewed separately, those issues containing a call feature ranged from 6.25 years in 1927 to a low of only 2.50 years in 1936. Many of the term bond issues with a 50-year life had a call date of 20 years.[13] There have been no studies during recent years; however, a casual examination of official advertisements in *The Bond Buyer* suggests that call provisions on serial bonds have been generally in the five- to 10-year range.

---

[12] For those readers interested in a more comprehensive statement on this point, see Moak, *Administration of Local Government Debt,* pp. 282–285.

[13] Committee on Municipal Debt Administration, Municipal Finance Officers Association, *The Call Feature in Municipal Bonds,* p. 24.

The Pattern of Call Premiums. Ordinarily, no call premium is payable on a bond called to conform to a *mandatory* obligation under the bond contract. The patterns of *optional* call premiums vary widely. Generally, when planned to obtain reductions in interest costs, call features fall within one of these four general patterns:

1. A uniform premium, applicable to all callable bonds, e.g., 3.00 percent
2. A uniform premium, applicable if the call is executed within a given span of years, e.g., 10th through the 14th year, with a different premium at other times
3. A schedule of premiums determined on the basis of the remaining life of the particular bond, e.g., a premium of $\frac{1}{4}$ of 1 percent for each remaining year of life from call date to maturity date, but with a ceiling on the maximum premium
4. One of the above, coupled with call at par after a given number of years, e.g., in a 30-year bond issue, call after the 17th year might be at par

Notice of Call. The bond contract ordinarily specifies that notice of call shall be publicly given to bondholders within a period at least 30 days and not more than 60 days prior to redemption date. The notice is required to be advertised—usually in a local newspaper and a journal of national circulation in the municipal bond field. For smaller communities, the requirement may also be for advertisement in a nearby metropolitan newspaper.

Order of Call

Each bond bears an identification number commencing with the first bond of the first maturity and progressing to the last bond of the final maturity. Thus, the bonds of the final maturity bear the highest numbers in the series. There are important differences in the order of call between serial bond issues and term bond issues. Within either, if portions of the bonds are required to be retired (in part or whole through exercise of a call option) prior to the normal maturity date, the order of call becomes of major importance.

Call of Bonds for Refunding. If the call option is to be used to refund serial bonds, the call should be in *inverse* order of the numbers assigned to the bonds. The importance of this option is illustrated in Chapter 21. In serial bond refunding to achieve interest savings, it is frequently inadvisable to call all of the outstanding bonds—due, in part, to the impact of the call premium and, in part, to the cost of issuance of the refunding bonds. If the refunding is in respect to term bonds, the order of call is of no consequence, inasmuch as it will be an all-or-none call in any event.

Call for Retirement from Excess Revenues. Many revenue bond contracts require allocations of excess net revenues to accelerate retirement of the debt. If the bonds are selling at below par, the issuer is usually permitted to discharge the obligation by purchase of bonds in the open market or through tender at below par. However, a failure to reserve this option can require pursuit of the more expensive course of redemption through the exercise of the call option. If the call is exercised, it is ordinarily required to be from the bonds with the longest maturity and by lot within such maturity. Thus, if $1,000,000 of serial bonds are to be redeemed and only $300,000 remain outstanding for the longest maturity, the issuer would call all of the $300,000 plus $700,000 drawn by lot from the next longest maturity outstanding. In the case of term bonds, all such calls are by lot inasmuch as all of the bonds have the same maturity date. Zero coupon bonds will require new patterns yet to be developed.

DENOMINATION OF BONDS

Prior to the 1960s, the primary denomination used in the sale of municipal bonds was $1,000. By the end of the 1960s, more than three-fourths of the issues, and almost all those of the larger issuers, were using a $5,000 denomination; while about 40 percent of the very small bond issues were still using the $1,000 denomination. A review of the "Sealed Bids Invited" column in *The Weekly Bond Buyer* currently shows an almost unanimous use of the $5,000 denomination in the sale of bonds by issuers of all sizes. The use of the higher denomination is necessary both to avoid needless multiplication of paper work and also to reduce the cost of handling per dollar of par value.

Some issuers permit the purchasing syndicate to place orders (before the bonds are printed) for larger denominations; however, the use of this option appears generally limited to issues of notes, rather than bonds.

Mini-Bonds

From time to time, various local governments have used mini-bonds as a means of helping to encourage broader distribution of bonds and expansion of the market. One of the earliest major uses of the mini-bond was by the City of New Orleans in the 1870s when it achieved success in marketing several million dollars of $20 denomination bonds carrying a simple interest rate of 4 percent, with payment of interest deferred until maturity. Maturity was by lot. Substantial premiums were also distributed at each semiannual drawing. Small denomination bonds were issued during the Great Depression. At various other times, governments have experimented with the use of mini-bonds. Thus, the law in Pennsylvania during the late 1960s sought to make these tax-exempt bonds available to buyers interested in $100 denomination securities. The School District of Philadelphia marketed $3,145,000 in such denominations in the years 1969–1974; a few other Pennsylvania jurisdictions issued considerable amounts of such bonds during a brief period of years.

The most recent sale of mini-bonds has been by East Brunswick Township, New Jersey. It marketed two small issues during 1978—$529,000 and $500,000 in denominations of $100, $200, and $500—although the township reports that the demand is usually for somewhat higher denominations. Sales are also reported for Framingham, Massachusetts, of $600,000 in March, 1979; Ocean County, New Jersey, of $1 million in April, 1979; and Union Township, New Jersey, of $574,000 in June, 1979.[14]

These and other sales indicate that there is a market for smaller denomination bonds. Two difficulties are encountered: (1) Providing an organized secondary market and (2) overcoming the high unit costs of issuance and processing. As noted, the high unit costs of processing have been largely overcome by New Brunswick through use of the micro-encoded, check-type coupon.

REGISTRABILITY OF BONDS

Only a small portion of municipal bond issues are registrable—either as to principal only or as to both principal and interest. On the other hand, a majority of the large issues permit registration. (This is in contrast to corporate bonds which are rarely issued in coupon form. In corporate practice, as ownership changes, registration on company records is made immediately by transfer agents. In this regard, corporate bonds are more attractive to some investors than municipal bonds.) For settlement, the bonds are usually prepared in fully negotiable form, with coupons attached. These are known as *bearer bonds,* inasmuch as ownership is presumed to rest with the person having possession of the bonds.[15]

---

[14] See L. Mason Neely, "Can the Municipal Bond Market be Broadened to Reach the Average Citizen?" *Municipal Management: A Journal,* 1978–1979, pp. 143–150.

[15] This is true in all cases except those in which the owner has lost the bonds or they have been destroyed by fire or other hazard. Normally, in such cases the owner can secure the issue of substitute bonds by filing an affidavit as to the circumstances under which the bonds were lost and also filing a surety bond with the issuing government to the effect that, should it subsequently appear that the person filing for the substitute bonds has misrepresented the facts and has sold, or otherwise legally disposed of, the original bonds, his surety will be liable for the face amount of the bonds and interest paid thereupon to the person filing the affidavit or to subsequent owners of the substitute bonds.

When interest is due upon a bearer bond, the owner clips the current coupon and presents it through commercial banking channels for collection from the issuer. The owner- ship of the bond is known only to the owner and sometimes to the bank to which he presents the coupons for collection.[16] Although bearer bonds are satisfactory to most owners, some investors prefer bonds registered as to both interest and principal.

A bearer bond that is to be registered as to principal and interest is surrendered to the issuer in exchange for a bond that is registered in the records of the issuer. A bond registered as to principal only is not negotiable; however, the coupons are handled in the same manner as those of a bearer bond. When registered as to both principal and interest, the issuer accepts the obligation of making prompt payment of interest when due.

There are several advantages to fully registered bonds. The owner receives his interest without the necessity of clipping the coupons and presenting them for payment. Further, he receives his interest as it becomes due—either on the due date or immediately following the due date. This avoids expensive delays involved in processing the coupons. In case of ownership of large blocks of bonds of a given maturity of an issue, registrability reduces the bulk of paper in the portfolio. And, finally, registration affords protection against theft or other loss; it avoids the necessity for posting surety in order to receive substitute bonds.

On the negative side, when a bond is registered as to both principal and interest, disposition of the bond is more difficult. The owner must obtain reconversion of the bond to bearer form. This process involves delays ranging from days to weeks, depending upon the importance the issuer attaches to the request for reconversion.[17] Ordinarily, the reconver- sion can be accomplished within a matter of days if there is an adequate stock of the original bonds in the hands of the firm which originally printed the bonds. If, however, the order for reconversion is in such quantity that a new printing is required, additional time is needed for the new printing and issuance of these bonds. For example, an institutional investor may accumulate several thousand bonds of a single government over a period of time and have all of them registered as to both principal and interest. At the point the investor decides to modify his investment portfolio, there is a need for immediate reconver- sion. The amount of work involved will be considerable and can involve delays that are both inconvenient and expensive.

When bonds are registered as to principal only, the bond remains intact and the coupons remain attached. The registrability as to principal protects the owner in case of theft or loss of the bond.

Although the process of registration and reconversion involves some additional out- of-pocket expense for the issuing government, it can produce benefits to the issuer that establish a record for sound, prompt, and dependable service in respect to registration and reconversion. A failure to maintain a record of promptness in handling registration and reconversion more than nullifies the original advantages sought.

Investors differ widely concerning the desirability of the registrability feature. Some prefer it as a means of reducing their paper work and expediting payment; others complain that the undue amount of time and inconvenience frequently involved in securing reconver- sion more than offset the advantages to be derived from this feature. Some large institutional holders believe that the registration and reconversion would be tremendously enhanced if:

---

[16] Ordinarily, the issuer has little interest in the ownership of its securities. However, marketability can frequently be increased by keeping investors informed concerning the financial affairs of the issuer, the economy of the region being served, and other factors pertinent to valuation of the credit. The list of owners of registered bonds constitutes one source for mailing of such information.

[17] A few issuing governments, e.g., Port of New York Authority, provide for overprinting of bonds at the time of initial issue and depositing these with the fiscal agent or leaving them in the hands of the bond printer to be used in reconversion. Some governments provide for retention of the original bonds when surrendered for registered bonds. Upon reconversion, the coupon bonds are taken from the vault, matured coupons clipped, and the original bond restored to the owner.

1. A suitable supply of bonds for reissue could be printed at the time of the original printing of the bonds. Alternatively, the coupon bonds can be retained and subsequently returned at reconversion.
2. The issuing government could designate a metropolitan bank in the nearest city with a Federal Reserve Bank to act as agent for registration and reconvertibility.

Some bond counsel and general counsel for issuers oppose the printing of a stock of bonds on the basis of problems of security. Such problems are genuine unless the bonds are deposited with dependable corporate paying agents under appropriate protective arrangements.

In conclusion, it appears that one of the major areas for improvement in the marketability of municipal bonds lies in the *concerted* action by state and local governments to provide a more acceptable method of full registrability accompanied by facilities for prompt transfer and/or reconversion of registered bonds.

Chapter 14
REVENUE BONDS: GOVERNMENTAL ENTERPRISE DEBT

It has been stated earlier that so-called revenue debt of state and local governments consists principally of three broad categories:

> Governmental enterprise debt
> Governmental lessee debt
> *On behalf of* debt

This chapter is concerned with governmental enterprise debt; other forms of revenue bonds are treated in Chapter 15.

Governmental enterprise debt is the oldest and largest of the categories of revenue debt. It is distinguished from the others by the fact that it is secured from revenues generated through governmental ownership and/or operation of facilities. These are frequently divided into (1) utility and (2) other enterprises, as follows:

1. *Public utilities*
   Water supply
   Sewers and waste water
   Electric light and power
   Gas supply
   Public transportation
2. *Other areas*
   Airports
   Docks and terminals
   Hospitals
   Higher education
   Recreation
   Convention halls and conference centers
   Bridges, roads and tunnels
   Parking facilities

Not all of the governmental enterprise debt is secured *exclusively* by the revenues of the enterprise. Portions are secured by a dual pledge of revenues and a full-faith-and-credit pledge; other portions are secured by the revenue pledge supplemented by access to various elements of the general revenues of governments exercising taxing power. Occasionally, revenue debt of a weaker governmental enterprise will be strengthened by access to excess revenues from more successful governmental enterprise operations. Some revenue debt is sold on the basis of provisions of law and ordinance alone. Other portions involve heavy reliance on the terms of contract, frequently known as an *indenture*. The investor looks to the security pledged to ascertain the viability of the debt.

BASIC SECURITY ARRANGEMENTS

When state and local government debt is supported directly or indirectly by the taxing power, the investor is concerned about the nature and extent of that power as well as the overall economic activity and wealth to which that taxing power can extend. By contrast, the owner of governmental enterprise debt focuses attention upon the operation of the enterprise, especially its capacity to generate the revenues needed to service the debt. The economy of the community served by the enterprise is of importance since it usually provides the patrons for the enterprise, but, the success of the enterprise also depends upon the strength of general management, the quality of money management, and the access of the investor to the moneys generated.

Among the factors considered by the investor are:

1. The feasibility study
2. The sources, magnitude, and reliability of revenues
3. Allocation of excess revenues
4. Mortgages of property
5. Maintenance of income, including rate adjustments
6. Conditions under which parity bonds can be issued
7. Segregation, character, magnitude, and protection of funds for debt service
8. Availability of reserve funds
9. Extent and character of external oversight of operations
10. Protection against encumbrance of assets

The Feasibility Study

Bonds secured by the revenues of a public enterprise may be sold only if the investor is convinced of the financial soundness of the enterprise. If an operating history is available, the record of both financial experience and management can be examined as a basis for determining the attractiveness of the proposed debt. If there is no past record, or if the proposal constitutes so vast a change that the past operations provide an inadequate base for projection into the future, reliance must be placed largely upon projections contained in feasibility studies covering demands for service, the rates to be charged, the operation and maintenance costs, and the debt service implicit in the new bonding program.

In the case of a new venture for this issuer, estimates depend on market surveys and the informed judgment of the consulting engineer, architect, or other specialist who uses comparable experience as a guideline. The formal feasibility study by a qualified independent consultant is needed. For the public utility group as well as for parking facilities, toll roads, bridges and tunnels, it is customary to engage a consulting engineer to prepare not only plans but also estimates of capital outlays, operation and maintenance costs, and debt service. The consulting engineer reviews the levels of probable use of the service, the service charges for various elements of service provided, and gross revenues to be generated. On the basis of these data, a pro forma operating and debt service statement is developed showing the relationship of revenues available for debt service to the estimated debt service requirements.

The preparation of feasibility studies in other public enterprise areas has increasingly been assigned to firms specializing in those services. The objective is to secure the opinion of qualified persons with acknowledged expertise in the service area under consideration. In this process, it is found that the financial advisor is being used due to his skill in arranging debt that can best harmonize with the estimated available revenue. Moreover, such advisor can bring an understanding of the impact of different kinds of reserve and other security pledges on the acceptance of the debt in the market.

Inasmuch as the feasibility report is critically important to the investor, the reputation of the feasibility consultants for soundness of projections is critically important. It is of especial importance to the investor that the revenue produced will be at least equal to that officially projected. When the estimates prove conservative, the investor is pleased with the greater security afforded. If realized revenue falls below the estimates, the investor's confidence in the consultant and the issuer is diminished.

The issuer has a different interest. The need is for the most realistic set of estimates possible—on both the revenue and the expenditure side. Overestimates of revenue may act to improve the interest rate for the initial bond sale but they impair the issuer's reputation and produce problems both in enterprise operations and any future funding. Conversely, if the feasibility study significantly underestimates the revenues, the issuer pays in terms of added interest costs on the original debt and in reduced flexibility.

Given the importance of the feasibility study, the issuer is obliged to make the best reasonable arrangements for the study and report. To this end, care in the development of the feasibility team is essential. Although the feasibility report can be developed and eventually signed by a single consultant, the issuer should require the feasibility consultant to work with the bond counsel, the financial advisor, the investment banker, and other persons assisting the issuer. A draft report should be required with sufficient time for careful scrutiny by the other consultants. The issuer should be prepared to challenge any portion of the draft report that fails to provide a comprehensive and accurate statement of the facts as well as any faulty element of the projection process. The report should be as realistic as possible in the circumstances.

The Revenues Pledged

The degree of latitude available to the issuer in pledging revenues varies widely from issuer to issuer and from time to time. In some cases, the issuer finds it essential to pledge all resources directly available in order to market the bonds; in other circumstances, the issuer can secure the needed capital at reasonable costs while preserving control over significant portions of revenues. In other cases, the project will prove feasible only if the total revenues of the issuer are supplemented by guarantees beyond the project revenues.

The available revenue pledges consist of: (1) Gross revenues, (2) net revenues, or (3) a junior position to pledges for senior debt. Beyond these are pledges of supplemental security.

The decision as to what is to be pledged extends not only to a choice among these alternatives but also to the disposition of excess revenues. The degree of flexibility is governed partly by pledges undertaken with respect to debt already outstanding. Usually, these can be overcome only by defeasing preexisting agreements. Alternatively, in some circumstances, new debt may be issued as junior debt.

Pledge of Gross Revenues. Although it is feasible to pledge gross revenues, by definition, governmental enterprise projects always involve operating and maintenance costs. Therefore, viability of the enterprise depends on the availability of money from other sources to pay for operating and maintenance costs. Otherwise, the gross revenue pledge becomes hollow because the enterprise is doomed. The alternatives under the gross revenue pledge are:

Gross Revenue. Under a full gross revenue pledge, the issuer agrees that all of the gross revenues of a project shall be used exclusively to pay debt service on a project. This implies that operating and maintenance costs will be paid from other sources. The issuer (or another government) may, for example, have other current income available that can be used for operating and maintenance charges, that is not available for capitalization. From the standpoint of the investor, the gross revenue pledge is likely to be very attractive.

First Lien on Gross Revenue. The pledge of a first lien on gross revenue differs from the pledge of full gross revenue in that it is assumed that the excess revenue generated *after* payment of debt service will be available for operation and maintenance. The first lien is appealing to many bondholders; however, there is still a need for assurance of funding of operating and maintenance costs in order to protect against substandard operation and decay that will result in reduced earning power.

Many investors prefer this pledge to that of net revenue even though it has potential hazards. It is an advantage to the issuer in that the sponsoring government with broader access to general revenue is likely to come to the aid of the governmental enterprise in order that the citizens may continue to enjoy the services involved.

The Net Revenue Pledge. The most frequently used pledge in governmental enterprise revenue debt is that of net revenue. Such a pledge assumes that the governmental enterprise will be operated on a level appropriate to the conduct of public business and that it will produce sufficient net revenue to meet debt service requirements, and provide a prudent safety margin.

From the standpoint of the user, this arrangement may help to assure that the service will be continued as a prior claim upon revenues, even though the revenue flow proves insufficient to produce net revenues to meet debt service costs, e.g., the users of the West Virginia Turnpike, which has not been able to meet its debt service requirements on a current basis. If there is a question as to the viability of the enterprise, the interest rates are likely to reflect the increased risks.

Junior Lien Pledges. The senior lien debt contract may prohibit the issuance of parity debt or it may impose restrictions on additional parity debt—usually by means of retrospective and/or prospective coverage tests. If there is a sufficient flow of residual revenue available after satisfying the senior debt obligations, the issuer may offer junior lien bonds supported by a pledge of these excess revenues. Many issuers have found junior lien debt useful in financing expansion of governmental enterprise facilities, especially when the indenture relating to the senior lien debt contains obnoxious restrictions governing the issuance of parity bonds. Although advance refunding can offer a means for defeasing that debt, that option involves additional costs arising from the issuance process. These costs must be balanced against the differentials in interest costs under the alternatives. Moreover, any sale of junior lien debt will doubtless have to be accompanied by a prohibition against the issuance of additional senior lien debt (which would have the effect of reducing the security being pledged for the junior lien debt).

Supplemental Security Pledged. Frequently, the security provided by revenues, either gross or net, is insufficient to enable the issuer to sell the bonds at a reasonable rate—or, perhaps, to sell them at all. This may arise from absence of sufficient past experience with the particular type of enterprise in the current setting or it may arise from other conditions of a temporary or permanent nature.

For example, a community may be entering into a redevelopment effort involving the erection of a downtown department store during a period when new department stores are being constructed only in suburban shopping centers. Although the downtown store subsequently proves profitable, investors are likely to be reticent to undertake the risks involved. Or, there may have been a demonstrated history of success in operation of off-street parking garages; however, crises in the 1970s over availability of petroleum may cause investors to require additional security as a prerequisite to purchase of the bonds. Or, a development such as the surgeon general's original report on the injurious effect of cigarette smoking may shake investor confidence in bonds supported by cigarette taxes. In such circumstances, a government with general taxing authority may bolster the security for the proposed debt. It may do so with the expectation that the debt will still be self-supporting; however, the government will have underwritten the liability. If the enterprise earns as planned, the government with taxing power may never be called on to provide any money. If the project turns sour, the investor has fall-back protection.

The Allocation of Excess Revenue

Regardless of the form of the basic revenue pledge, a critically important policy decision is involved in design of the provisions of the bond contract that govern the disposition of revenues in excess of those required for debt service—whether under a gross or a net revenue pledge. Most investors prefer that all excess revenues be dedicated to additional security for the bonds to be used to accelerate retirement or to accumulate added reserve funds. However, many issuers have discovered that such a preclusive pledge of future revenues can be costly and burdensome in the development of subsequent capital financing. When confronted with needs for additional capital, they have found it necessary to defease the existing bond contracts—frequently, at considerable expense.[1]

Therefore, issuers find it prudent to examine with great care the implications of each provision involving the allocation of future excess revenues.

Creation of a Debt Service Reserve Fund. A debt service reserve fund is highly desirable in revenue bond financing in order to provide a source of funds from which debt service requirements may be met in case of temporary shortfalls in cash flow in the enterprise. A great many contemporary indentures require the creation of such a fund from the proceeds of the bond issue. Others require its development from net revenues in the early years of operation. The choice of method has important effects upon indicated coverage—a subject discussed later in this chapter in relation to Table 42.

Replenishment of Debt Service Reserve Fund. When any portion of the assets of the debt service reserve fund has been temporarily used to meet debt service requirements, available revenues are immediately used to replenish the fund.

Acceleration of Debt Retirement. After meeting the requirements relating to debt service and the debt service reserve fund, a decision is required as to the allocation of the residual excess revenue. The decision may be to allocate the moneys to accelerated debt retirement or to the development of reserve funds subsequently to be applied to debt liquidation. All of these decisions must be made at the time the bond contract is developed. Inasmuch as different courses of action may have an impact on the interest rates as well as on the future operation of the issuer, the entire process requires astute appraisal by the issuer. The indenture will specify the allocation among such purposes as:

1. Acceleration of retirement of the debt
2. Creation of additional reserve funds for eventual debt retirement
3. Creation of maintenance reserve funds
4. Capital outlay financed directly from excess revenues
5. Creation of capital outlay reserve funds
6. Use of excess for servicing of junior lien debt

Mortgage of Property

The use of a conventional mortgage as a part of the security for debt is frequently found in enterprise debt financing. Mortgages are required in some states; optional in some; and prohibited in others. The primary advantage of the conventional mortgage lies in the protection it affords in case of bankruptcy and foreclosure. In the absence of a mortgage, the bondholders' rights are generally restricted to money from revenues with no entitlement to the proceeds of forced liquidation. The types of conventional mortgages differ in their effect from state to state. They must be carefully examined in the light of the laws in effect in the state where issued.

Another type of mortgage is known as a *statutory mortgage.* The effect of the statutory mortgage is limited and constitutes a deterrent to the issuer from placing other encumbrances on the property. It does not, however, give the bondholder right of foreclosure in case of default.

Rate Covenants

The governmental enterprise bond contract ordinarily includes a pledge by the issuer to establish and maintain rates and charges at levels at least sufficient to meet debt service

---

[1] Thus, the Delaware River Port Authority in the 1960s was obliged to call outstanding low coupon debt and replace it with higher cost bonds in order to be able to issue additional bonds to construct two new toll bridges.

and coverage requirements. In the case of gross revenue bonds, the provisions are rather simple; in the case of net revenue bonds, the pledge is for rates that will provide for operation, maintenance, and debt service (including certain reserve funds). Basically, the objective is to place the issuer under contractual obligation to adjust the rates upward to the extent necessary for security of the debt. Such covenants can usually be enforced by judicial process. These provisions are subject to reviews by state utility commissions in many cases and, in recent years, have been the subject of much litigation as the courts have extended their concepts of protecting the public interest. So-called "public interest" legal services and consumer protection agencies are frequently in the courts challenging the rates established under the rate covenant provisions of bond indentures. Regardless of the rate covenants, conditions sometimes arise in which no increase in rates (even in quasi-monopoly situations, e.g., the West Virginia Turnpike Commission in the 1960s and early 1970s) will produce additional net revenues. Thus in the case of public transit, rate increases have frequently resulted in decreases in net revenue.

From the standpoint of the investor, it is necessary to ascertain whether the issuer has the legal authority to enter into effective rate covenant agreements. Thus, for many years, it was assumed that roads and bridge tolls were governed only under such covenants. Recently, the federal government has asserted authority over such tolls as a part of its interstate commerce powers. Absent such authority in the issuer, investors frequently refuse to purchase the bonds. However, in most cases, the issuer does have broad authority in this respect and the rate covenant becomes a principal element of security for the bonds, emphasizing its importance both to the issuer and the investor.

Additional Bonds

The issuer is ordinarily circumscribed as to the amount of additional revenue bonds that may be issued and conditions precedent to such issue. These conditions may take one or more of these forms:

> As to senior bonds: Outright prohibition
> As to parity bonds: One or more of these:
> 1. Outright prohibition
> 2. Limitation to amount required to complete defined work
> 3. Limitation in terms of specified dollar amounts
> 4. Requirement of retrospective and/or prospective coverage ratios
> As to junior bonds: Retrospective and/or prospective coverage ratios

Each of these can act to provide elements of security for the bonds being currently issued. Coverage limitations usually take the form of conformity to certain retrospective and/or prospective ratios of earnings to debt service requirements. Thus, additional parity bonds may require a retrospective coverage ratio of $1\frac{1}{2}$ or 2 times debt service on existing senior bonds and a prospective coverage of $1\frac{1}{4}$ or $1\frac{1}{2}$ times the debt service on combined old and new parity debt.

This means that the issuer is obliged to establish a good earnings record from the operation of the facilities before it is permitted to expand the facilities through the issuance of additional parity debt. Moreover, there will be a need to produce additional income which will bring combined coverage to an acceptable level.

Inability to comply with these conditions forecloses issuance of parity debt. However, the issuer may still have authority to issue junior lien debt if there are sufficient excess revenues. Even here, however, the investor in the senior bonds has an interest in protection against potentially unwise practices in the future; because, a default in the junior lien bonds may adversely affect the market position of the senior debt. Moreover, the mere existence of the junior lien bonds can mean that moneys the issuer would otherwise have had available are now committed.

On the other hand, investors know that many public enterprises are viable operations; they tend to grow to satisfy needs and, in due course, require additional capital investment. Moreover, additional investment is sometimes required to maintain the earning power of the original facility, e.g., widening of roads and bridges to accommodate larger vehicles. To restrict narrowly the avenue for financing growth may result in an overtaxing of the existing facilities and even an accelerated depreciation in those facilities to the point they will wear out before the currently outstanding debt has been amortized. Hence, flexibility is provided in most bond contracts.

Segregation of Funds

Although many state laws and local charters establish patterns of segregation of funds, it is customary in most bond contracts of governmental enterprise operations to require a full segregation of the moneys of the enterprise from the other moneys of the issuer. This segregation may be only on an accounting basis; however, it is more likely to involve total segregation of cash assets into separate bank accounts and the investments held for the enterprise by identified name of the enterprise accounts. The segregation may provide some improvement in the administration of the proceeds of the bonds; however, the primary purpose of a segregation requirement is to avoid use of the revenue of the enterprise for general operations or other purposes of the government. This is particularly important with new enterprises or those on a larger scale than that typified by comparable issuers.

For governments that have great financial strength, this pattern is of minor importance for the present; however, even in these governments, the segregation is deemed by most investors to afford protection in case of a change in circumstances and, therefore, to add strength to the security of the bonds. For governments which are weak, the segregation is viewed as a more important element of protection to the investor and it may be reflected in the market position or rating of the bonds. Even though there may have been a long history by the issuer of prompt repayment of any internal loans between the immediate enterprise and other funds, the investor has an alternative view. The issuer must evaluate the advantages to be gained through use of consolidated cash and other consolidated asset management vs. the costs associated with the alternative pattern of segregation. This, of course, is very different from the typical private corporate practice (and much general obligation debt practice) in which almost all moneys, except those held by trustees, are kept in a common corporate treasury.

Reserve Funds

Contemporary enterprise revenue bond indentures are likely to provide several funds to accommodate the flow of revenues and to specify the order of application of moneys. Among the funds most frequently used are:

1. *A gross revenue fund* is used to accept receipt of all of the pertinent gross income.

2. *An operating fund* pays the necessary operating expenses. Ordinarily, operating expenses (including current maintenance) constitute a first charge upon the gross revenue fund. The remainder of the revenues are usually defined as net revenues.

3. *A debt service fund* is one into which the moneys required for the next interest payment (or both interest and principal payment) are placed.

4. *A debt service reserve fund* is used to hold money and securities as a reserve to pay the debt service in case of a temporary shortage of net revenue. The amount of such debt service reserve funds varies; but, frequently, it is set at the highest year's debt service. Or, in some cases, it is set at the greater of this amount or twice the highest year's interest costs.

5. *A sinking fund* is one in which amounts are accumulated to make payment of the principal or *a debt retirement fund* where funds are accumulated for mandatory or optional acceleration of the maturity of debt.

6. *Maintenance and/or equipment renewal funds* are used for mandatory or optional accumulation of funds to meet extraordinary maintenance items (e.g., a new surface on a bridge roadway) or replacement of major equipment (e.g., transit cars or motor buses).

Maintenance of Debt Service Reserve Fund Levels

The maintenance of debt service reserve fund levels is ordinarily only a matter of bringing the fund back to its original level following a period during which revenues have not been available to meet debt service on a timely basis. However, during periods of high interest rates, the market value of debt securities usually shrinks. If the debt contract requires maintenance of debt service reserve funds at given levels in *market value terms,* the issuer may be confronted with the necessity of bringing the funds up to required levels by deposit of additional money or securities. Thus, a fund required to be maintained at the $1,000,000 level may have initially purchased U.S. Government bonds due in 25 years at a 7.50 yield basis. When rates rise to the point that the yield is 12 percent for a remaining life of 20 years, the market value of the original holdings will have decreased to $742,000. Under a maintenance of market value agreement, the issuer would be obliged to deposit an additional $258,000. The possibility of such a development and its disruptive effects on operations and on junior debt arrangements should be dealt with in the indenture— perhaps by placing a limit on the amount that the issuer must set aside in any one year to meet such shrinkage.

A corollary provision is appropriate to govern the rate of withdrawal of assets from the debt service reserve in case of rising market value of securities held. Alternatively, if funds are invested in short-term securities changes in the market will have only a modest price impact on the statement of value for reserve fund holdings.

External Supervision and Oversight

Unlike general obligation debt where the issuer is ordinarily fully responsible for administration of the debt, many governmental enterprise debt contracts vest various responsibilities for supervision, management, and oversight in persons outside the government— primarily in trustees and consulting engineers but, occasionally, also in others. These assignments are most likely to be found in the enterprise debt contracted under separate indenture executed by the issuer. Nonindentured governmental enterprise debt may provide for performance of some responsibilities by the trustee and/or a consulting engineer; however, in such circumstances, their roles are likely to be severely limited.

These arrangements seek to increase the security for the debt; however, such external supervision is frequently beneficial both to the investor and to the issuer. It helps to regularize the administration of the enterprise—especially in circumstances where combined judgment may be superior to the sole judgment of the issuer.

The Trustee. Under bond indentures, a corporate trustee (usually a bank or trust company) is designated to receive the proceeds of the bonds and to supervise their use for the purposes and in the manner specified in the bond contract. The trustee may also assume a number of other responsibilities incident to general supervision of the handling of the revenues generated by the enterprise. Thus, the trustee may be obliged to see that the enterprise is operated within the framework of approved budgets; that provision is made for the maintenance necessary for optimum operation of the facility; that all of the revenues are administered in accordance with the terms of the indenture; that legal action is instituted in the name of the bondholders should the issuer fail to comply with terms of the indenture; and act as fiscal agent in the servicing of the debt.

Upon the selection of the corporate trustee depends some part of the confidence reposed by bondholders in the bonds. Therefore, it is desirable that the trustee be one with recognized soundness and integrity and with sufficient independence and objectivity to avoid being swayed by exigencies to approve actions not in full accord with the contract. In the selection of the trustee, it is desirable that the designation take into account acceptability to investors rather than being guided solely by parochial considerations.

The Consulting Engineer or Alternate. In many instances, the work of the feasibility consultant is ended with the issuance of the bonds; however, in other circumstances he performs a continuing role. Historically, this has been performed only in projects where a civil engineering background was required; however, a number of the responsibilities involved extend deeply into other areas. Thus, the feasibility consultant may be required to approve the issuer's proposed operating budget—to assure that sufficient funds are allocated for appropriate operations and to forestall unwise use of moneys; to provide general supervision of not only the initial capital construction but also of additions, maintenance, and replacement of structures and equipment; and to review rate schedules for conformity to bond covenants or to take the initiative in upward adjustment of rate schedules in order to obtain required revenue.

In some matters, the trustee and feasibility consultant report to the management or governing body of the governmental enterprise; however, in other matters, their obligation is directly to bondholders, especially in periods of financial difficulty. Certain of their reports are required to be available at all times to bondholders. Ordinarily, full current disclosure both to bondholders and financial journals is imperative if confidence in the issuer is to be maintained.

Restrictions on Encumbrances

The avoidance of encumbrances that significantly adversely affect the security for the bondholders is a point of major importance. If encumbrances can be created that have the effect of lowering the level of entitlement of the bondholder to the income from the property or from sale or other disposition of a portion of the assets, the value of the bondholder's securities is diminished. Accordingly, the indentures usually provide stringent restrictions governing the conditions under which the issuer may create such encumbrances. Although it is not in the interest of the investor to impose rigidity in the operations of the issuer, there must be an insistence upon a proper protection. Accordingly, independent consulting engineers, trustees, or others are frequently required to give their assent as a prerequisite to the creation of such encumbrances.

Competitive Facilities

Another type of protection sought by the investor is a protection against the development of competitive facilities. Although the number of competitive facilities that have interfered significantly with income anticipated by bondholders are few, they occasionally do develop. Thus, in the case of the $101 million of Calumet Skyway Bridge Bonds issued by the City of Chicago as revenue bonds in 1955, the State of Illinois constructed a free road nearby that diverted much of the traffic thereby reducing anticipated revenues. The Skyway bonds have been in default almost from the opening of the facility. Although the issuer can agree to forego construction of competitive facilities, binding guarantees concerning actions by other governments may be made only when state law specifically permits. Hence, the investor undertakes a risk that competitive facilities may be developed by governments with concurrent jurisdiction.

In Review

A review of the foregoing security arrangements indicates that, in a few circumstances, the interests of the issuer and the investor are more or less parallel. In such instances, the decision-making process is relatively easy for the investor. But, in most circumstances, these matters involve an adjustment of the competing interests of the issuer and the investor. At least at the time of the sale of the initial bonds, or at the time of defeasement of an existing covenant, the issuer has an opportunity for making significant policy decisions. If the position of the issuer is financially strong and if the bonds can be sold at competitive sale at good interest rates, the resolution is made on a basis that appeals to the judgment of the issuer.

If the public enterprise does not have a record of successful operation, the debt will probably be on a negotiated basis. In such negotiations, the issuer needs the best knowledge and assistance available in order to make wise decisions. Thus, the issuer seeks to provide protection sufficient to command a reasonable interest rate; however, in doing so it is difficult to retain sufficient freedom for future management. Skillful negotiation is required by the issuer.

PLANNING THE BOND ISSUE

In previous chapters, especially in Chapter 11, different aspects of the planning of bond issues have been discussed. Most of these observations relate not only to general obligation debt but also to governmental enterprise revenue debt. On the other hand, the genuine governmental enterprise revenue bond issue has a number of factors unique to it beyond those of security considerations explored earlier in this chapter. Most of these are concerned with the terms under which money can be borrowed in relation to the security from the flow of net revenues which may be available. The immediate concern here is the structuring of a bond issue which will take into account the manifold considerations that bear upon marketability and upon the terms under which marketability is best achieved.

Structuring the Bond Issue

A critical element of consideration by the investor is the indicated degree of coverage for debt service from the revenues pledged in support of the debt. Within any given degree of creditability of the revenue and expenditure projections, the investor is more comfortable with a high coverage ratio than with a lower one. However, he also has an eye to the relationship of the outstanding debt to the depreciated value of the facility, i.e., the status of patrimony accumulation at different times during the life of the facility. Although the investor may be willing to tolerate indicated net negative patrimony accumulation during some of the early life of the facility, the feasibility study must give assurance that the situation will right itself as the years pass. Otherwise, the investor is without any reasonable expectation of securing interest on funds advanced and timely repayment of principal.

Table 42 provides two illustrations of relationship of debt service to net revenues available for servicing of debt based on Patterns B and E of Appendix Table A. A study of the table will show that in a low level interest market characterized by a high incidence in the yield curve (Pattern B), net revenues commencing at $1,128,000 per year will provide an initial debt service coverage of 1.50 under Pattern B, with bonds being issued under an equal annual 30-year amortization period. Assuming that the net revenues increase at a compound annual rate of 2.5 percent, the coverage ratio continues to increase, reaching 2.17 in the 16th year and 3.07 in the final (30th) year in which the bonds are initially scheduled to be outstanding, for an average of 2.19 over the life of the issue. Assuming good feasibility estimates, this type of funding will be easily marketable.

By contrast, financing under Pattern E presents genuine difficulties. In the first place, the average net interest cost will be in the magnitude of 13 percent, regardless of how the bond issue is structured. At the outset the annual interest costs will be about $1.3

Table 42

Illustrative Debt Service Patterns for a
$10,000,000 Governmental Enterprise Revenue Bond Issue

(amounts in thousands of dollars)

Year	Pattern B Yield Curve Low Interest Level: High Incidence				Pattern E Yield Curve High Interest Level: Moderate Incidence			
	Net Revenues	Maturi- ties	Debt Service	Coverage Ratio	Net Revenues	Maturi- ties	Debt Service	Coverage Ratio
	(1)	(2)	(3)	(4)	(5)	(6)	(7)	(8)
1	1,128	145	752	1.50	1,730	35	1,348	1.28
2	1,156	150	753	1.54	1,773	40	1,354	1.31
3	1,185	155	752	1.58	1,818	45	1,350	1.35
4	1,215	160	751	1.62	1,863	50	1,350	1.38
5	1,245	170	754	1.65	1,910	55	1,350	1.41
6	1,276	175	753	1.69	1,957	65	1,354	1.45
7	1,308	180	749	1.75	2,006	70	1,351	1.48
8	1,341	190	751	1.79	2,056	80	1,353	1.52
9	1,374	200	751	1.83	2,108	90	1,354	1.56
10	1,409	210	751	1.88	2,161	100	1,353	1.60
11	1,434	220	750	1.91	2,215	115	1,356	1.63
12	1,480	235	753	1.97	2,270	130	1,357	1.67
13	1,517	250	755	2.01	2,327	145	1,356	1.72
14	1,555	260	750	2.07	2,385	165	1,358	1.76
15	1,594	275	750	2.12	2,444	185	1,359	1.80
16	1,634	295	754	2.17	2,505	210	1,358	1.84
17	1,675	310	751	2.23	2,568	235	1,355	1.90
18	1,716	330	752	2.28	2,632	265	1,354	1.94
19	1,759	350	752	2.34	2,698	305	1,359	1.99
20	1,803	375	755	2.39	2,765	345	1,359	2.03
21	1,848	395	751	2.46	2,835	390	1,358	2.09
22	1,895	420	751	2.52	2,906	440	1,357	2.14
23	1,942	450	754	2.58	2,978	500	1,358	2.19
24	1,990	480	755	2.64	3,053	565	1,357	2.25
25	2,040	510	753	2.71	3,129	640	1,357	2.31
26	2,091	545	754	2.77	3,207	715	1,347	2.38
27	2,144	580	753	2.85	3,288	825	1,366	2.41
28	2,197	620	754	2.91	3,370	935	1,362	2.47
29	2,252	660	752	2.99	3,454	1,060	1,362	2.54
30	2,308	705	753	3.07	3,540	1,200	1,360	2.60
Total	49,522	10,000	22,573	2.19	75,952	10,000	40,659	1.87

million before any provision is made for debt retirement. It is immediately obvious that the debt cannot be serviced unless the net available revenues can be markedly increased. Inasmuch as the Pattern E illustration occurs during a period with high interest rate levels [and probably high inflation rates], it may be feasible to increase the charges substantially. Whether these increases can be sufficient to produce the net revenues required in Column 5 of Table 42 will depend upon the circumstances then prevailing. If net revenues can be so increased—that is by about 50 percent—above those shown in Column 1—and if a compound growth rate of 2.5 percent per annum can be reasonably projected, a scheduling of debt service can be arranged under the requirements indicated in Column 7 of Table

42. However, it is emphasized that, in the development of the debt service under Column 7, only $35,000 is scheduled for maturity in the first year and that it is not until the 10th year that annual retirements reach the $100,000 level. By the end of the 20th year only about 27 percent of the debt will have reached initially scheduled maturity dates. Therefore, based upon any reasonable depreciation schedule, the residual capital value of the facility after depreciation would be less than the scheduled outstanding debt. In other words, unless the excess coverage is achieved there would be a negative patrimony accumulation throughout almost the entire life of the bond issue.

Excess Coverage Is the Key

Obviously, the excess coverage becomes the key to viability of the entire transaction. Absent a good showing of excess coverage, the market would not accept the debt under Pattern E. Under these conditions the investors will doubtless require that the full amount of the excess coverage be allocated as additional protection throughout the life of the bonds. If the revenues available for debt service materialize as indicated in Column 5 and if these were applied exclusively to acceleration of maturity of the debt, it would be found that by the end of the first decade about two-fifths of the debt would have been retired. This would go far toward overcoming the negative patrimony accumulation to which reference has been made above.

Debt Service Reserve Fund for Enterprise Debt

The development of a debt service reserve fund for governmental enterprise revenue debt constitutes a problem of some dimension. As has been stated previously, the availability of a debt service reserve fund is highly desirable. The quickest way in which to achieve this objective is to sell sufficient excess bonds to facilitate the creation of the debt service reserve fund from the proceeds of the bond issue. The alternative is accumulation over a period of years from the revenues anticipated to be developed from excess coverage achievement.

However, in tight market situations where the coverage ratio is already relatively low, it will doubtless be difficult to increase the size of the loan to provide for creation of the debt service reserve fund from bond proceeds. Although these funds will be invested, provision must be made in the debt service schedule for their orderly amortization. This will adversely affect the statement of debt service coverage in most circumstances.

Under the pattern of gradual accumulation of the debt service reserve, both the issuer and the investor face the possibility that circumstances may arise under which the issuer has no funds with which to meet the full debt service during the very early years of operation—when revenues are in the process of being developed to projected levels. This would trigger a default and would therefore be a great problem both to the issuer and the investor. In these circumstances, the issuer will do well to attempt to fund out the creation of the debt service reserve fund from the initial bond issue unless the coverage ratio then becomes so thin that it is intolerable. This can be overcome largely through deferring the amortization period for the amounts involved in the debt service reserve fund.

MORAL OBLIGATION BONDS

In addition to bonds supported by different kinds of contractual obligations (primarily through lease arrangements), several states have issued bonds that are described as "moral obligation" debt of the state. This type of debt has been largely associated with housing and other types of development in areas of economic importance to the public but, ordinarily, not for facilities operated as governmental activities. The State of New York has been the largest issuer of "moral obligation" bonds through the New York Housing Finance Agency and the New York State Urban Development Corporation. Essentially, the pattern is one in which the state legislature creates a public agency and authorizes it to issue debt for specified purposes with the proviso that, under certain circumstances, the legislature will come to the aid of the debt by annual appropriations—generally in the form of restoring debt service reserve funds that have been partially depleted during the year because the enterprise revenues have not been sufficient to meet the debt service payments.

When legislative bodies authorize this type of debt, they have ordinarily placed limits upon the amount of debt that can be issued under the "moral obligation" pledge. The decision at each legislative session to appropriate or not to appropriate funds sufficient to replenish debt service reserve funds does not constitute a contractual obligation of the state. Each legislature makes its own decision to appropriate or not to appropriate. The bondholder has no recourse to compel such appropriation or payment by the state. A failure to make the appropriation does not constitute default by the state; however, states have ordinarily made appropriations in recognition of the "moral obligation" incurred in the authorization of the debt.

SUPPLEMENTAL SECURITY ARRANGEMENTS

The bulk of this chapter has been devoted to the basic security for revenue bonds to be derived from pledges of the revenues and/or property of governmental enterprises. It is not feasible to issue debt (or to do so on reasonable terms) for all governmental enterprises based solely upon the income and property of that enterprise. Whereas a new water system can usually be financed from the outset from bonds secured solely from the revenues of the enterprise, it is not feasible in many other circumstances. Even a new water system may be accompanied by uncertainties resulting in investor reluctance to lend capital funds unless supplemental security pledges are forthcoming. Moreover, a new governmental enterprise has no local performance record. The investor will usually seek supplemental security or may require extremely high interest rates for the bonds. In either circumstance, the sponsoring general governmental unit with taxing authority may be confronted with a decision either to provide supplemental security from the general revenues or to forego development of the facility. These supplemental pledges of security can range from the full-faith-and-credit of the general purpose government to much more restrictive involvement. Among the alternatives is the use of governmental lessee debt to be discussed in Chapter 15.

When a special purpose agency is multifunctional, e.g., the Port Authority of New York and New Jersey, it may have excess revenues available from some of its enterprises that can be pledged in support of other enterprises that will not attract favorable attention in the debt market. Either consolidated debt or other supportive arrangements may be in order. The design of such arrangements calls for a high degree of staff competence—usually involving a combination of in-house and consultant services.

MANDATORY CALL PROVISIONS

Closely associated with security arrangements for governmental enterprise revenue bonds and other nongeneral obligation bonds is the use of excess revenues to provide for immediate retirement of portions of the outstanding debt—after a minimum number of years, e.g., five or more. The convenants take many forms, depending on the design of the bond issue and the negotiations between the issuer and the syndicate involved in the purchase.

One form of the requirement is that, after meeting required operating, maintenance, and debt service costs, all excess moneys will be used either to purchase or to call outstanding bonds. Such a provision has the effect of using all of the "coverage" moneys to accelerate the maturity of bonds. This early redemption has the benefit to the issuer of reducing the amount of outstanding debt and the annual interest charge on the accelerated redemptions. Conversely, it denies to the issuer alternative use of the funds—especially their use for achieving higher rates of return in the marketplace. It is likely also to produce unrealistically high market prices for bonds obliged to be purchased by the issuer in order to meet contractual obligations for debt reductions.

From the standpoint of the investor, the benefits are mixed with disadvantages—depending largely on whether the bonds are selling above or below par. Illustrative of the effects for the investor are:

1. *If the Bonds Are Selling Above Par.* If the bonds are callable and their yield rates have decreased below the coupon rates, the bonds will generally be priced on a basis assuming they may be called at the next interest payment date as a part of a refunding operation. Therefore, the pricing will take account of only that interest payable between the date of the sale of the bonds in the secondary market and the next interest payment date. Under these circumstances, the investor is at risk in two ways: (1) all of the bonds may be called in order to execute a full refunding, or (2) some of his bonds may be called to facilitate the operation of the mandatory call feature. Moreover, given the pricing to the next call date, the investor cannot expect to sell the bonds on the basis of capitalizing the potential future excess interest. Although the acquisition of additional bonds by the issuer provides a welcome support for the market, once the initial call date has arrived, the investor profits by having the bonds continue outstanding rather than by having them called under a mandatory call provision.

2. *If the Bonds Are Selling Below Par.* When the yield is above the coupon rate, a different set of factors is at work. The issuer's use of excess funds to accelerate maturity reduces the average life for the remaining outstanding bonds. Thus, assume that the pro forma debt service schedule provides for redemption in a manner that produces an average remaining life of 13.0 years and that the projected revenues will result in an acceleration of retirements to the point that the actual average remaining life will be only 8.0 years. If the bonds bear a coupon rate of 4.00 percent, they would be priced at $845.39 per $1,000 par value under an assumed yield of 5.70 percent for 13 years. But, they would be priced at $934.72 under a 5.00 percent yield for 8 years. Therefore, the operation of the mandatory call provision would have the effect of increasing the market price by $89.33. Thus, the investor would benefit materially either through sale to the issuer under mandatory call or through sale to another investor.

Moreover, if the issuer finds that it cannot purchase a sufficient number of bonds to meet the mandatory call provision, it must call some of the bonds. The investor holding such bonds would benefit further as there would be a total gain of $151.61 vis-á-vis the probable market price in the absence of the mandatory redemption provisions.

For these reasons, the issuer should seek bond indenture provisions giving the issuer the option of redemption or of retaining the excess moneys either as additional reserves to support the debt or for capital improvements. Thereby, the issuer is able to avoid the problems incident to mandatory call and also to invest in securities with a higher yield than could be obtained by either purchase of the tax-exempt securities or exercise of the call provision.

OTHER COVENANTS

Beyond the foregoing indenture covenants directed to security of the bonds, it is customary that other kinds of covenants be included. Most of these affect the security for, and therefore the value of, the bonds; however, none is likely to have the same impact as the items already discussed.

Use of Bond Proceeds

The public enterprise bond contract contains explicit provisions concerning the use of the proceeds of the bonds. Among the cost categories ordinarily addressed are:

1. Organization and preliminary expenses
2. Issuance expense
3. Interest during the development period
4. Site acquisition
5. Construction and development

These kinds of costs have been discussed in Chapter 11. The typical official statement and bond contract apportion bond proceeds among these categories; however, in some cases the list is more detailed and in a few, categories are consolidated. It is the responsibility of the issuer to apply the bond proceeds in the manner set forth, subject to such flexibility as may be afforded in the bond contract. In some contracts, consulting engineers, trustees, and others are also assigned responsibilities for oversight in the use of the proceeds of the bonds. The contract ordinarily permits some interchangeability in allocations. Excess proceeds are usually allocated to debt service reserve account or bond retirement.

Insurance

Of importance to both the issuer and the investor is the maintenance of appropriate insurance. For many years, public enterprise operations benefited under the doctrine of sovereign immunity. They were able to restrict their insurance programs largely to fire, windstorm, floods, and other damage to their own property. As the doctrine has been progressively reduced in its application, state and local governments have been obliged to expand their insurance programs to cover possible harm to others, especially in their governmental enterprise operations. Bondholders have an interest in the maintenance of adequate insurance coverage inasmuch as failure to do so may place their loans in jeopardy. To that end, it is not unusual for the bond contract to require the maintenance of appropriate insurance and to provide for independent participation by the feasibility consultant or the trustee in the determination of adequacy.

Audit and Reporting

Historically, many state and local governments did not have independent audits. Provision for audit was by separately elected officials or by auditors appointed by the legislature or other governing bodies. Since 1975 it has become increasingly common for local governments to engage independent certified public accountants to perform audit functions. State governments still rely largely upon either an elected state officer or officers appointed by the legislature. In order that investors have periodic information concerning the status of the financial affairs, the issuer is typically required to provide annual financial reports with certificates of independent certified accountants. Copies are available to the public and also are filed with the consulting engineer and the trustee in governmental enterprise bond issues involving them. The standards of reporting are discussed in Chapter 20.

Reduced Service Charges

Government operates in a political environment. As a result, various users of the services of public enterprises form pressure groups for the purpose of securing free or discounted rates for the services being rendered by those enterprises. Cities may demand free water for both general and fire hydrant purposes. Special inducements for development may be extended to new industries by means of preferential water and sewer rates.

Pretermitting considerations of the social policy, the investor is obliged to take into account the effects of such free service or service at discounted rates upon the security for the bonds. In some cases, this makes little difference; in others (where rates are already reaching a point of economic difficulty impinging upon the production of gross revenue), substantial free or discounted services can produce a financial crisis for the governmental enterprise. Therefore, the bond contract may prohibit or regulate discount practices.

Enforcement of Collection

One of the elements of attractiveness of many governmental enterprise operations has been the rigorous collection policies followed by most such enterprises—much the same as those of the privately owned public utilities. During the 1970s the attitude of public utility commissions and the courts softened substantially in respect to the right of operators to withhold delivery of utility services as a penalty for nonpayment. The result has been that many of these utilities find it more difficult to enforce collection through interruption of service to delinquents.

Some indentures have attempted to deal with this problem; however, the basic views of the courts appear to be that they will not enforce such contractual provisions if they constitute a threat to the public health and safety, or in cases in which the court is prepared to grant special privilege to the complaintant. The long-term effect is either to shift the costs to the other consumers or gradually to diminish the ability of the public enterprise to cope with its financial problems.

Callability and Refunding

In governmental enterprises, the use of the term bond with mandatory call features makes it essential that, when acceleration of maturity arises from use of excess revenues, there will be no call premium payable. Otherwise, the issuer is paying an unnecessary penalty. In fact, except to help assure a market for outstanding bonds, there is little economic justification for the mandatory call. The option of developing reserves dedicated to ultimate retirement of the debt should be sufficient. There is, however, the viewpoint of the U.S. Treasury to take into account. Some of its regulations appear to attempt to force a use of any excess funds for debt service purposes into the channel of accelerated retirement by seeking to prevent the investment of the excess revenues at rates higher than those that would be payable on the outstanding debt. Decision as to the current practice, as well as the original design of the issue, must take into account the prevailing regulations.

Default Procedures

The indenture will include provisions covering the steps to be taken in case of default. These ordinarily involve more stringent supervision by the trustee than under other circumstances. It is the responsibility of the trustee to have kept abreast of developments and to take actions from time to time, either independently or in conjunction with the consulting engineer, when the financial situation first begins to turn adverse. Timely intervention and effective action at an early stage will frequently foreclose the occurrence of the impending default. If default becomes inevitable, the indenture sets forth the manner in which available moneys shall be used. Ordinarily, all payment of principal of bonds is suspended. If moneys are not sufficient to pay the full amount of interest as it becomes due, provision is made for use of moneys to pay accrued interest on an equitable basis among bondholders.

In the planning of the default provisions, the issuer again finds that steps must be taken to protect the public interest as far as feasible within the context of providing reasonable protection to the bondholder.

Investment of Funds

The bond indenture is likely to contain provisions generally governing the investment of various reserve funds of the enterprise. Usually, the corporate trustee is vested with broad authority and responsibility in this connection. Even so, inasmuch as governmental funds are involved, responsibility is still imposed on public officials. The issuer has the implicit duty not to delegate power in a manner that would permit the improvident management of public funds. Hence the selection of the trustee becomes a significant responsibility. Moreover, the question must be confronted as to what liability the issuer retains should the trustee default in any obligations to the bondholders, especially in case of default arising out of financial mismanagement by the trustee.

Chapter 15
OTHER FORMS OF GOVERNMENTALLY SUPPORTED DEBT

Beyond the debt of state and local governments supported through direct pledges of either the full faith and credit of the issuer or from designated revenues of the issuer, as discussed in Chapter 3, there are a number of kinds of debt supported through indirect pledging of governmental revenue. The principal form of this type of debt is that which has come to be known as *governmental lessee debt*. Also of importance are various forms of *moral obligation debt* discussed in Chapter 14. In some cases the states have gone further by pledging their general credit in support of debt of local governments issued through bond banks or other state agencies. Other states are using *municipal bond banks* or their equivalent. There is also the long-standing classification of *special assessment debt*. There is *federally guaranteed debt* issued by state and local governments as tax-exempt debt under guarantees supplied by the United States, especially in areas of housing and urban renewal. Although this is not offered as an exhaustive list, the remaining categories of tax-exempt debt supported indirectly by the revenues of state and local governments are statistically unimportant.

The subject of *on behalf of debt* including federally supported, low-income housing debt is discussed in Chapter 16.

GOVERNMENTAL LESSEE DEBT

Governmental lessee debt is debt secured by the lease rental payments by one governmental entity (the lessee) to another governmental entity acting as issuer (the lessor). The practice of issuing governmental lessee debt appears to have commenced in the 1930s with the creation of the Pennsylvania General State Authority. The legislation provided for the creation of a special state agency which was given the power to contract with the Pennsylvania Department of Property and Supplies for furnishing facilities needed to conduct the affairs of the state. The General State Authority was authorized to market debt secured by lease rentals payable by the Department for the use of such property. Payment of the rentals was contingent on the legislature making annual appropriations to the Department for that purpose. Absent such payments, the state would no longer have the use of the facilities.

The purpose was to avoid the restrictive provisions of the Pennsylvania constitution governing the creation of debt by the Commonwealth of Pennsylvania. The matter was litigated extensively in the Pennsylvania courts, with the State Supreme Court finally upholding the validity of the bonds and declaring that they did not constitute a debt of the Commonwealth within the meaning of the constitutional prohibitions.[1] Following that decision, the use of governmental lessee debt expanded greatly, not only in Pennsylvania but also in a number of other states.

---

[1] For a fuller discussion of the development of the public authority and governmental lessee debt, see Tina V. Weintraub and James D. Paterson, *The "Authority" in Pennsylvania: Pro and Con.*

Typically, the system involves the creation of a governmental authority or nonprofit corporation that acquires, through purchase or construction, facilities that are leased to a general governmental unit with general taxing powers or other dependable revenue sources. Security for the governmental lessee debt is the rental payable to the issuer by the lessee government. In some instances, rentals are payable to the same lessor by a group of lessees for a number of different facilities. For purposes of financing, a suitable number of such facilities are consolidated into single bond issues. [One of the more significant operations of this type is that of the Pennsylvania State Public School Building Authority.]

Governmental lessee debt is distinguished from governmental enterprise debt by the fact that, in enterprise debt, the issuer is ordinarily engaged in the delivery of services for which charges are made to nongovernmental users. In most instances, enterprise debt does not involve reliance upon the general revenues (especially tax revenues) of general purpose governments. Most governmental lessee debt does not produce service charge revenues; it relies on access in an indirect manner to the revenues of general purpose governments, especially to their tax resources.

Governmental lessee debt is different from *governmentally supported development debt* ("moral obligation" debt) as the former provides facilities for use in the performance of governmental operations whereas the latter is to provide financial support from general revenue sources for various kinds of development activities in which the ownership and/ or operation of the developments are largely, or wholly, carried out by private persons.

Governmental lessee debt is distinguished from *on behalf of* debt by the fact that governmental lessee debt is for the purpose of providing facilities for *use by another governmental unit.* By contrast, *on behalf of* debt is defined as debt issued by a governmental entity for acquisition of capital assets that are financed by and are for the use of nongovernmental profit or nonprofit corporations. Governmental lessee debt does not include facilities constructed under financing guarantees of other governments for capital facilities to be used by the issuer, e.g., low-rent public housing facilities.

Since World War II governmental lessee debt has been used by the various state authorities that issue debt for construction of public school buildings that are leased to local school districts, e.g., Georgia, Virginia, and Pennsylvania. Also, a number of the states have created authorities for financing of such facilities in such fields as highways, bridges, public transport, and state-operated colleges and universities, e.g., New York and New Jersey.

Finally, a number of the states have authorized their local governments to create authorities, nonprofit corporations, or other entities to facilitate governmental lessee financing, e.g., Illinois and Indiana.

The Lease Arrangements

Typically, under governmental lessee financing, the user government enters into a contract with the issuer to construct or otherwise acquire facilities or equipment that may be needed by the user government (under agreed plans and specifications). The issuer may secure bids for the construction involved and arrange for supervision of construction, or the issuer may delegate this to the lessee. Ordinarily, the lessee has full responsibility for operation and maintenance of the leased facilities.

If the capital asset sought is a single facility, e.g., a school building, the lessor-issuer may execute all of the contracts on the same day—the lease, the construction contract, the bond sale, and other necessary agreements. If the issuer is financing a series of facilities with the same user (e.g., a number of road projects for the same highway department), a master lease agreement may be executed with the individual projects being developed over a period of time. In like manner, the issuer may consolidate a number of facilities for different lessee governments (e.g., buildings for several school districts) under a single financing arrangement. Also, the issuer may execute leases with each of the user (lessee) governments but the elements relating to security and administration of the debt are likely to be identical from one agreement to the next. These lease agreements tend to be both complex and lengthy, containing most of the kinds of provisions that have been discussed in the preceding chapter concerning governmental enterprise revenue financing. However, in the case of lessee financing, the amounts of the lease rental take the place of earned revenue in governmental enterprise debt.

Inasmuch as the debt service required to finance the facilities is already known, the lease will specify the amount and timing of the lease payments. Customarily, the financing includes most of the elements of costs that have been set forth earlier in Table 27 (Chapter 11). A debt service reserve fund is frequently set aside from the proceeds of the bond issue. If not, it is likely to be accumulated from excess lease rentals payable under terms of the contract.

The agreement ordinarily provides for payment by the lessee of amounts sufficient to meet the administrative and related expenses of the issuer. Many lease agreements provide for rental payments sufficient only to meet the actual debt service and administrative costs; others provide for payment of rentals that produce excess coverage to be used in the manner discussed later in this chapter.

Governmental Lessee Debt and Interest Costs

When first introduced, governmental lessee debt was usually assigned a significantly lower credit position both in the market and by the rating agencies than that provided to general obligation debt of the lessee government. As the governmental lessee device has become more widespread, investors and analysts have been better able to assess experience. As a result, there appears to have been a significant narrowing of the differential in interest costs between well-designed and well-secured governmental lessee debt and the general obligation debt of the lessee. Moreover, some governmental lessee debt arrangements have provided access to the market for numerous lessees on more favorable terms than could have been obtained through their own general obligation bonds, especially those communities with severely limited economic resources. Thus, smaller school districts in some states have effectively pooled their credit with other districts and produced lower borrowing costs than would have been available under individual school district financing.

In some of the pooled governmental lessee financing, essentially the same kinds of results have been obtained as would have been attainable through use of a state bond bank. In a few circumstances, the state governments have enacted laws that give added security by providing that, if the local government fails to meet its obligations in a timely manner, the issuer may cause state officials to pay the delinquent rentals out of the next moneys due from the state to the delinquent lessees. This type of provision has greatly strengthened the credit position for the debt involved, especially when coupled with strong credit of the state government itself.

Effects of Leasing Arrangements on Control of Debt Issuance

The abuses in the issuance of state and local government debt in the period immediately following the Civil War gave rise to the enactment of the constitutional and statutory restrictions on the creation of debt in most of the states. Many of the states went so far as to prohibit the creation of state debt in any form; others established debt limits which proved unrealistically low. The governmental lessee device was introduced as a method of evading constitutional debt limits and/or requirements for referenda on debt proposals. Some of the states have adopted more realistic debt provisions; however, the habit derived in the preceding decades has tended to maintain governmental lessee debt practices, even under revised debt limits.

The governmental lessee arrangements effectively nullify conventional debt limits for

public facility debt in most states where permitted. They generally avoid referenda requirements unless the constitution redefines debt in a manner to foreclose these possibilities.

Operation of Excess Rental Arrangements

Many governmental lessee arrangements call for payments of rental that are in excess
of the *pro forma* debt service requirements. It is not unusual for the lease rental to be at
110 or 120 percent of the *pro forma* debt service requirements. The excess rentals are
ordinarily applied first to the creation of a debt service reserve fund (unless this has been
created from bond proceeds) and, secondly, either to the liquidation of debt in advance
of stated maturity or to the accumulation of excess reserve funds.

One pattern is to provide for bonds to be callable after a few years—usually within
the range of five to 10 years—for purposes of redemption from excess revenues without
a call premium. This means that after the debt service reserve fund has been created, the
excess revenues are accumulated until the designated anniversary in a debt redemption
fund, unless the bonds are purchased at advantageous prices on the open market in the
interim. Commencing with the designated anniversary, the excess moneys available (including the interest on the debt service reserve fund and debt redemption fund) are applied
to redemption of outstanding bonds (ordinarily, with call in inverse order as to maturity
and by lot within each maturity).

To illustrate this use of excess coverage rental funds, Table 43 is presented, based
upon Pattern B yield curve in Appendix Table A. [Although the yield curve is from 1979
experience, the principles illustrated are applicable with equal force to both high and low
levels of interest if there is a substantial incidence to the curve.] It is apparent from the
table that the debt is scheduled on an equal-annual-debt-service basis over a 25-year period,
with debt service being calculated at approximately $804,000 per year on a *pro forma*
basis. Rentals are calculated on the basis of 120 percent of debt service, or $964,000.
The excess rentals are estimated to earn 7.50 percent per annum interest, compounded
annually. (To avoid complications implicit in semiannual computations, variations which
would arise therefrom are ignored on assumption that dates of payments of rentals and
intrayear income are assumed to produce the equivalent of a 7.50 percent per annum
net income on the Debt Service Reserve Fund.)

The actual debt service operation is reflected in Columns 9–13; the excess rentals
are accumulated in the debt service reserve fund until they have reached one full year's
debt service under the *pro forma* schedule (Column 7). Thereafter, until the end of the
10th year, the excess is accumulated in the bond redemption fund. By the end of the
10th year, $1,470,000 has been accumulated in that fund, when it is used to liquidate a
portion of the debt outstanding (as shown in Column 11). Further acceleration of redemption
is possible from the $964,000 annual lease rental payment and the annual interest on the
debt service reserve fund. Principal retired in the 11th year becomes $646,000 as compared
to scheduled retirement of $329,000 under the *pro forma* schedule. By the end of the
17th year, sufficient funds are in hand to retire all the outstanding debt and to reduce
the annual rental for the year from $964,000 to $885,000. Under the "actual" debt service
illustrated, total interest paid amounts to $7,198,000 and total rental to $16,314,000.

This type of arrangement is quite attractive to many investors. It provides a partial
hedge against price depreciation arising from generally higher interest levels in the market.
As has been shown in Chapter 14, such a practice acts to elevate the market price for
bonds with yield rates higher than coupon rates. For those whose bonds are redeemed
through tender or call, even greater advantage is likely to be forthcoming.

Comparative Costs under Serial Bond Issue

As an alternative to the use of excess rentals, it would be feasible to develop either
a straight serial bond issue without a debt service reserve fund or to provide for such a

Table 43

Nominal and Actual Debt Service Projected on a $10,204,000 Governmental Term Bond Issue Where Rental Is 120 Percent of Nominal Debt Service

(amounts in thousands of dollars)

Year	Nominal Debt Service					Annual Rental	Debt Service Reserve Fund	Bond Redemp-tion Fund	Annual Rental	Actual Debt Service			
	Out-standing 12/31	Pattern B Coupon Rate	Maturity	Interest	Debt Service					Out-standing 12/31	Principal	Interest	Debt Service
	(1)	(2)	(3)	(4)	(5)	(6)	(7)	(8)	(9)	(10)	(11)	(12)	(13)
1	9,990	3.20	215	589	804	964	160	—	964	9,990	215	589	804
2	9,768	3.50	221	582	804	964	334	—	964	9,768	221	582	804
3	9,539	3.80	229	575	804	964	519	—	964	9,539	229	575	804
4	9,301	4.10	238	566	804	964	719	—	964	9,301	238	566	804
5	9,054	4.35	248	556	804	964	804	130	964	9,054	248	556	804
6	8,795	4.60	258	545	804	964	804	361	964	8,795	258	545	804
7	8,525	4.80	270	533	804	964	804	609	964	8,525	270	533	804
8	8,242	5.00	283	520	804	964	804	875	964	8,242	283	520	804
9	7,945	5.20	297	506	804	964	804	1,162	964	7,945	297	506	804
10	7,632	5.25	314	491	804	964	804	1,470	964	6,171	1,783	491	2,274
11	7,302	5.50	329	474	804	964	804	—	964	5,525	646	378	1,024
12	6,955	5.60	347	456	804	964	804	—	964	4,840	686	339	1,025
13	6,588	5.70	367	437	804	964	804	—	964	4,114	727	287	1,024
14	6,201	5.80	388	416	804	964	804	—	964	3,343	771	253	1,024
15	5,790	5.90	410	393	804	964	804	—	964	2,526	819	206	1,025
16	5,356	6.00	434	369	804	964	804	—	964	1,658	869	156	1,025
17	4,895	6.10	460	343	804	964	804	—	885	—	1,643	105	948
18	4,407	6.20	489	315	804	964	804	—	—	—	—	—	—
19	3,888	6.30	519	285	804	964	804	—	—	—	—	—	—
20	3,336	6.35	552	252	804	964	804	—	—	—	—	—	—
21	2,750	6.40	588	217	804	964	804	—	—	—	—	—	—
22	2,126	6.45	624	180	804	964	804	—	—	—	—	—	—
23	1,461	6.50	664	139	804	964	804	—	—	—	—	—	—
24	754	6.55	708	96	804	964	804	—	—	—	—	—	—
25	—	6.60	754	50	804	964	804	—	—	—	—	—	—
Totals			10,204	9,887	20,091	24,109		16,314	16.4		10,204	7,198	17,403

Table 44

Debt Service on a $10,204,000 Governmental Lessee Serial Bond Issue Maturing Over a Period of 17 Years

(amounts in thousands of dollars)

Year	Outstanding 12/31	Pattern B Coupon Rate	Maturities 12/31	Interest	Debt Service	Increase (or Decrease) Over Table 43 Values[1] Outstanding	Annual Rental
	(1)	(2)	(3)	(4)	(5)	(6)	(7)
1	9,789	3.20	415	526	941	(195)	(23)
2	9,360	3.50	429	513	941	(408)	(23)
3	8,916	3.80	444	498	941	(623)	(23)
4	8,456	4.10	461	481	941	(845)	(23)
5	7,977	4.35	479	462	941	(1,076)	(23)
6	7,476	4.60	500	441	941	(1,319)	(23)
7	6,953	4.80	523	418	941	(1,572)	(23)
8	6,405	5.00	548	393	941	(1,837)	(23)
9	5,829	5.20	576	366	941	(2,115)	(23)
10	5,223	5.25	606	336	941	(939)	(23)
11	4,586	5.50	638	304	941	(929)	(23)
12	3,913	5.60	673	269	941	(916)	(23)
13	3,203	5.70	710	231	941	(899)	(23)
14	2,452	5.80	751	191	941	(879)	(23)
15	1,658	5.90	794	147	941	(854)	(23)
16	816	6.00	841	100	941	(827)	(23)
17	—	6.10	816	50	866	—	(19)
Total			10,204	5,725	15,929		(385)

[1] Comparison in Column 6 is with Column 10 of Table 43; comparison in Column 7 is with Column 9 of Table 43.
NB: Details may not add to totals due to rounding.

fund but avoid the excess coverage requirements. Table 44 compares the results of the operation under Table 43 with a serial bond issue not involving excess coverage or a debt service reserve fund. If the bonds could be sold as a regular serial issue at the same rates for the same maturity years, it would be feasible to liquidate the debt in 17 years. The annual rental payable under Table 44 requirements would be $941,000 compared to $964,000 under Table 43. Over the life of the issue, total rental costs under Table 44 would be about $385,000 less than under Table 43—a savings of about 2.4 percent.

However, the straight serial bond issue illustrated here does not contain any reserve provisions. The investor is obliged to depend on the timely full payments by the lessee in order to avoid default. This may be translated by investors into assumption of higher risk; however, a debt service reserve fund reduces the degree of such risk. The result could be high coupons that would nullify, or more than nullify, the advantages seemingly available under Table 44 vis-à-vis Table 43 unless other protections are present.

A final point in the comparison is concerned with the earnings rate assumption for the debt service fund and the bond redemption fund under Table 43. The assumption is a rate of 7.50 percent which is probably on the low side inasmuch as the bonds issued under Table 43 have a maximum coupon rate of 6.60 percent; however, for the bond redemption fund, an investment rate would probably have to be at the average rate for the bond issue to comply with arbitrage regulations, or somewhat below 6.00 percent.

In any event, debt managers will wish to make such comparisons at the time of planning governmental lessee bond issues in order to determine the impact of the excess annual rental on the interest rates likely to be payable. Doubtless the straight serial bond issue with a debt service reserve fund will prove to be advantageous in some circumstances—especially with issuers with a high credit position and/or strong secondary support, e.g., diversion of revenues from the state government. In other circumstances, the advantages to be derived from the coverage will overshadow the benefits to be derived under the serial bond issue.

Another factor to be considered is the amount of debt outstanding at any given time. It is noted that, under the serial bond issue, the outstanding debt is generally below that of the projected actual debt service in Table 43. With the outstanding debt being as much as 20 percent lower in some years and at least 8 percent in all years, consideration must be given to the impact of this process upon the total market for the debt of the issuer as well as the lessee. It is probably relatively small; however, it is a factor with which to contend in judging overall market effects.

State Support of Governmental Lessee Debt

In the original governmental lessee debt, there was a careful separation of support of such debt from the general revenues of state and local governments beyond that afforded by the lease-rental payments. This pattern was noted in the early court decisions as support for the view that the governmental lessee debt did not constitute debt within the meaning of constitutional provisions governing the amount and method of authorization of debt of state and local governments. The basic assumption was that to extend additional support would have the effect of causing this debt to become debt within the general meaning set forth in the constitutional prohibitions in the various states. However, as the concept has matured, there have been a number of changes in the positions of the states vis-à-vis governmental lessee debt. For example, in Georgia in 1960, a constitutional amendment was adopted which made it mandatory for the legislature to appropriate the debt service on lessee debt. Although not extending full faith and credit to the lessee debt, this provision came very close to producing such a result.

In Pennsylvania, a different approach was taken. In respect of the lessee debt of local school districts placed with the Pennsylvania State Public School Building Authority, the legislature provided that, in case of default by a local district on a lease rental payment, the Authority could obtain rental payment by a diversion from the next moneys due to the district by the Commonwealth for any school purpose of an amount sufficient to cure the deficiency. Similar provisions have subsequently been made in respect to lessee debt of school districts to local school authorities in Pennsylvania.

The State of New Jersey authorizes the issuance of "qualified bonds." Under this program, if bonds of municipalities are certified as "qualified" within standards established by law and administrative action, additional security is provided for the debt by causing the state treasurer to pay over from business personal property tax replacement revenues (provided by the state) the debt service on such qualified bonds.[2]

There is no comprehensive study of the full extent of the use of governmental lessee debt in its different forms nor of the extent to which various states using governmental lessee debt have adopted back-up provisions for one type or another of local government debt.

EQUIPMENT LEASING

State and local governments have historically made wide use of leasing of computers and some other types of equipment from private owners. Some of them have operated internal equipment rental funds to facilitate their accounting operations and to spread the costs of equipment acquisitions over a period of years. During the 1970s the practice became somewhat more widespread and a few governments commenced acquisition programs under various types of leasing arrangements which involved the use of tax-free interest and occasionally some benefits to the lessors in respect to depreciation or other benefits. Also in the 1970s some jurisdictions established special arrangements under which an authority or other tax-exempt mechanism was used to acquire the equipment with the use of tax-free bonds and thereupon lease it to the general government, with the lease-rental payments being the security for the notes or bonds issued by the leasing authority.

Finally in 1981 Congress enacted legislation under which very special arrangements were possible in the case of certain mass transportation equipment. In these circumstances the government was able to secure benefits arising both from tax-free interest and from depreciation which in effect was sold off to a taxable entity that could benefit therefrom.

MUNICIPAL BOND BANKS

Municipal bond banks have been established in Maine, New Hampshire, New York, Vermont, and Alaska. Essentially, the municipal bond bank operations in those states consist of the sale by local governments of their securities to a state bond bank. The state bond bank derives its capital from issuance of securities to the public. The Vermont bank was the first established (1969) and includes as security the bonds purchased from local governments which are secured, in turn, by local property taxes. Additionally, the Vermont statute seeks to impose upon the legislature the obligation to appropriate such sums as may be necessary to replenish the debt service reserve fund to the pledged level— if default by local governments in their payments has resulted in a diminution in the amount in the fund from the previous year. Thereby, the bonds become moral obligations of the state government.

The Maine bank, established in 1973, is similar to that of Vermont; however, it may purchase not only tax-supported debt of local governments but also their revenue debt. A similar "moral obligation" pledge is provided in the law under which state legislative appropriations to restore the reserve fund are required. The Alaska bank, established in

---

[2] *Laws of the State of New Jersey, 1976*, Chapter 38, approved June 28, 1976.

1975, provides for direct purchase; however, it does *not* carry a "moral obligation" pledge of state legislative support for restoration of the reserve fund. The New York State Municipal Bond Bank Agency was established under 1976 legislation which contains a specific prohibition against any pledge of state moneys in support of the debt of the Agency. The New Hampshire Municipal Bond Bank entered the field in 1979 with the sale of some bonds backed by the state's guarantee and some on a revenue bond basis.

The advantages of the state bond bank arrangement lie in (1) a pooling of credit, thereby lending strength to the bonds for many participating governments; (2) the marketing advantages to be derived from issuance of medium and/or large sized issues rather than a large number of smaller local issues; (3) development of central staff capacity for the planning, issuance, and administration of the debt; and (4) when applicable, state government support through general or "moral obligation" pledges.

In each of the states having bond banks, local governments are free to continue their independent sales of bonds and the state bond bank managers are free to reject bonds of individual local governments; however, it appears that matters of comity foreclose rejection, except in extreme circumstances.

Direct State Support

The Texas Water Development Board has authority to issue *general obligation* bonds of the State of Texas within limits of constitutional authorizations for either (1) direct development of water resources or (2) purchase of bonds of local water development agencies. In the exercise of the second function, the Board becomes a type of bond bank for the participating local water development agencies. However, inasmuch as the bonds of the Board are state general obligation bonds, the only revenue bond aspect of this operation is that of accepting local water development revenue bonds as part of the portfolio of the Board and obtaining debt service payments thereon, as due.

Another form of state assistance is marketing debt with tax proceeds destined for local governments. The Municipal Assistance Corporation for the City of New York was created in 1975 to market debt for the city following the city's inability to raise moneys in the credit markets. In that case, certain revenues of the City of New York were assigned to the Municipal Assistance Corporation and the corporation has, from time to time, issued debt with these dedicated revenues as security. In the meantime, the City of New York has issued its direct long-term debt only to its pension funds. The New York Municipal Assistance Corporation differs from the bond banks in that it is limited to a single city and the bonds are secured not by contracts with the city but by the dedication of a portion of the city's revenues. Therefore, these are, in fact, special tax bonds.

The State of Florida issues two types of debt for local governments which also fall within the special tax classification—those issued for local school districts and those issued for road purposes within the counties. In each case, the bonds are secured by certain state taxes allocated to educational or road purposes but under provisions of the state constitution which permit the issuance of debt for these local governments with portions of these tax revenues pledged as security.

SPECIAL ASSESSMENT DEBT[3]

Prior to 1933 one of the major sources of capital funds for municipalities and special districts was special assessment bonds with a large proportion of the streets and some

---

[3] Inasmuch as the use of assessment debt has receded as a portion of total state and local government debt, it is deemed appropriate to limit the discussion here to a summary statement. For those concerned with special assessment debt, attention is called to Moak, *Administration of Local Government Debt* (1970), in which a full chapter is devoted to the subject (pp. 423–440). See also A. M. Hillhouse, *Municipal Bonds: A Century of Experience*, pp. 106–142; 450–454.

other improvements in newly developed areas being financed in this manner. The prevailing pattern of land subdivision and development at that time was for the owners of the land to subdivide property and secure capital for streets and water mains (and, perhaps, also for sewers, sidewalks, and other amenities) by inducing local governing authorities to issue special assessment bonds. Thereby, the land in subdivisions was made marketable. The residential or other lots were then sold subject to the liabilities represented by the special assessments. In many portions of the nation—especially in Florida and in a few large midwestern suburban areas—subdivision and sale of land went forward well in advance of the time that the new owners were prepared to construct homes on such land.

When the Great Depression came, owners generally defaulted on the lots they had purchased on a time payment plan. Although some of the land reverted to the developers, it did so along with the special assessment obligations. Short of capital themselves, they defaulted and huge proportions of outstanding special assessment debt in the United States also defaulted.

In much the same manner, many developed areas lacked amenities of urban living. As the municipalities proceeded with pavement of streets, installation of water services, construction of sewers, and provision of street lighting, it was customary to assess the cost of these improvements against the abutting or adjacent property owners. In addition to these facilities of immediate concern to the property holder, other types of improvements were sometimes fully or partially assessed under the theory that those public improvements that benefited the land should be paid for by the benefited owners, rather than the entire community. These, too, went into default.

An indication of the importance of special assessment debt in the local government debt picture in 1932 was the fact that almost 10 percent of the $15.3 billion of total long-term local government debt then outstanding was special assessment debt. In the same year, special assessment revenue accounted for $295 million, or an amount equal to about 7 percent of all revenue derived from local taxes.[4] In municipalities, the percentages were much higher.

Commencing in the late 1930s, many states adopted laws requiring the developer to install streets and other amenities as a part of the privilege of development. The costs of these improvements became a part of the cost of the completed housing to be paid in cash or financed through the mortgage market. As a result, the use of special assessment debt in relation to new developments decreased rapidly. Use of special assessments to finance improvements in established neighborhoods continued for many years as an important aspect of financing these kinds of facilities. However, with the broadening of local revenue sources, special assessment financing assumed a lesser role. Even so, for all local governments, revenues from special assessments in 1980 were reported at the $1.3 billion level, which was equivalent to about 1.5 percent of total local tax revenues ($84.4 billion). In the case of city governments, special assessments amounted to $717 million, or about 2.3 percent of their tax revenues in 1980 ($31.3 billion).[5] With fiscal pressures increasing, the use of special assessments is likely to expand.

In 1977 (the most recent year for which data are available on a state by state basis for special assessments), special assessments were of even greater importance to special districts. In that year, special assessment revenues for these districts were $147 million, equivalent to 8.4 percent of tax revenues for those governmental units.[6]

---

[4] U.S. Bureau of the Census, *Statistics of State and Local Governments: 1932*, pp. 7, 51.

[5] U.S. Bureau of the Census, *1977 Census of Governments, Compendium of Governmental Finances,* Vol. 4, No. 5, p. 24; *Governmental Finances in 1979–80*, p. 17; and *City Government Finances in 1979–80*, p. 7.

[6] U.S. Bureau of the Census, *1977 Census of Governments, Compendium of Governmental Finances,* Vol. 4, No. 5, pp. 134–143.

General Procedure

The general procedure in the levy of special assessments is for the governing body to designate an area to constitute a special improvement district or area for specified public improvements. The initiative for such designation may be from property holders through a petition or it may arise from public officials. The kinds of improvements contemplated are described and preliminary cost estimates developed. A basis for allocation of such costs is determined, usually with maps from which property owners can determine what is proposed and the probable cost to each. Public hearings are held following which the governing body makes a determination as to whether to proceed with the proposed improvements. If the decision is to proceed, detailed plans and specifications are prepared and competitive bids sought. A determination is made as to whether the project will be fully assessable or whether portions of the costs will be borne from the community treasury. At a designated meeting, the bids are tabulated and unit costs are also determined. Assessments are determined based on the project costs and the prescribed formula for apportionment of the costs.

Different jurisdictions have different procedures as to the method of payment to contractors, depending, in part, upon the method of funding that is used. In some cases, the contractor is obliged to accept the assessments as part of his bid price for the work done. In such cases, the contractor is likely to make advance arrangements with a lending institution for discounting the entire set of assessments he has agreed to accept. The amount of such discount is added to the amount of the bid he would ordinarily enter if he were assured of full and timely payment.

In other cases, the contract for the work is made at the same time the assessment bonds are sold. Unless the sale brings a sufficient amount to finance the work to be done, the project is likely to be cancelled. In still other cases, the sponsoring government effectively underwrites the special assessment process, thereby enabling the contractor to bid in the same manner as on other public works projects. This step, however, tends to convert the special assessment obligations to a higher level of security—sometimes approaching the general obligation level.

At the conclusion of the work, the property owners in jurisdictions that have funded a portion of the cost of the project through special assessment debt are usually given the opportunity to pay the full amount of the special assessment or to make arrangements for payment over a period of years. For those jurisdictions in which the contractor is given the assessments as all, or part, of his compensation, the contractor presents the assessments to the property holder demanding payment. If the property owner is unable or unwilling to pay, the unpaid notes are discounted to lending institutions who work out a discharge of the lien with the property owner.

The Future of Special Assessment Debt

Since the 1930s there has been a general decline in dependence on special assessment debt, due, in part, to the changes noted earlier in the method of financing facilities required for new land development, and, in part, to the general prosperity of local governments which has enabled them to absorb through the general budget many of the costs once charged to assessments. The current pressures on tax revenues at all levels of government make it clear that local governments are turning more and more to service charges as a source of income to offset rising costs. In these circumstances, it will not be surprising if a part of the former popularity of special assessments and special assessment debt returns—both as a means of relieving direct pressures on the general treasury and as a means of discouraging some of the pressures for public improvements.

SPECIAL DEVELOPMENT DISTRICT (TAX INCREMENT) BONDS

Within a few states the practice has arisen under which special development districts are permitted to be organized. Essentially the pattern is one in which an area [frequently in center city] is selected for renewal, with the financing for the renewal activities including proceeds from tax increment bonds. The pattern varies from state to state; however, the basic outlines are similar.

Under the tax increment bond practice, all units of local government are limited, for a defined period of years, in the amount of taxes they may derive from the district being redeveloped. If, as a result of the urban renewal activities the property values within the district rise and this produces additional tax revenues at the rates being generally levied by districts active in the defined area, the incremental element of tax yield is earmarked for the servicing of the tax increment bonds. This device has been especially popular in California and some other western states.

Chapter 16
ON BEHALF OF REVENUE DEBT

The final general classification of tax-exempt debt to be considered is that designated as *on behalf of* financing. It is so designated because the states and/or their local governments are acting only as agents in the issuance of this debt, being careful not to extend their credit in support of the debt in either a direct or indirect manner. Essentially, the states and/or their local governments provide facilities for the issuance and servicing of the debt and, thereby, the interest on the debt becomes tax-exempt—subject to the regulations issued under Section 103 of the Internal Revenue Code. The bulk of this debt is issued as long-term debt for either profit or nonprofit corporations. That issued for profit corporations falls generally within the categories of industrial development and pollution control. The debt issued on behalf of nonprofit corporations falls primarily into two general categories: (1) Institutions of higher learning, (2) hospitals and other selected health facilities. Debt for housing is for both profit and nonprofit entities.

TAX-EXEMPT DEBT FOR INDUSTRY

One of the major purposes of *on behalf of* debt issued by state and local governments is promotion of the economy of the area served by the issuer. Although the present type of financing used to encourage economic development dates largely from the program initiated in Mississippi in 1933 [the Balance Agriculture with Industry—BAWI—program], the roots of governmental financing for economic development lie in early America. Some of the efforts apparently predate the American Revolution. The first major efforts came in the building of canals during the first several decades of the 19th Century, followed by a broad participation in railroad financing both before and after the Civil War.

Most of the early financing was based upon the use of general revenues and the general credit of the state or its local governments. Various questions of "public purpose" punctuate the legal history in both the state and federal courts and are too voluminous to recount here.[1]

Contemporary tax-exempt debt for economic development rests first upon the provisions of the Internal Revenue Code, especially the provisions of Section 103. For purposes of simplification, the Code provides in Section 171(d) a comprehensive definition of the term "bond" to include all forms of interest-bearing debt.[2]

---

[1] For a comprehensive statement of the history of state and local government involvement in the issuance of debt designed to improve their economic development prior to 1936, see Albert M. Hillhouse, *Municipal Bonds: A Century of Experience,* especially pp. 143–199, and also see Mark Rollinson, *Small Issue Industrial Development Bonds,* pp. 7–25.

[2] United States Internal Revenue Code, Section 171(d) reads as follows: For purposes of this section, the term "bond" means any bond, debenture, note or certificate or other evidence of indebtedness, issued by any corporation and bearing interest (including any like obligation issued by a government or political subdivision thereof), but does not include any such obligation which constitutes stock in trade of the taxpayer or any such obligation of a kind which would properly be included in the inventory of the taxpayer if on hand at the close of the taxable year, or any such obligation held by the taxpayer primarily for sale to customers in the ordinary course of his trade or business.

Therefore, at the outset it is essential to realize that the term "bond" is very broadly defined. This use of the term is frequently overlooked by those who seek to differentiate between different elements of the debt issued for economic development.

In Section 103 the Code undertakes to establish categories of economic development obligations and establishes two broad categories of interest here:

1. *Exempt Debt.* Exempt activities of state and local governments for these purposes are deemed to include debt created to provide:
   a. Residential real property for family units
   b. Sports facilities
   c. Convention or trade show facilities
   d. Airports, docks, wharves, mass commuting facilities, parking facilities, or storage or training facilities directly related to any of the foregoing
   e. Sewage or solid waste disposal facilities or facilities for the local furnishing of electric energy or gas
   f. Air or water pollution control facilities, or
   g. Facilities for the furnishing of water, if available, on reasonable demand to members of the general public
2. *Small Issue Exempt Debt.* In addition to the economic development debt that may be issued under the preceding paragraph, small issue debt may be sold under one of two limitations:
   a. Up to $1,000,000 may be issued for the benefit of a given corporation, generally with few restrictions
   b. Up to $10,000,000 may be issued over a period of five consecutive years for any corporation

IDB vs. IRB

Among the distinctions one must keep in mind in relation to industrial tax-exempt debt is one that is not made in the law. It is the difference between Industrial Development Bonds and Industrial Revenue Bonds:

Industrial Development Bonds is a term generally reserved to the type of debt in which the issuer is a taxing authority and in respect to the debt of which the issuer pledges its resources—sometimes in limited amounts and sometimes as full-faith-and-credit pledges.

Industrial Revenue Bonds is a term generally used to indicate tax-exempt debt that is secured by the revenues of the property or properties that are being financed—without any pledge of the general revenues of a tax-levying governmental entity.

The original BAWI bonds issued in Mississippi were of the IDB type of security and the State of Mississippi and its local governments continue to issue such bonds on many occasions. In like manner a number of other states and their local governments issue such debt, including Arkansas, Connecticut, Delaware, Maryland, and New Jersey. In a number of the other states, only the IRBs are permitted.

The IDBs are direct debt of the state or local government issuer and generally fall outside a strict definition of *on behalf of* debt of these governments. They tend to fall more within the concept of a tax-supported, or partially tax-supported, general obligation bond of the issuer than within the revenue classification, although much of the data on sales and outstanding debt is organized in a manner that lumps these with IRBs, which are squarely within the *on behalf of* classification. Given this fact, one is obliged to view with care data on such debt issued or outstanding.

Pollution Control Bonds

Pollution control bonds issued by state and local governments may be either for direct action by these governments in controlling air and water pollution or for providing a vehicle through which tax exemption is extended to certain bond issues in respect to which the proceeds are remitted to private corporations for pollution control purposes, and in respect to which bonds the security is likely to lie with the corporation involved, rather than on more general governmental revenues.

Sale of Debt

IDBs are likely to be sold in substantially the same manner as the general purpose debt of the issuer. Pollution control debt for the benefit of private corporations and a large portion of the IRBs are marketed in much the same manner as other revenue debt, i.e., in the form of bonds and/or notes sold through either competitive or negotiated sale through bond dealers and dealer banks. However, in the case of the IRBs there is a very large market through which the debt is placed directly with commerical banks or other lenders without the use of underwriters. The typical pattern is one in which the industrial development agency negotiates the terms of the financing between the corporation and the lender, with the industrial development corporation taking title to the property and mortgaging it to the lender. The private corporation enters into a lease/purchase agreement which constitutes the primary [or entire] security for the specific debt involved.

Volume of Debt Sold

Both *The Bond Buyer*[3] and the Public Securities Association[4] develop data concerning sales of industrial bonds and of pollution control debt. Their information for recent years may be summarized as follows:

	(in billions of dollars)				
Year	Industrial Tax-exempt Debt Issued			Industrial Pollution Control Debt Issued	
	The Bond Buyer	Public Securities Association	Congressional Budget Office	The Bond Buyer	Public Securities Association
1968	1.6	1.6	na	na	na
1969	.01	.05	na	na	na
1970	.05	.1	na	na	na
1971	.2	.2	na	na	na
1972	.5	.3	na	na	na
1973	.3	.5	na	1.8	1.7
1974	.3	.5	na	1.7	1.7
1975	.5	na	1.3	2.1	na
1976	.4	.5	1.5	2.1	2.3
1977	.5	2.1	2.3	3.0	2.6
1978	.6	.9	3.5	2.8	2.7
1979	1.3	1.7	7.1	2.5	2.1
1980	1.5	1.6	8.4	1.5	2.2

---

[3] *The Daily Bond Buyer,* (Special MFOA Conference Supplement No. 2), June 2, 1980, pp. 1, 11; The Weekly Bond Buyer, January 18, 1982, pp. 1, 42–44; The Bond Buyer, *Statistics on State and Local Government Finance,* Vol. 12 (May 1974), pp. 40–41; Vol. 13 (June 1975), pp. 42–43; Vol. 14 (June 1976), pp. 41–45; Vol. 15 (June 1977), pp. 37–39; Vol. 16 (June 1978), pp. 41–45; Vol. 17 (June 1979), pp. 41–44; Vol. 18 (1980), p. 44; Vol. 19 (1981), p. 8.

[4] Investment Bankers' Association, *Municipal Statistical Bulletin,* 4th Quarter, 1970, p. 3; Securities Industries Association, *Municipal Statistical Bulletin,* 4th Quarter, 1972, p. 3; Securities Industries Association, *Municipal Market Developments,* February 28, 1975, Table 2; Public Securities Association, *Municipal Market Developments,* April 21, 1977, Table 2; March 29, 1978, Table 4; February 15, 1979, Table 4; March 18, 1980, Table 4; and February 11, 1981, Table 4.

From this tabulation it is apparent that the three sources have widely differing views concerning the volume of industrial tax-exempt debt being issued. The major differences are with the Congressional Budget Office which has taken into account many of the small issue and direct placement loans with investors that do not regularly come to the attention of either *The Bond Buyer* or the Public Securities Association which depend largely upon investment bankers to provide basic information.

HOUSING BONDS

The use of tax-exempt bonds for housing has dated primarily from 1938, although there may have been relatively limited use in some states prior to that time. Under the Federal Housing Act of 1938, federal agencies were authorized to contract with public housing agencies (according to the provisions of state law) for the purpose of providing housing to families with low incomes. Successive laws, especially the Housing Act of 1949, as amended, have expanded and modified these powers. In the exercise of these powers, contracts were executed with local housing agencies providing guaranteed revenues sufficient to pay the debt service on housing debt issued by the local public housing authorities. This debt was tax-exempt inasmuch as it was issued for a public purpose by a state government or a local government or governmental agency authorized by the state laws to function in this field. Provision was made for loans by the appropriate federal agency during construction or for support of such loans as might be issued by the local public housing agencies.

Acting under this legislation, most of the public housing projects in urban communities were developed and financed. Large amounts of this debt were issued in the years 1938–1974 when the original program was substantially closed out; in some years more than $1 billion in such financing was issued.[5] These bonds have long been considered to be risk free due to a ruling of the Attorney General of May 15, 1953, which held that the faith of the United States had been solemnly pledged in support of the housing contracts and, therefore, in support of the debt service on these bonds.[6] In a sense, these bonds tend to follow the principle involved in governmental lessee financing where one government contracts with another to perform a function and the second government issues debt secured by the moneys payable under the contract. Although the federal payments are grants and not lease payments, the substance of the action is similar to governmental lessee financing in this respect.

The earlier program was gradually phased out insofar as the creation of new debt was concerned as the thrust in the early 1970s moved to provision of low-rent housing to economically non-self-sufficient families was shifted away from "project" financing to the scattered housing program. Different authors have developed different classification systems for housing debt. The summary provided by Standard & Poor's Corporation[7] is one of the better and more succinct of these which uses four broad categories for description of housing debt:

> **Direct Loan Program Issues.** Under this type of program, the public agency, generally a state housing finance agency, will provide a direct mortgage loan to a for-profit or a not-for-profit developer. Bonds are issued to provide construction and/or permanent financing for a portfolio of projects. The projects are generally multiunit for low- and moderate-income families or elderly tenants, and receive federal subsidy

---

[5] As of September 30, 1978, HUD reported outstanding obligations of local housing authorities in the hands of private investors to be $14.7 billion, of which $8.3 billion were bonds and $6.4 billion were project notes. U.S. Department of Housing and Urban Development, *1978 Statistical Yearbook*, p. 265.

[6] For a fuller statement of the legislative history, see Moody's Investors Service, *Municipal & Government Manual, 1977*, pp. 4405–4409.

[7] Standard & Poor's Corporation, *Municipal and International Bond Ratings: An Overview*, pp. 44–45.

payments. The bonds are payable from mortgage repayments, including subsidy payments.

Mortgage Purchase Issues. This type of program generally provides mortgage money for single family homes. The bonds are issued to provide funds to purchase mortgages from lending institutions either out of portfolio or on a newly originated basis. These programs are generally oriented to moderate income families or individuals who must meet generally accepted mortgage underwriting standards, and the only form of subsidy involved is the use of tax-exempt financing. The bonds are payable from mortgage repayments from the loan portfolio. This type of program was initially developed by state housing and mortgage finance agencies, but has recently seen use at the local level by cities and redevelopment agencies.

Section 11(b) Local Housing Authority Issues. Section 11(b) refers to the federal regulations providing for tax-exempt financing of individual Section 8 subsidized projects by local housing authorities or their agencies and instrumentalities. These projects for low- and moderate-income tenants are for the elderly or families, or may involve mixed projects containing both families and the elderly. The bond issues provide permanent financing only, and the bonds are payable from mortgage repayments including the federal subsidy payments. The mortgages on these projects may or may not be federally insured.

Loans-to-Lenders Programs. While strictly defined as revenue bonds, these issues, which use bond proceeds to make collateralized loans to lending institutions which in turn make mortgage loans and which are payable from loan repayments by the lending institution, are treated as collateralized issues. They are analogous to the mortgage-backed bond issues seen in the private sector, and have generally been issued by state housing or mortgage finance agencies. They have recently become less popular as the agencies have turned more to the mortgage purchase program. The collateral may consist of U.S. Government securities at a level of approximately 110% of the loan or conventional mortgages at a ratio of approximately 150%. Upon default on the loan by any lending institution, the collateral may be liquidated. Our ratings are based on the quality and the level of collateralization.

Under the current programs, the amounts of housing debt have increased significantly. Thus, the Public Securities Association has reported sales of tax-exempt bonds in recent years for housing purposes as follows:[8]

	(millions)
1976	$ 2,695
1977	3,698
1978	5,691
1979	12,124
1980	15,139

During the latter part of 1978 and during part of 1979, there was a flurry of single-family housing debt issued by state and local governments to facilitate the financing of such housing. The City of Chicago sold the first issue and, within a few months, very large aggregate amounts of financing were being undertaken. Shortly, the U.S. Treasury and the U.S. Congress became concerned about this development as opening the floodgates of tax-exempt financing. Steps were taken to abort new sales in mid-1979 and, as of the

[8] Public Securities Association, *Municipal Market Developments,* April, 1977, Table 2; March 29, 1978, Table 4; February 15, 1979, Table 4; February 11, 1981, Table 4.

spring of 1980, Congress had adopted no legislation to permit a return to single-family, tax-exempt financing of privately owned housing.

BONDS TO AID NONGOVERNMENTAL INSTITUTIONS OF HIGHER LEARNING

Financing Facilities

The development of programs of higher education among the states has been quite different from one region to another. The New England and Middle Atlantic states historically depended largely on privately financed colleges and universities. In most of the remainder of the nation, the governmental institutions of higher learning have predominated—at least during the past half century. The rising cost of facilities and the decrease in the buying power of endowments have curtailed the ability of nongovernmental colleges and universities. This led to the creation in many states of special financing agencies to enable these institutions to borrow at tax-exempt rates. Again, the concentration has been in the Northeast, although a number of other states also have active programs.

No comprehensive data are available concerning the volume of this financing. Much of the financing has been directed toward university housing; however, in some cases, it has extended to various types of instructional facilities. In the case of the housing facility loans, the security is sometimes limited to the revenues of such facilities, combined with a mortgage. In other situations, the bonds are supported by a general pledge of the revenues of the institution. In the issuance of these bonds, some states have sold bonds secured by the direct pledges of single borrowers; in others, a number of borrowers have been brought together in what amounts to pooled financing. Generally, the states have not pledged any of their revenues in support of such debt; however, the more recent move toward "state-related" institutions has resulted in indirect state assumption of some of the debt.

Student Loan Programs

As the cost of higher education increased in the 1960s and 1970s, it became obvious that many worthy students would be deprived of the opportunity for higher education unless loans were available to assist them in financing educational and living costs incurred in their attendance. A considerable portion of this program is underwritten by the federal government. After major expansion throughout the 1970s, the Reagan Administration in 1981 and 1982 sought markedly to curtail the program.

HOSPITAL AND HEALTH FACILITY BONDS

State and local governments have a long history of ownership and operation of hospitals and other health facilities. In some cases, such hospitals have generally been limited to the medically indigent; in others, they have been operated as broad-based health facilities to protect the public health, e.g., the system of special tuberculosis hospitals before discovery of modern treatment for that disease. In a few states, special hospital districts have been created, with limited taxing authority, to provide the principal hospital service for the community's acutely ill. These hospitals are frequently supported largely by patient charges and payments from third party sources, with only a relatively small portion of the financing coming from local tax contributions.

Alongside these governmental hospitals, the system of private nonprofit hospitalization has carried out broad health care programs. For many years these were financed through a combination of patient fees and private philanthropy. Following World War II the expanded emphasis upon the need for hospitals and other health facilities led to a federal program of assistance, largely through the Hill-Burton Act. That program contributed significant portions of the costs of financing capital outlays, although local personal and corporate philanthropy was still a major factor in financing. Gradually, hospitals began to charge interest and depreciation as elements of reimbursable expense. As Medicare became operative and as state/federal programs of medical assistance increased, large amounts of capital funds began to be derived by hospitals from loans, rather than from capital grants and contributions.

Commencing in the 1930s, prepaid hospital care became widespread first through the use of Blue Cross and later by use of other types of health and hospital insurance. In the 1960s Blue Cross organizations recognized the need for including depreciation and interest as elements of cost to be reimbursed with Medicare and medical aid plans acting in similar manner. The combination of interest and depreciation charges produced a stream of revenue which made possible much broader financing of hospital facilities through the anticipation of these revenues by use of bonds. Some of this was done through conventional mortgages; however, the use of lower rates afforded through tax-exempt financing meant that the same stream of revenues could be capitalized to provide greater amounts from debt financing. Therefore, the 1970s witnessed a great growth in financing of hospital and other health care facilities through tax-exempt bonds as more states and local governments adopted laws and created agencies to carry out these objectives. The amounts of such financing are significant, and a number of the investment banking firms have established separate divisions or subsidiary corporations for this type of financing.

Typically, the loans are on the basis of mortgages for the properties involved, with a pledge by the institutions of the revenues to be developed from the operation of the new facilities or from both old and new facilities. In some cases, the institutions have pledged other resources, e.g., endowment funds, to provide additional support for the hospital and other health facility bonds. The indentures ordinarily provide for a strong role to be played by the trustee and sometimes include heavy commitments of the full amounts set aside for depreciation as well as other revenues of the institutions involved. The variations are too numerous to permit meaningful generalizations.

A principal prerequisite for access to the tax-exempt market is a well-developed feasibility study by a consultant recognized as an expert—by the rating agencies and others.[9] These feasibility reports must be prepared under generally accepted accounting principles and the financial statements for the recent fiscal years must be certified by independent certified public accountants.

The Bond Buyer has reported sales of bonds for both governmental and nongovernmental hospitals and health facilities in recent years as follows:[10]

	(in millions)		
1974	$1,292	1978	$3,123
1975	1,959	1979	3,471
1976	2,726	1980	3,560
1977	4,731	1981	5,045

[9] In this regard, Standard & Poor's has stated: "The feasibility study should be prepared by a nationally recognized firm with expertise in hospital consulting. In this respect, S & P cannot recommend firms nor does it publish a list of acceptable firms. Our concern is that the firm have sufficient resources and experience; if we are unfamiliar with the firm that has been retained we will ask for a presentation to review the firm's credentials and to discuss the scope of the opinion and methodology of preparation." Standard & Poor's Corporation, *Municipal and International Bond Ratings: An Overview.* Undated, ca 1978, p. 39. For those interested in the approach to rating of hospital bonds, this is an especially valuable reference inasmuch as it outlines in a succinct manner information required and procedures employed in examination of proposed issues. Ibid., pp. 38–44.

[10] The Bond Buyer, *Statistics on State and Local Government Finance,* vol. 12, pp. 40–41; vol. 13, pp. 42–43; vol. 14, pp. 41–45; vol. 15, pp. 37–39; vol. 16, pp. 45–52; vol. 17, pp. 45–50; *The Daily Bond Buyer,* January 24, 1980, p. 1; *The Weekly Bond Buyer,* January 25, 1982, p. 26.

The amounts reported do not segregate the refunding amounts from the new money issues. It is known that considerable portions of the 1977–1979 financing were for advance refunding of earlier bond issues. Of the amounts reported above for the final three years, general obligation bonds accounted for $484 million in 1977; $184 million in 1978; and $148 million in 1979.

The volume of hospital and health care financing increased, in part, because of the insured mortgage bonds that were permitted until early 1979. An act providing for an additional $5.8 billion in housing financing signed December 21, 1979 prohibited a continuation of collateralized hospital financing coupled with tax-exempt financing. A report late in 1979 by the Congressional Budget Office opposed a continuation of the unrestricted use of tax-exempt financing for hospitals, pointing to losses in federal revenue estimated at $400 million in fiscal 1980.[11] This report raises the basic question that is implicit in all *on behalf of* tax-exempt financing: Is it more efficient for the Congress to provide direct subsidies than to provide for a reduction in costs through the use of tax-exempt bonds?

---

[11] *The Daily Bond Buyer,* January 24, 1980, pp. 1, 16.

Chapter 17
PREPARATION FOR MARKETING THE BONDS

In 1970 your author wrote the following paragraphs as an introduction to a chapter on marketing of municipal bonds:

> For more than three decades prior to 1966, local government officials tended to take the bond market for granted. A whole generation of local government finance officers and other officials had found a ready market for good and even poor quality securities. Few of them understood the fundamentals of the operation of the market upon which they depended for the cash to build their public facilities. They might be irritated about the price they paid for the use of money, but they had come to believe that all one had to do was to advertise, receive, and tabulate the bids, and make settlement with the purchasers of their securities.

> The warning contained in the abrupt changes in the 1966 "crunch"—especially short-term money—was quickly forgotten by some and brushed aside by some others.

> By mid-1969 almost everyone understood that the term "marketing of municipal securities" had some connotations which had been overlooked by many through three decades of relatively easy access to capital in the amounts required and at the time desired. In other words, competition heightened for use of the investor's dollar. Suddenly bond sales were postponed because bids were coming in at near record high interest costs. Promptly on the heels of this situation, there were displacements because of the inability of local governments to secure any bid within the interest limitations that had been imposed by law or administrative action in relation to the projected sales.

> Local government officials found that they indeed had to market their securities if they were to secure the funds required. They found the banks were not anxious to provide funds for either short-term or long-term requirements. In fact, they found that many banks were making no new purchases of local government securities, were allowing their holdings to run off, and in some instances were actively in the secondary market disposing of municipal security holdings at interest yields higher than the local governments were willing or able to pay in the sale of new securities in the primary market.

> They found that the bidding syndicates and the ultimate investors were much more discriminating as to the quality of the instruments they were willing to purchase and that the interest rates were at all-time highs. To those who already knew the market well, these were signals to do an even better job of acquainting both investment bankers and investors with the favorable features of their bonds. They found that it paid off to have good credit ratings. They found that keeping the investment bankers informed of their plans was useful. They learned once more the importance of providing full information on their financial situation to investors.

> If these lessons learned during the 1969 credit crunch are put to good use when the market is once again able to absorb the "normal" output of securities by state

and local governments, the temporary difficulties—at least it is hoped that they are temporary—will have served local governments well.

When those paragraphs were written, most of those interested in the issuance of municipal bonds thought that the combination of experiences from the Great Depression, World War II, and the difficulties of the late 1960s had about covered the gamut of adversities with which they would be obliged to cope.

Little did they realize that 1975 was on its way with the problems triggered by the inability of the City of New York to continue to market its notes and bonds. That development, coupled with the problems arising from the Cleveland default, the near-default of the Chicago Board of Education, and the continuing impact of inflation threw long shadows that will have continuing effects for many years. But these impacts were still relatively small in relation to the effects of the unprecedented high interest yield curves that predominated in part of 1980 and during all of 1981.

Against this backdrop, this chapter is concerned with two general areas relating to marketing of bonds: (1) The decision between competitive and negotiated sale and (2) selected procedural aspects of the sale of bonds.

COMPETITIVE VS. NEGOTIATED SALE

In most states, there is little choice available to local governments as to method in the sale of general obligation bonds, inasmuch as the law requires sale to the best competitive bidder. The only significant exception to the general rule in those states is when the issuer fails to receive two or more bids, thereby triggering the availability of the negotiated procedure—under adverse circumstances. Only Pennsylvania permits negotiated sale of general obligation bonds by almost all of the local governments.

Characteristics of the Two Systems

The general characteristics of competitive and negotiated sales may be summarized as follows:

Competitive Bid. The sale of bonds to the best bidder at competitive sale involves a predetermination by the issuer of the detailed characteristics of the bond issue, the circulation of a draft of the disclosure document, public advertisement, receipt and tabulation of bids, award of the bonds, issuance of the final draft of the disclosure statement, and settlement with the purchaser. The law ordinarily spells out the key elements of the procedures to be followed as well as the discretion available to the issuer as to the features of the bonds.

Negotiated Sale. The negotiated sale commences with the issuer inviting one or more dealers to develop and manage a syndicate to negotiate for purchase of the contemplated bonds. Once the management group has been designated, the issuer works with the manager(s) in the development of the details of the sale. The features of the bond issue are gradually determined and the disclosure statement is prepared jointly by the issuer and the syndicate, and their legal advisors. At the appropriate time, the syndicate presents a proposed schedule of reoffering yield rates. When approved, in original or amended form, the syndicate tests the market by having syndicate members approach their customers to determine the amount of bonds that can be sold at the rates tentatively approved. During and prior to this time, syndicate members will have informed potential customers about the forthcoming issue, seeking to develop interest and potential sales of the bonds.

Also in advance of the circulation of the tentative reoffering schedule, the issuer and the syndicate will have made presentations to the rating agencies and will have sought tentative ratings for the bonds. These significantly affect investor interest and the interest rate levels at which the bonds are likely to be accepted by investors. Moreover, it is customary to have one or more informational meetings with dealers and larger potential buyers to explain the issue and update knowledge concerning the affairs of the issuer.

When the syndicate management has received replies to the initial offering scale, the results are tabulated and presented to the issuer. Should the issue have been oversubscribed at the rate schedule offered, the interest rates will be reduced and the process repeated. Should relatively few bonds have been spoken for, a full new schedule will have to be prepared and tried again through the same process. Should most of the maturities have been fully subscribed with only a few remaining unsold, negotiations between the issuer and the syndicate management may result in a modification of the schedule for the maturities. This can result in readjustments in the schedule of reoffering yields, adoption of one or more groups of block-term bonds, or an increase in the commission payable in respect of these difficult-to-sell maturities. Concurrently, there will have been negotiations concerning the elements of gross profit to be provided the syndicate in case of a successful sale. In a successful negotiation, these various elements are finally brought together in a sales contract between the issuer and the syndicate.

Evaluation of Factors in Choosing the Method of Sale

Neither method offers the best answer for all occasions. If the issuer has a choice of methods, systematic evaluation of the two methods is required. This is a complex process for which no convenient score card exists. It is a judgment call. Among the principal factors to be taken into account are those discussed below.

Developing Investor Interest and Knowledge. Given the wide variety of securities always available to the investor, it is axiomatic that the issuer is operating in a competitive environment. Therefore, it is necessary for the issuer to secure the interest of a reasonable number of investors if the sale of the bonds is to be successful and at rates commensurate with the security being pledged. Information concerning the bonds reaches investors principally through an informal sales network—accompanied by some formal aspects.

In competitive sales, the more important information channels are: (1) Official actions, e.g., the official advertisement, official statements or circulars, and perhaps the preliminary draft of the disclosure statement; (2) media coverage, through trade journals and the general local and regional press; (3) informational meetings with dealers and investors; and (4) dealer discussions with their customers. In negotiated sales, substantially the same techniques are used; however, there is likely to be more emphasis *before* the sale upon informational meetings and upon dealer contacts with potential buyers than in the competitive sales.

One of the central problems in the informational process is commanding the attention of the dealers in a manner that will encourage them to devote a sufficient portion of their limited energies and time to this bond issue. The attention of the dealer and of the investor is critical to success of the sale. It is a type of competition in which the typical issuer engages only infrequently. The issuer is likely to have relatively little knowledge as to how to assure the desired focus on the issuer's bonds. In periods of low and moderate volume, the competition for attention is relatively low, but, in periods of high volume, it is great.

In theory, the institutional investor maintains a staff of sufficient size and capability to know what is being offered and to comprehend the relative attractiveness of different securities. In practice, this is true for only a limited number of institutional investors. The work load for the staff analysts again produces competition for attention. Many issues do not receive a thorough analysis and processing, with resultant narrowed interest in some issues.

Individual investors rarely have either the time or the skill to make meaningful comparisons and decisions. Only a very few have knowledge in sufficient depth. As a result, they operate in considerable degree upon the recommendations of others, primarily the recommendations of customer representatives. There is a need for penetration by the issuer of the sales organizations of dealers to be able to secure reasonable presentation of the issuer's bonds to a sufficient number of investors. It is axiomatic that the price will depend on the market for the securities. Inasmuch as the mix of investors changes within fairly wide ranges under different market conditions, there is a need for continual adjustment in the strategy of the issuer to assure appropriate accessibility to the market.

Thus, during periods in which individual investors have to be sought out by the dealers because institutional investors are temporarily restricting their purchases of new bonds, it is essential that dealers be encouraged to allot sufficient amounts of time to the smaller individual customers to provide support for the market of the issuer's bonds. During these periods, the dependence upon the ratings accorded the bonds by the rating agencies becomes much greater. The efforts which have been devoted over a period of years to promotion of a proper understanding of the financial affairs of the issuer will doubtless pay dividends.

If the customer representative knows enough about the availability of the bond issue to discuss it with his customers only after it has been purchased by the syndicate (as must be the case in competitive sales), he may have only a very short period of time in which to gain information and develop sales—particularly if the issue proves to have broad acceptability. He cannot have invested much time in advance of the sale—either in developing knowledge or in developing investor interest in bonds that may not be available to him to sell. On this score, it appears that the negotiated sale offers a better opportunity to develop the representative's knowledge and investors' interest. This is less important for a well-established issuer inasmuch as the new issue is but a part of a continuum of well-established bonds with identical security.

New Market Instruments. Closely allied with the matter of information is the subject of introduction of new market instruments. Both the primary and secondary markets function primarily on bonds in respect to which the security is well-known by dealers and many investors. Therefore, the introduction of each new credit instrument into the market requires an extraordinary amount of development by both issuer and dealer. The dealer, and his customer representatives constitute the channel through which most of the information concerning a new market instrument reaches his customers, regardless of the effort by the issuer in other aspects of the informational effort.

It is unrealistic to expect that the dealer will spend substantial amounts of time to understand a new market instrument unless there is a reasonable degree of likelihood of being able to translate his time investment into sales. The negotiated sale provides an excellent vehicle for identification, prior to the sale, of the dealers who are to participate. It also affords the sophisticated issuer an opportunity to insist that dealers develop a good sales campaign for the new issue. In the course of this process, the dealers become better acquainted with the security being offered and thereby are in a position to provide a genuine thrust in placement of the bonds.

The competitive sale method can and does produce customers; however, a greater input is required by the issuer and the reoffering yield schedule can be moderately higher because of the uncertainties confronted by the dealer. Conversely, if the issuer is unsophisticated, yields can rise in the negotiated sales as higher yields make the sales task of the dealer easier.

The Size of the Issue. The size of the issue (vis-à-vis the capacity of the market easily to absorb the particular bonds) is an important factor in the choice between competitive and negotiated sales. In large issues, the negotiated sale permits the organization of a syndicate representing a larger part of the total distribution strength of the investment banking community. In competitive sales, total market strength is divided between two or more syndicates, thereby reducing the capacity of each. If the market is sufficiently strong to support such a pattern, this competitive process is likely to work to the advantage of the issuer. However, if the market is thin, each of the bidders may be obliged to raise the level of the par yield curve being used—to the detriment of the issuer, regardless of which syndicate is successful. Therefore, in sales that are large for this issuer, it is appropriate to consider whether there is sufficient available distribution strength to sustain beneficial competition between two or more syndicates. If this cannot be reasonably established, a negotiated sale is probably indicated; if the market strength is there, a competitive sale is indicated.

In sales of more moderate size, and therefore less demanding on the market, the likelihood of receipt of two or more strong bids is greatly increased. The issuer is likely to benefit from the competitive atmosphere of the sale.

The Par Reoffering Yield Curve. The interest cost of the loan is determined primarily by the par yield curve used in development of the successful bid. In concert with the coupon rates, it will determine the prices at which the bonds are to be reoffered. Whether in negotiated or competitive bidding, each syndicate is obliged to operate on a par yield curve on which it plans to reoffer the bonds. Such curve is developed in the light of its appreciation of the general market conditions and the level within that market at which this bond issue should be pegged.

Differences of opinion among syndicate members and between different syndicates concerning the appropriate configuration of the curve and the level at which it is to be set represent the acme of professional judgment by underwriters and other specialists in the municipal bond market. Competitive bids generally show a high degree of similarity in terms of the par yield curves on which the bids are based. They are not identical but the curvature will be observed to be extremely similar in most such bids. The matter of the *level* at which the curve is placed is likely to be different among bidders, reflecting each syndicate's appreciation of the lowest level at which the bonds can be successfully marketed. In the process of developing the par yield curve for syndicates making competitive bids, only a limited sampling of customers is made. Ordinarily, such inquiry takes the form of asking whether a given investor may be interested in a block of bonds at a given yield level. A member of one syndicate may ask if the bonds would be acceptable at a 10.50 percent yield; a competitor dealer might ask if there would be an interest at 10.30 percent. Both may get a favorable answer because, in fact, the investor is willing to accept them at a yield as low as 10.20 percent; however, the investor obviously does not volunteer the lowest rate at which purchase would be made as this would tend to foreclose the possibility of higher yield.

In negotiated sales, there are a number of formal and informal contacts between the members of the syndicate and potential buyers as to the willingness of the buyers to purchase at explicit yield levels. These discussions frequently become negotiations themselves in terms of the dealer seeking to secure informal commitments as to the amounts of securities that might be purchased at a given yield level. As a result of these contacts, the members of the syndicate have a much more precise knowledge of the attitude of the investors. Therefore, when the syndicate comes to the table offering the issuer a preliminary reoffering scale, this is usually done with greater appreciation of the potential receptivity of the bonds. It is at this point that the skill of the issuer is tested in terms of reaching agreement on a tentative schedule that will (1) enable the syndicate to sell the bonds and (2) produce the lowest feasible scale of costs to the issuer.

A number of studies have attempted to determine whether there are any significant differences in the reoffering yields used in competitive and negotiated sales. Some of these have concluded that there is a significant advantage in the competitive sale; others have concluded that no significant demonstrable difference is observable. One of the problems with the studies is that each has been obliged to rely on the rating agencies for quality ratings that are then used as a basis for comparison in the studies.

Those who have studied the typical par reoffering yield of bonds issued in comparable municipal bond markets for bonds bearing identical ratings find a wide spread between the levels of yield at which the identically rated bonds are reoffered—regardless of whether sold at competitive or negotiated sale. Moreover, they are struck by the huge degree of overlap of the reoffering yield curves of bonds in one grade by those in another grade.

As a result, the use of such grading for the purpose of making these comparisons (a purpose never intended by the rating agencies) may produce an Achilles' heel for this type of study.

Despite sincere efforts to develop meaningful matched pairs or other groupings to eliminate bias, a significant bias may persist due to the mere process of selection of the method of sale by the issuer. Thus new types of instruments are more likely to come to market by negotiation; they are also likely to have moderately higher yields. *On behalf of* bonds are more likely to be negotiated, also at higher yields. Established general obligation credits are more likely to be by competitive sale. Difficult-to-sell credits are more likely to appear in the negotiated category even though their ratings may not reflect the selling difficulty.[1]

None of these points necessarily negates conclusions reached; however, they raise important questions concerning the validity of these conclusions.

Risk Bearing. Closely affiliated with the foregoing point is the matter of risk bearing by the syndicate. In competitive sales, none of the bonds can be sold in advance of their being purchased by the syndicate. The process of sale must go forward at a rather hectic pace as soon as the syndicate knows that it has purchased the bonds. At the moment of sale, the syndicate in the competitive sale owns the bonds and is fully at risk as to the number of bonds that can be sold at the established prices. A faulty judgment of the market or sharp change in the market can result in the bonds being easier or more difficult to sell than anticipated. There is a risk that the bonds will not go well and that the members of the syndicate will be obliged eventually to take a loss.

The risk in negotiated sales is usually less for the syndicate. Ordinarily, it will have received a substantial number of firm orders at given yield levels before the sale is consummated and will have accepted these on a conditional basis. It will have determined the placement of a large portion of the issue before purchase. Theoretically, this reduced risk should reflect itself in better pricing because the syndicate's hedge against possible loss is less. On the other hand, the syndicate will attempt to keep the yield level moderately high as this enhances the ease of sale and further reduces the risk of loss.

The skill of the issuer at negotiation coupled with a knowledge of the market will largely determine whether this reduction in risk is translated into an advantage for the issuer or given to others.

Penalty Yield Considerations. Penalty yields frequently occur in competitive sales; they should almost never be present in negotiated sales. In the competitive sale, the issuer may have established bidding conditions that make penalty yields unavoidable. Once determined, these features can be retracted only if the sale is cancelled and a new sale package offered. This is frequently true of some aspects of bonds sold on a negotiated basis; however, better knowledge by the issuer and the closer liaison between the issuer and the syndicate can almost always foreclose penalty yields.[2]

Spread between Purchase and Sales Prices. Another major element in the cost of the bonds to the issuer is the spread between the price at which the syndicate purchases the bonds and the prices at which they are reoffered (and hopefully sold) to investors. The gross profit of the purchasing syndicate is determined by such spread. The spread on different bond issues varies widely. In 1979 spreads were observed well below $10.00 in some sales and above $25.00 per $1,000 par value in others. In competitive issues, competition helps to keep the spread low; in negotiated issues, this is a matter for negotiation. Spreads also tend to reflect unstable market conditions and also excessively high volumes which tax the ability of the system easily to absorb the aggregate amounts being offered.

Various studies firmly establish the fact that the spread in the case of negotiated

---

[1] Among the studies appropriate for review are several listed in the bibliography which, by their titles, indicate relevance here.

[2] See discussion of penalty yields in Chapter 12.

sales is higher than the spread in competitive sales. The issuer pays this spread either in discount or coupon rates in excess of the yield curve. The amount of the spread is a part of the negotiation and the issuer must bear the responsibility for agreeing to spreads that are greater in the typical negotiated sale than similar competitive sales. Among the factors to be taken into account are the differences in services provided to the issuer in the competitive and negotiated sale. In the former, the only service ordinarily payable from the spread is the cost of underwriting and marketing the bonds. In the latter case, the syndicate will doubtless have provided fairly extensive advisory services in the course of the negotiation and will have used its facilities to provide information that may not have been otherwise available to the issuer. Moreover, in a negotiated sale, the added costs of informational meetings and promotion are likely to be paid by the syndicate from the moneys developed from the spread.

It is obligatory upon the issuer that a careful evaluation of these matters be made in coming to a conclusion as to the level of spread to be authorized in the negotiated sale. There are instances in which the issuer may find it appropriate to insist upon a greater, rather than a lesser, spread in order to provide greater sales impetus for certain maturities. In others, a good case can be made for reducing the spread relating to certain maturities because of the obvious ease with which they may be marketed.

Cover Bids. A risk factor in competitive sales arises from the differential in average interest costs between the successful bid and the second bid—frequently referred to as a "cover bid." There was a time in which complimentary cover bids were sometimes encountered in sales of municipal bonds; however that process has now largely disappeared. Assume that there are four bids in a competitive sale with the first three providing effective average interest costs (TIC) of 6.554, 6.559, and 6.563 percent, respectively. The market would likely conclude that the successful bidder had properly priced the bonds because two other syndicates had made bids that confirmed the judgment of the winner.

Alternatively, assume that in another circumstance the three lowest bids were: 6.554, 6.702, and 6.710 percent, respectively. The market would conclude that the 6.554 percent bid was too high in price (i.e., too low in yield), probably inasmuch as the second and third bidders had agreed that the market was in the 6.70 range rather than the 6.55 range. The successful bidder may thereby be obliged to cut the price of the bonds and take a substantial loss in the underwriting because the bid was "off the market." This exposure is always a potential in competitive bidding; it is never present in negotiated sales.

Sophistication of Issuer. The sophistication of the parties in any negotiation affects the results. If one party is an expert and the other is ignorant, the latter is at a significant disadvantage. He will be largely at the mercy of the other party. When the syndicate is sophisticated and the issuer represented by good citizens who are well-meaning but poorly informed, one can hardly dignify the transaction as a *negotiation.* One sets the condition and the other merely submits. On the other hand, if both sides are represented by sophisticated negotiators and back-up personnel, a genuine negotiation ensues and the issuer is likely to be able to develop a contract in which the public interest is well protected, frequently producing better results than could have been secured through competitive sale, but not always. At the outset, it is frequently difficult for the issuer's officials to accept the fact that they do not have sufficient knowledge, experience, and ability to negotiate on equal terms with the syndicate. Skillful representations by syndicate leaders frequently play upon the cupidity of the unsophisticated representatives of issuers. Thereby, they seek to continue the practice of negotiation in situations in which competitive sales would better serve the issuer.

From the standpoint of the issuer, the problem is also one of securing sufficiently expert assistance to conduct an effective negotiation and to secure this at a reasonable cost. It is unfortunate that the dearth of excellent talent in this field results in very high prices for the assistance of the genuinely competent and talented negotiators. Even for the issuer willing and able to pay for such service, the lack of technical knowledge by public officers responsible for making the choice among those offering their services is more difficult and hazardous. Competitive sales tend to obviate this problem; however, as is pointed out elsewhere, the competitive sale also has elements of adversity for the issuer.

Credit of the Issuer. The security supporting the bonds offered affects the matter of competitive vs. negotiated sale. The stronger the credit position, the less the likelihood of need of negotiation. Placement of bonds that are weak, or perceived to be so, is much more difficult than placement of strong bonds. If the bonds are extremely weak, they may attract no bid at a competitive offering. Such a failure will further adversely affect their market position.

The marketing of these weaker bonds involves a much greater sales effort than stronger bonds. This is likely to be reflected in the larger gross profits involved in marketing such bonds.

Flexibility in Features. A great deal has been written by proponents of negotiated sales emphasizing the greater degree of flexibility available under the negotiated sale. This has led to an overemphasis on the flexibility factor. The number of elements of flexibility that have any practical effect upon the sale are few. However, in some cases, these differences are of major significance to the issuer. The most important is the opportunity to adjust coupon rates, maturities, and security pledged.

Timing, Pace, and Delays. In competitive sale, the date of the bidding is determined in the specifications and is fixed once the first advertisement is made—unless the sale is withdrawn and a new one advertised. In negotiated sales, the timing of the sale is announced as an objective; however, the date of the sale can be changed as required. A cancellation of a sale in advance of the time for receipt of competitive bids constitutes some inconvenience but is not of great significance—unless the issuer has a demand for moneys on a certain date, e.g., redemption of bond anticipation notes or meeting of capital costs where bills are due.

A major adverse market development immediately prior to a competitive sale date may force the cancellation of the sale; the same development may engender only a few days' delay in the negotiated sale. The delay may be of little importance, or, it may result in considerable change in cost to the issuer.

Related to the matter of timing is the pace at which the sale goes forward, especially the distribution of the bonds after sale. The competitive sale provides a rather rigid calendar in advance of the sale and an accelerated pace of sales effort immediately afterwards because all of the bonds are unsold at the hour of sale. The competitive sales schedule provides a discipline requiring certain matters to be concluded by given dates in advance of the sale, e.g., the preparation of the official statement. The negotiated sale proceeds at a somewhat more relaxed pace, permitting flexibility in negotiation should unforeseen developments occur. It affords an opportunity to place a considerable portion of the bonds (on a conditional basis) in advance of the formal sale date. It also permits adjustments in the sale date in case of temporary disturbances in the market. Conversely, such flexibility can be used as a basis for inordinate procrastination by indecisive officials. In a declining market this is likely to prove very expensive.

Rejection of Bids. In competitive sales, the issuer reserves the right to reject all bids. In such cases, the rejection is usually followed by a readvertisement of the bonds in original or amended amounts and specifications. The market will respond to occasional reofferings; however, it becomes impatient with the issuer that indulges in the process with some frequency. Therefore, the de facto opportunities for rejection of bids and reofferings are few. By comparison, in negotiated sales, the issuer can make modifications in the composition of the bond issue—within the authorization—and can also reject preliminary offers of the bidder without jeopardizing the continuation of the negotiation. Of course, this process cannot be carried on ad nauseam but greater flexibility is present. Even in the case when the issuer and syndicate working in close concert cannot produce an acceptable sale, the likelihood is a recess—rather than a termination—of negotiations, pending better opportunities.

No-Bid and Single-Bid Situations. In the competitive process, the law usually authorizes the issuer to reject a single bid and to proceed to negotiation. In no-bid situations, further advertisement is a theoretical possibility; however, there is usually little indication of success unless either the specifications can be significantly changed or a significant shift to lower interest rates occurs. No-bid and single-bid situations are widely interpreted as a demerit for the issuer—regardless of the factors that led to the situation. During periods of market stress, the risk of encountering no-bid or single-bids increases. For elected officials, there may be adverse local public relations or political consequences. Negotiation goes far in eliminating the risk involved from the no-bid and single-bid situations.

Development of the Disclosure Statement. In a competitive sale, it can be more difficult to work out the contents of the disclosure document. Each syndicate may insist on its own counsel. One or more may refuse to participate in deliberations prior to the sale. This increases the pressure in development of the final statement.

In negotiated sales, the issuer can insist that the members of the syndicate select an underwriter's counsel and that all firms included in the syndicate agree in advance that they will abide by the advice of such counsel. In fact, it is essential that the issuer demand such a condition. In the months following New York City's problems in early 1975, it was not unusual for each of the firms in the management group to have its own counsel in the sessions preparing the disclosure statements. The result was a great deal of unnecessary conflict, bordering at times on pandemonium. Moreover, it is essential that members who have made such agreements—explicitly or tacitly—be under great pressure to honor them. They should not be permitted to use the excuse of "advice of counsel" at the last moment to withdraw when such withdrawal will significantly adversely affect the interest of the issuer. Should they persist in their action, despite the pressure of the issuer, they should never be allowed again to participate in the underwritings of the issuer.

Expansion of Market Area. Generally, the broad scope of operations of some of the members of most syndicates assures a fairly wide distribution of bonds to different portions of the nation. However, national firms must operate through local offices and these offices sometimes have priorities that supersede the sale of the bonds of a particular issuer. At the same time, many regional firms have easier access to important local investors than do local offices of national firms. In order to secure optimum access to the market, the issuer will find it desirable, from time to time, to undertake a deliberate expansion of its market into regions in which sales have heretofore been minimal. One of the means of developing such accessibility is to include in the management group for a negotiated sale a firm that is strong in the region sought to be penetrated. This issuer must not only include the firm but also see that a suitable block of bonds is allocated to this regional firm. Otherwise, the remaining members of the syndicate management can nullify the objectives of the issuer. Expansion of market is particularly important to issuers in regions with a declining economy. Such regions have limited internal supplies of capital and therefore must attract capital from elsewhere.

Politicalization of the Process. In competitive sales, the issuer has no authority and usually can exert no significant influence on the composition of a syndicate. In negotiated sales, the issuer has almost full authority and responsibility for the membership of the management group and may also influence the general composition of the syndicate. The issuer can also have an effect on the distribution of bonds among the members of the syndicate. It may not be wise for the issuer to go beyond determining the management group but the authority is presumably there for a determined issuer and its exercise is sometimes essential to protection of the issuer's long-term interest.

The exercise of this influence is usually solely in the public interest; however, under some circumstances, it becomes politicalized by the issuer insisting that favored positions be awarded firms with political connections to the administration. This imposes a weakness in the process of negotiation. Officials responsible for the conduct of the negotiation ordinarily cannot be oblivious to these political realities. As a result, they may be obliged to yield on some critical points, including the price paid for the bonds as well as the approved spread.

Investment Banker Relationships. Good secondary market positions for the issuer's bonds increase the likelihood of sale of new bonds on favorable terms. Good secondary market positions do not "just happen." They develop, in part, because of overall market factors but they are also maintained, in part, by the implied obligation of the dealer selling the bonds to service his customer in case the customer wishes to sell the bonds. In like manner, the management group in a negotiated sale understands that future relationships with the skillful issuer can be conditioned by the extent to which the underwriters help maintain a viable secondary market.

In competitive sales, the local banks that are members of historic syndicates are likely to help provide such a relationship with the issuer; however, there is not the same degree of likelihood as in negotiated sales. Moreover, in many cases, the local bank may not have the necessary expertise to help sustain the market. The distant head of the syndicate may not be inclined to make significant service available, as this will not affect the composition of future competitive syndicates.

The issuer using negotiated bidding should carefully evaluate and exploit this potential for improving the secondary market.

Conclusions in Respect to Competitive vs. Negotiated Sale

The decision between the use of competitive and negotiated sale is one of the most important in debt administration. Moreover, it is one in which there are no universally "right" answers. Each sale warrants an independent decision (where the option is present). Reliance on past patterns of selection may be useful; however, they do not constitute a wholly satisfactory basis of decision inasmuch as both the general market conditions and the local factors are in continuous states of flux. Issuers will do well to develop their own checklists and other elements of criteria for decision making and to review each item with care in advance of the decision as to how the next bond issue is to be handled.

Genuine negotiation subsumes substantial capability on each side of the table. Otherwise, the dice are too heavily loaded in favor of the one or the other party. In almost no case are syndicate members inadequately represented at the table. The buying and selling of securities is their profession. The price of inability is bankruptcy and elimination from the market. The issuer has many other reasons for existence and is only occasionally in the market. Almost by definition, the issuer depending solely on the knowledge and capability of its own staff is at a disadvantage. In many so-called negotiations, the issuer does not engage in meaningful negotiation; it merely accepts the last offer of the syndicate. Even when the issuer seeks to buttress in-house capabilities by engaging outside consultants, the question arises as to the extent of qualifications of the issuer to make wise selections. On the other hand, there are numerous circumstances in which genuine negotiation results in a better sale for the issuer than would likely have been obtainable through competitive sale of the same issue. The choice must lie with the issuer; however, the wise issuer seeks an outside evaluation from time to time of just how well the process is working.

THE DATE OF THE BOND ISSUE

Each bond issue bears a *date of issue.* This date serves to help identify the issue and establish the date from which interest on the bonds accrues. Although the issuer may choose a different annual date for maturity, the date of issue frequently serves as the anniversary date on which maturities occur as well as one of the semiannual coupon payment dates. Most issuers select a date at, or near, either the date of sale or delivery of the bonds. If the bonds are dated as of the settlement and delivery date, adjustments arising from settlement of accrued interest are obviated. If the issue date results in other than a six-months' period between such date and the first interest payment date, the initial coupon is adjusted to take this into account.

To the extent that the date of issue is permitted to govern the maturity date, the dating will impinge on the factors discussed below under *due dates*. Occasionally, there is a requirement in the bond authorization that fixes the issue date. If, in such a case, a considerable delay occurs between the issue date and settlement date, the expired coupons are detached before delivery of the bond.

THE DATE OF SALE

The *date of sale* for competitive sales is defined by the Municipal Securities Rulemaking Board as the date on which bids must be received [Rule G-11 (a) (ii)]. In negotiated sales the date of the sale is the date on which the issuer and underwriting syndicate sign an agreement of sale. In such negotiated sales there is no necessity for a formal advanced setting of the sale date inasmuch as this is determined at the time the parties reach the logical point for execution of the sales agreement. A target date for the sale may have been established early in the negotiations; however, this can be altered through agreement.

Among the factors to be considered in the selection of a date for receipt of competitive bids are:

1. The general condition and near-term prospects of the municipal bond market
2. The status of competitive bond sales, the major syndicate balances for those likely to bid on the current bonds, and *The Blue List* offerings of bonds of this issuer
3. The time of the year, with special reference to holiday and vacation periods
4. The time of the week
5. The time of the day

General Market Conditions

Much has been written concerning the need for issuers to take into account the general market conditions in selecting a date for a bond sale. Some of these writings—usually with the benefit of 20:20 hindsight—have criticized selected dates inasmuch as the market happened to take a turn to lower interest rates shortly after the sale. Few criticisms of this character are warranted. Any person who can consistently foretell the pattern of interest rates is a soothsayer whose talents are misdirected when applied as criticism. He can make a great deal of money in a brief period of time in the market.

At any given time, there will be a considerable range in the opinions of market specialists as to the outlook for the immediate future; the range of differences broadens with the distance in time. These differences help to maintain an active market. Given these differences, governments generally should neither defer nor accelerate sales on the presumption that they are able to select a more favorable market or to avoid an unfavorable one. If the debt officer guesses accurately, little note is taken; if he guesses wrong, censure may be immediate. This is not to suggest that an issuer should proceed blindly in execution of each sale on the initially scheduled date; however, it is to assert that the decision should be based primarily on other factors—not attempting to foretell the market.

Yet, there are times when it is advisable not to proceed. If the market is visibly disturbed due to some monetary or economic crisis, delay for a few days to await stabilization is in order. Major crises cause many investors to avoid new long-term commitments for the present. During such periods, available money is likely limited and only at premium rates. Situations to be avoided are revaluations of major national currencies; periods of outbreak or impending outbreak of international hostilities; decided breaks in the stock market and bond market; major changes in rediscount rate or other money supply policies of the Federal Reserve System; unexpected default of a major issuer; inability of a major issuer to market its securities; or the death, injury, or serious illness of the President of the United States.

In periods during which the Federal Reserve System is imposing unusual restraints on monetary supply, short-term interest rates are likely to increase sharply and long-term rates may also increase, but not to the same degree. Avoidance of such periods for major borrowing is usually in the best interest of the issuer.

Three other general market factors require evaluation: (1) The visible supply of new municipal bonds, (2) the status of major syndicate balances, and (3) the magnitude of offerings in *The Blue List.* A heavy calendar of offerings suggests that market absorption is likely to be somewhat reduced. Of especial importance in this regard are other offerings known to be directly competitive to the issuer's bonds, e.g., large issues within the same state or large issues bearing ratings and market attraction similar to the bonds about to be offered. Large syndicate balances, especially in bonds competitive to those under consideration, will usually produce higher interest rates for the new issue. The amount of the bonds being offered in the secondary market, as measured by *The Blue List* (after elimination of any syndicate balance bonds in the list), is important—especially the amount of bonds of the issuer.

It is axiomatic that when extraordinary amounts of unsold bonds are in the primary or secondary market, pressure develops for an increase in yields to facilitate absorption. Conversely, when the market supply is low, the yields are likely to move to lower levels. Periods of relative stability in the market are sometimes ended by abrupt changes. The issuer should keep abreast of the market not only in advance of advertisement but also as the day of sale approaches, with the final review on the day preceding the sale or even the morning of the sale.

Major Competitive Offerings

Although maintenance of general knowledge of the market is useful, an individual issuer is in competition for the attention of the investor for a specific portion of the market. The greatest competition is likely to be from within the state in which the bonds are issued, especially if the tax system in the state makes these bonds particularly attractive to residents. If cooperative arrangements can be worked out with other jurisdictions, there is likely to be a better overall response to the issue. A system such as that in North Carolina affords an opportunity for full coordination inasmuch as all of the bonds are sold by the Local Government Commission and it can develop schedules to help reduce the adverse effects of competition among issuers within the state.

Competition also comes from outside the state. It is ordinarily not feasible to work out any cooperative arrangements with those issuers; however, dealers and good investment advisors know of large impending competitive issues and can provide guidance in the light of such conditions. Bonds under negotiation are more difficult to take into account. Even when it is known that such a sale is pending, the precise sales calendar is not known.

Time of Year

Before air conditioning and jet travel, there was a heavy absence of investors during the summer months. This resulted in a discernible decrease in sales during the summer period, especially in July and August. In recent years, some summers have been characterized by heavy market activity—due, in part, to changing vacation patterns. Still to be avoided, or handled with extreme care, are the weeks in which major holidays fall, as the workweek is shortened and the opportunity to dispose of the bonds may be lessened.

Time of Week

Within any normal week, the rhythm of the market makes it inadvisable to sell at competitive sale on Mondays or Fridays or on the days immediately preceding or immediately following major national holidays. Most dealers and investors want some time following a holiday or weekend in which to ascertain and evaluate developments. In like manner, few investment bankers wish voluntarily to purchase bonds on Fridays or on the day before a holiday because of the uncertainties of developments over the weekend or holiday. Especially to be avoided are days in advance of long weekends.

Accordingly, it is best to carry out competitive sales on Tuesday, Wednesday, or Thursday. Within this middle-of-the-week syndrome, Tuesday is perhaps the best day for most issuers with Wednesday as second choice.

Time of Day

As to the time of the day—for the Eastern time zone 11:00 A.M. is generally preferable. This varies somewhat as one goes west. The 11:00 A.M. hour provides sufficient time for the syndicate to make a last minute review of market conditions during the morning while leaving a sufficient portion of the day for selling. An 11:00 A.M. sale which has not resulted in disposition of a significant portion of the bonds before the close of that business day is likely to be in trouble. The most successful offering is one in which all of the bonds are placed on the day of sale.

Hour of sale considerations also govern sales in the Central, Mountain, and Pacific time zones; however, if there is an expectation of considerable distribution in the East, an earlier local time for the sale warrants consideration.

DUE DATES

The selection of the due dates, i.e., dates for payment of principal and semiannual interest, has both debt management and budgetary implications. The principal factors are:

1. *Investor Convenience.* In its self-interest the issuer needs to facilitate investor convenience, thereby enhancing the ease with which securities may be traded in the secondary market. In terms of direct convenience, selection of due dates should take into account the times at which investors may prefer to receive payment, e.g., just in advance of major tax payment dates. Also, investors holding bonds or coupons due on January 1 almost always lose some interest in settlement of accounts. Generally, payment dates should be on the first day of the month in order that investors may schedule the processing of their portfolios for submission of coupons or matured bonds. The middle of the month is second-best, and odd days should be avoided.

2. *The Issuer's Cash Flow.* For general obligation bonds, maturity dates should be scheduled in the light of the rhythm of cash flow for the issuer. This is likely to be less true in revenue bonds because many revenue bond contracts require monthly deposits with the trustee for debt service purposes. Within recent years interest earnings on temporary balances have become important to issuers. In some cases, the arbitrage potentials are sufficient to take them into account in determining the maturity dates because these requirements may affect the application of U.S. Treasury arbitrage regulations.

3. *Budgetary Impact.* Budget officers are usually concerned with the impact of new debt issues on the requirements for operating budget appropriations during the first year or two of the life of the bonds because this is a new item of expense to be taken into

Exhibit C
Significant Information to be Provided in Bidding Specifications

Item	Information Provided
1. Name of Issuer	The Commonwealth of Massachusetts
2. Title of issue	General Obligation Bonds of the Commonwealth of Massachusetts
3. Date of issue	July 1, 1979
4. Time of sale	11:00 A.M. Tuesday, July 10, 1979, Eastern Daylight Time.
5. Place of sale	Office of State Treasurer, Room 227 State House, Boston, Massachusetts 02133
6. Amount of issue	$55,000,000 (composed of six independent authorizations, with statutory citations for each)
7. Maturity schedule	Serial maturities due July 1, 1980–1999 in indicated amounts for each year
8. Security	General obligation bonds of the Commonwealth of Massachusetts and full faith and credit pledged for payment of principal and interest
9. Denomination	$5,000
10. Registrability	May be exchanged for registered bonds; may not be re-exchanged
11. Interest payment dates	July 1 and January 1
12. Payment form	Clearing house funds in the State Treasury or at the principal office of Bankers Trust Company, New York, or The First National Bank of Chicago
13. Redemption prior to maturity	Optional by issuer at any interest payment date on and after July 1, 1989, upon payment of indicated redemption premiums. Redemption in inverse order or by lot within a maturity if less than full maturity is redeemed in any call
14. Notice of redemption	Not less than 30 days nor more than 60 days by publication as specified
15. Interest rate	In multiples of $\frac{1}{20}$ or $\frac{1}{8}$ of 1 percent; no rate shall be less than that for any earlier maturity; highest rate may not exceed lowest rate by more than 2.00 percent; and no more than one rate for any maturity
16. Basis of award	Single unit; TIC method under computing program of the Center for Capital Market Research of the University of Oregon
17. Form of bid	To be submitted on official bid form; sealed envelope
18. Security deposit	2 percent of principal amount
19. Rejection	Right reserved to reject any or all proposals and to waive any irregularity or informality with respect to any proposal
20. Legal opinion	Mintz, Levin, Cohn, Glovsky and Popeo

Source: Official advertisement of the Commonwealth of Massachusetts in the sale of $55 million of general obligation bonds dated July 1, 1979.

account. The timing of the sale may have an impact on the timing of the maturities and interest payment dates. These impact the near-term budgetary picture. This is especially true in cases in which the budgeting of debt service is on a cash basis. In enterprise accounting, there is a greater likelihood that it will be on an accrual basis, and timing of the issue (and particularly of the first payment date or the first maturity date) may be of only nominal importance, especially as debt service during the construction period is usually paid from bond proceeds.

BIDDING SPECIFICATIONS FOR COMPETITIVE SALES

For bonds to be sold at competitive sale it is necessary to provide detailed specifications for use by bidders. The specifications may be contained in the official advertisement, official circular, or the preliminary draft of the official statement. Regardless of the manner in which issued, certain elements of policy must be succinctly stated in the specifications.

Given the importance of these specifications, a review is required not only by the debt officer but also by bond counsel. It is useful to have them reviewed by the underswriter's counsel if such counsel has been selected in advance of the publication of bid specifications. The list of items for which specifications are required is impressive both by its length and complexity. Exhibit C sets forth a paraphrasing of those specifications on most of the points usually covered in official announcements of specifications. The details vary; however, the substance of the requirements is indicated by the exhibit.

If the issuer wishes to take advantage of the benefits of "original issue discount" in relation to any maturities, special attention is required at the time of preparation of the specifications. Otherwise the issuer will be confronted with unnecessary capital gains tax implications. This may become of major importance for those issuers contemplating the use of zero coupons for part of their future bond issues.

Chapter 18
OFFICIAL STATEMENTS AND DISCLOSURE

Investors are interested in information that enables them better to comprehend the risks associated with their investment activities; citizens and taxpayers are interested in obtaining information about the operation of their public services. Throughout the history of municipal bonds there has been some flow of information to investors. In some cases, this has been adequate, well-organized, timely, regular, and accurate; in others, it has been insufficient, disorganized, outdated, irregular, and/or inaccurate. Occasionally, it has been deliberately misleading; on a relatively few occasions, it has been fraudulent.

The quality and quantity of financial reporting have improved significantly in recent decades, partially because effective debt officers have insisted upon better ways in which to enhance public and investor understanding of the financial affairs of their governments. A large portion of this reporting has been through the budgetary process and periodic financial statements, especially through the annual financial report. The form and content of these reports are prescribed by a combination of law, custom, and, to an increasing degree, by accounting, auditing, and reporting standards commenced by the Committee on Municipal Accounting in the 1930s and carried forward by the National Council (formerly Committee) on Governmental Accounting (NCGA). During the 1970s the General Accounting Office (GAO) of the United States and the American Institute of Certified Public Accountants (AICPA) intervened in this process.[1]

Reporting of information concerning the finances of local governments is usually directly by such governments; however, in a few states, compendiums of data on the financial affairs of local governments are issued by units of the state governments, e.g., state departments of community affairs for municipal and county governments and state departments of public education for school districts.

The principal national sources of organized financial information concerning state and local governments have been the two principal rating agencies. *The Bond Buyer* and some other national and regional newspapers assist by publication of information of current interest as well as by publication of composite data on an annual or other periodic basis. The Bureau of the Census publishes annual volumes on the finances of state governments, county governments, public school systems, and selected municipal and township governments. It also publishes national data and estimates on an annual basis in its *Governmental*

---

[1] Since 1979, the Financial Accounting Foundation (FAF), American Institute of Certified Public Accountants, Municipal Finance Officers Association, National Council on Governmental Accounting, National Association of State Auditors, Comptrollers and Treasurers, the U.S. General Accounting Office, and the public interest groups concerned with state and local government have been conducting discussions to create a Governmental Accounting Standards Board (GASB). These groups issued a report dated October 13, 1981, recommending that a separate and independent GASB be created under the oversight of the FAF.

Early in 1982 the Financial Accounting Foundation created an implementation committee to develop the structural and operational aspects of GASB. It is anticipated that the GASB will be formed late in 1982. It will be financed in much the same manner as the Financial Accounting Standards Board and will maintain an advisory group upon which professional accounting groups and associations of state and local government officials will be represented. The function of GASB would be to develop, promulgate, and interpret principals of accounting and financial reporting for state and local governments.

Finances series. Since 1962 the Bureau has published its in-depth quintennial surveys of the financial (and some other) aspects of all governments in its *Census of Governments* series.

The Development of Formal Disclosure

Prior to 1933 the regulation of corporate securities was solely in the domain of the states. Irregularities in the 1920s and early 1930s led the Congress to enact laws in 1933 and 1934 establishing the Securities and Exchange Commission and to give it broad powers over various aspects of issuance and trading in securities. Although an effort was made at that time to encompass the operations of state and local governments, the provisions of these federal laws relating to these governments were limited to those involving fraud.

From time to time the Securities and Exchange Commission and others sought to secure broader federal regulation of the issuance of securities by the states and their local governments; however, they have not been successful. Such an effort was in process in early 1975 when New York City found itself unable to borrow, due in part to alleged irregularities in the financial reporting by the City. This situation, abetted by the problems of default temporarily on some of the State of New York "moral obligation" bonds, resulted in a drive for full federal oversight of state and local debt issuance. As legislation moved through the Congress, it appeared at one point that the Municipal Securities Rulemaking Board (MSRB) being created would have plenary authority, in concert with the SEC and others, in the municipal securities field. At the last minute, however, the conference commitee adopted the "Tower Amendment" that excised the state and local governments from most provisions of the act. The MSRB does require those dealing in municipal securities to make available to investors such information as the dealers may have concerning the securities and the financial and other affairs of their issuers.

The principal means used by the SEC through the years for disclosure in the case of corporate securities has been a formalized statement setting forth prospective and retrospective information about the operations of the corporation seeking to issue securities. The statements have not been attractive and have generally been directed to sophisticated readers only. They have been developed by attorneys for the issuer confronting attorneys for the SEC. The result is a technically correct, uninteresting, and frequently difficult-to-comprehend statement. The printing is crowded, in small type, and not very widely read.

For many years prior to 1975 it was customary in the sale of many governmental enterprise bond issues of state and local governments to provide official statements setting forth information similar to that contained in the SEC-type statement, but not subject to the same requirements. These governmental enterprise statements varied widely in format, content, reliability, and methods of presentation. General obligation bonds were frequently issued either solely on the basis of an official advertisement or the advertisement accompanied by a very brief official statement containing selected information on the operations of the government. They were clearly a "best foot forward" type of presentation and did not ordinarily meet the SEC corporate test of calling forcibly to the attention of the reader the adverse and potentially adverse factors. In the period between 1950 and 1975, this practice of providing official statements in respect to general obligation bonds expanded on a voluntary basis, but at a very slow rate. Gradually, debt officers learned that these statements were useful in placing before investors, rating agencies, and credit analysts a better picture of pertinent financial, demographic, and economic factors of interest to investors. The statements continued to differ widely in format, content, and utility.

The problems of New York and the associated clamor for more disclosure led to a totally new era. Whereas the earlier statements were basically positive, the new atmosphere placed emphasis on disclosure of actual and potentially adverse factors that could be identified. The large cities and numerous other jurisdictions were confronted with dealer demands for comprehensive disclosure statements and "comfort letters" as prerequisites to purchase of municipal bonds and notes. This reaction was triggered by a combination of the numerous legal actions instituted or threatened by investors against underwriters and other security dealers as well as by the general atmosphere produced by publicity about the alleged dangerous financial condition of a number of local governments. Despite the remarkably low historical rate of default on tax-supported state and local government debt after the 1930s, the emphasis was almost totally on the side of repealing *caveat emptor.*

Issuers were obliged virtually to prove the correctness of any statement of fact; they were frequently foreclosed from neutral interpretation on the prospects for the future; and they were sometimes pressured to include unrealistically negative forecasts or interpretations of the future. The new person at the table was the underwriter's counsel, usually drawn from the ranks of lawyers with long experience in SEC work. The underwriter's counsel brought to the table the general atmosphere that had come to characterize the offering of corporate securities—a practice that tends to emphasize the risks being undertaken by the investor. The underwriter's counsel was there to protect the underwriter who was being frequently attacked in court in litigation alleging that the underwriter had failed to disclose potential risks to the investor and was, therefore, liable for damages arising from losses being incurred by some investors.

In this position, the underwriter's counsel insisted upon the inclusion of all adverse facts and potential financial difficulties. From the standpoint of the issuer, this was emphasis on the negative. Official statements frequently included a "special factors" section consisting almost wholly of highlights of the negative. The shock effects of these developments upon public finance officers who theretofore had a free hand in development of their official statements was profound. The whole process was carried off in the post-Watergate period when public officials tended to be more than usually suspect. In a few communities, it became a field day for critics resulting in unwarranted adverse effects on the credit position of issuers.

In 1974 MFOA anticipated the need for more effective disclosure and commenced a program of work that led to the publication entitled *Disclosure Guidelines for Offerings of Securities by State and Local Governments.*[2] This publication found wide acceptance and promptly became the "bible" for many issuers and attorneys acting as underwriter's counsel. It was updated in 1979, taking into account experience gained in the intervening years. The eight sections of this work cover these areas:

1. *Cover Page of Disclosure Statement.* Substantially the items listed at the end of the preceding chapter as specifications for competitive bidding are to be included on the title page.

2. *Introduction to the Official Statement.* A summary is given of the salient information identifying the issuer, legal base, and purposes of the securities; the security pledged and methods of payment of debt service; and other factors of importance to the investor.

3. *The Securities Being Offered.* This section contains a comprehensive description of the securities being offered; the law, purpose, and security; flows of funds; creation, maintenance, and application of reserve funds; and maintenance of insurance on the properties. Also included are purposes of, and conditions under which, additional parity debt may be issued; the fiscal agency and trustee arrangements; and applicable jurisprudence affecting the bonds.

4. *The Issuer and the Enterprise.* This section details the legal base of the issuer; a succinct but comprehensive description of the community served; identification of principal officials; functions of the issuer and the governmental services performed; relationships with other governments; demographic data; and economic data for the service area of the issuer.

If governmental enterprise debt is involved, a comprehensive statement is made of

---

[2] Municipal Finance Officers Association. *Disclosure Guidelines for Offerings of Securities by State and Local Governments* (1976) and *Disclosure Guidelines for State and Local Governments* (1979).

the history of the enterprise, information concerning its past operations, the proposed use of the bond proceeds, and other factors concerning the operation of the enterprise that may impinge upon its revenues and capacity to meet debt interest and retirement payments. Of substantial importance are contingent liabilities and off-balance sheet financing for which the issuer has a responsibility.

If *on behalf of* debt is involved, the data are largely concerned with the private enterprise acting as guarantor for the debt.

5. *Debt Structure.* The description includes a comprehensive statement of outstanding short-term and long-term debt; authorized but unissued debt; debt service schedules; and prospective debt that may be required either for general purpose governmental activities or, in the case of enterprises, to maintain viability of the current undertaking. When appropriate, it includes information concerning debt limits, limitations upon the power of the issuer to impose taxes or charges offered as security for the debt; obligations undertaken to maintain rates at suitable levels; and other pertinent information.

6. *Financial Information.* The general description of financial practices shows results of recent operations, including comparative summaries of income, outgo, and balance sheet data; accounting practices; budgetary processes; detailed revenue data, especially that pledged for the debt being issued; revenue administrative practices; results of revenue operations, including history of delinquencies; data concerning assessed value and market value of property subject to ad valorem taxation; cash flow anticipated for the current year and perhaps the succeeding year; projected plans for conversion of bond anticipation notes to long-term bonds; status of deferred obligations, including accrued liabilities, unfunded accrued liabilities, and methods of funding. Uniformity in presentation of financial information and consistency with the applicable accounting principles are essential.

7. *Legal Matters.* Among the matters to be reported are the pending legal proceedings that may materially affect the ability of the issuer to perform obligations to the holders of securities being offered; a copy, or summary, of the opinion of bond counsel; tax status of securities and interest thereupon; and, in the final edition of the statement, a copy of the no-litigation certificate.

8. *Miscellaneous.* Other information appropriate for inclusion in the disclosure statement includes data concerning ratings by Moody's and Standard & Poor's; the financial interest, if any, of certain persons named in the official statement; and any other pertinent information that will facilitate the exercise of judgment by the investor.

THE CONTEMPORARY DISCLOSURE STATEMENT

The combined work of MFOA, bond counsel, and underwriter's counsel have had significant impact upon the scope and general character of disclosure statements. Many of these statements now follow the MFOA outline rather closely; many others cover the same materials but under different organizational patterns.

For most local governments, disclosure statements have produced substantial additional information for the investor. They have organized into a single statement information previously available from local financial statements and other documents into a cohesive whole. They have included most of the information previously required by rating agencies in connection with issuance of ratings. Generally, the information is more nearly up-to-date at the time of bond issuance than was previously the case. However, at the state level, the broad decentralization of the governments has frequently resulted in relatively less information than that for the more cohesive local governments. In those areas where patterns of local governments are highly fragmented among the municipality, school district, county government, overlapping special districts, and quasi-independent authorities, the disclosure statements have generally not provided a comprehensive picture of the relationship of local governmental finance to the economy of the area.

The 1981 MFOA publication, *Official Statements for Offerings of Securities by Local Governments—Examples and Guidelines*[3] will doubtless result in a higher degree of standardization in the content and style of presentations.

The Costs

The costs of preparation of the disclosure statements have not yet been fully identified or anlayzed. They include expanded staff time, added legal fees for both bond counsel and underwriter's counsel, probably some increase in the spread required by underwriters to compensate for additional time of their staff in developing the statements, and costs of printing and distribution of the statements. The likelihood is that these additional costs are in the range of $1 to $3 per bond for issues in the $10 million–$25 million range, with perhaps lesser unit costs in the larger issues. The costs have included increased difficulty in marketing in some instances due to media misinterpretation of facts or unbalanced treatment of the information presented.

The Benefits

At least four kinds of benefits have been forthcoming from the broadened disclosure statement procedures:

1. *Access to Market.* Investment bankers have been more comfortable with the new practices. In many cases, this has enabled them to continue participation in distribution of the bonds when their attorneys would otherwise have advised against such participation.

2. *Expanded Information to Investors.* Investors and investment analysts have generally received information that otherwise would not have been available. This is especially true of any adverse factors. It is less true of the favorable factors necessary to balanced judgment. The additional data have afforded a basis for more informed conclusions than was previously feasible for the debt of many issuers.

3. *Cash Flow Statements.* One of the greatest contributions has been to emphasize the cash flow of the issuer. Prior to 1975 attention of most taxing jurisdictions was centered upon budgetary and accounting factors. There was a more or less automatic assumption that operating capital either was available or could easily be secured through short-term loans in anticipation of the realization of current revenues. The new information required has forced many public finance officers to give more attention to matters of cash flow.

4. *Improved Accounting, Reporting, and Auditing.* Although the National Council on Governmental Accounting has long since offered good standards for the guidance of state and local governments in their accounting, auditing, and reporting, many of these governments did not meet acceptable standards. Many still do not; however, the emphasis on these matters has resulted in marked improvement in many jurisdictions during the last half of the 1970s and is likely to produce even greater improvement during the 1980s.

STRENGTHENING DISCLOSURE

For those governments which have not achieved accounting systems complying with the standards set forth by the NCGA and recommendations of the Municipal Finance Officers Association, the first step in improving disclosure is to bring the accounting systems into full compliance with these standards—both as to accounting and as to reporting. Beyond this step, there is a need for interim reporting (especially for the larger local

---

[3] Municipal Finance Officers Association, *Official Statements for Offerings of Securities by Local Governments—Examples and Guidelines* (1981).

governments and for state governments) which will provide interim data at quarterly or semiannual intervals in order to keep the investor and the community informed.

Some accounting firms have strongly urged the inclusion of information of a much more comprehensive character concerning elements of deferred compensation. Data on pension system finances is becoming more widespread although the systems of actuarial valuation lack the degree of standardization necessary to establish comparability in data from one jurisdiction to the next and sometimes one period to the next within the same jurisdiction. Information about accrued liabilities for vacation, sick leave, and other elements of separation pay may prove useful for inclusion in financial statements and in disclosure statements; however, the cost of such systems of data will doubtless be significant, and the data may not prove particularly valuable.

Perhaps the weakest points in the current disclosure statements are those relating to demographic and economic conditions and trends. The federal and state agencies that gather information about these subjects tend to develop them on bases that are generally of limited use in the case of most local governments. Except for the decennial census data, most of the reports are limited to the county level or to the large city level. The smaller cities and special governmental units find it difficult to secure timely data. In the case of the decennial census data, this quickly is outdated. The next step appears to be to urge state and federal data-gathering and reporting services to make information available in a manner that would be more useful in this connection. Perhaps the most useful data potential in this respect is the information on employment (establishment data) developed by state employment security agencies.

Projections

Much of the information in disclosure statements for governmental enterprise debt is derived from the feasibility report made by consultants. If the enterprise is an established one, the feasibility report deals with both retrospective and prospective operations; if it is a new enterprise, the report can deal only with prospective operations. One of the weaknesses of the ordinary feasibility reports for established enterprises is the failure to comment upon the extent to which prior projections have proved correct. The meaning of such reports to investors would be substantially strengthened by providing data necessary to evaluate the degree of accuracy of prior projections. In other words: How accurate have previous projections proved?

Although the information in feasibility reports for governmental enterprises deals largely with prospective data, the tendency in tax-supported operations has been either fully to ignore the future or to limit comments to the current year's operations, or to the current and succeeding years. Perhaps the time is at hand in which longer-term projections are in order. They could serve several purposes:

1. Providing assurance that officials are giving reasonable attention to planning for the future
2. Documenting the fact that the effects of operating costs and debt service costs arising from the new undertakings have been taken into consideration
3. Ascertaining the effects of overall expenditure and tax policies upon the community
4. Providing a benchmark against which to judge the degree of reliability in the projective processes

Greater Balance in the Disclosure Statement

The disclosure statements developed immediately following the 1975 problems in New York reflected a transfer to governmental finance of the SEC practice in respect to private finance. Although some of this may have been appropriate, it is to be remembered that, in a federal system of government, it must be presumed that the states and their local governments are as much concerned with the protection of the public interest as are federal officials. Therefore, it is not in the public interest for these governments to be obliged to give undue and unbalanced presentations in the offering of their debt instruments to investors. In the years since 1975, the official statements have reflected the views of underwriter's counsel as to how much of a negative character must be "disclosed" and how much of a positive character may be included in the disclosure statements. Given their responsibilities to the underwriter, it is understandable that they have tended to overemphasize the negative; however, many issuers have not been sufficiently aggressive in insisting upon reasonable balance in the presentations. Their own general counsel and their bond counsel have frequently settled for less than could have been secured by skillful and determined representation of the issuer's position.

Except for issuers in a genuinely hazardous position, the record is clear over decades that the exposure to potential default is much less than has been implicit in some of the negative presentations in recent years. It is not in the interest of equity between the community's taxpayers and the investors to produce costs that are excessive in relation to the genuine risks involved. These risks can be properly evaluated only in the light of a balanced presentation of the evidence—not in the light of an unbalanced negative emphasis. A better balance will be achieved only at the insistence of the issuer and by testing whether the underwriter is really willing to forego the potential profits in the sale if the issuer insists upon a more balanced presentation.

Format of the Disclosure Statement

There is a major opportunity to improve the format of the disclosure statements. As they are frequently presented they seem to have been specifically designed to discourage readership. Only the most determined investor or analyst is likely to persevere. Some good lessons could be learned from book publishers and others skilled in the arts of communication. There is no reason why the cover should be so unattractive merely because this has been customary in SEC-controlled offerings. There is no reason why the tables have to be so detailed or why the use of charts and other illustrations should occur so infrequently. There is no reason why some aerial photography and cartography should not be included. And, especially, it is not necessary that the statements be written by lawyers, rather than by specialists in effective communication—not salesmanship, but rational communication. The *Wall Street Journal* has long since learned that it can convey information in a manner that invites, rather than discourages, readership. Some of the talents of effective financial journalists could be profitably introduced into the official presentation of debt proposals.[4]

Distribution of the Disclosure Statement

Under the provisions of Regulation G-2 of the Municipal Securities Rulemaking Board, the final disclosure statement must be distributed by the dealers to customers at the time of confirmation of the sale. Distribution of the preliminary copies is largely in the hands of the syndicate in the case of negotiated sales. For competitive sales, the issuer—with the advice of the managers of the syndicates likely to bid—should provide for distribution to any persons requesting the statement as well as to potential customers in the sale about to take place. Availability of the statement should be clearly set forth in the official announcement and other materials inviting bids.

---

[4] Issuers will find useful the Municipal Finance Officers Association publication entitled, *Guidelines for Use by State and Local Governments in the Preparation of Yearly Information Statements and Other Current Information* (1978).

Conclusion

The disclosure statement is here to stay. The challenge is to bring balance into an unbalanced picture; to bring order into basically haphazard presentations; to substitute attractive and readable statements for the current presentations; to enhance understanding—not to destroy it by obscuring the key pertinent facts through presentation of so much that is irrelevant.

In short: Humanize the statement without sacrificing its utility.

Chapter 19
SALE AND DELIVERY OF BONDS

This chapter is concerned with the principal elements of sale and delivery of tax-exempt debt. The procedures relating to competitive sales are discussed first, followed by a review of steps in negotiated sales and a number of other elements of the sales process that are generally common to both competitive and negotiated sales.

COMPETITIVE SALES

The competitive sale process commences with a formal offering of the bonds for sale by means of an *official notice of sale*. This notice constitutes an invitation to bid and outlines the rules under which bids will be received, tabulated, and the award of the bonds made. The official notice may be solely by an *official advertisement* or it may be by an *official statement* (sometimes called the *official circular*) to which attention is called by an official advertisement. Bidding should be solely by use of an *official bid form* made available to bidders on request.

Official Notice of Sale

Competitive sales are conducted under the provisions of applicable law supplemented by the rules contained in the official notice of sale. If the formal offering is by use of an official advertisement, the advertisement must be sufficiently comprehensive to contain all appropriate specifications. If the offering is by an official statement, an abbreviated official advertisement is in order to assure that interested persons are advised as to where information and bidding forms may be obtained. The content of the official advertisement has been set forth in Exhibit C. The issuer's debt officer should maintain a comprehensive checklist of items that must be made available to the bidder—both to conform to the law and to encourage bidding in proper form. The general counsel and bond counsel should verify the adequacy of the checklist. Although the issuer's general counsel and debt officer have basic responsibility for the correctness of the content of the official notice of sale, it is to the bond counsel's opinion that the syndicate and investor look for assurance that each required step has been taken.

Placing Official Advertisements

The law under which the issuer operates ordinarily specifies the minimum number of insertions of the official advertisement and their timing as well as the number and type of journals to be used. Whether required by law or not, the official advertisement should appear at least once in *The Bond Buyer* and in a newspaper of general circulation in the community. Beyond meeting requirements for advertising, it is appropriate to send a news release to all local news media, *The Bond Buyer,* the *Wall Street Journal,* and nearby metropolitan dailies. Such news release should include the basic details concerning the offering, a few sentences about the most recent sale of similar bonds, and an indication as to the probable date of the next sale of this type of bond.

Failure to comply strictly with the state and local laws in giving notice of the sale is likely to require the bond counsel either to withhold his opinion or to issue a qualified opinion. It can also constitute a basis for legal action by opponents of the bond issue. Refusal by the successful bidder to accept delivery of the bonds is likely to result. Unless the law prescribes a different schedule, the first date of insertion of the notice should be about two weeks before the sale, with the final insertion a few days in advance of the sale if multiple insertions are required. The news release should precede bid opening by about three weeks.

Information Supplied Directly

Before 1975 it was customary for many debt officers to provide information on an informal basis to dealers, investors, or others interested in the projected bond sale. Such practices continue; however, debt officers are now obliged to be much more precise in their statements, especially as to financial information. The officers of the issuer should offer one comprehensive, cohesive statement setting forth the issuer's recent and current financial condition, a projection of financial prospects for the remainder of the current year (and, if the budget has been adopted, for the succeeding year).

Public Information Campaigns. It is appropriate for the issuer to provide general information concerning its financial and other affairs at times that do not correspond to bond sales. As a matter of fact, well-designed and well-executed information programs carried on independently of bond offerings are effective means of keeping investors informed.

The Official Bid Form

In order to discourage deviations from the terms of bidding set forth in the official notice of sale and also to facilitate detection of any deviation therefrom, the issuer should furnish an official bid form on which bids must be submitted. The essential elements of the bid form are:

1. Incorporation, by reference, of all of the terms and provisions of the official notice of sale

2. Provision for schedule of maturities (in sales in which the maturities are established in advance) or space for the bidder to insert the amount of each maturity (in sales in which the bidder is to establish the maturity pattern in order to develop predetermined patterns of debt service)

3. Provision for the coupon rate bid for each maturity

4. Description of the good faith deposit, i.e., bank, amount, etc. (When feasible, the bid form should state the minimum amount of the good faith deposit required in order to minimize the potential of error by bidders. Only in those cases in which the bidder is permitted to bid on less than the full amount of the securities being offered should the determination of the minimum amount of the good faith deposit be left to the bidder to insert.)

5. The aggregate amount bid, i.e., the amount to be paid for the bonds at settlement, taking into account the good faith deposit as well as any premium or discount

6. The name of the manager(s) and space for signature of the authorized representative of the bidder

7. The membership of the bidding group

8. In a portion of the official bid document clearly marked as:

"FOR INFORMATION ONLY: NOT A PART OF THE BID"

provision should be made for the bidder to record the bidder's computations of:

(a) The gross interest costs

(b) The amount of the premium offered, if any

(c) The amount of the discount sought, if any

(d) The average effective interest cost rate *calculated on the basis of the formula provided in the official offering statement*

The issuer will make the official determination of the amount of interest payable under each bid and the average effective interest costs, based on the maturity schedule and the coupon rate schedule. In case of bonds sold under equal annual or other specified debt service limitations, the issuer will make the official determination as to whether the specifications have been met. Information provided under paragraph "8" above is solely for information purposes.

The Draft Indenture Summary. When bonds are offered under an indenture, the official statement should contain a summary of the indenture, with the summary being approved by bond counsel. Copies of the draft indenture and the feasibility report should be available to potential bidders, investors, and other interested persons.

Receipt and Reading of Bids

The official announcement will have established the precise hour (including whether by daylight or standard time) by which all bids are to be received, along with the precise place at which they are to be received. The place selected for receipt of bids should be an easily accessible, well-known address in order to avoid failure to receive bids being delivered by persons unfamiliar with the community. Bidders should be permitted to submit more than one bid but each must be accompanied by a good faith deposit unless the specifications shall have authorized the submission of alternative bids and have authorized a single good faith deposit check to suffice. Usually, there is little reason for a second bid unless the specifications have afforded alternative bases for bidding, e.g., both callable and noncallable bonds.

In most cases, bids are presented to the appropriate officer only a few minutes in advance of the closing hour.[1] All bids should be submitted in sealed envelopes and the time of receipt of each bid noted on the envelope by the official in charge. The specifications should prohibit withdrawal of a submitted bid.[2] Once a bid is delivered at the public place for its acceptance (assuming it is delivered within the hour preceding closing), it should be kept in public view and in the custody of the designated officer until opened in the presence of witnesses. It is important that the receiving officer be at the precise place at which bids are to be received at least a short time in advance of the closing hour in order that no technical violation of the rules occurs. Within the final minute before the closing time, the officer should remind the audience of the approach of the closing time and should refuse to accept any bid delivered so much as a second after the closing hour.

The bids should be opened promptly after the closing time and a designated officer should publicly read the following elements of each bid:

1. The name of the bidder

2. The coupon rate for each maturity

3. In cases in which the amount of each maturity shall have been proposed by

---

[1] Although bids may be accepted by mail in advance of closing, there is little likelihood of such presentations under existing practices in municipal bond operations.

[2] Some authorities take the opposite view. They believe the bid is the property of the bidder until the closing minute and that the representative of the syndicate should have the right to withdraw the bid any time prior to the closing hour. Given this potential for disagreement, the point should be resolved in advance by appropriate language in the bidding specifications.

the bidder, the amount of the bidder's proposed maturity for each maturity year should be read
4. The amount of the bid, including amount of premium offered or discount sought
5. The amount of the good faith deposit
6. The average effective interest cost as computed by the bidder—preferably in both NIC and TIC

Representatives of the syndicates present may be anxious to report promptly whether it appears that they have submitted the successful bid.[3] Therefore, there should be no avoidable delay in opening and reading the bids. There should also be a minimum feasible lapse of time between opening and award of the bonds.

Preliminary Examination

The initial examination should disclose whether the bid conforms to the specifications in such matters as form, the minimum amount of bonds to be purchased, and amount of the security deposit. Bids found deficient on their face should be declared informal (preferably with the concurrence of bond counsel). It is appropriate to offer to return the deposit check as soon as a bid is disqualified. At the conclusion of the preliminary examination of the bids, it is in order to announce the *apparent* rank order of the bids; however, it is essential that no statement be made declaring a winning bid until verification of the effective interest costs of each bid and confirmation of compliance by the lowest bidder to the specifications. At the close of the session, the officer in charge should state the place and approximate time at which it is intended that the award be announced and the time and place at which unsuccessful bidders may reclaim their deposits.

Tabulation of Bids and Award of Bonds

Once the bid opening session has been adjourned, qualified personnel (or agents) of the issuer as well as bond counsel should examine each bid carefully for conformity to the specifications. Bids found to be in order should thereupon be tabulated. Computations of effective interest costs should be by use of computer programs previously announced publicly and entered in the computer memory. Only the information concerning the interest rates, premiums, discounts, and, where variable maturities are permitted, the amounts of maturities need be entered. Results should become available immediately. The use of portable units for computer input and output make it feasible to use computers from almost any point of sale. Results can be obtained in a matter of minutes from input under either NIC or TIC. Agreement with (or exceptions to) the results provided by the bidders should be noted. The officially determined effective interest costs should be entered on the face of the bid along with the signature of the person in charge of the tabulation of the bids. Copies of computer printouts should become a part of the official proceedings. If any bid appears to have failed to meet the specifications, that bidder should be informed immediately in order that any error in the preliminary official findings can be called to official attention by the bidder in advance of the official announcement of the results of the sale and the award of the bonds.

Once these reviews have been completed, the debt officer should prepare the formal entry of record in the proceedings showing the name of each bidder, the coupon rate bid

---

[3] In most circumstances, this is not the case due to the fact that copies of the bids will have been submitted to the wire services at about the time the bid is being delivered. Information as to content of the bid may have been distributed by the wire service before the time it is being read at the official opening. (In some cases, this has occurred in advance of the opening, resulting in significant disputes; however, the current policy is not to distribute results by wire in advance of the closing hour.)

for each maturity, the premium offered or discount sought, the amount of the average interest cost for each bid as determined under the bid specifications, and the name of the bidder to whom the award is made.[4] The award should be made in writing and be signed by each of the officers formally conducting the sale. Each other bidder should be provided with a copy of the official determination of the effective interest costs. If any bid shall have been rejected, the record should state explicitly the reasons therefor. The bidder should be advised in writing of the rejection and provided a copy of the statement of the reasons therefor. Bond counsel should review and approve such communication before it is issued. The checks of unsuccessful bidders should be returned as soon as the award is made.

Public announcement by means of a press release should then be made concerning the official award of the bonds; the good faith check accompanying the successful bid should be given to the treasurer for deposit.

Acceptance of Bid for Less Than Full Amount Offered

If one or more bidders comply with the bidding specifications, either the best bid should be accepted or all bids should be rejected. If no bid is received for the full amount of the bonds offered but one or more bidders submit bids for less than the full amount, the question arises as whether it is appropriate for the issuer to accept partial bid or bids. Authorities differ as to what constitutes desirable practice in such a circumstance. The issuer may wish to reject the bids and make another effort to secure full financing; however, circumstances may make it desirable to accept a bid for less than the full amount of the bond issue being offered. For example, in periods of highly unsettled markets, the issuer may need whatever cash that can be raised currently with the remainder to be raised through a subsequent sale. Advice of both general counsel and bond counsel is required in such circumstances.

If the market is sufficiently disturbed at the time the bonds are being offered, it may be appropriate to reserve the right to sell less than the full amount of the bonds being offered (if the law permits); however, this constitutes something of an advanced admission of difficulty of securing access to the market on a favorable basis, and the action will have to be weighed in the light of its potential impact upon bidding.

No-Bid Situations

Fortunately, the no-bid situation arises infrequently in the municipal bond market; however, when interest rates are high or ascending at a rapid rate, one finds large numbers of "displacements." These displacements may be due to: (1) a lack of bids, (2) a decision by the issuer to delay a planned financing due to general market conditions, or (3) withdrawal of the invitation to bid due to the likelihood of either no bids or only unacceptable bids. If no bid is received, a thorough analysis is in order to determine the causes and probable effects.

The Causes

Among the factors most frequently responsible for failure to receive bids are:

1. *Market Conditions.* The general market may be disturbed due to economic or political factors. A drive by the Federal Reserve System to tighten money supply can result in a

---

[4] In the unlikely event of a tie bid, the issuer should offer to divide the bonds among the tied bidders. If this is not acceptable, the award should be by lot. No preference should be shown on the basis of the time of receipt of bids.

dire shortage of money, especially long-term money. Such periods may be limited or protracted. Periods of marked depression and liquidation of problem loans by commercial
banks, e.g., 1974–76 and 1980–81, can lead to a drying up of large portions of the normal
supply of funds for purchase of municipal bonds. Shifts from a profit to a loss position
by major purchasers not only is characterized by shortages of money but also by greatly
reduced attractiveness of tax-exempt securities. A general reduction in income tax rates,
such as those adopted in 1981, can significantly reduce investor willingness to purchase
tax-exempt securities—or, alternatively, make major modifications in the terms under which
he participates in purchase. If there is a widespread depression, the effects on the market
are accelerated. Also, the political situation may become disturbed in a manner that adversely
affects the market, e.g., serious illness or death of a president, international frictions, or
impending major military conflict.

2. *Credit Position of Issuer.* The credit position of the issuer may prove unacceptable—
either in general or in respect to the particular bonds being offered. Adverse media treatment
of the issuer acts to negate investor confidence. Actual or alleged mismanagement, corrup-
tion, fraud, or official misconduct destroys confidence of many investors, thereby weakening
the market. The credit position of the issuer can also be adversely affected by a lack of
confidence in the bond counsel, the fiscal agent, the trustee, the authors of the feasibility
report, or the soundness of the security being pledged in support of the bonds.

3. *Technical Factors.* No-bid situations are sometimes produced by technical factors
involved in the offering, especially by either overall interest rate ceilings or ceilings placed
on particular maturities. If the bonds are callable, the combination of the call feature
and requirements for equal annual debt service arrangements in periods of high interest
rates can result in an inability of the syndicate to devise a bid which meets the specifications
and, simultaneously, the requirements of the market.

4. *Size of the Issue.* Another major factor is the size of the issue. There is always a
maximum size beyond which any given issuer will probably be confronted with a no-bid
situation on a given day. The determination of the maximum feasible size is a professional
judgment of the highest order of importance to the issuer, albeit one which the issuer is
usually unable to assess accurately. On a day when the market will find it feasible to
accept $200 million in bonds of one issuer, it may not be able to accept at any reasonable
price an issue of $25 million of another issuer, because there are not a sufficient number
of buyers willing to purchase the smaller issue. Moreover, if there is an overhang in the
secondary market of a large amount of the outstanding bonds of the issuer, flotation of
additional securities in large amounts may not be feasible.

The Effects

Along with the study of the causes of a no-bid situation, there is need for analysis
of the effects of a failure to sell the bonds. These effects are likely to fall within one or
more of these three broad categories:

1. *Debt Default.* If the redemption of BANS is contingent on the sale, a default is
likely unless a roll-over of the BANS can be accomplished—a task made much more
difficult because of the no-bid. If the cash anticipated from the bond sale is to be used
(through a consolidated cash account) to help meet current debt service payments temporarily, a debt default may be triggered.

2. *Capital Program Disruption.* To the extent that payment of capital outlay obligations
is contingent on the availability of the bond proceeds, the execution of the capital program
is jeopardized. The determinations required at this juncture include identification of work
that can be forestalled at minimum cost, the timetable for interruption of work-in-progress,
and the penalty costs arising from interruption and subsequent start-up of work.

3. *Operating Budget Impact.* If the consolidated cash account relies significantly on
bond proceeds the impact of the loss of this anticipated cash requires evaluation.

Meeting the No-Bid Challenge

Depending on the causes identified and the effects likely to flow from a no-bid situation, action may be required immediately on a near-crisis basis or may be deferred under more leisurely procedures. The first avenue to be explored is that of the possibility of a negotiated sale. Ordinarily, the law permits such a sale when no bids are received; sometimes it permits a negotiated sale if only one bid has been received, inasmuch as the objectives of competition have not been achieved. Some laws controlling competitive sales suspend many of the competitive sale specifications; other laws lift few specifications. The issuer must know the precise parameters under which negotiation can be conducted and proceed as promptly as feasible to initiate the negotiation process—ordinarily, relying on some combination of the syndicate membership that has shown interest in the issue on a competitive basis. If early explorations show that it is not feasible to sell long-term bonds within the limits permitted, or that the terms of such sale are so adverse as to make it desirable to seek an alternative, the first step is to determine whether BANS can be sold, pending more favorable conditions for sale of the bonds.

If relaxation of specifications is not sufficient to enable the issuer to sell either BANS or bonds at negotiation, the issuer is confronted with the unpleasant task of rearranging the pattern of execution of the capital program and, in some cases, of negotiation of short-term revenue anticipation loans to avoid default in payment of debt service or other obligations due. If the bond fund is a member of a consolidated bond account or a consolidated cash account, an exploration of sale of bonds or notes by other funds with the cash being made available to the bond fund is in order. The comments below indicate some of the actions that can be taken to facilitate the bond sale depending on the factors responsible for the no-bid occurrence.

1. *Coupon and Average Cost Limitations.* If the failure to receive a competitive bid arose from inability of the bidders to present viable bids within the interest rate limitations imposed by the specifications, the issuer may find one of these steps feasible:

a. When the yield curve is significantly inclined, a marked shortening of the average life may lower average rates sufficiently to bring them within limits. That is, the average interest costs may drop sufficiently to overcome any narrow margin by which the receipt of a bid was missed. On the other hand, if the yield curve is almost flat, inverted, or humpbacked, relief from this action is unlikely.

b. If the coupon rate limitations for the bonds maturing in advance of the first call date have produced high penalty yield problems, lengthening or abandoning the call option may provide relief.

c. If unrealistic limitations have been imposed by local action, efforts at liberalization should be immediately instituted, and a liberalization of statutory limits sought.

2. *Credit Position and Security Pledge.* There is a tendency to confuse the independent concepts of (a) the credit of the issuer and (b) the security pledged for bonds being offered.

An individual heavily in debt in relation to his income or wealth is a poor credit risk. But, at the same time, if the individual has assets that are free and clear of encumbrance, these may provide security for a loan and guarantee access to the market. This distinction is not fully appreciated as applied to issuers of tax-exempt securities.

If the no-bid situation has been actuated by the poor credit position of the issuer, the solution is likely to require a long period for rehabilitation. It will involve adjustments in the revenue structure and program levels, tighter management, and/or supplemental state government absorption of some local responsibilities. On the other hand, it may be feasible to improve security arrangements without undue difficulty. This can take the form of a pledge of additional assets of the issuer, or it can be in the form of support of the debt by another government.

Closely associated with the basic support of the bonds is the cash flow of the issuer within the fiscal year. The prudent investor knows that a prompt payment of debt service due is contingent upon availability of cash. Governments with strong positive cash flows throughout the fiscal year or with a record of significant working capital funds, need have little concern about payment. Governments with minimal working capital and/or revenue calendars under which large amounts of payments must be met prior to realization of the year's revenue are frequently dependent on the annual negotiation of working capital loans to meet their obligations in a timely manner. Aside from revisions in the revenue calendar, two kinds of action can help to overcome this problem as it relates to debt service: (1) The use of debt service reserve funds or (2) the creation of a working capital fund through issuance of bonds for that purpose.

Legal Actions Pending

Community life has become increasingly characterized by legal actions—sometimes to achieve their stated purposes and sometimes to provide leverage to the plaintiff in some unrelated activity. At the time of the sale of bonds, there may be pending legal actions of importance and relevance to the issue. The bidding may not be affected inasmuch as the issuer is obliged to deliver a "no-litigation" certificate satisfactory to the buyers at the time of settlement. However, if bidders consider the grounds on which the litigation is brought to be sound, the syndicate may refuse to bid. They know that, in order to bid, they are obliged to make a good faith deposit. For the successful bidder, this deposit is retained until the bonds are delivered and it bears no interest while held. Even though the deposit is eventually returned, the bidder loses the use of these funds during the period. Moreover, if there is a legal action over whether settlement will be made, the purchaser is confronted with still further costly delays and may be joined in the litigation. Although the issuer is powerless to prevent the initiation of such legal actions, prompt resolution can be vigorously sought. Moreover, in order to discourage frivolous litigation, the issuer can seek legislation imposing elements of financial responsibility on the plaintiffs for losses that may be incurred by the issuer.

NEGOTIATED SALE OF BONDS

At this point it is appropriate to repeat, in summary form, some of the points made in Chapter 17 concerning negotiation in order to provide emphasis. Thus, the sale of bonds through negotiation has some significant market advantages when there is a genuine negotiation, i.e., bargaining between sophisticated, knowledgeable, and skillful parties.

If there is to be genuine negotiation, the issuer must be represented effectively. To do this, those handling the negotiations for the issuer must have knowledge concerning numerous aspects of the market; the position which the bonds can command, the significance of yield curves and the fitting of them to different grades of securities, the most effective and reasonable patterns of compensation for the syndicate, the alternatives available in construction of bond issues to fit current market requirements, the kinds of promotion required to secure the best market, and other pertinent aspects of negotiation of bond sales. Given their other responsibilities, few public finance officers have an opportunity to develop and maintain these kinds of skills. For most of them, an effort to do so would involve a significant inefficiency in the use of their time and energies. This does not suggest any lack of ability on their part. Rather, it addresses the matter that such a high degree of specialization in a highly complex (but often quite limited) portion of their responsibilities may not be worth the price required. Under these circumstances, reliance on others becomes essential.

Among the more critical aspects of negotiation is the capacity of the issuer to affect the following in a meaningful manner:

1. The fixing of the yield curve to be used in the sale vis-à-vis the basic market yield curve
2. Development and execution of an informational and promotional campaign appropriate to the offering
3. Obtaining a bona fide effort by the syndicate in promotion and placement of the bonds
4. Fixing of the compensation of the syndicate in a manner that is fair but, at the same time, encourages the customer representatives of the syndicate members to push the bonds
5. Adjustments of terms of the bond issue for the final sale to take into account the information developed in the preliminary sales effort

When the issuer is in a position effectively to negotiate these matters, the community is likely to be well served by negotiation. When the issuer is not in a position to conduct a sophisticated negotiation, reliance on competitive bidding (if feasible) is likely to produce better results.

The sale itself is a simple act. Following one or more tests of the market, the underwriter makes an offer (in the light of negotiations to date) to purchase the bonds. The issuer makes a decision as to whether to accept this offer constituting the best that can be obtained under the circumstances, defer sale, or discontinue the negotiation in favor of competitive sale. Not all negotiations result, or should result, in sales. On some occasions, it is not feasible to develop a package that can be marketed at all or marketed at reasonable terms. This may not reflect adversely upon either the issuer or the syndicate but may be instead a measure of market and/or economic circumstances beyond the control of either.

The experiences of 1981 and 1982 shed new light on negotiation vis-à-vis competitive bidding. It was found that volatility was so great that many of the most sophisticated managers of competitive bid accounts were confronted with major losses because the market performed in a manner to which they were not accustomed. Thus bond issues purchased at record interest rate levels for an issuer sometimes proved to be unacceptable to investors. Frequently it became necessary to dissolve the syndicates and distribute the remaining bonds among the members. In turn they were obliged to take significant losses due to the price cuts required to dispose of the bonds.

The ultimate effect of this upon the market is not determinable in any precise manner. However, it inevitably led to uncertainty by dealers and to aggressiveness by the investors as to the terms upon which they would accept the bonds. During the same period negotiated sales could proceed in a somewhat more orderly fashion because it was easier for the syndicates to determine the degree of interest among their customers *before* they bought the bonds. Many in the market came to believe that in these circumstances the negotiated sale served both dealers and issuers—and perhaps even the investors—by lending a degree of stability that could not be provided in the competitive bid market.

SALES OF BONDS TO OTHER GOVERNMENTS

Under a number of circumstances, sales of bonds by local governments to state or federal agencies constitutes the best available method of obtaining funds. Moreover, the use of governmental lessee debt may afford the most efficient manner in which to raise needed capital.

Sales to the Federal Government

Commencing with the Public Works Administration in the early 1930s, the federal government has, from time to time, offered financing for various types of state and local government capital facilities. One of the more notable of these through the years has been the federal guarantees or purchase of notes and bonds of local public housing agencies and, for the years prior to 1976, to proceed with various types of advances, loans, and loan guarantees in conjunction with community development activities.

Recently one of the major programs is through the program of the Farmers Home Administration,[5] which has been used extensively by some states, to secure moneys at more favorable rates than were available in the general market. Although the aggregate amounts of such loans is relatively small, this provides a useful source to many local governments.[6]

Sales to State and Local Governments

There is no full catalog available of the sale by state and local governments of their securities to various special funds held by such governments. At December 31, 1980, the Board of Governors of the Federal Reserve System estimated that holdings of state and local government securities by state and local government pension funds amounted to $4.1 billion.[7] In addition the general funds of state and local governments (primarily of state governments) held $6.5 billion at December 31, 1980.[8]

The Bureau of the Census reported that at fiscal year-end in 1979–80, holdings of state and local government securities by state government funds (other than insurance trust funds) amounted to $4.7 billion and by local governments, to $1.7 billion.[9] With adjustments for the time differential, this would accord with the *Flow of Funds* statement. The distribution of these holdings by the "general funds" of state governments (i.e., all funds other than insurance trust funds) showed these states had the largest holdings at the end of their 1980 fiscal years:[10]

	(amounts in millions of dollars)				
Alaska	367	Michigan	117	Virginia	385
California	116	New York	1,789	West Virginia	327
Connecticut	66	Oregon	70	Wyoming	120
Florida	469	Tennessee	88	Subtotal	4,419
Iowa	76	Texas	218	All other	293
Maine	155	Vermont	56	Total	4,712

In some of these states, the holdings were apparently by state bond banks. In some others, e.g., Texas, these represented largely holdings by a state agency which acted substantially as a bond bank for limited purposes, e.g., water development or for purchase of certain public school district bonds by special state educational reserve funds. Again, the predominance of the State of New York in this picture distorts the data when stated only on a

---

[5] See provisions of Section 306, Public Law 92–49, 7 U.S.C. 1926.

[6] A number of other federal departments and agencies make advances to state and local governments for specialized purposes. One of the most frequently used sources is in the loans from the U.S. Department of Labor to state employment security agencies for that program. The full range of these loans and grants is set forth in various editions of the *Catalog of Federal Domestic Assistance,* issued frequently by the Executive Office of the President.

[7] At fiscal year end in 1979–80, pension funds of the City of New York owned $3.5 billion of city and MAC securities. Bureau of the Census, U.S. Department of Commerce, *Finances of Employee-Retirement Systems of State and Local Governments in 1979–80,* pp. 5–8, 23.

[8] Board of Governors of the Federal Reserve Fund, *Flow of Funds Accounts: Assets and Liabilities Outstanding, 1957–1980* (September, 1981), pp. 15, 27.

[9] Bureau of the Census, U.S. Department of Commerce, *Governmental Finances in 1979–80,* p. 54.

[10] Bureau of the Census, U.S. Department of Commerce, *State Government Finances in 1980,* pp. 59–62.

national basis. Although the potential is apparently small in most states, it is appropriate to pursue these sources—especially when money is difficult to obtain directly from the credit markets.

Sales of Bonds by State Governments and Agencies on Behalf of Local Governments

The past three decades have been characterized by a variety of methods under which state governments have sold bonds *of* or *for* their local governments. The systems have varied widely but can be classified generally under the following headings:

1. *State as Sales Agent.* A state government officer or agency sells local government securities secured by individual local governments, e.g., the North Carolina Local Government Commission.

2. *State Bond Banks.* A state government creates a state bond bank or special agency to acquire securities of local governments, with payment from proceeds of bonds sold by the bond bank—with or without state government participation in security for bond bank debt.

3. *State as Funding Agent.* A state government creates a funding agent to develop capital for local governmental entities with the security pledged being dedicated revenues collected and administered by the state government, e.g., Florida.

4. *Governmental Lessee Debt.* As noted in Chapter 15, a state government may create authorities, building commissions, or other special agencies authorized to enter into contracts with local governmental entities under which the state unit issues debt in its own name secured by leases with local governments. In some instances this involves state government support of debt through "moral obligation" covenants, or, in some cases, through potential or actual diversion of certain state appropriations to the local governments in support of the debt. Each of these is discussed earlier in this volume. The procedures vary from state to state and are not appropriate for further discussion here. The state agency sells its own bonds either at competitive or negotiated sale under procedures outlined previously in this chapter.

PRINTING THE BONDS AND COUPONS

As soon as bonds are sold, an order for printing is placed with the bond printer selected in advance of the sale. The pattern of printing—whether to be in conventional form or in postdated, check-encoded form—will have been determined in advance. The bond and coupons will have been designed, leaving the printed bonds showing denomination and number of each bond and the denomination of each of the coupons.

The widespread use of computers and other processing techniques led to the creation of the Committee on Uniform Security Identification Procedures (CUSIP), which developed a system of numerical identification for all known outstanding series of bonds—corporate and municipal. New CUSIP numbers are assigned for new bond issues and can be printed on the face of each bond and coupon. The *CUSIP Directory* is published by Standard Statistics Company, Inc., a subsidiary of Standard & Poor's Corporation. This system provides for an effective and efficient means of identification in sales transactions and record keeping.

If the bonds are registrable as to principal or as to principal and interest, arrangements may be made between the issuer and the purchasing syndicate for delivery of bonds in registrable form for those who prefer them; or, the bonds may be delivered as coupon bonds and then offered by the owner for registration.

When delivery of definitive bonds cannot be made within a reasonable number of days following the sale or when settlement is needed before permanent bonds can be prepared, temporary bonds may be offered to the purchasers. These are printed in simple form without coupons and are exchangeable within a few days for permanent bonds. If temporary bonds are contemplated, this option should be noted in the official offering. Delivery of the temporary bonds is accompanied by the legal opinion of bond counsel. As soon as the permanent bonds are available, notice is given to the underwriters and to the various journals and advisory services of the availability of the permanent bonds in exchange for the temporary bonds. In any event, the permanent bonds must be available before the first interest payment date in order to assure prompt payment of interest due.

SETTLEMENT

The final step in the sale of the bonds is settlement—accomplished by delivery of the bonds to the purchaser in return for the remainder of the purchase price (price less good faith deposit) and the interest which has accrued between the date of the bonds and settlement date.

In the period between the sale date and settlement date, the bonds will have been printed and validated or authenticated by the bank or other agent designated for this purpose. Usually, at least one manuscript signature is affixed by special multiple pen arrangements; others are likely to be facsimile only.

At settlement, the issuer delivers to the purchaser necessary contract documents—ranging from a few for general obligation bonds to many for most revenue bonds. Illustrative is the list of items promised by the Commonwealth of Massachusetts in its $55 million general obligation bond issue in 1979.

1. *Legal Opinions.* Approving opinions of the attorney general and bond counsel to the effect that the full faith and credit of the Commonwealth was pledged to payment of principal and interest and that the interest was tax-exempt for federal income tax purposes and exempt from taxation imposed by the laws of Massachusetts except in certain inheritance and corporate taxes

2. *No-Litigation Certificate.* A certificate of the attorney general to the effect that there is no litigation pending or known to be threatened seeking to restrain or enjoin the issuance, sale, execution and delivery of the bonds or contesting their validity or repayment

3. *Official Statement.* A signed copy of the official statement relating to the bonds to be dated on or about the date of sale and which shall be in substantially the same form as the preliminary statement, subject to such changes as the Commonwealth deemed appropriate

4. *Comfort Letters.* A certificate of the state treasurer and secretary of administration and finance to the effect that to the best of their knowledge and belief:

   a. The preliminary official statement and the official statement contain no untrue statement nor fail to disclose any material fact, the absence of which would cause the statements made to be misleading

   b. That there had been no material adverse change in the financial condition and affairs of the Commonwealth during the period from the date of the official statement to and including the date of delivery of the bonds which was not disclosed or contemplated in the official statement

5. *Bond Counsel Additional Certificate.* A statement by bond counsel that, within the scope of their knowledge in the preparation of the official statement, no facts had come to their attention that would cause counsel to believe any statement was misleading or that any adverse material had been omitted

In the closing for general obligation bonds, the list also includes other documents, e.g., an "authentication of bonds" letter and an arbitrage certificate. In the closings for revenue bonds, the list of the documents is extended, depending on the type of revenue bond involved and the complexity of the transaction. Additional documents may include:

1. The indenture
2. The feasibility study
3. Resolutions of governing authority authorizing the bonds, construction contracts, and related matters
4. Statements concerning the planned use of the proceeds
5. Certified copies of proceedings of officers or agencies with regulatory or supervisory authority
6. "Comfort letters" from independent certified public accountants

With all required statements in hand, the bonds are exchanged for the purchase money. The actual delivery of the bonds is usually by a bank in the city in which settlement is made.

No-Litigation Certificate and Authentication of Bonds

In order to facilitate the delivery of bonds, it is essential that there be a certificate to the effect that no litigation is pending which, if successful, would invalidate the bonds or adversely affect the security being pledged. In some states, the no-litigation certification is made by the chief legal officer of the issuer, the attorney general, and/or the bond counsel. In any event, the bond counsel must be satisfied as to the validity of this statement in order to issue an unqualified opinion. As a protection to bondholders, the laws in many states require that any action brought to test the validity of the bonds (including any actions concerning authorization and approval) must be brought either prior to, or shortly after, the date of the sale of the bonds. Although such legislation has the effect of reducing the rights of citizens and taxpayers subsequently to raise legal points not tested prior to sale or delivery, the legal protection to the bondholder is in the public interest inasmuch as investors hesitate to purchase bonds if their validity could be subsequently challenged. The investor is unwilling to accept the risk arising from legal actions brought months, or years, after the sale.

Litigation concerning the validity of bond issues occurs infrequently but it must be handled quickly when it does occur. Challenges range from those based on alleged procedural irregularities in authorization of the bonds to such fundamental issues as the status of the borrowing capacity of the issuer. If litigation has not come to the attention of bidders prior to sale, or if the litigation is instituted in the period between the date of sale and contemplated date of settlement, there is likely to be a delay in delivery unless the legal issues are resolved immediately. If the litigation should result in a significant reduction in the security for the bonds, it may not be feasible to complete delivery in a timely manner. (In a few cases, the issuance is permanently restrained.) Even if the bonds are eventually delivered, litigation usually results in losses by the syndicate as a result of expense incurred in marketing or, perhaps, legal costs as to whether the syndicate is obliged to complete the transaction. The ability of the issuer to deliver a no-litigation certificate is critical.[11]

Method of Payment

The method of payment is important to the issuer. Usually purchasers prefer to make payment in funds that are immediately good in only certain financial centers. For issuers maintaining accounts in the bank upon which the payment check is drawn, this means the immediate availability of money. On the other hand, a day or more may be required in order to make these funds available to the issuer as good moneys in their own banks,

---

[11] See Arthur J. Kalita, "The Effects of Unforeseen Developments on Competitive Sales," *The Daily Bond Buyer:* PSA Supplement, October 8, 1979, pp. 7–9.

i.e., time for clearance of the check through the banking system. When short-term interest rates are at the 10.00 percent level on a $25,000,000 bond issue, with a 2 percent good faith deposit, this means that the issuer loses $6,712 in interest for each day of delay in investment of the proceeds. The issuer should insist upon settlement in funds available to the issuer for investment on the day of settlement.

SALE OF SHORT-TERM DEBT

A vast amount of short-term debt is issued by state and local governments each year. All of this is sold in the same sense that bonds are sold, albeit the procedures are frequently much more informal.

Issuance of Short-term Notes

Negotiable short-term debt is usually evidenced by notes. These may be in relatively simple form, or they may be similar to bonds. Notes issued by governments are usually in larger denominations than bonds. Many governments borrow only from commercial banks—either from a single bank or from a consortium of banks. Others routinely depend on the public sale of notes to the general, tax-free market or negotiate with a few lenders. Some regularly pursue only a single course; others use the forms selectively depending upon conditions. One readily identifies the competitive sale and the negotiated sale as the two general processes by which short-term debt is issued. The direct loan from the bank is a *form* of negotiated sale; it is also a private placement.

Competitive Sales. In the competitive sale of short-term notes, the procedures are similar to those described for competitive sale of bonds. Ordinarily, notes that mature within one year of date of issue provide for payment of interest at maturity; notes with a longer life usually require interim interest payments.

The disclosure and advertising procedures are similar to those for sale of bonds. The method of award of the notes may be similar to the award of bonds, i.e., an all-or-none basis; however, some issuers allow the bidders to offer to purchase portions of the notes being offered. The use of this procedure makes it possible for larger investors to bid directly for portions of the notes rather than pay commissions by purchasing them through investment bankers. When there is a good market for the issuer's notes, this procedure can produce a lower effective interest cost to the issuer with good market access than an all-or-none requirement. Yet, the issuer is running a risk because there may be a reluctance of investment bankers to bid—knowing some of their potential customers are able to purchase notes directly from the issuer. The issuer using this type of sale must be fully informed as to the sufficiency of demand from the market for the type of short-term investment being offered.

Negotiated Sales. Typically, a person making a loan from a bank does not look on this as a negotiated transaction; however, it is in the sense that the borrower (issuer of the loan) usually can secure the loan from more than one place. Some banks make it appear that, when they name a rate for a tax-exempt issuer, the rate is nonnegotiable. Occasionally, this is true; frequently, it is not. The skillful public debt officer knows that the terms of a loan to a governmental entity are usually subject to substantial flexibility as to rate. Unless the government has no practical alternative, it can (when armed with proper information) confront banks with the facts about the market level vis-à-vis the rates being offered.

After adjustment for the cost of issuance of notes to the general securities market, the issuer can negotiate with the confidence that, unless the banks are willing to provide loans at reasonable rates, the general market will accept the note issue. This should be a negotiation—not a dictation of terms by one party. Of course, governments with a poor credit position are like poor debtors everywhere; the lender may name the terms. Among the categories of issuers frequently paying high short-term rates on commercial bank loans are the smaller jurisdictions. Community relationships are involved. The issuer may make no exploration of alternative sources or may not be sufficiently sophisticated to conduct an effective negotiation. Officers of issuers of short-term loans should either become fully acquainted with these matters or obtain professional assistance in the negotiation.

In periods of very tight money or in periods when money markets are quite uncertain, it is desirable for the issuer to have optional available sources of borrowing for short-term purposes. Accordingly, medium-sized and larger jurisdictions that may be required to come into the short-term market will find it advisable to have established their position both with the commercial banks and in the larger municipal market through having issued notes there from time to time. Moreover, it may be appropriate to have utilized both the competitive and the negotiated procedures as each has its place in periods of extreme market pressure and lack of experience with either may place the issuer at a disadvantage.

Internal Financing

Many state and local governments depend, at least partly, on loans within the government to meet cash requirements. This can be accomplished through direct loans by one fund to another or by the operation of a consolidated cash account. The extent to which internal loans are used may depend on the policies of the government concerning the maximization of interest income from treasury cash. Frequently, it is less expensive for Fund A to invest its assets in short-term taxable securities and for Fund B to borrow at tax-exempt rates from the credit markets than it is for Fund A to lend to Fund B. For smaller loans or very short-term loans, interfund loans are likely to be much simpler; in some cases, this is the only feasible approach as this may be the only viable source of credit for Fund B.

The use of the consolidated cash account in private business is well understood and very widely practiced in most corporations. There is usually only one treasury (except for sums kept with trustees). However, as the fund concept has developed in public business, there is a tendency for legislative bodies and pressure groups to look on each fund as a monetary as well as accounting and budgetary entity. Pursuing that concept, the assets of each fund are required to be kept in separate bank accounts and the moneys are not to be mingled with other current assets of the governmental entity involved. This concept has denied many governments the opportunity for maximization of investment and earnings on available balances. The problems of cash management tend to grow geometrically in relation to the number of bank accounts involved. Whether the loans from the creditor to the debtor funds are direct or through use of a consolidated cash account, accurate records of the interfund transactions should be maintained. The government should have a fixed policy concerning the manner in which interest is to be charged and credited in the use of such moneys in order to maintain equitable relationships between the creditor and debtor funds.

Intergovernmental Financing

There has been a great increase in recent decades in the amount of money collected by one government and paid to another. These intergovernmental payments fall into three categories:

1. Revenue sharing and basic support
2. Cost sharing and categorical grants
3. Purchase of services

In the revenue sharing and general support category, senior governments make payments that are available for budgeting by the recipient as a part of its general revenue structure. Ordinarily, these payments have few strings attached. The federal general revenue sharing program is the largest single operation, but there are also many such programs at the state level.[12] Cost sharing programs occur frequently in health, welfare, and education. In these programs, recipients are usually expected to perform the services under jointly financed programs. The purchase of services concept should involve payment of the full cost of the services to the provider government.

The question always arises as to the *time* of the payments from the senior governments vis-à-vis the time of disbursements by the provider governments. Many of these programs developed on a reimbursement basis, i.e., the provider government paid out the cash and then requested a reimbursement of the amounts due from the senior governments. As new programs developed, different patterns of timing of payments also developed. In some programs, advances correspond roughly to the schedule for the outlays; in many others, significant delays occur between the time of outlay and reimbursement. Interest on the funds involved has usually been ignored. This is unfortunate. The time value of money is as much an element of cost as is the payment for goods or services. Yet, bureaucracies of the senior governments have generally refused to take interest into account for two reasons: (1) The added cost of the interest and (2) the leverage available in assessing a penalty on the provider government for failure to yield to the pressures of the senior government bureaucracy.

This is piracy!

When the provider governments are denied the right to include interest as an element of cost, they shoulder more than their agreed, or contemplated, shares of the costs of these programs. Conversely, when provider governments fail to credit net interest earned on advances, they are overpaid.

The provider governments are frequently less able to obtain working capital than the senior governments. The excess demands for working capital can adversely affect the credit position of the provider government, thereby adding appreciably to the cost of not only this financing but also that of other debt financing. In no small degree, this problem helped precipitate the New York City financial crisis in 1975. Provider governments are generally powerless at the administrative levels to correct this problem; however, by acting in concert with other providers they can do a great deal at the political level.

Warrants

The use of warrants was the historic manner of payment of claims on state and local government. Warrants constituted forced loans.

For the issuer, warrants offer a relatively painless manner in which to borrow money. However, most vendors quickly adjust their prices to reflect the estimated cost of discounting the warrants. Thereby, the issuer is paying interest at taxable rates. Moreover, the delays and costs involved are likely to discourage many vendors from continuing sales to the government. This lack of competition is likely to impose further costs. In adjusting prices, vendors tend to add a premium charge for the nuisance involved. Inasmuch as the vendor may not know the length of period of discount involved—especially when the contract extends over a period of time—an additional safety factor for this item is likely to be involved. Some jurisdictions maintain noninterest bearing compensating balances from other funds in the banks as a method of encouraging them to accept warrants at par, pending their redemption by the issuer.

---

[12] In history now generally forgotten, one finds that in the 1920s and 1930s the local governments in many states levied and collected their own motor fuel taxes. The function of collection was taken over by the states in the 1930s so that the revenues are now usually classified as state revenues although they are, in fact, state-collected, local taxes.

Chapter 20
ADMINISTERING OUTSTANDING DEBT

In planning for the administration of state and local government outstanding debt, each aspect needs to be identified and responsibility for it assigned. Concurrently, a system of coordination among those to whom functions are assigned should be designed and placed in operation. The administration of one type of debt may be similar in broad outlines to another; however, there are significant differences–depending on the type of debt involved, the terms of the bond contract, and the law.

In the administration of conventional, general obligation debt, the primary responsibilities are concentrated in designated governmental offices. By contrast, a number of elements of administration of enterprise, lessee, and *on behalf of* debt, assigned to agents, trustees, engineers, and others outside the government may overshadow the role of public officials. In smaller governments, the chief financial officer working in concert with the paying agent may perform most of the steps of debt administration. In larger governments, these responsibilities are spread among a number of other officers—the treasurer, a comptroller, a sinking fund commission, and others.

Establishing Control Records

Immediately prior to the delivery of bonds, a record should be created showing:

1. The number, denomination, and maturity date of each bond or note
2. The number of coupons attached, the amount of each coupon, and their due dates
3. The aggregate amount of maturities scheduled for each maturity date
4. The aggregate amount of interest due on each payment date

If the primary record is in computer storage, a copy should be prepared and stored in a separate, secure place.

Accounting for Bond Sale Proceeds

The settlement record should reflect the full amount of all cash received from the purchaser—including the good faith deposit. It should reflect any discount or other noncash items. A copy of the settlement record is furnished to the accounting officer who makes the entries in the general ledger and other appropriate accounting records.

Treatment of Premiums and Discounts

The accounting for premiums and discounts will be in accordance with the basic accounting system of the issuer. Discounts are ordinarily related to the payment of issuance costs. Premiums are used almost entirely to adjust the effective interest cost, although they constitute a present value (PV-1) amount whereas the interest is in terms of future value.

The NCGA in 1968 recommended that premiums be transferred to the debt service reserve fund. It recognized that, theoretically, discounts should be similarly handled; however, it stated:

> In actual practice, this may be impossible because of legal prohibitions or may be impractical because, during its early years at least, a Debt Service Fund will not have moneys over and above current principal and interest requirements out of which to make such a transfer. Accordingly, discounts are ordinarily imposed by debiting the *Revenues* account and crediting the *Discount on Bonds* account. . .[1]

Accrued Interest at Settlement

Accrued interest paid to the issuer at the time of settlement should be credited to the debt service fund that will be used to pay the interest on the bonds. It can be recorded as a general revenue, or, under more precise accounting concepts, it should be offset against the first interest payment that is due in order that the record of interest costs will reflect only the net amount of interest from the date of settlement to the first interest payment date.

Investment of Bond Proceeds

The procedures to be followed in the investment of bond proceeds will depend, in large degree, on the general practices followed by the issuer in its cash management program. Thus, if there is a consolidated cash account and the proceeds of the bond issue are deposited therein, the management of this cash becomes part of the overall cash management program. If the proceeds of this bond issue are consolidated only with the proceeds of other bond issues into a consolidated bond fund, the management of the cash will be developed in the light of cash flows from prior, current, and prospective bond sales within the period that cash is available from the immediate bond sale. If the proceeds of each bond issue are obliged to be kept fully segregated, a separate investment program is required for each bond fund. When general consolidated cash accounts or consolidated bond funds are maintained, good cash flow forecasting and continuous monitoring of the performance are essential. When the proceeds of each bond issue are segregated, the issuer must maintain larger account balances in cash in order to meet obligations as they fall due.

When the yield curve is sharply inclined, the short-term rates at which the bond proceeds may be invested are likely to be less than the average cost of the long-term money borrowed. In such circumstances, good cash management practice suggests that bond proceeds balances be somewhat restrained. On the other hand, when the yield curve is flat, inverted, or hunch-backed, substantial sums can be gained through arbitrage in most governments. These considerations are important, both in the timing of the sale of bonds and in the planning of the investment program. The investments (aside from being used for interfund loans) will ordinarily be kept in the highest quality credit market instruments. The term of investments must be such as to assure availability of cash as needed.

Arbitrage

The whole matter of investment of bond proceeds is much impacted by the rulings of the U.S. Treasury in respect of arbitrage. Under existing regulations, an issuer is ordinarily permitted arbitrage on bond proceeds for a period of up to three years on that portion

---

[1] National Committee on Government Accounting, *Governmental Accounting, Auditing, and Financial Reporting* (1968), pp. 43–44; Municipal Finance Officers Association, *Governmental Accounting, Auditing, and Financial Reporting* (1980), pp. 57–58.

of the proceeds that is to be used to pay capital costs. On proceeds to be used for establishment of debt service reserve funds, there is no limit as to the amount or duration of arbitrage if the amount of such funds does not exceed a reasonable amount (generally interpreted to be 15 percent of the net proceeds of sale, i.e., gross proceeds less cost of issuance). When proceeds of each bond issue are kept segregated, there are few problems in working out a response to the arbitrage regulations. If proceeds are maintained in consolidated bond accounts or general consolidated cash accounts, suitable accounting is required to assure conformity to arbitrage regulations.

Use of Interest Earned on Bond Proceeds

Interest earned on bond proceeds during the construction period may be used in a variety of ways:

1. To offset interest costs on the bond issue from which the funds are provided
2. To provide an increment to the bond proceeds, thereby increasing the amounts of money available for capital project construction costs
3. To be added to the general revenue of the fund from which debt service is to be paid in due course

Each of these has considerable logic. The use of interest earned to offset interest paid during construction seems most logical.

Management of Debt Service Reserve Funds

The investment of debt service reserve funds required under revenue bond indentures may be the responsibility of the issuer, the trustee, or the two acting jointly.

From the standpoint of the issuer, investment should meet the tests of soundness and production of the highest yield compatible with soundness. The trustee and issuer have a compatible interest in the soundness of the investment; however, the trustee may have a much greater concern with the market value of the securities than with income. The trustee knows that, in periods of rising interest costs, the market value of securities is likely to decrease. Moreover, the longer the term of such securities the greater the risks of market price decline. Thus, $1,000,000 in 25-year U.S. Treasury Bonds purchased at par to yield 7.50 percent will drop in value to $785,511 if, on the fifth anniversary, interest yields have increased to 10 percent for 20-year treasury bonds. The trustee knows that should such decline coincide with a crisis in net revenues for the issuer, the de facto security originally provided by the debt service reserve fund will have decreased by more than 20 percent—unless interim augmentation has been feasible. From the standpoint of the issuer, demands for supplementary deposits to maintain the debt service reserve funds at the original value levels may compound an already difficult operating income situation.

Had the funds been invested in short-term securities, the issuer would have received a reduced current yield but would have avoided the serious impact arising from changed market conditions. Moreover, reinvestment at the end of five years is accomplished at higher rates. It is, of course, beyond the scope of this volume to offer investment advice; however, it is necessary for both the issuer and the trustee to contemplate these kinds of potential developments. In any event, maintenance of a portion of the reserves in short-term debt is advisable to provide a hedge against temporary short-falls of revenue needed to meet current debt service requirements unless other dependable cash flow is available.

In somewhat the same vein, a decision is required during periods of falling interest rates—especially when the reserve funds are invested in long-term, high-yield securities. Thus, if $1,000,000 is invested in 25-year bonds yielding 10 percent and the yield drops to 7.50 percent at the fifth anniversary, this will produce a market value of $1,256,887. The question arises as to whether the excess value should be withdrawn from the debt service reserve fund through sale of some of the securities or retained as an additional protection for the present and a hedge against future adverse market fluctuations.

Budgeting, Appropriations, and Revenue

The funds for payment of debt service are ordinarily derived from one or more of the following sources:

1. Appropriations from general revenue
2. Taxes separately levied for debt service
3. Gross or net revenues of governmental enterprise operations
4. Lease payments under governmental lessee arrangements
5. Payments by nongovernmental obligors in *on behalf of* financing
6. Special assessments
7. Revenues provided under contract by other governments (other than governmental lessee financing)

Except in *on behalf of* financing and special assessments, moneys are likely to be paid under appropriations or resolutions of governing bodies. The annual budgets ordinarily include provision for debt service although paying officers are frequently under obligation to make payments under bond contracts with or without current appropriations. Even so, the annual executive budgets should request moneys for debt service and governing bodies should make required appropriations. In order that the budget contain proper authorizations, the principal debt officer should make comprehensive determinations of the amounts needed for principal and for interest on the bonded debt and also for interest payable on tax or revenue anticipation notes. If the payment of debt service is contingent upon an annual levy of a special tax sufficient to meet requirements, the principal debt officer should make determinations of the amounts required and the tax levy necessary to provide the moneys. Inasmuch as delinquencies in collections can upset payment schedules, provision will have to be made for such contingency through either reserve funds or excess levy sufficient to provide cash as needed.

For governmental enterprise debt, the bond contract ordinarily requires the issuer to adjust charges to assure production of gross and/or net revenues sufficient to meet the debt service costs. Studies should be made at least annually to determine any needed adjustment in rates. When changes in rates are indicated, the finance officer should recommend rate changes and present an estimate of yields under the proposed rates, together with their impact upon operations of the enterprise. Should the finance officer fail to take the initiative in a timely manner, the consulting engineer and/or trustee should initiate the actions necessary to achieve adjustments in rates and operating budgets to meet debt service costs. The issuer should act with such dispatch that an initiative by the trustee is unnecessary, inasmuch as delay to the point that the trustee must act ordinarily produces adverse investor reaction. In recommending rate changes, account must be taken of the impact of projected changes on the use of the services being provided. There are points at which no amount of increase in rates is likely to produce additional net revenue. Thus, if a parking facility fails to attract sufficient patronage, an increase in rates may result in a decrease—rather than an increase—in both gross and net revenues. Studies by the finance officer will identify these problems long before default is confronted. In such circumstances, it is incumbent upon the finance officer to make timely disclosure to investors, the public, and the underwriters of the bond issue(s) for which default is likely. Such disclosure may facilitate the working out of a plan that will both avoid default and provide a better long-term operating and/or debt service pattern.

Although some jurisdictions enjoy the flexibility associated with general consolidated cash accounts, many bond contracts (particularly enterprise revenue bond contracts) restrict such flexibility. Consistent with provisions of the bond contract, moneys in debt service funds should be appropriately invested.

In the administration of governmental lessee debt, the issuer should maintain a continual review of the performance of the governmental lessee rental payments to prevent delinquencies. Even though debt service reserve funds may be available to avoid current default, the credit of the issuer is affected by the quality of business management. For *on behalf of* debt, the governmental issuer must keep continual checks on the lessees to assure a proper flow of money in a timely manner. To this end, not only is attention required to the timely payment of amounts due but also the evolving financial condition of each underlying lessee. The issuer should be among the first to know of any difficulties likely to result in delays in payments by the lessees. Frequent financial reports to the issuer are necessary. Moreover, the issuer should make continual reviews and evaluations of the result of operation of each lessee.

Payment of Principal and Interest

Payment of principal and interest may be exclusively by the issuer's treasurer, a special governmental agency, a corporate paying agent, or the trustee. If the newer procedure of micro-encoded, post-dated checks is used, reliance is on routine banking processes. Historically, treasurers of many issuers performed the full range of paying responsibilities. With the increase in volume and tempo of the market, delegation to corporate agents or representatives (usually corporate trust departments of commercial banks) has become the prevalent pattern for most jurisdictions. The issuer is ultimately responsible for the prompt payment of both principal and interest. Even if the bond contract has delegated certain aspects of the operation to others, the issuer remains fully responsible for oversight—seeing that the designated agents or representatives perform in an appropriate manner. If the trustee or paying agent fails, the issuer should move immediately to void the trustee contract and arrange for a suitable substitute.

Definition of Responsibilities

Regardless of the extent of delegation, a single official of the issuer should be assigned overall responsibility for seeing that the obligations of the issuer are met fully and in a timely manner.

Avoidance of Temporary Default. Although the law under which the issuer operates may specify procedures for ordinary payments, the law should also stipulate that the designated official have sufficiently broad authority and responsibility to assure the timely payment of principal and interest as due. Failure to make timely payment by so much as a single day constitutes default. As has been stated earlier, the word *default* is the most awesome (some say gruesome) word in the entire vocabulary of debt management. Therefore, if a default arises out of failure to take necessary actions in a timely manner, responsibility for such failure must be firmly and undeniably fixed with a single official. Such actions discourage inadequate performance. Yet, it is to be remembered that a default is a default by the government itself—not merely by its agents. A default shakes investor confidence as do few things. The memory of investors, investment analysts, and all others is elephantine on this point.

If paying responsibilities are fully or partially delegated to agents or representatives, one of the best protections against a temporary default is a regular flow of communication between the debt officer and the paying agent. It is essential that there be personal acquaintance at several levels between the issuer's officials and their counterparts in the paying agent. Only in this manner is continual contact preserved and encouraged.

The responsible public officer should furnish a faithful performance bond in substantial amount to the issuer. Although the premium should be paid by the issuer, the official's personal responsibility should also be emphasized.

All the parties representing the issuer must understand that in the municipal bond market there is no such thing as an "informal" default. If payment is not made in a timely manner, there is *default*—by definition. There is no middle ground! Failure to make timely payment is not acceptable, except where payment is enjoined by a court of competent jurisdiction. It matters not whether the failure was due to the inability of a messenger to reach the paying agent with funds or whether the issuer is bankrupt and unable to pay. It is still *default!* Performance of the obligations of contract constitute performance. Failure constitutes *default!*

Funds for Making Payments

When either bonds or interest are payable in more than one place, the issuer makes payment to a single paying agent, with a reminder of the copaying agency arrangements in order that appropriate interbank arrangements can be made in a timely manner.

If the treasurer of the issuer is the paying agent, the payment may be made either in the form of a check or a cashier's check; however, with the advances in electronic transfers of money, the new method offers the best alternative.

Timely Remittances to Paying Agents

Moneys must be in the hands of the paying agent not later than the opening hour on the date at which payment is due. This can be accomplished through a variety of means. In order to avoid the loss of income from the temporary investment of these funds, the issuer can work out appropriate arrangements with the banks assuring availability of money at the proper place and time while simultaneously obtaining the income from temporary investments.

Remittance Advice. A remittance advice should accompany the remittance to the paying agent specifying:

1. The exact legal name of the governmental unit making the deposit and should the payment be made in connection with debt originally issued by an annexed or consolidated government, the name of the original issuer
2. The purpose for which the money is to be used, i.e., the specific bond issue; the number of the bonds to be redeemed; and/or the number, date, and dollar amount of the coupons to be paid; and the CUSIP number, if available
3. The portion of the remittance to be used to cover the fee, if any, of the paying agent
4. Instructions for crediting any interest due the issuer on temporary balances

Such remittance advice creates a record for the issuer and for the paying agent as well as defining the uses to which the moneys may be put.

Reconciliation by Paying Agent

For all bonds and for the coupons bearing identification numbers corresponding to the bonds, it is now appropriate for the paying agent to be required to maintain computerized controls and make periodic reports to the issuer as to the bonds that have been paid and those outstanding. The reports should also provide information as to the specific bonds on which coupons have been paid and the bonds on which coupons that have matured have not been paid. A number of the larger paying agents, e.g., the Bank of America, have had such systems in effect for some time and smaller paying agents should be required to maintain such records and make monthly reports to the issuer concerning the status of the account on each bond for which there has been a transaction during the month.

Annual reports should be made concerning the status of all bonds that compose a bond issue. Such reports may be in the form of hard-copy reports for smaller issuers and in the form of either hard copy or computer tapes for the large issuers. The reports should show the amounts of cash retained in each payment account and the earnings on temporary balances unless the issuer shall have surrendered these as all, or part, of the paying agent compensation. Cancelled bonds and coupons should be retained by the paying agent pending audit and cremation.

Payment of Interest on Registered Bonds

When a coupon bond (or a block of coupon bonds of the same issue and maturity) have been surrendered in exchange for a fully registered bond, the issuer agrees to forward to the owner the interest on the bonds as it becomes due. Accordingly, the treasurer or the paying agent must review the records of registered bonds sufficiently in advance of each coupon due date for principal or interest in order that the payments for interest due may be made in a timely manner. Ordinarily, checks for the interest due should be dated on the due date and mailed before the day on which such interest is due unless the owner has indicated that payment will be picked up from the office of the treasurer or the paying agent and credited directly to the issuer's account.

Payment of Principal

Payment of principal is made only upon surrender by the owner of the bond—whether in registered or bearer form.

Compensation for the Paying Agent

The paying agent is entitled to compensation for services rendered. This compensation may be in terms of a specified fee or it may consist of interest earned on remittances pending disbursement. In some cases, it consists of a combination of the two. There are delays in presentation of many matured bonds and coupons to the paying agent. Substantial moneys are likely to be in the hands of the paying agent for a few days and smaller amounts for longer periods of time. Such balances have significant economic value. Therefore, the issuer will wish to take such earnings into account in fixing the compensation arrangements with paying agents.

Cancellation of Bonds and Coupons

As soon as bonds or coupons are paid, they should be cancelled by perforation, preferably with the word "cancelled" or "paid" together with the date on which cancelled. For decades it was the custom to file cancelled bonds and coupons—frequently, in large books into which they were affixed. Files and vaults of treasurers or other debt officers were filled with such paper. Although this system may still be appropriate for issuers with small amounts of debt, it is no longer appropriate for governments with large volumes of debt. Under contemporary practice, most governments provide for the audit and destruction of cancelled bonds and coupons. A certificate of cremation provides the basis for answering almost any question as to which bonds and coupons have been paid. There is a risk that the payment was for a fraudulent bond or coupon and that, subsequently, the bona fide instruments will be presented for payment. Holding cancelled bonds and coupons for a reasonable period, e.g., one year, seems to provide a reasonable safeguard. Only in the case of securities previously reported lost should cancelled instruments be held for long periods of time.[2]

Lost or Destroyed Bonds and Coupons

Municipal bonds are sometimes lost or stolen; occasionally, they are destroyed by fire, flood, or otherwise. The customary manner of dealing with this situation is to:

1. Require the owner to file a sworn affidavit as to the loss, identifying the series of the security, and, if possible, the number as well as the CUSIP number
2. Require the owner to post a surety bond in an amount sufficient to indemnify the issuer should both the original and duplicate bond be presented for payment

Upon the filing of the affidavit and surety bond, the issuer should provide a substitute bond which is clearly marked as such. The issue of the substitute should be noted in the records of the issuer and the paying agent. If both the original and duplicate bonds are presented for payment, or if duplicate coupons are presented for payment, an investigation (and perhaps litigation) is required to ascertain which of the holders' claims should be recognized as valid.

Early Retirement of Debt

The retirement of debt in advance of its scheduled maturity occurs under these circumstances:

1. Voluntary acceleration of retirement
2. Mandatory acceleration of maturity of a portion of the debt
3. Exercise of call options for the purpose of refunding outstanding debt

The first two are treated here; the final eventuality is discussed in the succeeding chapter.

Voluntary Acceleration of Maturity

Voluntary acceleration of the maturity of bonds, except to exercise a call option to facilitiate refunding, is not generally undertaken. Although it can be used in order to reduce outstanding debt and eliminate interest thereon, under most circumstances, the money can be invested to yield a greater return than the amounts of interest payable on outstanding tax-exempt bonds. However, issuers that have funds available for investment or debt reduction should carefully explore the relative advantages and disadvantages of the two courses of potential action.

Another circumstance in which voluntary acceleration is used is the purchase of bonds to help provide support for the market—especially when the issuer is contemplating the issuance of additional bonds. On occasion, support of the market may reduce future borrowing costs in amounts to warrant this use of available funds. In the exercise of optional or mandatory procedures involving accelerated debt retirement, it is appropriate for the debt officer to consult both bond counsel and general counsel to assure that planned steps are in full accordance with the provisions of both law and contract provisions.

---

[2] A number of the commercial banks now offer special services in the processing of coupons and making reports to issuers concerning the status of payment and cancellation of coupons and bonds. The service of the Bank of America in this field has been one of the most complete and effective.

Mandatory Acceleration of Maturity

The mandatory acceleration of maturity of debt refers to acquisition and cancellation of a greater amount of bonds than those shown for redemption each year in the pro forma schedules distributed at the time of the bond sale. The moneys for accelerated maturity may come from fixed excess rentals (as in the case of governmental lessee debt and *on behalf of* debt), from excess earnings from governmental enterprise operations, or from accelerated payments by other obligors (as in the case of special assessment bonds).

As has been discussed in Chapter 13, the inclusion of bond contract provisions requiring acceleration of maturities should be very carefully evaluated before agreeing to the bond contract. If included, the debt officer and the trustee are obliged to work within that framework. If the bonds are selling in the market at yield rates below the coupon rates, the issuer ordinarily has available only the option of exercise of the call provisions relating to such mandatory acceleration because it is unlikely that the bonds can be obtained in the market at a lesser price. However, if the bonds are selling below par, the issuer and the trustee will do well to monitor the market with a view to acquisition of the bonds at prices below par. The actual pricing will be a function of the willingness of the owners to dispose of the bonds at prices below par. Generally, the bonds are traded at yields prevalent for the grade of security involved, priced to reflect the estimated *average* remaining number of years of life of the bonds. However, if the bonds are closely held, only a few bonds may be available in the market. Thereupon, the owners of large blocks of bonds may withhold them from the market in an effort to force the price toward par or to require the issuer to call the bonds at par.

Debt Administration Records

The proper administration of outstanding debt requires the maintenance of suitable accounting records and also supplementary records needed for budgetary and other aspects of financial administration. Insofar as the accounting records are concerned, the reader is directed to the current statements of generally accepted accounting principles as promulgated by the National Council on Governmental Accounting. Beyond the accounting records, there is the need for records useful in the administration of the general financial affairs of the issuer. The comments below are directed to general requirements although these impinge upon some aspects of accounting.

Records of Individual Bond Issues

A comprehensive record of each bond issue is needed, including the kinds of sale documents referred to at numerous points in the foregoing chapters. These individual bond issue records will include:

1. *A Bond Register.* The register should show the record of each bond of the issue from the time of sale until retirement. It should also show the payments of coupons relating to each bond if the number of the bond appears on the coupons. This record should be computerized and maintained by the paying agent. Copies should be regularly filed with the issuer in the form most useful to the issuer in maintaining required records and also in overseeing the work of the paying agent.

2. *Transactions with Paying Agent.* A comprehensive file of all transactions with the paying agent concerning each bond issue should be maintained, including remittance advices, reports from the paying agent, interest earned, and disposition of interest earned on deposits with the paying agent.

3. *Register of Lost Bonds and Coupons.* A register should be maintained to reflect all lost bonds and coupons that have been reported to the issuer. Information concerning

the issuance of substitute bonds and coupons and surety that may have been posted should be a part of this group of records.

4. *Registration and Reconversion of Bonds.* If the bonds are registrable either as to principal only or as to both principal and interest, a record of all such transactions is necessary. If the registration process involves the interim custody of the original bearer bonds, appropriate records of the disposition of these bearer bonds and their coupons is needed.

5. *Sinking Fund Accounts.* If bonds are issued as term bonds, with invested sinking funds, the record of the bond issue will include each official determination of the rate at which the issuer shall make deposits to the sinking fund; the acquisition, disposition, and holdings of securities by the fund; the earnings of the fund; and the status of the fund balances in the light of the approved annuity assumptions.

6. *Projections of Debt Service Costs.* For noncallable serial bonds, the maintenance of the debt service schedule by payment period is a simple record, albeit a necessary one. For bonds with mandatory redemption or other features that are likely to result in changes in the projections from time to time, a review should be made following each interest payment date to determine that the new projection of debt service costs is accurate.

Projections of debt service costs on individual issues should be compiled in ways that are meaningful for management purposes, e.g., by fund and by month or other period needed for administrative purposes.

7. *Status of Receivables.* For *on behalf of* debt, governmental lessee debt, and occasionally in other situations, there is a possibility of delinquency in payment of amounts required under the bond contracts by the users of property involved. The record of the payments due, payments made, and payments due but not paid are essential elements of the responsibility of the governmental unit charged with the administration of these kinds of debt. Frequently, the issuer is obliged under the law or bond contract to enforce collection of these moneys. In others, advice to other public officials is required in order that moneys otherwise due to the obligor are paid over to the issuer promptly.

8. *Debt Service Reserve Funds and Other Debt Offsets.* The magnitude of debt service reserve funds and other debt offsets have risen to the point that they dwarf the imagination of those dealing with outstanding debt only a relatively few years ago. Although always important for accurate accounting, the mere growth in size emphasizes the importance of the most accurate and comprehensive records of these assets.

9. *Status of Official Borrowing Capacity.* For debt that is subject to constitutional or statutory debt limits, it is necessary that suitable records be maintained for periodic calculation of the amounts of pertinent gross debt, allocable debt offsets, and net debt applicable to the debt limits.

Reporting

Perhaps the most important aspect of administration of outstanding debt—other than meeting debt service payments promptly—is comprehensive, accurate, periodic reporting. Although the annual financial report for smaller agencies is sufficient if it meets the NCGA standards, separate reports are in order for large issuers of debt. These reports should contain the balance sheet, appropriate summaries of the principal operating statements, detailed information concerning outstanding debt, debt that is authorized but unissued, statement information concerning the available borrowing capacity for general obligation debt, the schedules of debt service for each of the future years in which debt service is payable, data concerning the status of sinking funds and debt service reserve funds, and other kinds of information that will present to the investor a proper and reasonable statement of the financial affairs of the issuer.

The content of the report should take into account the known current views of the rating agencies and major investors and investment analysts as to the kinds of information most useful to them in maintaining their studies of the debt of the issuer.[3] These reports should be issued annually and, when feasible, should be certified by the independent certified public accountant. The distribution list should be comprehensive to the extent that the issuer has reason to know who may be interested in the financial affairs of the issuer as an investor. They should be made available both to the local press and also to *The Bond Buyer* and other periodicals that have a special interest in tax-free debt.

---

[3] See Municipal Finance Officers Association, *Guidelines for Use by State and Local Governments in the Preparation of Yearly Information Statements and Other Current Information.*

Chapter 21
REFUNDING AND REORGANIZATION OF DEBT

This chapter is concerned primarily with the refunding of outstanding debt; it also discusses some aspects of debt reorganization. Simply stated, refunding of debt is the substitution of one set of credit market instruments for another. Thus, one who has issued a note secured by a mortgage on his home at 15 percent interest may find that mortgage money is now available at 10 percent. If he has a right to pay off the old mortgage, he may be in a position to save considerable interest—depending on the penalty (premium) he may be obliged to pay for the privilege of accelerating payment on the previous mortgage. With such a wide spread between the 15 and 10 percent interest levels, savings of magnitude can be achieved; however, if the spread is small and the penalty is high, it may not be advantageous to proceed. The penalty in the initial contract constitutes a protection to the investor who holds a desirable mortgage (property right) and does not wish to forfeit this without compensation beyond par payment.

In municipal bond practice, this type of transaction occurs frequently. However, in conventional terms, it can occur only if the issuer has reserved a call option, i.e., a right to accelerate the maturity of the outstanding bonds. Without such a reservation of right, the bonds are noncallable and there can be no conventional refunding.

During the 1970s a new type of refunding became popular with issuers of tax-exempt bonds. It is known as *advance refunding*, i.e., refunding of outstanding bonds in advance of the date on which they can be called. As the process developed, advance refunding was applied not only to callable bonds but also to outstanding noncallable bonds in some circumstances. Thus, an entire issue of outstanding noncallable bonds could be *advance refunded*. This type of refunding is of major importance in the process of *defeasing* outstanding bond indentures. By depositing money with a trustee in amounts sufficient to pay all monies to bondholders as they become due—with or without accelerating the maturity of the debt—restrictive covenants are no longer applicable.

There are two basic purposes of refunding from the point of view of the issuer:

1. A reduction in debt service costs, through lower interest rates to enable the issuer to reduce total debt service
2. The defeasement of a current indenture

In some instances, refunding is also used as a means of reorganization of outstanding debt.

REFUNDING DEBT TO ACHIEVE INTEREST SAVINGS
—Through Conventional Use of Call Premium

Savings through refunding operations occur under one or more of these circumstances:

1. A basic repositioning of the yield curve to reflect lower interest rates
2. A reduced average remaining life of outstanding debt, enabling the issuer to take advantage of the lower average rates in the early years of most yield curves

3. An improvement in the credit position of the issuer vis-à-vis the general tax-exempt market

These refundings can be made through either conventional refunding, i.e., call and issue of substitute bonds, or through advance refunding.

Illustrative Conventional Refunding

To illustrate a conventional refunding Table 45 has been developed to show the debt service on the original bonds sold[1] under the following assumptions:

1. Par value of issue $13,520,000
2. Term 30 years
3. Debt service pattern Equal annual debt service
4. Denomination of bonds $5,000
5. Yield curve assumption Pattern B, Appendix Table A
6. Coupon rate assumption Same as yield rates
7. Call features 10th anniversary @ 103

Under these assumptions, Table 45 reflects an aggregate debt service of $30,504,373 of which $16,984,373 is interest. The interest payable in the first five years of the life of the bond issue amounts to $4,033,835 and during the first 10 years to $7,818,565, leaving interest payable after the initial call date of $9,165,808. Principal payable during the first five years is $1,055,000; during the first 10 years, $2,350,000; and, during the final 20 years, $11,170,000.

Table 46 illustrates a pattern of comparative debt service for refunding bonds under these assumptions:

1. All $11,170,000 of outstanding bonds will be called as of the 10th anniversary
2. A call premium totaling $335,100
3. Sufficient refunding bonds will be issued to redeem the outstanding bonds and to pay call premiums and issuance costs of $199,900
4. The coupon rates and the reoffering yield rates will be approximately 80 percent of the rates shown in Pattern B, Appendix Table A, for years 1–20

Under these assumptions, refunding bonds in the amount of $11,705,000 will be required. The total debt service payable on the refunding bonds will amount to $18,090,000, which will be $2,246,000 less than the $20,336,000 payable on the outstanding original bonds for the years 11–30. This savings in current dollars of $2,246,000 translates into a present value savings of $1,474,000 when each semiannual amount of savings is discounted to present value (PV-3) by using one-half the annual rates shown in Column 6, Table 46.

Should these circumstances exist on the 10th anniversary, it would be appropriate for the issuer to proceed with the refunding. On the other hand, the market may be different and the patterns of the yield curve quite different in configuration as well as in level on the scale. Thus, Table 47 has been developed to illustrate the debt service under three other sets of assumptions as to the yield curve with approximate equal annual debt service

---

[1] This illustration is deliberately chosen to represent a period of low interest rates. Although the advance refunding would also operate under Patterns A, C, and D of Appendix Table A, it is doubtful that a successful advance refunding could be achieved under Pattern E—especially for other than the very high quality municipal bonds. This arises from the fact that in advance refundings it is necessary to be able to invest the proceeds of the refunding bonds in highly acceptable securities at rates at least equal to the rates payable on the outstanding bonds. When the original bonds have been issued in a very high rate interest market, it becomes very difficult to anticipate availability of acceptable securities [usually U.S. Government Bonds] which enable one to so invest the proceeds of the refunding bonds. Absent such an opportunity, the advance refunding for purposes of achieving interest savings becomes much more difficult.

Table 45

Debt Service on $13,520,000 Equal Annual Debt Service Bonds

Year	Bonds Outstanding 1/1/—	Maturities 12/31/—	Coupon Rate	Interest	Debt Service
	(1)	(2)	(3)	(4)	(5)
1	13,520,000	195,000	3.20	821,860	1,015,860
2	13,325,000	205,000	3.50	814,620	1,019,620
3	13,120,000	210,000	3.80	807,445	1,017,445
4	12,910,000	220,000	4.10	799,465	1,019,465
5	12,690,000	225,000	4.35	790,445	1,015,445
6	12,465,000	235,000	4.60	780,658	1,015,658
7	12,230,000	245,000	4.80	769,848	1,014,848
8	11,985,000	260,000	5.00	758,088	1,018,088
9	11,725,000	270,000	5.20	745,088	1,015,088
10	11,455,000	285,000	5.25	731,048	1,016,048
11	11,170,000	300,000	5.50	716,085	1,016,085
12	10,870,000	320,000	5.60	699,585	1,019,585
13	10,550,000	335,000	5.70	681,665	1,016,665
14	10,215,000	355,000	5.80	662,570	1,017,570
15	9,860,000	375,000	5.90	641,980	1,016,980
16	9,090,000	395,000	6.00	619,855	1,014,855
17	9,090,000	420,000	6.10	596,155	1,016,155
18	8,670,000	445,000	6.20	570,535	1,015,535
19	8,225,000	475,000	6.30	542,945	1,017,945
20	7,740,000	505,000	6.35	513,020	1,018,020
21	7,245,000	535,000	6.40	480,953	1,015,953
22	6,710,000	570,000	6.45	446,713	1,016,713
23	6,140,000	610,000	6.50	409,948	1,019,948
24	5,530,000	645,000	6.55	370,298	1,015,298
25	4,885,000	690,000	6.60	328,050	1,018,050
26	4,195,000	735,000	6.65	282,510	1,017,510
27	3,460,000	785,000	6.70	233,633	1,018,633
28	2,675,000	835,000	6.75	181,088	1,016,088
29	1,840,000	890,000	6.75	124,675	1,014,675
30	950,000	950,000	6.80	64,600	1,014,600
Totals					
1– 5	65,565,000	1,055,000		4,033,835	5,088,835
1–10	125,425,000	2,350,000		7,818,565	10,168,565
11–30	139,515,000	11,170,000		9,165,808	20,335,808
1–30	264,940,000	13,520,000		16,984,373	30,504,373

on the refunding bonds and with the other assumptions being the same as those used in development of Table 46.

The coupon rate assumptions for the three alternatives illustrated in Table 47 are developed as follows:

Alternative Plan VI-B   At the same levels as those prevailing at the time of the initial sale for years 1–20

Table 46

Debt Service on $11,170,000 Callable Portion of Original Bond Issue and $11,705,000 Refunding Bond Issued to Accomplish Redemption on 10th Anniversary of Original Sale

(amounts in thousands of dollars)

Year	Plan VI: Original Bond Issue				Under Alternative Refunding Plan VI-A				Gain (Loss) from Refunding	
	Maturities	Coupon Rate	Interest	Debt Service	Maturities	Coupon Rate	Interest	Debt Service	Current Dollars	Present Value at Sale Date[1]
	(1)	(2)	(3)	(4)	(5)	(6)	(7)	(8)	(9)	(10)
11	300	5.50	716	1,016	415	2.55	502	917	99	98
12	320	5.60	700	1,020	415	2.80	491	906	114	109
13	335	5.70	682	1,017	425	3.05	479	904	112	104
14	355	5.80	663	1,018	445	3.30	466	911	106	95
15	375	5.90	642	1,017	455	3.50	452	907	110	94
16	395	6.00	620	1,018	470	3.70	436	906	109	89
17	420	6.10	596	1,016	485	3.85	418	903	113	88
18	445	6.20	571	1,016	510	4.00	400	910	106	78
19	475	6.30	543	1,018	525	4.15	379	904	114	80
20	505	6.35	513	1,018	545	4.20	358	903	115	77
21	535	6.40	481	1,016	575	4.40	335	910	106	67
22	570	6.45	447	1,017	595	4.50	309	904	112	67
23	610	6.50	410	1,020	620	4.55	283	903	117	66
24	645	6.55	370	1,015	650	4.65	254	904	111	59
25	690	6.60	328	1,018	675	4.70	224	899	119	60
26	735	6.65	283	1,018	710	4.80	192	902	115	54
27	785	6.70	234	1,019	745	4.90	158	913	115	51
28	835	6.75	181	1,016	775	4.95	122	893	119	50
29	890	6.75	125	1,018	820	5.00	84	904	111	44
30	950	6.80	65	1,015	850	5.05	43	893	122	46
Totals 11–30	11,170		9,166	20,336	11,705		6,385	18,090	2,246	1,474

[1] The calculation of present value (PV-3) of the gain (loss) from refunding is done on each semiannual amount of debt service at one-half the coupon rate shown in Column 6. For the final year, the refunding bonds have a life of 20 years. The debt service payable in the 39th and 40th periods and the present value of each is as follows:

Semiannual Period for Refunded Bonds	Semiannual Discount Rate		Debt Service			Present Value
			Principal	Interest	Total	
39	2.50	Original bonds	—	33,300	33,300	
		Refunding bonds	—	21,250	21,250	
		Gain			12,050	4,600
40	2.50	Original bonds	950,000	33,300	981,300	
		Refunding bonds	850,000	21,250	871,250	
					110,050	40,986
Total for Year 20 of Refunding Bonds					122,100	45,586

Table 47

Debt Service on $11,705,000 in Refunding Bonds Under Alternative Coupon and Yield Assumptions

(amounts in thousands of dollars)

Year	Alternative Plan VI-B			Alternative Plan VI-C			Alternative Plan VI-D		
	Maturities	Coupon Rate	Debt Service	Maturities	Coupon Rate	Debt Service	Maturities	Coupon Rate	Debt Service
	(1)	(2)	(3)	(4)	(5)	(6)	(7)	(8)	(9)
11	365	3.20	999	350	4.85	978	285	6.30	1,151
12	380	3.50	1,002	370	4.90	982	305	6.45	1,153
13	390	3.80	999	385	4.95	979	320	6.55	1,148
14	405	4.10	999	400	5.00	975	345	6.65	1,152
15	420	4.35	998	425	5.05	980	365	6.80	1,150
16	440	4.60	999	440	5.10	973	390	6.90	1,150
17	460	4.80	999	465	5.15	976	420	7.00	1,153
18	480	5.00	997	490	5.20	977	445	7.15	1,148
19	510	5.20	1,003	515	5.20	976	480	7.25	1,152
20	535	5.25	1,002	545	5.25	980	515	7.30	1,152
21	560	5.50	999	570	5.30	976	550	7.35	1,149
22	590	5.60	998	600	5.35	975	595	7.40	1,154
23	630	5.70	1,005	635	5.40	979	640	7.50	1,155
24	660	5.80	999	665	5.45	974	685	7.55	1,152
25	700	5.90	1,000	705	5.50	978	740	7.60	1,155
26	740	6.00	999	745	5.55	979	795	7.65	1,154
27	785	6.10	1,000	785	5.60	978	855	7.70	1,153
28	830	6.20	997	825	5.65	974	920	7.75	1,152
29	885	6.30	1,000	870	5.70	972	990	7.80	1,151
30	940	6.35	1,000	920	5.75	973	1,065	7.85	1,149
Total	11,705		19,994	11,705		19,356	11,705		23,032

Alternative Plan VI-C   At approximately 85 percent of the levels shown in Pattern A, Appendix Table A, for years 1–20

Alternative Plan VI-D   At approximately 130 percent of the levels shown in Pattern A, Appendix Table A, for years 1–20

On the basis of these, the comparative debt service on the original bonds and the refundings for years 11–30 under the different plans may be summarized as follows:

(in thousands of dollars)			
	Under Original Bond Issue	Under Refunding Plan	Gain (Loss)
Alternative Plan VI-A	20,336	18,090	2,246
Alternative Plan VI-B	20,336	19,994	341
Alternative Plan VI-C	20,336	19,536	799
Alternative Plan VI-D	20,336	23,032	(2,696)

If an issuer found conditions outlined under VI-A existed, it would be advisable to proceed with the refunding inasmuch as a current dollar savings of $2,246,000 could be obtained and this reflected a present value saving of $1,474,000.

On the other hand, the issuer would exercise a conventional refunding under Plan VI-D only if obliged to use it in order to defease one or more obnoxious contract provisions. Ordinarily an issuer would not refund under conditions illustrated under VI-B and VI-C inasmuch as the reduction in costs may not be deemed sufficient to warrant the undertaking.

The Importance of Present Value Determinations

Most of the illustrations in this chapter are based on a level annual debt service for both the original bonds and the refunding bonds. Before leaving the subject of refunding, however, it is necessary to emphasize the importance of reducing all values to a present value being sure to use the same discount rates for this work. From time to time, one encounters a refunding in which there is a gain in current dollars but a substantial loss in terms of present values. Table 48 has been developed to illustrate the point. Although one rarely encounters a case quite as blatant as the illustration, it does occasionally occur when a dealer finds an opportunity to develop a comfortable gross profit on a transaction that appears to the unsophisticated to be a useful step but, in fact, constitutes a major loss to the issuer.

In Table 48, the life of the refunding bonds has been reduced from that covering a period of 20 years to a 15-year period. The gross debt service charges for the outstanding bonds amount to $20,336,810. By reducing the life of the bonds sharply, it appears that the issuer will be able to reduce overall debt service costs to $19,657,585, producing an indicated saving of $679,225. In terms of current dollars, this is true as is shown in Column 7 of the table. On the other hand, it is noted that, during the first 15 years, the issuer would be obliged to pay debt service charges ranging from $289,000 to $305,000 greater than those on the outstanding bonds. All of the indicated current dollar gain is in the final five years. When these losses and gains are reduced to present value for each semiannual period through discounting at one-half the coupon rates shown in Column 5, the issuer will have sustained a $1,315,000 present value loss through the transaction.

Table 48

Present Value Determinations in Refunding Operations

Year	Outstanding Bonds			Refunding Bonds			Gain or (Loss) (3) − (6)	
	Maturities	Coupon Rate	Debt Service	Maturities	Coupon Rate	Debt Service	Current Dollars	Present Value Dollars[1]
	(1)	(2)	(3)	(4)	(5)	(6)	(7)	(8)
11	300,000	5.50	1,016,085	470,000	6.30	1,308,652	(292,568)	(276,786)
12	320,000	5.60	1,019,585	505,000	6.15	1,314,043	(294,450)	(260,903)
13	335,000	5.70	1,016,665	530,000	6.55	1,306,470	(289,805)	(240,135)
14	355,000	5.80	1,017,570	570,000	6.65	1,311,755	(294,185)	(227,466)
15	375,000	5.90	1,016,980	600,000	6.80	1,303,850	(286,870)	(206,096)
16	395,000	6.00	1,014,855	645,000	6.90	1,308,050	(293,195)	(195,656)
17	420,000	6.10	1,016,155	695,000	7.00	1,313,545	(297,390)	(183,964)
18	445,000	6.20	1,015,535	750,000	7.15	1,319,895	(304,360)	(173,497)
19	475,000	6.30	1,017,945	790,000	7.25	1,316,270	(288,325)	(151,632)
20	505,000	6.35	1,018,020	850,000	7.30	1,308,975	(290,975)	(141,588)
21	535,000	6.40	1,015,953	910,000	7.35	1,306,945	(290,993)	(130,841)
22	570,000	6.45	1,016,713	980,000	7.40	1,310,160	(293,348)	(121,755)
23	610,000	6.50	1,020,948	1,055,000	7.50	1,315,650	(292,893)	(111,253)
24	645,000	6.55	1,015,298	1,130,000	7.55	1,308,415	(293,118)	(102,576)
25	690,000	6.60	1,018,050	1,225,000	7.60	1,318,110	(300,050)	(96,552)
26	735,000	6.65	1,017,510	—	7.65	—	1,017,510	307,735
27	785,000	6.70	1,018,633	—	7.70	—	1,018,633	283,211
28	835,000	6.75	1,016,088	—	7.75	—	1,016,038	259,423
29	890,000	6.75	1,014,675	—	7.80	—	1,014,675	237,671
30	950,000	6.80	1,014,600	—	7.85	—	1,014,600	217,789
Total	11,170,000		20,336,810	11,705,000		19,657,585	679,225	(1,314,871)

[1] Present values computed by discounting actual semiannual amounts at one-half the annual rates shown in Column 5.

Effects of Debt Service Reserve Funds

Most bond issues, other than general obligation bonds, are now sold on the basis of creation of a debt service reserve fund, either from the proceeds of the bonds at the time of sale or from the excess revenues in the early years of the operation of the debt service reserve fund. In developing a plan for refunding such bonds, it is necessary to take fully into account the effect which the liquidation of the existing debt service reserve fund and the creation of the new fund will have on the gain or loss arising from the transaction. Inasmuch as such calculations depend on a number of factors that vary from time to time, no calculations are presented here; however, the general factors to be taken into account are: (1) The relative size of the debt service reserve funds, (2) the rates at which the old fund is invested and at which the new funds are to be invested, and (3) the provisions of the debt contract concerning the current use of any interest earned by the fund.

REFUNDING TO ACHIEVE INTEREST SAVINGS
—Through Advance Refunding

The use of the advance refunding technique enables the issuer to sell refunding bonds and execute a refunding today even though the refunding does not become fully operative until a future date. The net proceeds of the refunding issue, together with earnings thereon, must be at least sufficient to meet debt service on the outstanding bonds through the first call date and any call premium involved (a net refunding), or the interest (all or a major portion) on the refunding bonds. The amount invested must be sufficient to pay the principal of and interest on the refunded bonds (a gross refunding).

The 1970s brought a huge expansion in the practice of issuing advance refunding bonds. At the outset of the decade, large fortunes were made by some well-situated persons through inappropriate use of advance refunding operations. Under 1968 legislation the U.S. Treasury gradually imposed various *arbitrage* regulations that had the effect of reducing these practices as well as others perceived by the Treasury to be abuses. The arbitrage regulations are complicated and lengthy; they regulate advance refunding by restricting the yield which may be obtained on the investment of the monies deposited in escrow with the trustee for the refunded bonds. In a sense, the regulations have gone beyond the elimination of abuses and have redefined the concept of interest to exclude the issuance costs in certain types of advance refunding operations—a cost heretofore always recognized as an element of interest. One objective has been to preclude the use of income from taxable securities in which bond proceeds are invested to pay the costs of the refunding. Essentially, the Treasury limits the yield rates on such funds to those paid by the issuer on refunding bonds and also restricts any such investments to the net proceeds of the refunding issue. The effect has been to require the issuer to absorb issuance costs of the refunding bonds, except to the extent that portions of this may be offset by excess earnings on any debt service reserve funds created from the proceeds of refunding bond issues.

For the issuer, the effect of advance refunding can be similar to the effect of a refunding executed at the time of redemption of the outstanding bonds under the exercise of a call option. It can also be somewhat different. Even when substantially the same in terms of present value (PV-1) considerations, the differentials in the timing of the operations may produce illusions that are quite different from the realities involved. (See especially the discussion below relating to Table 49.) Advance refunding for the purpose of achieving interest savings offers a tool by which the issuer can take advantage of a beneficial prevailing market. Although it is possible that a future market will be as good (or even better), the issuer may conclude that, all factors considered, it is appropriate to proceed with the advance refunding now in order to assure the reduced costs implicit in it, rather than risk higher interest rates at the call date which preclude profitable refunding.

Table 49

Debt Service Requirements in Respect of $11,170,000 Original Bonds Callable at 10th Anniversary and $12,400,000 in Refunding Bonds Required to Accomplish Advance Refunding on 5th Anniversary

(amounts in thousands of dollars)

Year	Original Bond Issue[1]				Refunding Bond Issue[1]				Gain (Loss) from Refunding	
	Maturities	Coupon Rate	Interest	Debt Service	Maturities	Coupon Rate	Interest	Debt Service	Current Dollars	Present Value at Sale Date[2]
	(1)	(2)	(3)	(4)	(5)	(6)	(7)	(8)	(9)	(10)
6	—	—	716	716	—	2.55	593	593	123	120
7	—	—	716	716	—	2.80	593	593	123	117
8	—	—	716	716	—	3.05	593	593	123	113
9	—	—	716	716	—	3.30	593	593	123	109
10	—	—	716	716	—	3.50	593	593	123	104
11	300	5.50	716	1,016	395	3.70	593	988	28	23
12	320	5.60	700	1,020	415	3.85	579	994	26	21
13	335	5.70	682	1,017	425	4.00	563	988	29	22
14	355	5.80	663	1,018	445	4.15	546	991	27	19
15	375	5.90	642	1,017	465	4.20	527	992	25	17
16	395	6.00	620	1,015	485	4.40	508	993	22	14
17	420	6.10	596	1,016	510	4.50	486	996	20	12
18	445	6.20	571	1,016	530	4.55	464	994	22	13
19	475	6.30	543	1,018	550	4.65	439	989	29	16
20	505	6.35	513	1,018	575	4.70	414	989	29	15
21	535	6.40	481	1,016	605	4.80	387	992	24	12
22	570	6.45	447	1,017	635	4.90	358	993	24	11
23	610	6.50	410	1,020	670	4.95	327	997	23	10
24	645	6.55	370	1,015	700	5.00	293	993	22	9
25	690	6.60	328	1,018	730	5.00	258	988	30	11
26	735	6.65	283	1,018	770	5.10	222	992	26	9
27	785	6.70	234	1,019	815	5.15	183	998	21	7
28	835	6.75	181	1,016	850	5.20	141	991	25	8
29	890	6.75	125	1,015	890	5.25	97	987	28	8
30	950	6.80	65	1,015	940	5.30	50	990	25	7
Totals 6–30	11,170		12,747	23,917	12,400		10,401	22,801	1,116	827

[1] Original maturities for years 6 through 10 remain outstanding. Debt service relating to those bonds is omitted from table.

[2] Present value (PV-3) is computed on basis of each semiannual amount of net debt service discounted at a rate equal to one-half that shown in Column 6.

Although the focus here is on the issuer, it is appropriate to note that, if the investments required or used in advance refunding are United States Government obligations, the prerefunded bonds usually trade at the level of triple-A rated bonds. As a result, the price of outstanding medium- and lower-grade serial bonds may increase dramatically when prerefunded. This can also occur in respect to term bonds; however, in some situations, refunding produces other effects explained later in this chapter.

Illustrative Advance Refundings to Achieve Interest Savings

To illustrate the results of advance refunding and to compare these with the results of refunding as of the first call date, several tables are presented. The first of these is Table 49 which provides for an advance refunding as of the 5th anniversary of the $11,-170,000 of bonds shown in Table 45 as maturing after the 10th anniversary of the initial issue. In the development of Table 49, these basic assumptions are applied:

1. The bonds maturing in the 11th–30th years of the original schedule are refunded as of the 5th anniversary
2. The present value (PV-1) of the call premium and the issuance cost on the refunding bonds are paid from the proceeds of the refunding bond issue
3. The coupon rates and yield rates are identical and roughly approximate 80 percent of the original coupon/yield rate for bonds of similar life
4. The refunding bonds are issued on the basis of approximately equal annual debt service for the 11th–30th years. For the 6th–10th years, the original bonds maturing in those years and interest thereon continue as originally issued. The interest on $11,170,000 of advance refunded bonds of $716,000 is recorded as the debt service for years 6–10 and the interest on the refunding bonds is recorded as costs during the same years at $593,000
5. The gain for each year under the refunding plan is recorded in current dollars in Column 9 and in present value (PV-3) dollars in Column 10

The amounts of refunding bonds required to be issued will be $12,400,000, determined in the following manner:

	Value in Current Dollars	Present Value (PV-1) @ Semiannual Rate of 2.445635 Percent*
Par value of bonds	$11,170,000	$ 8,772,403
Value of Interest in 6th–10th year on outstanding bonds	3,580,425	3,142,432
Call premiums	335,100	263,172
Issuance costs	221,993	221,993
Total	$15,307,518	$12,400,000

* The discount rate will be determined by making an assumption as to a TIC rate, working through the details of debt service on the new bonds on a trial basis. This will be repeated until a semiannual TIC rate is determined that will satisfy the requirements of the search for a par value of the new bond issue. At the end, the issuance cost amount will have to be slightly overstated with the remainder treated as a premium.

The proceeds of the sale allocated to the redemption of the bonds, the payment of the call premium, and payment of the interest on the outstanding bonds will be invested at a rate approximating the semiannual present value discount rate. These proceeds will equal the amount required on the various interim interest payment dates and the refunding date.

The details of the debt service on the original bonds are shown in Columns 1–4 of Table 49 and of the advance refunding in Columns 5–8. In terms of overall debt service, the advance refunding produces a gain of $1,116,000 in current dollars. Reduced to present value (PV-3) as of the 5th anniversary, the amount becomes $827,000. The values in Table 46 and Table 49 can be appropriately compared only by bringing them into a present value relationship as of a given date, e.g., the 5th anniversary, which shows:

	Table 46	Table 49	Excess of Table 46 over Table 49
Present value of savings as of 5th anniversary for Table 46 (PV-1 from 10th to 5th anniversaries)	$1,239,000*		
Present value (PV-3) of savings for Table 49 @ 5th anniversary		$827,000	
Differential of savings as of 5th anniversary			$412,000

* Based upon a present value savings (PV-3) at 10th anniversary for Table 46 of $1,474,000.

Under these circumstances, the issuer would be expected to obtain a greater gain at the 10th anniversary; however, inasmuch as none can foretell what rates the market may bring at that time, an advance refunding at the 5th anniversary would be quite defensible in light of the $827,000 present value gain. If the market continued to prevail at the 10th anniversary, there would probably be no reason to seek a further refunding in light of the call premiums and issuance costs that would be attendant on such further refunding activity.

Gain through Market Operations

For certain types of bonds, especially for low-coupon outstanding bonds, it may be feasible to execute refunding plans that enable the issuer to engage advantageously in the open market or tender purchases of bonds at a financial advantage to the issuer. This type of operation is especially appropriate where the issuer is required by the bond contract to liquidate outstanding bonds under a stipulated schedule, coupled with a preexisting practice of acceleration of redemption of bonds (in addition to the required redemption) by using all, or part, of the excess revenues.

As initially executed, this type of refunding involves the likelihood of a net cost approximating the issuance costs on the refunding bonds. However, it may be that through a stabilization of the amounts of bonds to be matured each year under the refunding the prices of the bonds will decrease to a point that the issuer can develop a considerable saving over the remaining life of the refunded bonds. The present value (PV-1) of such savings may be sufficient fully to offset the issuance costs on the refunding bonds and to provide a net savings to the issuer.

PRELIMINARY FEASIBILITY TEST

Before engaging in extensive work concerning the feasibility of refunding outstanding bonds, it is desirable to apply a relatively simple test of feasibility. This can be done by determining the amounts of principal supportable through capitalization of the debt service on the outstanding debt at prevailing yield rates likely to be applied to refunding bonds under consideration. The general method has been described in an earlier chapter.[2] The steps involved in such a preliminary test are those involved in determining PV-2, i.e.,

1. Determine the amount of debt service payable in each year in relation to the outstanding bonds
2. Select a par reoffering yield curve at which it is believed that refunding bonds could be marketed if sold at the time of the preparation of this estimate
3. Determine the amount of principal supportable by the debt service in (1) using the reoffering yield curve in (2)
4. Determine the issuance cost for new bonds and the present value of call premiums
5. Determine net value by subtracting (4) from (3)

A comparison of the net value (5) with the par value of the outstanding debt will show the approximate amount of savings (or increased costs) likely to arise from the refunding operation. Based on this information, a quick preliminary determination can be made as to whether there appears to be sufficient flexibility to warrant a more comprehensive examination of the refunding or whether the margin is so low (or even negative) as to show that this is not a good circumstance in which to proceed further.

To illustrate this type of preliminary examination, Table 50 has been prepared. The debt service on the outstanding bonds has been chosen as that shown in more detail in Table 45 (Col. 5). In Table 50, the results of an examination under four different sets of assumptions are shown. Under all of the four, it is assumed that the examination is being made immediately in advance of the 10th anniversary of the bonds shown in Table 45. The four different market circumstances under which examination is presumed to have been made are:

Pattern A-1   Market is at about 80 percent of yield curve for Pattern B, Appendix Table A, years 1–20. (Same as shown in Table 46, Columns 5–8.)

Pattern B   Market is at the identical pattern that prevailed when the bonds were initially issued under Pattern B, Appendix Table A, years 1-20.

Pattern C-1   Market is at about 95 percent of yield curve for Pattern A, Appendix Table A, years 1–20.

Pattern A-1a   Market is irregularly higher than that shown in Pattern A, Appendix Table A, years 1–20—generally, in the range of 22 to 30 percent higher.

The outcome of this testing shows indicated savings under conditions assumed: for Pattern A-1 of about $1,439,000 on $11,170,000 in outstanding bonds (almost 13 percent); for Pattern B, $201,000 (1.8 percent); and for Pattern A-1a, a loss of $1,366,000 (12.2 percent). Under conditions illustrated as Pattern C-1, the savings would be about $480,000 or 4.3 percent. In these circumstances, an issuer would pass up further exploration under Pattern A-1a unless obliged to refund in order to defease indenture. The low amount of savings under Pattern B would indicate a wait until hopefully better times; Pattern C-1 is somewhat marginal, although perhaps appropriate for fuller exploration. Pattern A-1 is clearly so much to the advantage of the issuer that full speed ahead in refunding is doubtless indicated. This type of analysis is essential as a preliminary step in consideration of refundability of bonds.

---

[2] The general method has been discussed in Chapter 12 and further information is presented in Appendix B in the discussion of PV-2.

Table 50

Capitalization of Debt Service on Outstanding Bonds under Alternative Yield Curves to Test Refunding Feasibility

(amounts in thousands of dollars)

Year	Debt Service on Outstanding Bonds[1]	Debt Supportable under Coupon Pattern A-1		Debt Supportable under Coupon Pattern B		Debt Supportable under Coupon Pattern C-1		Debt Supportable under Coupon Pattern A-1a	
		Coupon Rate	Principal Supportable	Coupon Rate	Principal Supportable	Coupon Rate	Principal Supportable	Coupon Rate	Principal Supportable
(1)	(1)	(2)	(3)	(4)	(5)	(6)	(7)	(8)	(9)
11	1,016	2.55	452	3.20	371	4.85	362	6.30	251
12	1,020	2.80	467	3.50	386	4.90	383	6.45	270
13	1,017	3.05	478	3.80	397	4.95	399	6.55	285
14	1,018	3.30	493	4.10	413	5.00	419	6.65	305
15	1,017	3.50	509	4.35	429	5.05	440	6.80	324
16	1,015	3.70	524	4.60	446	5.10	460	6.90	344
17	1,016	3.85	545	4.80	468	5.15	484	7.00	369
18	1,016	4.00	565	5.00	490	5.20	509	7.15	394
19	1,018	4.15	590	5.20	517	5.20	538	7.25	425
20	1,018	4.20	615	5.25	543	5.25	566	7.30	456
21	1,016	4.40	639	5.50	570	5.30	593	7.35	487
22	1,017	4.50	668	5.60	602	5.35	625	7.40	524
23	1,020	4.55	700	5.70	639	5.40	662	7.50	566
24	1,015	4.65	728	5.80	671	5.45	693	7.55	603
25	1,018	4.70	765	5.90	712	5.50	734	7.60	652
26	1,018	4.80	800	6.00	754	5.55	774	7.65	701
27	1,019	4.90	840	6.10	800	5.60	817	7.70	756
28	1,016	4.95	878	6.20	846	5.65	861	7.75	811
29	1,015	5.00	920	6.30	898	5.70	908	7.80	874
30	1,015	5.05	966	6.35	954	5.75	959	7.85	942
Total Principal Supportable (PV-2)			13,144		11,906		12,185		10,339
Bonds Redeemed			11,170		11,170		11,170		11,170
Call Premiums			335		335		335		335
Issuance Costs on Refunding Bonds			200		200		200		200
			11,705		11,705		11,705		11,705
Indicated Savings			1,439		201		480		(1,366)

[1] Amounts shown are the rounded amounts shown in Table 45, Column 5. Actual amounts are capitalized (PV-2) and rounded totals shown in Columns (3), (5), (7), and (9).

REFUNDING TO DEFEASE LIEN

The foregoing discussion concerns refunding directed to reduction of overall debt service costs. There may be, however, terms in the indenture under which revenue bonds are issued which prove unsatisfactory to the issuer. These are of two general types: (1) Administrative requirements, e.g., relationships with the trustee or consulting engineer; or (2) substantive restraints, e.g., coverage requirements prerequisite to issuance of parity bonds. Indentures frequently contain protections against the dilution of the security pledged for outstanding bonds. These may be outright prohibitions against additional parity bonds or they may be stated in terms of a prospective and retrospective coverage test. Assume that the bonds issued under Table 45 contained a five-year retrospective and prospective coverage test of 1.40 (or 140 as stated in the trade). This would mean that the issuer could not increase debt service beyond the point at which the average combined debt service for the original and supplemental bonds could exceed 71.4 percent of the average net revenues available for debt service during the past five years (1 ÷ 1.4). Therefore, if the net revenues during the past five years averaged $2,500,000, the debt service could not exceed $1,785,000. Inasmuch as the debt service on the outstanding bonds is averaging about $1,118,000, the debt service on the new bonds could not exceed $667,000.

If the market were such that the issuer could sell long-term bonds with an average interest rate of about 4.90 percent, a $10,000,000 new loan (including issuance costs) would result in a debt service cost of about $643,000, which would just fit within the limitation of $667,000. On the other hand, if the need for new capital came at a time when the interest costs were significantly higher, e.g., 7.75 percent, the annual debt service cost on a $10 million new loan would be $867,000, which would forestall the loan under the existing indenture. At that point, the issuer would be obliged either to drop his new capital loan to $7,690,000 or to defease the existing indenture.

If the decision were to issue refunding bonds and if the market required yield/coupon rates shown in Column 6 of Table 51, the issuer would be obliged to increase the annual debt service costs relating to the refunding bonds by an aggregate current dollar amount of $2,512,000, or a present value (PV-3) cost of $1,100,000. If the debt service costs on the new bonds amounted to $867,000 and on the refunding bonds to $1,117,000, the total of $1,984,000 would have a retrospective coverage of 1.26. This, together with prospective earnings from the additional capital facilities, would make the refunding and new capital issues quite viable. If, on the other hand, it were important for other reasons to defease the indenture and if the market permitted refunding under Pattern A-1 shown in Columns 2–4 of Table 51, a net interest savings of $380,000 with a present value of $218,000 could simultaneously be achieved.

BONDS NOT TO BE REFUNDED

In the previous illustration concerning the exercise of the call option for the purpose of saving interest charges, it has—for purposes of simplicity—been assumed in each situation that all of the outstanding bonds subject to call would be called and refunded. This assumption is not necessarily appropriate in all circumstances. As a matter of fact, in each bond issue in which the bonds are callable in inverse order, an examination should be made of the early maturities in order to determine which maturities can be advantageously refunded and which should be allowed to remain outstanding. (Of course, if the objective is defeasement of a contract provision, all outstanding bonds must be refunded or prerefunded in order to overcome the obnoxious restriction.)

This examination consists of determining the amounts of debt service payable on the outstanding bonds of a given maturity vs. the amount of debt service payable in respect to that maturity should the bonds be refunded. In other words, looked at on a maturity-

Table 51

Debt Service on Advance Refunding Bonds to Defease Bond Contract

Year	Debt Service: Original Bonds	Under Coupon Pattern A-1			Under Coupon Pattern A-1a		
		Maturities	Coupon/ Yield Rates[1]	Debt Service	Maturities	Coupon/ Yield Rates[1]	Debt Service
	(1)	(2)	(3)	(4)	(5)	(6)	(7)
6	1,015,658	330,000	2.55	959,408	190,000	6.30	1,117,000
7	1,014,848	340,000	2.80	960,992	200,000	6.45	1,115,800
8	1,018,088	350,000	3.05	961,473	215,000	6.55	1,117,900
9	1,015,088	360,000	3.30	960,797	230,000	6.65	1,118,817
10	1,016,048	375,000	3.50	963,918	245,000	6.80	1,118,523
11	1,016,085	385,000	3.70	960,792	260,000	6.90	1,116,862
12	1,019,585	400,000	3.85	961,548	275,000	7.00	1,113,923
13	1,016,665	415,000	4.00	961,148	295,000	7.15	1,114,725
14	1,017,570	430,000	4.15	959,547	320,000	7.25	1,118,580
15	1,016,980	450,000	4.20	961,703	340,000	7.30	1,115,380
16	1,014,855	470,000	4.40	962,802	365,000	7.35	1,115,560
17	1,016,155	490,000	4.50	962,123	395,000	7.40	1,118,733
18	1,015,535	510,000	4.55	960,072	425,000	7.50	1,119,502
19	1,017,045	535,000	4.65	961,868	455,000	7.55	1,117,628
20	1,018,020	560,000	4.70	961,990	490,000	7.60	1,118,275
21	1,015,953	585,000	4.80	960,670	525,000	7.65	1,116,035
22	1,016,713	615,000	4.90	962,590	565,000	7.70	1,115,872
23	1,020,948	645,000	4.95	962,455	610,000	7.75	1,117,368
24	1,015,298	675,000	5.05	960,528	655,000	7.80	1,115,092
25	1,018,050	710,000	5.10	961,440	705,000	7.85	1,114,003
26	1,017,510	745,000	5.20	960,230	765,000	7.85	1,118,660
27	1,018,633	785,000	5.15	962,235	825,000	7.90	1,118,607
28	1,016,088	825,000	5.20	961,808	890,000	7.90	1,118,433
29	1,014,675	865,000	5.25	958,007	960,000	7.90	1,118,122
30	1,014,600	915,000	5.30	963,495	1,035,000	7.95	1,117,283
Total	25,415,538	13,765,000		24,034,537	12,235,000		27,927,400

Reduction in Interest Cost in Relation to Original Bonds	381,001	
Reduction in Interest Cost in Relation to Original Bonds		(2,511,862)
Approximate Present Value Based on Coupon/Yield Rates (PV-3)	218,000	(1,100,000)

[1] Coupon/Yield Rates are from Table 50, Columns 2 and 8.

by-maturity basis, one is dealing with the present value (PV-1) of the debt service on an outstanding bond plus the debt service on the refunding bond, provided that refunding bond includes its pro rata share of the call premium and the issuance cost of the refunding bonds. Table 52 illustrates the effect of potential refunding upon maturities originally scheduled for Years 11, 12, and 13 of bonds issued under Pattern B of Appendix Table A.

For Year-11, in current value dollars, if the bond is allowed to remain outstanding, the cost will be $1,055.00 (Line 5) compared to $1,076.08 (Line 13). In current dollars, this would, therefore, represent a loss of $21.08 per $1,000 par value of outstanding Year-11 bonds ($1,055.00 − $1,076.08). In present value terms (PV-1) at one-half of the rate

Notes to Table 51

In determination of the amount of the advance refunding bond issue, it is necessary first to make an assumption as to the TIC level at which the new bonds will be sold. One-half of this annual rate is then used to reduce to present value those elements of debt service or redemption of outstanding bonds which occur after the refunding date. The calculations in Columns 2–7 of Table 51 are based on the following calculations.

	Current Dollars	Present Value Dollars	
		A-1	A-1a
Semiannual discount rate (percent)		2.4213	3.8672
Principal payable 11–30 maturities	11,170,000	8,793,311	7,655,020
Call premium	335,100	263,799	229,650
Interest on 11–30 maturities in 6th–10th years	3,580,425	3,157,812	2,925,706
Debt service on bonds maturing in 6th–10th years	1,499,302	1,303,960	1,205,964
Subtotal	16,584,827	13,518,882	12,016,340
Totals for Columns 2–4 Allowance for issuance cost on refunding bonds	246,118	246,118	
Total	16,830,945	13,765,000	
Totals for Columns 5–7 Allowance for issuance cost of refunding bonds	218,660		218,660
	16,803,487		12,235,000

Table 52

Testing for Profitability of Refunding of Individual Maturities

Line	Year-11	Year-12	Year-13
Amounts in Current Value Dollars Original Bonds			
1 Par value	1,000.00	1,000.00	1,000.00
2 Coupon rate	5.50	5.60	5.70
3 Years to maturity	1	2	3
4 Interest payable [1] × [2] × [3]	55.00	112.00	176.00
5 Total payable [1] + [4]	1,055.00	1,112.00	1,176.00
Refunding Bonds Par value			
6 Called bond	1,000.00	1,000.00	1,000.00
7 Call premium	30.00	30.00	30.00
8 Issuance costs	19.32	19.32	19.32
9 Subtotal	1,049.32	1,049.32	1,049.32
10 Coupon rate	2.55	2.80	3.05
11 Years to maturity	1	2	3
12 Interest payable [9] × [10] × [11]	26.76	58.76	96.01
13 Total payable [9] + [12]	1,076.08	1,108.08	1,145.33
Amounts in Present Value Dollars (at one-half rates on Line 10)			
14 Original bonds	1,028.75	1,054.09	1,075.42
15 Refunding bonds	1,049.32	1,049.32	1,049.32
16 Gain (Loss)	(20.57)	4.77	26.10

shown in Table 52, Line 10, the loss would amount to $20.57. Under these circumstances, the issuer should not refund the Year-11 maturities. On the other hand, under the circumstances assumed here, it would be marginally profitable to refund Year-12 maturities and distinctly profitable to refund the Year-13 maturities.

REORGANIZATION OF DEBT

Reorganization of the debt of a state or local government may occur on a voluntary basis; reorganization of the debt of a local government may also occur on an involuntary basis under default due to bankruptcy. Voluntary reorganization is carried out solely under state legal processes; involuntary reorganization may be under state auspices or under federal municipal bankruptcy laws, with the consent of the state government involved.

Voluntary Reorganization

Almost every state or local government refunding operation constitutes a reorganization of debt in the sense that there is some change in the patterns of principal and interest payments; however, the term is ordinarily reserved to circumstances in which the objective is to provide for *major* changes in debt service arrangements. These usually occur in one of two situations: (1) a requirement for extension of the term of outstanding debt (especially enterprise debt) in order to accomodate the issuance of additional bonds under favorable coverage indications, or (2) a much less frequently used pattern of readjusting outstanding debt service for the purpose of providing a more equitable distribution of the amortization of debt outstanding on a physical plant to be used over a long period of time.

Extension to Provide for Debt Service Stabilization. From time to time, governmental agencies find themselves with very large debt service costs during the next several years, but with relatively little in the way of capital requirements of a major character in the near future. This has been especially true of many of the major central city school districts during recent years. They had constructed large numbers of new buildings to accomodate bulging enrollments during the 1950s and 1960s; but, by the end of the 1970s, they found markedly decreased enrollments due not only to declines in birth rates but also to net decreases in overall population. In these circumstances, they began to explore various means of adjusting their financial affairs, including the readjustment of debt service charges.

One of the methods by which such stabilization can be achieved is by sale of a special bond issue that will yield proceeds from which a part of the current debt service can be paid during the early years of the schedule as well as capitalizing the interest on the stabilization bonds during such period. Under such plans, the requirements from current revenues can be deferred until later years.

The specific plan of debt stabilization bond issues must be tailored to the circumstances in which the debtor finds itself. Ordinarily an issuer that is confronted with such problems during periods of abnormally high interest costs and basic disorganization of its own finances will find it necessary to obtain some special form of assistance in order to be able to sell debt stabilization bonds. This may take the form of the right to levy a special tax earmarked to support the stabilization bonds; it may take the form of the New York Municipal Assistance Corporation under which certain revenues of the issuer were assigned to a special agency that was then able to issue bonds required to avoid default by the City of New York. It can take the form of some special state assistance or guarantees.

Extension to Accomodate Issuance of Additional Debt. A simple illustration suffices to indicate the advantage of reorganization to facilitate sale of new debt. Assume that a governmental enterprise has outstanding $25,000,000 in 6.00 percent term bonds that are required to be amortized on the basis of equal annual debt service over the next five years. It is confronted with the need for a major addition to its facilities estimated to require $100,000,000 in new financing.

Assuming that the new debt required will also be marketable at 6.00 percent with a proper coverage, the results of alternative patterns would be as follows:

	Combined Debt Service Costs (in thousands)			Revenues	Coverage
	Outstanding Bonds	New Bonds	Total		
Alternative A Retain $25,000,000 and issue $100,000,000 in additional bonds to be amortized over					
25 years: First 5 years	$5,935	$7,823	$13,758	$15,000	1.09
Remaining 20 years	—	7,823	7,823	15,000	1.92
Alternative B Retain $25,000,000 and issue $100,000,000 in ad- ditional debt, paying only interest during first five years					
Annual costs for 5 years	5,935	6,000	11,935	15,000	1.26
Final 20 years	—	8,718	8,718	15,000	1.72
Alternative C Issue $100,000,000 in new money bonds and refund remainder through issuance of $25,773,000[1] in refunding bonds—all to be amortized over					
25 years	- - - - - -9,838- - - - - -			9,838	15,000	1.52

[1] To provide for issuance costs on refunding bonds, $773,000 is added to the bond issue. It is presumed that the bonds would have been callable at par.

Under these circumstances, the issuer doubtless would find it appropriate to follow Alternative C inasmuch as it is the only alternative that provides a fully attractive coverage to the investor. Alternative B would provide sufficient coverage in some circumstances; however, the coverage would not be so attractive during the first five years. Alternative A would not be attractive at all during the first five years.

Involuntary Debt Reorganization

The number of defaults in tax-exempt debt secured by governmental *taxing power* have been few since the Great Depression of the 1930s. Most of the defaults that have occurred in relation to tax-exempt debt has been occasioned through failures of either *on behalf of* debt or industrial development debt.

The subject of default and its remedies is a much too complex subject to be treated definitively in this volume.[3] As a governmental entity is confronted with the probability of default in its debt, the assistance of specialists in these fields is required *immediately*. Time is an indispensable ingredient if the default is to be avoided. Or, if it cannot be avoided, time is again of maximum importance in seeking early remedial actions.

---

[3] See Wade S. Smith, *The Appraisal of Municipal Credit Risk* (1979), pp. 243–253, for an excellent discussion of the more important aspects of this problem.

In the search for remedies, bondholders turn first to the exercise of rights they have under the terms of the bond contract, especially under governmental enterprise or governmental lessee debt. They move directly, or through the trustees, to seek to enforce those rights likely to provide adequate remedy. This may include court mandated increases in service charges, levy of taxes, segregation of moneys, tighter budgetary operations for enterprise operations, requirement for diversion of state moneys due to local governments, or other actions.

The debtor government may seek to avoid default by issuance of refunding bonds at a time when it still has access to the market. Such refundings may be undertaken under an announced plan or may be undertaken piecemeal by the local government. Under some circumstances, local banking institutions have come to the temporary rescue to help avoid default and, on occasion, state governments have been induced to assist in such efforts. Other efforts are made, from time to time, through sale of bonds to pension funds or, as in the case of New York City in 1975, through the creation of a special agency by the state to take over a part of the city's revenues and issue funding bonds to provide required cash to avoid default.

In 1934 the Congress adopted the first federal legislation designed to provide relief to local governments confronted with bankruptcy. This legislation was of a temporary character designed to expire in two years; however, it was terminated by adverse holdings by the Supreme Court in May, 1936. The original legislation emphasized its mandatory character. In 1937 new legislation was adopted emphasizing the voluntary character of municipal bankruptcy actions. This legislation is now included as Chapter IX of the Federal Bankruptcy Act (11 USC, paragraphs 901–946). Under the provisions of this legislation, local governments which have the prior authority under the laws of their respective states, may seek a reorganization of their debt under protection afforded by a federal court action.

More recent changes in federal legislation concerning municipal bankruptcy appear to raise substantive questions concerning its viability. Some students hold that it has provided so many procedural defenses to the state and local governments that the legislation is virtually unworkable. Only protracted litigation will demonstrate whether in fact these laws become enforceable or whether there will be a reversion to earlier laws under certain saving clauses.

Appendix A
APPENDIX TABLES

Five appendix tables are presented here. Given the length of two of these it was inappropriate to attempt to incorporate them into the text. The function of the appendix tables, especially Appendix Table A, is to provide a framework for reference in many of the illustrative tables appearing in the text. A few notes concerning the individual tables is appropriate here.

Appendix Table A. Presented in this table are five specimen patterns of reoffering yield rates covering a period of 100 years. The rates for years 1–30 have been taken from actual reoffering schedules appearing in recent years. For the bonds in the 31–40 maturity range, very few reoffering yield patterns have been found and for the years after the 40th year no maturities have been reported in the literature examined. Accordingly, the yield rates shown beyond the 30th year are largely arbitrary in that they represent the author's assumptions of conditions which may have prevailed had such longer issues have been sold.

The five rates illustrate different market conditions as follows:

A and B illustrate rates during a period of generally low interest levels. The difference between A and B is that A offers a moderate level of incidence, i.e., percentage increase in the rate from one year to the next while B offers a high incidence of change from year to year.

C and D illustrate the same differentials in incidence patterns but occur at a time when the levels of interest rates were at an intermediate level of the overall patterns in 1979–80.

E illustrates conditions which existed during the record levels of 1981 and early 1982. The incidence rate was on the moderate to high level but is characterized as moderate in the table.

Appendix Table B. The function of this table is to illustrate the operation of a sinking fund, assuming that there were no Internal Revenue Service arbitrage restrictions upon the issuer. The right of the IRS to issue such regulations is being challenged in the courts; however, it may be some time before a resolution of the point is made by the U.S. Supreme Court and until that time it will not be feasible for issuers to utilize the conventional term bond issue with the accumulation of a sinking fund as was customary in the years prior to 1940.

Appendix Table C. This table is a companion to Appendix Table D. It illustrates in detail the maturities to be achieved through the capitalization of $1,000,000 per year for 20-year and 30-year periods. The total amounts of capitalization for the two periods correspond to the amounts found at the 20th and 30th years in Col. 7 of Appendix Table D.

Appendix Table D. This appendix table is something of a *tour-de-force*. The objective here is to illustrate the extent to which extension of the life of an equal annual debt service bond issue provides additional capitalized money-in-hand for the issuer. Six patterns of calculations are presented: The five patterns illustrated in Appendix Table A plus a Pattern F from the January public power sales in January 1982 when the issuance of bonds for a 40-year period actually produced negative accumulations of capitalized value in the final 10-year period. The only justification for such a long period of capitalization lay in the fact that this was necessary in some cases in order to sell the bonds—regardless of its diseconomy.

Appendix Table E. Illustrates the differentials in capitalized value as of the selected date for bonds carrying different credit ratings.

Appendix Table A

Specimen Reoffering Yield Patterns

Year	Low Interest Levels		Intermediate Interest Levels		High Interest
	Moderate Incidence Pattern A	High Incidence Pattern B	Moderate Incidence Pattern C	High Incidence Pattern D	Level: Moderate Incidence Pattern E
1	5.10	3.20	5.95	4.40	10.25
2	5.15	3.50	6.00	4.65	10.50
3	5.20	3.80	6.05	4.90	10.75
4	5.25	4.10	6.15	5.15	10.90
5	5.30	4.35	6.20	5.25	11.00
6	5.35	4.60	6.25	5.55	11.25
7	5.40	4.80	6.30	5.75	11.50
8	5.45	5.00	6.35	5.95	11.65
9	5.50	5.20	6.40	6.10	11.80
10	5.55	5.25	6.45	6.25	12.00
11	5.60	5.50	6.50	6.40	12.20
12	5.65	5.60	6.55	6.55	12.40
13	5.70	5.70	6.60	6.65	12.60
14	5.75	5.80	6.65	6.75	12.80
15	5.80	5.90	6.70	6.85	13.00
16	5.85	6.00	6.75	6.95	13.10
17	5.90	6.10	6.80	7.05	13.15
18	5.95	6.20	6.85	7.15	13.20
19	6.00	6.30	6.90	7.25	13.20
20	6.05	6.35	6.95	7.35	13.25
21	6.05	6.40	7.00	7.45	13.25
22	6.10	6.45	7.05	7.50	13.25
23	6.10	6.50	7.10	7.55	13.25
24	6.15	6.55	7.15	7.60	13.30
25	6.15	6.60	7.20	7.65	13.30
26	6.20	6.65	7.20	7.70	13.30
27	6.20	6.70	7.25	7.75	13.30
28	6.20	6.75	7.25	7.80	13.30
29	6.25	6.75	7.30	7.85	13.35
30	6.25	6.80	7.30	7.90	13.35
31	6.25	6.80	7.30	7.90	13.35
32	6.30	6.80	7.35	7.95	13.35
33	6.30	6.85	7.35	7.95	13.35
34	6.30	6.85	7.35	8.00	13.40
35	6.30	6.85	7.35	8.00	13.40
36	6.35	6.85	7.35	8.00	13.40
37	6.35	6.90	7.40	8.05	13.40
38	6.35	6.90	7.40	8.05	13.40
39	6.35	6.90	7.40	8.05	13.45
40	6.35	6.90	7.40	8.05	13.45
41	6.40	6.95	7.45	8.10	13.45
42	6.40	6.95	7.45	8.10	13.45
43	6.40	6.95	7.45	8.10	13.45
44	6.40	6.95	7.45	8.10	13.45
45	6.40	6.95	7.45	8.10	13.50
46	6.40	7.00	7.50	8.15	13.50
47	6.40	7.00	7.50	8.15	13.50
48	6.40	7.00	7.50	8.15	13.50

Appendix Table A
(continued)

Year	A	B	C	D	E
49	6.40	7.00	7.50	8.15	13.50
50	6.40	7.00	7.50	8.15	13.50
51	6.40	7.00	7.50	8.20	13.55
52	6.40	7.00	7.50	8.20	13.55
53	6.40	7.00	7.50	8.20	13.55
54	6.40	7.00	7.50	8.20	13.55
55	6.40	7.00	7.50	8.20	13.55
56	6.45	7.05	7.55	8.25	13.55
57	6.45	7.05	7.55	8.25	13.55
58	6.45	7.05	7.55	8.25	13.55
59	6.45	7.05	7.55	8.25	13.55
60	6.45	7.05	7.55	8.25	13.55
61	6.45	7.05	7.55	8.25	13.55
62	6.45	7.05	7.55	8.25	13.55
63	6.45	7.05	7.55	8.25	13.55
64	6.45	7.05	7.55	8.25	13.55
65	6.45	7.05	7.60	8.30	13.55
66	6.45	7.10	7.60	8.30	13.60
67	6.45	7.10	7.60	8.30	13.60
68	6.45	7.10	7.60	8.30	13.60
69	6.45	7.10	7.60	8.30	13.60
70	6.45	7.10	7.60	8.30	13.60
71	6.45	7.10	7.60	8.30	13.60
72	6.45	7.10	7.60	8.30	13.60
73	6.45	7.10	7.60	8.30	13.60
74	6.45	7.10	7.60	8.30	13.60
75	6.45	7.10	7.60	8.30	13.60
76	6.50	7.10	7.60	8.30	13.60
77	6.50	7.10	7.60	8.30	13.60
78	6.50	7.10	7.60	8.30	13.60
79	6.50	7.10	7.60	8.30	13.60
80	6.50	7.10	7.60	8.30	13.60
81	6.50	7.15	7.65	8.35	13.65
82	6.50	7.15	7.65	8.35	13.65
83	6.50	7.15	7.65	8.35	13.65
84	6.50	7.15	7.65	8.35	13.65
85	6.50	7.15	7.65	8.35	13.65
86	6.50	7.15	7.65	8.35	13.65
87	6.50	7.15	7.65	8.35	13.65
88	6.50	7.15	7.65	8.35	13.65
89	6.50	7.15	7.65	8.35	13.65
90	6.50	7.15	7.65	8.35	13.65
91	6.50	7.15	7.65	8.35	13.65
92	6.50	7.15	7.65	8.35	13.65
93	6.50	7.15	7.65	8.35	13.65
94	6.50	7.15	7.65	8.35	13.65
95	6.50	7.15	7.65	8.35	13.65
96	6.50	7.15	7.65	8.35	13.65
97	6.50	7.15	7.65	8.35	13.65
98	6.50	7.15	7.65	8.35	13.65
99	6.50	7.15	7.65	8.35	13.65
100	6.50	7.15	7.65	8.35	13.65

Appendix Table B

Illustrative Values in Operation of a Sinking Fund for 60 Semiannual Periods with Investments at 1½ Times Rates Shown in Pattern A, Appendix Table A

Line	Item	Period Number					
		1	2	3	4	59	60
1	Deposit on final day of period	$1.0000	$1.0000	$1.0000	$1.0000	$ 1.0000	$ 1.0000
2	Investment rate applicable to investment made on final day of period	.046875	.046875	.046875	.046875	.038625	.039250
3	Earnings realized on final day of period from investment made in prior period	—	.0469	.0490	.0513	.4385	.4510
4	Earnings realized on final day of period on investments made before the prior period	—	—	.0469	.0959	10.3524	10.7909
5	Total earnings in this period (Line 3) + (Line 4)	—	.0469	.0959	.1472	10.7909	11.2419
6	Total amount available for investment on final day of this period (Line 1) + (Line 5)	1.0000	1.0469	1.0959	1.1473	11.7909	n.a.[1]
7	Total earnings to close of this period (Line 7 of prior period) + (Line 5 this period)	—	.0469	.1428	.2901	211.3679	222.6098
8	Total deposits to close of this period (Line 8 of prior period) + (Line 1 of this period)	1.0000	2.0000	3.0000	4.0000	59.0000	60.0000
9	Total in fund at close of period (Line 7) + (Line 8)	1.0000	2.0469	3.1428	4.2901	270.3679	282.6098

[1] This is not applicable inasmuch as principal will be used at end of period to retire debt.

Appendix Table C

Differential in Value from Capitalization of $1,000,000 Per Annum under Pattern B of Appendix Table A for 20 years and for 30 Years under PV-2

Year	Capitalization for		30 Year Period
	Coupon Rate	20 Year Period	30 Year Period
	(1)	(2)	(3)
1	3.20	365,704	192,730
2	3.50	377,406	198,897
3	3.80	390,615	205,859
4	4.10	405,459	213,681
5	4.35	422,983	222,442
6	4.60	440,443	232,118
7	4.80	460,704	242,796
8	5.00	482,817	254,450
9	5.20	506,958	267,173
10	5.25	533,320	281,066
11	5.50	561,319	295,822
12	5.60	592,192	312,092
13	5.70	625,355	329,569
14	5.80	661,000	348,354
15	5.90	699,338	368,559
16	6.00	740,599	390,304
17	6.10	785,035	413,722
18	6.20	832,922	438,959
19	6.30	884,563	466,175
20	6.35	940,291	495,544
21	6.40	—	527,011
22	6.45	—	560,740
23	6.50	—	596,908
24	6.55	—	635,707
25	6.60	—	677,345
26	6.65	—	722,050
27	6.70	—	770,067
28	6.75	—	821,661
29	6.75	—	877,123
30	6.80	—	936,329
Total		11,708,134	13,395,267
NIC		5.8145	6.4106

Appendix Table D

Values Derived from Capitalization of $1,000,000 per Period for 1 to 40 Periods under PV-2

(amounts in thousands of dollars)

Period	Pattern A				Pattern B				Pattern C			
	Yield Rate	Capitalized Value Gained by Addition of This Period	Cumulative Capitalized Value	Percent Gain by Addition of Period	Yield Rate	Capitalized Value Gained by Addition of This Period	Cumulative Capitalized Value	Percent Gain by Addition of Period	Yield Rate	Capitalized Value Gained by Addition of This Period	Cumulative Capitalized Value	Percent Gain by Addition of Period
	(1)	(2)	(3)	(4)	(5)	(6)	(7)	(8)	(9)	(10)	(11)	(12)
1	5.10	951	951	na	3.20	969	969	na	5.95	944	944	na
2	5.15	904	1,856	95.0	3.50	933	1,902	96.3	6.00	890	1,834	94.2
3	5.20	859	2,715	46.3	3.80	894	2,796	47.1	6.05	838	2,672	45.7
4	5.25	815	3,529	30.0	4.10	850	3,646	30.3	6.15	787	3,459	29.4
5	5.30	772	4,301	21.9	4.35	806	4,453	22.0	6.20	740	4,199	21.3
6	5.35	731	5,032	16.8	4.60	760	5,213	17.0	6.25	694	4,893	16.5
7	5.40	691	5,723	13.7	4.80	715	5,929	13.7	6.30	651	5,544	13.2
8	5.45	653	6,376	11.4	5.00	670	6,599	11.3	6.35	609	6,153	10.9
9	5.50	615	6,991	9.7	5.20	624	7,223	9.4	6.40	570	6,723	9.2
10	5.55	580	7,571	8.3	5.25	590	7,813	8.1	6.45	532	7,255	7.9
11	5.60	545	8,116	7.2	5.50	541	8,353	6.9	6.50	496	7,751	6.8
12	5.65	512	8,629	6.3	5.60	504	8,857	6.0	6.55	462	8,213	5.9
13	5.70	481	9,110	5.6	5.70	468	9,326	5.2	6.60	430	8,643	5.2
14	5.75	450	9,560	4.9	5.80	434	9,760	4.6	6.65	399	9,041	4.6
15	5.80	421	9,981	4.4	5.90	401	10,160	4.1	6.70	369	9,411	4.0
16	5.85	393	10,374	3.9	6.00	368	10,539	3.6	6.75	342	9,753	3.6
17	5.90	366	10,740	3.5	6.10	337	10,866	3.2	6.80	315	10,968	3.2
18	5.95	341	11,081	3.2	6.30	307	11,173	2.8	6.85	290	10,359	2.8
19	6.00	316	11,397	2.9	6.30	279	11,452	2.4	6.90	267	10,625	2.5
20	6.05	293	11,690	2.6	6.35	257	11,708	2.2	6.95	245	10,870	2.3
21	6.05	275	11,966	2.4	6.40	236	11,944	2.0	7.00	223	11,093	2.0
22	6.10	255	12,221	2.1	6.45	216	12,159	1.8	7.05	204	11,297	1.8
23	6.10	240	12,461	2.0	6.50	197	12,356	1.6	7.10	185	11,482	1.6
24	6.15	220	12,681	1.8	6.55	179	12,535	1.4	7.15	167	11,649	1.4
25	6.15	207	12,888	1.6	6.60	162	12,697	1.2	7.20	150	11,799	1.2
26	6.20	189	13,077	1.5	6.65	146	12,843	1.1	7.20	140	11,940	1.1
27	6.20	178	13,255	1.4	6.70	131	12,974	1.0	7.25	125	12,065	1.03
28	6.20	168	13,423	1.3	6.75	116	13,090	.89	7.25	117	12,182	.95
29	6.25	152	13,574	1.2	6.75	109	13,199	.83	7.30	103	12,285	.84
30	6.25	143	13,717	1.1	6.80	96	13,295	.72	7.30	96	12,381	.78
31	6.25	134	13,852	1.0	6.80	90	13,385	.67	7.30	90	12,471	.72
32	6.25	120	13,972	.87	6.80	84	13,469	.63	7.35	78	12,548	.62
33	6.30	113	14,084	.81	6.85	72	13,542	.53	7.35	72	12,621	.57
34	6.30	106	14,190	.75	6.85	68	13,609	.50	7.35	67	12,688	.53
35	6.30	99	14,290	.70	6.85	63	13,673	.46	7.35	63	12,751	.49
36	6.35	87	14,377	.61	6.85	59	13,732	.43	7.35	58	12,810	.45
37	6.35	81	14,459	.56	6.90	49	13,781	.36	7.40	49	12,858	.37
38	6.35	77	14,536	.53	6.90	46	13,827	.33	7.40	45	12,903	.35
39	6.35	72	14,608	.50	6.90	43	13,870	.31	7.40	42	12,945	.32
40	6.35	68	14,676	.46	6.90	40	13,910	.29	7.40	39	12,984	.30

Appendix Table D (continued)

Values Derived from Capitalization of $1,000,000 per Period for 1 to 40 Periods under PV-2

(amounts in thousands of dollars)

Period	Pattern D				Pattern E				Pattern F			
	Yield Rate	Capitalized Value Gained by Addition of This Period	Cumulative Capitalized Value	Percent Gain by Addition of Period	Yield Rate	Capitalized Value Gained by Addition of This Period	Cumulative Capitalized Value	Percent Gain by Addition of Period	Yield Rate	Capitalized Value Gained by Addition of This Period	Cumulative Capitalized Value	Percent Gain by Addition of Period
	(13)	(14)	(15)	(16)	(17)	(18)	(19)	(20)	(21)	(22)	(23)	(24)
1	4.40	958	958	na	10.25	907	907	na	11.00	901	901	na
2	4.65	913	1,871	95.3	10.50	819	1,725	90.	11.15	809	1,710	89.8
3	4.9	866	2,737	46.3	10.75	735	2,461	42.6	11.30	725	2,435	42.4
4	5.15	817	3,554	30.0	10.90	659	3,121	26.8	11.40	648	3,083	26.6
5	5.25	773	4,327	21.7	11.00	592	3,913	19.0	11.50	579	3,662	18.8
6	5.55	720	5,047	16.6	11.25	523	4,236	14.1	11.70	512	4,174	14.0
7	5.75	671	5,718	13.3	11.50	460	4,696	10.9	11.90	450	4,624	10.8
8	5.95	623	6,340	10.9	11.65	406	5,102	8.6	12.00	397	5,021	8.6
9	6.10	578	6,915	9.1	11.80	356	5,458	7.0	12.30	341	5,361	6.8
10	6.25	534	7,453	7.7	12.00	308	5,766	5.6	12.50	293	5,655	5.5
11	6.40	492	7,944	6.6	12.20	264	6,030	4.6	12.70	250	5,905	4.4
12	6.55	450	8,394	5.7	12.40	224	6,255	3.7	12.90	211	6,116	3.6
13	6.65	414	8,809	4.9	12.60	188	6,443	3.0	13.05	179	6,295	2.9
14	6.75	380	9,188	4.3	12.80	155	6,598	2.4	13.20	149	6,444	2.4
15	6.85	347	9,535	3.8	13.00	125	6,724	1.9	13.35	123	6,567	1.9
16	6.95	315	9,851	3.3	13.10	105	6,829	1.6	13.50	100	6,667	1.5
17	7.05	285	10,136	2.9	13.15	90	6,920	1.3	13.65	79	6,746	1.2
18	7.15	257	10,393	2.5	13.20	77	6,997	1.1	13.80	61	6,807	.90
19	7.25	230	10,623	2.2	13.20	67	7,064	.96	13.90	47	6,854	.69
20	7.35	204	10,828	1.9	13.25	57	7,120	.80	14.00	35	6,889	.52
21	7.45	180	11,007	1.7	13.25	50	7,170	.70	14.25	16	6,906	.23
22	7.50	162	11,169	1.5	13.25	44	7,214	.61	14.25	14	6,919	.20
23	7.55	146	11,315	1.3	13.25	39	7,253	.53	14.25	12	6,932	.18
24	7.60	131	11,445	1.2	13.30	31	7,285	.42	14.25	11	6,942	.15
25	7.65	116	11,561	1.0	13.30	28	7,312	.37	14.25	10	6,953	.12
26	7.70	102	11,663	.88	13.30	25	7,336	.33	14.25	8	6,960	.10
27	7.75	89	11,752	.76	13.30	21	7,358	.29	14.25	7	6,967	.10
28	7.80	77	11,828	.65	13.30	16	7,373	.21	14.25	6	6,973	.09
29	7.85	66	11,895	.55	13.35	14	7,387	.18	14.25	5	6,983	.08
30	7.90	56	11,951	.46	13.35	12	7,399	.16	14.25	5	6,983	.06
31	7.90	52	12,003	.43	13.35	11	7,410	.14	14.50	(11)	6,972	(.16)
32	7.95	43	12,045	.35	13.35	10	7,420	.12	14.50	(10)	6,963	(.14)
33	7.95	33	12,085	.32	13.35	8	7,428	.11	14.50	(8)	6,955	(.13)
34	8.00	31	12,115	.26	13.40	4	7,432	.05	14.50	(9)	6,947	(.12)
35	8.00	29	12,144	.23	13.40	4	7,436	.04	14.50	(6)	6,941	(.09)
36	8.00	26	12,170	.21	13.40	3	7,439	.04	14.50	(6)	6,935	(.08)
37	8.05	19	12,189	.15	13.40	3	7,442	.03	14.50	(5)	6,931	(.07)
38	8.05	17	12,207	.14	13.40	2	7,444	.03	14.50	(5)	6,926	(.07)
39	8.05	17	12,223	.13	13.45	2	7,446	.02	14.50	(4)	6,922	(.05)
40	8.05	15	12,237	.12	13.45	2	7,448	.02	14.50	(3)	6,919	(.03)

Appendix Table E

Illustrative Differentials Arising from PV-2 Capitalization of $1,000,000 Per Annum for 20 Years Using Specimen Yield Rates Typifying Differentials Between Security Grades at a Selected Time

Year	Aaa Rated		Aa Rated		A and A-1 Rated		Baa-1 and Baa Rated	
	Coupon Rate	Capitalized Value	Coupon Rate	Capitalized Value	Coupon Rate	Capitalized Value	Coupon Rate	Capitalized Value
	(1)	(2)	(3)	(4)	(5)	(6)	(7)	(8)
1	4.20	382,360	4.35	372,478	4.40	358,081	4.55	344,422
2	4.35	398,419	4.45	388,681	4.55	373,836	4.70	360,093
3	4.45	415,750	4.55	405,977	4.70	390,896	4.85	377,017
4	4.55	434,251	4.65	424,449	4.80	409,216	5.00	395,303
5	4.65	454,009	4.75	444,186	4.90	428,858	5.10	415,068
6	4.70	475,121	4.85	465,285	5.00	449,872	5.20	436,236
7	4.75	497,451	4.90	487,851	5.10	472,366	5.30	458,921
8	4.80	521,080	4.95	511,756	5.15	496,456	5.35	483,243
9	4.85	546,092	5.00	537,088	5.20	522,024	5.40	609,097
10	4.90	522,578	5.05	563,943	5.25	549,169	5.45	536,588
11	4.95	600,635	5.10	592,422	5.35	578,001	5.55	565,832
12	5.00	630,366	5.15	622,635	5.40	608,924	5.60	597,236
13	5.10	661,884	5.20	654,701	5.45	641,806	5.70	630,681
14	5.15	695,640	5.25	688,745	5.55	676,784	5.80	666,630
15	5.20	731,465	5.35	724,905	5.60	714,346	5.85	705,295
16	5.25	769,502	5.40	763,687	5.65	754,349	5.90	746,555
17	5.30	809,901	5.45	804,926	5.75	796,970	5.95	790,601
18	5.40	852,825	5.55	848,795	5.80	842,796	6.00	837,642
19	5.45	898,878	5.60	895,903	5.85	891,678	6.10	887,901
20	5.50	947,867	5.70	946,073	5.95	943,841	6.15	942,063
Totals		12,296,082		12,144,496		11,900,227		11,686,433
NIC		5.1867		5.3365		5.5847		5.8066
Decrease in capitalized value from Aaa rated bond				152,324		395,855		609,649

Appendix B
PRESENT VALUE SYSTEMS

For the public finance officer concerned with the administration of state and local government debt, it is useful to have a comprehensive understanding of the methods by which present value may be calculated. The function of any present value calculation is to ascertain the amount of money in hand that can be obtained now in return for a payment, or series of payments, promised to be made at a future date, or series of dates.

The system of present value most familiar to citizens is the purchase of United States Government Series E Savings Bonds. The buyer surrenders a given amount of money today in return for the promise of a given amount of money to be paid at a future date. If the rate of interest is known, the amount payable at the future date is discounted to present value by *Equation A* presented below in the discussion of PV-1. The function of this appendix is to identify four patterns of present value which have been designated in the text as PV-1, PV-2, PV-3, and PV-4, and to illustrate the manner in which present value is calculated under each of the three patterns.

PV-1: Constant Discount Rate

For determining the present value of an amount due on a single date and for which there is a single discount rate, *Equation A* is used:

$$PV = \frac{1}{(1+i)^n} \times A$$

When: $i =$ the discount rate per period
$n =$ the number of periods
$A =$ the par value of the amount due

Thus, a Series E Savings Bond having a maturity value of $100.00 that is due in seven years and offered to yield 7.00 percent per annum, compounded semiannually, the expression becomes:

$$PV = \frac{1}{(1+.035)^{14}} \times \$100.00 = \$61.78$$

Therefore, if the U.S. Government offered to sell a bond due in seven years to yield 7.00 percent, the buyer would pay $61.78 now in return for the promise to pay $100.00 seven years from date.

If, on the other hand, an investor held $14,000 par value of such bonds, each in $1,000 denomination and each bearing 7.00 percent interest, with one bond maturing at each six-month interval for seven years, the value of the $14,000 in bonds could be expressed in *Equation B,* which measures the present value of 1 per period:

$$PV = \frac{1 - \frac{1}{(1+i)^n}}{i} \times A$$

341

When: i = the discount rate per period
n = the number of periods
A = the amount due per period

Applying the equation, the values become:

$$PV = \frac{1 - \dfrac{1}{(1 + .035)^{14}}}{i} \times \$1,000 = \$10,920.52$$

When PV-1 is applied to determining the value of a bond due at a future date, in respect to which the interest is payable semiannually, the value (price) of the bond becomes the sum of the present value of the principal and the present value of the interest, determined under *Equation A* and *Equation B,* respectively.[1]

Use in Determining TIC (True Interest Cost). When the average effective interest cost rate is being determined under TIC, the objective is to find a rate for use under *Equation A* which, when applied to the amount payable at each semiannual date, will produce a total of all values precisely equal the amount received as cash in hand in return for promised future payments. In such use of *Equation A,* the rate is a constant while the number of periods and the amounts for each period are variable from period to period under most bond issues. In comparing results among bond issues the differences in the number of periods also become significant.

Use in Pension Fund Valuations. Equation A of PV-1 is also frequently used in pension fund valuations. Ordinarily, such valuations are made under an officially determined interest rate assumption. Estimated liabilities are valued under *Equation A* when the amount of the liability is payable in lump-sum amount. If the liability is payable in periodic equal installments, *Equation B* of PV-1 is used. And, in some systems, for the valuation of pension fund assets, it is required that a single rate be determined representing the composite "internal rate of return" of the securities held. This process is similar to the determination of TIC; however, it is much more complex inasmuch as all of the values involved in all of the securities must be taken into account.

PV-2: Capitalization through Issuance of Serial Bonds

A somewhat different problem is posed by the governmental unit which has a revenue-producing facility estimated to produce a variable amount of net income available for debt service from year to year throughout the life of the bonds. After allowing for any amount required to be set aside as excess coverage, the objective is to ascertain the amount of principal which the available debt service will support. In order to do this, the calculation commences with the final semiannual period and proceeds from period to period until all of the available amounts have been capitalized. The par reoffering yield rates are used as coupon rates for this purpose, with adjustment being made to the total debt supportable for the issuance costs.

Equation C is used for this purpose:

$$\begin{array}{l}\text{Amount of}\\\text{Bonds for}\\\text{"n" period}\end{array} = \frac{\left(\begin{array}{l}\text{Amount of Debt}\\\text{Service Available}\end{array}\right) - \left(\begin{array}{l}\text{Interest Payable in this Period on}\\\text{Bonds Maturing in Subsequent Periods}\end{array}\right)}{(1 + i)}$$

When: i = the semiannual yield rate

---

[1] See Rules G-12 and G-15 of the Municipal Securities Rulemaking Board for methods it has prescripted for calculation of price, accrued interest, yields, value of odd coupons, and day count.

"Interest payable in this period on bonds maturing
in subsequent periods" is the sum of such semiannual interest
payable on those bonds

In the first calculation (for the final period), there would be no interest payable on account of bonds maturing at a later date. Therefore, the amount of bonds supportable for the final period would be as follows if the amount available for debt service in the final period were \$600,000 and the rate 7.00 percent.

$$A = \frac{\$600,000 - \$0}{(1 + .035)} = \$579,710.15$$

The interest carried foward to the next period would be \$20,289.85 (579,710.15 × .035).

For the penultimate period, the calculation would be as follows, if the amount available were \$600,000 and the rate were 7.00 percent:

$$A = \frac{\$600,000 - \$20,289.85}{(1 + .035)} = \$560,106.43$$

The interest carried forward to the next period would thereupon become \$39,893.57.

For the next period, assuming a 6.95 percent annual interest rate and the amount of \$590,000 available for debt service, the calculation would be as follows:

$$A = \frac{\$590,000 - \$39,893.57}{(1 + .03475)} = \$531,632.35$$

This process is repeated until all amounts available for debt service have been used. The sum of the values of "A" for each semiannual period thereupon becomes the amount of debt supportable by the estimated amounts available for debt service. After deducting the estimated issuance costs, the resultant amount is the net the issuer could expect in return for the debt service pledged under the bond contract. (See Table 40 for example.)

PV-3: Present Value of Series of Amounts Discounted at a Series of Rates

The third pattern for determining present value occurs in circumstances in which amounts payable at different dates in the future are discounted at a series of rates, each applicable to different time periods. *Equation A* is used for such discount; however, different rates are applied to the amounts payable at the respective time when due.

PV-4: Present Value of Series of Amount Capitalized under Combinations of PV-2 and PV-3

The pattern of a combination of serial bonds and zero coupon bonds introduced into the municipal bond market in March, 1982, provides a still further method of determining the present value of a stream of money. The present value of the stream becomes the sum of the amounts determined under PV-2 and PV-3.

Appendix C
GLOSSARY

Note. The definitions contained in this glossary have been derived from three well-known sources together with a number of definitions prepared by the author. In some instances, the author has appended a comment to such definitions, labelled as *comment*. Where definitions have been taken from other sources, those sources have been identified by the number of asterisks indicated. The principal sources are as follows:

*Municipal Finance Officers Association. *Governmental Accounting, Auditing, and Financial Reporting.* Chicago: Municipal Finance Officers Association, 1980, Appendix B, pp. 53–77. A definition attributed to that source is transcribed verbatim, except that internal references within the work are indicated by *italicized* type, rather than bold face type. [These definitions generally follow those contained in National Committee on Governmental Accounting, *Governmental Accounting, Auditing, and Financial Reporting.* Chicago: Municipal Finance Officers Association, 1968, pp. 151–157.]

**The definitions of the Bureau of the Census of the U.S. Department of Commerce are taken from the *Governmental Finances* and associated series cited in Appendix D or from the Bureau's *Classification Manual, Governmental Finances* issued March 1976, in conjunction with the preparation of data for the *1977 Census of Governments.*

***Securities Industry Association, *Fundamentals of Municipal Bonds.* 9th. ed. New York: Securities Industries Association, 1981, pp. 193–201.

Definitions not preceded by an asterisk have been prepared by the author.

Words or phrases within a definition that are italicized refer to words or phrases defined in the glossary. Materials enclosed by [brackets] have been inserted by the author for clarification.

Accrued Interest on Investments Issued. Interest for the period between the *date of issue* and the *settlement date.*

Accrued Interest on Investments Purchased. Interest accrued on investments between the most recent interest payment date and the date of acquisition. The account is carried as an asset until the first interest payment date after date of purchase.

*Actuarial Basis.** A basis used in computing the amount of contributions to be made periodically to a fund or account so that the total contributions plus the compounded earnings thereon will equal the required payments to be made out the fund. The factors taken into account in arriving at the amount of these contributions include the length of time over which each contribution is to be held and the rate of return compounded on such contribution over its life. A Pension Trust Fund for a public employee retirement system is an example of a fund concerned with actuarial basis data.

> *Comment.* The concept is also used in determination of the amount of semiannual contributions to be made to a fund to retire a bond issue or to build an annuity. The formula for determining the amount of the contribution required is:

$$A = \frac{i}{(1 - i)^n - 1} \times P$$

When: i = semiannual earnings rate
n = number of semiannual periods
A = amount of semiannual deposit
P = principal of fund at maturity

Ad Valorem Tax. A tax based on the value of taxable property, usually the assessed valuation but, in some cases, an adjusted assessed valuation.

*Advance Refunding Bonds. Bonds issued to refund an ousstanding bond issue prior to the date on which the outstanding bonds become due or callable. Proceeds of the advance refunding bonds are deposited in escrow with a fiduciary, invested in U.S. Treasury Bonds or other authorized securities, and used to redeem the underlying bonds at maturity or call date and to pay interest on the bonds being refunded or the advance refunding bonds.

After-tax Yield. The annual percentage earnings rate reflected in the *yield to maturity rate,* adjusted for the effect of any capital gains tax estimated to be payable at maturity.

All-or-none Bid. A bid basis requiring the issuer either to award all of the bonds being offered to the successful bidder or to make no award to any bidder.

*Amortization. (1) Gradual reduction, redemption, or liquidation of the balance of an account according to a specified schedule of times and amounts. (2) Provision for the extinguishment of a debt by means of a *debt service fund.*

>   *Comment.* Rather than the use of a *debt service fund,* the use of a *sinking fund* appears more expressive of contemporary practice.

Arbitrage. The profit derived from the more or less simultaneous purchase and sale of governmental securities.

>   *Comment.* Certain regulations of the U.S. Treasury have redefined the word to mean the gain which may be obtained by borrowing at a tax-exempt rate and investing at a taxable rate by a tax-exempt investor. Moreover, the regulations redefine *interest* in conjunction with the definition of arbitrage so as to exclude the spread between the price at which the investment banker purchased and sold the security.

Auction Sale. A *competitive sale* of securities at which bidding and award is on an *all-or-none* basis. [See also: *Dutch Auction.*]

Authentication. The action of a bank or trust company in certifying that the signature and seal of an issuer which appear on the instrument are true and correct.

>   *Comment.* In some circumstances the authenticating agency may also supervise the printing of the securities and otherwise safeguard against fraud, counterfeiting, or overissue. Also known as *certification* or as *validation.*

*Authority. A government or public agency created to perform a single function or a restricted group of related activities. Usually such units are financed from service charges, fees, and tolls, but in some instances they also have taxing powers. An authority may be completely independent of other governments or partially dependent upon other governments for its creation, its financing, or the exercise of certain powers.

*Authority Bonds. Bonds payable from the revenues of a specific authority. Since authorities usually have no revenues other than charges for services, their bonds are ordinarily *revenue bonds.*

>   *Comment.* Authority bonds currently also include governmental lessee bonds and *on behalf of* bonds.

Average Effective Interest Cost. The average rate determined to express the average interest rate for a bond issue, including the cost of issuance. Used primarily in determining the lowest of two or more bids in a competitively bid sale of bonds or notes; also used to compare the differentials in costs of two or more bond issues. The average effective interest cost is determined under one of two methods: (1) *NIC-Net Interest Cost,* or (2) *TIC-True Interest Cost* [also known as Internal Rate of Return].

Average Life of Bond Issue. The aggregate life of all bonds (in years) divided by the number of bonds.

Award Date. The date on which the issuer makes an award of bonds or notes.

BANS. See: *Bond Anticipation Notes.*

Basis Book. A book of mathematical tables used to convert *yield to maturity rates, coupon rates,* and the *term* of bonds to a dollar price. [The term is now largely outdated due to contemporary reliance upon computers.]

Basis Point. One-one hundredth of one percent [0.0001]. Used in the pricing of bonds and in discussions of the yield of a bond.

*****Basis Price.** The price of a security expressed in yield or percentage of return on the investment.

*****Bearer Security.** A security that has no identification as to owner. It is presumed to be owned, therefore, by the bearer or the person who holds it. Bearer securities are freely and easily negotiable since ownership can be quickly transferred from seller to buyer.

Bid. An offer to purchase securities at a given price or under other stipulated conditions. A bid may be submitted in either a competitive sale or a negotiated sale of municipal bonds.

Bid Date. The day and hour not later than which bids must be submitted in a competitive sale of securities.

Blanket Lien. A claim held by the owners of special district obligations against all properties situated within the district. If some properties are delinquent in payment of their assessments, the amount of the arrearage must be raised by an additional levy applicable to all properties.

Block-term Bonds. A portion (block) of a serial bond issue that has been combined into a single maturity, usually with the requirement that specified amounts of such bonds be redeemed on specified dates prior to the maturity date.

Blue List. A daily publication of The Blue List Publishing Company [a subsidiary of Standard & Poor's] entitled, *The Blue List of Current Municipal Offerings.* It contains a list of municipal, government, and selected other securities offered for sale by dealers. Information ordinarily includes the name of the issue, maturity date, coupon rate, and yield rate (or price) at which offered.

***Bond.** A written promise to pay a specified sum of money, called the face value [par value] or principal amount, at a specified date or dates in the future, called the maturity date(s), together with periodic interest at a specified rate. The difference between a note and a bond is that the latter runs for a longer period of time and requires greater legal formality.

Comment. The term *bond* has a second meaning in municipal bond finance, namely the par value of $1,000. Although bonds may be issued in any denomination, municipal bond dealers and others use the term to mean $1,000 par value, regardless of the actual denomination. Thus, a $25,000 bond would be referred to as "25 bonds." Many transactions, e.g., the spread between the purchase and sales price by investment bankers, are expressed in terms of the "amount per bond," i.e., per $1,000 par value.

Bond and Interest Record. The permanent record maintained for each bond issue sold showing the amounts of interest and principal due on each payment date, the bond and coupon numbers, and other pertinent information. Sometimes referred to as the *Bond Register.*

*Bond Anticipation Notes [BANS]. Short-term interest-bearing notes issued by a government in anticipation of bonds to be issued at a later date. The notes are retired from the proceeds of the bond issue to which they are related.

> *Comment.* BANS may also be retired from current revenue, or even from proceeds of other BANS or bonds under some conditions.

Bond Authorization. See *Bond Resolution.*

Bond Buyer. A publication issued in New York in two editions: (1) *The Daily Bond Buyer* which is issued each business day except on major holidays and (2) *The Weekly Bond Buyer,* issued each week. The journal is devoted solely to the municipal bond market and related developments. It contains substantially all of the news concerning activities relating to the sale, refunding, and related information on such bonds.

*Bond Discount. The excess of the face value of a bond over the price for which it is acquired or sold. The price does not include accrued interest at the date of acquisition or sale.

*Bond Fund. A fund formerly used to account for proceeds of general obligation bond issues. Such proceeds are now accounted for in a *Capital Projects Fund.*

> *Comment.* The *Capital Projects Fund* is primarily an accounting entity. The indentures of many revenue bond issues identify the "Bond Fund" as the fund into which proceeds for capital projects are deposited, managed, and disbursed. The term Bond Fund is also a term used to refer to a mutual investment fund consisting of bonds. See *Consolidated Bond Account.*

Bond Ordinance. See *Bond Resolution.*

*Bond Premium. The excess of the price at which a bond is acquired or sold over its face value [*Par Value*]. The price does not include accrued interest at the date of acquisition or sale.

Bond Ratings. See *Ratings.*

Bond Resolution. An action of a governing body of a state or local government, or agency thereof, authorizing a bond issue. The bond resolution may be self-operative, or it may require further approval, e.g., by the electorate or by other governmental officials, before bonds can be sold thereunder. The resolution may be in the form of an amendment to a state constitution; an act or resolution of the state legislature; a local law or ordinance; or a resolution of the governing body of the issuer.

Bond Retirement Fund. See *Debt Service Fund.*

Bond Revenues. Revenues, including special taxes, levied or collected for the purpose of providing for payment of the debt service on outstanding bonds.

*Bonded Debt. That portion of indebtedness represented by outstanding bonds. See *Gross Bonded Debt* and *Net Bonded Debt.*

*Bonds Authorized but Unissued. Bonds which have been legally authorized but not issued and which can be issued and sold without further authorization. This term must not be confused with the term "margin of borrowing power" or "legal debt margin," either one of which represents the difference between the legal debt limit of a governmental unit and the debt outstanding against it.

> *Comment.* The laws of the states treat bonds authorized but unissued differently in determining the legal borrowing margin. Many treat such debt as outstanding for this purpose.

*Callable Bond. A type of bond which permits the issuer to pay the obligation before the stated maturity date by giving notice of redemption in a manner specified in the bond contract. Synonym: *Optional Bond.*

Call Option. The right to accelerate the redemption date of a bond which is reserved by the issuer at the time of sale. It is subject to the conditions included in the bond contract.

Call Premium. The amount the issuer has promised to pay in excess of par value when bonds are redeemed in advance of their maturity date.

*Capital Budget. A plan of proposed capital outlays and the means of financing them. See *Capital Program.*

> *Comment.* A capital budget embraces only those funds subject to appropriation by the governing body of the governmental unit. Moreover, the capital budget is (or should be) the sole instrument by which appropriations for capital facilities are made.

*Capital Program. A plan for capital expenditures to be incurred each year over a fixed period of years to meet capital needs arising from the long-term work program or otherwise. It sets forth each project or other contemplated expenditure in which the government is to have a part and specifies the full resources estimated to be available to finance the projected expenditures.

*Capital Projects Fund. A fund created to account for financial resources to be used for the acquisition or construction of major capital facilities (other than those financed by proprietary funds, *Special Assessment Funds,* and *Trust Funds*).

Casualty Insurance Company. An insurance company predominately involved in insurance against risks other than those covered by life insurance.

Certification. See *Authentication* and *Validation.*

*Check. A bill of exchange drawn on a bank and payable on demand; a written order on a bank to pay on demand a specified sum of money to a named person, to his or her order, or to bearer out of money on deposit to the credit of the maker. A check differs from a warrant in that the latter is not necessarily payable on demand and may not be negotiable. It differs from a voucher in that the latter is not an order to pay. A voucher-check combines the distinguishing characteristics of a voucher and a check; it shows the propriety of a payment and is an order to pay.

*Combination Bond. A bond issued by a government which is payable from the revenues of a governmental enterprise but which is also backed by the full faith and credit of the government.

Commercial Paper. See *Municipal Commercial Paper.*

Competitive Bid. A bid submitted for bonds or other evidences of indebtedness sold at a competitive sale.

Competitive Sale. A sale of securities to the bidder offering the best bid in open competitive bidding. [See also *Auction Sale* and *Dutch Auction Sale.*]

Concession. The allowance that an underwriter or syndicate allows a nonmember of the account; sometimes referred to as a dealer's allowance.

Consolidated Bond Account. An account into which assets of two or more bond funds are pooled in order to facilitate the investment of proceeds temporarily held. Also used to provide a basis for advances of cash derived from the sale of one issue of bonds to the credit of an unissued group of bonds, pending their sale. [See also *Consolidated Cash Account.*]

Consolidated Cash Account. An account to facilitate cash management by having two or more operating funds merge their cash balances into a consolidated account for the current management of such balances, including temporary investment thereof. In some governments, the consolidated cash account membership includes not only operating funds but also capital funds.

*Contingent Liabilities. Items which may become liabilities as a result of conditions undetermined at a given date, such as guarantees, pending law suits, judgments under appeal, unsettled disputed claims, unfilled purchase orders, and uncompleted contracts. All contingent liabilities should be disclosed within the basic financial statements, including the notes thereto.

> *Comment.* As applied to bonded debt, the term relates to debt in respect to which the government is not the issuer but in respect to which it has undertaken some form of contingent guarantee of the bonds or other debt.

Conversion. Exchange of a coupon bond for a registered bond, or vice versa.

Convertible Coupon Bonds. Coupon bonds which, at the option of the holder, may be converted to registered bonds.

Coupon. That part of a bond which evidences interest due. Coupons are detachable and, as they become due, they may be presented for payment.

Coupon Bonds. Bonds issued with coupons attached.

*****Coupon Rate.** The interest rate specified on interest coupons attached to a bond. The term is synonymous with nominal interest rate.

    Comment. Many coupons specify the amount of interest to be paid, rather than the rate at which the bond bears interest. See *Nominal Interest Rate.*

Coverage. The extent to which revenues pledged for a bond issue exceed (or are expected to exceed) the debt service requirements expressed either in terms of the highest year or average year's debt service. Thus, a bond issue with a debt service of $1,000,000 per year that has pledged revenues expected to produce $1,400,000 per year is said to have a 140 [percentage] or a 1.4 times coverage.

****Current Yield.** The ratio of interest to the actual market price of the bond stated as a percentage. For example, a $1,000 bond that pays $80 per year would have a current yield of 8%.

    Comment. The term is also used to connote the current yield to the owner of a security, based on the cost of acquisition. [See also *Yield to Maturity Rate* (YTM).]

****CUSIP.** The Committee on Uniform Security Identification Procedures, which was established under the auspices of the American Bankers Association to develop a uniform method of identifying municipal, U.S. government and corporate securities.

*****CUSIP Numbers.** Numbers assigned to securities under the system developed by *CUSIP.*

(The) *Daily Bond Buyer.* See *Bond Buyer.*

Date of Issue. The date assigned as the issuance date of a security.

    Comment. It may be the date on which the security was, in fact, issued or another date, i.e., "as of" date. Interest to the first interest payment date is calculated from the date of issue. Prices of the security at the time of initial sale are calculated from date of issue to maturity date.

*****Debt Limit.** The maximum amount of gross or net debt which is legally permitted.

*****Debt Offsets.** Offsets to long-term debt comprise cash and investment assets of sinking funds and other reserve funds, however designated, which are specifically held for redemption of long-term debt. This includes bond reserve funds, deposits held by fiscal agents for redemption of uncanceled debt, balances in refunding bond accounts held pending completion of refunding transactions, and any credit paper or other assets of credit funds which are pledged to ultimate redemption of debt incurred to finance loan activities of such funds.

    Assets held for redemption are included up to the amount of the specific debt for which they are accumulated. Any excess of assets over the amount of such debt, and any separately recorded amounts held for future interest payments are excluded . . .

    Comment. To the extent that the term is used in ascertaining net debt for purposes of determining the available margin for borrowing under a debt limit, appropriations made for service of specific debt for the current year, and occasionally for the succeeding year, are considered elements of debt offsets.

Debt Service. The amounts of money necessary to pay interest and principal requirements for a given year or series of years. The term may relate to a single bond issue or to a group of bond issues.

    Comment. The term is frequently used in a budgetary and reporting sense to comprehend rentals payable on governmental lessee debt.

*****Debt Service Fund.** A fund established to account for the accumulation of resources for, and the payment of, general long-term debt principal and interest. Formerly called a *Sinking Fund.*

Comment. Also used, on occasion, to denote a debt service and sinking fund or bond fund; however, not in the sense defined in this glossary.

*Debt Service Fund Requirements. The amounts of revenue which must be provided for a *Debt Service Fund* so that all principal and interest payments can be made in full on schedule.

Debt Service Rentals. See *Lease Rentals.*

Debt Service Reserve Fund. A fund created from the proceeds of a bond issue and/or the excess of applicable revenues to provide a ready reserve to meet current debt service payments should moneys not be available from current revenues.

    Comment. The amount of such debt service reserve fund is frequently established at the average annual debt service level; however, in some cases, it may be at the highest annual debt service amount or, in others, at twice the annual interest costs.

***Default. Failure to pay principal or interest promptly when due.

    Comment. It is also used to refer to a specific violation of other covenants made in respect to an issue of debt.

Defeasance. The process by which an issuer of securities is able to *defease* the lien created by an indenture or other form of contractual provision relating to a bond issue.

Defease. To discharge the lien of an ordinance, resolution, or indenture relating to a bond issue and, in the process, rendering inoperative restrictions under which the issuer has been obliged to operate.

    Comment. Ordinarily an issuer may defease an indenture requirement by depositing with a trustee an amount sufficient fully to pay all amounts under a bond contract as they become due.

*Deferred Serial Bonds. Serial bonds in which the first installment does not fall due for two or more years from the date of issue.

Definitive Bonds. The bonds delivered as the final bonds to complete the obligations of the issuer in a bond sale. When delivery of definitive bonds is not feasible on settlement date, interim certificates are sometimes issued pending the preparation of the definitive bonds.

Delivery Date. See *Settlement Date.*

Denomination. The face value or par value of a bond or note.

*Direct Debt. The debt which a government has incurred in its own name or assumed through the annexation of territory or consolidation with another government. See *Overlapping Debt.*

Disclosure Statement. See *Official Statement.*

Discount. See *Bond Discount.*

Displacement. A term used by municipal bond professionals to connote the fact that bonds planned to be sold have not been sold in accordance with the original schedule for such sale. Delays ordinarily arise from unexpected changes in market conditions which would result in higher than anticipated interest rates or litigation or other unforeseen events.

***Dollar Bond. A bond that is quoted and traded at dollar prices rather than in terms of yield.

    Comment. Frequently associated with term maturities in large amounts, especially revenue bonds which often have mandatory acceleration redemption provisions.

Dutch Auction. A competitive sale of securities, usually with all maturing on the same date, at which individual bids may be submitted and award made for less than the full amount of securities being offered. Contrasts to auction sale.

*Effective Interest Rate. The rate of earning on a bond investment based on the actual price paid for the bond, the coupon rate, the maturity date, and the length of time between interest dates, in contrast with the nominal interest rate.

Comment. The term is sometimes also used to connote the *true interest cost* for a bond issue. [See also *Yield to Maturity.*]

Enterprise Debt. Debt which is to be retired primarily from the earnings of publicly owned and operated enterprises. [See also *Revenue Bonds.*]

*Enterprise Fund. A fund established to account for operations (a) that are financed and operated in a manner similar to private business enterprises—where the intent of the governing body is that the costs (expenses, including depreciation) of providing goods or services to the general public on a continuing basis be financed or recovered primarily through user charges; or (b) where the governing body has decided that periodic determination of revenues earned, expenses incurred, and/or net income is appropriate for capital maintenance, public policy, management control, accountability, or other purposes. Examples of Enterprise Funds are those for water, gas, and electric utilities; swimming pools; airports, parking garages; and transit systems.

Equal Annual Debt Service Bond Issue. See *Serial Annuity Bonds.*

Equal Annual Maturity Bonds. Serial bond issues in which the amount of principal payment for each year is equal, or substantially equal, to the amounts payable for each other year. Also known as *Straight Serial Bonds.*

Comment. Some bond sales consist of bonds being sold under different bond authorizations, each with its own requirements. In such cases, each portion may have equal annual maturities, but, the issue, taken as a whole, may appear to provide a different pattern.

Fiscal Agent. An entity (usually a commercial bank or trust company) designated by an issuer to act for it in one or more designated capacities in the sale, administration and payment of bonds and coupons. Usually includes the functions of the *Paying Agent* and sometimes includes signing bonds for the issuer.

Fixed Debt. A term used to differentiate that portion of the debt that is funded debt from that portion that is floating debt.

*Floating Debt. Liabilities other than bonded debt and time warrants which are payable on demand or at an early date. Examples are accounts payable, notes, and bank loans.

Comment. The inclusion of notes and bank loans in this group is significant inasmuch as most floating debt is temporarily financed in this manner.

*Force Account. A method employed in the construction and/or maintenance of fixed assets whereby a government's own personnel are used instead of an outside contractor. This method also calls for the purchase of materials by the government and the possible use of its own equipment, but the distinguishing characteristic of the force account method is the use of the government's own personnel.

Forced Refunding. An involuntary refunding in which bondholders are obliged to accept refunding bonds in exchange for bonds being held. Such refunding is ordinarily accomplished only under court supervision.

Full-Faith-and-Credit Debt. Two definitions presented.

    *A pledge of the general taxing power for the payment of debt obligations. Bonds carrying such pledges are referred to as general obligation bonds or full faith and credit bonds.

    **All long-term obligations for which the credit of the government, implying power of taxation, is unconditionally pledged. This category is further subclassified under two headings as follows:

    (a) *General obligations.* Full-faith-and-credit debt other than that payable initially from nontax revenue (but including debt payable in the first instance from particularly earmarked taxes).

    (b) *Debt payable initially from specified nontax revenue.* Long-term debt amounts payable in the first instance from some specific source of nontax revenue (such as pledged toll highway revenues, recoupment of loans made in credit operations, or particular intergovernmental revenue sources) but payable from taxes or other available resources if the pledged sources are insufficient.

> *Comment.* [See also *Nonguaranteed Debt* and *Revenue Bonds.*]

*Funded Debt. Same as *Bonded Debt,* which is the preferred term.

> *Comment.* Some types of long-term debt may be funded but may be referred to in terms other than bonded debt, e.g., special assessment bonds secured in the first instance by special assessments but accepted as contingent liabilities by the issuer.

*Funded Deficit. A deficit eliminated through the sale of bonds issued for that purpose. See *Funding Bonds.*

> *Comment.* A deficit may also be funded through a long-term bank loan for which bonds are not issued.

*Funding Bonds. Bonds issued to retire outstanding floating debt and to eliminate deficits.

*General Long-term Debt. Long-term debt (other than special assessment bonds) expected to be repaid from governmental funds. See *Long-term Debt.*

General Obligation Bonds (or Debt) Three definitions.

> *Bonds for the payment of which the full faith and credit of the issuing government are pledged.

> **Full faith and credit debt other than that payable initially from nontax revenue (but including debt payable in the first instance from particularly earmarked taxes).

> ***A bond secured by the pledge of the issuer's full faith, credit and, usually, taxing power.

Good Faith Deposit. The amount of money that a bidder is obliged to deposit with an issuer to guarantee acceptance of the bonds awarded to him should the issuer conform to all of the conditions of the bond contract precedent to delivery of the bonds.

Governmental Enterprise Debt. See *Enterprise Debt.*

Governmental Lessee Bonds. Bonds issued by one governmental agency based upon the security provided by leases executed with other governments or governmental agencies as lessees.

*Gross Bonded Debt. The total amount of direct debt of a government represented by outstanding bonds before deduction of any assets available and earmarked for their retirement. [See also *Direct Debt.*]

Gross Debt. The sum total of a debtor's obligations.

Gross Refunding. An advance refunding in which the earnings on the deposited proceeds of the refunding bonds are sufficient to pay a portion, or all, of the interest on the refunding bonds with the principal of the investment being sufficient to pay principal of and interest on the refunded bonds to maturity, or earlier call date.

Housing Bonds. Bonds issued by a governmental unit to provide money for financing housing construction.

> *Comment.* For decades, the principal portion of housing bonds was known as *New Housing Bonds* issued by local public housing agencies under guarantee by the United States Government. More recently, housing and other agencies also issue a wide variety of bonds to facilitate the financing of housing which do not carry a federal guarantee.

Humped Backed Scale. A reoffering yield curve where points in some middle maturities are higher than those preceding and succeeding them.

Indenture. The formal agreement between a group of bondholders, acting through a trustee, and the issuer as to the terms and security for the debt. Ordinarily, it involves the placement of a lien upon either the income, property, or both, being acquired from expenditure of the proceeds of the bond issue.

*Industrial Revenue Bonds. Bonds issued by governments, the proceeds of which are used to construct facilities for a private business enterprise. Lease payments made by the business enterprise to the government are used to service the bonds. Such bonds may be in the form of general obligation bonds, combination bonds, or revenue bonds.

>*Comment.* Many loans for industrial aid purposes are made by banks and are reported as mortgage loans rather than bonds.

***Interest.** Compensation paid or to be paid for the use of money. Interest is generally expressed as an annual percentage rate.

>*Comment.* It may be paid at periodic intervals or at the maturity of the loan that has been discounted at the time of issuance to provide for all, or a portion, of the interest payable. Ordinarily, interest comprehends the full range of costs other than repayment of the loan received as money in hand at the time of issuance; however, the U.S. Treasury arbitrage regulations have redefined interest in a manner that excludes from the total interest payable that portion represented by the issuance costs.

*Interim Borrowing.** (1) Short-term loans to be repaid from general revenues during the course of a fiscal year. (2) Short-term loans in anticipation of tax collections or bond issuance. [See also *Bond Anticipation Notes* and *Tax Anticipation Notes.*]

Interim Certificates. Temporary certificates issued by a governmental unit to the purchaser of a bond issue pending the ability of the issuer to deliver definitive bonds. Also commonly called "temporary bonds."

Internal Rate of Return. The rate which when applied to a series of amounts of interest and principal due at different dates will result in the determination of a present value (PV-1) which precisely equals the amount received at the time a loan is made.

*Internal Service Fund.** A fund used to account for the financing of goods or services provided by one department or agency to other departments or agencies of a government, or to other governments, on a cost-reimbursement basis.

Inverted Scale. A reoffering yield curve on which the yield to maturity rates are higher in some earlier years than those for later years.

Issuance Costs. The costs incurred by the issuer of securities incident to the planning and sale of securities.

>*Comment.* These costs include the spread for underwriters, feasibility studies, printing, advertising, the fees of counsel, costs of presentations to potential investors, and the value of staff time and facilities required in the planning and sale of the bonds. They ordinarily do not include the costs of holding elections, when required as a part of the process of authorization.

Issuer. The governmental unit in the name of which securities are issued.

Joint Account. An account formed by two or more dealers for the purchase of securities.

Lease Rental. The amount payable by a lessee to a lessor for the use of property. As applied to governmental lessee debt, it relates to the amounts payable as lease rentals by the governmental lessee.

Legal Debt Limit. See *Debt Limit.*

*Legal Investments.** (1) Investments which savings banks, insurance companies, trustees, and other fiduciaries (individual or corporate) are permitted to make by the laws of the state in which they are domiciled, or under the jurisdiction in which they operate or serve. The investments which meet the conditions imposed by law constitute the legal investment list. (2) Investments which governments are permitted to make by law.

*Legal Opinion.** (1) The opinion of an official authorized to render it, such as an attorney general or city attorney as to legality. (2) In the case of governmental bonds, the opinion of a specialized bond attorney as to the legality of a bond issue. [See also *Qualified Legal Opinion* and *Preliminary Legal Opinion.*]

Level Annual Debt Service. See *Serial Annuity Bonds.*

*****Limited Tax Bond.** A bond secured by a pledge of a tax or category of taxes which is limited as to rate or amount.

Local Government. A term used to denote, on a collective basis, all of the units of government in the United States other than the federal government and the 50 state governments. It includes municipalities, townships, towns, school districts, other special districts, local authorities, corporations, and any other units of local government serving citizens on a local basis.

> *Comment.* As used by the Bureau of the Census, it includes Washington, D.C., but excludes local governments in Puerto Rico and possessions of the United States.

Local Improvement Tax. See *Special Assessment.*

***Long-term Debt.** Debt with a maturity of more than one year after the date of issuance.

MAC. See *Municipal Assistance Corporation for the City of New York.*

Marketability. Connotes ability of the issuer to sell a security in the marketplace on reasonable terms.

*****Maturity [Date].** The date on which the principal amount of a security becomes due and payable.

Micro-encoded Bonds and Coupons. Bonds and coupons printed in check size and upon which selected information commonly appearing on the face of checks is printed in a manner to facilitate processing on an automatic basis, through the banking system or otherwise.

Moral Obligation Bonds. Bonds in respect to which a government, especially a state government, has asserted the intent of the legislative body to make appropriations sufficient to cure any deficiency in moneys required to meet debt service for specified bonds but in respect to which the legislative body has no legally enforceable obligation to pay.

***Mortgage Bonds.** Bonds secured by a mortgage against specified properties of a government, usually its public utilities or other enterprises. If primarily payable from enterprise revenues, they are also classed as revenue bonds. See *Revenue Bonds.*

Municipal Assistance Corporation for the City of New York. A corporation established by the State of New York to issue bonds secured by certain revenues of the City of New York assigned to the Corporation.

***Municipal Bond.** A bond issued by a state or local government.

> *Comment.* Known as "municipals."

Municipal Commercial Paper. A form of short-term tax-exempt debt of state and local governments, usually maturing within a short period from the date of issue but in no event more than 365 days. It may be secured or unsecured, as in the case of commercial paper of corporations.

***Municipal Corporation.** A body politic and corporate established pursuant to state authorization for the purpose of providing governmental services and regulations for its inhabitants. A municipal corporation has defined boundaries and a population, and is usually organized with the consent of its residents. It usually has a seal and may sue or be sued. Cities and villages are examples of municipal corporations. See *Quasi-Municipal Corporations.*

Negotiated Sale. A sale of securities in which the terms of the sale are determined through negotiation between the issuer and the purchaser without competitive bidding. Includes sales of securities directly to commercial banks or consortiums of commercial banks as well as to investment banking firms or syndicates, private placements by issuers, or other sales to investors on other than a competitive basis.

***Net Bonded Debt.** Gross bonded debt less any cash or other assets available and earmarked for its retirement.

> *Comment.* In cases in which net debt is determined for the purpose of ascertaining available borrowing capacity, appropriations may be taken as offsets if made for the current year, and in some jurisdictions, if made for the succeeding year.

Net Interest Cost (Rate) (NIC). The average interest cost rate on a bond issue calculated on the basis of simple interest. Involves a fraction in which the numerator is the gross amount of interest to be paid over the life of the bonds plus the amount of discount or minus the amount of premium at the time of sale and the denominator of which is the average life of the bond issue times the par value of the bond issue.

Net Refunding. An advance refunding in which the net proceeds of the refunding issue are deposited with a trustee and invested with the earnings on such investments supplementing the principal to pay the principal, premium (if any), and the interest on the refunded bonds until their call date or subsequent maturity.

New Housing Bonds. Bonds issued by local public housing agencies [prior to 1976] that are secured by the full faith and credit of the United States.

New Issue Market. The market for newly issued bonds. [See also *Secondary Market.*]

NIC. See *Net Interest Cost.*

*****Nominal Interest Rate.** The contractual interest rate shown on the face and in the body of a bond and representing the amount of interest to be paid, in contrast to the effective interest rate. See *Coupon Rate.*

> *Comment.* For most bonds, the nominal interest rate is the same as the coupon rate. Also see *effective interest rate.*

******Nonguaranteed Debt.** Long-term obligations payable *solely* from pledged specific sources, such as earnings of plants or activities, special assessments, and which do not constitute obligations against other resources of the government if pledged sources are insufficient. Includes "revenue bonds" payable *solely* from earnings of toll highway facilities, college dormitories, utilities, sewage disposal plants, and the like.

Nontax Bonds. Bonds redeemable from revenue sources other than taxes.

Odd Lot Dealers. Bond dealers who purchase and sell municipal bonds in lots less than the prevailing trading quantities.

> *Comment.* In 1980, for example, the typical trading lot was $25,000; those dealers regularly trading in lesser amounts were considered odd lot dealers.

Official Advertisement. An advertisement placed by a governmental authority announcing an impending sale of securities of the issuer in a competitive sale. [See also *Official Notice* and *Official Circular.*]

Official Circular. A document setting forth the terms of the bonds being offered and the terms of the sale. The official offering may be by means of an official circular or by means of an official advertisement.

Official Notice. A notice in the form of an official advertisement of the forthcoming sale after competitive bidding of the securities of a governmental issuer.

> *Comment.* An official notice may be limited to formal advice of the impending sale whereas an official advertisement normally includes a description of all of the more significant terms of sale.

Official Statement. A statement issued by a governmental authority at the time of sale of its bonds or notes setting forth the pertinent facts concerning the issuer, the issuer's financial condition, the security pledged for the securities being offered, the projected use of the proceeds of the sale, and other facts deemed necessary to enable the investor fairly to judge the quality of the securities being offered. Also known as the *Disclosure Statement.*

On Behalf of Bonds. Bonds issued by a governmental entity to acquire facilities for nongovernmental entities, e.g., nongovernmental profit or nonprofit corporations, and the security for which is promised payments by the users of such facilities.

Optional Bond. See *Callable Bond.*

Original Issue Discount Bonds. Bonds which are a part of a bond issue sold at a discount at the time of original sale.

> *Comment.* If original issue discount bonds are sold to investors at discount, the capital gain thereon is considered a part of the tax-exempt interest.

Overlapping Debt. Two definitions.

*The proportionate share of the debts of local governments located wholly or in part within the limits of the reporting government which must be borne by property within each government. Except for special assessment debt, the amount of debt of each unit applicable to the reporting unit is arrived at by (1) determining the percentage of the total assessed value of the overlapping jurisdiction lies within the limits of the reporting unit, and (2) applying this percentage to the total debt of the overlapping jurisdiction. Special assessment debt is allocated on the basis of the ratio of assessments receivable in each jurisdiction which will be used wholly or in part to pay off the debt to total assessments receivable which will be used wholly or in part for this purpose.

***That portion of the debt of other governmental units for which residents of a particular municipality are responsible.

Comment. The MFOA definition of overlapping debt expresses a narrow view of such debt. Essentially, the objective is to determine the economic burden to be borne by the economy of a geographical area. Taxing systems that rely to a relatively modest degree upon property taxes have the effect of negating the narrower concept expressed by MFOA.

***Over-the-Counter Market (OTC).** A securities market that is conducted among dealers throughout the country through negotiation rather than through use of an auction system as represented by a stock exchange. [See also *Secondary Market.*]

Par Bid. A bid which must be in an amount at least equal to the par value of the debt instruments upon which the bid is submitted.

Par Value. The face value or amount of the principal of a bond or note.

Par Yield (Rate). The yield rate of a given bond if traded at a price equal to the par value of the bond.

Par Yield Curve. A curve developed by connecting the points of an arithmetical chart that represents the par yield applicable to securities of the same issue maturing at different times.

Patrimony. The net assets, especially the net depreciated value of fixed assets after taking into account outstanding debt in relation thereto, transferred from one "generation" to the next.

*Pay-as-You-Go Basis.** [Pay-as-You-Spend.] (1) A term used to describe the financial policy of a government which finances all of its capital outlays from current revenues rather than by borrowing. A government which pays for some improvements from current revenues and others by borrowing is said to be on a partial or modified pay-as-you-go basis. (2) Failure to finance retirement obligations on a current basis.

Comment. The phrase "pay-as-you-spend" is more descriptive of the process than the phrase "pay-as-you-go."

Pay-as-You-Use. A term used to describe the financial policy of a governmental unit which finances its capital outlays by allocating costs among the users of each "generation." It seeks to maintain a zero or near zero accumulation of patrimony as to each fixed asset acquired and used under the pay-as-you-use basis.

Paying Agent. A commercial bank or other institution acting as agent for the issuer in the payment of interest or principal on a bond or note.

Penalty Yield or **Penalty Yield Rate.** A yield in excess of the par yield for a bond or other security.

Comment. Normally, penalty yields arise from either large premiums, e.g., in excess of five percent of the par value of the bond, or from provision for the payment of the projected capital gains tax for bonds acquired at a discount.

Penalty Yield Increment. The difference between the par yield rate and the penalty yield rate.

Preliminary Legal Opinion. A draft of a legal opinion presented by a bond counsel in advance of the completion of all of the steps incident to sale. It offers an indication of the language likely to be included in the legal opinion to be issued at the time of the delivery of the bonds.

Premium. The excess of the price at which a bond is acquired or sold over its face value.

> *Comment.* The price does not include accrued interest at the date of acquisition or sale.

Present Value. The amount of money in hand delivered in exchange for promises to pay principal and/or interest at a future date or dates.

> *Comment.* For a discussion of present value, see Appendix B.

Primary Market. The market in which new issue securities are initially sold to investors.

Principal. The par value or face value of a bond, note, or other fixed amount security, excluding accrued interest.

Private Placement. Bonds or notes issued by state or local governments sold directly to investors but not reoffered to the public.

> *Comment.* Ordinarily term is used only in relation to the entire issue of the securities.

Production. A term used by investment bankers to indicate the spread between the price at which a bond issue is purchased and the price at which the bond issue would be sold should all bonds be sold at the initial reoffering yield rates.

PV-1, PV-2, and **PV-3.** Different methods of determining present value.

> *Comment.* See Appendix B for discussion.

Qualified Legal Opinion. A legal opinion containing conditional, as distinguished from unconditional, affirmations concerning the legality of an instrument used in borrowing and/or concerning the tax status of the interest on a debt instrument.

*Quasi-Municipal Corporation. An agency established by the state primarily for the purpose of helping the state to carry out its functions; for example, a county or school district. Some counties and other agencies ordinarily classified as quasi-municipal corporations have been granted the powers of municipal corporations by the state in which they are located. See *Municipal Corporation.* [See also *Municipal Assistance Corporation for the City of New York.*]

RANS. See *Revenue Anticipation Notes.*

Rate Covenant. A provision in a bond indenture under which the issuer agrees to adjust rates charged for services being rendered in order to produce sufficient revenue to meet obligations under an indenture.

Ratings. Designations of the quality of bonds or notes issued by state and local governmental units. Ratings are provided by agencies or corporations that seek thereby to render a professional judgment concerning the quality of the security being rated, e.g., Moody's Investors Service, Inc. and Standard & Poor's Corporation.

> *Comment.* See Appendix D for a discussion of ratings.

Redeemable Bond. See *Callable Bond.*

*Refunding Bonds. Bonds issued to retire bonds already outstanding. The refunding bonds may be sold for cash and outstanding bonds redeemed in cash, or the refunding bonds may be exchanged with holders of outstanding bonds. [See also *Advance Refunding Bonds.*]

*Registered Bond. A bond whose owner is registered with the issuing government [or its bank or trustee agent] and which cannot be sold or exchanged without a change of registration. Such a bond may be registered as to principal and interest or as to principal only.

*Registered Warrant. A warrant which is registered by the paying officer [or agent] for future payment due to present lack of monies and which is to be paid in the order of its registration. In some cases, such warrants are registered when issued; in others, when first presented to the paying officer by the holders. See *Warrant.*

*Regular Serial Bonds. Serial bonds in which all periodic installments of principal repayment are equal.

Reoffering Yield Curve. The curve that results from connecting the points on an arithmetic chart that are derived from plotting the reoffering yield rates for each year in a serial bond issue. See Appendix E.

Revenue Anticipation Notes (RANS). Notes issued in anticipation of the receipt of revenues, generally nontax revenues—especially revenues receivable from other governments.

*Revenue Bonds. Bonds whose principal and interest are payable exclusively from earnings of an *Enterprise Fund*. In addition to a pledge of revenues, such bonds sometimes contain a mortgage on the *Enterprise Fund's* property.

    Comment. The term revenue bonds is currently used in the municipal bond market to comprehend almost all bonds other than general obligation bonds.

Sale Date. The day on which a contract is executed between the issuer and the purchaser of an issue of securities.

    Comment. If competitively bid, the bonds ordinarily bear the same date as the bid date although it may be a different date. The execution of the contract is presumed to occur at the time of the acceptance of the bid, whether in competitive or negotiated sale.

Scale. See *Reoffering Yield Curve.*

*Scrip. An evidence of indebtedness, usually in small denominations, secured or unsecured, interest-bearing or noninterest-bearing, stating that the government, under conditions set forth, will pay the face value of the certificate or accept it in payment of certain obligations.

Secondary Market. The market in which bonds are sold at a time following the initial sale in the new issue market.

*Securities. Bonds, notes, mortgages, or other forms of negotiable or non-negotiable instruments.

*Self-Supporting or [Self-] Liquidating Debt. Debt obligations whose principal and interest are payable solely from the earnings of the enterprise for the construction or improvement of which they were originally issued. See *Revenue Bonds.*

*Serial Annuity Bonds. Serial bonds in which the annual installments of bond principal are so arranged that the combined payments for principal and interest are approximately the same each year.

*Serial Bonds. Bonds whose principal is repaid in periodic installments over the life of the issue. See *Regular Serial Bonds, Deferred Serial Bonds, Straight Serial Bonds,* and *Serial Annuity Bonds.*

    Comment. [See also *Equal Annual Maturity Bonds.*]

Settlement Date. The day on which the securities are exchanged by the issuer for the purchase price, after taking into consideration the security deposit and the accrued interest on the bonds.

*Short-term Debt. Debt with a maturity of one year or less after the date of issuance. Short-term debt usually includes floating debt, bond anticipation notes, tax anticipation notes, and interim borrowing.

    Comment. It also includes revenue anticipation notes.

*Sinking Fund. See *Debt Service Fund.*

    Comment. The term sinking fund derives from the concept of "floating a bond issue." The sinking fund was the fund created to accumulate moneys to "sink" the debt at its maturity.

*Sinking Fund Bonds. Bonds issued under an agreement which requires the government to set aside periodically out of its revenues a sum which, with compound earnings thereon, will be sufficient to redeem the bonds at their stated date of maturity. Sinking fund bonds are usually term bonds.

Sinking Fund Requirements. See *Actuarial Basis.*

*****Special Assessment.** A compulsory levy made against certain properties to defray part or all of the cost of a specific improvement or service deemed to primarily benefit those properties.

*****Special Assessment Bonds.** Bonds payable from the proceeds of special assessments. If the bonds are payable only from the collections of special assessments, they are known as special assessment bonds. If, in addition to the assessments, the full faith and credit of the government are pledged, they are known as general obligation special assessment bonds.

Special District. Two definitions.

> *****An independent unit of local government organized to perform a single governmental function or a restricted number of related functions. Special districts usually have the power to incur debt and levy taxes; however, certain types of special districts are entirely dependent upon enterprise earnings and cannot impose taxes. Examples of special districts are water districts, drainage districts, flood control districts, hospital districts, fire protection districts, transit authorities, port authorities, and electric power authorities.

> **All entities other than the four categories listed above [counties, municipalities, townships, and school districts], authorized by State law with sufficient administrative and fiscal autonomy to qualify as independent governmental units and known by a variety of titles, including districts, authorities, boards, commissions, etc., as specified in the enabling State legislation, and which are authorized to provide only one or a limited number of designated functions.

*****Special Lien Bonds.** Special assessment bonds which are liens against particular pieces of property.

*****Special Tax Bond.** A bond secured by a special tax, such as a gasoline tax.

> *Comment.* Occasionally confused with a limited tax bond.

Spread. See *Production.*

*****State Government.** The State government in each case consists of the legislative, executive, and judicial branches of government and all departments, boards, commissions, and other organizational units thereof. It also includes any semiautonomous authorities, institutions of higher education, districts and other agencies that are subject to administrative and fiscal control by the State through its appointment of officers, determination of budgets, approval of plans, and other devices. As to all such agencies, financial information included in Census reports represents their gross transactions with the public and other governments, rather than only the net effect of such transactions on central State funds. Each data item for a State government consists of the sum of the amounts of the type described for all funds and accounts—including not only the general fund but also special revenue funds, sinking funds, public trust funds, bond funds, and all other special funds.

*****Straight Serial Bonds.** Serial bonds in which the annual installments of bond principal are about equal.

*****Syndicate.** A group of investment bankers and commercial banks who buy (underwrite) a new issue from the issuer and offer it for resale to the general public.

*****Take-Down or Take-Down Concession.** The discount from the list price allowed to a member of an underwriting account on any bonds he sells.

TANS. See *Tax Anticipation Notes.*

*****Tax Anticipation Notes** (TANS). Notes (sometimes called warrants) issued in anticipation of collection of taxes, usually retirable only from tax collections, and frequently only from the proceeds of the tax levy whose collection they anticipate. [Also known as "tax anticipation warrants."]

Tax Bonds. Bonds redeemable from the proceeds of tax levies. Distinguished from revenue bonds that are secured from sources other than taxes.

Tax Delinquency Notes. Interest-bearing, short-term obligations issued in anticipation of the collection of delinquent taxes.

Tax-Exempt Bonds. Bonds in respect to which the interest is exempt from federal income taxes under Section 103 of the Internal Revenue Code of the United States or other federal legislation, e.g., housing acts.

>   *Comment.* Tax exemption is also ordinarily extended by state and local governments to the income from municipal bonds owned by residents of the state of issue. In some cases, such bonds are also exempt from other state and/or local taxes.

>   The exemption does not extend to capital gains derived from the difference between the purchase price and the par value, except in the case of original issue discount bonds for bonds kept until maturity or to profits between the purchase price and sales price for bonds sold prior to maturity.

Tax Increment Bond. A bond secured by the excess yield of specified taxes after taking into account the historic yield of such taxes for a specific area—ordinarily for an area that is being or has been redeveloped.

*Tax Liens. Claims which governments have upon properties until taxes levied against them have been paid. This term is sometimes limited to those delinquent taxes for the collection of which legal action has been taken through the filing of liens.

*Tax Notes. See *Tax Anticipation Notes.*

*Tax Rate Limit. The maximum rate at which a government may levy a tax. The limit may apply to taxes raised for a particular purpose, or to taxes imposed for all purposes, and may apply to a single government, to a class of governments, or to all governments operating in a particular area. Overall tax rate limits usually restrict levies for all purposes and of all governments, state and local, having jurisdiction in a given area.

>   *Comment.* Frequently, governments functioning under a tax rate limit for operating purposes are empowered to issue bonds secured by an unlimited tax to the extent required to pay debt service on bonds.

Temporary Bonds. See *Interim Certificates.*

*Temporary Loans. Short-term obligations representing amounts borrowed for short periods of time and usually evidenced by notes payable or warrants payable. They may be unsecured, or secured by specific revenues to be collected. See *Tax Anticipation Notes.*

Tender. An offering of securities to a governmental unit. Tenders may be made in response to invitations which contain specifications as to amounts and prices or which may be open-ended.

Term (of a Bond Issue). The term of years for which the bonds are issued. Usually related to the number of years from date of issue to date of final maturity.

*Term Bonds. Bonds the entire principal of which matures on one date.

>   *Comment.* The reference to sinking fund bonds implies a requirement for the accumulation of a sinking fund sufficient to pay the debt at its maturity. [See also *Block-term Bonds* for a description of bonds frequently called term bonds but which are not encompassed by the NCGA concept of term bonds.]

The Blue List. See *Blue List.*

TIC. See *True Interest Cost.*

*Time Warrant. A negotiable obligation of a government having a term shorter than bonds and frequently tendered to individuals and firms in exchange for contractual services, capital acquisitions, or equipment purchases.

True Interest Cost (Rate) (TIC). A rate which when used to discount each amount of debt service payable in relation to a bond issue will produce a present value (PV-1) precisely equal to the amount of money received by the issuer in exchange for the bonds.

Trustee. An individual or corporation designated as custodian of funds under a bond contract, ordinarily with additional responsibilities as specified in the bond contract for the purpose of protecting the financial interest of the bondholders.

*Unamortized Discounts on Bonds Sold. An asset account used to reflect that portion of the excess of the face value of bonds over the amount received from their sale which remains to be amortized over the remaining life of the bonds.

*Unamortized Premiums on Bonds Sold. A liability account used to reflect that portion of the excess of bond proceeds over par value and which remains to be amortized over the remaining life of such bonds.

Unlimited Tax Bond. A bond secured by a pledge of taxes that may be levied at an unlimited rate or amount.

Unqualified Bond Counsel Opinion. A bond counsel's opinion which contains no qualifications or exceptions concerning the legality of the bond issue or its tax-exempt status.

Utility Debt. Revenue bonds of a publicly owned utility.

Validation. Required approval of a bond issue by a state official or state agency. Conditions precedent to approval by such official or agency are set forth in state law.

*Warrant. An order drawn by the legislative body or an officer of a government upon its treasurer directing the latter to pay a specified amount to the person named or to the bearer. It may be payable upon demand, in which case it usually circulates the same as a bank check; or it may be payable only out of certain revenues when and if received, in which case it does not circulate as freely. See *Registered Warrant.*

Weekly Bond Buyer. See *Bond Buyer.*

*Working Capital Fund. See *Internal Service Fund.* [See also *Consolidated Cash Account.*]

Yield. See *Yield to Maturity Rate.*

Yield Curve. See *Reoffering Yield Curve.*

Yield to Maturity Rate (YTM). The percentage rate of return an investor will receive taking into account the dates of purchase and maturity of the bond, the coupon rate, and the price paid for the bond. [See also *After-tax Yield* and *Current Yield.*] See Appendix E.

Appendix D
RATING GRADES AND DESCRIPTIONS STANDARD & POOR'S AND MOODY'S INVESTORS SERVICE

The following rating symbols and descriptions are used by Standard & Poor's Corporation for municipal bonds[1]:

AAA Bonds rated AAA have the highest rating assigned by Standard & Poor's to a debt obligation. Capacity to pay interest and repay principal is extremely strong.

AA Bonds rated AA have a very strong capacity to pay interest and repay principal and differ from the highest rated issues only in small degree.

A Bonds rated A have a strong capacity to pay interest and repay principal although they are somewhat more susceptible to the adverse effects of changes in circumstances and economic conditions than bonds in higher rated categories.

BBB Bonds rated BBB are regarded as having an adequate capacity to pay interest and repay principal. Whereas they normally exhibit adequate protection parameters, adverse economic conditions or changing circumstances are more likely to lead to a weakened capacity to pay interest and repay principal for bonds in this category than for bonds in higher rated categories.

BB
B
CCC
CC Bonds rated BB, B, CCC and CC are regarded, on balance, as predominately speculative with respect to capacity to pay interest and repay principal in accordance with the terms of the obligation. BB indicates the lowest degree of speculation and CC the highest degree of speculation. While such bonds will likely have some quality and protective characteristics, these are outweighed by large uncertainties or major risk exposures to adverse conditions.

C The rating C is reserved for income bonds on which no interest is being paid.

D Bonds rated D are in default, and payment of interest and/or repayment of principal is in arrears.

Plus (+) or Minus (−): The ratings for "AA" to "BB" may be modified by the addition of a plus or minus sign to show relative standing within the major rating categories.

Provisional Ratings: The letter "p" indicates that the rating is provisional. A provisional rating assumes the successful completion of the project being financed by the bonds being rated and indicates that payment of debt service requirements is largely or entirely dependent upon the successful and timely completion of the project. This rating, however, while addressing credit quality subsequent to completion of the project, makes no comment on the likelihood of or the risk of default upon failure of such completion. The investor should exercise his own judgment with respect to such likelihood and risk.

NR Indicates that no rating has been requested, that there is insufficient information on which to base a rating, or that S&P does not rate a particular type of obligation as a matter of policy.

---

[1] Standard & Poor's Corporation, *Municipal and International Bond Ratings: An Overview*, pp. 69–70.

The following rating symbols and descriptions are used by Moody's Investors Service, Inc., for municipal bonds[2]:

Aaa Bonds which are rated Aaa are judged to be of the best quality. They carry the smallest degree of investment risk and are generally referred to as "gilt edge." Interest payments are protected by a large or by an exceptionally stable margin and principal is secure. While the various protective elements are likely to change, such changes as can be visualized are most unlikely to impair the fundamentally strong position of such issues.

Aa Bonds which are rated Aa are judged to be of high quality by all standards. Together with the Aaa group they comprise what are generally known as high grade bonds. They are rated lower than the best bonds because margins of protection may not be as large as in Aaa securities or fluctuation of protective elements may be of greater amplitude or there may be other elements present which make the long term risks appear somewhat larger than the Aaa securities.

A Bonds which are rated A possess many favorable investment attributes and are to be considered as upper medium grade obligations. Factors giving security to principal and interest are considered adequate but elements may be present which suggest susceptibility to impairment sometime in the future.

Baa Bonds which are rated Baa are considered as medium grade obligations, i.e., they are neither highly protected nor poorly secured. Interest payments and principal security appear adequate for the present but certain protective elements may be lacking or may be characteristically unreliable over any great length of time. Such bonds lack outstanding investment characteristics and in fact have speculative characteristics as well.

Ba Bonds which are rated Ba are judged to have speculative elements; their future cannot be considered as well assured. Often the protection of interest and principal payments may be very moderate and thereby not well safeguarded during both good and bad times over the future. Uncertainty of position characterizes bonds in this class.

B Bonds which are rated B generally lack characteristics of the desirable investment. Assurance of interest and principal payments or the maintenance of other terms of the contract over any long period of time may be small.

Caa Bonds which are rated Caa are of poor standing. Such issues may be in default or there may be present elements of danger with respect to principal or interest.

Ca Bonds which are rated Ca represent obligations which are speculative in a high degree. Such issues are often in default or have other marked shortcomings.

C Bonds which are rated C are the lowest rated class of bonds and issues so rated can be regarded as having extremely poor prospects of ever attaining any real investment standing.

Con. (. . .) Bonds for which the security depends upon the completion of some act or the fulfillment of some condition are rated conditionally. These are bonds secured by (a) earnings of projects under construction, (b) earnings of projects unseasoned in operating experience, (c) rentals which begin when facilities are completed, or (d) payments to which some other limiting condition attaches. Parenthetical rating denotes probable credit stature upon completion of construction or elimination of basis of condition.

---

[2] Moody's Investors Service, *Moody's Bond Record,* Vol. 48, No. 9 (September, 1981), pp. 1–2, 129, 191.

Rating Refinements: Those bonds in the Aa, A, Baa, Ba and B groups which Moody's believes possess the strongest investment attributes are designated by the symbols Aa 1, A 1, Baa 1, Ba 1, and B 1.

In addition to its ratings of municipal bonds, Moody's provides ratings of short-term loans to which it assigns one of four ratings:

MIG 1. Loans bearing this designation are of the best quality, enjoying strong protection from established cash flows of funds for their servicing or from established and broad-based access to the market for refinancing, or both.

MIG 2. Loans bearing this designation are of high quality, with margins of protection ample although not so large as in the preceding group.

MIG 3. Loans bearing this designation are of favorable quality, with all security elements accounted for but lacking the undeniable strength of the preceding grades. Market access for refinancing, in particular, is likely to be less well established.

MIG 4. Loans bearing this designation are of adequate quality, carrying specific risk but having protection commonly regarded as required of an investment security and not distinctly or predominately speculative.

Beyond the foregoing, Moody's also carries a set of ratings for commercial paper; however, these ratings have heretofore been largely applied to taxable issuers and, therefore, are not included here even though some nontaxable issues have apparently been included in its rating activities.

Appendix E
CAPITAL GAINS TAXATION
OF TAX-EXEMPT BONDS

The interest on state and local government bonds is generally tax free for purposes of federal income taxation and also for state and local income taxation within the state of issue of the bonds. On the other hand, such income as is derived in the form of a gain between the price at which the bond was acquired and the amount received either at sale prior to maturity or at redemption of the bond is considered a taxable capital gain under most circumstances. The only significant exception is in relation to bonds sold under terms qualifying for "original issue discount" (OID) as discussed later in this Appendix.

The calculation of the yield rate for municipal bonds subject to capital gains taxation is likely to be in dual terms: (1) the gross yield to be derived and (2) the after-tax yield. Appendix Table E-1 illustrates the manner in which these two yield rates are related and in which the calculations of the pre-tax yield is derived in principle. In the development of the table it has been assumed that a bond is being purchased (in either the primary or secondary market) which bears a coupon rate of 4.50 percent, is due 18 years from date, and that the transaction occurs in a market which would produce a 6.20 tax-free yield should the coupon rate and the yield rate be identical: In other words, for a 6.20 coupon bond purchased at par.

On Line 5 it is noted that the price of the bond would be $817.16 assuming that there were no capital gains tax to be paid. However, from Line 7 it is noted that for any taxable investor a capital gains tax would be payable, with the amount depending upon the taxable position of the investor. Under existing legislation for the individual, long-term capital gains are taxable at one-half the rate at which current income is taxable. By law, however, certain advantages are provided which establish the maximum long-term capital gains rate at 20 percent. Therefore in Column 2 the amount of the capital gains tax is estimated at $36.56 for the individual. For those who would be entitled to a lesser maximum income tax rate, the capital gains tax presumed to be payable at maturity would be at a correspondingly lesser amount.

On the other hand capital gains for profit-oriented corporations are taxed at the rate for ordinary income [subject to certain refinements not required for exploration here]. As a result in Column 3, Line 7, it is noted that the capital gains tax presumed to be payable at maturity for the bond would amount to $84.11. The present value of the capital gains tax (for the initial calculation only) appears on Line 8 as being $12.18 for the individual and $28.02 for the corporation when computed at the semiannual rate of 3.10 percent (one-half the after tax yield rate on Line 2). However, given the fact that the taxable investor would be confronted with this as a potential present value diminution of his invested capital, the calculation of the capital gains tax must now be extended to this amount in the second round on Lines 9 and 10, producing a further present value of $0.81 for the individual and $4.30 for the corporation. This process is repeated in successive rounds and it is finally determined that the present value of the total capital gains tax presumed to be payable becomes $13.04 for the individual and $33.10 for the corporation. Thus the total discount which would be involved in order to maintain the after-tax yield objective in the original transaction becomes $195.88 for the individual and $215.94 for the corporate investor.

Appendix Table E-1

Illustrative Calculation of Impact of Capital Gains Taxation on Yields and Prices of Tax-free Municipal Bonds

(based upon a $1,000 par value bond)

Line	Item	Tax-Exempt Purchaser	Highest Bracket Individual Taxpayer	Corporate or Financial Institution Taxpayer
		(1)	(2)	(3)
1	Maximum tax rate for purchaser	—	20.00	46.00
2	After-tax yield rate for par bond	6.20	6.20	6.20
3	Coupon rate for bond	4.50	4.50	4.50
4	Years to maturity	18	18	18
5	Price before accounting for capital gains tax	817.16	817.16	817.16
	Initial Round: Capital Gains			
6	Capital gain at maturity: $1,000 − (5)	182.84	182.84	182.84
7	Capital gains tax at maturity	—	36.56	84.11
8	Capital gains tax: Present value	—	12.18	28.02
	Second Round: Capital Gains			
9	Capital gains tax on Line 8	—	2.44	12.89
10	Capital gains tax: Present value	—	.81	4.30
	Third Round: Capital Gains			
11	Capital gains tax on Line 10	—	.15	1.98
12	Capital gains tax: Present value	—	.05	.66
	Fourth Round: Capital Gains			
13	Capital gains tax on Line 12	—	—	.30
14	Capital gains tax: Present value	—	—	.10
15	Total present value of capital gains taxes payable (8) + (10) + (12) + (14)	—	13.04	33.10
16	Total discount (6) + (15)	182.84	195.88	215.94
17	Adjusted price $1,000 − (16)	817.16	804.12	784.05
18	Approximate adjusted gross yield corresponding to price on Line 17	6.20	6.34	6.56
19	Penalty yield	—	.14	.36
20	Price penalty (17) − (6)	—	13.04	33.10
21	Price penalty as percent of nonpenalty price (20) ÷ (6)	—	1.60	4.05

The gross yield to the investors would thereupon continue at 6.20 for the nontaxable investor if he should acquire the bond at $817.16 (Line 17). For the taxable individual assumed here, the adjusted price would become $804.12 (Line 17) with an adjusted gross yield of approximately 6.34 percent. For the corporate investor, the yield would be 6.56 percent before taxes if the bond could be purchased at $784.05.

Penalty yields would normally have to be assumed by the holder of the bond inasmuch as the purchaser would presumably have access to other securities of equal value at the market tax-free yield of 6.20 percent. Therefore he would suffer a 0.14 percent decrease in YTM at sale if to the individual and 0.36 percent decrease in YTM in the case of the corporate investor.

Of course the market is not this finely tuned for the ordinary transaction. When the bond is offered in either the primary or secondary market it is offered at a stated yield or price. The seller therefore determines the type of investor toward whom he is prepared to make his offer. This does not preclude other investors more fortunately situated as to taxes from taking advantage of the situation and deriving a better after-tax yield.

The major point is that in the case of bonds sold in the primary market which involve the likelihood of eventual payment of a capital gains tax, the issuer is likely to be obliged to absorb the present value of that tax calculated under the principles illustrated in Appendix Table E-1. Accordingly it is to the advantage of the issuer to avoid such penalty yields when feasible, and well-designed issues under appropriate specifications can almost always avoid this type of penalty yield.

Original Issue Discount

The only way in which the issuer can avoid the type of prepayment of the present value of the capital gains tax on such maturities as are reoffered at penalty yields arising from coupon rates being substantially below reoffering yield rates is under the "original issue discount" rule. Under this rule the Internal Revenue Service permits the original discount to be amortized as nontaxable interest, except to the extent that it represents issuance cost. In negotiated sales this is relatively easy to arrange by specifying in the purchase contract that certain bonds are being sold by the issuer as an original issue discount. This is considerably more difficult to arrange in competitive sales and exceedingly few issuers have developed and used bid specifications which make this feasible.

Where the original issue discount is in a form acceptable to the Internal Revenue Service, the owner is permitted to claim the capital gain as payment in lieu of coupon interest and to treat it as nontaxable income.

Implications for Zero Coupon Bonds

There is a major implication here for zero coupon bonds. If a zero coupon bond is a part of a general bond issue sold at competitive sale where the specifications do not permit application of the OID rule, then the capital gains tax is presumably applicable and inasmuch as the capital gains, especially on the longer term bonds, would be tremendous, the issuer would be obliged to make a huge prepayment of the projected capital gains tax to be payable at maturity. This should essentially foreclose its use in that circumstance.

On the other hand in negotiated sales and in appropriately designed competitive sales this liability of the zero coupon bond would not be present.

Appendix F
BIBLIOGRAPHY

A. General Works and Articles

Advisory Commission on Intergovernmental Relations. *Federal Approaches to Aid State and Local Capital Financing.* Washington: U.S. Government Printing Office, 1970.

————. *Significant Features of Fiscal Federalism: 1976–1977 Edition, Volume II—Revenues and Debt.* Washington: U.S. Government Printing Office, 1977.

————. *State Technical Assistance to Local Debt Management.* Washington: U.S. Government Printing Office, 1965.

Anderson, Lynn F. *A Debt Manual for Texas Cities.* Austin: Bureau of Municipal Research, University of Texas, 1949.

Ayres, Robert Moss. "The Procedures for Underwriting New Issues of Municipal Obligations." Master's thesis, University of Pennsylvania, 1952.

Beerman, Albert L. "How Much Disclosure Do Municipal Bond Investors Really Want?" *Banking* 70 (1978):66 ff.

Berenyi, John. "Financing Governmental Activities in the United States: With Special Reference to the State and Local Markets: A Private Banker's View of the Public Capital Markets." *Local Finance* 3 (1974):3–9.

Bierwag, G. O. "Optimal TIC Bids on Serial Bond Issues." Mimeographed. Eugene, Oregon: University of Oregon, 1974.

Bierwag, G. O.; Hopewell, Michael H.; and Kaufman, George G. "TIC Coupon Optimizing Program." *The Daily Bond Buyer,* October 2, 1974.

Boyles, Harlan E. "Marketing Municipal Bonds in Today's Full-Disclosure Environment." *Popular Government* 43 (1978):7–9.

Brazer, Harvey E., ed. *Essays in State and Local Finance.* Ann Arbor, Michigan: University of Michigan Press, 1967.

Brealey, Richard A., and Pyle, Connie, compilers. *A Bibliography of Finance and Investment.* Cambridge, Mass: The MIT Press, 1973.

Brown, Fraser. *Municipal Bonds: A Statement of the Principles of Law and Custom.* New York: Prentice-Hall, Inc., 1922.

Browne, Alan K. "Misuse of Public Credit to Aid Private Enterprise: The Case Against Municipal Industrial Revenue Bonds." In *State and Local Taxes on Business.* Princeton: The Tax Institute, 1965.

Browne, Lynn E., and Syron, Richard F. "Big City Bonds After New York," *New England Economic Review,* July/August, 1977, pp. 3–15.

Bureau of National Affairs and Institute for Professional and Executive Development. *Tax Exempt Mortgage Bonds for Single Family Housing: Opportunities, Pitfalls and Public Policy Directions.* Washington: Bureau of National Affairs, 1979.

Burnham, J. A. *Law of Municipal Bonds.* Chicago: (privately published), 1889.

Burwell, James M. "Borrowing and Investment by Municipal Governments: In an Attempt to Cope with Tomorrow's Demands for Improved Service, Where Should the Municipal Administrator Look for Capital Funds to Finance the Construction and Maintenance of New Service?" *Chartered Accountant* 101 (1972):37–40.

Buse, A. "Expectations, Prices, Coupons and Yields," *Journal of Finance,* September 1970, pp. 809–18.

Cagan, Philip. "The Interest Saving to States and Municipalities From Bank Eligibility to Underwrite All Nonindustrial Municipal Bonds," *Governmental Finance* 7 (1978):40–48.

Calvert, Gordon L. ed. *Fundamentals of Municipal Bonds.* New York: Securities Industry Association, 1972.

Carr, Frank C. "Municipal Bond Insurance." In *Municpal Finance Officers Association Special Bulletin 1972C.*

Chase, Davis and Bryson, Charles. *Bank Participation in Municipal Revenue Bond Underwriting: Impact on Securities Industry Revenues.* Washington: Securities and Exchange Commission, 1979.

Chatters, Carl H. and Hillhouse, Albert M., *Local Government Debt Administration.* New York: Prentice-Hall, Inc., 1939.

Clark, John C. "Local Government Bond Ratings: The Changing Scene." *Popular Government* 34 (1968):20–24.

Clark, Joseph F. "Observations Concerning the Rating of Municipal Bonds and Credits," In *Municipal Finance Officers Association Special Bulletin,* February 1972.

Coe, Charles K. and Stallings, C. Wayne. *A Debt Management Handbook for Small Cities and other Governmental Units.* Municipal Finance Officers Association, 1978.

Commerce Clearing House, Inc. *Municipal Securities Rulemaking Board Manual.* Chicago: Commerce Clearing House, Inc. 1980.

Continental Illinois National Bank and Trust Company. *State Housing Finance and Mortgage Finance Agencies.* Chicago: Continental Illinois National Bank and Trust Company of Chicago, 1977.

Coopers & Lybrand. *Financial Disclosure Practices of American Cities: Closing The Communications Gap. II.* New York: Coopers & Lybrand, 1978.

Cronson, Robert G. and Touche Ross & Co. *Program Audit of the Management of State Long-Term Debt.* Springfield (Illinois): Office of the Auditor General, 1978.

Daley, Joseph C. *A Guide to Municipal Offering Statements.* New York: Harcourt Brace Janovich, 1981.

Danforth, Louis F. "Analyzing Municipals and Other Credits." *Bankers Magazine* 155 (1972):91–95.

Darst, David M. *The Complete Bond Book: A Guide to All Types of Fixed-Income Securities.* New York: McGraw-Hill, 1975.

Doty, Robert W. and Petersen, John E. "The Federal Securities Laws and Transactions in Municipal Securities." *Northwestern University Law Review* 71 (1976):283–412.

Dyl, Edward A. and Joehnk, Michael D. "Refunding Tax Exempt Bonds," *Financial Management* 5 (1976):59–66.

Dyl, E. A. and Joehnk, M. D. "Competitive versus Negotiated Underwriting of Public Utility Debt." *Bell Journal of Economics,* 7:680–689.

Etter, Wayne E. and Fraser, Donald R. "Broadening the Municipal Market: A Neglected Issue." In *Municipal Finance Officers Association Special Bulletin 1974.*

Farnham, Paul G. and Cluff, George. *The Municipal Bond Rating Process: Implications for Local Government Decisions.* Atlanta: Georgia State University, 1981.

Financial Accounting Standards Board. *Objectives of Financial Reporting by Nonbusiness Organizations.* High Ridge Park (Stamford, Connecticut): Financial Accounting Standards Board, 1979.

_____. *Statements of Financial Accounting Standards No. 22: Changes in the Provisions of Lease Agreements Resulting From Refunding of Tax-Exempt Debt* (an amendment to FASB Statement No. 13). High Ridge Park (Stamford, Connecticut): Financial Accounting Standards Board, 1978.

Financial Publishing Company. *Financial Net Yield Table After 48% Tax on Discount for Tax Exempt Discount Bonds.* Boston: The Financial Publishing Company, 1970.

Fitch, Lyle. *Taxing Municipal Bond Income.* Sacramento: University of California Press, 1950.

Forbes, Ronald W., and Petersen, John E. *Building a Broader Market.* Report of the Twentieth Century Fund Task Force on the Municipal Bond Market. New York:McGraw-Hill Book Company, 1976.

_____. *Local Government General Obligation Bond Sales in Pennsylvania: The Cost Implications of Negotiation vs. Competitive Bidding.* Washington: Municipal Finance Officers Association, 1979.

Fortune, Peter. "Tax-exemption of State and Local Interest Payments: An Economic Analysis of the Issues and an Alternative." *New England Economic Review,* May/June 1973, pp. 3–31.

Galper, Harvey and Peterson, George F. "The Equity Effects of A Taxable Municipal Bond Subsidy." *National Tax Journal* XXVI: 611–624.

Gobar, Alfred J. "Avoiding Limits on Local Borrowing." *Business Review* 24 (1967): 6–8.

Haley, John F., Jr. "A Study of State-Imposed Municipal Bond Validation Requirements." In *Government Financial Management Resources in Review.* Washington: Municipal Finance Officers Association, 1979.

Harris, Alfred T. "Deep Discount Tax Exempt Bonds: Who Buys Them—Why?" *The Daily Bond Buyer,* November 30, 1964, pp. 40, 42–43.

Hastie, Larry. "Determinants of Municipal Bond Yields." *Journal of Financial and Quantitative Analysis* 7 (1972):1729–1948.

Havemann, Joel. "Cities, States Aren't Buying Proposals to Shore Up Bond Market [Response to Bills Before the Congress to Strengthen the Municipal Bond Market by Requiring More Disclosure of Financial Information and to Allow Governments to Issue Taxable Bonds]." *National Journal* 8 (1976):394–399.

Healy, Patrick. "The Assault on Tax-exempt Bonds," *Tax Policy* 36 (1969):2–16.

_____. "Further Comments on Proposed Capital Financing Alternatives." *Tax Policy* 37 (1970):1–12.

Heins, A. James. *Constitutional Restrictions Against State Debt.* Madison: The University of Wisconsin Press, 1963.

_____. "Constraints on NIC Bidding: Discussion and Recommendations." Mimeographed. Eugene, Oregon: University of Oregon, 1974.

Hempel, George H. *Measures of Municipal Bond Quality.* Ann Arbor: The University of Michigan Press, 1967.

_____. "Quantitative Borrower Characteristics Associated With Defaults on Municipal General Obligations," *Journal of Finance* 28 (1973):523–530.

Hillhouse, A. M. *Municipal Bonds: A Century of Experience.* New York: Prentice-Hall, Inc., 1936. Reprint. New York: Arno Press, 1975.

Homer, Sidney and Leibowitz, Martin L. *Inside the Yield Book: New Tools for Bond Market Strategy.* Englewood Cliffs, N.J.: Prentice-Hall, Inc., and New York: New York Institute of Finance, 1972.

Hopewell, Michael H. and Kaufman, George G. "The Cost of Inefficient Coupons on Municipal Bonds." *Journal of Financial and Quantitative Analysis,* March 1974, pp. 155–164.

_____. "Cost to Issuers of Using NIC in Competitive Bond Sales." *The Daily Bond Buyer,* June 24, 1974.

_____. "Costs to Municipalities of Selling Bonds by NIC." *National Tax Journal,* December 1974, pp. 531–541.

Hopewell, Michael H.; Kaufman, George G.; and West, Richard R. "'Lowest' Bond Bid

Costs Minnesota Extra One Million Dollars." Mimeographed. Eugene: Oregon: University of Oregon, 1972.

Huefner, Robert P. "Municipal Bonds: The Costs and Benefits of an Alternative." *National Tax Journal* 23 (1970):407–416.

_____. *Taxable Alternatives to Municipal Bonds.* Boston: Federal Reserve Bank of Boston, 1972.

Illinois, Office of the Auditor General. Program Audit of the Management of State Long-Term Debt. Springfield: Office of the Auditor General, 1978.

Jarrett, James E. and Hicks, Jimmy E. *The Bond Bank Innovation: Maine's Experience.* Lexington, Kentucky: Council of State Governments, 1977.

Joehnk, Michael D. and Hays, Patrick. "Reducing Interest Costs on Municipal Bond Issues [by Improving the Procedures Used to Award Bond Issues]." *Colorado Business Review* 50 (1977):2–4.

Joehnk, Michael D. and Kidwell, David S. "Comparative Cost Study Favors Competitive Bidding over Negotiation." *The Daily Bond Buyer–PSA Supplement,* October 8, 1979, pp. 16–19.

_____. "Determining the Advantages and Disadvantages of Private Municipal Bond Guarantees; Local Finance Officers Can Evaluate Properly the Decision to Purchase Private Municipal Bond Insurance with the Aid of a Managerial Model which Considers Both the Benefits and Costs of the Guarantee Decision Over Time." *Governmental Finance* 7 (1978):30–36.

Kalita, Arthur J. "The Effects of Unforeseen Developments on Competitive Sales." *The Daily Bond Buyer* (PSA Supplement), October 8, 1979, pp. 7–9.

Katzmann, Martin T. "Measuring the Savings from State Municipal Bond Banking." *Governmental Finance* 9:19–25.

Kaufman, George G. "Implications of Couponing Municipal Bonds in NIC Bidding." In Fisher, Donald E., ed. *Proceedings of the 1973 Annual Meeting of the Eastern Finance Association.* Hartford: University of Connecticut, 1973.

Kaufman, George, and Hopewell, Michael. *Improving Bidding Rules to Reduce Interest Costs in the Competitive Sale of Municipal Bonds: A Handbook for Municipal Finance Officers.* Eugene: Center for Capital Market Research, University of Oregon, in cooperation with the Municipal Finance Officers Association. 1977.

Kaufman, George G. "Improving Competitive Bidding Procedures for Municipal Bonds." *Governmental Finance* 3 (1974):22–27.

_____. "State and Regional Effects on the Interest Cost of Municipal Bonds in the United States." *Local Finance* 5 (1976):19–23.

_____. Experience with TIC Bidding," *The Daily Bond Buyer—SIA Supplement,* October 2, 1974.

Keir, Peter M. and Kichline, James. "Interest Cost Effects of Commercial Bank Underwriting of Municipal Revenue Bonds." *Federal Reserve Bulletin* 53 (1967):1287–1302.

Kelley, Peter P. Jr., et. al. *Municipal Bond Insurance: An Evaluation.* New York: Merrill Lynch Pierce Fenner & Smith, Inc., 1980.

Kessel, Reuben. "A Study of the Effects of Competition in the Tax-Exempt Bond Market." *Journal of Political Economy,* July/August 1971, pp. 706–738.

Kidwell, David S. "Characteristics of Call Provisions on State and Local Government Bonds." *Economics and Business* 15 (1976):63–70.

_____. "Saving Interest on Municipal Bonds." *Indiana Business Review* 51 (1976):1–6.

Kirk, John. "What You Ought to Know About Escrowed Municipals." *Banking* 59 (1967):10 ff.

Klapper, Byron, "Facing Up to Facts: SEC is Suing Lawyers for Failing to Uncover Municipal Bond Frauds." *Wall Street Journal* 190, July 26, 1977, p. 1.

Klapper, Byron and Pappas, Vasil. "Tell and Sell: Wall Street is Forcing Cities to Disclose

More When Floating Bonds: Underwriters Hold Up Issues to Back New Guidelines." *Wall Street Journal* 189, June 30, 1977, p. 1.

Lalley, Francis A. "Marketing Municipal Bonds: The Philadelphia Plan." *Municipal Finance Officers Association, Special Bulletin, 1962.*

Lamb, Robert, and Rappaport, Stephen P. *Municipal Bonds: The Comprehensive Review of Tax Exempt Securities and Public Finance.* New York: McGraw-Hill Book Company, 1980.

Lawson, Herbert G. "Fishy Finance Investors Lose Millions on a California Swamp Called Quimby Island." *Wall Street Journal* 191, January 4, 1978, p. 1.

Lerner, Allan C. and Nathanson, Philip D. *Forecasting Municipal Rates and Spreads by Monitoring Trends in Other Markets.* New York: Bankers Trust Company, 1978.

London (Ontario), Department of Finance. *Municipal Debt Carrying Capacity Study.* London (Ontario): City of London, [1979].

Ludeman, Douglas H. *The Investment Merits of Big City Bonds.* Boston: Financial Publishing Company, 1973.

Madrick, Jeffrey G. *Fundamentals of Municipal Bonds.* New York: Public Securities Association, 1981.

––––––. "The Municipal Funds Are no Sure Thing." *Business Week,* November 29, 1976, p. 60.

Malkiel, Burton G. *The Term Structure of Interest Rates.* Princeton: Princeton University Press, 1966.

Mangnusson, Jon. "Lease-Financing by Municipal Corporations as a Way Around Debt Limitations." *George Washington Law Review* Vol. 25, No. 3 (March 1957), pp. 41–60.

Mann, Bettie. *State Constitutional Restrictions on Local Government Borrowing and Property Taxing Powers.* Albany (New York): Governmental Affairs Foundation, 1965.

Maxwell, James A. *Financing State and Local Governments.* Washington: The Brookings Institution, 1969.

May, Eleanor G. *Bond Banks: Their Role in Assisting Municipalities in Obtaining Funds for Public Improvement Purposes, with Particular Application to the Commonwealth of Virginia.* Charlottesville: University of Virginia, 1973.

Miralia, Lauren M. "Municipal Bond Insurance Gaining Acceptance." (American Bankers Association) *Banking Journal,* 172:63 ff.

Mitchell, William E. *The Effectiveness of Debt Limits on State and Local Government Borrowing.* New York: New York University, 1967.

Moak, Lennox L. *Administration of Local Government Debt.* Chicago: Municipal Finance Officers Association, 1970.

Moak, Lennox L. and Killian, Kathryn W. *A Manual of Suggested Practice for the Preparation and Adoption of Capital Programs and Capital Budgets by Local Governments.* Chicago: Municipal Finance Officers Association, 1964.

Moak, Lennox L. and Hillhouse, Albert M. *Concepts and Practices in Local Government Finance.* Chicago: Municipal Finance Officers Association, 1975.

Moody's Investor Service. *Pitfalls in Issuing Municipal Bonds.* 4th edition. New York: Moody's Investor Service, Inc., 1982.

Morris, Frank E. "Restructuring the Municipal Bond Market." *New England Economic Review* January/February, 1971, pp. 47–52.

Mumy, Gene E. "Issuers' Cost and Competition in the Tax-Exempt Bond Market." *National Tax Journal* 31 (1978):81–91.

––––––. "Impact of Monetary Policy on State and Local Governments: An Empirical Study." *The Journal of Finance* 15:233.

Municipal Finance Officers Association. "Costs Involved in Marketing State/Local Bonds: A Survey." Chicago: Municipal Finance Officers Association, 1973.

––––––. *Disclosure Guidelines for Offering of Securities by State and Local Government.* Chicago: Municipal Finance Officers Association, 1976.

_____. *Disclosure Guidelines for State and Local Governments.* Chicago: Municipal Finance Officers Association, 1979.

_____. *Governmental Accounting, Auditing, and Financial Reporting.* Chicago: Municipal Finance Officers Association, 1980.

_____. *Guidelines for Use by State and Local Governments in the Preparation of Yearly Information Statements and Other Current Information.* Chicago: Municipal Finance Officers Association, 1978.

_____. *Official Statements for Offerings of Securities by Local Governments—Examples and Guidelines.* Chicago: Municipal Finance Officers Association, 1981.

_____. *Procedural Statements in Connection with the Disclosure Guidelines for Offering Securities of State and Local Governments and the Guidelines for Use by State and Local Governments in the Preparation of Yearly Information Statements and Other Current Information.* Chicago: Municipal Finance Officers Association, 1978.

_____. *The Call Feature in Municipal Bonds.* Chicago: Municipal Finance Officers Association, 1933.

_____. *Watching and Counting: A Survey of State Assistance to and Supervision of Local Debt and Financial Administration.* Chicago: Municipal Finance Officers Association. 1979.

_____. "State Bond Banks." *Municipal Finance Officers Association Special Bulletin, 1972.*

Municipal Finance Officers Association, Governmental Research Center. *Governmental Financial Management: Resources in Review,* Vol. 4, No. 1 (January 1981).

Mussa, Michael. *Competition and Borrowing Costs in Municipal Revenue Bond Market: An Appraisal of the Evidence.* Chicago: Privately published by author from Graduate School of Business of the University of Chicago, 1979.

_____. "The Taxable Bond Option: Appraisal of its Economic Effects." *The Daily Bond Buyer: MFOA Supplement,* May 15, 1979.

Mussa, Michael L. and Kormendi, Roger C. *The Taxation of Municipal Bonds: An Economic Appraisal.* Washington: American Enterprise Institute for Public Policy Research, 1979.

National Association of Supervisors of State Banks, Committee on Municipal Obligations. *Municipals.* Washington: National Capital Press, 1941.

National Committee on Governmental Accounting. *Governmental Accounting, Auditing, and Financial Reporting.* Chicago: Municipal Finance Officers Association, 1968.

National Conference of State Legislatures and Municipal Finance Officers Association. *Guidelines for Single-Family, Tax-Exempt Mortgage Revenue Bonds.* Chicago: Municipal Finance Officers Association, 1980.

National Council on Governmental Accounting. *Statement I: Governmental Accounting and Financial Reporting Principles.* Chicago: Municipal Finance Officers Association, 1979.

_____. *Statement 2: Grant, Entitlement, and Shared Revenue Accounting and Reporting by State and Local Governments.* Chicago: Municipal Finance Officers Association, 1980.

National Institute of Municipal Law Officers. *Report of Committee on Municipal Bonds. NIMLO Municipal Law Review, 1963.* Washington: National Institute of Municipal Law Officers, 1964.

National Municipal League. *Model Municipal General Obligation Bond Law.* New York: National Municipal League, 1970.

_____. *Model Municipal Revenue Bond Law.* New York: National Municipal League, 1970.

Neely, L. Mason. "Can the Municipal Bond Market Be Broadened to Reach the Average Citizen?" *Municipal Management: A Journal* 1:143–150.

Nichols, F. Glenn. "Debt Limitations and the Bona Fide Long-term Lease with an Option to Purchase: Another Look at Lord Coke." *Urban Lawyer, The National Journal of Urban Law,* Vol. 2, No. 2 (Spring 1977) pp. 11–28.

New Jersey Tax Policy Committee. *The Use and Costs of Public Credit.* Report No. 4. Trenton: New Jersey Tax Policy Committee, 1972.

Oldman, Oliver and Schoettle, Ferdinand P. *State and Local Taxes and Finance: Text, Problems and Cases.* Mineola (New York): The Foundation Press, Inc., 1974.

Oregon, University of. *Improved Bidding Rules to Reduce Interest Costs in Competitive Sale of Municipal Bonds: A Handbook for Municipal Finance Officers.* Eugene: University of Oregon, 1977.

———, Center for Capital Market Research, in cooperation with the Municipal Finance Officers Association. *Improving Bidding Rules to Reduce Interest Costs in the Competitive Sale of Municipal Bonds.* Chicago: Municipal Finance Officers Association, 1977.

———. *Local Government Bonding in Oregon.* Eugene: University of Oregon, 1972.

Peacock, Thomas P. "A Review of Municipal Securities and Their Status under Federal Securities Laws as Amended by the Securities Acts Amendments of 1975." *Business Lawyer* 31 (1976):2037–2061.

Peaslee, James M. "Limits of Section 102(c): Municipal Bond Arbitrage After the Invested Sinking Fund." *Tax Law Review* 34:421–471 (1978).

Petersen, John E.; Doty, Robert W.; Forbes, Ronald W.; and Borque, Donald D. "Search for Standards: Disclosure in the Municipal Securities Market." *Duke Law Journal* 1976:1178–1204.

Petersen, John E. and Doty, Robert W. *Regulation of the Municipal Securities Market and Its Relationship to the Governmental Issuer.* Chicago: Municipal Finance Officers Association, 1975.

Petersen, John E. "Small Borrowers in the Municipal Bond Market: Does Size Matter?" In *Conference on Non-Metropolitan Community Services Research,* proceedings of a conference sponsored by the U.S. Senate Committee on Agriculture, Nutrition and Forestry. Washington: U.S. Government Printing Office, 1977.

Petersen, John E.; Spain, Catherine Lavigne; and Laffey, Martharose F., eds. *State and Local Finance and Financial Management: A Compendium of Current Research.* Washington: Municipal Finance Officers Association, 1978.

Petersen, John E.; Stallings, Wayne; and Spain, Catherine Lavigne. *State Roles in Local Government Financial Management: A Comparative Analysis.* Washington: Municipal Finance Officers Association, 1979.

Petersen, John E.; Cole, Lisa A.; and Petrillo, Maria. *Watching and Counting: A Survey of State Assistance to and Supervision of Local Government Debt and Financial Administration.* Chicago: Municipal Finance Officers Association and National Conference of State Legislators, 1977.

Peterson, George E. with Cooper, Brian. *Tax-Exempt Financing of Housing Investment.* Washington: The Urban Institute, 1979.

Phillips, Almarin. "The Banks' Case for Underwriting Tax-Exempt Revenue Bonds." *The Daily Bond Buyer—MFOA Supplement,* June 4, 1979.

Porter, Richard J. "Factors Influencing the Cost of State and Local Borrowing in Kentucky." Lexington (Kentucky): University of Kentucky, 1965.

———. "Underwriter's Price Policy for Municipal Serial Bond Offerings.' Ph.D. dissertation, University of North Carolina, 1965.

Priest, Ivy Baker. "The Case Against Taxable Municipal Bonds." *Governmental Finance* 2 (1973):6 ff.

Public Securities Association, *Fundamentals of Municipal Bonds.* New York: Public Securities Association, 1981.

Rabinowitz, Alan. *Municipal Bond Finance and Administration.* New York: Wiley-Interscience, 1969.

Ratchford, B. U. *American State Debts.* Durham (North Carolina): Duke University Press, 1941. Reprinted New York: AMS Press, Inc., 1966.

Reeves, H. Clyde, "A Case for Industrial Revenue Bonds." In *State and Local Taxes on Business.* Princeton: Tax Institute, 1965.

Reilly, James F. *Too Good For The Rich Alone.* Englewood Cliffs (New Jersey): Prentice-Hall Inc., 1975.

Renshaw, Edward and Forbes, Ronald. "The Case for Zero Coupon Bonds." *The Daily Bond Buyer,* May 30, 1972, pp. 43–44.

Richardson, Pearl. *Small Issue Industrial Revenue Bonds.* Washington: Congressional Budget Office, 1981.

Robinson, Roland I. *Postwar Market for State and Local Government Securities.* Princeton: Princeton University Press for The National Bureau of Economic Research, 1960.

Roden, Peyton Foster. "Economic Implications of Taxing Municipal Bonds." *Business and Economic Review* 4 (1973):13–17.

Rogers, Harold E., Jr. "Municipal Debt Restrictions and Lease-Purchase Financing." *American Bar Association Journal* 49:31–37.

Rogowski, Robert J. "Commerical Banks and Municipal Revenue Bonds [Overview of the Events that Led to the Prohibition of Commercial Bank Underwriting of Municipal Revenue Bonds]." *Banking Law Journal* 95 (1978):155–172.

Rollison, Mark. *Small Issue Industrial Development Bonds.* Chicago: Capital Publishing Corporation, 1976.

Rothwell, Jack C. "The Move to Municipals." *Bulletin of the Federal Reserve Bank of Philadelphia,* September 1966, pp. 3–7.

Rubinfeld, Daniel. "Credit Ratings and the Market for General Obligation Municipal Bonds." *National Tax Journal* 26 (1973):17–27.

Ryan, William J. "Trick Coupons Lower Net Interest Costs But Complicate Issuer's Fiscal Affairs." *The Daily Bond Buyer,* October 7, 1964, p. 15.

Shapiro, Harvey D. "The High Price of Bargain Rate Pollution Control." *New Leader* 60 (1977):9–12.

Silber, William L. "Municipal Revenue Bond Costs and Bank Underwriting: A Survey of the Evidence." Paper prepared for the American Bankers Association and the Dealer Bank Association, September 28, 1979.

Sims, Kent. "Municipal Bonds and Public Needs." *Bulletin of the Federal Reserve Bank of San Francisco,* July, 1970, pp. 135–147.

Sims, William B. *Utility Revenues versus Full Faith and Credit: The Security of Municipal Bonds.* New York: Herbert J. Sims and Co., Inc., 1976.

Smith, Wade S. *The Appraisal of Municipal Credit Risks.* New York: Moody's Investors Service, 1979.

Snyder, Linda. "Municipal Bonds: Investors Can't Get Enough of Them." *Fortune* 96 (1977):89–90.

Sorenson, E. H. "A Study of Negotiated Municipal Bond Issues and the Impact of Negotiation Upon Interest Cost." Ph. D. dissertation, University of Oregon, 1977.

Staats, William F. "Commercial Banks and the Municipal Bond Market." *Bulletin of the Federal Reserve Bank of Philadelphia,* February 1967, pp. 11–14.

———. "A New Package of Municipal Bonds." *Bulletin of the Federal Reserve Bank of Philadelphia,* November 1966, pp. 18–21.

Stanback, Thomas M. Jr. and Knight, Richard V. *The Metropolitan Economy: The Process of Employment Expansion.* New York: Columbia University Press, 1970.

Standard & Poor's Corporation. *Municipal and International Bond Ratings: An Overview.* New York: Standard & Poor's Corporation, undated (ca. 1979).

Stanfield, Rochelle I. "The Securities Market Is a Different Place Now for Cities in the Wake of the New York City Financial Crisis." *National Journal* 9 (1977):300–302.

Stiess, Alan Walter. *Local Government Finance.* Lexington (Massachusetts): Lexington Books, D. C. Heath and Company, 1975.

Surrey, Stanley S. "The Tax Treatment of State and Local Government Obligations—Some Further Observations." *Tax Policy* 36 (1967):3–16.

Tallman, G. D.; Ruch, D. F.; Melicher, R. W. "Competitive Versus Negotiated Underwriting Costs for Regulated Industries." *Financial Management,* Summer 1974, pp. 49–55.

Thompson, F. Corine and Norgaard, Richard L. *Sinking Funds: Their Use and Value.* New York: Financial Executives Research Foundation, 1967.

Tinsley, W. E. and Speer, Paul D. "Debt Administration." *Municipal Finance Officers Association Special Bulletin 1968.*

Trimble, Gerald M. "Tax Increment Financing for Redevelopment: California Experience Is Good." *Journal of Housing* 31 (1974):458–63.

Twentieth Century Fund, Task Force on Municipal Credit Ratings. *The Rating Game.* New York: The Twentieth Century Fund, 1974.

Tyler, Walter H. "Municipal Bond Ratings: Symbolic Terms Used by Rating Firms Express the Odds Against Possible Losses to the Investor in any Particular Issue." *Michigan Municipal Review* 35 (1962):285–287.

U.S. Congress Congressional Budget Office. *Small Issue Industrial Revenue Bonds.* Washington: U.S. Government Printing Office, 1981.

U.S. Department of Agriculture, Economics, Statistics and Cooperative Service in cooperation with the Department of Agricultural and Applied Economics, University of Minnesota. *Issuing Municipal Bonds: A Primer for Local Officials.* Washington: U.S. Government Printing Office, 1977.

U.S. Congress Joint Economic Committee. *Changing Conditions in the Market For State and Local Government Debt.* Washington: United States Government Printing Office, 1976.

_____. *State and Local Facilities and Financing.* Washington: United States Printing Office, 1966.

United States Congress, House Committee on Interstate and Foreign Commerce, Subcommittee on Consumer Protection and Finance. *Municipal Securities Full Disclosure Act of 1976: Hearings, August 31, 1976, on H.R. 15205.* Washington: United States Government Printing Office, 1977.

United States Congress, House Committee on Ways and Means. Summary of Testimony on the *Tax Treatment of State and Local Bond Interest at Public Hearings, February 18 to April 24, 1969, on the Subject of Tax Reform.* Washington: United States Government Printing Office, 1969.

Van Horne, James C. *Functions and Analysis of Capital Market Rates.* Englewood Cliffs (New Jersey): Prentice-Hall, Inc., 1970.

Wallison, Frieda K. "Self-Regulation in the Municipal Securities Industry." *Securities Regulation Law Journal* 6 (1979):291–344.

Weingartner, Martin H. "The Generalized Rate of Return." *Journal of Financial and Quantitative Analysis,* September 1966, pp. 1–29.

West, Richard. "Determinants of Underwriter Spreads on Tax Exempt Bond Issues." *Journal of Financial and Quantitative Analysis,* September 1967, pp. 241–263.

_____. "Federal Disclosure Law Is Unnecessary: Much of What Was Documented in the SEC's Report on New York City Finances Has Been Known in General Terms for More than Two Years and Has Already Set in Motion Developments which Are Increasing Financial Disclosure by Issuers of Tax Exempt Bonds." *Wall Street Journal* 190 (1977):10.

_____. "The 'Net Interest Cost' Method of Issuing Tax Exempt Bonds: Is It Rational?" *Public Finance,* Fall 1968, pp. 346–358.

_____. "On the Non-Callability of State and Local Government Bonds: A Comment." *Journal of Political Economy* LXXV (1967):98–99.

Weston, J. Fred and Brigham, Eugene R. *Managerial Finance.* 5th ed. Hinsdale (Illinois): The Dryden Press, 1975.

B. Serial Publications of Special Interest to Municipal Bond Field

The Bond Buyer. *The Bond Buyer's Municipal Finance Statistics: Statistics on State and Local Government Finance.* New York: The Bond Buyer.

    An annual publication providing succinct statistical data concerning numerous aspects of state and local government finance, with special emphasis on debt.

————. *The Daily Bond Buyer.* New York: The Bond Buyer.

A newspaper published each weekday, with the exception of some holidays. It is the most comprehensive publication available on a daily basis reporting news and data concerning debt of state and local governments.

————. *The Weekly Bond Buyer.* New York: The Bond Buyer.

A newspaper published each week. Contains most of the important items included in *The Daily Bond Buyer,* with some items being in condensed form.

Blue List Publishing Company. *The Blue List of Current Municipal Offerings.* New York: The Blue List Publishing Company, a division of Standard & Poor's Corporation.

A daily publication issued each weekday, except some holidays. It contains a comprehensive listing of municipal bonds and some other types of bonds which are announced as available for purchase. Includes the name of each bond being offered, its coupon rate, maturity date, yield or price at which offered, and name of dealer making listing.

Moody's Investors Service. *Municipal & Government Manual.* New York: Moody's Investors Service.

This serial is published annually, usually in two volumes. It contains a comprehensive listing of all principal bond issues outstanding by state and local governments, to the extent that information is made available to the publisher. It also includes information on debt of the United States and its agencies as well as that of many foreign governments. Considerable information concerning state laws relating to debt and the revenues by which it is secured in state and local governments is presented.

Public Securities Association. *Municipal Market Developments.* A monthly statistical report of long-term and short-term municipal debt sales with a number of interesting classifications of data not available elsewhere.

C. Serial Publications of the United States Governmental Agencies

United States Department of Commerce, Bureau of the Census. The Bureau of the Census offers a number of important documents for those concerned with debt and other aspects of the financial affairs of state and local governments. The basic publication is *Census of Governments.* This series commenced in 1957 but with antecedents in other selected years, including 1902 and 1932. It provides comprehensive information concerning the structure of state and local governments in the United States as well as information about their finances and personnel. It is dated at five-year intervals, the most recent being for 1977. A very important aspect of the *1977 Census of Governments* was the *Classification Manual, Governmental Finances* issued by the Bureau of the Census. This work contains the basic definitions of concepts used in the gathering, tabulation, and reporting of data.

On an annual basis, the Bureau of the Census publishes the following reports of interest to those concerned with municipal debt (in the following titles, the "*19xx–19xx*" is meant to designate successive years, i.e., 1970–1971; 1971–1972; etc.):

Governmental Finances in 19xx–19xx. A comprehensive summary of data and estimates.

State Government Finances in 19xx. A comprehensive set of data concerning the finances of state governments for the fiscal year ending in the calendar year shown in the title.

City Government Finances in 19xx–19xx. Contains individual city data for cities of over 50,000 population and estimates for those with populations of less than 50,000.

County Government Finances in 19xx–19xx. Contains individual county data for counties with populations of 100,000 and over and estimates for those with populations of less than 100,000.

Finances of Public School Systems in 19xx–19xx. Contains data on finances of individual school systems with enrollment of 20,000 or over and estimates for those with enrollment of less than 20,000.

Local Government Finances in Selected Metropolitan Areas and Large Counties, 19xx–19xx. Individual data for 74 major SMSA's and their county areas and for local governments in county areas of 200,000 or more outside the 74 SMSA's.

County Government Employment in 19xx.

City Government Employment in 19xx.

These two publications provide continuing data concerning results of annual employment surveys of city and county governments.

Local Government Employment in Selected Metropolitan Areas and Large Counties: 19xx.

Finances of Employee-Retirement Systems of State and Local Governments in 19xx–xx.

Of more general interest is the annual volume entitled:

Statistical Abstract of the United States: 19xx. This publication contains a wealth of information on a huge range of topics, including summary data concerning public finances and debt.

Finally, there is the historical compendium:

Historical Statistics of the United States: Colonial Times to 1970. The two volume set offers summary data on almost all aspects of American life.

There are many others of importance; however, the foregoing constitute the more important recurring reports of interest here.

U.S. Department of Housing and Urban Development. *Statistical Yearbook.* A handy reference of data on numerous programs of interest to state and local governments.

United States Secretary of the Treasury. *Statistical Appendix to Annual Report of the Secretary of the Treasury of the State of the Finances.*

Broad information concerning the finances of the United States government, including some data of interest concerning state and local government debt.

Federal Reserve System, Board of Governors *Flow of Funds.*

This publication appears in both annual and quarterly editions and under a number of titles. The principal title is: *Flow of Funds Accounts.* Some editions have subtitles to facilitate identification.

Federal Reserve System, Board of Governors; Federal Deposit Insurance Corporation; and Office of the Comptroller of the Currency. *Assets and Liabilities: Report of Income for Commercial and Mutual Savings Banks.*

This annual report sets forth income and certain balance sheet information for commercial and mutual savings banks as of December 31 of each year. This annual report was discontinued after 1977 in favor of individual reports by the several agencies. Generally these are not available in printed form for 1978 and subsequently but information may be secured from the individual agencies.

Notation Concerning Bureau of the Census Financial Data

The Bureau of the Census financial data for governments is ordinarily on a fiscal year basis. Inasmuch as fiscal years vary widely among governments, it is appropriate to note the following:

1. Federal government data is for the fiscal year ending within the year to which reference is made. Thus, data for 1960 would be for the year ending June 30, 1960; for 1970–71, for the fiscal ending June 30, 1971.
2. For state governments data is for the fiscal year ending within the year to which reference is made, e.g., *State Government Finances in 1979* contains data for fiscal years ending in 1979. For that year, all states had fiscal years ending June 30 except for New York (March 31), Texas (August 31) and Alabama and Michigan (September 30).
3. For school districts, data is ordinarily for the year ending June 30, however in Alabama and Texas school fiscal years end in September and August, respectively. Therefore, data reported in this volume under heading *1978* would relate to the fiscal year ending in the summer of 1978 and would therefore actually be for the 1977–78 academic year.
4. For other local governments the rules were modified in 1962:
   a. For 1962 and prior years, data connotes fiscal years ending at any time within the calendar year. Thus, a municipality on a June 30 fiscal year would have had its 1958–59 finances reported as *1959* and a municipality on a calendar year fiscal year would also have been reported as *1959*.
   b. For 1962–63 and following, local government financial data relates to fiscal years ending at any time during the period July 1, 1962, through June 30, 1963. Thus, for a municipality on a June 30 fiscal year in 1969 would have had its 1968–69 data reported as *1969* whereas one on a calendar year fiscal year would have had 1968 calendar data reported as *1969*.

INDEX